Norman Foster Works 6

The Deutsche Bibliothek
holds a record for this
publication in the Deutsche
Nationalbibliografie;
detailed bibliographical
data can be found under
http://dnb.ddb.de

Library of Congress Control
Number:

2009921379

©2013, Foster + Partners,
London, and Prestel Verlag,
Munich · Berlin · London ·
New York

Prestel Verlag
A member of Verlagsgruppe
Randomhouse GmbH

Prestel Verlag
Neumarkter Str. 28
81673 Munich
Germany
Tel +49 (089) 4136-0
Fax +49 (089) 4136-2335
www.prestel.de

Prestel Publishing
900 Broadway, Suite 603
New York NY 10003
USA
Tel +1 (212) 995-2720
Fax +1 (212) 995-2733

Prestel Publishing Ltd
14 - 17 Wells Street
London W1T 3PD
UK
Tel +44 (020) 7323-5004
Fax +44 (020) 7323-0271
www.prestel.com

Printed in Italy
on acid-free paper
ISBN 978-3-7913-3259-8

Norman Foster Works 6

Contributors

Chris Abel
Gavin Blyth
Edward Bosley
Peter Buchanan
Francis Duffy
Norman Foster
Joseph Giovannini
Paul Goldberger
Simon Inglis
Nicola Jackson
Annette LeCuyer
Thomas Leslie
Kenneth Powell
Libby Sellers
Deyan Sudjic
Thomas Weaver
Richard Weston

Editor

David Jenkins

Prestel   Munich · Berlin · London · New York

Editor's Note

This volume is the sixth
of a series devoted to the
complete works of Foster
+ Partners. It details projects
undertaken largely from
the late-1990s to the
mid-2000s. As with previous
volumes, it is organised
broadly chronologically.
However, within that
chronology some projects
have been grouped into
'themes' or 'families' in
order to facilitate a better
understanding of their
underlying ideas, to represent
a body of work with a
particular client, or to enable
the study of a series of
projects in one location.

Running along the top of
each page is a strip – which
has come to be known as
the 'film'. This provides an
additional commentary on
the relevant project or essay,
and takes the form of 'visual
footnotes', ephemera and
'voices off'. It is hoped that
this material will add to the
reader's enjoyment and aid
those who wish to research
the work of the Foster
studio further.

In editing this volume,
as ever, I am particularly
grateful to Norman Foster,
whose support and
enthusiasm have been
unfailing. I would also like to
thank Per Arnoldi, who first
helped to shape the concept
of the series; Thomas Manss,
and Keira Yang for designing
this and other books in the
series; Rebecca Roke, Gavin
Blyth and Matthew Foreman
for invaluable editorial and
research support; Kathryn
Tollervey and Gayle Mault,
who together with Katy Harris
mined the office archive; Julia
Dawson and Oliver Pawley
for proofreading the text;
Hilary Bird for indexing;
Martin Lee and John Bodkin
for coordinating production;
the numerous people in the
Foster studio – past and
present – who have provided
help in researching a number
of the projects included
here; and finally the many
contributors who have helped
to make this book such
a pleasure to put together.

David Jenkins
London, June 2013

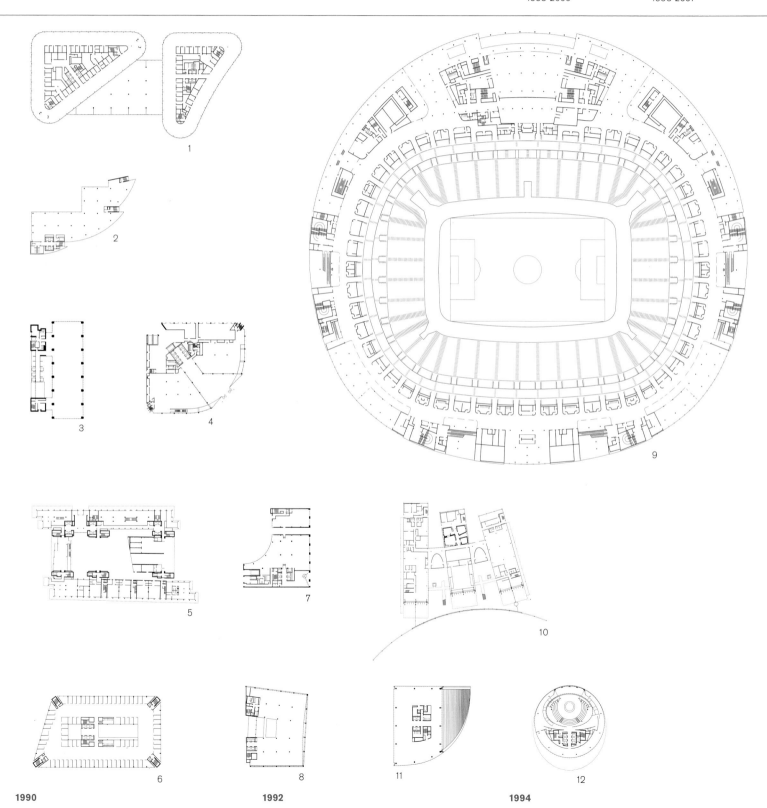

1

2

3

4

9

5

7

10

6

8

11

12

1990

1992

1994

10. Electronic Arts
European Headquarters,
Chertsey, England
1997-2000

11. Moorhouse,
London, England
1997-2004

12. City Hall,
London, England
1998-2002

13. Petronas University
of Technology,
Malaysia
1998-2004

14. Albion Riverside,
London, England
1998-2003

15. Riverside One,
London, England
1998-1999

16. Grandstand, Newbury
Racecourse,
Newbury, England
1999-2000

17. La Voile, St Jean Cap
Ferrat, France
1999-2002

18. McLaren Technology
Centre,
Woking, England
1998-2004

19. Beijing International
Airport, China
2002-2006

20. London City Racecourse,
London, England
2000-2004

21. Capital City Academy,
London, England
2000-2003

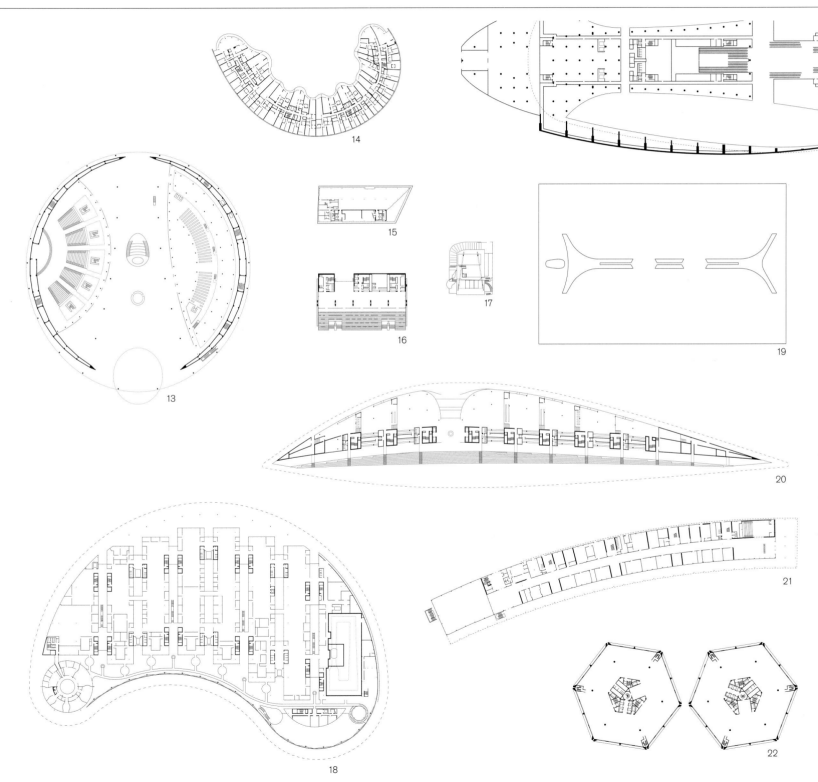

1996   1998   2000

Contents

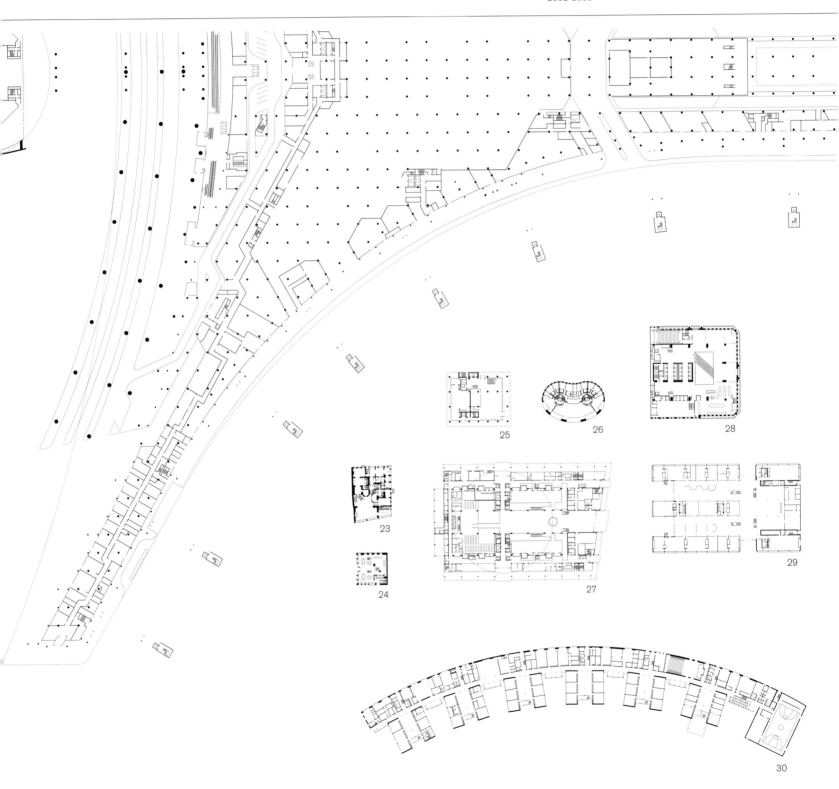

22. World Trade Center,
    New York, USA
    2002-2003
23. Asprey,
    London, England
    2001-2004
24. Asprey,
    New York, USA
    2002-2003
25. Leslie L Dan Pharmacy
    Building,
    Toronto, Canada
    2002-2005

26. Chesa Futura,
    St Moritz, Switzerland
    2000-2004
27. Supreme Court,
    Singapore
    2000-2006
28. Hearst Headquarters,
    New York, USA
    2000-2006
29. Business Academy,
    Bexley, England
    2001-2003
30. West London Academy,
    London, England
    2002-2005

25

26

28

23

24

27

29

30

2002

2006

2004

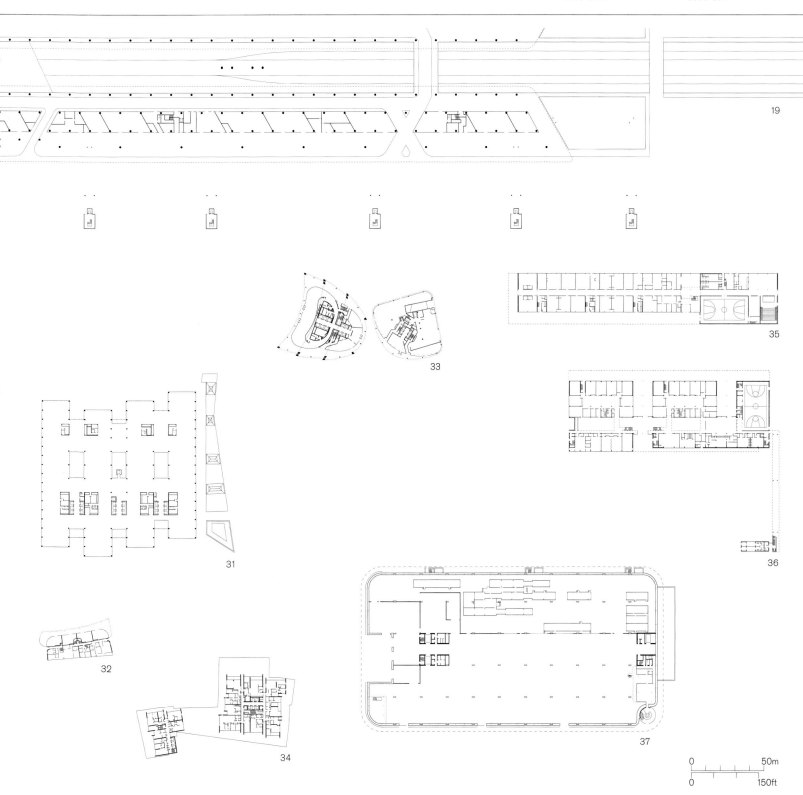

31. Bishops Square,
    London, England
    2001-2007
32. The Murezzan,
    St Moritz, Switzerland
    2003-2007
33. 51 Lime Street,
    London, England
    2001-2007
34. Regent Place,
    Sydney, Australia
    2003-2007

35. Djanogly City Academy,
    Nottingham, England
    2002-2005
36. London Academy,
    Edgware, England
    2002-2006
37. McLaren Production
    Centre,
    Woking, England
    2009-2011

19

31

32

33

34

35

36

37

0   50m

0   150ft

2008   **2010**   **2012**

Timeline of Plans

Preface
Norman Foster

This volume is the sixth chronological instalment in the continuing series of books on our work. As before, I say 'our' conscious of the fact that architecture is essentially rooted in teamwork – there are so many people involved, both in the foreground and behind the scenes. A large number of those people have contributed to this book, some in the form of sketches and drawings done at the time, others by offering their thoughts and recollections – all of which you will find as you explore.

As we selected the projects described here it became clear that the past few years have witnessed huge social and technological transformations. It might be said in this context that the only constant is change. However, if I had to summarise, I would say that reviewing our work highlights concerns that have guided us consistently from the beginning, and you see those concerns projected forward as points of continuity.

Design for me is all encompassing. It is about values. To design is to question and to challenge. I believe that we have a moral duty to design well and responsibly, whether that is a chair or an airport; and interestingly both those scale extremes are represented here.

Design can explore the new and build on the past. It can transform patterns of living and working. One example of that is the family of new schools we have completed in the UK, beginning with Bexley Business Academy, and these are featured here. The Academies represent a new direction in secondary education. Often replacing failing schools in under-privileged areas, they are designed to create inspirational environments in which to teach and to learn. The first schools have been open long enough to prove the point that an uplifting environment can have a tangible impact on patterns of pupil behaviour and achievement.

A willingness to challenge accepted solutions is another theme that has always underpinned our work. It means asking the right questions, allied with a curiosity about how things function – whether that is an organisation or a mechanical system. I have characterised this tendency to work from first principles as 'reinventing'.

Often that is a process that unfolds through a series of projects. If you take an early building from the 1970s, such as the headquarters for Willis Faber & Dumas – which virtually reinvented the concept of workplace, introducing an unprecedented range of staff amenities – you see how it sparked ideas that underpin many of the office projects included here, whether that is a low-rise complex for Electronic Arts or McLaren, or a high-rise headquarters for the Hearst Corporation in New York. There, the lobby with its restaurant is conceived on the scale of a town square – a social focus for the Hearst community.

On other occasions, reinventing involves a steep learning curve, as it did with Wembley Stadium. A new London landmark, the Wembley arch symbolises the rebirth of 'the cathedral of football'. Wembley is significant in another sense too, part of a London renaissance that has brought with it a new generation of public buildings such as Tate Modern, the London Eye and the Great Court at the British Museum. Indeed, London is a city that figures prominently in this book, with projects as diverse as City Hall, the refurbishment of HM Treasury, the Central London masterplan and the transformation of Trafalgar Square.

Our approach to architecture is rooted in the belief that it is not only individual buildings but also their wider urban context that affects our wellbeing. The masterplan for Central London is an example of that. It made detailed proposals for the improvement of Trafalgar Square, Parliament Square and Whitehall in the ceremonial heart of London. Its goals were to enhance pedestrian access and enjoyment of the area, to address public transport and to create more sympathetic settings for the city's historic buildings and monuments. I have characterised that task as a 'balancing act' – a search to promote a genuinely integrated solution able to satisfy the often conflicting needs of residents and visitors. That is something that holds true for any historic urban environment attempting to sustain contemporary activities.

This leads me to another theme: how new architecture can be the catalyst for the revitalisation of old buildings. We opened that dialogue with the Sackler Galleries at the Royal Academy, and you see it again in the Treasury and the courtyard of the Smithsonian Institution in Washington DC. The enclosure of the Smithsonian's courtyard has helped to transform the visitor experience and makes the point that just as the perception of a city can be enriched when old and new complement one another, so can that of a building.

One of the things that most excites me about our approach to practising architecture today is the mobility we enjoy, not just in moving around the world, but also in our ability to respond quickly to new challenges. That is illustrated in both senses by Beijing Airport, a project that moved very fast indeed. We were commissioned in mid-November 2003; by the end of that month we had set up an office in Beijing; over the next four months the team completed 2,500 preliminary design drawings in time for the groundbreaking on 28 March 2004. At the peak of construction there were 50,000 workers on site. Consider that this is a building of 1.3 million square metres, capable of handling up to 50 million passengers per annum, providing under one roof all the facilities provided by five terminals at Heathrow – plus another 17 per cent of that total. Yet remarkably it was commissioned and completed in a little over four years – a pace inconceivable in the West.

All the projects I have described so far are rooted in sustainable design strategies. This highlights another consistent theme in our work, though many of the 'green' ideas that we explored in early projects are only now becoming a reality because of new technologies at our disposal. Today we have computer-modelling techniques that allow us to research and design structures in greater depth and more rapidly than ever before. You see that in the design of the Chesa Futura apartment building in the Swiss Alps, which marries advanced computer-aided design tools with state-of-the-art timber construction techniques and handcrafted shingles to create a building that is environmentally benign and visually of its place.

Chesa Futura shows that by building at greater densities in urban centres we do not have to encroach on land at the fringes of towns and cities, and suburbanise nature. It also illustrates the importance of studying the 'whole life' energy patterns of buildings – not just how much energy they consume, but how much is embodied in their fabric. It is a low-energy structure not just in terms of its consumption, but also terms of the materials used. Wood is a renewable resource and it absorbs carbon dioxide during its growth cycle. Additionally, in this part of Switzerland, building in timber is culturally sympathetic and contributes to the ecology of harvesting older trees to facilitate forest regeneration.

In a very different context, Hearst Tower takes bold steps in terms of sustainability, beginning with its construction. Its diagrid skeleton uses 20 per cent less steel than a conventionally framed structure and 85 per cent of that steel is recycled. A host of passive environmental measures, including the use of natural ventilation, ensures that its energy consumption is 25 per cent better than the standard set by state and city energy codes. As a result, it was the first new tower in Manhattan to be awarded a gold rating under the US Green Building Council's Leadership in Energy and Environmental Design Program (LEED).

Taken together, the projects described here raise another important issue: how do we optimise the potential of new buildings and infrastructure for progressive change, not only for the private world of the occupants but also in the public domain. Part of the answer to that question lies in objective research. In that sense, the practice mirrors an international consultancy, which will typically begin by exploring the detailed workings of the client organisation. That approach is fundamental to the way we work. In another sense, the studio is close in spirit to a school of architecture, which is open around the clock and thrives on a jury system, with incisive critics guided by a shared design ethos – I am thinking especially of Yale, where I was a student. Good design is rooted in creative discourse, whether that is with one's colleagues, the consultants – particularly engineers of diverse skills – or the client, without whom, of course, nothing is possible.

That brings me back to teamwork. Over the years, my close colleagues and I are fortunate to have had the support of a fantastic team and many generous collaborators. This book records and celebrates their many different creative contributions. Finally, as anyone who has been involved in putting together a book will understand, like designing a building it is very much a team effort. I would like to thank all those who have helped to bring this book to fruition. As always, I am especially grateful to David Jenkins who conceived and edited this and previous volumes in the series; to Per Arnoldi, Thomas Manss and his team, who established the graphic discipline; and to the distinguished writers – far too many of them to acknowledge individually – who together have offered fresh insights into our work.

An Unfolding Project
Paul Goldberger 2012

To Norman Foster, Modernism is not a social crusade. It is not a means to some imagined Utopia, and neither is it a quaint period piece, an aesthetic to be viewed as the subject of affectionate revivals. For Foster, Modernism is more of an unfinished experiment, and it is ongoing. The most important thing to be said about the work of Foster + Partners is that it emerges from the belief that Modernism is *now*. Foster's architecture is set firmly in the present, not only in the sense that it takes advantage of the latest technologies, but also in the way in which it seeks to develop new models. For all that Foster's work owes to the Modernism of the first half of the twentieth century, it bears only the most distant resemblance to any of it. Foster has little interest in following his Modernist forebears literally. He pays homage to them in his relentless determination to reinvent Modernism, his eagerness to prove that its possibilities, far from being exhausted, are only beginning to be discovered.

The notion that the potential of Modernism is yet to be realised, and that the structural technologies and architectural programmes of the twenty-first century provide more fertile grounds than those of the twentieth, bespeaks an earnestness that could seem, at first glance, out of keeping with the highly organised, multifaceted operation that Foster + Partners has become. There is no question that Foster's office today represents the kind of model of corporate practice that Skidmore, Owings & Merrill did for several decades in the middle of the twentieth century, the firm whose reputation is based to a significant degree on its ability simultaneously to execute highly complex projects, please corporate clients, and represent an advanced, not to say cutting-edge, aesthetic position.

The most striking thing about that aesthetic position is not the surface appearance of Foster's buildings – their almost insistent elegance, the way they look light and sleek – or even the way in which they seem intended to prove that minimalism need not be incompatible with visual interest. It is, rather, the way in which Foster has woven urbanism, sustainability, and inventive responses to programmes together, joining all three of these things to the Modernist tradition in a way that makes their connection seem not only logical, but completely natural.

This is no small achievement, given the extent to which orthodox Modernism, in practice if not in theory, has often devalued urbanism, ignored context, paid scant attention to issues of energy consumption, and contorted programmes to meet aesthetic demands. Foster's reinvention of Modernism represents, at least as much as anything else, a desire to correct these shortcomings and to demonstrate that this can be done at no cost to sheer visual beauty. In Foster's best work, reason and logic share pride of place with physical allure. Foster's buildings exert a visceral attraction as pure objects, but they never depend on beauty alone. There are always brains, in other words, somewhere in the equation.

That is all the more remarkable when one considers the scope of the firm's work: from airports to football stadiums, from office buildings to factories, from bridges to door handles to a new version of the London double-decker Routemaster bus, in almost every case creating a virtually new paradigm. Foster + Partners' output is so large and diverse that one wonders how it can be achieved.

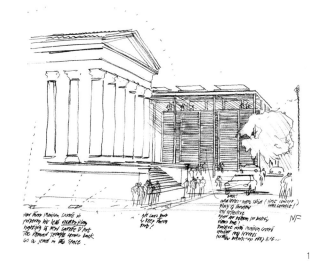

1

2

The only real power the architect has is that of advocacy – fighting for a cause, whether that is the quality of construction or innovative design. The popular image of the architect as an all-powerful form-giver is very far from reality. Today we operate in a very complex environment. Working on projects around the world means that we have to deal with many different constraints – cultural, legal, political and environmental. Bureaucracy has grown wherever you turn. And somewhere, through this tangle of conflicting pressures, we practise our art as architects, trying to push the envelope of creativity. Norman Foster, in conversation with the editor, 2012

The answer lies in the way that the firm is organised. Despite its international presence, it is highly centralised, with all major design decisions emanating from the senior partners, led by Mouzhan Majidi, Spencer de Grey and David Nelson, who work together with Norman Foster in the sprawling, Thames-facing London studio at Riverside – a workplace that itself embodies the pristine elegance the firm is known for, not to mention its sweeping and occasionally grandiose ambitions. Most importantly, the studio, in which everyone from partners to assistants works together in a single, vast open space, symbolises the commitment to the notion of architecture as a collaborative effort.

For Foster, Modernism is not a constant but, rather, an evolving language, a language within which new ideas can be expressed and new things made.

If Norman Foster's work represents an attempt to bring Modernist sleekness into accord with urban context, environmental responsibility, and the demands of complex programmes – to take Modernism to a higher level of sensitivity, one might say, and to make it less self-referential – its most subtle achievement, surely, is the deference it shows to older buildings. Foster's ability to create Modernist interventions in older buildings that project an air of comradeship rather than defiance is nothing short of remarkable, given the way in which his interventions invariably bear no direct resemblance to the older buildings to which they have been added.

Foster adds sleek new sections to venerable and distinguished buildings in such a way as to make them feel entirely natural, almost inevitable. He has no desire to create the illusion that an addition or renovation has been there all along, which in Foster's terms would be disingenuous at best, as well as highly unlikely to succeed. There is never any confusion as to what was there before, and what Foster has added. But neither is there a sense that an old building has been violated. Rather, Foster deals in juxtaposition. However different his work may be visually from what lies beside it, there is a harmonic balance – not the simple connection of imitation, but the subtle and complex balance of true counterpoint. Foster's juxtapositions of new and old are almost always enticing and energetic dialogues, in which two architectural generations engage each other discretely, making manifest the richness of time.

This aspect of the practice began with a pair of projects conceived in the mid-1980s: the Carré d'Art in Nîmes, France, designed in 1984 and finished in 1993, and the Sackler Galleries of the Royal Academy of Arts in London, designed in 1985 and completed in 1991. The Carré d'Art is not, technically, an addition, but an entirely new and freestanding building in the historic centre of Nîmes, immediately adjacent to the Maison Carrée, a fully intact Roman temple. But it was clear that this project, a combination of arts complex and public library, would always be seen in conjunction with the Maison Carrée; indeed, that its visual identity would be created in large part by its immediate neighbour, and that it could never be viewed wholly on its own. How, then, to acknowledge both its independence and its role as a centre of information technology without offending the extraordinary structure beside it?

3. An early sketch study of the cupola of the Reichstag (1992-1999), by Norman Foster. The transformation of the Reichstag was rooted in four related issues: the Bundestag's significance as a democratic forum, an understanding of history, a commitment to public accessibility, and sustainability. The cupola brings these themes together. Symbolic of rebirth, it is also fundamental to the building's natural lighting and ventilation strategies. Now an established Berlin landmark, its viewing platform is one of the city's most popular destinations.

4. The Great Court at the British Museum (1994-2000). The courtyard at the heart of the museum was one of London's long-lost spaces. This project was about its reinvention: as a new focal point for visitor circulation within the museum and a social hub – a cultural square. In this respect, the Great Court resonates beyond the confines of the museum, forming another link in the pedestrian route from the British Library to Covent Garden, the river and the South Bank.

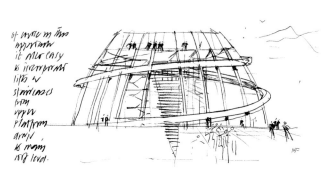

3

4

For me, every building is an intervention in a historical setting, because the present will be history tomorrow – in that sense, history is always relative … Every project has to be sensitive to its historical setting and in the tradition of history as I see it, every age makes its own contribution, makes its own mark. And if you take that approach, there can be no place for pastiche. Norman Foster, lecture in Mexico City, 26 April 1996

You don't get ponderous architecture out of Norman Foster's office and that goes back to discussions he had way back in the 1960s with legends like Buckminster Fuller whose question always was: 'How much does a building weigh?' It was the notion that a building could almost be like a bubble sitting in the landscape. If you look at some of the buildings from the earliest to the latest – from the Sainsbury Centre to Beijing Airport terminal – they are just extraordinary enclosures of space, now almost becoming capable of having whole towns inside them. I think Foster is moving towards that Buckminster Fuller vision of the city beneath a bubble. Hugh Pearman, 'Front Row', BBC Radio 4, 28 December 2007

If you have the responsibility to give a historic building a new lease of life by upgrading it, you are confronted by a range of options or possibilities. Do you preserve the old simply because it is old? Perhaps the oldest part is ugly – perhaps it obscures something which is later in age but more beautiful? What do you preserve or reveal? Maybe you can add something of today which is even more beautiful. The sense of awareness of history is often heightened by the context of the new. Norman Foster, in conversation with the editor, 2012

1. One of the newly landscaped courtyards in Her Majesty's Treasury (1996-2002). Most early twentieth-century office buildings are not naturally suited to modern working practices. However, the best of them add to the architectural wealth of our cities and can be restructured to fit contemporary needs. The Treasury is such a building. In refurbishing it, the goal was to transform a labyrinthine and under-utilised set of spaces into an efficient and enjoyable working environment.

2. The Smithsonian Institution Courtyard (2004-2007). The Smithsonian occupies a structure that Walt Whitman described as 'the noblest of Washington buildings'. The enclosure of its courtyard has transformed the public's experience of the Smithsonian's galleries and given the Institution one of the largest event spaces in the capital. The fluid form of the glazed roof develops structural and environmental themes explored in the Great Court at the British Museum, bathing the courtyard with natural light.

Foster's solution was to put five of the building's nine storeys below ground so as to keep the roofline below the top of the Maison Carrée. Above ground, he placed a glass box, set within a white steel frame and covered largely with white metal louvres. The box is under an overhanging roof supported on slender columns. The building's scale, its proportional system and its rich texture relate to the Maison Carrée, but with utter deference; no element mimics the classical building, but every modern piece is designed in clear response to it. What the new building lacks entirely is any hint of the anxiety and brittleness that marks many modern buildings. It is serene, without in any way being soft. Foster has responded to the strength and clarity of the Roman temple with a building that bespeaks order and a quiet grace.

Foster's ability to create Modernist interventions in older buildings that project an air of comradeship rather than defiance is nothing short of remarkable.

At the Royal Academy, the Foster practice moved beyond Nîmes to the challenge of a direct intervention in an existing building. But the principle remained the same: to use modern materials and details and to assemble them into a balanced composition that suggests clarity, strength and understatement. As at Nîmes, Foster and his partner Spencer de Grey – who has overseen much of the firm's historical work – sought juxtaposition and balance. They took their cues from the original fabric, as if they were engaged in a form of dance in which the existing building was always the lead partner.

These were followed by two of the firm's most celebrated interventions in historic structures, the Great Court at the British Museum, completed in 2000, and the renovation of the Reichstag in Berlin, completed in 1999. The solutions grew somewhat bolder in both of these projects, but the principles remained the same.

At the British Museum, Foster covered the central court, once an area filled with bookstacks, with a glass roof patterned almost like a spider's web, and restored the famous round Reading Room of the British Library in the middle of the courtyard. It is a spectacular public space that manages, for all the panache and visual power of its roof, to allow the Reading Room to continue to occupy pride of place as the major visual focus. The Great Court gives the museum an internal 'town square', but it also fulfils an equally valuable function, rationalising circulation throughout a building whose sequences of galleries once appeared to lack any clear order.

If the British Museum could benefit from a freshened image, the Reichstag desperately needed one: it had been damaged during the war and subsequently altered with little sympathy for its grandiose nineteenth-century architecture. The challenge was to restore the building and update it so that it would be both a functioning seat of government and an apt architectural symbol for a unified Germany. Foster opened up the interiors and created a large assembly hall for the Bundestag and replaced the lost dome with a cupola of glass. The cupola is lined with helical ramps that lead to an observation platform, and the space is visually open to the Bundestag chamber below: as powerful a symbol of transparency as the dome itself. Because the dome is traditional in profile, it is not visually jarring atop the heavy, Germanic mass of the Reichstag; it seems like a light, transparent version of a classical element, which is precisely what it is. As at the British Museum, Foster has managed to engineer an intervention that at once respects a historic building's past and yet departs from it radically.

1

2

The theme of simultaneously injecting a strongly Modernist element and expressing, at least abstractly, some degree of historical continuity continues in more recent work, such as the Robert and Arlene Kogod Courtyard at the Smithsonian Institution in Washington, completed in 2007. It is an orthogonal space, covered by a glazed canopy, whose shape is fixed in the form of undulating waves, as if it were billowing in the wind. The key thing here is the way in which the curving profile of the roof provides a perfect counterpoint to the more rigid lines of the courtyard of the Greek Revival building, which was erected starting in 1836 – not long after the British Museum – as the United States Patent Office, and more than a century later transferred to the Smithsonian for use as both the National Portrait Gallery and the Smithsonian American Art Museum. The roof is not only light, it is lyrical, and it yields a space below that possesses both grandeur and softness.

The same thing might be said of certain interventions that are not, strictly speaking, even architecture, such as the witty entry canopies to the Metro in Bilbao – glass bubbles whose form as well as their materials is designed to play off against the rest of the cityscape, or the Millennium Bridge in London, the pedestrian bridge across the Thames designed in association with the sculptor Anthony Caro and engineers Arup and completed in 2000. The Millennium Bridge is a suspension bridge whose cable structure, rather than hanging from high towers, is thrust out to the side of the deck. The bridge's towers are a pair of concrete supports in the shape of the letter Y, with the deck set into the middle of the Y, and the cables supported from its points, which project laterally from the deck. The result is a low and graceful shape, from a distance a thin form slicing its way in a gentle arc across the Thames. On the bridge, the sideways-projecting cable structure gives the bridge what one might call discreet monumentality, grandeur without enclosure, with a wide-open vista of the city unimpeded by hanging cables. And the bridge enters into a cordial dialogue with an earlier technological achievement that lies directly opposite its northern terminus: the dome of St Paul's Cathedral.

Surely the most extensive of the firm's Modernist interventions into historical context is an architectural project that, paradoxically, has almost no external visibility at all – the six-year renovation of the Treasury complex in Westminster, adjacent to Parliament Square. The project is, in a sense, the un-Reichstag, a thorough reconstruction of a sprawling government building undertaken entirely to improve internal workings, not to provide a conspicuous public symbol of newness and change. The Treasury was completed in 1917, and it bears all of the strengths and weaknesses of the Edwardian period: very clearly the counting-house of an empire, it is grandiose, more than a little bombastic, and yet it possesses an unmistakable degree of classical dignity at the same time. It is a relic of a day when government buildings were expected to be neither welcoming to the public nor particularly comfortable or efficient for the bureaucrats toiling within them.

The building stretches for the equivalent of several city blocks and has numerous light-wells, some small courtyards and one enormous, drum-shaped courtyard in the centre. Spencer de Grey observes that the building contains as much space as the Commerzbank Tower in Frankfurt, one of Foster's tallest skyscrapers, and describes the challenge of the renovation as 'making this a horizontal building with gardens, as the Commerzbank is a vertical building with gardens.' The brief was somewhat less romantic – it was to reorganise the interiors completely, to find more usable space, and to make it more energy efficient. Nonetheless, de Grey's comparison is apt, since one of the key decisions was to landscape the two largest courtyards and, working with the landscape architect Kathryn Gustafson, to turn them into private gardens for the use of the staff.

3. The Millennium Bridge (1996-2000), looking towards Tate Modern on Bankside. A creative collaboration between architecture, art and engineering, the bridge was developed with sculptor Anthony Caro and engineers Arup. London's only dedicated pedestrian bridge, it is a key element in the city's pedestrian infrastructure. A vital new artery into Southwark, in the south, it has also brought increased numbers of visitors to the northern embankment and St Paul's Cathedral.

4. One of the distinctive 'Fosterito' canopies on Line 1 of the Bilbao Metro (1988-1995). A metro system is an excellent demonstration of how a city's infrastructure can influence the quality of people's lives. Bilbao Metro is unusual in that it was conceived as a totality: architectural, engineering and construction skills were integrated within a shared vision. A major investment in a city that hitherto had no underground system, the Metro has transformed the visitor experience of Bilbao and underpinned its economic renaissance.

3

4

Trafalgar Square is fundamentally a very simple scheme although the process was highly complex and the challenges great. We discovered that the key to unlocking the potential of the square was subtle intervention. We learnt that grand gestures and expensive solutions are not necessarily what make a successful urban environment. Often it is the smaller interventions that make a city enjoyable. Similarly, the Millennium Bridge was driven by a desire to minimise the impact of the bridge on the river and to celebrate the existing fabric of the city – the views and the possibilities for new links and connections. Spencer de Grey, speech at the Forum for the Built Environment, London, 28 November 2008

With Trafalgar Square we showed how relatively modest steps can lead to significant change. The effect has been to turn the square from an isolated traffic island into a truly generous urban space. New facilities, such as a café, have been inserted beneath the upper terrace, looking on to the square. I remember going there with the team when we began our studies and the central part of the space was virtually deserted. Go there now and it's thronged with people. There is a programme of hugely popular outdoor events and concerts, and tens of thousands of visitors and Londoners visit every year. The transformation has been extraordinary. Norman Foster, in conversation with the editor, 2012

1. An aerial view of the remodelled Trafalgar Square (1999-2003). Dominated by Nelson's Column, the square is lined by fine buildings, including the National Gallery to the north. Yet, despite its grandeur, by the mid-1990s it had become choked by traffic, the central area visited only by those willing to risk life and limb. Proposals were developed as part of the Central London Masterplan. The scheme reflects a balancing act between the needs of traffic and pedestrians, the ceremonial and the everyday, the old and the new. Many of the changes are subtle. The big moves were to close the northern side of the square to traffic and to create a broad terrace in front of the National Gallery, linked via a new flight of steps to the body of the square. A once hostile urban environment has been restored as a truly civic space.

The smaller light-wells were covered with translucent PTFE 'pillows' and turned into interior spaces that might benefit from large scale and natural light, such as cafeterias and lounges. The changes in the offices were more subtle – new lighting, for example, that emphasises the profile of the long, barrel-vaulted corridors – and in almost every instance the details of the original building are not supplanted by Foster's interventions but enhanced by them. Security considerations prevented the firm from carrying out one of the most appealing parts of its plan, which was to turn the round central courtyard into public space and a pedestrian passageway connecting Parliament Square to the Foreign and Commonwealth Office to the north. However, Foster did manage to replace the tarmac surface of the court with elegant paving stones, which give the courtyard the air of a tiny, hidden European piazza, its new beauty making its isolation from the public all the more saddening.

The success of the renovation of the Treasury underscores the extent to which the Foster office seems comfortable deferring to older architecture, invariably accepting it as a starting point and frequently allowing existing structures, rather than any new element, to stand as the predominant visual image of a project. That is certainly the case with the renovation of Trafalgar Square, which Foster + Partners reorganised significantly, re-directing traffic, closing the street that ran in front of the National Gallery, extending a new pedestrian island at the south end and cutting a wide staircase through the balustrade at the northern end.

The result is not Trafalgar Square changed so much as Trafalgar Square realised: made finally into a square that is attractive to enter, appealing to linger in, and inviting to saunter across, rather than just an unapproachable podium for Nelson's Column or an austere front yard for the National Gallery. Trafalgar Square is now woven far more gracefully into the urban fabric of the city. But for all the changes in the way it works, it seems visually almost the same. This and the Treasury demonstrate one aspect of Foster's work that is surely the least known, given the self-assuredness that underscores so much of the architecture: a willingness in some circumstances to be so discreet as to barely leave a mark.

Collectively, Foster's work has had a different and more subtle impact on London than its most famous buildings would suggest.

At its best, this is discretion being the better part of architectural valour, since the rationale that underlies such understatement is not hesitation or timidity but the recognition that sometimes existing pieces of architecture possess iconic status that genuinely cannot be improved upon, and that there is no architectural benefit in trying to do so. The Treasury and Trafalgar Square might be made better, in other words, but their iconic status cannot, and so the challenge is to fix them without significantly changing the image they project.

It is a view that isn't really, in the end, as inconsistent with the rest of Foster's work as it might appear, since all of the firm's work is based on the belief that architecture emerges less from a theoretical construct than from a set of problems to be solved, and a set of conditions to be met. Often enough, and particularly in the case of protected historical buildings, the problem is defined from the beginning as determining how to make significant change almost invisible. But it is part of the ethos of Foster + Partners that the firm knows the difference between problems with older buildings that are solved by understatement, as at the Treasury, and problems that are solved by bold gestures, as at the British Museum. If the best solution to a problem is merely to tweak what is already there, then Foster tweaks with gusto.

1

Our approach to urban design is manifested in London, where we have a large body of work – both realised and unbuilt schemes – that dates back to the earliest days of the practice. It ranges across the spectrum, from masterplans, transport interchanges and a bridge, to office buildings and museums. Despite the diversity of that work, there is a strong common thread. In each of the projects there is an emphasis on the social dimension and the recognition that an individual building can work to enhance its broader urban context. Norman Foster, in conversation with the editor, 2012

A good city should comprise mostly subtle and modest interventions, combined with a select number of imposing architectural statements. Perhaps the emphasis for London as we look to the future, therefore, should be about upgrading and improving the quality of the infrastructure to enhance the human experience, rather than the grand-statement design. Spencer de Grey, speech at the Forum for the Built Environment, London, 28 November 2008

Structures like the Swiss Re tower at 30 St Mary Axe (the 'Gherkin'), the London City Hall and the Millennium Bridge define the firm in the minds of many, certainly so far as its work in London is concerned. But Foster's oeuvre in the practice's home city suggests that these memorable shapes are the exception, not the rule, and that collectively the work has had a more subtle impact on London than the iconic buildings would suggest. Over the last two decades, Foster + Partners has completed a number of buildings in the City of London as well as on the South Bank and elsewhere that manage to combine the finesse characteristic of the firm with a committed, not to say generous, degree of contextualism. They are hardly anonymous structures, but in each case they are deferential to a broader urban fabric, and even the largest of them can fairly be called background buildings.

These London buildings vary considerably in size, materials, shape and overall configuration; though none departs from the firm's Modernist vocabulary, there is a wide range of volumes, skins, and public open space, generally in response to the existing context. Some of the buildings, such as 10 Gresham Street and 50 Finsbury Square, occupy relatively conventional sites and fit quietly into the streetscape, distinguishable from their neighbours more by a refinement of detail and an overall sleekness than anything else. The same might be said of the three-part tower at 51 Lime Street, the London headquarters of Willis, the firm formerly known as Willis, Faber & Dumas, whose 1975 building in Ipswich probably did more than any other single project to establish Foster as an architect of international note.

The differences between the Ipswich building and the London one are considerable. Where Ipswich is an elegant, shimmering object of glass, seemingly weightless and looking, at first glance, as if it had come from another world, 51 Lime Street is rooted firmly in the City of London site, and the design takes its cues from what is around it. The building shows its deference as much by means of its stepped-down profile as its footprint, since the lower section of the tower is placed so as to avoid crowding the building's immediate neighbour to the west, Richard Rogers' celebrated 1986 tower for Lloyd's of London, as well as to keep vistas open to Foster's own 30 St Mary Axe to the north. At the eastern end of the site, distinct from the tower, there is a ten-storey block designed to match the scale of the smaller buildings on Fenchurch Avenue.

It would be a mistake, however, to think of these buildings as opposites, of London as representing compromise and Ipswich as standing for the ideal. Much of the importance of Ipswich comes from its footprint, and the way the subtle curves of the plan relate closely to the unusually shaped site; in its way, the earlier building is every bit as site-specific as 51 Lime Street; and Lime Street, for its part, is far less a conventional developer's building than an exceptionally inventive response to a highly complex and contradictory context – one might even call it a mature response to a context that thirty years ago might have frustrated Foster. As much as anything else, the evolution from Ipswich to Lime Street is a progression from relatively simple solutions to more intricate and internally complex ones, a quest to acknowledge and embrace a broader set of contextual influences without sacrificing the elegance and inventiveness that the practice has always sought.

2. Located in the heart of the City of London, 51 Lime Street (2003-2007) is a high-rise project that interacts strongly with the traditional grain of the city at street level. A new pedestrian route has been created through the site – in the spirit of the City's courts and alleyways – and café and restaurant seating helps to animate the space.

3. Bishops Square (2001-2005) completes the regeneration of the historically important Spitalfields neighbourhood, which bridges the City and the East End, and provides a major new public space for London – larger than the piazza at Covent Garden. Comprising offices, retail space, apartments, community facilities, cafés and restaurants alongside a new covered market area, the scheme has transformed a former wholesale fruit and vegetable market into a thriving urban quarter.

2

3

What's evolved through the history of the practice in looking at towers in particular – offices in the sky – is how taller structures can be integrated into existing cities. They're all studies in how one can integrate the vertical, usually private world of a tower, with the horizontal public world of the city. That, for us, is a fascination and over the years we've become increasingly more aware of that interface between people and the building. David Nelson, in conversation with the editor, 2012

Londoners have taken to the Foster tower because it is shapely and recognisable from a distance – whether seen from the heights of Camberwell or the flat expanse of the East End – and sensational at close range, a defining landmark. But the glamour of the project should not obscure its genuine radicalism. The inherently conservative City of London has not seen innovation on this level since the completion of Lloyd's nearly two decades ago. It is only hoped that 30 St Mary Axe has established a measure of quality for new City buildings that will inspire others. Kenneth Powell, *The Architects' Journal*, 25 November 2004

As a building, Swiss Re embodies many of the core values that we as a practice have championed for more than forty years. It sets out to humanise the workplace, to conserve energy, to democratise the way people communicate within a building, and to respond positively and sensitively to the urban realm. At ground level it is much more than just an office building. There are shops and a café to serve the local working community, and the building is set within a new public piazza – an urban shortcut or a place to just sit and relax. Norman Foster, in conversation with the editor, 2012

1. One of a series of townscape sketches that Norman Foster made to study the urban impact of the Swiss Re building at 30 St Mary Axe. The 'City within a city' has always been full of surprises, as he observes.

2. The forty-one storey Swiss Re Headquarters (1997-2004). London's first ecological tall building and an instantly recognisable addition to the skyline of the City. Conceptually, the tower develops ideas explored in the Climatroffice (1971), a theoretical project with Buckminster Fuller, its energy-conscious enclosure resolving walls and roof into a fluid, triangulated skin.

If a site facing Lloyd's on one side and the dense, old cityscape of Fenchurch Avenue on the other offers one kind of contradiction, Spitalfields, the site of Foster's Bishops Square project, offers another. An East London neighbourhood on the edge of the City toward which the City was inevitably marching, Spitalfields contains, in addition to blocks of venerable townhouses, a well-known public market and one of the greatest ecclesiastical landmarks of London: Christ Church Spitalfields by Nicholas Hawksmoor, dating from 1729. The challenge was to find a way to accommodate the City's growth without either destroying Spitalfields or turning it into an ersatz version of an old London quarter. The solution here was to create a office building in the form of four long fingers, ranging from five to eleven storeys in height, set parallel to each other with atria and gardens in between. The fingers step down in response to the historic section of Spitalfields, and they have elaborate roof gardens. The project includes significant new public spaces, including pedestrian walkways to enhance the connection to the neighbourhood's older streets, and it is tied into a restored Spitalfields Market.

As the Treasury building did almost a century earlier, Bishops Square manages to include an enormous amount of square footage without either rising too high or interrupting the street pattern of the district, and functions as a kind of horizontal skyscraper, complete with both internal and external gardens.

Great size and demanding contemporary programmes, in other words, do not have to mean overwhelming scale and violent intrusion. Bishops Square's most important contribution, however, is an even more general one: a reminder that Modernism need not be inconsistent with urbanism, and that the Modernist aesthetic can be used to enhance rather than disrupt traditional urban patterns.

Bishops Square was completed in 2005. A decade earlier, in 1992, the office began work on another large-scale office project intended to integrate into the streetscape of the City rather than challenge it – Tower Place, adjacent to the Tower of London. Tower Place replaces an earlier project of the same name but significantly different form: a sixteen-storey tower that blocked views of St Paul's Cathedral, the Tower of London, the Monument and Greenwich. Foster's Tower Place is much lower – a pair of seven-storey buildings with slightly curved rooflines – and more thoughtful in plan, opening up not only the main view corridors but also creating a new public piazza in front of All Hallows' Church.

The buildings are triangular in plan, and they contain one striking innovation, a huge, glass-roofed atrium that is on the outside of the buildings rather than the inside. The atrium, like the buildings, is triangular in shape, and two of its walls are exterior walls of the office buildings. To make the third side, tension cables are stretched between the two buildings and a glass curtain wall hung from them, raised just high enough to walk beneath. It is a striking space that relates well to the street pattern around it, though its abstract geometry means that its relationship to the City perhaps lacks the subtlety of Bishops Square. Compared with the development it replaced, however, it is an urbanistic triumph.

Moor House, a nineteen-storey office tower completed in 2005, is another replacement of a roundly disliked post-war office building, although in this case Foster responded to context with a more striking geometry still, a building that forms a quarter arc in both plan and section. That could seem to be more of a parlour trick than a considered architectural solution, since it is difficult to think of such a form being seen as contextual anywhere other than, perhaps, in a sculpture garden by Ellsworth Kelly.

The "City within a city" has always been full of surprises!

1

2

The city of the future has to be sustainable. Whether it is predominantly high-rise or of mixed height, it will be high density with a high quality of urban lifestyle and a wide variety of choices. In this approach, buildings and infrastructure will be more closely integrated. Increased mobility between cities is also likely to continue and drive the present trend toward higher-quality public transport: itself a key to sustainability. Norman Foster, in conversation with the editor, 2012

Still, this eye-catching shape is not without its logic, since the context of Moor House is defined largely by ungainly post-war towers – buildings that it would have made little sense to echo – and a more neutral form would have been overwhelmed by the harshness of that context. The larger post-war buildings are mainly to the south and west of Moor House, however, and there are more remnants of the City's older urban fabric to the east, which is a further justification for the shape, since the building's taller side is on the west, rising vertically to face the towers, while the side that curves downward faces east, diminishing in scale to meet its neighbours.

30 St Mary Axe needs to be seen not in isolation, but in conjunction with Foster's other buildings in the City of London, since together they constitute foreground and background.

Moor House is positively conventional, of course, compared with 30 St Mary Axe, which since its completion in 2004 has been one of the best-known skyscrapers in the world, and surely Foster's most celebrated tower since the Hongkong and Shanghai Bank nearly two decades earlier. The two are sharply different – the Hong Kong building a powerful and brilliantly fresh expression of structure raised to monumental grandeur; London a smooth and instantly recognisable shape, circular in plan and gently bowing out as it rises. No one could sum up the Hongkong Bank building in simple terms, but the entire world was calling 30 St Mary Axe 'the Gherkin' before it was even finished.

It is not surprising, therefore, that there is a certain temptation to think of Hong Kong as a rich and complex solution, and of London as a more rhetorical one, paralleling the view that the Willis, Faber & Dumas building in Ipswich offered a degree of both intellectual and aesthetic promise that was not fulfilled by its admittedly more commercial descendant in London.

However, the argument is no more valid in this case than it was with the Willis structures, not only because there is far more going on at St Mary Axe than the simple shape would suggest, particularly in the realm of the building's response to environmental issues, but also because the form of the London building, unlike that of its predecessor in Hong Kong, truly can be said to play a key role in the wider urban context.

The 30 St Mary Axe tower might be thought of as the campanile of the City of London, the spire of its commercial age. As such, its form needs to be understood not in isolation, but in conjunction with Foster's other buildings in the City of London, since together they constitute foreground and background. The profile of the City was once determined by the steeples of Christopher Wren's churches, the Monument to the Great Fire, St Paul's Cathedral and the Tower of London. As the commercial buildings rose ever higher in the twentieth century, their boxy forms managed to block these classic elements without offering anything new of comparable symbolic power. Until 30 St Mary Axe, then, there was no modern skyline to give the City a real identity above street level; even Richard Rogers' building for Lloyd's, for all its importance, failed to establish itself as a true symbol of the City.

3. Moor House (1997-2005) replaces a building completed in 1960 as the first of a series of office slabs that constituted the post-war reconstruction of London Wall. The challenge was to restore the traditional life of the City at street level and create a building that would mediate between the harsh, rectilinear geometry of London Wall and the more varied grain of the townscape to the south and east.

4. City Hall (1998-2002) houses the chamber for the London Assembly and the offices of the mayor and staff of the Greater London Authority. It forms the focal point of the More London development, a new working community on the South Bank next to Tower Bridge. More London integrates a mix of uses within a new network of streets and public spaces that forge links between the activity of the waterfront and the residential community of Bermondsey.

3

4

1. Sketch study of the Swiss Re building by Norman Foster. Atria formed between the radiating fingers of each floor link vertically and spiral up the building. These spaces are a natural social focus and function as the building's 'lungs', distributing fresh air drawn in through opening panels in the facade. This system reduces the tower's reliance on air conditioning and, together with other sustainable measures, means that it consumes only half the energy of a conventionally air-conditioned tower.

2. At fifty-three storeys, the Commerzbank Headquarters (1991-1997) explores the nature of the office environment, developing new ideas for its ecology and working patterns. Central to this concept is a reliance on natural systems of lighting and ventilation. Winter gardens spiral up around a central atrium to become the visual and social focus for four-storey, village-like office clusters.

And while it may seem odd to consider the 'Gherkin' to be contextual, its uniqueness underscores Foster's recognition that this kind of formal gesture only makes sense once, and thus ties this foreground building inevitably to its background neighbours, both those designed by the practice and those of other architects. Seen from all over the neighbourhood, 30 St Mary Axe serves as an orienting device as well as a symbol. And the open space its tapered form yields at ground level provides welcome public area of a sort that makes great sense once or twice in a neighbourhood, but if done constantly would destroy the streetscape.

It works here to a large degree because the street walls that face 30 St Mary Axe are tightly defined, successfully creating a sense of enclosure and allowing Foster's building to indulge in what might be called counterintuitive contextualism, breaking away from the street and away from conventional response to context only to reinforce the power of the street, and the value of the overall context. The paradox here – using an element that doesn't appear to fit as a way of strengthening the overall cohesion of a district – is the sort of reverse move that an architect can only get away with on rare occasions. Part of Foster's gift lies in knowing just when that occasion should be.

The office space within the tower is distinctive not only for its shape, but for the absence of columns, since structural support is provided by diagonal bracing behind the glass facade. The bracing creates lines that appear to spiral up the building; they also establish a pattern that begins to give the unusual shape a degree of scale. It all culminates in a remarkable space at the top, which is in effect a glass dome, unencumbered by columns or even mechanical equipment, which is set below. The triangular pattern becomes the only enclosure, around and above, framing extraordinary views in every direction. But for all the emotional impact of the building's crown, which is occupied by a private restaurant-club, the most significant element of the interior is surely the series of atrium gardens that are set at the perimeter of each floor, spiralling upwards behind the facade.

The gardens develop ideas the practice began to study long ago with Buckminster Fuller and experimented with in the Commerzbank Tower in Frankfurt and refined further in the tower for the Jiushi Corporation in Shanghai. Here, however, their connection into a spiral moving around the building brings the concept to a new level of accord with the building's overall aesthetic. The gardens serve both as social spaces and as distributors of fresh air, reducing the load on the building's air-conditioning system. As atria joining together groups of floors, they also reduce the vertical isolation that is common in skyscrapers, as well as weaving a green presence all the way through the tower.

The foreground-background relationship between 30 St Mary Axe and Foster's other, lower buildings around the City of London is replicated across the Thames, where City Hall on the riverfront serves the same iconic function and a series of other buildings known as More London Riverside function as background. City Hall, a rounded glass building that curves in both plan and section, has a highly complex shape that looks simple from a distance – something like an egg tilted to one side – and is easily recognizable as a symbol of the city's new local government. Within, its debating chamber is surrounded by a spiral ramp and is open to views of the river, creating as spectacular a governmental room as any city has built for its business in a long time.

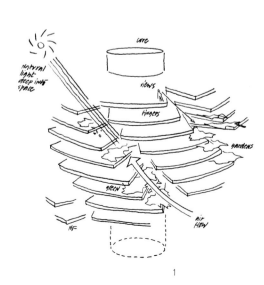

1

2

Not all of the firm's work, of course, connects to the issues of streetscape, history and urban context that have become part and parcel of its work in London. But the willingness to create new models is an aspect of the Foster + Partners approach that can fairly be said to extend to all realms of the practice's output. Nowhere is it more striking than in three building types – airports, bridges and sports stadiums – that are quite different indeed from commercial buildings in a dense urban quarter. In the last few years the office has completed the largest airport terminal in the world, in Beijing; one of the most spectacular bridges ever built, over the gorge of the River Tarn in southern France; and one of the most expansive sports facilities anywhere, the stadium at Wembley. Each is notable not only for the success with which it brings the Foster aesthetic to a building type that has historically been resistant to high architectural ambition, but also for the extent to which it involves a fundamental rethinking of the standard model.

Beijing Airport is a descendant of Chek Lap Kok airport in Hong Kong, itself based in part on the terminal for Stansted Airport north-east of London. Architects who try to reinvent the airport usually fail, and most tend not to try, instead limiting themselves to adding a greater degree of visual sophistication or making some personal mark on the conventional airport layout. Foster, however, beginning with Stansted, has managed to rethink the airport and make it work. At Beijing he eliminated the long concourse fingers that mark most airports, stretching gates out for distances that can approach half a mile, and laid out the airport as a pair of triangles whose points face each other and are connected by a long line.

The sides of both triangles curve inwards and their roofs swell upwards in a generous swoop. One triangle is the main terminal, and it has the sensuous curves of a sloop, rising gradually to monumental scale; the other contains international gates, and it offers arriving passengers as well as departing ones a chance to experience the airport's triumphant architectural space.

Beginning with Stansted, Foster has managed to rethink the airport and make it work.

The triangular plans function like funnels at either end, sending departing passengers in the landside terminal wing and those arriving in the airside wing toward the central spine of the building, where they pass through security or passport control. At every juncture the entire building is organised into a pattern that is clear enough so that passengers instinctively know where they need to go. While the size of the programme prevents the building from having the concise organisation or intimacy of an older airport, there is never a sense that it sprawls endlessly, as do so many airports, new and old. It is vast, but tight. The real achievement of this building is not just clarity, however, but exhilaration, a rare quality in air travel in the twenty-first century.

3. Millau Viaduct (1993-2004). Located in southern France, the bridge spans a gorge between two high plateaux to complete the motorway route from Paris to Barcelona. Bridges are often thought to belong to the realm of the engineer, but the architecture of infrastructure has a powerful impact on the environment and the viaduct illustrates how the architect has a role to play in the design of bridges, helping to resolve the relationship between function, technology and aesthetics in a graceful structural form.

4. The architecture of infrastructure in a different context: Beijing International Airport (2003-2008). The largest building in the world, it is capable of handling an estimated 50 million passengers per annum by 2020. Its design expands on the new airport paradigm created by Stansted and Chek Lap Kok, in which passenger experience, operational efficiency and sustainability are paramount.

3

4

1. A cutaway drawing of Wembley Stadium (1996-2007). The stadium's retractable roof is supported structurally by a soaring arch that rises 133 metres above the pitch. Floodlit at night, it is an apt symbol for the new stadium and a new London landmark.

In Beijing, as in Hong Kong, the tight plan comes at no cost to generosity of space, and there is also an unusual amount of natural light and wide-open views of the airfield, both of which add significantly to the sense of uplift. All of Foster's airports, Beijing most of all, stand as reminders that the concept of a monumental gateway to the city that offers sumptuous space and civic grandeur did not end with train stations, but can be achieved in the most modern, technologically advanced airport.

Beijing Airport is a product of basic logic, engineering skill, and an unusual degree of what can only be called Modernist lyricism. That combination surely marks the Millau Viaduct, a bridge structure of breathtaking beauty. It is quite different from the Millennium Bridge over the Thames: where London was a relatively modest pedestrian bridge, this is a vast, soaring roadway stretching for 2.5 kilometres. But in France as in London, structure and aesthetics are joined so closely that it is impossible to say where one ends and the other begins.

This is a very long bridge between two high plateaux, which also happens to span a relatively narrow river. Foster realised that the conventional solution, to build a structure that expressed a relationship to the river, would have a far greater visual impact in the landscape than a slender, masted structure that could span the entire valley at the level of the plateaux.

The result is an exceptionally elegant cable-stayed bridge with seven thin towers, carrying the road high – in some cases as much as 235 metres – above the ground level. It prances lightly over the landscape, quite literally a skyway, since the bridge deck is so elevated that it sits above the cloud line. Probably not since the Golden Gate Bridge in San Francisco has a bridge built in the midst of a dramatic natural landscape so enhanced its setting. As with the Golden Gate, it is now practically impossible to imagine the Gorges du Tarn without the bridge: here, man-made structure is not nature's adversary, but its partner.

Foster deals in juxtaposition, not violation, and however different his work may be visually from what is beside it, there is a harmonic balance.

A vast football stadium makes as many functional demands as an airport or a bridge, and would seem, at first glance, to offer as few opportunities for a freshness of approach. The dimensions of the pitch cannot be changed; the number of seats is more or less fixed, and the need to move tens of thousands of people around efficiently without bottlenecks dictates much of the design, just as the need to move aircraft around determines much of an airport's layout. With Wembley Stadium – one of the most celebrated sports venues in the world – there was the added challenge of history. The old stadium with its famous twin towers was revered, however dysfunctional it had become, and there were many who viewed the very notion of a new stadium with hostility.

Foster, working with HOK Sport and the Lobb Partnership as the World Stadium Team, produced a plan that ceded nothing to nostalgia, least of all the retention or replication of Wembley's towers. Instead, he offered a potent architectural alternative in the form of a vast, arched truss, soaring high over the stadium as both structural support for the partly retractable roof and iconic element on the skyline. The arch is both tough and nimble, an apt image for football, one might say. Rising to 133 metres, the arch is canted, which adds to its drama; and floodlit at night it is visible from across London – a steel rainbow arcing across the sky.

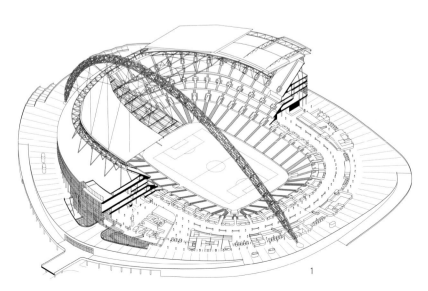

1

Wembley has enhanced the visibility of Foster + Partners not only across London, but around the world. Then again, the international impact of the firm at this point seems to be beyond question, with projects such as the Hearst Tower in New York, the Supreme Court in Singapore and the Deutsche Bank Place tower in Sydney assuring that the sun never sets on the Foster empire. The quantity of the firm's work is less of an achievement, however, than its consistency and commitment to innovation. Hearst, for example, is a tour de force of both structural inventiveness and stylistic juxtaposition, and it made for a particularly striking debut in New York, a city noted more for preaching about innovative architecture than for building it.

The tower is perched atop the Hearst Corporation's old headquarters, an essay in flamboyant, highly theatrical classicism by the architect Joseph Urban and completed in 1929. The six-storey corporate palazzo was intended as the base of a larger tower, which was never designed, and Urban's building is such a strong presence that until Foster came along it was difficult to imagine how it could be built upon unless an architect were to try to imitate Urban's quirky style, or retreat to an entirely neutral Modernist glass box.

Foster would never have considered the former, but he avoided the latter in favour of a building that meets Urban's showiness with some drama of its own in the form of a forty-storey glass and stainless-steel missile that all but shoots out of Urban's stone launching pad. The tower's most prominent feature is the geometric pattern of its structural frame, which the architect calls a 'diagrid': a diagonal grid of supporting trusses. The diagrid articulates the facade into a series of four-storey-high triangles and makes up much of the building's supporting structure. It does it with impressive economy, using 20 per cent less steel than a conventional post-and-beam skyscraper frame would require.

It is an engineering trick exploited for aesthetic pleasure. The triangles give the building a jubilantly jagged shape. Foster started with a box, then sliced off the corners and ran triangles up and down the sides, pulling them in and out – a gargantuan exercise in nip and tuck. The result resembles a many-faceted diamond. The corners of the shaft slant in and out as the tower rises, and the whole form shimmers.

The shaft would make an elegant tower on its own, but its energy comes from the way in which it relates to Urban's old building, which it manages somehow to violate and dignify at the same time. Foster has hollowed out the Urban structure, turning it into a vast atrium at the base of the new tower, making its interior like the nave of a cathedral, with several storeys of windows visible one atop the other. It is his most assertive juxtaposition of new and old by far. The old building is turned into something else altogether. But it is not discarded, any more than were the older sections of the Royal Academy or the British Museum. Instead, it is cajoled into a new existence, evincing how much the new depends on the old and vice versa and how much richer the cityscape can be when it does not deny complexity and inconsistency and the presence of the past, but embraces them.

Hearst, like so much of Foster + Partners' work, also demonstrates a commitment to structural innovation, a belief in the logic of planning, and a profound respect for the issues of sustainability. Most of all, however, it represents a determination to make of the Modernist aesthetic something ever new. That, in the end, is what distinguishes all of the work of the firm – the belief that Modernism is capable of continued reinvention, and that the Modernist aesthetic can still yield fresh paradigms for structures ranging from skyscrapers to airports, from sports stadiums to bridges. For Foster, Modernism is not a constant but, rather, an evolving language, a language within which new ideas can be expressed and new things made, bringing forth an architecture that can be as different from the modern buildings of the last century as those buildings were from the architecture of the nineteenth.

2. Hearst Tower (2000-2006) has quickly established itself as a landmark in a city where novelty is commonplace. Structurally, the tower has a highly efficient triangulated form which, with the corners cut back between the diagonals, creates a distinctive faceted silhouette.

2

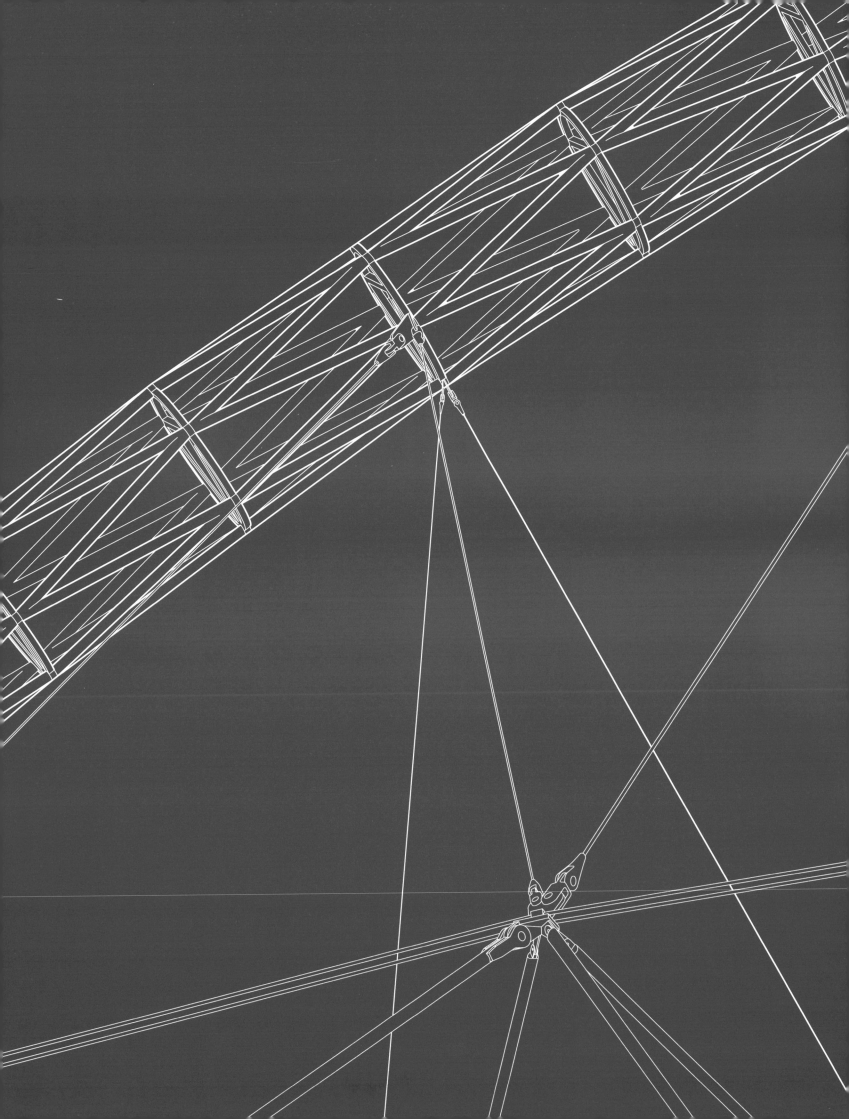

Wembley Stadium
London, England 1996–2007

Wembley is Britain's leading sports and entertainment venue. The challenge in reinventing it was to build on its heritage, yet create a stadium that would be memorable and special in its own right. With 90,000 seats, standing almost four times the height and covering twice the area of the old stadium, the new Wembley is the largest arena of its kind in the world. A retractable roof ensures that the spectator experience is always comfortable, the geometry of the seating bowl gives everyone an unobstructed view, and the seats are located as close to the pitch as possible to recreate the intimate atmosphere for which the old Wembley was famous. Floodlit at night, the arch that soars overhead has become a new landmark on London's skyline. Importantly, though it is ideal for football, the stadium has been 'future proofed', with the ability to host track and field athletics events to Olympic standard if required.

Norman Foster

Wembley has arisen with its great pavilions as a shrine of Empire: it has become the natural meeting-place for the peoples of the British nations in every corner of the globe. Every day sees an increase in the crowds of people from London, from all over these islands, from the Dominions and Colonies, and from foreign parts who flock through the gates, and for each section of visitors the Exhibition has its special lesson.
The Times, 24 May 1924

Left: An original pass to the British Empire Exhibition. The admission fee was just one shilling and sixpence. Right: The Duke and Duchess of York, later King George VI and Queen Elizabeth, in a cable car at the Wembley Exhibition, 1925.

Previous pages: The Red Arrows soar overhead before kick-off for the 2007 FA Cup Final.

1. Her Majesty Queen Mary is shown around the British Empire Exhibition on the opening day, 23 April 1924.

2. A visitors' map of the British Empire Exhibition. The Exhibition covered 87 hectares and was intended to showcase the best of industry, engineering and the arts from Britain and its 'Dominions and Colonies'.

1

As a venue for football and concerts, as a profitable commercial operation, but more especially in the popular imagination, the old Wembley Stadium held a place in world sport virtually unrivalled by any other venue. It was the one commission every stadium architect longed to secure. But it was also one that came heavily laden with issues and constraints. Glorified for its place in footballing history, it was itself the ultimate political football. So when it came to rebuilding Wembley Stadium, it was inevitable that Norman Foster and his colleagues would take on far more than a mere design brief.

From its first match in April 1923, when a crowd of 240,000 overwhelmed a stadium designed for half that number – famously requiring the efforts of a white police horse, Billy, to clear the pitch – the Empire Stadium as it was then, made headlines. Simply in its role as the venue for English football's annual showcase, the FA Cup Final, a match first contested in 1872 and today watched by a television audience of some 400 million, Wembley garnered for itself a unique aura, as an El Dorado of passion, escapism and symbol of national identity.

To the Cup Final must be added Wembley's hosting of the 1948 Olympics, the 1966 World Cup Final, the Live Aid concert of 1985, and the 1996 European Championships. Woven into this narrative may be added countless other historic moments. Thus in the iconography of twentieth-century Britain, the name Wembley transcended its locational identity, becoming, like those other London institutions, 'the City', 'the Palace' or 'the West End', as much an abstract notion as a physical entity.

Significantly, Wembley Stadium was always a neutral venue. Unlike the majority of countries where the national stadium hosts at least one football club, Wembley has never had a resident team. For most club supporters, therefore, a visit to the old Wembley was often a once-in-a-lifetime event.

For followers of the England team, Wembley represented the nation's fortress, while for overseas players it was the stadium in which they most aspired to play. As the legendary Brazilian, Pelé, commented in 1995: 'Wembley is the cathedral of football, it is the capital of football, and it is the heart of football.' But churches crumble, capitals fall and hearts grow weak, and in reality, in its final years the old Wembley had become a national embarrassment as a venue. Only its emblematic twin towers inspired any real affection.

Especially deflating was the stadium's setting. Originally parkland, the site had been laid out to host the 1924 Empire Exhibition, of which the stadium formed the centrepiece. In 1934 the stadium was joined by the wonderful Empire Pool (now the Wembley Arena). But otherwise, as suburbia rose up on its borders throughout the 1930s, and the exhibition halls were demolished, destroying the integrity of the original masterplan, the stadium itself was left isolated. Compared with the grandeur surrounding Rome's Olympic Stadium, or the magisterial cohesion of Munich's Olympiapark and stadium, Wembley appeared unplanned and unloved.

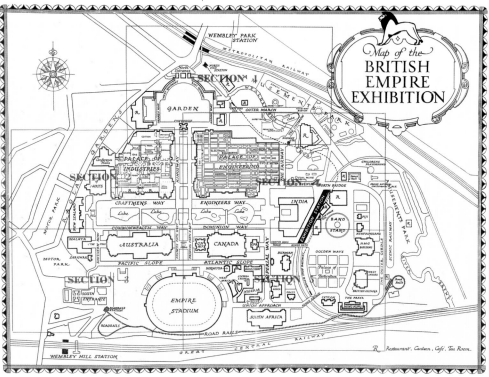

Map of the BRITISH EMPIRE EXHIBITION
2

Inside there was a mass of people and I realised I'd been separated from my father. I didn't feel frightened, though I didn't like being squashed … I was carried along by the crowd and then I remember a chap behind me shouting: 'There's a young lad here, let's give him a hand.' And someone else said: 'Pass him down to the front.' So they passed me over the heads until I found myself sitting on the grass by the touchline. The pitch was in front of me, but it was covered by a huge wave of people. You couldn't imagine how they could have played a game of football.
Denis Higham, who attended the 1923 Cup Final, aged eight, interviewed in *The Independent*, 18 May 2007

Left: The legendary 'White Horse' FA Cup Final of 1923 – the first to be held at Wembley. Some 200,000 fans crowded into a stadium designed to accommodate 126,500. When His Majesty King George V took his place in Wembley's royal box, three-quarters of the field was covered with fans. Here, mounted police – among them PC George Scorey on his white horse Billy – attempt to clear the pitch. Play commenced forty-five minutes late and Bolton Wanderers defeated West Ham United 2–0.

But most damaging of all to Wembley's image were its inadequacies as a spectator venue. Neither the original architects, John Simpson and Maxwell Ayrton, nor the engineer, Owen Williams, had any experience of stadium design. Consequently, for all its innovative use of reinforced concrete, the building suffered a number of basic flaws, not least appalling viewing standards for up to a quarter of its 126,500 capacity (most of which was standing), cramped concourses, and grossly inadequate toilet provision. Nor did successive remedial works ease these shortcomings. So the old Wembley Stadium was loved and hated, revered and reviled in almost equal measure.

From its inaugural match in April 1923 … Wembley garnered for itself a unique aura, as an El Dorado of passion, escapism and symbol of national identity.

No one doubted that it needed replacing. But with what, by whom, and how might this be achieved? In the end it took twelve years of planning, design and construction to unlock this conundrum, during which time Wembley's future fell subject to more detailed scrutiny than surely any other stadium in history. In the media Wembley became a national obsession, fuelled for the most part by commentators with pre-defined agendas and no real knowledge of large construction projects or stadium design. Consequently there are two quite separate, though parallel narratives attached to the emergence of the new stadium.

The first, if recounted in full, would occupy a book twice the size of this one. Criticism of the project flew in from every angle and on almost every aspect – its cost, location, ownership and operation, contractual arrangements and funding.

Arising from this, three parliamentary reports and two independent consultants' reports were commissioned. At least six major figures associated with the project from various public and private bodies either resigned or were ousted. It can also be argued that the careers of two government ministers suffered as a result of their interventions. (The English, it should be noted, have a long tradition of denigrating major building projects, going back to St Paul's Cathedral, the Houses of Parliament and more recently the Millennium Dome. All three, of course, are now popularly regarded as iconic structures.)

Then there is a second possible narrative. Almost inevitably in the prevailing atmosphere of point-scoring, this aspect of the development received virtually no coverage until the building was completed. But it is the one that concerns us here, and is the story of the new stadium's design. Not that this tale is any less complex.

3. An aerial view of the Empire Stadium, as it was then known, with the Australian Pavilion in the foreground.

4. The pavilions for the British Empire Exhibition, nearing completion. Behind the Indian Pavilion, from left to right, are those of Canadian Pacific, Canada and Australia. The stadium occupied the highest part of the site.

3

4

Left: A poster for the 1948 Olympic Games. The hands of the Big Ben point to 4 o'clock, the time at which the opening of the Games was planned. The statue in the foreground is Discobolus, the discus thrower from Ancient Greece. Despite the fear of Britain's rationed athletes appearing as 'scarecrows in running shoes', the Games proved a welcome distraction from post-war austerity. Right: The cover of the official programme for the Olympic athletics events, 7 August 1948.

1

1. Fanny Blankers-Koen of The Netherlands – nicknamed the 'Flying Housewife' – takes the last flight of hurdles to win the 80-metre race in a world record time of 11.2 seconds. The mother of two, who listed 'housework' among her hobbies, became a favourite figure of the 1948 Olympic Games.

2. An aerial view of the men's 100-metre final won by Harrison Dillard from the USA. Inspired by Jesse Owens, Dillard is the only American male to have won Olympic titles in both sprinting and hurdling to date.

2

Almost since its opening in 1923 architects and engineers had puzzled over strategies to improve Wembley Stadium. But as the building's fabric deteriorated, and as the commercial and social role of stadiums changed so radically from the 1970s onwards, these efforts took on a greater urgency. Two practices with stadium experience tried their hand in the early 1990s, the Lobb Partnership and Arup Associates. Each incorporated into their speculative designs the stadium's twin towers, on the assumption that the Grade II-listed structures were inviolable. Each assumed that the stadium and its surroundings – totalling some 70 acres – would remain in single ownership, if not necessarily in the hands of long-term owners Wembley plc.

However, neither scheme left the drawing board. The football industry had yet to gain the riches it would later accrue from television and sponsorship. Equally, since the abolition of the Greater London Council in 1986, there existed within the capital no single administrative body that might coordinate a redevelopment strategy for Wembley. The local planning authority, Brent, had certain powers but no access to funds.

In the meantime, Wembley was about to find its role as the de facto national stadium under threat from provincial rivals. After failed Olympic bids by Birmingham (in 1986) and twice by Manchester (in 1990 and 1993), Britain's sporting bodies agreed that if, in future, a British city was going to bid for an Olympiad, it would be London. For its part, Manchester concentrated on gaining the right to stage the 2002 Commonwealth Games. In the process of preparing that bid, Manchester not only secured public funding for an indoor arena, a velodrome and an aquatic centre, but its City Council argued that its proposed Commonwealth Games stadium should receive similar grant aid, and that, furthermore, it should become a replacement for Wembley.

Tired old Wembley, in leaderless London, thus had to face up to genuine competition for the first time in its history. But at least there was one possible source of funding to kick-start Wembley's renaissance – the National Lottery, introduced in November 1994.

When the Briton thinks of the Olympic Games he thinks of the Running … and Mrs Blankers-Koen from Holland, with her orange shorts and her fair floating hair, striding home time and again to victory, with all the irresistible surge of the great men sprinters, and stealing half their thunder.
The Times, 18 August 1948

Left: The thirty-year-old Fanny Blankers-Koen with three of her four gold medals for the 100- and 200-metre running finals and the 80-metre hurdles. Her training success was put down to a healthy diet, two hours training and three pints of milk daily.
Right: The cover of an Olympic Games special issue of *Picture Post*, August 1948.

3

4

5

Under the terms of the National Lottery Act, funds for sport-related projects are distributed via a government agency, Sport England, originally known as the Sports Council. However, its remit prevents the Council from inviting applications for lottery grants from any one bidder. Nor could Wembley plc apply, as commercial entities are barred from the lottery process. Thus, in April 1995 the Sports Council found another means of starting the bidding, by holding a competition for the creation of an 80,000-capacity National Stadium – one capable of staging three main sports: football, rugby league and athletics.

For stadium designers, the provision for athletics was by far the most problematic. Beyond Britain there are hundreds of stadiums featuring athletics tracks, with a pitch for football or rugby in the centre. But none is popular with spectators of football or rugby. Viewing distances are extended and intimacy is lost. Moreover, apart from the World Athletics Championships and the Olympics – events unlikely to be staged at any one venue more than once or twice in a fifty-year cycle, if at all – few athletics meetings attract significant attendances.

For that reason, only publicly subsidised stadiums can justify the retention of a track. Certainly in Britain the combination of track and field has long been regarded as anathema, as a result of which there are no athletics stadiums in the country with a capacity greater than 25,000, and none of those is shared by senior football or rugby clubs.

Nevertheless, the Sports Council insisted that if the proposed Lottery grant of £120 million was to be forthcoming – the largest sum for any sports-related project to date – there had to be provision for athletics. It conceded, however, that the minimum capacity for an athletics event could be 65,000, rather than 80,000, to allow greater flexibility. (The Council based this calculation on the experience of the Stade de France in Paris, where the lower tier of seats retracts 15 metres from football and rugby mode to reveal a track underneath. Although it was expensive, wasteful in terms of space, and resulted in compromised sightlines and viewing distances, the Sports Council's view was that if it could work for Paris then it could work for England's new stadium.)

3. Athletes parade around the Empire Stadium during the opening ceremony of the Olympic Games, 28 July 1948. The Games hosted a record-breaking 5,980 athletes and officials from sixty nations, though Germany and Japan were not invited. No new facilities were available for athletes; the men were housed in army barracks and the women in dormitories close to Wembley.

4. Runners leave the stadium at the start of the 1948 Olympic marathon. The race concluded in a heart-breaking finish for the leader, Étienne Gailly of Belgium, who failed in spectacular fashion half a lap short of gold.

5. 1,500-metre winner Henry Eriksson of Sweden is congratulated after a tough race on a wet and heavy track. Eriksson contributed to Sweden's impressive forty-five medal tally.

Left: The cover of the 1924 FA Cup Final programme and souvenir. It was the first all-ticket match FA Cup Final held at Wembley, lessons having been learned from the preceding year's mayhem.

1

1. An aerial view of Wembley in the late 1920s. As completed, the stadium accommodated 126,500 spectators, the great majority of them standing. Covered stands on the north and south sides of the stadium contained seats for 25,000.

2. The 1953 FA Cup Final – Blackpool versus Bolton Wanderers. Blackpool's Stan Mortensen hammers in his first goal on his way to a hat-trick. Blackpool beat Bolton Wanderers 4-3.

3. An aerial view of Wembley Stadium towards the end of its active life. Although by 1963 it was entirely roofed, and by 1990 had become an all-seat venue, with a maximum capacity of 78,000, accommodation standards were extremely tight and the facilities it provided were very poor.

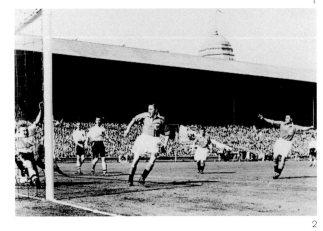

2

Shortly after the Sports Council's brief was announced, Huw Thomas of Foster + Parters called on Bob Heaver, Wembley Stadium's development director. Huw Thomas had been involved in the masterplanning of Manchester's Olympic bid, and argued that if Wembley was to have any success in outbidding Manchester for Lottery funding as the national stadium, its management would have to prepare a cogent plan.

The Foster team drew up a masterplan that embraced the Wembley site as a whole. Its aim was to create a vast new public open space around the stadium that borrowed from the Centre Beaubourg and its piazza in Paris, and the National Gallery and Trafalgar Square in London. 'What was it', asked Huw Thomas, 'about Beaubourg, for example, that allowed a building with ostensibly no ground floor interface to interact with a public space? Similarly, we looked at the way the Campo in Siena transforms itself by populating the edge of its square with temporary structures. This led us to the idea of the stadium concourse being part of both the stadium itself and the public space.'

Within this masterplan the stadium shifted northwards to create space around its southern perimeter (itself bound by a railway cutting, too wide to bridge economically). To the north a range of sport, music and leisure outlets were linked to the stadium via an elliptically shaped piazza on two levels. Further commercial developments between this part of the site and the existing mixed-use developments opposite Wembley Park Underground station flanked Olympic Way, the main approach to the stadium. The idea was to create a new urban complex, while also using commercial development to help fund the stadium's reconstruction.

Meanwhile, in addition to Wembley, four cities submitted proposals for the new national stadium: Birmingham, Bradford, Manchester and Sheffield. After three months of lobbying, in October 1995 the bids from Birmingham, Bradford and Sheffield were rejected by the Sports Council, leaving Wembley to fight it out with Manchester. Finally, in December 1996, Wembley was selected.

Any second now, it will all be over. Thirty seconds by our watch and the Germans are going down and they can hardly get up. It's all over I think. No, it's … And here comes Hurst, he's got … Some people are on the pitch they think it's all over. It is now … it's four! Kenneth Wolstenholme, BBC commentator, 30 July 1966
Left: Champions of the World! The cover of the *Evening Standard*, 1 August 1966; Bobby Moore holds the coveted Jules Rimet World Cup trophy aloft.

I remember craning my neck to watch players that looked like ants, a large pillar obscuring half the pitch, and queuing for ages to use a toilet that had me wishing I'd worn Wellington boots. Ethan Mroz-Davies, describing match day in the old stadium, *Sunday Mirror*, 20 May 2007

In truth, of course, the ultimate decision rested less with the Sports Council or with any pro-London lobbyists and more with the Football Association. For the FA, the Wembley tradition and the stadium's undoubted pulling power were powerful factors.

Wembley plc was now able to appoint its architects. Having established a strong working relationship with the practice, Foster + Partners was a clear favourite. But the practice had no stadium experience, and therefore opted to join forces with two other firms, HOK Sport and the Lobb Partnership.

Based in Kansas, HOK Sport (now known as Populous) are the world's most prolific stadium and arena designers. For their part the smaller London-based Lobb Partnership, led by Rod Sheard, had a solid track record in the UK. They were also working on Stadium Australia, the venue for the 2000 Olympic Games in Sydney and on Cardiff's Millennium Stadium, Britain's first venue with a retractable roof. Huw Thomas recalls a meeting at Foster's Battersea studio to settle this tripartite agreement. 'After we had all declared our various expertise and renown, Norman said that if we were that good, why not call ourselves the World Stadium Team. The name stuck and we put in a bid as WST.'

The strategy worked: WST was appointed in May 1998. From Foster + Partners the team comprised Norman Foster, Ken Shuttleworth and Huw Thomas, with Alistair Lenczner (a structural engineer recruited from Arup, where he had worked on the Stadio San Nicola in Bari), and Angus Campbell who, with Lenczner, would see the project through to completion. They would be joined by Mouzhan Majidi, who led the project after completing Chek Lap Kok airport in Hong Kong.

From HOK's office in Kansas City David Manica was brought in to work on the design of the seating bowl, while from Lobb, in addition to Rod Sheard, Ben Vickery took a lead role. Appointed at the same time were structural engineers Mott MacDonald and Connell Wagner, and Stephen Morley from Modus Consulting Engineers, who had worked with Lobb on several UK stadiums.

3

For nearly eighty years the old Wembley Stadium was the premier sports venue in Britain. The new stadium builds and expands upon that rich heritage. It has huge presence – it has become *the* place to experience the passion and magic in football, sports and music.
Norman Foster

4

4. Geoff Hurst is ecstatic after scoring the contentious third goal during the World Cup Final, 1966. The Russian linesman famously gave the goal allowing England to go on to win 4-2 in extra time.

Wembley Stadium is sacred to football fans around the world. It is the major soccer venue in Britain. Bringing a major social focus like this up to modern international standards requires a radical approach, both architecturally and strategically in terms of urban design, transport connections and so on. We began by looking at the surrounding public spaces, the railway and Underground connections – the connective tissue if you like – that allow a stadium on this scale to be fully integrated into the life of the city. Norman Foster, lecture at the Madrid Conference on Urban Regeneration, 24 October 1996

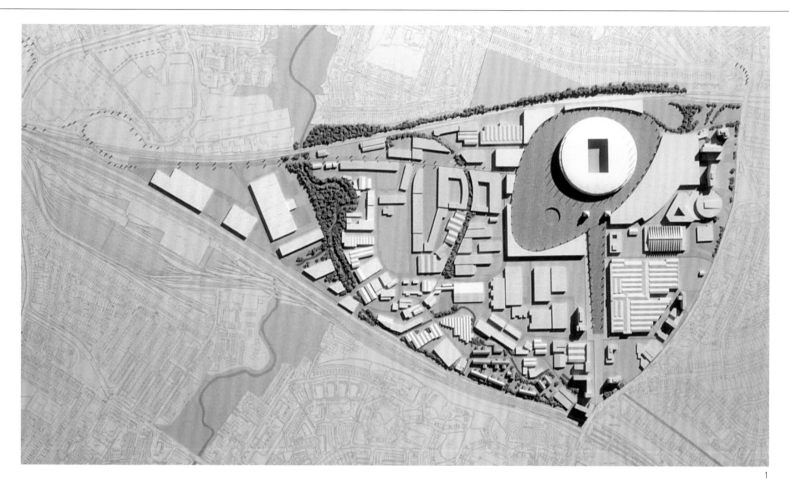

1

1. The first masterplanning model of the stadium and its surroundings, dating from 1996. These proposals were never adopted. In 1999 the English National Stadium Development Company (ENSDC) took formal possession of the stadium and 24 acres of adjacent land, the purchase price being £106 million. The remaining land around the stadium, including the Wembley Arena and large areas of car parking, was on offer for £25 million, but the FA declined to bid for it – a fact now viewed as a strategic error.

However, while all seemed settled on the design front, in the corridors of power there were mighty stirrings. Because Lottery funds could not be given to Wembley plc (a commercial entity), a non-profit body called the English National Stadium Trust had been established to oversee the design and construction of the stadium. The plan was for the Trust to hire Wembley plc to manage the stadium on its behalf on a twenty-year lease. But as the Trust struggled to find an acceptable mechanism for this arrangement, only weeks after WST's appointment, in July 1998 an extraordinary turn of events transformed the situation. The FA, driven by one of the highest-profile figures in English football, the then Chelsea chairman Ken Bates, announced its intention to buy the stadium outright.

Bates' reasoning was that since football was providing most of the events it should take the lion's share of the profits. (It should be noted that the FA's previous deals with Wembley plc had been absurdly weighted in Wembley's favour.) The FA formed a subsidiary, Wembley National Stadium Limited (WNSL), to build and run the new stadium, with the English National Stadium Trust being given a place on WNSL's board to safeguard the public interest. It was a remarkable and quite unexpected coup. With Wembley Stadium firmly in football's hands – purchased for £106 million in March 1999 – Bates drove forward his vision of how a modern stadium should be planned and financed.

In a match played in the driving rain, England failed to rise to the occasion ... it was a miserable end to seventy-seven years of magical memories.
Glen Isherwood, *Wembley – The Complete Record 1923-2000*, 2001
Left: Bedraggled fans walk along Olympic Way towards the stadium for the England versus Germany match, 7 October 2000.
Right: Germany, Wembley's most successful foreign team, inflicts a final 1-0 defeat on England at the old stadium in a World Cup qualifier, 2000. It was the final competitive game played at Wembley before the old stadium closed.

2

3

2. A new Wembley Stadium, as first envisaged by the Foster team in 1995. This scheme retained the twin towers as a gateway to an extended stadium piazza leading to an arena with a cable net structure. The principal approach was from the north, with new facilities accommodated on land to be acquired behind the old stadium. This would have required a significantly larger site than was ultimately available.

3. The World Stadium Team's first design for the new Wembley Stadium, presented publicly in 1999, was for a masted structure that retained the old stadium's east-west axis. It was obvious to the design team that retaining the twin towers for any reason other than sentiment was illogical and would have considerable cost implications.

At his own stadium at Stamford Bridge, Bates had masterminded the creation of an entirely novel form of development. Called Chelsea Village, this placed the stadium at the centre of a commercial hub that incorporated a hotel, restaurants, a health club, visitor attraction and banqueting suites – a facility that could be used 365 days a year, rather than simply on match days. Bates sought to repeat this formula at Wembley, expanding the stadium brief to include a 2,000-seat restaurant, a hotel and office space – in effect, a 'Wembley Village'.

Joined by a new WNSL chief executive, Bob Stubbs – who had first acted as a consultant to the Sports Council on the National Stadium project – Bates now dominated proceedings, with meetings held not at Wembley but at Chelsea.

Norman Foster quickly grew to respect Bates' no-nonsense approach, his capacity to absorb detail and his determination to make things happen in the face of all manner of obstacles. Bates also shared Foster's vision for a stadium that connected practically and economically with the surrounding urban infrastructure.

Once asked to nominate his favourite building, Norman Foster selected a Boeing 747. In one important respect, a modern stadium provides a similar business model. Although designed to hold the maximum number of economy passengers, the aircraft's economic viability depends on revenues from the passengers flying in business and first class. Reflecting this approach, Bates and Stubbs determined that Wembley would hold 90,000 seats, rather than 80,000, but of those, the entire middle tier (eventually consisting of 16,000 seats) would be devoted to executive boxes and club seats.

When we launched the scheme it was a masted structure. But I don't think I was alone in thinking that the image it presented wasn't special enough to Wembley. The Saturday after our press conference I was in Bayreuth. I am a passionate cyclist and it was while I was out cycling that day I decided we had to do better. That was how the arch began. Over the course of that weekend there was a frantic exchange of faxes with Alistair Lenczner in London. I sketched images relating to the symbolic quality of such an arch, and Alistair, an engineer, explored how it might be built. Remarkably, he anticipated its eventual height to within a metre. Norman Foster, in conversation with the editor, 2012

On the Monday after the first unveiling, and following a frantic weekend of faxed exchanges between the office and Norman in Germany, we decided to go ahead with the new design. But we first had to talk to other members of the design team and so we made a really quick, crude foam model, and took it to Rod Sheard at HOK. To his great credit, Rod wasn't upset that we were having second thoughts about the scheme and immediately supported the new design. Mouzhan Majidi, in conversation with the editor, 2012
Right: Norman Foster and Ken Bates present the arch scheme to FIFA, as part of England's bid for the 2006 World Cup.

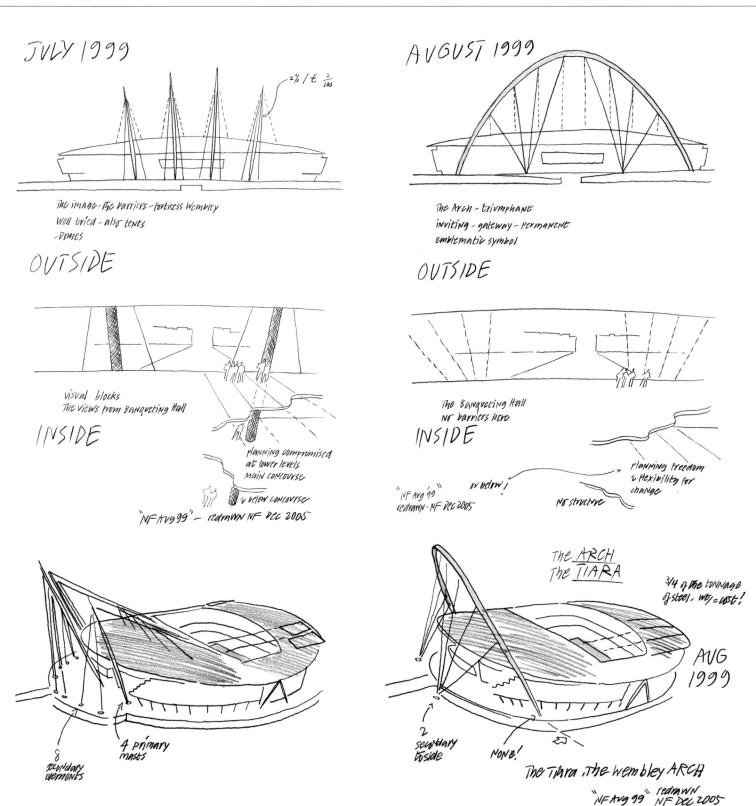

In this way, roughly two thirds of ticketing revenue would be earned from one-fifth of the total capacity. (The 747 analogy would later be extended to the stadium toilets, whose numbers are provided in the same, if not a higher ratio than on a passenger jet.)

A further key design issue concerned the retention or otherwise of the stadium's twin towers. The old stadium was originally configured with terraces for mostly standing spectators; only a small proportion were seated. Over the years this ratio changed. Conversion to an all-seated configuration in 1990 resulted in a drop in capacity to 80,000, but depended on extremely narrow seat tread depths of 640mm, and below average seat widths of 410mm. By the early 1990s the standard was for tread depths of 760mm and seat widths of 500mm. For Wembley, based on the experience of Stadium Australia, the design team opted for still more generous dimensions of 800mm and 500mm respectively, thereby allowing each spectator 30 per cent more room than in the old stadium. Crucially, this decision extended the new stadium's footprint considerably – to 300 metres east to west, and 280 metres north to south – on what was already a confined site. As there was no room on the southern flank of the site (bound as it is by the railway cutting), that meant expansion could only take place on the northern side; but that was where the towers stood.

Throughout 1999 speculation mounted as to the towers' fate. As listed structures, demolition required consent from English Heritage. But what if the towers could somehow be moved and incorporated within the new design? Rallying to the cause, one engineer proposed sliding the towers on platforms to another part of the site. Another option was to jack them on steel frames so that they might be incorporated into the new stadium structure (which would otherwise dwarf the towers at their original height).

Significantly, English Heritage agreed with the design team that the presence of the towers would be an unnecessarily inhibiting factor. That said, it was incumbent on the team to come up with a similarly iconic feature to take the towers' place.

Another factor was the provision of an athletics track. Studies by Lobb concluded that the design solution adopted at the Stade de France, using retractable seating, wasted space and offered few benefits for spectators in either athletics or football mode. Instead, Rod Sheard suggested that if and when Wembley was ever to stage an athletics event, a temporary platform could be built over the pitch and the first few rows of seating, and an athletics track laid on top of it. Originally it was thought that this platform would need precast concrete supports, but in time the team came to favour a more lightweight and cost-effective steel-framed solution.

Whichever modular system might eventually emerge, the geometry would be the same. A temporary platform would allow the front row of lower tier seats, in football and rugby mode, to be placed within a more intimate range of 9-17 metres from the touchlines, compared with a range of 11-29 metres at Stade de France. Moreover, although a temporary platform would reduce the stadium's seating capacity from 90,000 in football mode to 72,000 in athletics mode, this was still above the 65,000 limit required by the Sports Council brief.

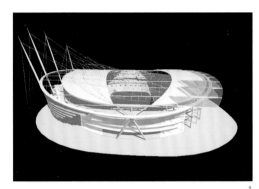

1

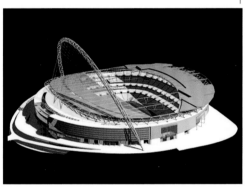

2

Opposite: Some of Norman Foster's more developed Wembley sketches in which he charts the evolution from a masted structure to an arch, and notes the advantages of the new structure.

1. A visualisation of the early, four-masted scheme.

2. This visualisation of the arched scheme shows the sliding roof panels on the south side, with the pitch oriented east-west.

3. Extracts from Norman Foster's early Wembley sketches. Here he begins to outline a landmark building, a triumphal arch and a strong symbol for Wembley.

3

The first thing that we as a team with the client asked ourselves was what constitutes the best of its kind in the world today? How can we create a new generation stadium? How can we learn from previous stadia? What form does that take? The project had to be conceptually robust and flexible enough to withstand many challenges – financial and political. Norman Foster, presentation at the Architecture Foundation, London, 22 May 2007

Ken Bates had based Wembley on the business plan at Stamford Bridge – a stadium with a hotel and office complex. However, at Wembley he didn't have a tenant and because WNSL was a new company it didn't have a credit rating so the banks pulled out and the project stopped in May 2001. Given his experience with stadiums in Australia, Multiplex chief executive John Roberts realised the importance of hospitality so brought in sports marketing company IMG. Together they got rid of the office and hotel and replaced them with more restaurants and boxes. On the basis of that, Roberts put a new business plan together and funding was secured. Angus Campbell, of Foster + Partners, in conversation with the editor, 2012

The American attitude towards stadiums was very important for us because it focused on their broader use. In contrast, at the Italia '90 World Cup, the stadiums were simply about football, not about 365 days a year use. It was important that everyone involved with the project understood what effect this change of the building typology was having. Huw Thomas, of Foster + Partners, in conversation with the editor, 2012

1. An early visualisation of the arch. Consisting of forty-one steel rings connected by spiralling tubular chords, the arch tapers at each end and is supported by concrete bases, founded on piles 35 metres deep. Inclined 68 degrees to the vertical, the arch is held in position by a series of cables tied to the main stadium structure.

Opposite: In these sketches, Norman Foster explores the arch's symbolism – 'glistening at night on the skyline, a jewel, a tiara' – and explains how the retractable roof allows sunlight to fall on the pitch: an essential factor in maintaining healthy grass.

This solution should have been welcomed. It was simple, low-tech, and took consideration of the fact that there might well be only one or two occasions in the building's entire life when such a platform would be needed. Yet the response from government and the athletics lobby could hardly have been more hostile. Ken Bates was accused of hijacking the stadium project for football's benefit (to which he responded that football was raising all the capital and providing all the guarantees). It was also claimed that Wembley would never be able to host an Olympics using the platform solution, because the minimum capacity demanded by the International Olympic Committee was not 65,000 but 75,000. For weeks these figures were contested (even among IOC members), but the original terms of the brief – in which no mention of Olympic capability had been mentioned – were a matter of record. (Interestingly, the IOC report on the 2012 Olympic requirements states that the minimum capacity requirement for athletics and ceremonies in the stadium is 60,000.)

Opponents of the platform scheme also tried to prove, without success, that sightlines for athletics at Wembley would be inferior to those for athletics at the Stade de France. Suddenly everyone was an expert, among them the newly appointed sports minister, Kate Hoey, whose first pronouncement was that, given the option, she would happily cancel the project altogether.

As the furore continued in the press, the first plans for the stadium were unveiled at Wembley on 29 July 1999. But it was the stadium's costs and the athletics issue which seemed to occupy most attention on the day. The design was barely commented on at all. Perhaps this was just as well, because even as the scheme was being unveiled, Norman Foster was harbouring second thoughts about a key element.

This concerned the support system for the stadium roof. A requirement of the brief was that the pitch had to consist of natural turf, rather than synthetic fibres (as has become common in North America), and that every effort should be made to guarantee the turf as much light and ventilation as possible so that pitch quality would not suffer as it has done at so many large modern stadiums with high-profile stands.

In order to achieve this, the design team came up with a system whereby sections of the roof over the south, east and west of the three-tier seating bowl are retractable, the moveable sections covering spectator areas only, not the entire pitch. To bear the load of the fixed northern side of the roof, the designers proposed erecting four 130-metre-high steel masts in front of the stadium's main facade, from which supporting cables would be suspended.

Not only did the arch suppress any lingering regrets about the loss of the twin towers, it also provided the new stadium with a powerful and instantly recognisable motif.

On the day of the unveiling very little was said about these masts, other than a comment by the England manager Kevin Keegan that they reminded him of the Stade de France. But within the design team there were almost immediate misgivings. Norman Foster recalled, 'My worry was that the mast structure was not in any way special to Wembley and in fact had a lot of associations with other building types – the circus tent, for example'. Mouzhan Majidi recalls, 'Norman was worried that the masts did not present a strong enough image. As a team we also had doubts about them from a structural standpoint. So it was that just a couple of days after the unveiling we were all sitting down trying to redesign it.'

The following weekend found Foster cycling near Bayreuth, where he had been attending the annual festival, and it was in the German countryside that the idea of a 'super arch' struck him. A rapid exchange of faxes ensued between Foster and Alistair Lenczner in London; Foster sending sketches, Lenczner working out how such a structure could be constructed and located on the tight site.

The stadium is dominated by Norman Foster's breathtaking 133-metre-high arch, a sight to leave the 38m of concrete that made up the old stadium's Twin Towers in the shade. At 315 metres long (three football pitches laid end to end), it is the longest single-span roof structure in the world, tall enough to roll the London Eye underneath and, at 7.4 metres in diameter, wide enough to carry a Channel Tunnel train.
The Mail on Sunday, 20 May 2007
Left: Lighting designer Claude Engle with an illuminated mock-up of the arch structure.

Sport is a huge phenomenon around the world. A big match like the FA Cup Final will have an international television audience of something like 450 million people. So it's not surprising that with numbers like these a lot of money flows into football – enough money to finance a building like Wembley. But if you're going to create a major new stadium it has got to have an image that people will recognise instantly when they tune in. That's what these buildings are about.
Rod Sheard, of HOK Sport, presentation at the Architecture Foundation, London, 22 May 2007

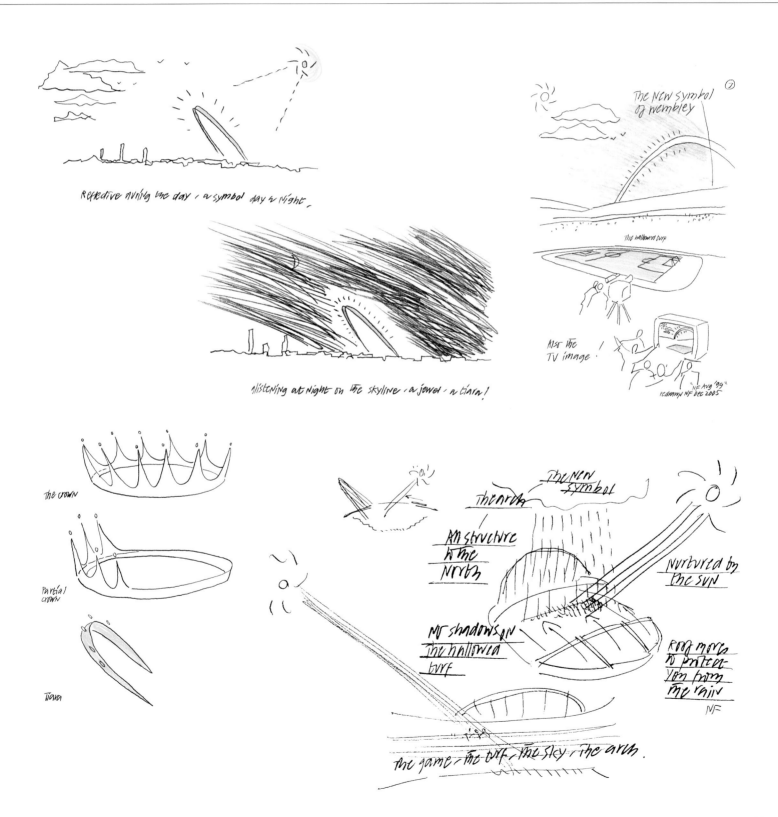

Around the time of the first presentation I had decided to increase the capacity from 80 to 90,000. Chris Smith asked me, 'why are you doing that?' And I said, 'because I can't get it up to 100,000' which is what I wanted. But I just wanted to make it bigger so that more ordinary punters could watch the game. You don't make more money on that last 10,000 – they have to be high in the air, so you have to widen the base of the stadium – but the extra capacity dramatically increases the feel and intensity of the place. Ken Bates in conversation with the editor, 2005

If you look at the size of the old twin towers at Wembley, which gave it its distinctive silhouette, you can see that they would have been dwarfed by the size of the new stadium's seating bowl. So even if we had kept them, they would have looked slightly ridiculous. In any case, I like to make the analogy that if you are buying a new Bentley, you wouldn't expect to have the mudguards and headlights of a 1920s model stuck on to it. Similarly, the old towers would have been out of place in front of the new stadium. Alistair Lenczner, of Foster + Partners, in conversation with the editor, 2012
Left: Alistair Lenczner with a model of the stadium.

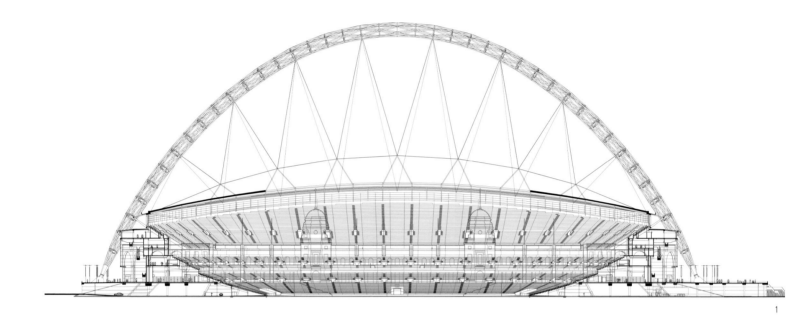

1

1. An east-west cross-section through the new stadium compared with an elevation of the old. Standing 133 metres high and spanning 315 metres, the arch is almost four times taller than the original twin towers. The longest single-span structure in the world, it is tall enough to roll the London Eye underneath and its 7.4-metre diameter structure is wide enough to carry a Channel Tunnel train. At 1,750 tonnes, the arch weighs as much as ten Boeing 747s.

2. A plan of the new stadium compared with the old. Twice the size of its predecessor, the new Wembley Stadium is among the most spacious and best equipped in the world. Every one of the 90,000 seats has clear sightlines, a marked contrast with the 20 to 25 per cent of seats whose views were obscured by the pillars in the old stadium.

Wembley's arch is conceived as a triumphal gateway – a heroic symbol for the new stadium. Floodlit at night, it is a new London landmark. You can see it soaring on the skyline from the very heart of the city.

Norman Foster

The Eiffel Tower was mocked as a brutalist metal Babel when it first touched the sky. Lovers of old St Paul's were never reconciled to Wren's vulgar new dome. But time lends enchantment to the townscape. The Gherkin and the giant Ferris wheel are becoming familiar friends. The new Wembley Stadium will become a neo-Colosseum for English football. *The Times*, 19 May 2007

Right: The Wembley arch compared with other London landmarks: 30 St Mary Axe, the London Eye, the BT Tower, Big Ben and Nelson's Column.

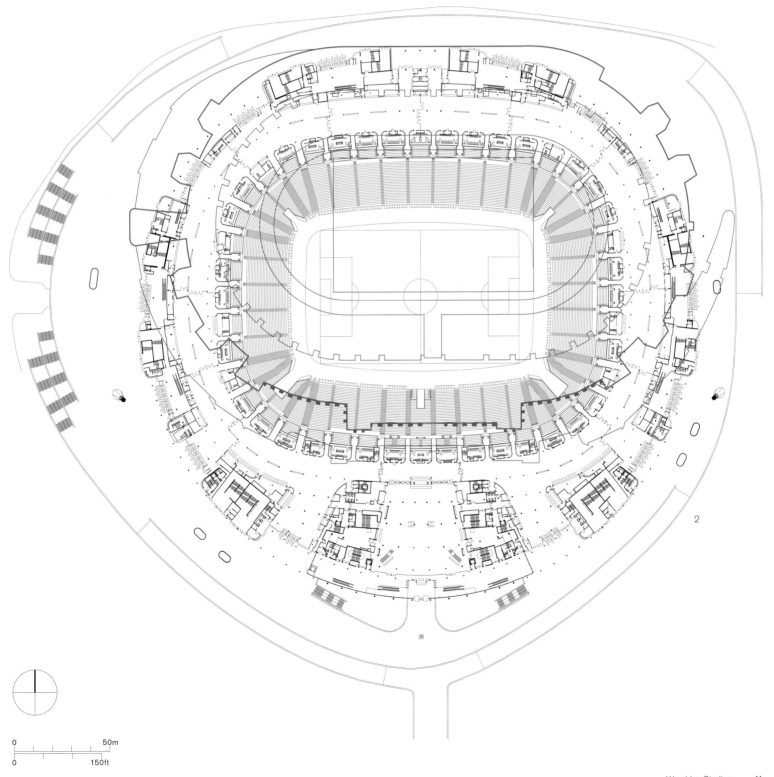

2

0   50m

0   150ft

A cutaway drawing of the stadium showing how the 'drum' of entertainment facilities and hospitality suites is arranged around the perimeter of the seating bowl. Escalators take spectators to the upper levels.

The demolition of the famous Wembley twin towers began at just after 2.00pm yesterday, the final act in a long drawn-out saga, and the most significant. Few could fail to spot the irony of a German excavator known as 'Goliath' being charged with the task. Alan Pattullo, *The Scotsman*, 8 February 2003

Left: Norman Foster interviewed against the backdrop of the stadium's last remaining tower, which was demolished on 7 February 2003.
Right: The giant German excavator 'Goliath' clears the site; the twin towers remain in the background – the last pieces to go.

2

3

1-6. This aerial sequence, taken from summer 2003 to shortly before the opening in 2007, tracks the entire construction process. With limited space available outside the stadium, the pitch became a fabrication space for elements of the arch and the perimeter truss. Simultaneously, the bowl grew up around it. At the peak of construction there were over 3,000 workers on site.

It quickly emerged that the determining structural factor would be the height of the arch, and that this height would have to rise so high above the London skyline that Wembley would gain an unparalleled visibility.

Recalling those hectic few days, Lenczner says, 'Immediately we were convinced that the arch was the way to go – that it could replace the twin towers with an incredibly powerful image. We were also confident that the engineers would agree that the arch was a better solution.'

First thing on the Monday morning Mouzhan Majidi briefed the Foster model shop to make a rudimentary model of the arch proposal, and as soon as it was ready it was taken to Rod Sheard at HOK Sport's offices. 'To his great credit,' Lenczner recalls, 'Rod wasn't upset that we were having second thoughts and immediately supported the new design.'

'The next step', Lenczner says, 'was for Norman to present it to the FA, or rather to Ken Bates. So he took a stack of sketches and walked over the river to Chelsea Village. Ken had no idea what the meeting was about and so had said to Norman, "Let's meet in the pub". And it was there that Norman took him through the reasoning behind the change. And again, like every other member of the team, Ken Bates went for the new version, and made the really big decision to change the design.' That one decision was to transform the public's perception of the project. Not only did the arch suppress any lingering regrets about the loss of the twin towers, it also provided the new stadium with a powerful and instantly recognisable motif.

Statistics relating to the arch's construction have become part of the Wembley lore. Its span of 315 metres is larger than any other arch in the world. It towers 133 metres above the pitch, almost as tall as the London Eye (the capital's favourite new icon). A double-decker bus or train could pass through its core. Best of all, it offers a vital focal counterpoint to the mass of the stadium bowl. And as Alistair Lenczner emphasises, the arch uses only 1,750 tonnes of steel, making it lighter and thus more economical than the mast solution.

The almost incredible statistics relating to the arch's construction have become part of the Wembley narrative.

It is a measure of how many other distractions there were at the time that hardly a single press report voiced any comment on this sudden change of plan. Instead, the press continued to concentrate on the sports minister's barrage of comments about the athletics track.

WNSL's 1,600-page planning application was submitted to Brent Council in November 1999. But the press continued to present the Wembley scheme as if it was doomed to failure. One could only hope that the architects were each issued with copies of Rudyard Kipling's poem 'If', with its stirring exhortation, 'If you can keep your head when all about you are losing theirs …'

During the design phase of the stadium we were always looking for a marketing symbol, and with the arch scheme we got one. The ability to see the building across the whole of London was really important – a visible statement, that was all about making Wembley a destination. The FA never grasped this – for them the stadium was simply where the cup final was played each year. I would upset FA board members by saying that the stadium has nothing to do with football, it just happens to be that people turn up to watch it at Wembley, and that's what gets played on the pitch. Bob Stubbs, former chief executive, Wembley National Stadium Ltd, in conversation with the editor, 2005

I have heard a lot of misinformation about the cost in the press. The facts are these: the cost of the building (the hardware) was £388 million. The only Lottery funding was £105 million for the purchase of the land. The rest was private money. If you take 388 and divide by 90,000 seats, it gives a figure of between £3,500 and £4,000 per place. That compares favourably with recent European stadiums, which do not offer the facilities we have provided here. Typically, in North America or Japan, you find that costs far exceed the £4,000 per seat threshold. Norman Foster, presentation at the Architecture Foundation, London, 22 May 2007
Left: Norman Foster and Alistair Lenczner inspect the newly raised arch.

4

5

6

Planning approval for the revised scheme came in June 2000. But that was by no means the end of Wembley's 'woes'. As plans were drawn up for the old stadium's final curtain call – the England versus Germany, FIFA World Cup qualification match – press reports said that the scheme's costs had risen to £600 million – almost twice the amount stated a year earlier. In fact, the additional costs – which included the £105 million purchase of the site, legal and administrative fees – were independent of the stadium construction costs, which had been fixed at a guaranteed maximum price of £326.5 million by the contractors Multiplex (the giant Australian firm that had built Stadium Australia). Even with later revisions, which took the total stadium cost to £388 million, the average of £3,900 per seat is still comparable with other major stadium developments in North America, Japan and Europe. But the press had no time for such distinctions. The story was that costs were spiralling and the stadium had to be part of the problem.

Old Wembley's final match turned out to be a dreadful let-down. Played in pouring rain on a grey October afternoon, an uninspired England were beaten 1-0, after which the crestfallen manager, Kevin Keegan, resigned.

Three months later there followed another high profile resignation. After the proposed hotel and office developments were dropped from the scheme and under increasing pressure from his counterparts at the FA, in December 2000 Ken Bates stood down from the chairmanship of WNSL. 'Even Jesus Christ suffered only one Pontius Pilate,' remarked the ever-caustic Bates: 'I had a whole team of them.'

Critics began to call for a scaled down project. There was even talk of Birmingham re-entering the fray. However, after detailed scrutiny of the costs, Bates' replacement at WNSL, Rodney Walker, announced in early 2001 that he saw no need to amend the plans further. Bates had been vindicated. The design stood; but it also remained on the drawing board. While WNSL's bankers, the German bank WestLB, sought to arrange the loan of £433 million needed to trigger the reconstruction, the old stadium remained boarded up and empty for two years: time aplenty for the press to maintain its barrage of negative reporting, time for a new chief executive to be installed at WNSL, and in government for the appointment of new culture secretary.

Back at Wembley, meanwhile, hope of a coherent masterplan for the site faded when, in August 2002, 41 acres of the adjoining site, containing the Wembley Exhibition Centre, the Wembley Arena, various car parks and access routes, were sold by a beleaguered Wembley plc to a development company, Quintain Estates, plus a further 11 acres comprising the two last plots of the 1924 British Empire Exhibition site. Thus ownership of the Wembley site was divided for the first time since 1923.

Finally, in late 2002, once the finance agreements had been signed, demolition of the old stadium commenced. It would take another five years before the new stadium was ready. Predictably, throughout this period scare stories concerning the construction gathered their own momentum.

A north-south cross-section through the stadium bowl. The seating bowl is made up of three main tiers. The lower tier, accessed from the lower concourse, seats approximately 35,000. The middle tier, including club seats, hospitality suites and the Royal Box (now approached by 107 steps) accommodates some 16,000. The top tier, reached by lifts, stairs and escalators (common in American stadiums but rare in Europe) seats approximately 39,000.

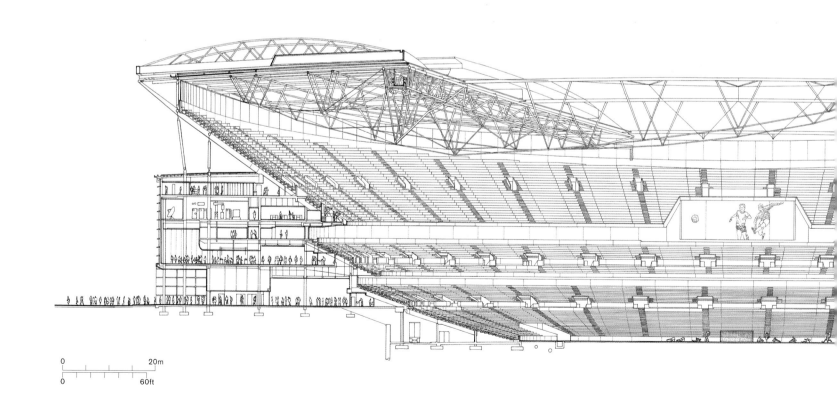

0   20m
0   60ft

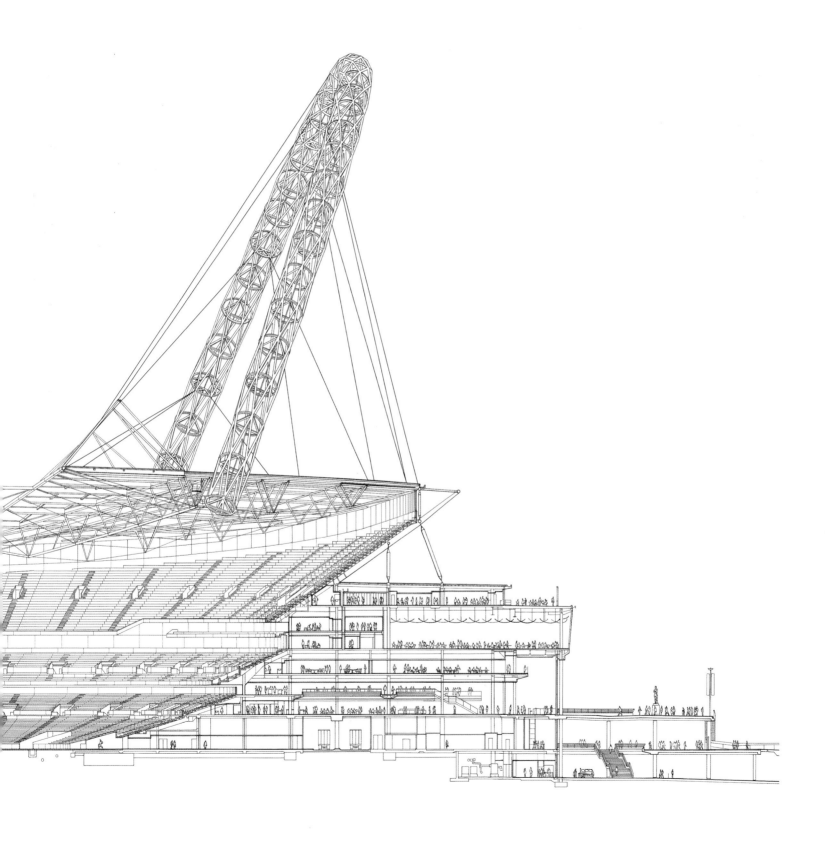

There was a big debate within the design team of us, HOK and Lobb, as to whether the stadium should have a big lower bowl or a big upper bowl, with smaller tiers below. HOK wanted the big lower bowl, and one of the guys from Lobb wanted a large upper bowl. We ended up in a crunch meeting at Chelsea Village. That was where Ken Bates was so effective. He said: 'You lot never say what you think. Those of you who want the larger lower bowl, hands up'. Nine hands went up. 'Right, who wants a larger upper bowl?' One hand went up. 'Well, you've lost, take it like a man'. Huw Thomas, of Foster + Partners, in conversation with the editor, 2012

One of the key generators of the design of the roof was the 'hallowed turf'. The turf requires constant nurturing. Without sunlight and fresh air the grass will not grow. The question was how do you protect all 90,000 spectators from the rain, but in fine weather still allow air and sunlight to reach the pitch? The answer was a retractable roof, which operates as a series of sliding panels. Norman Foster, presentation at the Architecture Foundation, London, 22 May 2007

We studied about twenty simplified generic options for the roof and seating bowl. Initially we worked with University College London using a computer program that could compare the light levels on the pitch of the existing stadium with those of the generic design options. These studies showed that the generic model which got closest to the existing stadium levels was one which was on an east-west orientation (as with the old stadium) and where the roof opened up to the south, east and west, maintaining the drip line on the north, but pulling the roof back beyond this on the three other sides. Alistair Lenczner, of Foster + Partners, in conversation with the editor, 2012

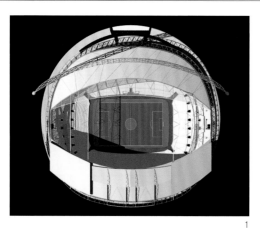

1

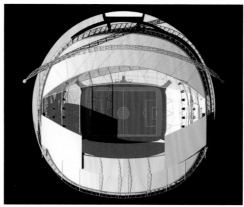

2

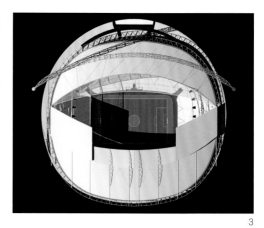

3

1-6. Extracts from a sequence of sunlight studies, modelled at regular intervals throughout the day, with the roof open and closed. The design challenge was to maximise the amount of light and air at pitch level, while protecting spectators from the rain. Essentially, this led to the idea of a retractable roof; one that would cover the seating when required but allow light and air to reach the turf and minimise shadow patterns on the pitch.

As was widely reported, Multiplex suffered financial losses in the process. There were disputes with subcontractors, problems with unions. Yet another chief executive at WNSL was appointed, as was a new chairman and another new chief executive at the FA. In February 2004 a third House of Commons report was published.

From the pitch outwards, there are no features that do not contribute to the stadium's ability to accommodate a full house, in maximum comfort, and with maximum visibility.

And all the while the stadium bowl rose up on the horizon, step by step, until in June 2004, as the arch began its ascent on the skyline, suddenly, but quite perceptibly, a change in the public mood could be discerned. The final remaining executive box leases were sold. Nearly all the 15,000 club seats were sold. At one point the box office was taking receipts of £1 million a day. Here, clearly, was no ordinary stadium. Here was a colossus – it only needed some physical manifestation of the design to have the public come flocking to its gates.

The world is full of anonymous stadiums that few people recognise but that function perfectly adequately. Equally there are numerous examples of eye-catching stadiums that are beloved by architectural critics, yet loathed by spectators. Considering how successful the Romans were in solving most of the geometric and structural issues inherent in the type – as evidenced by the Colosseum – it is remarkable how frequently twentieth-century architects managed to sacrifice function for form. Tony Garnier at the Stade Gerland, Lyon (1920), Pier Luigi Nervi at the Stadio Comunale, Florence (1932), Frei Otto's undulating acrylic, tent-like canopy at the Olympiastadion, Munich (1972); each was acclaimed by the critics, yet remained flawed as a mass-spectator facility.

Where Foster and the World Stadium Team parted from this trend was in their determination to ensure the pure functionality of the design. From the pitch outwards, there are no features that do not contribute to the stadium's ability to accommodate a full house, in maximum comfort, and with maximum visibility.

At the centre of this design matrix lies the pitch, 4 metres below the level of the old Wembley turf and layered on a substructure of sand and soil, interlaced with piped systems for drainage, ventilation and under-soil heating. These systems allow air to circulate to promote root growth, and for warm water pipes to provide protection against frost.

In the early days, we used an old image of the stadium which showed a group of guys sitting on a bench in the stands, with their hats on, watching a game. Today, the spectators demand some kind of protection. But when they've gone the roof has absolutely no purpose – in fact it has a detrimental impact, stopping sunlight and air getting to the grass. So from the outset we were committed to a moving roof that could protect the fans, even give them the opportunity to sit under the sun on a nice day, and also to protect the pitch by retracting when the place is empty. Huw Thomas, of Foster + Partners, in conversation with the editor, 2012

One bugbear of mine is the shadowing of the pitch in many modern stadiums. With the old Wembley I loved the fact that if the Cup Final was played on a sunny day, then at kick-off the pitch would be cast in sunlight. Only towards the final whistle did a little bit of shade encroach. In Cardiff, the Millennium Stadium is orientated north-south, so at kick-off one side of the pitch is in sunlight and the other is in shade. If you consider that most people watch the game on TV, then this contrast causes a lot of problems. We were determined that at Wembley, with the help of the retractable roof, the tradition of sunlit FA Cup Finals would be retained. Alistair Lenczner, of Foster + Partners, in conversation with the editor, 2012

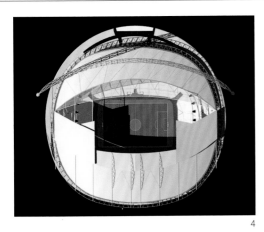

4

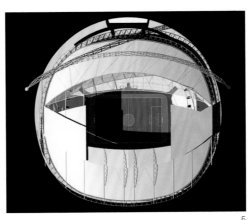

5

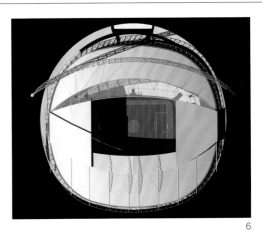

6

To allow the maximum amount of daylight to fall on the pitch, moveable panels in the roof can be adjusted to meet varying conditions. As photographs taken after the stadium's completion confirmed, the predictions on which these designs were based turned out to be almost 100 per cent accurate. At 3.00pm on a May afternoon (the traditional date for the FA Cup Final), the variation in shade recorded turned out to be within half a metre of the computerised model.

However, no computer model was able to predict the exceptionally wet summer that coincided with Wembley's completion. That, combined with the effects of an American gridiron football match, tested the new pitch systems to the full during Wembley's first months and refinements have since proved necessary. But most stadium pitches take several years to bed down and mature, and in that sense, the insistence on a natural turf pitch for Wembley will always require extra vigilance and care.

Of course, nowadays a stadium pitch is not only for sport, but for accommodating concert audiences. At Wembley there is provision for up to 20,000 people to stand on the pitch, not on the turf but on a protective system of moulded and interlocking panels, which can remain in place for several days without damaging the grass. Wembley's in-house sound system can be similarly geared towards those on the pitch, as well as those in the stands.

Around the pitch stands the six-storey 'drum', consisting of seating tiers on the inner rim, and concourses and hospitality areas on the outer. At basement level a service road provides 360-degree vehicle access (for television and concert trucks as well as service vehicles). This road also provides a secure point of entry for players, performers, officials and VIPs. Once again, the statistics for these 'back-of-house' areas have been repeatedly cited. But the fact that there are more than 2,600 lavatories – more than any other stadium in the world – becomes more meaningful when one considers that this is six times the number in the old stadium.

Similarly, that there are restaurant facilities for up to 15,000 diners at a single sitting has to be seen in the context of the capital's already vast corporate hospitality market. Wembley, as Ken Bates hoped it would, has London's largest banqueting room, seating 1,900 guests. This room, and three of its other restaurants, are indeed the city's four largest.

But what of the seating bowl itself? Given the number of elliptically shaped stadiums in the world it might be imagined that few variations in design are possible. Yet the possibilities are infinite, with each bowl exhibiting a subtle interplay of aisles, gangways, vomitories and barriers. At Wembley, the architects had no choice over the colour of the tip-up seats. These had to be the same red as used in the old stadium. But look closely and you see that the design team took great care with spacing each row of seats to avoid the awkward gaps that so often appear in the corners of stadiums.

Overleaf: The stadium at night. Wrapped by a kilometre of internal concourse, each of the three tiers of seating anticipates capacity crowds. In total the stadium can accommodate 90,000 people. Placed end to end, the seats stretch to a distance of 54km and each seat is 25 per cent wider than those in the old stadium.

The arena itself is breathtaking. A vast undulating wave of sculpted concrete, set about with 90,000 red plastic seats, each with plenty of leg room and uninterrupted views, it shelters beneath a gigantic yet unobtrusive roof, all 11 acres and 7,000 tonnes of it supported by Foster's 133-metre high, 315-metre long 'tiara' of steel. Although it might be hard to fall in love with such a colossus, the new stadium will surely come to be seen as a worthy successor to its hugely familiar, twin-domed predecessor. Jonathan Glancey, *The Guardian*, 9 March 2007

Before the game, Wembley officials were at pains to honour the stadium's illustrious past, kicking off proceedings with a parade of former players who had starred in previous Wembley Cup Finals. The England legend Sir Geoff Hurst said the new stadium was 'absolutely magnificent. We invented the game of football. We deserve to have the best stadium in the world and now we have got it by far'. Simon Hart, *The Sunday Telegraph*, 20 May 2007

We spent a huge amount of time discussing how we would maintain the drama of the old stadium. One of the things that struck me about the old place was how the pitch was illuminated but that everything else appeared quite dark. It was like going to the theatre. We decided to keep it dark in the stands, so as to maintain this theatrical quality. Bob Stubbs, former chief executive, Wembley National Stadium Ltd, in conversation with the editor, 2005

The 133-metre-high arch works not only structurally but also as an icon: it is an enormously successful London landmark and a worthy successor to the stage-set architecture of the old twin towers (on which the clients are to be congratulated for having the un-English guts to demolish). Guide to the RIBA Awards, 2008

The new Wembley Stadium bowl is a truly magnificent space. To emerge through one of its vomitories on a match day is to experience spatial 'compression and release' at an ultimate level. One must marvel at just how effortless it all seems, this sophisticated geometry of radiused tiered seating set out to create the spectacle of a continuous sea of humanity ... to behold the Mexican Wave in this arena is an architectural delight. Neven Sidor, *Architecture Today*, May 2007

If some of the world's larger football stadiums are sometimes referred to as cathedrals, then Wembley is the Vatican. John Carlin, *El País Semanal*, 22 January 2000

On the Saturday after we presented the scheme I was in Bayreuth. I was talking about the project and saying that the quality of the finishes at Wembley would be better than you would find in the average opera house. Quite rightly, the person I was speaking to said: 'Why not? I mean this is a cultural building in every way.' Norman Foster, presentation at the Architecture Foundation, London, 22 May 2007

Right: The 6-metre-high statue of Bobby Moore by sculptor Philip Jackson pays tribute to one of England's greatest footballers. Moore made 108 appearances for England, 642 appearances for West Ham and was Footballer of the Year in 1964, Sports Personality of the Year in 1966 and was awarded the OBE in 1967. The plaque at his feet reads: 'Immaculate footballer. Imperial defender. Immortal hero of 1966. First Englishman to raise the World Cup aloft. Favourite son of London's East End. Finest legend of West Ham United. National Treasure. Master of Wembley. Lord of the game. Captain extraordinary. Gentleman of all time.'

1

2

1. Fans queue for admission at the turnstiles.

2. Broad and spacious, the lower concourse circulation for general admission easily accommodates a thronging football crowd.

3. The FA Cup Final comes home as Chelsea and Manchester United meet at Wembley on 19 May 2007. Framed by the Wembley arch, rival fans bring Olympic Way alive with colour.

3

One of the key business strategies behind our vision for the new Wembley was that given its uniqueness as an event space how were we ever going to make any money to repay the loans to build the new stadium. What we came up with was a concept borrowed from the airline industry – we were going to make 80 per cent of our profits from 20 per cent of the customers. So like the first-class lounge of a plane, the whole stadium was designed around our corporate hospitality requirements. Without these, the stadium would never have paid its way. Bob Stubbs, former chief executive, Wembley National Stadium Ltd, in conversation with the editor, 2005

When the stadium opened for the FA Cup I walked down Olympic Way with Norman, who was being interviewed at points along the route. As he went, there was a realisation among the fans of who he was and they came out to greet him which was amazing because you don't normally get that kind of attention as an architect. It's still a great experience to go to Wembley and see a match just as it's nice to see any of your projects once they're finished, but how many projects do you complete which regularly have 90,000 visitors? Angus Campbell, of Foster + Partners, in conversation with the editor, 2012
Right: Angus Campbell (foreground) with other members of the Foster office in a box at Wembley.

4

5

6

Normally, when you go to a stadium, if you are lucky you queue up and eventually get something to eat. You watch the game and then you're out of there as fast as possible. But Wembley is completely different – it's a day out.

Mouzhan Majidi

7

8

4. Looking along the main public concourse at Level 00.

5. One of the 163 corporate boxes; each holds up to twenty guests and all have spectacular views of the pitch.

6. As London's largest banqueting space, the Great Hall seats up to 2,000 guests and overlooks Olympic Way. It is complemented by five other premium venues, each of which offers a high standard of service and dining at Wembley.

7. Hospitality areas flank the north side of the pitch and open to the corporate boxes.

8. Wembley's twelve restaurants range in size from 500 to 2,000 seats and are serviced by ninety-eight kitchens – the largest is one-third the size of the pitch.

On Saturday I went up to Wembley on the tube with the Manchester fans. As you pass Neasden you catch a glimpse of the arch. I could tell when it came into view because everybody who was standing in the middle leaned down to look out of the window. These Mancunians had been jibing each other the whole trip. But suddenly they went silent. Then I heard: 'Oooohhh, it makes you proud to be English doesn't it?' Rod Sheard, of HOK Sport, presentation at the Architecture Foundation, London, 22 May 2007

Wembley has a special magic, and it is going to be the most spectacular stadium in the world. It will be hugely important in its own right, but it is also very important to our Olympic bid for 2012. It shows we can build the biggest and the best there can be. Prime Minister Tony Blair, speaking at the ceremony to mark the topping out of the Wembley arch, 1 September 2004
Left: Prime Minister Tony Blair and England captain David Beckham teamed up to celebrate progress on the construction of the stadium. They triggered a spectacular firework display over the new stadium's arch.

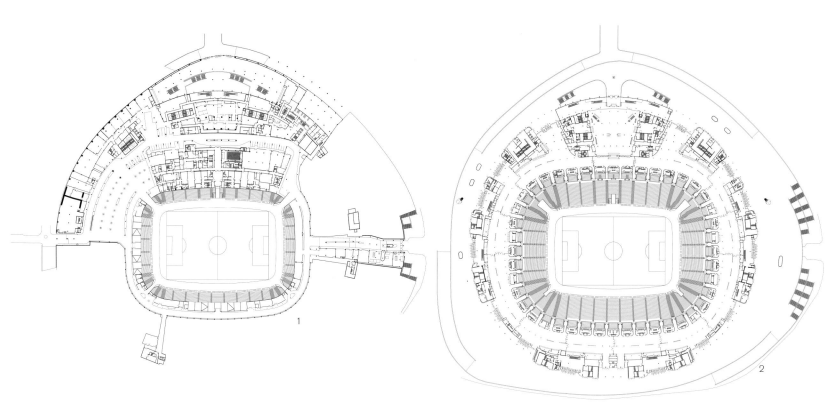

1. Plan at Level B2, corresponding with the pitch.

2. Plan at Level 00, the lower public concourse.

3. Plan at Level 02, the Club Wembley concourse.

4. Plan at Level 03, hospitality boxes.

5. Plan at Level 04, hospitality boxes and WNSL offices.

6. Plan at Level 05, the public concourse.

7. Plan at Level 06, the highest seating tier, showing the full seating bowl.

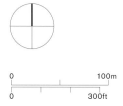

0   100m

0   300ft

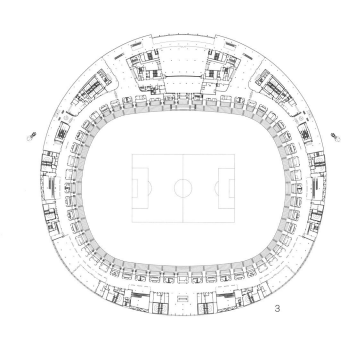

Wembley was our first stadium and it involved a very steep learning curve. But that experience broadened our knowledge base and helped us to win the commission to design the Camp Nou Stadium in Barcelona just four months after Wembley's opening. Again, more recently, Wembley led us to Doha and the design of the Lusail Stadium, which will be the focal point of the 2022 World Cup celebrations in Qatar.

Mouzhan Majidi, in conversation with the editor, 2012
Right: An aerial visualisation of the 100,000-seat Camp Nou Stadium, Barcelona (2007-).
Far right: A visualisation of the Lusail Stadium, Doha (2009-), which accommodates 86,000 spectators and has been designed to perform in extreme climatic conditions.

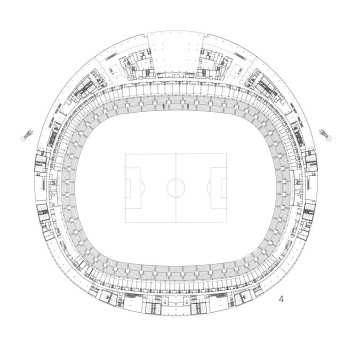

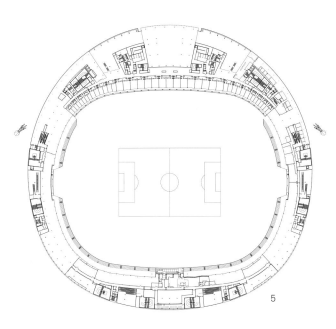

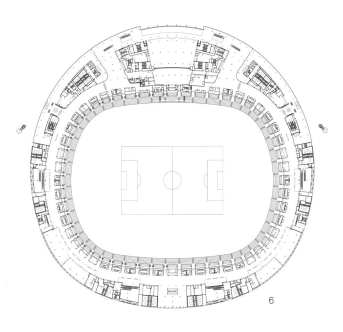

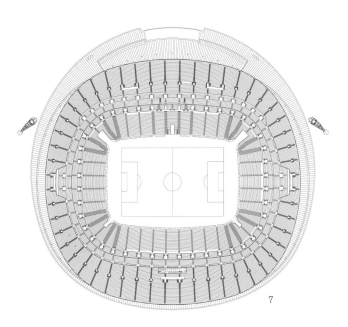

The return of the FA Cup Final to north-west London had been a long time coming and, despite the goose-bumps generated by the atmosphere inside the new Wembley, it was well worth the wait. Seven years after the bulldozers moved in on the stadium that Pelé once described as 'the church of football', 89,826 customers finally had the chance to pay homage to the national game at the gleaming, arched cathedral that replaced it. They were not disappointed. Simon Hart, *The Sunday Telegraph*, 20 May 2007

The new Wembley project was a bit like picking the England team. Everyone thought they could do it better than you. Bob Stubbs, former chief executive, Wembley National Stadium Ltd, in conversation with the editor, 2005

Left: A ticket to the first international match in the new stadium, on 24 March 2007. England took on Italy in an Under-21 friendly in front of over 55,000 fans. England and Italy drew 3-3.

Right: England team shirts hanging in the dressing room at Wembley, ready for a match.

Far right: The English and Brazilian teams file out of the Wembley tunnel prior to the first full international in the new stadium, 1 June 2007.

1

1. Play commences in the first FA Cup Final to be played in the new stadium, 19 May 2007. Chelsea beat Manchester United 1-0. Chelsea has the distinction of winning the last FA Cup Final at the old Wembley and the first in the new stadium.

2. Jubilant Manchester United fans reignite the famous 'Wembley roar'.

3. The England flag spread out on the pitch before the first full international match in the new stadium on 1 June 2007. England and Brazil drew 1-1.

2

3

The crowd will chant its name in time-honoured fashion: 'Wem-ber-ley!' – three roaring syllables evoking the boisterous spirit of our national football ground, and the Anglo-Saxon settlement from which it rises. What they will see, and experience, is a Wembley of sporting dreams, although nothing like its predecessor. The swooping, smooth concrete arena is wrapped around with five levels of atriums, walkways, cafés, bars, shops and restaurants. These wide and lofty interiors feel more like some stupendous airport – Foster's Chek Lap Kok at Hong Kong, perhaps – than the inside of a sports stadium.
Jonathan Glancey, *The Guardian*, 9 March 2007

This seamless quality adds greatly to the uniformity of the bowl, and therefore to the visual impact of the three concentric levels. Of these, the lowest tier seats 34,303; the centre tier, including club seats and 160 hospitality suites and the Royal Box, accommodates 16,532; while the upper tier seats 39,165.

Stadium designers frequently debate the relative merits of having small lower tiers and larger upper tiers, or vice versa. Here the equilibrium between the two and the absence of a large overhang over the central tier means that the bowl has a unity that is rare in stadiums of more than 50,000 capacity. Crucially – because at a stadium the crowd is as much a part of the spectacle as the performers – this allows spectators in almost every part of the stadium to see from their seat as much of the other spectator accommodation as is possible.

This geometry does mean, however, that instead of winning captains having to climb thirty-nine steps to receive their cup and medals from the Royal Box, as in the old stadium, they must now ascend 107 steps. But again, this was part of the design brief. The presentation of honours from a centrally placed Royal Box was part of the old Wembley's appeal, whereas at other modern stadiums the ceremony is usually performed on platforms placed on the pitch. Not the Wembley way at all.

But the ultimate test for any new stadium is how the spectator responds to it as a building. Often commentators use the expression 'wow factor'. By this they mean a stadium's ability to excite and inspire, and also its visual identity. Put simply, what can it offer that another stadium cannot? Because of its history and the events staged there, Wembley has a cachet that other stadiums cannot match. But what the old stadium never had was comfort or amenity levels commensurate with its status, a situation that has changed completely.

4

5

4. A St George's Cross formation celebrates England's national pride during the first international match against Brazil at the new stadium, 2007.

5. Denying England a debut win at Wembley, Brazil's late equaliser saved their unbeaten seventeen-year run against the Three Lions.

Sophisticated physical and computer modelling ensured that the electric atmosphere of the old Wembley – including the famous 'Wembley roar' – was retained and even enhanced.

Norman Foster

People are dying NOW! Give us the money now, Give ME the money NOW! Fuck the address, just give the phone, here's the number … Bob Geldof, musician and Live Aid organiser, 13 July 1985
Right: The crowd at the Live Aid concert at Wembley Stadium on 13 July 1985. Seen on television around the world, Live Aid raised funds to help relieve severe famine in Ethiopia. The organisers' initial expectation to raise £1 million was dwarfed by the final figure of £150 million.

Before the old stadium was torn down I went to meet with Noel Jeffs, the operations manager, to look at how they allowed whole tanker trucks full of beer to drive on to the pitch, park up behind the mixer desk area, and supply the crowd through long pipes. On concert nights the crowd would drink a whole tanker dry. Noel and I were walking across the pitch while roadies for the Rolling Stones were setting up for a concert. About halfway across, Mick Jagger got on the thrust stage and with no one else around but Noel and me, sang an acoustic version of 'Route 66'. Noel said that Jagger would go crazy if he saw us stop to listen, so we just had to walk on. Huw Thomas, of Foster + Partners, in conversation with the editor, 2012

1

1. Muse make their stadium debut, 16 June 2007.

2. The Concert for Diana marked her 46th birthday on 1 July 2007. Many of her favourite pop artists appeared, followed by a performance of Swan Lake, Act Four, which recalled her love of ballet.

2

The stadium works as well for concerts as it does for football or rugby. It's fully wired for sound, everyone has a great view, and the atmosphere is quite intimate, despite its size.
Mouzhan Majidi

Even through the thickness of the prison walls at Robben Island, Pollsmoor, Victor Verster, Pretoria, Kroonstad, Diepkloof and elsewhere, we heard your voices demanding our freedom. Nelson Mandela, speaking at the Nelson Mandela International Tribute at Wembley Stadium shortly after his release from prison, 16 April 1990
Left: Preceded by a six-minute-long ovation, Nelson Mandela addressed an ecstatic Wembley crowd, just a few weeks after his release from prison in Cape Town on 11 February 1990. Over a billion people across five continents watched on television as Mandela took the stage, prior to a concert by performers from across the globe.

The real skill in designing a stadium is not the technical stuff – it's designing a building that bottles emotion. Norman Foster, quoted in *Reader's Digest*, May 2007

That the new stadium stands resplendent on the north-west London skyline, its arch a towering statement of engineering finesse; that its amenities have been praised by both spectators and athletes; that its high standards of materials and finishes far outstrip popular expectations, confirms what all its backers argued from the beginning. That design excellence must override all other considerations, and that, bluntly, the end will justify the means. But what a struggle it was.

Wembley's turnstiles opened for its first trial match, an England Under-21 friendly against Italy, on 24 March 2007. The first full house of 90,000 spectators, for the FA Cup Final between Manchester United and Chelsea, followed on 19 May. Alas for John Roberts, the chairman of Multiplex, the opening came too late. The man described by Norman Foster as one of the two key individuals in bringing the project to fruition died a year earlier. The other, Ken Bates, had in the meantime moved on to become chairman of another football club, Leeds United.

Wembley, it might be argued, is a true creation of the twenty-first century. Wired for sound and light, plugged into the digital world, marketed as a brand and hired out for one use or another on almost every day of the year, its ultimate function is part live theatre and part television studio. Once the players of clubs like Manchester United and Chelsea take centre stage, the architects, engineers and the legions of contractors who pieced it together can only look on from the sidelines.

In the stadium's first three months it hosted six major football matches, one Rugby League Challenge Cup Final, seven concerts (featuring such stars as George Michael, Elton John, Status Quo, Duran Duran, Genesis and Madonna) and a regular series of exhibitions and corporate events. It was even used to host a mini motor-racing circuit, laid on tarmac above the pitch. And should there ever be a need to stage an athletics event the plans for a platform are ready and waiting to be implemented – all as planned.

Simon Inglis

3

4

3. George Michael plays Wembley's first concert, 9 June 2007. The new Wembley event stage is London's ultimate big-name music venue.

4. A temporary platform is erected above the pitch for concert events, bringing fans as close as possible to the stage.

Overleaf: Illuminated to celebrate the first FA Cup Final, Wembley Stadium's arch is seen reflected in the waters of Brent Reservoir.

An Interview with Ken Bates
Thomas Weaver 2005

The easiest place to meet Ken Bates these days is in Monte Carlo, as far from the world of English football as it's possible to imagine. A maverick former chairman and major shareholder of Chelsea FC, and the current chairman of Leeds United, he is still widely regarded as a 'controversial figure'. But it was as a very energetic member of the Football Association Executive and founding chairman of Wembley National Stadium Ltd (WNSL) that he really made his mark. Without him, there would probably have been no new Wembley Stadium – and certainly not a stadium of the same scale and ambition.

The Wembley story was 'a very British set-up', he says. 'Sport England had set up a trust to hold the money for the stadium. They then decided that this trust would set up a company to manage the new stadium. I didn't think too much about it, until I got a letter from Graham Kelly, the secretary of the FA, asking me to join the board and advise them on Wembley.

'Basically, they didn't know what they were doing. The FA was going to take a ninety-five-year lease from Wembley plc; pay a huge rent, plus give them a management contract, plus take out a twenty-five-year agreement, undertaking to play all the England games there. All the TV money and admission revenues would be pre-agreed with the Trust Board. They were going to take the FA's covenant to the City to bargain with to build the stadium. It would have been a disaster.

'So I said to the FA "I'll only get involved if I am chairman of the FA's National Stadium Board." The FA board was basically happy for me to just get on with it. The whole history of football not owning its own National Stadium was my point from the start. My intention was for us to buy Wembley and rebuild it ourselves. All the profits would stay within the FA, within the game itself. And this, of course, was before the advent of the huge TV deals for football, before the Premier League.

'Someone had come up with the figure of £180 million for the cost of the stadium. I remember asking Bob Stubbs – who was then working for the National Stadium Trust – how that figure was arrived at. He said they took the cost of the Millennium Stadium in Cardiff, and said allow for this, and allow for that, and call it £180 million. It was laughable.

'The first thing Bob and I did was to have the old place valued – at £106 million – a figure that seemed amazing to me. This sale price was put to the Wembley plc board. The board was split and there was huge opposition from the shareholders. I said "If you don't sell us Wembley we won't renew our lease." They thought I was bluffing. But the FA went along with my threat. Eventually the Wembley board had a poll vote, and it went our way.

'That's when the fun started. It was about this time that I first met Norman Foster. I remember getting a call from him and he invited me to lunch. From the start we got on very well. We actually had a bloody good relationship. He, I'm sure, had never met anyone like me before, with my very particular sense of humour, and I for sure had never met anyone like him before, with his painstaking attention to detail.'

How did you respond when he suddenly introduced the arch? 'Well, I'd decided that the new stadium should have a 1,000-seat restaurant, looking down Olympic Way. But on the day Norman made his big presentation to the press, I looked at the model and thought, hang on, how big are these masts? I can't have these bloody great things blocking the view of my restaurant. Anyway, a few days later, out of the blue, I got a phone call from Norman, asking if he could come over. He walked over to the Stamford Bridge stadium bar, ordered a bottle of champagne, and pulled out some sketches of a new scheme – with the arch. He said, "What do you think?" I was gobsmacked. It was so much better. But then I thought, what's the cost implication? He said, "It's neutral". So I said, "Let's do it". It was as simple as that.'

1

Having worked out the basic design, you had to choose a contractor. 'It was very interesting. Everyone knows that there's a "you scratch my back and I'll scratch yours" kind of mentality in the construction industry. Typically they give a price; the architect delivers a design and makes changes; then they're hit with fees for extras. If they don't make changes they get banged for extras anyway. And so it goes on. But John Roberts of Multiplex said from the outset that he'd give me a fixed-price contract. "The day you sign the contract", he said, "is the day I start building, and the price of the contract is the price that you will pay me". So obviously I warmed to the fellow.

'But there were other firms interested in the job too. We whittled it down to about a dozen. Rather than seeing them all, we prepared a contract on the basis of what Roberts was proposing. After that, most of them dropped out: only Multiplex and Bovis were left. But in talking to Bovis, every time we asked for something they added another £5 or £10 million to the price. This went on until it reached £390 million. It was crazy.'

The whole history of football not owning its own National Stadium was my point from the start. My intention was for us to buy Wembley and rebuild it ourselves.

Had you already decided to increase the capacity from 80,000 to 90,000? 'Yes. Chris Smith asked me, "Why are you putting it up to 90,000?" And I said, "Because I can't get it up to 100,000" which is what I wanted. I wanted to make it bigger so that more ordinary punters could watch the game. Because you don't make any more money on that last 10,000 – they have to be high in the air – so therefore you have to widen the base of the stadium. The other thing I insisted on was that everybody should have as good a view as the Queen gets.

'I also spent money on escalators, because I've seen what happens at Newcastle and Manchester United where you nearly suffer a heart-attack climbing the stairs. I remember when Touche Ross came in to tell us how we could save £100 million from the project. The first things they wanted to get rid of were the escalators. I told them to get lost – they would have ripped the guts out of the place. Eventually I signed off on the contract at £326.5 million plus £8 million for the directors – so the total price for the stadium was £334.5 million.

'The biggest obstacle was the government. We had to make presentation after presentation. They were pointless – Chris Smith even fell asleep in one of them. We had had Tony Banks before that, who was 100 per cent behind us – a football man – but then he resigned. Then came Kate Hoey, who was determined that Wembley should have a running track. How many times had the old stadium's track been used since 1948? Almost none – and it completely messed up the sightlines. But it was in our remit.

'Hoey wanted a track with retractable seating. I looked into that and it doesn't work because anything mechanical corrodes – so all the hydraulics and electrics, which are hardly ever used, just fail. The other problem is the space into which the track retracts is completely wasted. In the new stadium we wanted the toilets and bars to be under the seating. But when you have a huge space for the track, they get pushed out into the concourse, which means you have to move the structure out too – all because of the track. Eventually we came up with a solution that involves building a temporary track on a concrete deck. You lose the first twenty rows or so, but it works.

'There were other problems too. I wanted Wembley to have restaurants and hotels – to be a 365-day-a-year operation, like Chelsea Village. But suddenly there was a story in the media that Chelsea Village was a flop, and that I was repeating the same mistakes at Wembley. Well, it wasn't a flop. Any new business takes time to build up. In the end, I took out the hotel, just to show that I could make a change. I was also keen for the FA to move in there – it took me three years to get that idea past them. I kept asking, "why are we paying huge rents on Soho Square, when we could move into our own building for free." But Adam Crozier was an advertising man – he liked Soho Square.

'We also had problems raising money. We originally got £120 million from the Lottery; £105 million was used to buy the ground, the other £14 million, plus the profits we made running the ground, was used to pay the architects' fees. Because of the money Wembley had been making after we took it over, people asked me why we shut the old stadium down when we did. I said, "Because we didn't have another game for nine months", so I saved nine months' operating expenses. But I also knew that if we didn't shut the old place we would never be able to build the new stadium. All these plans just to refurb it would have taken over.

'Anyway, all's well that ends well. And the ends justified the means … and we've got our stadium. And it's the most fantastic stadium in the world. And it could never be built anywhere else. It's unique.'

Newbury Racecourse Grandstand
Newbury, England 1999–2000

1

2

**The grandstand is a
simple, almost industrial
building – all the colour
and drama comes from the
action on the racecourse.
On race days, the
atmosphere is electrifying.**

Norman Foster

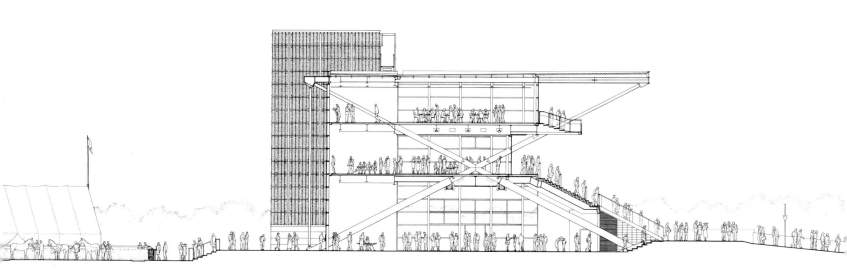

Here we are talking about a people's stand, a genuine attempt to break down the barriers, and to offer a top-of-the-range service to 'ordinary' race-goers. Cornelius Lysaght, *The Times*, 10 November 2000

Left: Several attempts were made to build a racecourse at Newbury from the end of the nineteenth century but all fell foul of the Jockey Club's strict criteria. In the end it took the endorsement of King Edward VII to get the go-ahead and the first meeting at Newbury Racecourse took place on 26 September 1905. The opening race, the Whatcombe Handicap, was won by Copper King, ridden by Charles Trigg and trained by Charles Marnes.

While Wembley was in the planning stage, the practice turned its attention to another sporting commission, albeit one on a much smaller scale. The brief was to design a replacement grandstand for Newbury Racecourse, home to one of the most important races in the UK National Hunt diary – the Hennessy Gold Cup. The importance of the cup was amply illustrated by the accelerated schedule: design, demolition and construction had to be completed between the dates of the annual race meeting, giving the team less than a year to complete the project.

Given the quick turnaround and the relatively small budget – £9 million – a simple, economical structure was needed. The result is a building based around six clearly articulated steel X-frames spaced at 12-metre intervals. These support the roof, restaurant and bar at the upper level and the terracing at the lower level. The cavernous betting hall, which also doubles as a conference or exhibition venue, is located beneath the terracing.

Both the bar and restaurant are fully glazed and offer panoramic views of the racecourse. The legs of the X-frame pierce the internal space at bar level, passing directly through the glass of the southern facade in a series of dramatic interventions. Spectators are also able to enter the bar from the terracing. Those in the restaurant can take advantage of a series of balconies which project out between the legs of the frames.

The plan is the same on each level with all the core elements – lifts, stairs, services and so forth – grouped together in a single spine of accommodation running along the northern edge of the building. In contrast to the southern, racecourse-facing elevation, this is clad in corrugated steel covered by a fine mesh. This otherwise opaque box is divided in two by a glazed slot that affords spectators views of the paddock behind. Further glazed slots to the west and east not only facilitate easy egress but also ensure that spectators enjoy a 360-degree view of the whole racecourse, enabling them to see everything from the jockeys saddling up, to the race and subsequent winner's presentation, all from inside the grandstand.

Philosophically and structurally the stand echoes the Reliance Controls Electronics Factory, completed by Team 4 in 1966. This, like Newbury, was realised in an incredibly short period – ten and a half months from brief to completion – and to a tight budget. Similarly, the use of repetition and prefabrication coupled with an economy of materials, are common to both structures. They also embody an egalitarianism usually lacking in buildings of their type. Reliance Controls led the way in accommodating both factory workers and management in one unifying space and similarly, Newbury is conceived as a true 'people's stand'. The facilities within it are open to all with none of the stuffiness or snobbery often associated with British racing and it is all the better for it.

Gavin Blyth

3

1-3. The grandstand offers uninterrupted views of both racecourse and paddock.

4. Cross-section through the grandstand and paddock. The building's structure is based on six X-frames that support terraces with tiered balconies above. The ground-floor betting hall can be used on non-race days for exhibitions, conferences and corporate entertainment; entrances to this space are located on all four sides to ensure maximum permeability in an extremely busy environment. All core elements – lifts, stairs, and services – are contained in a spine running along the northern edge of the building.

4

0   5m

0   15ft

London City Racecourse

London, England 2000–2004

1. The grandstand accommodates half of the racecourse's visitor capacity of 20,000 people. The organic, curving form of its metallic roof swells and tapers along its length. The form of the grandstand is generated by the logical concentration of spectators around the home stretch and the finishing line. It is possible to watch every aspect of the racing ritual from within the building – either from one of the stepped terraces or from a table in one of the restaurants on the upper levels.

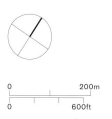

```
0          200m
0          600ft
```

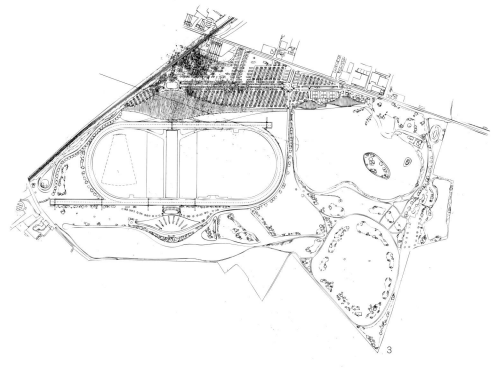

The commission to design an entirely new racecourse in north-east London came shortly after the completion of the Newbury grandstand. The brief was to develop a 2km oval track, complete with facilities for 20,000 spectators. Had it been built, not only would this have been the first racecourse to be completed in the UK since 1927, it would also have been the country's first all-weather track and the first to offer floodlit evening races.

Racecourses in the UK have generally developed piecemeal, in some cases over more than 300 years. The result is often a haphazard collection of buildings which impede views and create congestion between the parade ring and the grandstand. With this in mind, the team planned London City so that everything would be visible from one integrated stand running the length of the final straight.

The grandstand itself is covered by a great sinuously curved roof which rises and swells as it gathers momentum along the track, reaching its peak at the finishing post before falling away again on the other side. The nose of the roof – which is 4 metres deep at its widest point – is glazed so that spectators have an unhindered view of the racecourse; commentators are well served from their vantage point in a glass bubble below the apex of the roof. Beneath the commentary box, a series of glass-fronted bars and restaurants ensure that diners can keep in touch with the activity of the track beyond.

The finishing post acts as a focal point for the whole racecourse. A processional route runs along its axis linking the stables on the far side of the track to the sunken parade ring below the grandstand. Horses are led to the parade ring alongside a reflective pool, only momentarily disappearing from view as they enter the tunnel that takes them under the track. Similarly, the race over, horses are led back down the other side to their stables. Beyond the parade ground lies a glass-fronted jockeys' weighing room, ensuring that even this ritual is visible. As a result, the crowd can see the entire spectacle unfold before them in a continuous piece of theatre culminating in the finishing line.

Gavin Blyth

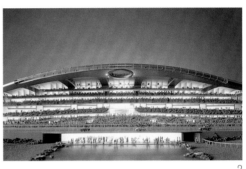

2

2. The cantilevered roof structure shelters spectators and the parade ring. The curve of the roof is designed to reflect sound into the interior, allowing spectators in the restaurants and bars to share the excitement of the racing experience. Visitors are also able to watch races from a viewing area high within the roof. This space is open to all members of the public, inverting the hierarchy of spectator accommodation found at most racecourses.

3. Plan of the racecourse. The stables are positioned directly opposite the grandstand to allow spectators to see the horses' route to the parade ring, which is sunk into the ground in front of the terraces, forming an amphitheatre. Other buildings on the site – stables, a crèche and a fitness club – share the grandstand's curved roof form.

1

The establishment of England's first new course since 1927 gave us the opportunity to rethink completely the layout and design of contemporary racecourse facilities.

Norman Foster

In Conversation with Ron Dennis
Kenneth Powell 2010

The McLaren Technology Centre at Woking, says Ron Dennis, is 'a building that has a lot of passion in it, and a lot of effort and attention to detail'. Dennis is certainly passionate about everything he does, and it shows. 'Infect people with your passion and pull them along and they become as committed to the objective as you are yourself', he says. It is this attitude that places him squarely among a series of clients whose collaborations with Norman Foster have generated outstanding buildings.

Dennis describes himself as 'a reasonably process-driven individual'. In the early 1990s he began the demanding process of finding a site for a new building that would accommodate all McLaren's manufacturing, research and management facilities, then inconveniently distributed among a collection of buildings in and around Woking. After a series of frustrating delays, including a planning inquiry, consent was finally obtained to build on the site outside Woking that now houses Foster's building. Dennis wanted a building that was not only practical and efficient but also memorable and inspiring and eventually appointed Foster + Partners to design it. 'I decided to work with Norman because he was passionate about things that I was passionate about', he says. 'He may have been seductive, you know, in perhaps saying what I wanted to hear, but I was convinced, and it quickly became a collaborative process.'

Ron Dennis's quest for an architect took him all over the world, looking at buildings in Europe, the USA and Japan designed by the six international practices he had shortlisted for the job. 'I asked a question that really floored most of them', he recalls. 'What is the building you are most proud of, and what is the building you are least proud of, because I want to see them both'. His visits were nothing if not thorough, with plant rooms a special interest – too often he found buildings which had 'a saloon frontage but with a chicken shed behind', suggesting a lack of coordination between the work of the architects and the structural and services engineers. 'For a building to work, it's not just about its being an architectural statement, it's about it really working, really having some defined parameters that determine a specification and that the building is compliant to that specification'. Good design, he insists, is 'not just an aesthetic statement, not just a functional statement – it's also a question of whether it fulfils the brief'.

Dennis admits that he was a 'high maintenance' client who is 'never sympathetic to those who can't deliver' – 'I wanted a phenomenal attention to detail that drove many people to the brink. But I don't think there was ever a time when I didn't say it as it was'. The rapport that Dennis found with Foster subsequently extended to David Nelson, as partner in charge, and to project architect Nigel Dancey and other members of the design team.

The relationship with the Foster team was nothing if not hands-on but was both creative and cordial – 'the whole project was relationship-led', says Dennis. Everyone involved, he says, became a friend. 'I'd like to feel that my contribution to the process was that we really stretched the boundaries of an architect/client relationship'. It was a relationship based on mutual respect. 'I think they respected the client's wishes but I think they also respected valid opinion', Dennis says. Foster + Partners' in-house resources certainly inspired confidence. 'When it came to consultants, we only had to go out of the Foster structure two or three times, other than obvious things like structural engineers signing off the structural issues. I needed that culture to have the confidence that the building was going to be sound and capable of performing'.

For me, this building is 95 per cent NASA and 5 per cent Disney. It's got that slight twist of entertainment, but at the same time it is absolutely up there in terms of technology.

Working with the Foster office has given Dennis a clear insight into its culture: 'I think you have to be able to put your work before your ego at Fosters, because your ego is not going to be easily satisfied'. But working there, he says, gives people 'the Foster DNA'. This is 'a cultural DNA which isn't linked to any one individual but which delivers performance and professionalism and, I think, cost effectiveness'. The Technology Centre cost £138 million, coming in at around £1 million below budget. ('Good design is design that actually achieves the cost objectives', Dennis believes.) But for that price McLaren got much more than a container for its activities – 'in that price there was every plug in the right place, the right type of electricity in the right place, the humidity and dust controls, the ecological cooling system, every floor was tiled …'

I'm very fortunate in that every day for many years now, when I wake up and go to work, I have enjoyed the experience. It's an experience that has given me the opportunity to be part of the history of McLaren. I often say the most important thing when you are running an organisation, irrespective of its size, is that you strive to be the chapter in the book of the company, not the entire book. Which means that you do not see your end in the company, but that you see your period in the company as being relevant, and that you can look back on it in retirement, and feel comfortable with your contribution. Ron Dennis, lecture in Florence, 15 May 2004

On the technical detail as well as the bigger picture Ron Dennis wanted to get involved with it, to really understand it. That reflects his character and approach. You also have to remember that McLaren makes things – there is a huge culture of designing and making. They design and manufacture to an incredibly high standard. In architecture you might talk about plus or minus 10mm; for them it's plus or minus a few microns. Not since the industrial projects back in the mid-1960s and early '70s have we really had a client who makes things in that same sense. This is an industrial project, but it also houses scientists, art galleries, offices and a museum. David Nelson, in conversation with the editor, 2012

Ron came with a number of ideas. Not so much about what the building should look like, but more about what the spirit of the building might be – its aspirations and social generators. Although neither of us probably realised it, there was a natural synergy between us in what we had both, in our very different fields, been trying to achieve. As architects, both I and my colleagues have been engaged for many years in meeting the challenge of constant social, technological and lifestyle changes and the way that they interlock. There is a constant quest for re-evaluating the workplace as a good place to be. Norman Foster, in conversation with the editor, 2012

Why are these details so important? 'Take floors', Dennis responds: 'spend the money on the right material and in ten years time it's in pristine condition.' In many instances, the details of the building reflect his personal ideas – using opaque glass, for example, rather than 'nasty vertical blinds' in meeting rooms, where the design of the tables also reflects his involvement. Dennis believes that this hands-on approach made for a better building. 'It was like that old carpenter's adage – "measure twice, cut once" – and it was that we brought to the programme. We were always challenging. Experts would come and talk about the way things had been done before and I would say: "I hear what you say, but I just don't believe it!"'

Far from being extravagant, Dennis says, the project was exactly tailored to McLaren's needs. And, in the end, the building was much more than a factory – 'it's a brand statement', he says. 'We don't have an advertising budget: this is what we're about. For me, this building is 95 per cent NASA and 5 per cent Disney. It's got that slight twist of entertainment, but at the same time it is absolutely up there in terms of technology and the technology of the building contributes to the products that we make'.

Over the last forty years, many Foster projects, from Reliance Controls on, have helped to reshape the workplace and redefine the nature of work. The McLaren Technology Centre is no exception and its architecture is in tune with the ethos of the organisation that occupies it. McLaren, says Ron Dennis, is fundamentally non-hierarchical. 'The bosses aren't on top of the building with the best view. We are down one end, looking at the same view as everybody else, on to the lake and trees'. Having an enjoyable environment in which to work is one way, Dennis says, in which people become passionate about their work – 'I'm a great believer in the idea that work has to be enjoyable'.

The environmental agenda of the project is also close to Dennis's heart. He loves the way in which the building dissolves into the landscape in a seamless transition. The idea was 'to have this quite formal building and then to dissolve this formality, to taper it, from the gardens into the surrounding nature of the countryside'. He hopes and believes that the building has actually enhanced the landscape in which it stands. The sophisticated servicing strategy of the building, which uses the water in the lake for cooling purposes, is also an aspect of the building of which he is proud, not least because it works well and provides a well-tempered environment for everyone who works there.

The building also has an incredible sense of calm. As Ron Dennis says: 'The difference between a productive building and a non-productive building is the fact that you've got human beings in one and not the other. And so if you are going to put people in it, why not ensure that you are designing for all their senses? Everybody, for example, can get their mind around the need for air conditioning; sometimes people get their minds around the importance of smell, but they rarely get their minds around noise. Noise is probably the biggest pollutant you can have of human thought. Many of the tortures that have been devised by man in the past relate to the systematic use of sound or the absence of sound. That is why this building is very calm. It's calm because we have designed it to suck the sound out of the system. Why should you work in an industrial environment that is noisy, when with modern materials you can absorb that noise and take away that contaminant.'

The Technology Centre project is a huge investment in the future: the building, Dennis says, has the flexibility to adapt to the likely future needs of the company. He hopes that the visitor centre – the Brand Centre as he has decided to call it – will be anything but an 'experience'. Among other functions, it will be a place for inspiring the young. 'What I want to do is bring young people in and excite them. I want to light the spark of enthusiasm for the sciences and particularly for those that relate to industry, to try and give people a real sense of purpose and point them or help them point themselves in a direction where their ambition and motivation is best served'. And everywhere you look in the McLaren building you sense that spirit.

1. Norman Foster with Ron Dennis in the Riverside studio. Design meetings were regular and intensive and every part of the building was considered in great detail.

1

Connections McLaren Technology Centre

Reliance Controls Factory Swindon UK 1965-6

In 1966 the idea of a democratic pavilion for all was a radical departure from the separate worlds (and buildings) for "management" and "workers". The typical factory of the time was an office block at the front of the site and a shed behind.

The McLaren Technology Centre continues a series of 'groundscrapers' that began with Willis Faber & Dumas in 1975. Willis Faber was low-rise – flowing to the edges of its site like a pancake in a pan – when a high-rise solution would have been the norm. That theme is taken up in a series of City of London buildings that have replaced insensitive 1960s slab blocks. Allied with that approach is the use of 'streets' as an organisational device within a densely organised, mat-like plan – there are links to unrealised projects such as Televisa and Paternoster Square. Overarching themes are the 'democratic workplace' and the 'integrated enclosure' – concepts embodied in the Reliance Controls Electronics Factory of 1966 and throughout the practice's work – in which every employee benefits from shared facilities and the same high standards of accommodation. The McLaren Technology Centre brings these themes to a new level of refinement.

Newport Comprehensive School

This started as a competition entry and developed into a research project. A rationalised lightweight steel frame formed an umbrella over classrooms and larger volume halls - served by an internal linear street. A regular pattern of roof glazing diffused natural light through a translucent glass ceiling over the entire floor plan.

Olsen Amenity Centre 1968-70

A pioneering project in Londons Milwall Docks - later demolished when the area was redeveloped as Canary Wharf. It brought together, for the first time, dockers and management in a single building with new social standards and innovative technology.

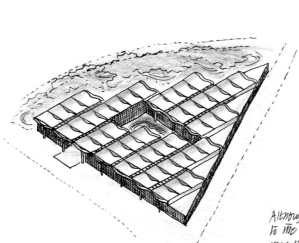

Televisa Headquarters, Mexico City · 1986

Paternoster Square - London - 1987

Although the scale and location of these three projects vary from Mexico to the City of London and the countryside beyond it - there is a repeating theme which unites them all. This is the communality and density offered by terraced fingers of work space interspersed by landscape or areas for social gathering.

willis faber - ipswich - UK 1971-5   Tower Place London 1992-2002   33 Holborn London 1993-2000

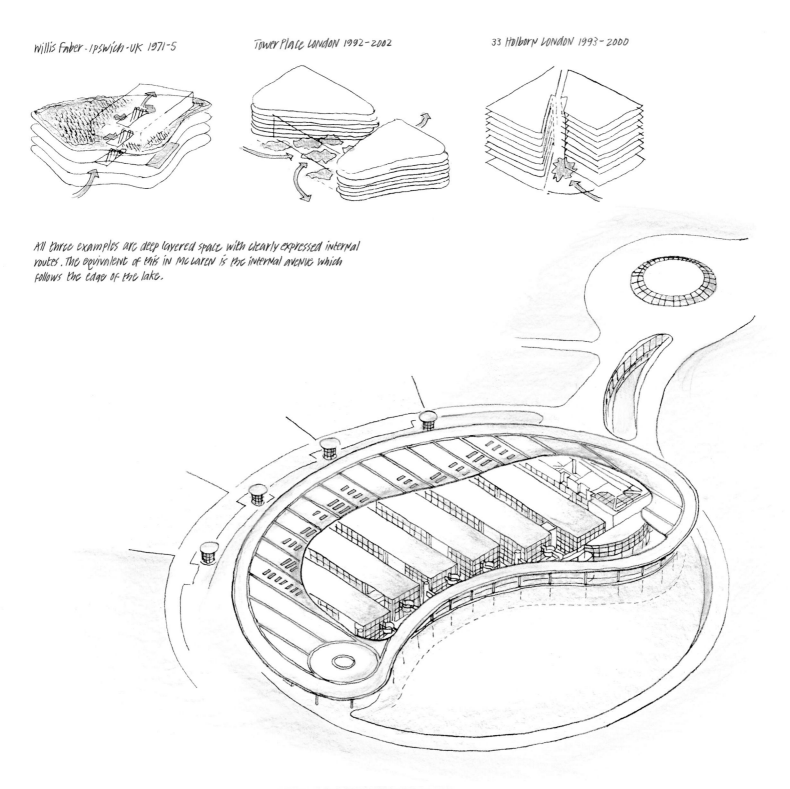

All three examples are deep layered space with clearly expressed internal routes. The equivalent of this in McLaren is the internal avenue which follows the edge of the lake.

McLaren Technology Centre Woking UK 1998-2004

The industry of car manufacture and research is associated with the image of dark satanic mills, smoke and pollution. The McLaren project with its dominance of landscaping and low profile presence is closer in spirit to an English country estate complete with artificial lake. It is in the practice tradition of blending the democratic workplace with high environmental standards and pioneering technology. The internal planning of terraced "buildings within a building" offers flexibility to express different divisions within the organisation, with the ability to change over time.

Electronic Arts European Headquarters 1997-2000

NF 2012

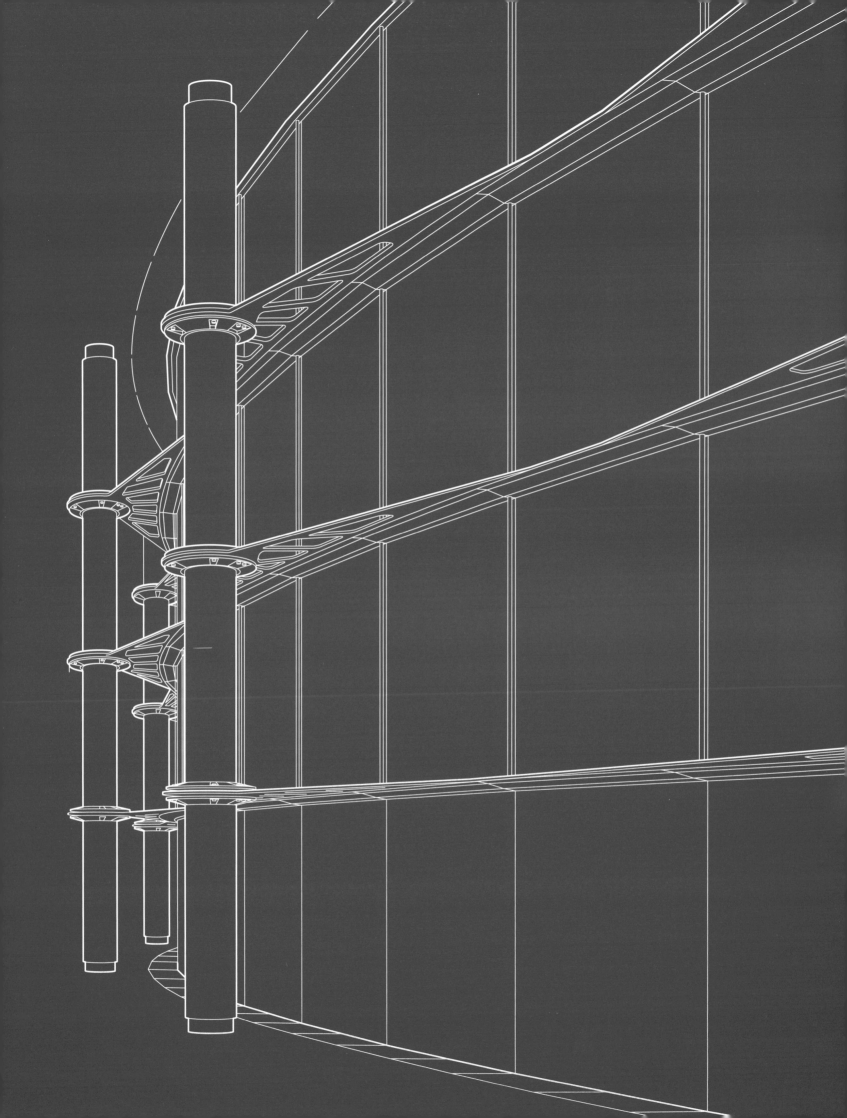

McLaren Technology Centre
Woking, England 1998–2004

The McLaren Group brings together extraordinary design and engineering expertise and the McLaren Technology Centre reflects that. The building includes design studios, laboratories, testing and production facilities for Formula 1 and road cars. In plan it is roughly semi-circular, the circle being completed by a formal lake, which forms an integral part of the environmental cooling system. The lakeside facade is a continuous curved glass wall, which we developed with the help of McLaren's technological input. The accommodation is planned around double-height linear 'streets', which articulate long fingers of flexible floor space. All the production and storage areas are placed on the lower levels, with toplit design studios, offices and meeting rooms above. Directly behind the facade is the 'boulevard', with its display of McLaren cars, which leads to a staff restaurant that looks out across the lake.

Norman Foster

Our aim has been to create an outstanding industrial building. But it doesn't matter how wonderful the box is, how shiny it is or how beautifully designed it is, if it is not also functional, inspirational and motivational. If we achieve the standards we have set for ourselves in all those respects, then we hope they will be something that other companies will wish to follow, once they see the benefits of providing **a better place to work.** Ron Dennis, quoted in *Icon*, November 2003

I have long been fascinated by so-called 'crop circles'. I remember coming across my first view of a 'formation' when piloting a helicopter one evening in Wiltshire. It was close to Silbury Hill, the largest man-made earthwork in Europe, whose origins are lost in antiquity. I was spellbound by the sheer beauty of the complex geometry that had been etched into the smooth table of wheat – dramatically thrown into relief by the setting sun. That image would come to mind again when we started to think about McLaren. Seen from above, the building seems to echo the abstract forms that have inspired crop formations over time. Norman Foster, in conversation with the editor, 2012
Left: A crop circle, incised in a green field of wheat.

Previous pages: Height constraints, the flood plain, public footpaths, the river and restricted land use combined to dictate a building that is low, curved and dug into the landscape in order to obtain the maximum floor area.

1, 2. Two views of the rural site, which is located on the edge of Horsell Common, outside Woking, in Surrey.

3. A series of site analysis sketches by David Nelson.

4. The organic plan form was further shaped by the fact that McLaren Racing – the Formula 1 division – required more space than the other businesses. The best way to resolve that was to push the facade forward at that point in the curve, so creating the 'yin and yang' shape interlocking with the lake.

5. Extracts from a sequence of preliminary planning studies by Nigel Dancey.

1

2

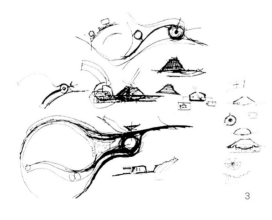

3

The foundations of Norman Foster's practice rest in part on what was once a neglected discipline for architects: the design of the industrial building. With a series of early projects for forward-looking clients, such as Reliance Controls, Fred Olsen, SAPA and Renault, Foster forged a reputation for innovation: architecturally and socially. Working with McLaren was an opportunity not only to reconnect with that discipline but to engage with a new generation of buildings set in a vastly changed industrial landscape.

The McLaren Technology Centre represents a remarkable blend of factory and corporate headquarters and a precise expression of the company's ethos. McLaren today is highly diversified. In addition to McLaren Racing, with its leading role in Formula 1, and McLaren Automotive, which produces road cars at the cutting edge of technology and performance, its divisions include McLaren Electronics and McLaren Applied Technologies, whose brief is to develop groundbreaking solutions across sport, medicine, and biomechanics through the application of McLaren 'know-how'.

The Vodafone McLaren Mercedes Formula 1 team can trace its roots back to 1963, when it was founded by New Zealander Bruce McLaren. Given a 750cc Austin Seven Ulster by his father, Bruce raced it while still a student. He not only became a successful Formula 1 driver, and winner of the Le Mans 24-hour race, but established a parallel career as a constructor. Tragically, he was killed at Goodwood in 1970, testing one of the Can-Am cars that bore his name.

The McLaren team continued after Bruce's death, merging in 1981 with Ron Dennis's Project Four Racing. Dennis first assumed the role of team principal before taking control of the company. The team is now one of the most successful in the history of Formula 1 and second only to Ferrari as the oldest active competitor. That incredible heritage is embodied in the design of McLaren's new building.

McLaren has long been based in Woking, in Surrey. Dennis wanted to stay in the town but faced the problem of finding a suitable site for a new complex, which was intended to replace a miscellany of buildings scattered across the locality. The site eventually selected was partly occupied by some nondescript glasshouses and sheds. However, it was located within the Green Belt, so there were numerous constraints on the scheme. For David Nelson, Foster's senior partner and Head of Design, who led the project with Nigel Dancey, this was simply 'one of the most difficult sites we've ever encountered.'

McLaren had already obtained outline consent for developing the site, although the application had been the subject of a public inquiry. Ron Dennis had commissioned the architect/planner Terence O'Rourke to draw up an outline design for submission to the inquiry, which resulted in approval for the development. At that point, Dennis began in earnest the search for an architect to design the building, which was intended to be the base for the five companies under the McLaren umbrella and accommodate some 900 staff.

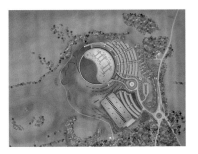

McLaren approached us to design a Production Centre for a new road car. One of the key things we had to think about was fitting the building sensitively into the landscape while maintaining a consistent architectural language with the existing centre. The new building is located to the south of the Technology Centre and has a north-south orientation. It's dug into the landscape and with trees and planting around it you can barely see it.
David Nelson, in conversation with the editor, 2012
Left: A site plan of the developed McLaren campus.

Dennis began the search by buying 'mountains of books' and identifying suitable practices. In due course, he drew up a shortlist of six international firms and visited buildings designed by each of them around the world. 'I arrived at a decision to work with Norman because he was passionate about some of the things that I was', Dennis says. Foster, for his part, recalls the 'natural synergy' that he quickly identified between the two men.

The McLaren Technology Centre represents a remarkable blend of factory and corporate headquarters and a precise expression of the company's ethos.

The ability to design seamlessly across the spectrum from urban planning, through all aspects of architecture to industrial design, has allowed Foster + Partners to develop a fully integrated approach that includes working closely with the people who make things – craftsmen, manufacturers and subcontractors – in order to gain a complete understanding of the construction process. With McLaren this collaborative methodology had the potential to develop enormously.

Dennis was to be as proactive and demanding a client as any the practice had worked with. 'Ron understands drawings: he doesn't need to be educated', Nelson observes. 'There must have been more than 200 meetings during the course of the project – some of them six hours long.' McLaren is a business where detail counts for a huge amount and Dennis naturally studied every element of the scheme.

McLaren's design expertise overlaps with Foster + Partners' work as industrial designers and there is a natural affinity between the two teams. However, never having designed at the scale of a headquarters building, McLaren might have expected the architects to assume control.

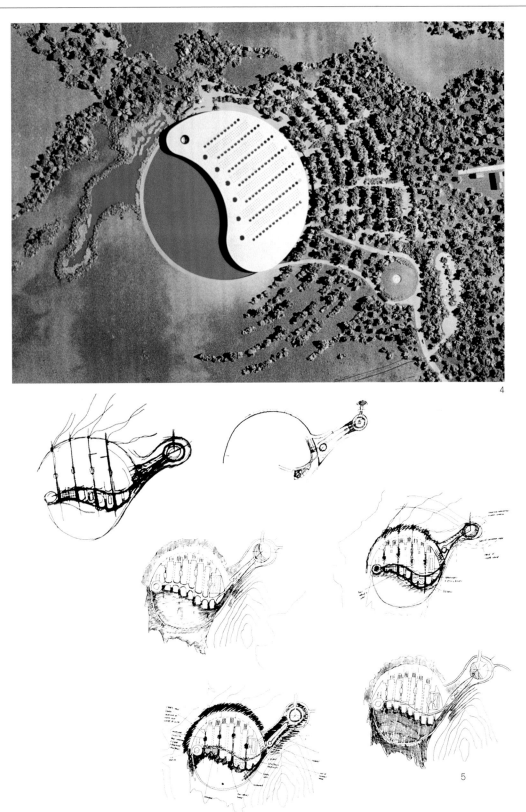

4

5

THE STATUS QUO

management box / workers shed
front / back
clean / dirty
posh / scruffy
we / they
white collar / blue collar

? OR

THE DEMOCRATIC PAVILLION

NF

In our earliest industrial and office projects, we sought to re-evaluate the design of the workplace, and to find ways to make it more democratic, sociable, flexible and responsive to developments in technology. In many ways this project was an opportunity to revisit some of those issues.
Norman Foster, in conversation with the editor, 2012
Left: In these sketches, Norman Foster sets out the thinking behind the Reliance Controls Electronics Factory (1965-1966).
Right: The Reliance Controls canteen, which was shared by white and blue-collar staff.
Centre: The Fred Olsen Amenity Centre (1968-1970).
Far right: Looking out across the roof garden of the Willis Faber & Dumas Headquarters (1971-1975).

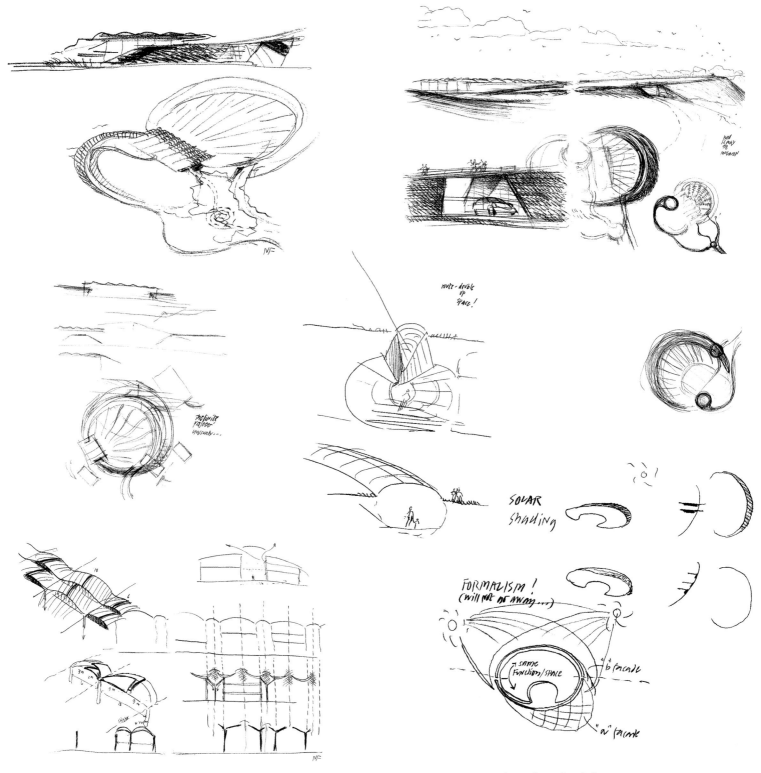

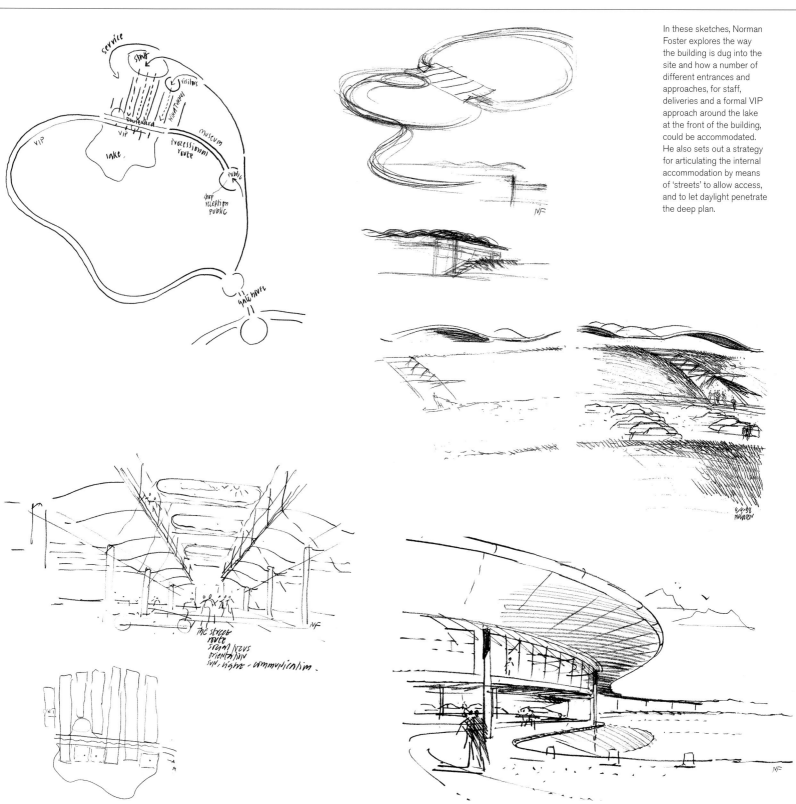

In these sketches, Norman Foster explores the way the building is dug into the site and how a number of different entrances and approaches, for staff, deliveries and a formal VIP approach around the lake at the front of the building, could be accommodated. He also sets out a strategy for articulating the internal accommodation by means of 'streets' to allow access, and to let daylight penetrate the deep plan.

We and McLaren also had Mercedes-Benz as a client. The design of the reception spaces and the handover area, where you go to specify your road car initially and where you then go to collect it, all had to be agreed with Mercedes. They wanted to be sure that the client experience was just right. Nigel Dancey, in conversation with the editor, 2012
Right: Nigel Dancey (left) in a design meeting with David Nelson.

From the beginning Ron Dennis had a very clear vision for the project. I remember he said he wanted it to be 95 per cent NASA and 5 per cent Disney. I think we all understood what he meant by that. He described the experience of coming to the building and going away. He talked about the 'aftertaste'. He wanted to control that aftertaste, so that when you leave you have an impression of somewhere that is scientific, technical, under control, but also has an element of fun. The Formula 1 experience has an element of the circus about it – there are lots of people gathered together in a spirit of excitement. Ron wanted to capture an element of that in the building. David Nelson, in conversation with the editor, 2012

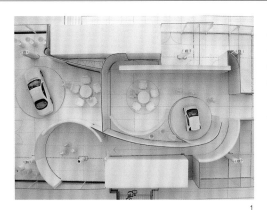

1. A model of the customer reception area. Sketch models such as this were used to explore the design of every part of the building.

2. Isometric drawing of the entrance to the restaurant; the stairs lead down to a fitness centre and pool.

3. An early drawing showing how services are distributed through the floor and ceiling voids. The mix of disciplines and the varying processes involved in each of the specialist industries dictated a structure that could allow for changing needs.

4, 5. Public areas have light fittings co-designed with the Italian company Targetti. All the companies that became technical partners on the project – AMEC, Schüco, Targetti, Pastorelli, Mapei, Instron and Grohe – went far beyond the notion of supply. They wanted to make sure that their technology was fully represented in what the design team was trying to ensure would be the most advanced work environment.

1

On the contrary, wherever possible the two teams combined their expertise, collaborating on the design of many of the key components and working together on space planning. Similarly, with the design of the handover area for the Mercedes-Benz SLR McLaren – the first road car to be assembled in the new building – a joint Foster McLaren team responded to Mercedes as client. It was a working relationship that forged a deep bond between the two organisations.

The brief for the Technology Centre included design studios, laboratories, research and testing facilities, electronics development, machine shops and prototyping and production facilities for Formula 1 cars and the Mercedes-Benz SLR McLaren. It also had to accommodate the 145-metre-long wind tunnel, used for testing half-size mock-ups of racing and road cars.

If the building had to be technically efficient, as much a 'machine' as the cars it produced, it also had to be an inspirational place to work. Dennis's aim is to communicate to everyone who works for the company the passion he feels for its products and heritage. He wanted the building to play a part in that – to leave an indelible impression on staff, visitors and customers alike.

The Foster team recognised that the project presented an opportunity to approach design in a different way: to consider a high level of integration and interdependency between architecture, design and engineering. Automotive design, particularly racing car design, focuses on reducing weight, which means increasing the efficiency of its components and integrating elements so that each does more than one job.

In the Technology Centre there is a high degree of integration. For example, the structural columns also double as rainwater pipes and absorb wind loads from the glazed lakeside facade. Similarly, sources of natural and artificial light, acoustics and cooling are brought together within the ceiling and roof build-up. Very thin water pipes are coiled and mounted directly behind the acoustically perforated metal ceiling panels, providing sound absorption and cooling within a very thin section. In each case, an integrated approach achieves 'more with less', suggesting new ways of conceiving high-performance buildings in the future.

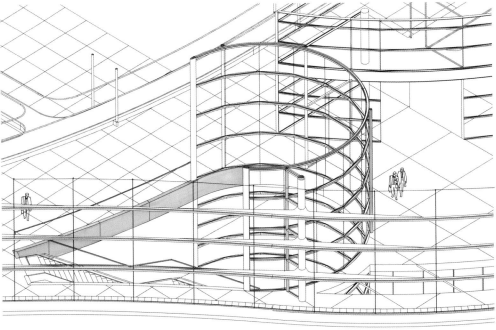

2

The roof is a story of integration between structure, services and daylight. It was all about developing something that lets the daylight in, has the cooling integrated and which allows the cooling surface also to work as a reflector. It's almost as if the roof is a mega-scaled light fitting. That level of service integration is what the practice is famous for. Stefan Behling, in conversation with the editor, 2012

The roof is penetrated to let light into the streets and office spaces. We took inspiration from Stansted where we had worked out that we didn't need much more than 5 per cent of the roof to be glass in order to light the floor space evenly. To help test this we made a half-size model of the roof which we placed in the office car park to study how the light would come in. The end result is quite a sophisticated design where the light enters through the roof before bouncing off the wind blades to be reflected back on to the curved ceiling. Nigel Dancey, in conversation with the editor, 2012

Working with Targetti and McLaren, Fosters designed a neat lighting system that combines natural and artificial light. Recognisably coming from the Foster stable, but with an added attention to visual detail that comes from Ron Dennis, the workplaces, whether an assembly line or office, exude a precise discipline that belies the intense intellectual effort that goes into the tasks. Jeremy Melvin, *Architectural Design*, January/February 2006

The first element of the building to be completed was the wind tunnel, which occupies an acoustically sealed, freestanding structure in order to minimise noise break-out and vibration. For operational reasons, the tunnel had to be up and running two years ahead of the rest of the building, which meant that its design had to be frozen before the overall plan had been finalised. A joint McLaren Foster team raced ahead with its development, giving special attention to the design of the services to ensure that they would be flexible enough to be adapted at a future date.

If the building had to be technically efficient, as much a 'machine' as the cars it produced, it also had to be an inspirational place to work.

The wind tunnel was one determining factor. The physical constraints of the 50-hectare site presented a further challenge. It was bisected by a river and subject to flooding; some polluted areas required decontamination; public footpaths had to be maintained; and the area where development was permitted was restricted to the 20,000-square-metre footprint previously occupied by sheds. Finally, any new building had to be low-rise, with a maximum height of 10 metres above datum.

The Technology Centre is a large building – 63,000 square metres – not much smaller than the terminal at Stansted Airport. Despite this, its presence is elusive. To accommodate the building, 450,000 cubic metres of soil was excavated and redistributed around the site to meet the restrictions on height and to create the subtly uneven landscape setting.

The building is arranged on three levels, including an extensive undercroft, which is largely occupied by services, in line with the strategy pioneered at Stansted Airport. Manufacturing, testing and storage facilities are located on the ground floor in 18-metre-wide fingers of accommodation separated by toplit 'streets'. The streets are circulation zones as well as areas for interaction, where the different McLaren 'families' meet. The upper level contains design studios, offices and meeting rooms.

4

5

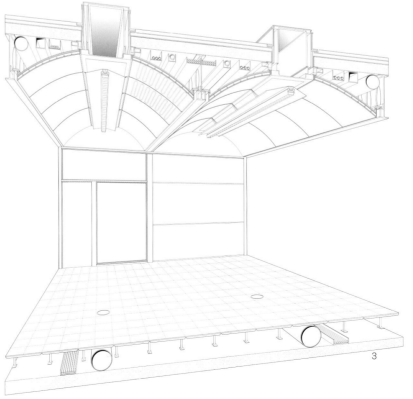

3

We worked very closely with McLaren's designers. Some things we designed jointly with them; other things – such as the workstations – they designed and made themselves. We also formed multi-disciplinary teams that worked on the design of all the big-scale equipment. That was done very late in the day. But that's part of their culture. They build things at the last minute because they need the maximum amount of time for development – for pushing until they get it right. Most people would have designed it two years earlier. But their argument is that if you do that, you end up with something that's two years out of date. It was quite staggering in many respects. David Nelson, in conversation with the editor, 2012

How does one deal with a kind of perfection? Certainly not by wibbling on about the fact that one is profoundly disappointed that the joints in the planar glazing panels weren't 2mm narrower. Or that the essential geometry of the headquarters might have been improved if the asymmetric radii involved had been 0.2 per cent tighter. The overriding architectural point about McLaren's headquarters is that one isn't talking about a building, but a somewhere that replaced nowhere and immediately became self-contained, sentient and completely purposeful. Jay Merrick, *The Independent*, 11 August 2004

Ron Dennis felt that the design of the building should be very integrated – like the components on a race car. If you have a wishbone, for example, that holds the wheel on, it's a key part of the suspension, but it's also part of the aerodynamics and it's a route for cables for sensors for the tyres. In car design one component does several things, but in architecture we tend to segregate everything: the structure is structure, the cladding is cladding; and services are separate from the structure and the cladding. So this project was a conscious attempt not to do that. The services and the structure are closely integrated. You will see components doing more than one job. David Nelson, in conversation with the editor, 2012

1. Section through an upper level studio space. Chilled ceilings provide cooling. Fresh air is introduced via floor-level grilles and extracted at ceiling level.

2. Environmental section. The potential of lake water to act as a cooling agent is exploited and expressed in a highly visible operating system. The lake receives storm-water run-off from the roof. It provides cooling through evaporation, while a 180-metre-long cascade is designed to vaporise the water into droplets, thus aiding the cooling process, oxygenating the water and introducing a white water visual effect. The lake water is pumped through a natural reed bed filtration system, followed by a cleansing biotope. Water can be drawn either from the lake or the biotope before being pumped to the heat exchangers. Water circulates through the system in a forty-eight hour cycle. Warm water is returned to the lake via the cascade, where the process begins again.

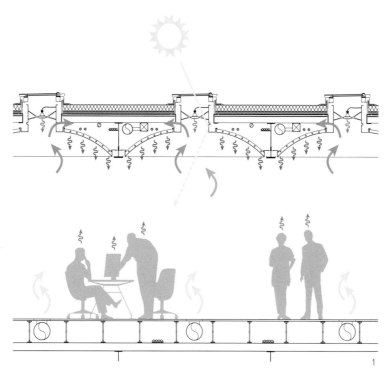

1

The visitor to the Technology Centre, if he or she has VIP status, approaches the building along a curving drive around a 2.9-hectare lake. Lake and building are contained within a perfect circle in the landscape. These two sinuous forms, united in this highly formal plan, recall the ancient Chinese symbol of the *taijitu*, the balance between the forces of yin and yang. The lake might indeed appear to be a formal gesture – like those created by Capability Brown in the parks of great country houses – but it also has a highly practical rationale. As well as assisting the drainage of the site, it is central to the project's environmental strategy.

Generally, the building has to be cooled, not heated, and lake water is used for cooling. Water is pumped through a filtration system (using the natural medium of reed beds) into heat exchangers. This water is stored in tanks inside the building and circulated on a forty-eight-hour cycle, so reducing the requirement for cooling towers. The cascade around the edge of the lake – another striking feature with historic resonances – cools warm water generated by the cooling system in the wind tunnel, the heat being dissipated directly into the air.

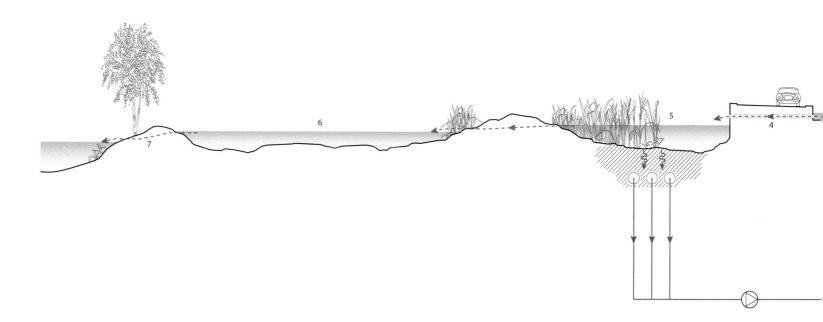

I am a person who pays great attention to detail … I surround myself with people who either try to assist me with achieving perfection, or guide me on the best way to achieve it. Of course, one of the principal guiding forces has been Norman Foster. I'd like to feel that he considers me as a sort of mixture of the paint and paintbrush, he being the artist. Ron Dennis, lecture in Florence, 15 May 2004

Left: Ron Dennis and Norman Foster discussing the project in the Foster studio at Riverside.

The flow of water from the lake into the reed beds allows natural filtration and the recirculation of water back into the building's main systems. Fish were introduced into the lake to control algae and the fish have in turn attracted herons, which now play their part in a natural cycle.

Practical though it is, the lake is also visually spectacular, extending right up to the building, which from certain viewpoints appears to float on the water. There are memories here, David Nelson suggests, of the Binnenhof Palace in The Hague: 'the relationship between the interior of the building and the lake is fundamental to the project – it's as if the water is flowing inside.'

The Technology Centre is not visible from the public road. A streamlined security lodge marks the point of entry to the complex. From here, the road bifurcates, with staff, service vehicles and non-VIP visitors using a route to the main car park. The building is entered via an imposing reception area leading directly to the full-height 'boulevard' that wraps along the lake frontage and leads to the staff restaurant and hospitality areas. An upper level walkway, following the curving line of the facade, provides an alternative through route; and the deeply cantilevered roof provides a high degree of shade.

With its fine views out and display of classic McLaren road and racing cars, the boulevard is designed to impress – here is the 'wow factor' at full throttle. Frequently used for social events and product launches, it feels very much front-of-house, with an obvious glamour.

Key to environmental section:
1 rainwater collection
2 formal lake (topped up from mains supply if required)
3 cooling by natural convection and evaporation
4 overflow from formal lake into biotope (rill)
5 cleansing biotope (rill)
6 balancing lake (environmental lake)
7 overflow into River Bourne
8 heat exchanger
9 cooling buffer tanks
10 chiller
11 supply to chilled ceilings
12 return heated water
13 cascade cools and aerates water before returning to lake

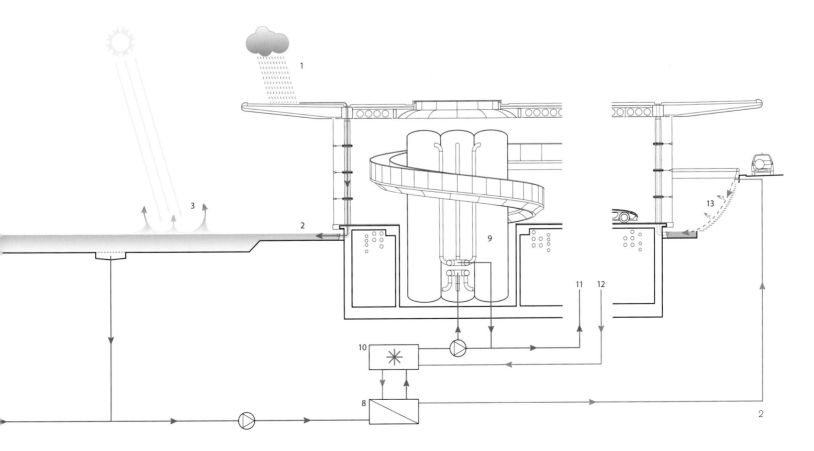

Cutaway drawing showing the two principal levels (there is another floor below ground, with some deeper undercroft areas in specific locations), and the arrangement of the underground museum and learning centre, seen here at top right. The main building brings together under one roof the different companies within the McLaren organisation, and supports all their research and manufacturing needs, including facilities to produce the Vodafone McLaren Mercedes Formula 1 cars, and a 145-metre-long wind tunnel. The challenge was to ensure that each of the studios, laboratories and other facilities would be kept separate and totally clean, but with good communications between the different areas. A 'galleria' in front of this accommodation looks out on to a newly created lake, which also forms an integral part of the building's cooling system.

It really is a Utopian vision in the unlikely setting of a field near the remarkably unlovely town of Woking. There is not the history of Maranello nor the ring to the name like Jaguar, but Dennis is on course to create his own paragon, a Manchester United of Formula One, in which success is not an accident but the result of long-term planning, financial care and vision. Kevin Eason, *The Times*, 29 January 2001

McLaren understood very quickly the curves and flowing lines of the building because there's hardly a straight line in anything they make – almost everything is a complex three-dimensional entity. We were mindful that we were in a definite cost range so we consciously stuck to what I call 1930s' geometry – circles and arcs and their interrelationship. If you get into more complex geometries there is a cost premium, so you have to have good reasons for doing it. There were a few things, like the curves on the underside of the walk bridge for example, which are more complex, but we kept them to a minimum. David Nelson, in conversation with the editor, 2012

For a long time I've been passionate about something the outside world often scratches its head about – what I call corporate hygiene. It means that the outside and inside of the building, the cleanliness and the maintenance – all have got to convey the message that at all times we are operating to the highest possible standards of efficiency. Ron Dennis, quoted in *The Financial Times*, 9 February 2000

1

2

1. Looking back from the approach road towards the gatehouse.

2. Water is extracted from the lake and used to cool the building. The water is returned to the lake via a system of waterfalls which gradually cools and oxygenates it.

However, that impression is balanced by views into the production areas beyond – there is no more 'back-of-house' at McLaren than there was in Foster and Team 4's Reliance Controls Electronics Factory, built four decades earlier.

The work carried out at Woking is far removed from the typical factory production line. The McLaren assembly line, if it exists at all in the conventional sense, is a collaborative craft operation with perfection being the goal: a mirror, perhaps, of the agenda behind the building itself. When the Mercedes-Benz SLR McLaren was built in the Technology Centre, no more than two were completed daily, while building a Formula 1 car takes a minimum of six weeks; and staff work in small, highly skilled teams. Throughout the production areas there is a strong sense of openness and transparency, though naturally some areas such as paint shops have to be sealed environmentally.

The design of the services was overseen by a joint multidisciplinary group, comprising members of the Foster and McLaren teams, the contractor and the M+E consultants. This dedicated 'team-within-a-team' was also responsible for sourcing the large-scale equipment incorporated into the building, a process that was undertaken late in the day to ensure that everything was state of the art.

Ron Dennis pressed for ventilation capacity in many areas to be increased above the accepted specification level, using a system more usually found in hospital wards. He also suggested depressurising the restaurant to ensure that cooking smells would not permeate the circulation spaces. Throughout, the focus was on achieving the best possible environment. As Ron Dennis says, 'once you've satisfied the salary of a mad scientist, the only way you can keep him is to give him the finest facilities and resources.'

The cascade around the edge of the lake – another feature with historic resonances – cools warm water from the cooling system in the wind tunnel.

McLaren does not just build cars: the technologies developed for advanced car production are being applied more widely than ever before and research partnerships have been developed with companies in fields ranging from paint to electronics. These associations were drawn on freely as the building project evolved, no more spectacularly than in the design of the curved lakeside facade.

3

4

To reinforce the visual connection with the water and open countryside beyond, it was vital that the glazing be as sheer as possible, with minimal structural support in evidence. However, the flat expanse of the lake generates wind loads beyond the average, which would normally demand substantial vertical posts and mullions. The search for an alternative involved close collaboration between the Foster and McLaren teams and the German glazing manufacturer Schüco – one of McLaren's long-standing corporate partners.

The design of the facade is a perfect example of what used to be called 'technology transfer', a recurring theme in Foster's early work and fundamental to his break with traditional methods of construction. Wind loads are absorbed by 12-metre long aluminium 'blades', their form inspired by the rear wing struts of the McLaren F1 GTR, which won the 1995 Le Mans 24 Hours race. These are connected to the columns by aluminium collars. Vertical loads are supported by elliptical 5mm stainless-steel tie-rods, as used to frame the bodies of McLaren's Formula 1 cars. The rods form a matrix on which 40 tonnes of laminated glass can be suspended from the roof with virtually no apparent means of support.

Norman Foster has described the facade as 'a light, almost gravity-defying wall that liberates the view and the relationship to the world outside' and it is certainly one of the most innovative glazing projects of recent years.

The demanding client brief meant that a high proportion of the fittings and furnishings were bespoke, reinforcing the image of the building as a hand-built machine in the McLaren mould. The concern for detail extended to the design of work clothing, which was made by Hugo Boss. Nothing in the building is incidental.

The lighting strategy was devised by Claude Engle, a seasoned Foster collaborator, who worked with the Italian manufacturer Targetti to develop innovative ways of lighting the building using an automatic control system to ensure ideal lighting conditions in working areas by day and by night. Light fittings were custom fabricated to a Foster design. Again, McLaren's associations with manufacturers kept costs relatively low. Natural light is controlled by bespoke diffusers, using low-iron glass 'wings' that baffle direct sunlight and soften the effect of the light permeating internal spaces.

3. Approaching the building from the car park. Distant views are deliberately screened, in accordance with planning requirements, but the visitor is in no doubt he or she is about to enter the special world of McLaren.

4. The entrance rotunda to the wind tunnel and Zone A; subsequent fingers of accommodation, which are named sequentially from B to G, are paired around three further rotundas, all approached from the car park.

Overleaf: Seen from across the lake, the building nestles in the landscape. Low-lying and compact it is shielded from view by 100,000 newly planted trees.

The McLaren complex is surely the most extraordinarily arranged high-performance car research, administration and production plant in the world. Can this place really have been constructed by men with tool belts? No: of course not. It must, instead, have spooled out of a specially modified VDU into the landscape, in a gelatinous bolus of hi-res pixels that, within seconds, solidified into a building … Jay Merrick, *The Independent,* 11 August 2004

When I considered the initial brief, I tried to portray the mind of the person leaving the facility to go home. In fact, I didn't even want them to go home. I wanted it to be such a great place that people would want to stay there. We've incorporated lots of different things to create an environment that not only motivates them, not only sends them home not smelling of the company and with a positive approach to life, but also tries to put a skip in their walk. Ron Dennis, speaking at the XXI World Congress of Architecture, Berlin, 26 July 2002

Having tried to effect the closest merger between the building and nature, the rolling countryside beyond the lake, and the sky, it was quite a challenge to find a way of almost 'dissolving' the wall that defines the building's edge to the lake. Norman Foster, in conversation with the editor, 2012

The landscape plays a vital part, creating a sense of surprise and delight for visitors when the building is finally revealed, viewed from an approach road across a lake. Even the water combines aesthetics and function. It reflects sunlight into the interior, and also helps with the cooling load, especially from the wind tunnel where car aerodynamics are tested and refined. Jeremy Melvin, *Architectural Design*, January/ February 2006

It is not by accident that everybody working in the company looks out over the lake and at the fields: **that's by design.** Ron Dennis, interviewed in *Profile 02*, 2004

By using the lake to cool the building we raise its temperature by about five degrees. I went to visit McLaren one morning in very cold weather. There was snow on the ground but the lake itself was steaming, not violently but it created an eerie mist. It was very beautiful — and a great demonstration of how well the system works. Iwan Jones, of Foster + Partners, in conversation with the editor, 2012

Normal workplaces just require desks, telephone systems, electricity and data systems. McLaren needs all this plus hydraulic systems, air pressure and vacuum systems, two types of electricity – three phase and single phase – and two levels of data systems to serve the administrative and technical sides of the company. And this had to be achieved whilst creating a psychologically uplifting environment, which was vital for the project to be successful. Ron Dennis, quoted in *Racing Line*, June 2004

Today they're building road cars in the factory space – and you can look in and see what's going on. But it's possible that at some point this might come to an end. In five years' time they might be building a different car, working with another engine supplier. Or they might be building parts for aerospace, which might require an increased level of security. So you have to be able to shut down different parts of the building when you want to and open them up when you can. It has to be very flexible. David Nelson, in conversation with the editor, 2012
Right: The design team with a model of the building, getting ready for a client presentation.

0   50m
0   150ft

1

Ron Dennis was anxious that there should be a whole range of experiences. He didn't just want to walk into one space, see it and that's all you got. Rather, he liked the idea of a gradual building which as you walk around unfolds more and more different spaces and that was what led partly to the double curve. Nigel Dancey, in conversation with the editor, 2011

If you imagine a person, male or female, sat in a dark office, perhaps having had a little alcohol, versus another person sat in a well-ventilated environment, drinking a glass of cool water, and you ask each of them to solve a problem, I don't think you have to be an Einstein to realise that the person in the better environment is going to be better equipped, with a better mindset, to take a more positive decision. The environment in essence, is more uplifting, more motivating, and of course it provides for the individual to be more focused. Ron Dennis, lecture in Florence, 15 May 2004

The McLaren Technology Centre is the most beautiful industrial building in the country. Firstly in its design and in its incorporation of majestic sweeps and curves, secondly in its lightness and airiness and thirdly its glorious space beside the Capability Brown-style lake that is essentially part of the enterprise. Lord St John of Fawsley, chairman of the Royal Fine Art Commission Trust, announcing the winner of the Building of the Year Award, 16 June 2005

1. Site plan, incorporating the first floor plan.

2. Ground floor plan

3. Lower level plan.

  1 car park
  2 service yard
  3 offices
  4 lake
  5 VIP dining
  6 wind tunnel
  7 visitor and learning
    centre
  8 production area
  9 boulevard
  10 restaurant
  11 storage
  12 swimming pool

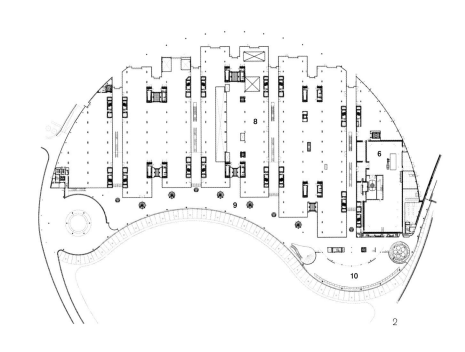

2

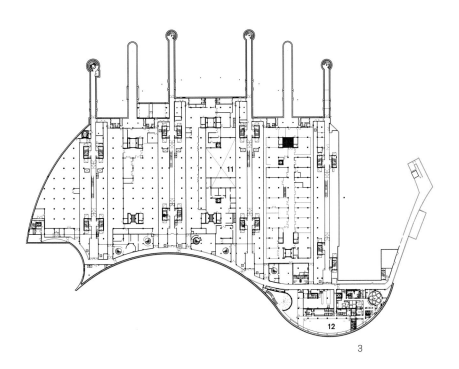

3

Winning the World Championship with the
**McLaren M23 was much harder than winning my
first one in 1972. Clay Regazzoni and I were on
equal points, and side by side on the grid, for the
last race, in the USA. I think it was the only race
where I didn't sleep well the night before. Clay too
probably. With so many good drivers around we
needed a real team effort, but I always felt that
McLaren was better prepared, and this was the
day it really showed.** Emerson Fittipaldi, Drivers' World
Champion 1974, *McLaren – The Cars*, 2008

**Other teams are driven by emotions and as long
as you perform they love you, but if you don't
perform you get sacked like anybody else. But
McLaren is the opposite, being a high-quality,
high-tech team, making the best racing cars
ever built and run with Ron's British coolness.**
Niki Lauda, *McLaren – The Cars*, 2008
Left: Four of McLaren's celebrated Formula 1 cars – some
of the many lined up on the building's opening day. From
left: the M26 of 1976-1977; the M23 of 1974, designed
by Gordon Coppuck – in which Emerson Fittipaldi won the
world championship; the M19C of 1972-1973; and
the M7C of 1969.

1

2

1. The assembly line
seen during production
of the Mercedes-Benz
SLR McLaren.

2. Since McLaren began
competing in Formula One
in 1966, it has become one
of the most successful teams
in the history of the sport.
Here, McLaren technicians
work on a MP4-20A car,
generally considered to
be the fastest car of the
2005 Formula 1 season.

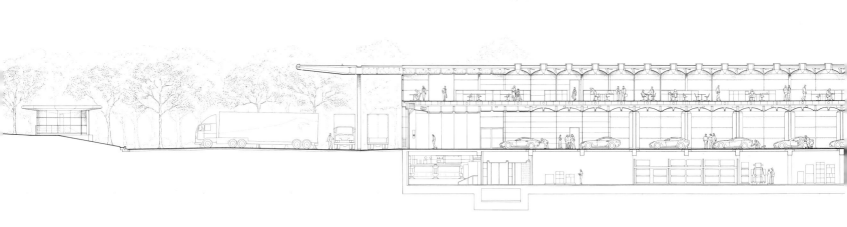

Another interesting thing about McLaren is how it transfers the technology of its F1 cars to the design of road cars. The Mercedes-Benz SLR McLaren was the first of its road cars to be constructed in the new building. But before that, there were other great cars: the McLaren F1 – the fastest production car in the world in 1998 – and the F1LM, which came out of McLaren's track experience with the F1. David Nelson, in conversation with the editor, 2012

Right: The Mercedes-Benz SLR McLaren. The bodyshell is built from carbon fibre composite and the engine is a 5439cc Mercedes-AMG V8 that delivers an astonishing 626bhp. Echoing the iconic Mercedes 300SL 'Gullwing' of the 1950s, the doors swing forwards and upwards.

The bays for examining Formula 1 cars when they return to the factory between races are closer to an operating theatre than the usual grime-coated inspection pit of a local garage. Even the assembly line for the road-going Mercedes-Benz SLR McLaren … where these third of a million pound toys are nursed into existence at the rate of three a day has something of a hospital about it. Jeremy Melvin, *Architectural Design*, January/February 2006

3

4

3. Internally, the building is organised around double-height circulation 'streets', which articulate 'fingers' of flexible accommodation.

4. A circulation 'boulevard' leads to areas for hospitality and to the staff restaurant, both of which look out across the landscape.

5. Cross-section through the Mercedes-Benz SLR McLaren assembly line, the 'boulevard' and the lake.

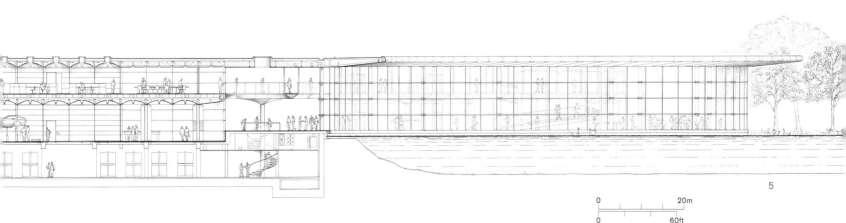

0		20m
0		60ft

5

The serpentine lakeside facade … that appears in some lights to touch the water, is composed of glass supported by aluminium wind blades and slim stainless-steel tie rods. The 12-metre perforated blades are modelled on the rear-wing support struts of the 1995 Le Mans winning McLaren F1 GTR and manufactured by a process similar, says McLaren, to that employed in the production of wing frames on Airbus jets by BAE Systems, one of the Woking firm's 'technology partners'. Jonathan Glancey, *The Guardian*, 13 October 2003

There are lots of parallels to Formula One. There has been the same search for perfection, the same search for performance, and the same demand for proven cutting-edge technology. We didn't want to be a guinea pig for technology, but we did want the latest and the best. Ron Dennis, quoted in *The Guardian*, 13 October 2003

McLaren had a number of designers who were very good and who had worked on the Formula 1 motor homes and they began working more closely with our team. For example, we originally anticipated that the wind blades would be made from solid steel but McLaren weren't happy with this at the mock-up stage and wanted much more of a celebrated junction, so we worked with them to refine the design. The resulting wind blades are made from aluminium which has been cut and milled so you can show the holes in the openings. We basically cut out the structure we didn't need to make them much lighter and more efficient. Nigel Dancey, in conversation with the editor, 2011

1

We combined aerospace and Formula 1 engineering technology to find the strongest and most transparent solution for the facade. We devised computer-cut aluminium 'wind-blades' to absorb the wind loads, while the vertical loads are supported by stainless-steel tie rods that are the same as those used to support the bodywork of a Vodafone McLaren Mercedes Formula 1 car.
Norman Foster, interviewed in *Profile* 02, 2004

Ron Dennis was very keen for us to learn about Lockheed Martin's legendary Skunk Works, in Burbank, California. It was established during the war, in June 1943, under the leadership of Clarence L 'Kelly' Johnson with a brief to design and build a new jet fighter in record time. Lockheed developed an airframe around the most powerful jet engine that the Allied Forces had access to at that time – the de Havilland Goblin – and the Skunk Works team designed and built a prototype XP-80 in just 143 days, beating the deadline by a week. The key to that achievement was communication – at all levels

– and the design and engineering teams were completely integrated, which greatly increased productivity. That level of collaboration really characterised the design process here. Similarly, in the finished building, the design departments are located alongside the production line so that the designers can walk over and talk to the engineers and vice versa. In practice, it works incredibly well. David Nelson, in conversation with the editor, 2012

The Technology Centre is one Foster building to which the adjective 'organic' is frequently applied, although the geometric synergies are relatively simple. To some degree the curvaceous form derives from the necessity to dig the building into the landscape in order to conform to planning restrictions and maximise the floor area on the site. Yet the geometry also evokes memories of early Modern Movement landmarks, such as Mendelsohn and Chermayeff's De La Warr Pavilion at Bexhill, even of Art Deco.

The design of the facade is a perfect example of what used to be called 'technology transfer'.

'The building has a unifying language of form', says Nelson. 'Its shape is the outcome of refining potentially conflicting geometries.' There are parallels with the Swiss Re tower, where the circular plan generates orthogonal floors; and equally with The Sage Gateshead music centre, where foyers and public circulation areas wrap sensuously around rectilinear performance spaces. In the Technology Centre, the glazed envelope acts as a wrapping for the rectangular strips of accommodation within, bursting out in the striking glazed enfilade along the lakeside. The balance between the rational and the expressive is as fine as in any Foster project.

At the time it was completed, the Technology Centre ranked as one of the largest private construction projects in Europe, in terms not only of the new building but equally of the associated landscaping (100,000 trees and shrubs were planted throughout the site, for example). Looking at it today, the scale of its ambition is matched by the built reality. Ron Dennis has stressed the need to motivate and inspire the people who work for McLaren. The building, he says, is 'a strong statement about a new kind of architectural approach which gives priority to caring about the employees and how they work'. It surely offers more than enough to send them home 'with a skip in their walk.'

Kenneth Powell

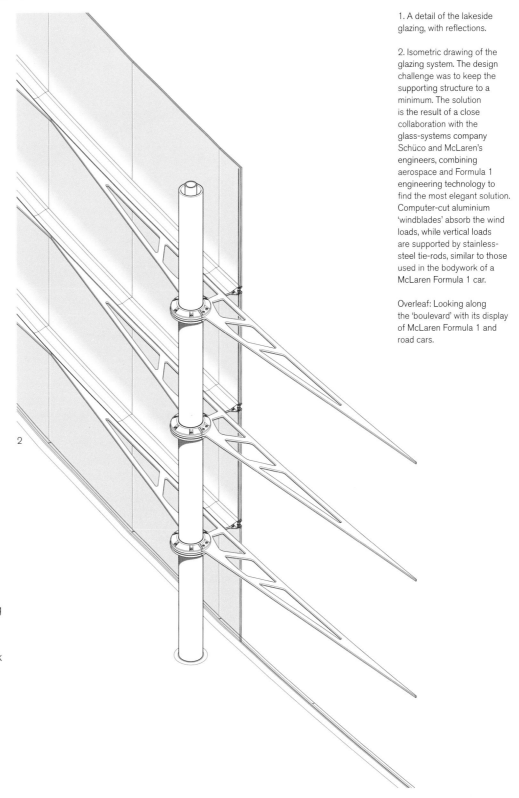

2

1. A detail of the lakeside glazing, with reflections.

2. Isometric drawing of the glazing system. The design challenge was to keep the supporting structure to a minimum. The solution is the result of a close collaboration with the glass-systems company Schüco and McLaren's engineers, combining aerospace and Formula 1 engineering technology to find the most elegant solution. Computer-cut aluminium 'windblades' absorb the wind loads, while vertical loads are supported by stainless-steel tie-rods, similar to those used in the bodywork of a McLaren Formula 1 car.

Overleaf: Looking along the 'boulevard' with its display of McLaren Formula 1 and road cars.

The technology centre is not a monument, it is above all else, designed to be a tool. It is designed to motivate, to uplift people's emotions, to try and capture within people's minds the thought that being at work is even better than being at home. It's a wonderful thing to achieve for an employer, if nobody wants to go home. Of course they do, but I think they are very happy to come back because the spaces are so uplifting. Ron Dennis, lecture in Florence, 15 May 2004

It is absolutely perfectly done. It's put together like a Swiss watch. It's not just that the joints line up it's that the joints between materials are all exactly the same width. Judge's comment, RIBA Stirling Prize 2005, *The Architects' Journal*, 12 October 2005

Why is it that the McLaren headquarters makes the Gherkin seem like just another office block? Answer: two perfectionists, and the small black vacuum cleaners parked next to each work station on the assembly lines … Here, the white ceramic floor tiles shine like polished milk. The guts and gubbins of the Formula One and sports cars are Flash clean. There is not a single smudge, a smear, an iota of dirt to be seen … nor is there a ghost of a smudge on the tubes of glass (pistons, of course!) that contain the bespoke lifts that hum smoothly upwards to the management level and the spectacularly sinuous double curve of the elevated walkway. Jay Merrick, *The Independent*, 11 August 2004

Whether the purpose of a visit to the centre is to pick up your SLR, or hand over a sum of many magnitudes greater as an F1 sponsor, you see the company's history in its products. The fastest production road car, cars that have won eleven constructors championships and taken eight drivers to individual glory, are laid out in front of you … Here technology is turned into spectacle – and it might even be turned into something of quotidian use. Jeremy Melvin, *Architectural Design*, January/February 2006

Left: HM the Queen and the Duke of Edinburgh meet members of the client and design teams before the formal opening of the building, 12 May 2004.

Right: The 'bollard' recording the opening date.

McLaren Production Centre

Woking, England 2009–2011

1

For Ron Dennis, the McLaren Technology Centre was not so much a building as 'a brand statement', its technical excellence mirroring that of the Formula 1 racing cars that are designed and built there. After thirty years as principal of the Vodafone McLaren Mercedes Formula 1 team, Dennis stood aside in 2009 to become executive chairman of McLaren Automotive – part of a long-term strategy of diversifying McLaren's business into new areas.

The Technology Centre was the first element in a growing campus being developed by the company on the edge of Woking, where McLaren is now the largest employer (2,000 staff and still recruiting). The Production Centre, conceived as a 'satellite' to the Technology Centre's 'mother ship', is designed for the assembly of sports cars – the ultra-high-performance MP4-12C being the first model to go into production.

The production hall is an all-white space with the ethos of a laboratory rather than a factory.

Launched in the summer of 2011, the MP4-12C has a lightweight chassis, based around an F1-style carbon-fibre tub. The car's appeal lies in its performance and its exclusivity. No more than 4,000 MP4-12Cs will be built annually. That is a fraction of the output of a typical car factory, but the Production Centre is hardly typical; and 4,000 represents a large number for McLaren, which previously made 350 Mercedes-Benz SLR McLaren cars a year.

The brief was far more straightforward than that for the Technology Centre and this is reflected in the contrast in form between the two buildings. The Technology Centre is curvaceous, organic, with expansive reception and circulation areas wrapping around rectangular fingers of production and research space. It is designed to make a strong impression on the visitor. The same visitor may barely notice the presence of the Production Centre, which lies behind trees close to the entrance to the McLaren campus.

The company's expansion in Woking was potentially controversial: the site lies within the Green Belt and the development of the Technology Centre only proceeded after a public inquiry. Even then, planners insisted that its environmental impact be kept to the minimum. The Production Centre, which was designed and constructed in just twenty months (compared with sixty months for the Technology Centre), extends that principle by being dug into its sloping site. The soil excavated in the process was re-used for landscaping, concealing the building still further.

In essence, the building is a very large shed, with a footprint measuring 200 x 100 metres and a net floor area of 34,500 square metres. It has antecedents in Norman Foster's early work, which extends back to the Reliance Controls Electronics Factory, designed while Foster was a partner in Team 4, and more specifically in his subsequent Advance Factory Systems studies of 1969, in which he explored the design of a flexible factory building, capable of integrating 'clean' industries within urban communities.

1. A view of the assembly line, showing the integrated services. The McLaren Production Centre shares a design philosophy with the adjacent Technology Centre, to which it has a direct connection via a 100-metre tunnel. That philosophy manifests itself in a rigorous attention to detail and a determination that the building will be highly flexible to ensure a long working life.

2. An axonometric study of a typical column-beam junction, showing how structure and services are fully integrated. A key element of the brief was to make the production hall adaptable to virtually any assembly scenario, so that McLaren can change its model line-up with ease.

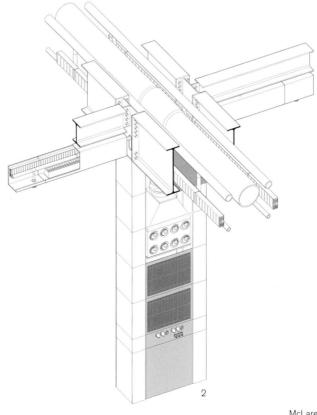

2

We are trying to use automation where it doesn't take away the quality of the finished product, hence the uniqueness of how we paint the cars in an environment that is more about giving birth to a car than making it. If we fulfil our objective, I would love to be considered the Swiss watchmaker of cars. If you look at the great watches, they are still put together by craftsmen who are very focused and dedicated to how they build them. There is virtually no automation in how the watch is made. Ron Dennis, quoted in *The Daily Telegraph*, 29 August 2011

1

2

1. A body shell in the paint shop. All the machinery for the 'noisy' or 'dirty' processes of manufacturing cars, such as painting, is contained within highly serviced, self-contained glass booths.

2. The production hall itself has a calm atmosphere. Everything in the general assembly area is designed to be no higher than 1.6 metres, so that from any one point you can see almost the entire production process.

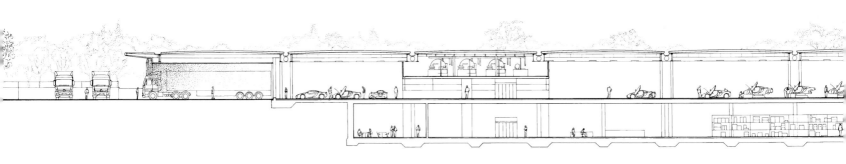

There is nothing above a height of 1.6m in the MPC, unlike mass-volume car plants where machines stretch from floor to ceiling and cars travel along the roof to the next production station. Indeed, with its sterile white walls, there is a noticeable lack of machinery. This is because McLaren wants as much of the car as possible to be produced by hand to ensure the highest levels of quality and finish. Graham Ruddick, *The Daily Telegraph*, 29 August 2011

McLaren's work is incredibly precise. In many ways, the production line is like an operating theatre and the architecture reflects this, with an industrial building of the highest quality. As well as drawing on the understanding we gained with the Technology Centre, the Production Centre echoes its aesthetic. Visually, they can be seen as a family, unified by a common language of finishes and a consistent palette of materials. David Nelson, in conversation with the editor, 2012

The MP4-12C has generally received strong reviews from critics, but where it has been criticised, McLaren has responded with upgrades. For example, some critics complained the engine was not loud enough as the car accelerated. So, McLaren developed technology to allow the driver to tune the volume. Graham Ruddick, *The Daily Telegraph*, 29 August 2011

3

4

3, 4. At peak production it is possible to build a McLaren MP4-12C in five days and for a new car to join the line every 45 minutes.

5. Cross-section north-south through the production hall; the linear arrangement of the structure mirrors the workflow of the production line. A basement level accommodates parts storage and plant.

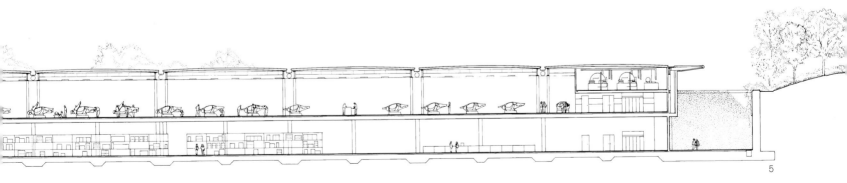

5

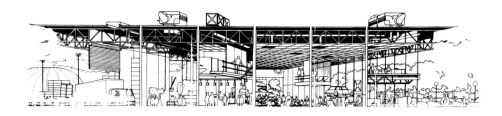

The Production Centre is a quantum leap forward in the evolution of industrial buildings, both socially and in terms of working conditions, and technologically – in its flexibility and its services integration. The scale and sophistication of the assembly hall is a fitting complement to the precision of McLaren's cars. Interestingly, from my perspective, it links back to the Factory Systems studies that I made in the late 1960s – so in that sense there are points of continuity.
Norman Foster, in conversation with the editor, 2012
Left: Norman Foster's perspective drawing of a fully flexible factory system (1969-1972). The double-height space can be adapted to suit a multiplicity of functions.

This is probably the first time anyone has developed a production facility around the car. Over the coming years it will allow us to expand the company. We're building around 1,000 cars a year now and that will grow to 4,000 within four years, adding at least 200 jobs just to build the cars. We will also be introducing new models, and entering new markets such as China, all of which will create a lot of investment on the engineering side as well. Antony Sheriff, McLaren Automotive Managing Director, speaking at the opening of the McLaren Production Centre, 17 November 2011

It is rare that you get to design two companion buildings for the same client and it was a great experience. While the Technology Centre took six years to design and build, the fast-track programme meant that the Production Centre was completed in a third of the time. The same team worked on both buildings and this continuity helped to make such an ambitious timescale possible. We were also able to draw on the wider capabilities of our studio: the Production Centre is a great example of integrated design, with all the services built into the structure to create a highly flexible space. Nigel Dancey, in conversation with the editor, 2012

By optimising structural spans to allow a largely clear floor space, we have essentially created a big empty box, with services integrated within the structural zones, wall and floor voids. This flexible form ensures that the building is also highly cost efficient – it will support McLaren's production needs today and far into the future. Iwan Jones, of Foster + Partners, in conversation with the editor, 2012

Through everything we do, McLaren strives to find the solution. We never stop. We exist to go faster; to be state-of-the-art; to innovate; to perform with belief, flair and passion; to be the absolute best at what we do. And everything that McLaren is has been built on the founding principles of good design and solid, seamlessly efficient engineering and manufacturing.
Ron Dennis, speaking at the opening of the McLaren Production Centre, 17 November 2011
Left: Ron Dennis, McLaren Group Chairman, introducing the McLaren Production Centre to the press.

1

Previous pages: Looking along the assembly line from the mezzanine at the northern end of the production hall.

1. Site plan, showing the relationship between the original Technology Centre, left, and the Production Centre. More than 800 trees were planted on the site, and 68 mature specimens replanted before the bird-nesting season, as part of the landscaping to screen the new building from view.

| 0 | 100m |
| 0 | 300ft |

Engineering does not get more complex than this – tens of thousands of components, aerodynamics that almost defy the laws of physics, cars that go from 0-300kmh in less than nine seconds. This team designs a new part for a car every twenty minutes across the season, that's how fast the innovation is. It's engineering so groundbreaking that when space scientists are looking for ideas they come to the brains in Formula 1. Prime Minister David Cameron, opening the McLaren Production Centre, 17 November 2011
Left: Ron Dennis introduces David Cameron to Vodafone McLaren Mercedes drivers Lewis Hamilton and Jenson Button at the start of the Prime Minister's visit to the McLaren Technology Centre.

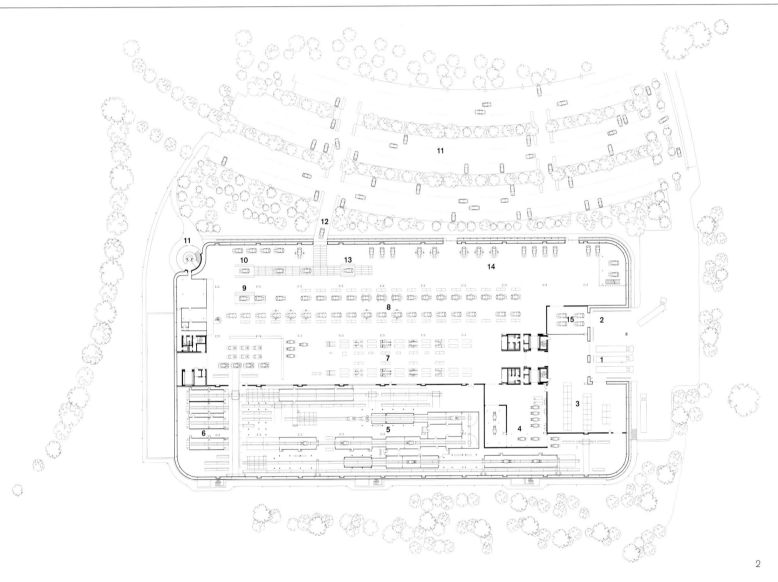

2

This is the workplace of the future. It is about human values, advanced technology and ecology. It creates an environment that encourages people to meet their full potential.

Norman Foster

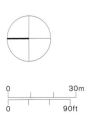

2. Plan of the production hall.

1 goods in
2 goods out
3 logistics
4 CMM control area
5 paint shop
6 re-work area
7 body assembly
8 general assembly
9 rolling road
10 monsoon wash
11 entrance rotunda
12 test drive
13 final wash
14 quality sign off
15 finished cars

1

2

1. The Production Centre is entered via a circular glass drum beneath the overhang of the roof canopy.

2. A glazed lift and spiral stair lead down to the production hall.

The great automobile factories of the first half of the twentieth century – for example, Ford's vast River Rouge Complex at Dearborn, Michigan – were places where all the components were manufactured and then brought together on an assembly line. The McLaren Production Centre, in contrast, is a symbol of a very different industrial era. It relies on a system of team working, to produce a technologically advanced, handmade product using components sourced globally.

The building is organised on three levels – basement, ground and mezzanine. The main production space at ground level is a steel-framed structure, with large spans for maximum flexibility and a generous head height of 5.5 metres. Mezzanines are located at the northern and southern ends, the latter containing offices.

The paint shop occupies an area along the western side of the building. A double-height enclosed space, extending down to basement level, its air filtration systems ensure a dust-free environment; and protective clothing is mandatory.

The basement, contained by shear walls of in-situ concrete, is almost entirely given over to storage and logistics – some 60,000 parts arrive here daily and are stored in linear racks. Staff facilities, including showers, are also provided at this level, but production staff, like all McLaren employees from management down, have their meals in the Technology Centre's restaurant.

The rationale behind the project was to create a highly flexible, economical building, driven by the logic of the assembly process. However, this did not preclude the need for stylistic continuity with the Technology Centre – the aim being to create a 'family' of details for the campus. For example, the overhanging roof of the Production Centre, with its bullnose edge, has an affinity with that of the Technology Centre; and the aluminium tubing used to clad two sides of the building provides a further point of reference.

Externally, however, the building gives little away: its drama is essentially internal. While its prime function is manufacturing cars, it is equally part of an 'experience' that McLaren offers to its customers.

Many buyers are keen to see their cars in the final stages of production. These VIPs, having been received in the Technology Centre, are taken to the Production Centre via a 100-metre-long tunnel. This all-white expanse leads to a glazed rotunda, where a lift takes them to the mezzanine overlooking the production floor. Here there is a dedicated space where visitors are given a presentation on the car's design and development, before screens are pulled back to reveal the vast expanse of the production hall. It is a remarkable *coup de théâtre*.

3

4

The production hall is an all-white space, with the ethos of a laboratory rather than a factory. The ceramic floor tiles are pristine, staff wear neat black uniforms, and racks for components and other items were all custom made. Cars are assembled on purpose-designed trolleys which move along the space as work progresses. This is as near to automation as the McLaren production process gets. Ron Dennis has stated McLaren's aspiration to become 'the Swiss watchmaker of cars' and the whole ensemble – building, cars and methodology – exemplifies this pursuit.

Externally the building gives little away: its drama is essentially internal.

Although the building is superficially a shed, albeit an exceptionally well-detailed one, it incorporates highly progressive moves in terms of its servicing. The enormous roof is drained using the siphonic system pioneered by Foster on the roof of the Stansted Airport terminal. It is designed to take solar panels; and given its scale it is theoretically possible for the building to generate its own power needs.

The sustainable agenda is one that McLaren is actively pursuing in the design of its cars – the MP4-12C boasts a higher horsepower to emission ratio than any other internal-combustion engine (592bhp to 279g/km).

The building may have distant roots in the High-Tech aesthetic of the 1970s but there is no exposed ductwork here. All services, including air-supply ducts, data and power cabling, lighting, sprinklers and smoke detectors, are integrated within the depth of the columns and beams that form the structure of the wide-span building, and in cast-in trenches in the floor slab. A low-energy displacement system provides ventilation. The overall result is an extraordinarily high degree of flexibility in use.

With the planned further development of the McLaren campus, Woking is emerging as a powerhouse of the new advanced-technology manufacturing economy in Britain, while the Production Centre marks McLaren's transition from the highly specialised world of Formula 1 into a far broader industrial scene. The building itself is clearly process-driven, tailored to very specific demands, yet it embodies a flexibility that reflects the dynamic nature of McLaren's evolving future business.

Kenneth Powell

3. The Production Centre is dug into the gentle incline of the site, to give it a discreet presence in the landscape.

4. The external detailing continues the spare formal language established by the Technology Centre.

Overleaf: An aerial view of the McLaren campus, with the Production Centre to the left and the Technology Centre to the right. The small circular building in the foreground is a visitor centre.

We built it for ourselves. I know how many hours people work, and frankly a large proportion of their life is spent at that office. So to put in little touches like a fireplace, a sports bar, a football pitch, as well as the best technology, the latest toys, the latest computing power, and a great restaurant – it was all part of saying to the staff, we can never really compensate you for all the work you do for the company in pure salary terms but we can make your life here more pleasurable and comfortable. David Gardner, former European Vice President and COO of Electronic Arts Worldwide Studios, in conversation with the editor, 2004
Left: David Gardner by the fireside in the new building.

'When we came to the UK, in 1986, the computer games industry was people chained to desks bought at second-hand shops – it was amazing how badly resourced everything was.' Like many young Americans before him, David Gardner's move to England in the mid-1980s came as a bit of a shock. Gardner had arrived in the UK as a twenty-year-old programmer, charged with setting up and running the European offices of Electronic Arts, soon to become the largest developer and distributor of computer games in the world. It was a company he had worked for since the age of seventeen as one of the first ten employees at its headquarters in Redwood City, California.

'We didn't intend to build – we planned to rent. But when we looked at what was available we were disappointed. If we wanted a world-class business, then we had to have a world-class building.'

Having established its European base, under Gardner's management Electronic Arts grew quickly. Increasingly conscious of the need to develop its own studio facilities, in 1995 Gardner oversaw the merger of Electronic Arts Europe with an English computer games design company, Bullfrog, which had a reputation for creating highly innovative games. The merger gave Electronic Arts Europe greater autonomy from its parent company in California, and allowed it to initiate, design, and market its own titles.

By 1996, Gardner had transformed Electronic Arts Europe into an ostensibly independent games design and distribution firm with a staff of over 400. In practice, however, the company comprised two groups housed in separate buildings located 20 miles apart – the marketing and distribution staff of Electronic Arts being in Langley, just outside Slough, and Bullfrog in Guildford.

Electronic Arts clearly had to find new accommodation, bringing everyone together, but at this early stage, its ambitions did not extend to commissioning an architect. However, that soon changed. As David Gardner describes it: 'We didn't intend to build, but when we saw what was available to rent we were disappointed. I knew that if we wanted a world-class business, we had to have a great building.'

The move to a purpose-designed building was also seen as important in dissolving the gentle rivalry that still existed between Bullfrog and Electronic Arts. Gardner's aim was to pull the old office model apart and encourage staff to 'reimagine' their working lives. The building would act as a catalyst to make the company work together; and ideally it would be located halfway between the two existing locations, so that the staff's commute would not be adversely affected.

Gardner discovered what he saw as the perfect site at Hillswood Business Park in Chertsey – a 100-acre park surrounding an eighteenth-century country house – and selected an area on the estate's former cricket pitch, bordered to the north by a man-made lake. The architects invited to enter a limited competition included a number from the UK, together with US firms Gensler and SOM, who were then completing Electronic Arts' Californian headquarters. When they all expressed an interest, Gardner was delighted:

Opposite: Looking along the street-like atrium that runs along the lakeside. As an animated showcase for Electronic Arts' work and the social focus of the building, the atrium provides primary circulation at ground level and forms an environmental buffer between the offices and the landscape.

1, 2. Staff relax together after work on the lakeside terrace.

3. Norman Foster's early concept sketches of the lakeside facade.

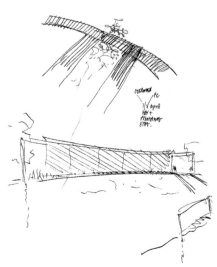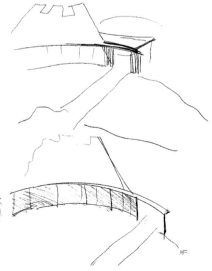

The brief was to improve communication for the company. The building we got pretty much follows our core values of communication, transparency and openness – it doesn't have things like offices or executive suites, but lots of play areas for all … Commissioning the place was one of those taste-changing experiences. I had no predisposition for modern architecture per se, but I felt that both mine and the architects' philosophy matched. I just had to say: 'Design an office you'd like', and I got one I liked. David Gardner, former European Vice President and COO of Electronic Arts Worldwide Studios, quoted in *Sunday Business*, 23 September 2001

The lovely dialogue between the building and the lake is very intentional – this was very much Norman's approach to the thing – to get this interaction, and an amazing composition. You can see this in his first concept sketch. Norman kept stressing the need to have a vision for the project and that the extension of the lake could provide an answer. Heightening, in his sketch, the importance of nature – the birds and the bees and the trees all interacting with the building, and there for everybody to enjoy – this was all contained within this first little drawing, and this is pretty much what we built. John Silver, formerly of Foster + Partners, in conversation with the editor, 2009

1. Ground floor plan.

2. First floor plan.

3. Second floor plan.

1 visitor entrance
2 open-plan studio/office
3 library
4 media centre
5 sound studios
6 bar
7 café
8 kitchen
9 street space
10 plant
11 boardwalk
12 barbecue deck
13 lake

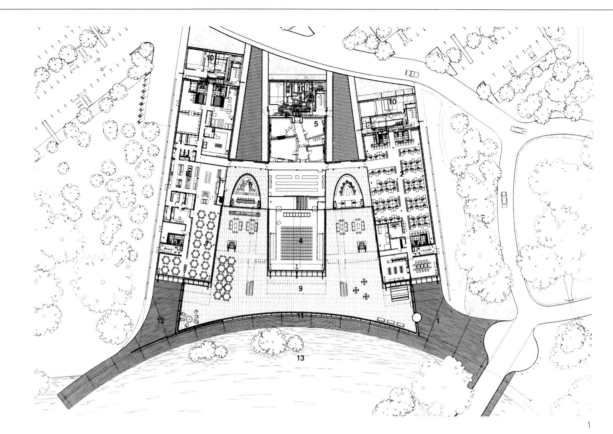

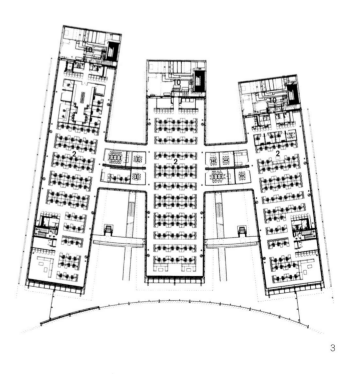

Beginning with Reliance Controls, we've consistently encouraged companies to adopt flexible, non-hierarchical working environments. Electronic Arts were fantastic in that they embraced this idea completely, so much so that we were able to set new standards in this fast-moving industry. We were also encouraged to incorporate an astonishing range of on-site facilities for their staff – something that really projected them into a different league. Norman Foster, in conversation with the editor, 2012
Left: This early model shows how the three 'fingers' that were built could be complemented by a further two, creating a total of 24,000 square metres of accommodation looking out on to the lake.

Companies that allow their staff to work flexibly reap handsome dividends. It is a case of a little going a long way. Employees who have even one morning or afternoon a week working from home are more content with management, and record much higher scores for fair dealing and personal growth. Alastair McCall, *The Sunday Times*, 2 March 2003
Electronic Arts was voted the ninth best company to work for in the 2003 *Sunday Times* 100 Best Companies – 'Dream Jobs' category.

'The most amazing moment was in our Langley office having Richard Rogers leaving as Norman Foster walked in the door – two great architects in our incredibly dumpy shed of a building, in an industrial park in Slough. It was then that I knew we were on the brink of something that could be great. We were very excited.'

The brief was simple: it was to be a building that would integrate itself within the landscape, and be a place in which people would enjoy working. The project also had to be organised in two phases, both of about 10,000 square metres, with the second phase dependent upon the projected growth of the company. As a caveat, and a reminder that this was still very much a commercial project, the brief also stipulated that the building had to have strong resale value. P&O, which owned the site and initially the building too (until Electronic Arts bought it on completion), did not want a space tailored to a specific tenant but a building that had obvious investment value.

Intuitively recognising this commercial discipline, in his competition presentation Foster dwelt more on the practicality of the building than the originality of its design. At the same time, he emphasised the importance of the architectural image – and that, despite being a two-stage project, the building had to look complete in both phases. The strategy worked.

In winning the commission, the practice was extending its family of business park designs – a series begun in 1987 with offices at Stockley Park, Britain's first architecturally driven business park. Leading the Foster team was John Silver. He drew up a plan based loosely upon the template of Stockley Park, comprising three office 'fingers', each 16.5 metres wide, with a 1.5-metre planning grid. This arrangement satisfied the brief but the architects still had to find a balance between the need for pragmatism and Electronic Arts' hopes for something striking and original. Working through a number of alternatives, the solution ultimately came not through looking at the internal spaces but at the landscape.

As Silver recalls: 'The key design meeting was with Norman, in the model shop, with the sketch model. He had the idea of changing the shape of the lake, extending it around the front of the building, and then placing a north-facing glass wall parallel to it. It was really a restatement of themes found in our own building, where the studio looks out over water.'

In fact, the image of the Foster studio became a model for Electronic Arts: 'When we visited the studio and saw how people worked there, we realised immediately that we could abbreviate the brief and just say, "build us something that you would like to work in,"' says Gardner.

4

4. Bound to the north by an eighteenth-century lake, and an atrium that lines the water's edge, the building comprises three 'fingers' of three-storey office blocks that look out into the landscape.

5. An early sketch by Norman Foster, imagining the building approached from across the lake.

5

We set out to create something very different from a regular office block. You expect a museum to be great, but you don't expect that from an office – which is a shame when you consider how much time we spend at work. David Gardner, former European Vice President and COO of Electronic Arts Worldwide Studios, in conversation with the editor, 2004

A couple of decades ago there were forecasts that the office as we know it, and all the paper it contained, would cease to exist as we became more dependent on computers. Well the office is alive and well – as is all the paper. In fact, the more we spend on computers the more paper seems to be generated. But I think the key thing is that the more technology allows us not to come to the office, the more significant the workplace becomes. But the emphasis has changed, and this is reflected in Electronic Arts, where the creative activity overlaps with, and takes place in, the social spaces, rather than being contained within the traditional workstation. Norman Foster, in conversation with the editor, 2012

The old Langley building was made up of two little speculative business park buildings that Electronic Arts had colonised and were bursting out of. You would go in and enter a very dark, highly personalised space. We're very used to this now – you look at the way Pixar Studios and companies like that have these wild and wacky spaces that they totally personalise and live in night and day as a world within a world – but back then it was quite a shock to me. For example, you'd walk in there, and at a guy's desk you would have a computer, a massive great amplifier, a bunch of electric guitars, a pile of other stuff, and that's the way they did things. John Silver, formerly of Foster + Partners, in conversation with the editor, 2010

1

2

3

Gardner also visited a number of other Foster buildings, including the Commerzbank in Frankfurt, which was presented as a vertical version of Electronic Arts' own building. Spiralling up around the tower are four-storey garden spaces. One consequence of these gardens is that people working in the offices, whether internal or external, can enjoy a view from their window, either directly outside or through the gardens. It offers a foreground experience in a high-rise building. Gardner instantly grasped the importance of this social diagram and with Silver began to re-imagine his own building as a series of office and studio spaces organised around a communal area – a kind of village green.

Eighteen months later, phase one of the building was finished. The speed of the project is a reflection both of the clarity of Gardner's direction and the relative simplicity of the plan. The office 'fingers' are arranged over three floors (colour coded yellow, green and blue), which accommodate marketing and studio spaces. The communal areas form the 'webbing' between the fingers and extend along an internal 'street' that looks out across the lake through a curving glass facade, which gives the building its sense of drama. This is heightened by the ability of two of its bays to slide open, seemingly dematerialising the wall.

Having established the line of the glass wall, the Foster team was keen to exploit the space behind it by enlarging the area of the street. However, the building's footprint had been agreed with the planners and could not be changed. The solution was to scoop away office space at the lakeside end of the fingers, at ground floor level, and to add it back higher up, giving the ends of the fingers a striking incline. As a result, the social spaces – including a restaurant, coffee bar and games room – flow freely from the street at ground level, while at the back of the plan are a gym, sound studios and computer rooms.

Electronic Arts' publishing arm is on the first floor, while the second floor provides open-plan studio spaces, which are laid out in sections, each devoted to a particular game. 'Touch-down' zones, with games consoles and plasma screens, offer areas for meetings and presentations. Originally, this kind of informal office thinking, characteristic of many recent dotcom offices, in which desk spaces are not allocated individually, was considered for the building as a whole.

Ultimately, though, the amount of computer hardware required by studio staff meant that desk layouts had to be fixed. The extent to which games designers customise their own spaces is also encouraged by the neutral backdrop of the partitioning system.

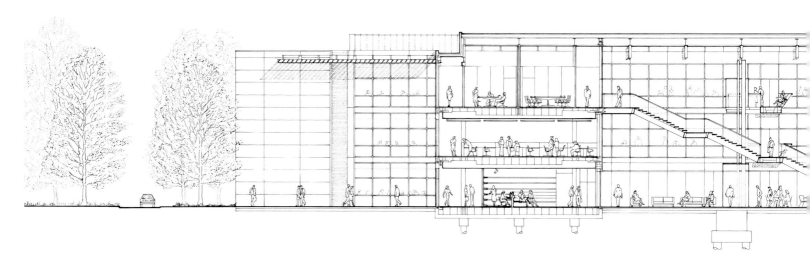

Facilities here have names like 'Room for Improvement' and 'The Bored Room' – so you know you are not in any conventional office setting. *Workplace,* January/February 2001

Left: *Catwoman,* one of Electronic Arts' most popular games. By 2003, Electronic Arts had amassed a revenue of over $3 billion, generated from the astonishing sales of computer games such as *The Sims, FIFA Football, Harry Potter* and *The Lord of the Rings* series.

Balancing a heavy demand for IT systems and services with the need to provide comfortable conditions for occupants has been an elusive goal, especially in any development with green aspirations. In this case, however, the design teams have worked hand-in-glove with the clients to ensure that lighting, air quality and temperature controls provide the right environment for employees. Here is proof that passive cooling techniques do have a place in IT-dominated buildings when applied sensibly and given an element of mechanical systems to lean on for support from time to time. *Workplace,* January/February 2001

Given the quantity of computer equipment, one would expect that extensive cooling systems would be required, but the reality is that much of the building adopts a low-energy environmental strategy, combining displacement ventilation with natural cooling from the high thermal mass of the building's exposed structure. When, on the hottest days, additional ventilation and cooling are required, people working at their desks can simply open a window or slide open the glass facade. Air conditioning is also available (in particular for the sound studios and other 'black-box' areas) but as with all the building's environmental systems, this can be specifically zoned and controlled.

The result is a building minutely designed to satisfy any environmental need, and one that not only provides the very best facilities for the staff's working lives but also amenities and comforts designed to enrich their social lives too. David Gardner has even lent this idea a name – rather than working from home, it provides all the amenities for 'homing from work'.

In this concept, as with the building as a whole, there are echoes of Foster buildings from the 1970s – the open-plan offices and social facilities at the Olsen Amenity Centre; and the heightened articulation of both in the Willis Faber & Dumas headquarters, which virtually reinvented the workplace in the UK.

Like Willis Faber, the provision of amenities at Electronic Arts is complemented by innovative and socially orientated space planning. The result is a building that has helped the company to establish its own strong sense of identity. As Gardner observes: 'When people come to hear us present our ideas and compete for games, the building puts us in a different league as a company. There's no doubt that it helped us to achieve our business objectives. I remember when our professional advisers said: don't spend £2 million on the glass wall because you'll never make it back; and I knew that if we didn't spend money on all the things that make it special then we would be missing an opportunity. Hilariously, after we had won an award from the same people who told us not to build it the way it is, not only did the value of the land and the building go up, but so too did the prosperity of the company.

'The first year after we occupied the building, we held a big party. It was a spectacular late summer evening. We had the place lit, we had the glass wall rolled back, we had people standing out by the lake, and food was being served, and I realised that we really were leading the industry. And the building played a major part in helping us to establish that lead.'

Thomas Weaver

4

1-4. Details of the work spaces, from informal games, meeting and eating areas through to the top-floor design studio. The building sets new standards in the fast-moving computer games industry.

5. Cross-section through the atrium, from the car-park entrance on the left, through office and studio spaces, the main staircase and 'street', to the lakeside terrace.

Overleaf: The building seen from across the lake.

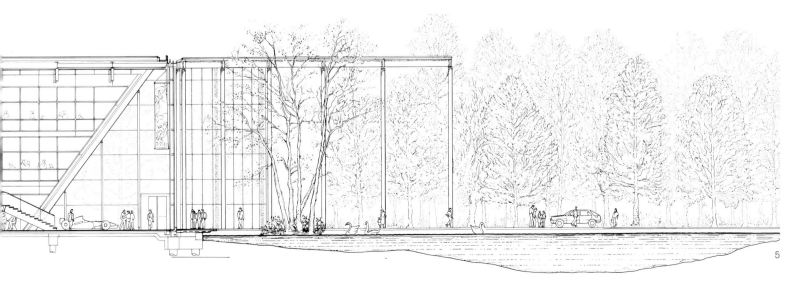

5

Riverside One

London, England 1998–1999

1. Looking west along the length of the living space. The apartment enjoys spectacular views across the river, framed by Albert Bridge in one direction and Battersea Bridge in the other. The wall piece, seen left, is by Richard Long.

2. A small roof garden at the eastern end of the apartment looks out across the river and Battersea Park. The timber deck accommodates a breakfast table.

2

From the apartment you look out across London and not down on it. London is an essentially low-rise city and the area of Chelsea we overlook is, by European standards, quite dense. But the contact with the sky and the weather is sublime. One surprise is the bird-life – for a wide variety of species the Thames seems like a play space and aerial highway. Although there is no doubt that one is in the midst of a city, the proximity of Battersea Park and the ease of being able to walk everywhere gives the area a village-like quality.
Norman Foster, in conversation with the editor, 2006
Right: The view north from the apartment.

Riverside, located on the south bank of the Thames at Battersea, was a pioneering example of mixed-use development in London, combining places to live and work in one location and, in the process, reviving a stretch of the waterfront that had virtually been abandoned. This penthouse on the eighth floor of the Riverside building replaces an earlier apartment, which was configured as two separate pavilions facing each other across a central garden.

Riverside One is conceived on a grand scale: it was in its time one of the most versatile entertaining spaces in London, with an unrivalled view north across the capital. The apartment has moments of spectacular spatial largesse, yet it is thoughtfully planned, equally capable of seating formal dinners for several hundred or being enjoyed by the Foster family as their private realm.

Riverside One is conceived on a grand scale: it was in its time one of the most versatile entertaining spaces in London.

Within the apartment's expansive frame, there are moments of intricately choreographed planning. One is the kitchen, which is located behind the scenes, with its own service access; for convenience, it can be entered from the living space through a pivoting 'secret' door in the library shelving. Another is the bathroom adjoining the master bedroom. With its mirrored walls and custom-designed appliances – including an elegant shower totem – the bathroom is detailed with exquisite precision. The doors and external glazing to these and other major spaces are all full-height, which adds to the sense of generosity.

In the living space, occasional pools of sunlight are introduced through a linear skylight at the back of the room, offering a dynamic counterpoint to the prevailing soft north light. Artificial lighting is discreet and has the flexibility to create moods that range from the subdued to the theatrical.

3. Sketch by Norman Foster, studying the form of the south-facing skylight that lines the rear wall of the living space.

4. The far corner of the living space looks out towards Albert Bridge and is configured for informal seating – a quiet spot in which to sit and read.

5. The master bathroom, with its mirrored walls and purpose-designed fittings, is intricately planned and precisely detailed.

I watched Richard Long make his wall piece for Riverside One. I was going to say 'paint', but the only painting involved was the black ground, which Richard marked out and painted with an assistant. The mud is applied as soon as the background is dry. He mixes it quietly by himself, getting it to the right consistency – I think it's an almost meditative experience. Then he applies it by hand, working with rapid, vigorous strokes. The piece took a morning to complete – it was incredible to watch. Tim Quick, formerly of Foster + Partners, in conversation with the editor, 2009 Right: Tim Quick with Richard Long at work in the apartment.

1. The wall piece by Richard Long occupies the long wall at the back of the living space. It was made with mud harvested from the banks of the River Avon, close to Long's native Bristol.

A step up in the centre of the ceiling plane articulates the fact that this is a new surface – spanning the area once occupied by the garden. In contrast to the existing flat plaster soffit on either side, here the supporting steel frame is expressed and celebrated. The flooring throughout the apartment is of pale ash with a resin finish – a Spanish system originally developed for use in art galleries, where durability and elegance go hand-in-hand.

The most striking element of the living space is a remarkable wall piece by Richard Long – made with Avon river mud, hand-applied over a black ground – which occupies the long southern wall.

Formally, the piece balances the framed view of the river and the London panorama opposite. It also engages in a dialogue with the garden, which anchors the eastern end of the plan, seeming to draw its organic forms deep into the room. The garden itself is populated by a dense copse of birch trees into which a small 'clearing' has been cut, its boarded deck large enough to accommodate a breakfast table. The view from here is across to the treetops of Battersea Park, which provides another link with nature.

David Jenkins

I live with my family on the eighth floor, a few minutes' walk from Battersea Park. It's a great place for a family with a two-year-old son and five-year-old daughter. The eighth floor is not high by London standards, but it's as high as I can get. I have a fantastic view across London, with sun and sky and an outdoor green space. For my family and me it's the ultimate in urban living. I would be happy to go higher still – if I were another twenty or thirty storeys higher I would only spend a few more seconds in the lift in the morning. Interestingly, when I am in a city like New York I choose a hotel that allows me to be high up in the city: it's a preference.
Norman Foster, lecture in Milan, 11 December 2003

1

2

3

2, 3. Richard Long began by painting a matt black ground; the liquefied mud was applied quickly in splashy strokes, working from left to right.

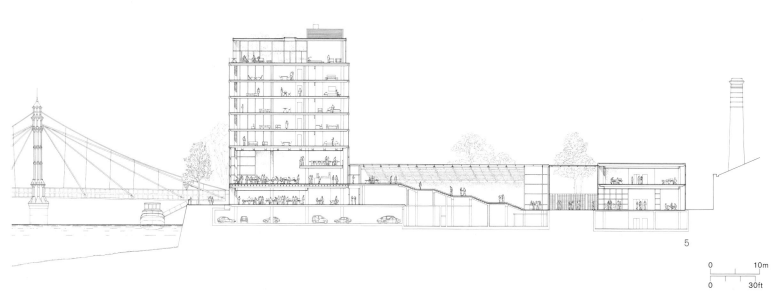

5

0   10m
0   30ft

Long conversations with Anish Kapoor took place over several months in his kitchen in Camberwell. This is the first time that Anish has explored the ambiguous relationship between book and sculpture. Drawings, maps, wooden prototypes and experimentation with shapes, colours and materials provoked the final *Wound*. Elena Ochoa Foster, Chairman and CEO of IvoryPress, in conversation with the editor, 2005
Left: Anish Kapoor signing *Wound*, which was published in an edition of twenty-five by IvoryPress in November 2005 and launched with a party in the Riverside One apartment.

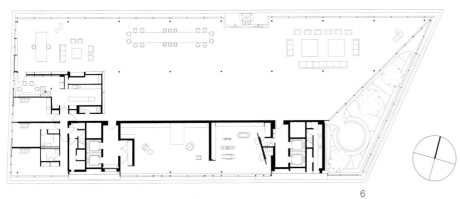

1

2

3

4

1-4. The apartment offered one of London's greatest entertaining spaces and was the scene for numerous parties and formal dinners.

5. Cross-section through Riverside, showing the apartment's relationship with the Foster studio below.

6. Plan of the principal level. The living space stretches the entire length of the building, looking out on to the river. The master bedroom and bathroom line the southern edge of the plan, with a kitchen and two-storey children's suites to the west.

6

0   10m
0   30ft

Albion Riverside

London, England 1998–2003

In 1990, when Foster Associates (as the practice was then) left Great Portland Street and moved south of the river, it was considered a 'brave' step. Although the new studio enjoyed spectacular views across the Thames to Cheyne Walk, Hester Road and the decaying industrial hinterland were decidedly down at heel. To approach the office then meant running the gauntlet of abandoned workshops and derelict sites. However, looking back it is clear that the move provided the catalyst for the transformation of Hester Road over the next ten years to the point where it has become a prestigious residential and business address.

Possibly uniquely in the capital, Albion Riverside provides a mix of living, working, shopping and leisure – with a wide range of options from affordable housing to luxury penthouses.

Foster's own building, which has seven storeys of apartments above the architects' studios and workshops, demonstrated that high-specification residential development could succeed south of the river. Over the course of the next decade, the Battersea riverside would be developed by others, the site immediately to the west of Foster's office being one of the few that remained unexplored. It was Hutchison Whampoa, a developer with significant holdings in the UK and Hong Kong, who finally saw the potential of Hester Road.

Albion Riverside comprises four buildings. The south side of Hester Road is lined with four-storey office blocks, which have services cores along the party walls to the south. The western site boundary is defined by a seven-storey block with a showroom at ground level and flats above, which have been designed for the Peabody Trust as affordable housing for essential workers.

The entrance to a single level of parking beneath the entire site is discreetly tucked under the raised garden terrace of this residential block, effectively removing cars and service vehicles from the street to ensure that the ground plane of this new precinct is dedicated to pedestrians.

The western building, which provides forty-two one- and two-bedroom affordable flats, is organised into three 9-metre-wide bands of space – a line of flats on the east, an open circulation zone in the middle, and a line of flats to the west. The apartments are entered from bridges, which are wide enough to be inhabited. The outward-facing zones of the units are given over entirely to living rooms with generous glazing and sliding doors that give these apartments a sense of connection to the civic realm.

The new office and residential blocks, together with the end elevation of Foster's own building and its extended two-storey entrance pavilion along the eastern boundary of the precinct, work together effectively as urban fabric that both adjusts to the scale of existing buildings around the site and creates a coherent new context for the freestanding figural building at the heart of the scheme. This eleven-storey structure consists of double-height retail and gallery spaces at ground level, with seven storeys of apartments above, capped by two-storey penthouses.

While it may appear sculptural, the form of this building is carefully considered. In real estate terms, the impact of making a crescent, stretching it to become asymmetrical and then expanding it again into an undulating line, has the effect of increasing river frontage on the site by 50 per cent. The curved block, at an average 22 metres wall-to-wall, is unusually deep for a residential building, and its high floor-to-wall ratio resulted in significant economies both in construction and projected operating costs. Although appearing formally as a single entity, it is organised as an ensemble of four party-wall buildings, each with its own lifts and a single escape stair.

1

Opposite: A detail of the southern facade, which is veiled in a fine net of aluminium rods and pierced by recessed balconies and windows.

1. The development of Albion Riverside reinforces a growing new community on the south bank of the Thames, alongside the Foster studio between Albert and Battersea Bridges. A mixed-use development, its ingredients are designed to promote a lively urban quarter where people can live, work and enjoy life in the heart of the city.

2. An early sketch study of the south facade by Norman Foster.

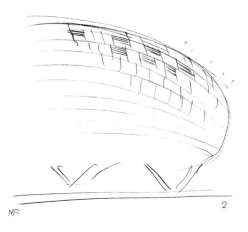

NF

2

Far left, left: Space Syntax, of University College London, was asked to analyse pedestrian access to the riverfront; these drawings show the 'before' and 'after' conditions. Previously, as pedestrian surveys and spatial integration analysis revealed, there had been little movement both along the riverfront, partly because of an indirect stair connection between Battersea Bridge and the riverside walk, and through the area between Battersea Bridge and Albert Bridge Roads, because no convenient through route existed. This was changed by creating a public space on the riverfront, whose activities extend inland from the water's edge to animate the hinterland. Pedestrian traffic along Elcho Street and Hester Road is connected to the riverside by a 'V' of diagonal routes that open up views of the river.

We didn't want to have any lift motors or plant sticking above the top of the building so we developed the roof as a series of hills. There are four cores and the roof gently undulates between them hiding their massing, so that when you see the building from a distance the roof's composition is always different depending on your approach. Andy Bow, of Foster + Partners, in conversation with the editor, 2012

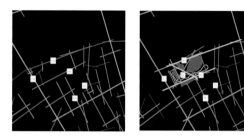

0   10m
0   30ft

1

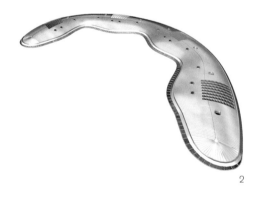

2

There are four to six units grouped around a pair of lifts on each floor, with the two at each end of the short corridor planned as through units and those in the centre having a single aspect, either north or south. The deep interior of the plan is filled by bathrooms and walk-in wardrobes.

Penthouses are interlocked in section so that bedrooms to adjacent units are stacked on the south side of the building, while double-height living spaces face the river. A high degree of flexibility is incorporated to allow purchasers the option of combining adjacent units. A maximum of 200 units is provided, ranging from one to five bedrooms. With a double-loaded corridor, this planning strategy enables more than two thirds of the flats to have a river frontage or a river view.

The form of the building was rationalised for construction so that it is composed of only three curves in plan and section. The north and south facades are distinctly different. The southern face, which curves externally in both plan and section, is a glass and metal curtain wall punctured by window openings, the entire composition shaded by a silver veil of horizontal aluminium rods.

The migration of windows within rooms from floor to floor, as well as terraces from unit to unit, produces a random composition that avoids the repetition of most housing developments. This curved face extends up and over to transform seamlessly into a roof that undulates in section to conceal the lift motor rooms.

The counterpoint to this predominantly solid shaded wall on the south is a totally glazed north facade overlooking the Thames, which is made of storey-height flat glass panels, both fixed and sliding. These create a faceted elevation that sparkles and alters colour as light and viewpoints change. The building's sinuous curve is delineated only by the projecting balconies, which vary in width, and by the curved glass balustrades.

These balconies wrap around to create spectacular units at the east and west ends of the building, terminating in a translucent glazed junction with the louvred skin of the south facade. The strong horizontal line of the projecting balconies defines an ordered civic facade and enables the recessed domestic elevation to absorb the clutter of inhabitation.

The design was based on spiral curves in both plan and section. Like Swiss Re this produced a recessive form, in which the mass apparently reduces as the building is approached. The facade was panellised with a torus patch solution, but the effect of double curvature was further enhanced by adding an outer skin of tubular rods to provide solar protection. The roof, however, was designed as an undulating form with a soft silhouette, rising smoothly over the service cores to enclose the plant rooms. Hugh Whitehead, formerly of Foster + Partners, in conversation with the editor, 2011

Albion Riverside belongs to a family of projects – City Hall, Swiss Re, The Sage Gateshead and the proposal for the roof of the arts district in Kowloon – that represent a moment when the office embraced complex geometries. Andy Bow, of Foster + Partners, in conversation with the editor, 2012 Right: A cross-section through a nautilus shell – one source of inspiration for Albion Riverside's complex double-curvature geometry.

1. Cross-section through the principal building on the waterfront. A typical floor in this building contains twenty-six apartments, arranged around four service cores. In total there are 183 apartments, ranging from one to four bedrooms, and twelve duplex penthouses. Balconies offer an extension of living spaces and are deep enough to encourage outdoor dining.

2. The roof continues the building's curving form, wrapping over and around in a single sweep.

3. An aerial view, looking east. Arcing back from the water's edge, the riverside building forms an asymmetric crescent to create a public space alongside the river walk.

4. Typical upper level plan. The scheme comprises three separate buildings linked by new public spaces and routes. Shops, business spaces, cafés and leisure facilities are grouped at ground level, with parking below and apartments, including low-cost housing, above.

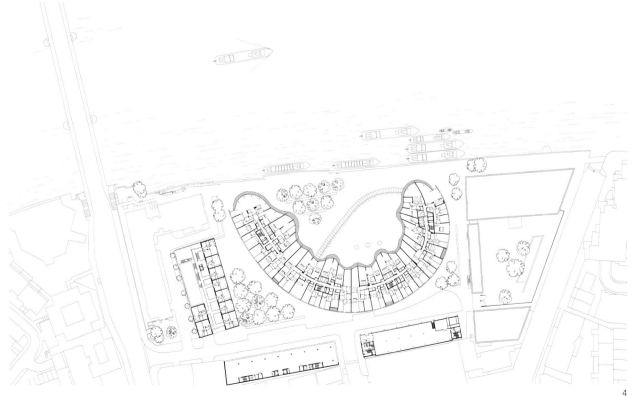

3

4

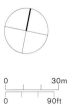

0   30m

0   90ft

The aim was to achieve total flexibility within the shell of a standard one-bed flat. By moving the sliding glass walls, the space can be configured to define areas for living, dining and sleeping; or you can create a large dining room or a generous bedroom or a spacious living room. The glass walls give glimpses from one area to the next, so it feels generous. We used high-quality materials – a stone floor, glass shelving and wardrobes by Molteni, and a custom-designed mobile plasma wall – so that it feels luxurious, even though the floor area is quite small. Graham Phillips, formerly of Foster + Partners, in conversation with the editor, 2012
Right, far right: Graham Phillips' remarkable pied-à-terre on the fourth floor.

1

The promenade at first floor level exploits the wonderful view across the river to Chelsea. Everyone gets to use and enjoy this space and the riverside garden – whether they own the grandest penthouse or the smallest apartment.

Norman Foster

The planning that produces many benefits on the residential floors of this central building also yields dividends on the ground, where the spiral geometry creates three public spaces – one along the Thames and two along Hester Road – that mediate between the central and perimeter buildings and open up oblique views of the river from deep within the site.

Above the shop and gallery spaces, loads from the concrete slabs and radial piers of the residential floors are picked up by curved concrete transfer beams, which are supported by two rings of canted V-shaped concrete columns. One ring runs parallel to the south facade to make a colonnaded entrance frontage to the commercial spaces.

When we first bought the flat we intended to move into it for a short period before renting it out but we found that we enjoyed it and liked the fact that we didn't have to commute. It's a great experience living there because you're able to move around London quite easily without having to hop in the car each time. I did the typical architect thing and removed all the internal walls. I rearranged the space and added sliding screens so it's more flexible and there's a much greater feeling of space and light. In many ways we redesigned the interior to a Foster specification. Chris Connell, of Foster + Partners, an Albion Riverside resident, in conversation with the editor, 2009
Right: Chris Connell's apartment on the sixth floor.

When we first saw Albion Riverside, it was very different to what we were used to. We looked at many modern developments, weighed up the pros and cons, of location, size, price, and of course architecture as everyone does. In the end, we always came back to Albion as our only choice. I am in property myself, and know London very well. Buying an apartment at Albion is a little like purchasing a Bang & Olufsen TV. Firstly you are led by your heart, the design works from every angle, and you know that although it's a little more than you'd like to spend, it ticks every box. Your choice is driven by your passion for the design and features. Sacha Rahbary, an Albion Riverside resident, in conversation with the editor, 2009

1. A view of the lobby, looking towards the concierge's desk. A broad staircase rises to a gallery at first floor level.

2. The first-floor gallery winds along the river frontage and provides access to the four banks of lifts that serve the apartment floors.

3, 4. All the apartments on the riverside enjoy striking views up- or down-stream.

5. A typical bathroom in one of the larger apartments; all the fittings are from the Foster-designed Duravit and Hoesch ranges.

Overleaf: On the river facade, curved balconies with clear glass balustrades are accessed through full-height sliding glazed panels, which allow the apartments to open out on to the water. The strong horizontal line of the balconies reinforces a sense of visual order, allowing the clutter of inhabitation to proliferate but not dominate. Public spaces are punctuated by long granite benches and clusters of trees – either flowering cherry or tall sculptural pin oaks.

2

3

4

5

The apartments share a double-height entrance lobby, with a grand stair up to a cloistered walkway held within the second ring of columns. This walkway is enclosed by a wall of glazing that looks out on to a garden terrace and provides a panoramic view of the river. From here, residents take the lifts up to their flats. As project architect Andy Bow notes: 'We created this sequence of shared entrance spaces so that everyone who lives in the building – even those with south-facing units – can enjoy the river view.' The cumulative effect of these various moves has been to energise this part of the city.

Possibly uniquely in the capital, Albion Riverside provides a mix of living, working, shopping and leisure – with a wide range of options from affordable housing to luxury penthouses – supported by free access to a new public space on the riverside, all designed and detailed to a very high standard. Just as Foster, in his early industrial work, sought to bridge the gap between blue and white collar workers by providing a single high level of accommodation for everyone, so Albion Riverside has transformed Hester Road into a better neighbourhood for all.

Annette LeCuyer

When we bought our apartment at Albion, it was the first time we had purchased within a new and modern development, and to a certain extent, we did not know what to expect or feel. It's only when you live there, that you grow to love it. There is a very definite sense of a community and neighbourly respect for one another, and for the first time, we have made many new and close friends, primarily through our Cavalier King Charles Spaniel, Max. Sacha Rahbary, an Albion Riverside resident, in conversation with the editor, 2009

The spiral geometry was all to do with maximising river frontage – if you make a crescent you get more and if you make it curve in and out you get even more still. The whole idea was that the facade would move in and out like a piece of string to maximise the amount of space and enable each of the north-facing apartments to be angled to give them an individually trained view of the river. Andy Bow, of Foster + Partners, in conversation with the editor, 2012

The terrace is a great communal space and we use it regularly. When it snowed quite heavily in February this year, people were out there making snowmen. It was quite surreal getting this thick carpet of snow which hadn't been trampled to a pulp right next to the Thames. Chris Connell, of Foster + Partners, an Albion Riverside resident, in conversation with the editor, 2012

Albion Riverside faces the Queen Anne and Georgian glories and rich foliage of Cheyne Walk, gazing with a huge, satisfied Cheshire-cat smile at the Albert Bridge, undisputedly the prettiest in London … The Chelsea Embankment traffic that trundles unceasingly and noisily up and down is for those of us on 'the other side' the ultimate child's Dinky Toy set, with cars and trucks and little red buses viewed in double-glazed silence from across the river, where a towpath walkway, dotted with lamps and trees and park benches at the water's edge, carries nothing noisier than a random jogger, young couples arm-in-arm and the occasional inline skater. Leslie Bricusse, an Albion Riverside resident, *The Sunday Times*, 12 June 2005

Gerling Ring Karree
Cologne, Germany 1995–2001

The project began with an approach from Gerling. In a previous life, one of their guys had spent months in the Mandarin Hotel in Hong Kong looking out of the window at the Bank and he had always wanted to work with us. They had a site in Cologne and wanted to develop it. But Cologne is quite a difficult place to do that – it's very traditional, it's hard to break new ground. Gerling recognised that the best way to move forward would be to think about mixing uses. Rather than just being office space, there might be other functions in there, possibly residential.
David Nelson, in conversation with the editor, 2012
Right: The site on Ringstrasse before redevelopment.

The project is set at the point where Cologne's medieval fortified wall used to run. Like many cities – Vienna a prime example – as the city expanded, and the fortifications were removed, it created a major thoroughfare on which all the city's grandest new buildings were located. The Ring in Cologne is like that. On one side the site faces a metropolitan-scaled street of six to seven-storey buildings, whereas on the other side it's more medieval in origin and probably only three or four storeys high. Our response was to mediate between the two, with taller, bigger buildings facing the Ring, and scaling down to the height of the adjoining buildings behind. Norman Foster, in conversation with the editor, 2012

Making a virtue of relative modesty, the Gerling Ring complex remains virtually unknown among architects – undeservedly so, since it is one of Foster + Partners' best urban schemes. Architects shaped by the architectural culture of the 1960s, with its enthusiasm for systems and flexibility, should applaud the project's embrace of these concepts. Indeed all architects should admire the rigorously systematic design, which adapts most aptly to its various relocatable functions, solar orientation and adjacent noise levels, while also enhancing its surroundings.

Matching the corresponding building heights on its long sides, it reinvigorates the streets and the square it faces, while between the side wings, three towers rise to address central Cologne. All this is achieved with a deadpan effortlessness and, unlike many earlier system buildings, which emphatically express an ungainly kit of parts, it exhibits a well-integrated and understated formal elegance.

Gerling, an insurance firm, is long established in Cologne as a major employer and architectural patron. Its headquarters expanded in phases that are all modern yet classical in inspiration and are intrinsic to Gerling's identity as a company. Nearby are other Gerling properties, built or bought as commercial investments.

The Gerling Ring Karree stands close to Gerling's headquarters and is named after the broad tree-shaded Hohenzollernring, on its long western edge, which circles the historic city core and demarcates the line where the city wall once stood. Edging the long eastern side of the site is Friesenwall, a narrow street with mixed uses: mainly housing above a ground level of shops and bars. On the south-west corner is Friesenplatz, where a city gateway once stood.

Although Gerling originally occupied part of the complex, it is essentially a commercial development. Because long-term trends in the city are unpredictable, and because offices and housing provide similar rental returns, the complex was designed so that the upper floors can be configured as either offices or flats – although only the wing on the residential street is currently housing. Such flexibility is more easily provided in Germany than in most countries because cellular offices are the norm. Also, as the country most committed to the green agenda, offices there, like housing, tend to be naturally lit and ventilated, and provide all staff with external views. As advocated for sustainability, Gerling Ring is a long-life, loose-fit, low-energy building, yet another reason for it to be better known.

Because long-term trends are unpredictable, the complex was designed so that the upper floors can be configured as either offices or flats.

Key to the design is the 12.1 metre-wide standard cross-section, used throughout, in alliance with the straightforward parti of lower wings edging the long sides and three towers rising between. Each elevation is then glazed and shaded according to orientation, noise and function. The key element of the section is the wavy, flattened 'W' of the white concrete ceiling slabs. In the side wings, these slabs are supported on regularly spaced concrete columns. The slabs of the towers span between vertical circulation shafts adjacent to the lower wings, so also freeing the floors from columns.

1

Opposite: Café tables fill the new square created at the southern end of the Gerling Ring Karree, on Magnusstrasse. South-facing elevations, as seen here, and those exposed to street noise have double-layered facades. Louvres in the cavity can be pivoted to deflect the sun, direct light into the offices, or absorb heat to warm the incoming air as required.

1. On the two long edges of the site, the blocks match the established building heights; the three towers address the larger city scale. The towers of Cologne Cathedral are visible in the background.

The adaptability of buildings is crucial in the pursuit of a sustainable architecture. If we design buildings that are purely monofunctional, for example a fully airtight office tower, even if it is perfect at the time of building, it will still become obsolete because future technologies will change just as people's desires and needs will change. Consequently, in a few years time such buildings will either have to be demolished or retrofitted into something else. The Gerling building was designed from the very start to allow for change. Adaptable buildings that can be offices one day and apartments the next are an intelligent way forward. Stefan Behling, Ivorypress conference on sustainability, Madrid, 17 September 2009

The idea of mixing uses was our starting point. But there was a moment when we thought: could we do that in the same building, as opposed to just the same location? Interestingly, in Germany, the nature of work and the nature of living, in terms of their expression in space, are quite close, because Germany's work patterns are more cellular. There are no deep-plan offices, and everybody has to be within 7 metres of a window. Often the scale of the space that you occupy within an office is not that dissimilar to what you live in. There were a series of parallels that really gave us clues. David Nelson, in conversation with the editor, 2012

The big difference between office and residential structures is the provision made for kitchens and bathrooms. The difference lies in the servicing and the section of the units. To overcome this we proposed a three-barrel system with columns and beams and a raised floor above, which basically creates a room-corridor-room arrangement. The raised floor above the corridor zone has a greater depth, which means that you can put your services in there; and because the ventilation is passive and there's no air conditioning there is plenty of room to accommodate plumbing for residential purposes. Paul Kalkhoven, of Foster + Partners, in conversation with the editor, 2012

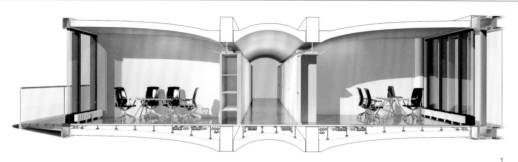

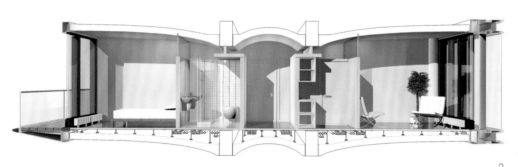

1, 2. Gerling Ring is a long-life, loose-fit, low-energy scheme. It responds to the fact that long-term demand for offices in Cologne is unpredictable, allowing the upper floors to be configured as either cellular offices or apartments. Interestingly, each provides a similar rental return. Such an approach is more easily argued in Germany, where cellular offices are the norm; with their shallow floor plates, like housing, they are predominantly naturally lit and ventilated. Floors are raised off the profiled structural slab, creating duct space for wiring and pipework.

The office wing along Ringstrasse is seven floors high and the housing wing is five floors with recessed penthouses. The seventeen-storey south tower and ten-storey north tower are set back between the ends of the lower wings, to enlarge the quiet, shaded Friesenplatz and, to the north, create a vehicular court in front of loading docks and the ramps to the basement parking. Where the lower wings project past these towers they terminate in balconies, with one strip of the standard section projecting further forward than the other, so animating the corners both formally and socially.

The offices in the middle tower begin on the third floor so a landscaped court, with its pool, stretches below it, between the two outer towers. The lowest offices of the southern tower are on the second floor, with a restaurant in the lofty, south-facing volume below. With its huge sliding doors open, the restaurant blends imperceptibly with, and enlivens the square. The court is visible through a glazed wall extending down, alongside a cascade from a large pool in the court fed by a natural spring, to light the basement extension of the restaurant.

The wavy ceiling slab is made of precast panels exposed to the floor below to exploit the thermal inertia of the considerable mass. The bottom, visible layer of the panels is of white concrete – white cement and limestone aggregate with an etched finish – above which is ordinary grey concrete. The central inverted trough defines a circulation zone from which the slab sweeps up to either side to admit maximum light and give generous headroom within a floor-to-floor height of only 3.3 metres. The circulation zone panels are 160mm deep by 2.7 metres wide by 8.1 metres long and are grooved above the centre of the storage wall partition between corridor and offices to receive glazing extending up from the height of the storage partitions. The panels over the offices are 200mm deep by 4.7 metres from corridor to perimeter by 4.05 metres wide and have grooves matching those between panels that can receive the heads of partitions at every 1.35 metres, which is the basic planning grid. Conversion of offices into housing is achieved by removing a vaulted central ceiling slab to accommodate lifts, stairs and drainage stacks.

Floors are raised off the structural slab, creating space for services. In the deeper space along the beams are water, power and data cabling, as well as chilled water for cooling units concealed within the storage wall, if required. Such units currently cool only conference rooms, where people may be formally attired. Waste pipes are also in this zone, sloping down from washrooms and kitchens to vertical stacks. Beneath the outer edge of the floor are hot water pipes for radiators located in front of the glazing and electrical and data cables to floor outlets. Only smoke detectors and escape signs are cast into the ceiling panels, along with limited provision for extra lighting; generally this is from uplighters and task lighting.

The two noisiest and sunniest elevations have a double facade with shading louvres in a cavity that is ventilated from horizontal bands of louvres between broad stretches of glazing. To serve as both inlet and outlet, air admitted from below is exhausted from the head of the stretch of cavity adjacent, so also avoiding exhaust air entering the cavity above. The inner skin is of inward opening, side-hung casements. Along Ringstrasse, which faces west, the louvres pivot vertically; those on the south elevation of the Friesenplatz tower pivot horizontally. Both kinds are white on one side and black on the other. This allows them to be pivoted to reflect the sun or act as light shelves into the offices, or to offer a black face to absorb heat to warm the cavity and incoming air.

Unlike many earlier systems buildings, which emphatically express an ungainly kit of parts, Gerling exhibits a well-integrated, understated formal elegance.

This solution also adds considerable animation to otherwise neutral facades. In use, the louvres are always arranged in syncopated patterns of patches of black and white and are angled differently to add further rhythmic articulation. Particularly in oblique views, the Ringstrasse elevation gains also from the reflections of the plane trees that line the street. Inside, the wavy white ceiling gives the offices a distinctive character, far better than a conventional suspended ceiling; and even the corridor is naturally lit.

All the other elevations have a single layer of inward-opening double-glazed units shaded by internal blinds. The south facades of the other towers are sufficiently quiet in outlook and shaded by the tower before them to obviate the need for an outer layer of glazing or shading.

The street elevation of the housing is more articulated, giving a scale and richness appropriate to function and location. Inward opening French windows are screened by balcony fronts of fritted glass. There are also two kinds of slatted screens. One is set outside a window which, because protected from rain and intruders, can be left open all night to cool the interior and is of the same aluminium tubes that screen the end balconies. The other, on a track inside, is of wooden louvres to be moved for shade and privacy, adding further animation.

Projecting from the elevation are three stacks of boxy bay windows, mirroring in size and form those across the street, which also mark the entrances to the housing. The street-level glazing is set back behind the precast columns, from which projects a steel canopy. Together these devices give an intimacy of scale and incident that creates an unusually satisfying urban presence. Entrances in the west wing to all the offices are marked by canopies set a little higher and projecting further than elsewhere.

All in all, this is a building of quiet assurance that generously does everything it should yet does not draw undue attention to itself. There is nothing gratuitous and yet it is in no way drab. It is easy to imagine that, like the best, somewhat generic historic buildings, it will last and be well used for hundreds of years. It sets a standard for function and urbanity, of uncontrived and effortless aptness that people simply accept. That is something which should be the norm, but is achieved very rarely.

Peter Buchanan

3

3. Where the lower wings – containing either offices or flats – project past the towers they terminate in balconies with glass balustrades. One half of the extruded section is pulled further forward than the other to animate the corner condition.

Gerling wanted an incredibly green building and part of their brief for this was concerned with embodied energy and the full life cycle of materials. From this we questioned why buildings get demolished and concluded that it wasn't necessarily because they decay but rather because their use changes. So we said if we can have the same section and the same plan across different uses then you could theoretically change office space into residential. The whole definition of what an office is may change in the longer term, so rather than demolish something why not have a structure which is capable of being converted into a different use. Paul Kalkhoven, of Foster + Partners, in conversation with the editor, 2012

We found that to go higher in the middle produced quite big towers, not large by Commerzbank standards, but nevertheless big buildings. But by setting them back inside the lower-level perimeter components, one could reduce the impact of that scale, particularly as a ground-level experience. And where you get the tallest building we created a public space right in front of it. And we oriented the towers so that you always get sunlight into the courtyards. We really took a largely commercial brief and tried to give it an urban dimension. David Nelson, in conversation with the editor, 2012

1. A typical mid-level plan. The block on Ringstrasse is configured as offices above shops and galleries; the block behind as flats. The towers provide offices, though this mix can change.

2. Plan at ground level; shops, cafés and showrooms line the two long street fronts.

0   20m

0   60ft

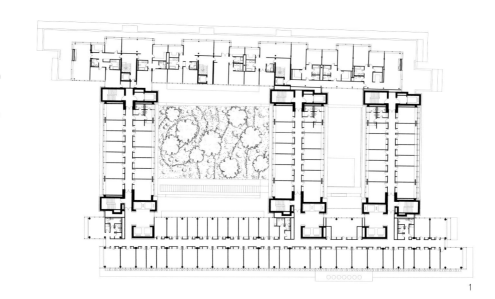

1

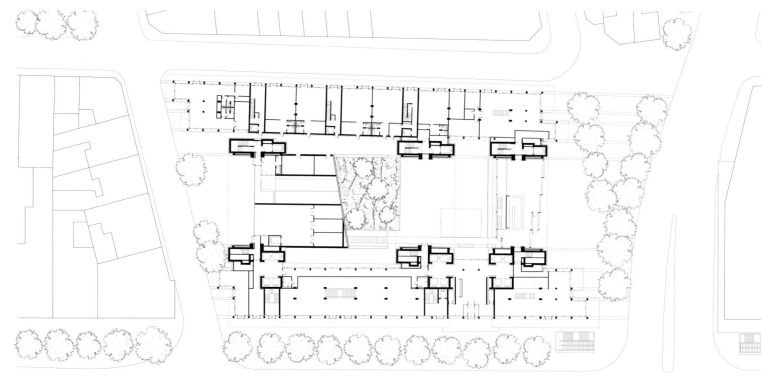

2

Because it is highly adaptable, this is a building that will last for a very long time. It is also a building that contributes on a city level. We believe passionately that the real test for architecture is when a building hits the ground – does it make the city a better place? Do you just want to pass by or would you rather stop and sit in the café? If the ground floor works and people come, then your building is on the right track to improving the public urban realm. Stefan Behling, Ivorypress conference on sustainability, Madrid, 17 September 2009

3

4

5

6

3-6. Lined with shops, bars, cafés and galleries, the scheme animates the street life in this quarter of Cologne. The restaurant beneath the southern tower overlooks the landscaped courtyard on one side and extends out into a shaded square on the other; in summer its tables are busy throughout the day.

Left: A model of the Shinagawa mixed-use development, Tokyo (1990).

Cross-section through the three towers and the underground parking. The office floors of the central tower begin on the third floor, allowing the landscaped courtyard and a pool to extend beneath it. The lowest offices of the southern tower are on the second floor, with a restaurant occupying the double-height volume below.

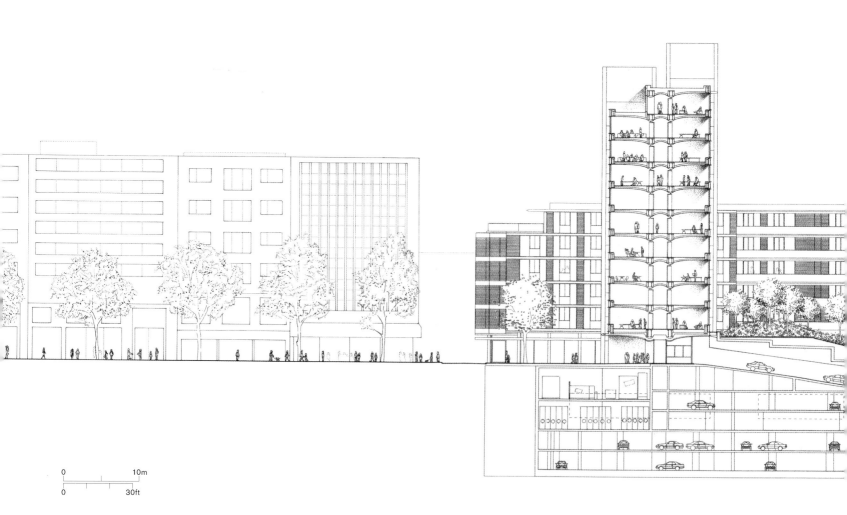

0   10m

0   30ft

Gerling Ring aims to be sustainable by being low-energy and highly flexible to ensure a long life. The same building blocks can provide either offices or apartments as either the market or society requires – and the change-over can be made easily and cheaply. I think a lot of intelligent developers will be taking a similar approach in the future. Norman Foster, in conversation with the editor, 2012

Because the Gerling Ring is situated on the site of one of Cologne's historic city gates we thought combining a tall tower with a bigger public space would be an appropriate vocabulary to celebrate a point of entry into the city. As a result, the tallest tower on the south side of the development is alongside what would have been, in medieval times, a city gate. Paul Kalkhoven, of Foster + Partners, in conversation with the editor, 2012

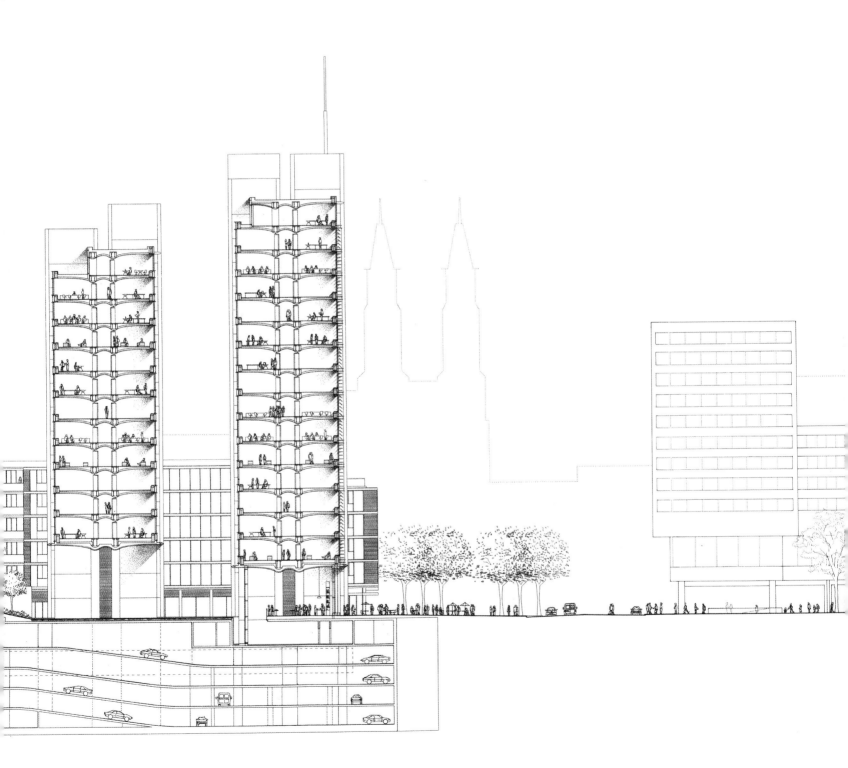

La Voile
St Jean Cap Ferrat, France 1999–2002

The coastline around St Jean Cap Ferrat is dotted with Modernist villas – by architects such as Le Corbusier, Eileen Gray and Oscar Niemeyer. The best of them fuse Modernist principles with the Mediterranean vernacular. With La Voile we aimed to build on this tradition, integrating the house within the landscape and using passive methods of environmental control. However, in this case there was a complicating factor. The villa lies in a protected area, which means that you are not allowed to build anything new, but nor can you demolish. Our only course was creative adaptation. Norman Foster, in conversation with the editor, 2012

Because much of the Mediterranean coastline is overbuilt the French government decided to take control of this area away from the local towns and administer planning controls from a central ministry. As a result the regulations are very tough and strictly enforced. However, I think for La Voile these rules produced the outcome and I think the outcome is very beautiful because of them. Restrictions always give architects reasons for studying alternative solutions and they usually make for a very interesting result. Juan Vieira, of Foster + Partners, in conversation with the editor, 2012

The St Jean Cap Ferrat peninsula on the French Riviera west of Nice – a vacation spot for royals and Rothschilds since the nineteenth century – is highly developed and deeply conservative by tradition. Every square metre of its coastline has long been spoken for, each parcel of land already occupied by a building that is either genuinely historic or effectively so because it is protected by law and perception. The architectural corollary of this cultural disposition is the community's resistance to change: despite the long and distinguished tradition of the abstract white villa in the Mediterranean, Modernism here need not really apply.

The villa may be called 'La Voile', as in the sail of a boat, but voile equally suggests *le voile*, that is, the veil that covers a face in modesty.

When Norman Foster started designing a house for a property on the south-east-facing slopes of this privileged enclave, he faced an impenetrable system of approvals and an immovable fact on the ground – an existing five-storey, stone-faced house dating from the 1950s. That this stolid structure, which was neither traditional nor modern, had no architectural merit did not constitute a valid argument for tearing it down and building anew. Says Foster, 'I couldn't build and I couldn't demolish – in the end, what I did was to transform.'

The typology of the existing house was basically that of a tower, its stump rising from a rocky slope that led down to the sea. It was not remotely characteristic of Foster's work, nor did it offer a very promising starting point. But Foster is a problem solver, not a stylist, and he accepted the givens and subjected the house to a rigorous, step-by-step analysis squared with the spatial, structural, technical and environmental criteria that he applies to any new building, working simultaneously from the inside out and the outside in.

Despite its location on a coast where the sea, sky and sun fuse into a daily spectacle, starting at sunrise, the existing house was closed in form, with boxy poorly lit rooms. This was partly because of the traditional language of masonry and partly because the footprint of the house was simply extruded from the ground up to the height of the roadway. Form and material both seemed to be working against the sea and the view.

The primary task was to liberate form, both inside and outside, to open the house up to the view and create a spatially generous interior that would draw the outside spectacle in. The existing house did not really have a 'heart' – in fact its spatial organisation was more like an office building, its accommodation stacked floor upon floor. Foster realised immediately that only by removing some of the intervening structure, and opening up the building vertically, would it be possible to admit sunlight and views and give the house a social focus.

By subtraction, Foster created the basic armature to which he would then begin to add new elements. He started by paring the building down to its core, stripping it of fussy 'suburban' elements, such as thin balconies and spindly railings, which encrusted the basic structure.

Opposite: Looking out to sea from the study area in the living room. All the living spaces are oriented towards views of the sea, some framed, others panoramic.

1. One of a sequence of preliminary drawings by Norman Foster, dating from June 1999, in which he story-boarded the transformation of the house, from a closed masonry box to a spatially fluid family house.

1

Left: The house was originally built in the mid-1950s as a simple three-storey masonry structure but had undergone major alterations that compromised its simplicity and undermined its vernacular Mediterranean character. However, building regulations governing the French coastline did not allow the house to be demolished, but it could be 'adapted'.

Right, far right: Only the external walls of the old house were retained; everything inside was scooped out and the windows combined to form a single large opening. The regulations demanded that the definition of the external volume had to be maintained at all times, so if structure was removed it had to be replaced immediately.

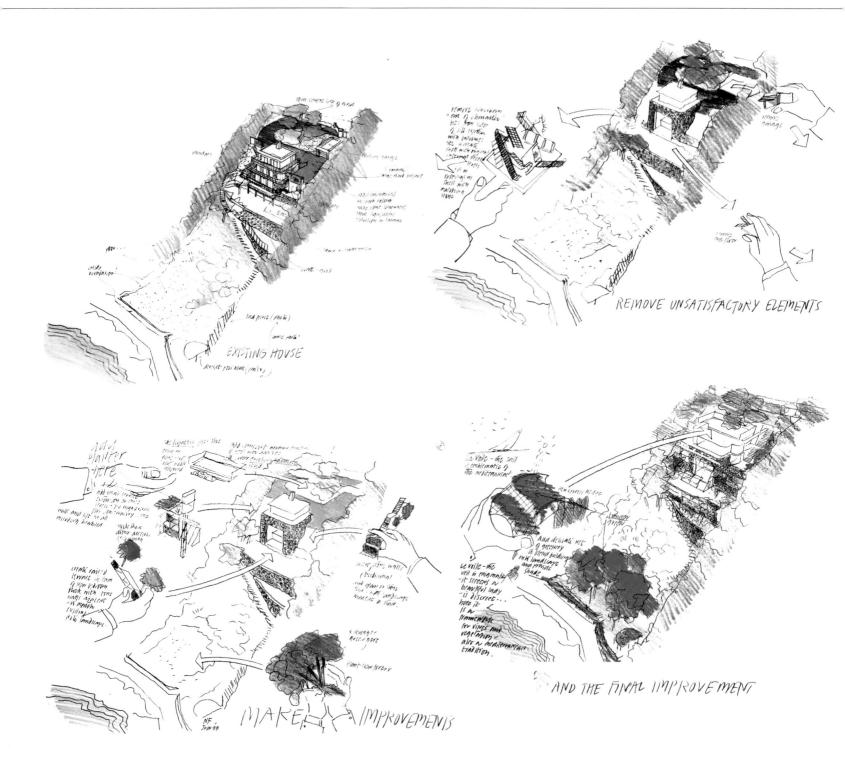

EXISTING HOUSE

REMOVE UNSATISFACTORY ELEMENTS

MAKE IMPROVEMENTS

AND THE FINAL IMPROVEMENT

What remained was a 'tower' element with rounded corners and faced in a honey-coloured limestone, with a single-storey, box-like penthouse on top, set in from the edge of the stone base. The structure revealed by this editing – two stacked volumetric elements – exhibited a strong, primary geometry and constituted Foster's point of departure.

His next step was to close apertures in the side walls, making the surface continuous and the masonry form more Platonic. Then he broke open the closed volume inside and out, merging nine windows on three floors of the main facade to create a single large aperture that confers a heroic scale on this domestic structure. The lower floor was removed entirely, and the upper two floors cut back to create a four-storey-tall interior that is open vertically from terrace level to the roof. Horizontally, it opens up to the great feature of the site: the sea and the limitless horizon.

'I couldn't build and I couldn't demolish – in the end, what I did was to transform.'

In many of his projects – particularly in his earlier work – Foster has built up his structures through componentry, from a kit of either custom-made or off-the-shelf parts. In the Cap Ferrat villa, he devised a variation of the same strategy, attaching a kit of elements to the basic core. It was a kit in which form, apparatus and programme were combined. The diagrams he drew of how the various components of the house would be assembled rival the simplicity of an IKEA diagram on how to put together a piece of furniture from its constituent parts, or a model aircraft kit of the kind he might have attempted in his youth.

Foster's organisational parti necessitated the clever packing of all the separate elements required to support modern living into the very limited space available. To the southern side of the house he attached a three-storey service core, including kitchen, laundry and staff rooms. Alongside them he placed a lift shaft, to connect all levels.

At the base he extended the lower floor out into the rough landscape – the garrigue – to create a suite of four bedrooms. The roof of these bedrooms forms a large terrace that extends the main floor of the living area through the heroic portal. At the top of the site close to the street, he removed the garage and appropriated the driveway, tucking a new garage beneath a swimming pool engineered into the wedge of space between the original house and a new driveway.

The steep slope of the site is used to full advantage. The top of the building is extended towards the street, and the bottom towards the sea, giving this formerly erect block a dynamic, Z-shaped profile. The structure extends out of plane at the top and bottom, east and west, backwards and forwards; the static 'tower' breaking out of its geometry and moving in space and light.

The design process was gradual and iterative. Foster worked the design as though it were a block of clay, adding and subtracting chunks, while smoothing out incidental irregularities. By emphasising the seaward exposure and saddling the sides with functions that he removed from the centre, he was able to give the interior direction, towards the sea and the view. The moves were big, confident and radically transformative.

Green concerns have long been a major consideration in Foster's approach to design, and he studied many environmental scenarios, through the day and through the seasons, in order to determine an appropriate architectural response. Surprisingly for an architect who has been characterised as High-Tech (incidentally, a label he rejects), Foster relied on several low-tech moves to establish environmental comfort and reduce dependency on mechanical systems.

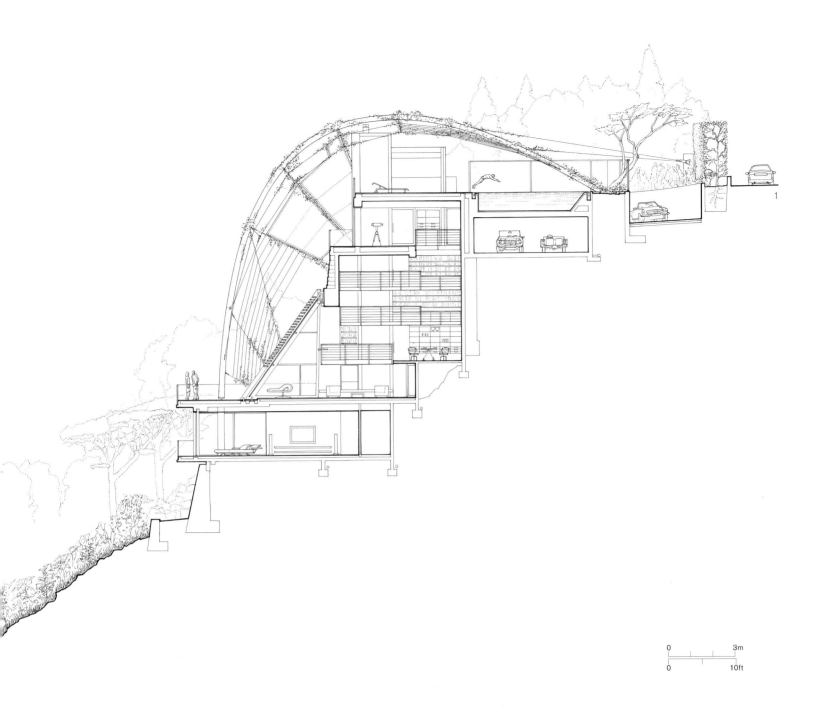

1. Longitudinal cross-section through the living space. The house is entered at high level, either via the terrace, or via the drive, which winds down along the side of the house to a garage located beneath the pool.

2. A detail of the study/look-out on the dining level.

3. Looking across the living space towards the library, from the vantage point of the staircase that connects the four levels.

Press a subtle button, announce your arrival and quietly, electronically a wall of steel slides to show the brightest and bluest sea. The eye travels straight to the horizon far away and, far below you as you stand almost on a cliff top, the house is below your feet – half eagle's nest, half cave cut into the hillside. This is a secret place, a resting place for the restless traveller, a place to escape to and, with your back to the rocks, a place to feel protected, isolated, reflective. Ben Johnson, in conversation with the editor, 2012

Sailing aficionados admire a yacht when she is yare – fast, right and quick to the helm. Foster has trimmed his design so that this Modernist house on the Mediterranean is everything it should be – light, bright, taut and ready to sail. She is *yare*.
Joseph Giovannini, *Architectural Digest*, October 2006

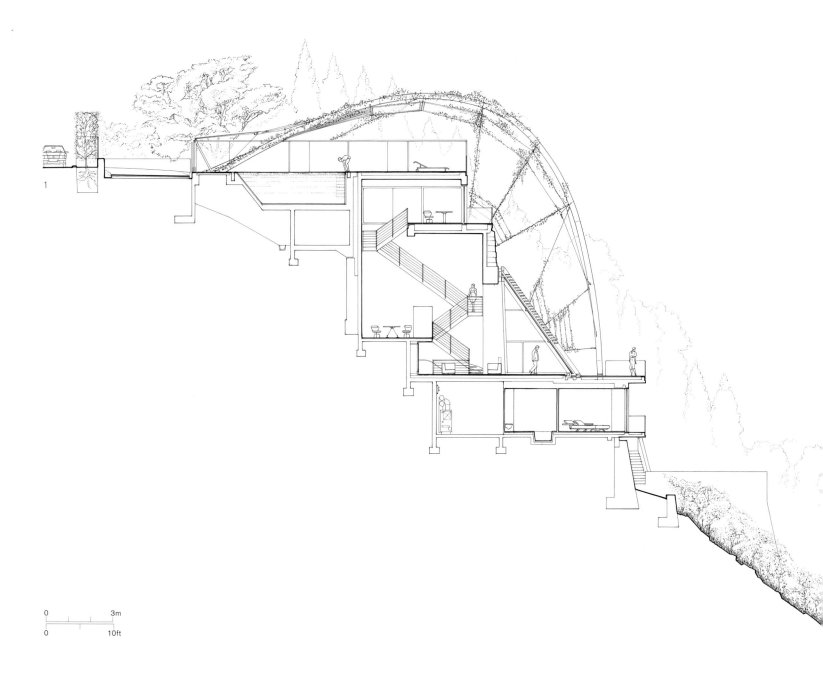

0 ———————— 3m
0 ———————— 10ft

Previous pages: Looking out
to sea from the poolside.

1. Longitudinal cross-section
through the living space,
looking towards the staircase.

2. A detail of the staircase
and the glass balustrade
on the dining level.

3. The corner of the living
space at terrace level.

2   3

First there is the road, neat and discreet, with walls that make even a glimpse of the Mediterranean subject to a private view invitation. Then there appears a high-tech shadow play on opaque glass. Plants dance, trees throw shapes and whimsical sculpture suggests a mythical goddess is being chased through the garden. Ben Johnson, in conversation with the editor, 2012

Our starting point was to de-clutter the building so that it could be better incorporated with the surrounding rough garrigue landscape. The new elements are offered as a counterpoint to the rugged masonry of the original house. We raised the retaining wall by one storey to create a new bedroom level, which is fully glazed, and unified the windows facing the sea to create one large double-height opening. The glazed screen in front of that aperture became in effect a winter garden, which you can slide open in warm weather. Norman Foster, in conversation with the editor, 2012

The brief was for a summer house. The house was designed for the use of a close family rather than for entertaining large numbers of guests. It is an intimate space. William Castagna, of Foster + Partners, in conversation with the editor, 2011

1. Looking up at the house from the garrigue of hardy indigenous shrubs that runs down to the sea.

2. Plan at pool level, corresponding with the entrance from the street. From here the house is entered via a lift.

3. Plan at garage level; the house and studio can both be entered via the garage.

4. Plan at second mezzanine level, corresponding with library and staff quarters.

5. Plan at first mezzanine level, corresponding with library and service areas.

6. Plan at dining level.

7. Plan at terrace level.

8. Plan at bedroom level.

1 entrance gate
2 swimming pool
3 entrance/lift
4 terrace
5 garage
6 plant room
7 office/studio
8 staff bedroom
9 staff living room
10 library
11 laundry
12 kitchen
13 dining room
14 living room
15 terrace
16 master bedroom
17 bedrooms

1

The planning regulations meant that we couldn't use a lift system which had a motor room at the top as this wouldn't have fitted within the existing envelope. We also couldn't use a conventional system because we had a number of stops which were closer together than the standard minimum of 2.5 metres. These factors meant that we had to get a system specially made by an Italian manufacturer and the end result is a very elegant glass lift which runs from the pool at the top of the house to the bedrooms at the bottom.

Juan Vieira, of Foster + Partners, in conversation with the editor, 2012

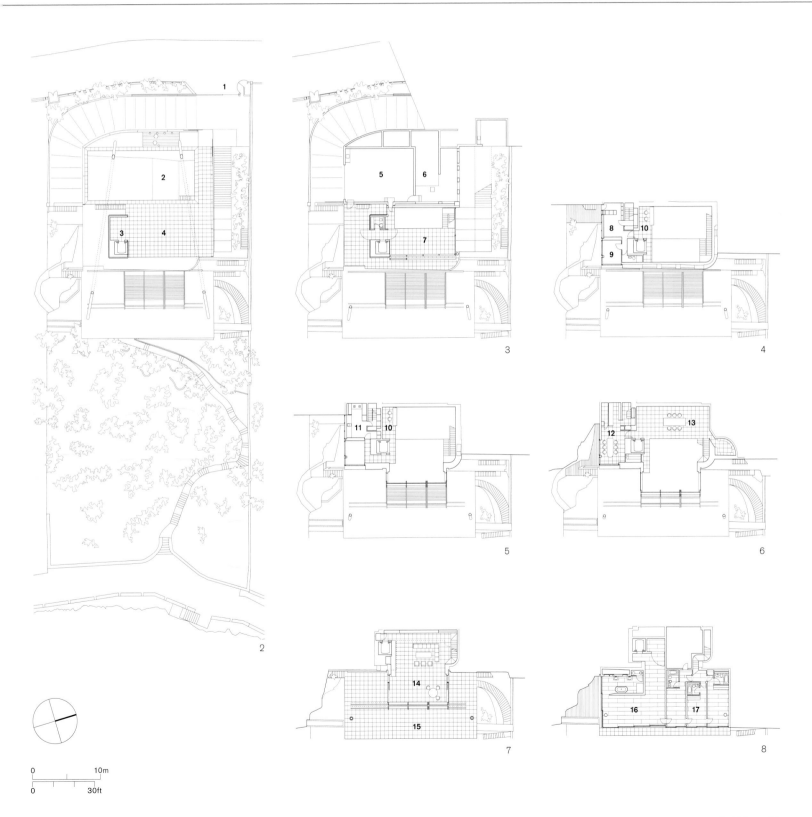

0   10m
0   30ft

Somebody asked me how long Richard took to do this piece, to which I replied: 'It must have taken about forty years.' I won't say how long it actually took, but to see Richard in action is very interesting. It is almost as if he goes into another world and uncoils an incredible energy. So there is a paradox between seeing the intensity of the work's creation and the experience of living with it. To live with Richard's work is incredibly moving and stimulating. It's an everyday spiritual experience. That's the true measure of the integration between art and architecture – when it works boy does it deliver. Do you feel better at the beginning and at the end of the day? Sure you do. Norman Foster, in conversation with the editor, 2012

Richard Long took an afternoon to complete his piece and it was incredible to see. It was a bit like watching a Kodo drummer because it's an amazingly physical process to cover such a huge area with just your bare hands. Andrew Thomson, formerly of Foster + Partners, in conversation with the editor, 2009

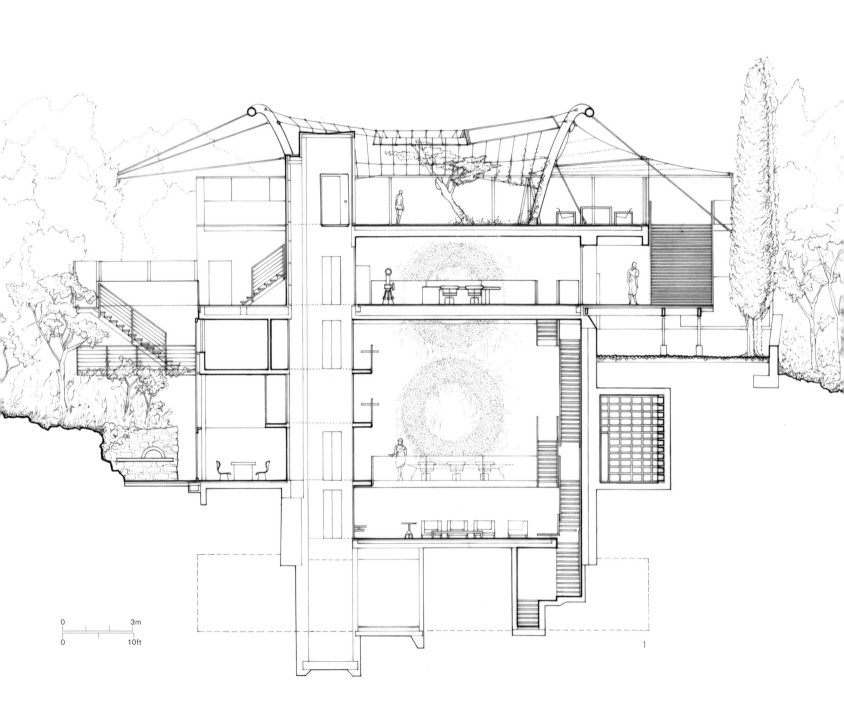

0   3m

0   10ft

1

Richard Long is an artist whose work I admire deeply – it is rooted in a profound understanding of nature and inspired by natural forms and materials. In his 'mud works' one senses this engagement in an almost visceral way – they convey an incredible sense of physical energy. They are literally 'hands on'. I have watched him produce such works in many different settings. Each time, though the process is similar, the result has been strikingly different. Looking at the fluid lines close up is akin to looking at fingerprints or snowflakes under a microscope – you begin to see an incredible diversity of forms. Norman Foster, in conversation with the editor, 2012
Left: Richard Long's wall piece in La Voile.

He conducted studies on thermal mass, air flow and passive cooling, always balancing benefits, liabilities and short- and long-term costs. By opening up the section of the house vertically, he created an interior volume with a stack effect that would conduct hot air out through the roof and work against daily heat build up. In summer, night cooling is used to refresh the structure; and in winter the huge window opening allows the concrete floor in the living space to work as a heat sink.

No architect working in the Mediterranean can ignore Le Corbusier's advocacy of the brise-soleil, and after studying a variety of sun screen options, Foster settled on a combination. The great environmental asset of the large portal in the facade was also its liability: while in the winter it would allow the sun to warm the concrete floor, in the summer it risked overheating the house. In response, Foster devised an inclined 7.5-metre tall, glass facade made of two framed panels that slide to either side to allow cooling breezes to move inside. At the push of a button, the two doors (together weighing 18 tonnes) part theatrically, the scale of the sliding window wall having the effect of making the tall, generous volume continuous with the terrace.

A slatted brise-soleil covers the doors. You can close or open either the sliding doors or brise-soleil, or both, in a total of six possible combinations, depending upon the season or the time of day. Residents can shade the house, and let breezes through, or shade it while keeping cold air out.

The major difference between traditional Mediterranean villas with shutters and Foster's house is that opening the brise-soleil and glass wall completely transforms the exterior form and interior space: it allows you to modify the environment and embrace the landscape in a very remarkable way.

To shade the rest of the house, Foster took the notion of the pergola, an ancient and effective Mediterranean approach to seasonal shading. He designed two curving steel beams that spring from the back of the house to the front in a single sweep. Between them, he stretched a series of canvas sails and a spider's web of stainless-steel cables. The sails provide specific areas of shade, particularly on the rooftop deck next to the pool, and the cables carry a veil of deciduous vines – a living sunscreen – up and over the house, effectively forming a secondary facade. Off season, without leaves, the house is warmed by the sun, and in season, the dense vines shade the upper deck and the pool while encouraging cooling breezes to flow through.

Foster has subordinated the notion of a building as object to the notion of the building as enclosure and space.

The gesture of the overarching beams, the sails and the stainless-steel bright work may be heroic, alluding to majestic sailing vessels, but it is also architecturally self-effacing, even self-erasing – a very effective piece of camouflage. The villa may be called 'La Voile', as in the sail of a boat, but voile equally suggests *le voile*, that is, the veil that covers a face in modesty. Beneath the lithe, minimal trapeze of steel and cables, fabric and vines, the 'architecture' virtually disappears.

Foster, then, did not demolish and build from the ground up, but he wrought a transformation that is so radical and thorough that the house might be effectively regarded as new. The surgery he performed basically changed the typology of the house from a layer-cake of repetitive floors into a composition with a section that is stepped with terraces inside and out. By carving out a continuous interior volume, opening levels to each other and allowing space to flow vertically as well as horizontally, he recast the house entirely.

2

1. Transverse cross-section through the living space and pool terrace. Staff quarters and service accommodation are stacked in mezzanines to the left (in this view) of the living space.

2. Looking into the living area at night through the aperture of the 'winter garden'. The wall piece, which commands the space, is by Richard Long.

As you enter it is hard not to be stunned: the view, the drop, the scale, the sense of theatre, where space is the subject and the main performer. You stand on a firm platform but are drawn to the edge to look down into this elegant and uncompromising vault. We are all used to entering architecture that impresses by means of height. Here we are turned upside down – it is the depth that takes the breath away. No sensible attempt to maximise usable space. Here drama brings joy. It is a very sensual house. Ben Johnson, in conversation with the editor, 2012
Left: Ben Johnson's *Far Horizons 1*, 2009 – one of a series of paintings by Johnson that were inspired by the view from the house.

1

1. A detail of the study area, located on the dining level, in the living space. This photograph is one of a series taken by the artist Ben Johnson on his visit to the house in the summer of 2007.

2. Looking down on to the dining area from the staircase which winds up through the living space.

2

By removing the multiple floors of the existing building and by cutting a large hole into the facade we were able to create a dramatic light-filled space which frames the view out to sea almost like a theatre or stage set. Juan Vieira, of Foster + Partners, in conversation with the editor, 2012

Our journey continues down. On the right wall descend five or six floors by safe enclosed lift or, on the left wall, adventure on the equally safe but much more challenging stairs. Hitchcock would certainly have wanted to use this house as a set. The stairs keep you in touch with your emotions. Closer to sea level (but still elevated) is the eating platform. There is a vast table large enough for the most extended family to feel comfortable and happy but also space for two to sit contentedly observing the beauty and power of nature. Sea and sky are experienced from a majestically engineered habitat. Ben Johnson, in conversation with the editor, 2012

A staircase zigzags down through the living space, lining one of the original 'tower' walls. It has stone treads and a stainless-steel balustrade with taut steel cables. In contrast, the living spaces, which look out to sea, have transparent glass balustrades. They relate to the vistas: they're parallel to the coast, and so they are expressed differently. Norman Foster, in conversation with the editor, 2012

3

4

5

An interior tower of space has replaced a tower of floors, and the vertiginous interior, whose drama is emphasised by a characteristic mural by Richard Long, now unifies what had been a spatially fragmented house. Functions such as the kitchen, laundry, lift, and service areas are located outside the original volume; and the bedrooms are located on the lower floor, so that the interior volume is an entirely social domain.

Although the house seen from a boat is arresting, especially in the transitional period before the green facade takes over completely, it is not a house that you look at, but rather look out from. Foster has subordinated the notion of a building as object to the notion of the building as enclosure and space. He has opened up the house to the outside and opened up the interior to itself. What it has in common with other much larger Foster structures is the sectional richness that cultivates a robust interior life. In this case, the section is scaled to the grandeur of the outside – to the sea and the far horizon.

Foster seldom designs single-family residences. If most of his buildings are used by hundreds if not thousands of people daily, what the Cap Ferrat villa reveals more clearly than larger buildings is the basic humanistic attitude of an architecture that cares for the individual: La Voile nurtures its occupants while keeping them in touch with the environment and revealing the spectacle of nature. The open character of the plan and section brings occupants into socialising spaces rather than keeping them apart, compartmentalised by room or by floor.

Although Foster has left High-Tech imprints on the design, particularly in the movable glass wall and the trapeze of cables that forms the pergola, the house resembles no other building in his repertoire. Foster has never designed by formula or signature but by analysis. He studied the original building and determined how best to approach the design within local restrictions. With his set of environmental concerns, he greatly expanded the range of the building's environmental response and behaviour. He did not design La Voile a priori, with a pre-existing set of forms imported to the commission. It is instead a resultant design, the product of discreet moves emerging from an analysis of environmental, structural, spatial and cultural considerations.

No architect working in the Mediterranean can ignore Le Corbusier's advocacy of the brise-soleil.

The result is the complete transformation of an undistinguished, but protected building into a stately new Modernist structure. Foster successfully worked within the restrictive rules without pandering to the authorities through feints of historicism or traditionalism. Through an ingenious but fundamentally modest and direct empirical process, he has created a building of invention, elegance and originality.

Joseph Giovannini

3-5. The living space looks out through an inclined glass 'winter garden' whose 'doors' can be slid apart to open the space up to the terrace and the sea. A slatted brise-soleil slides into place to screen the glass doors – or to provide shade when the doors are open – as required. The combination of these elements allows occupants to 'tune' the space in response to changing temperature or wind direction.

6. Norman Foster's sketch of the multi-level living space.

Overleaf: Looking out to sea at dusk.

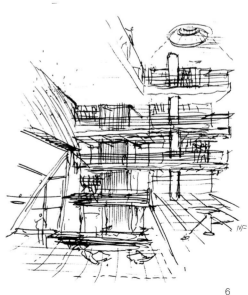

6

To experience this house is to experience fundamental aspects of ambition. It is a suitable retreat for a privileged person; it is uncompromising in design; it is very tactile; it awakens the senses. It shows what we can do when we challenge the norm. It shows how we can respect, appreciate and work with our environment. It expresses the ingenuity and creativity of the individual. Ben Johnson, in conversation with the editor, 2012

The house appears to hang suspended in space, hovering. From the living space or the dining level, it has been described as a cross between the deck of a ship and a helicopter. Norman Foster, in conversation with the editor, 2012

Asprey

London, England 2001–2004

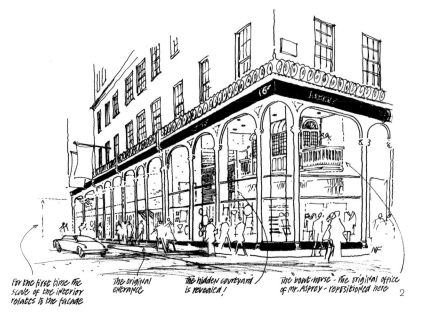

For the first time the scale of the interior relates to the facade

The original entrance

The hidden courtyard is revealed!

The 'boat-house' - the original office of Mr. Asprey - repositioned here

Asprey is an established British luxury goods brand with a worldwide reputation. The challenge was to promote the timelessness, values and craftsmanship associated with Asprey's goods through the medium of contemporary design.

Norman Foster

Left: The Asprey shop on Bond Street, photographed in 2001. In 2000, when the parent company Asprey & Garrard was sold, its new owners decided that Asprey & Garrard would demerge, Garrard returning to Albemarle Street, leaving Asprey to have free rein in Bond Street. The refurbishment of the Bond Street shop was spurred by Asprey's desire both to broaden its market and bolster its cachet as an exclusive brand.

Our intention was to create a strong family identity for Asprey – first in London and New York, and then in stores in other cities – that would communicate all the values of a major luxury brand. Like all families there would be differences between individual stores, but there would also be strong common features. Norman Foster, in conversation with the editor, 2012

Asprey, the English luxury goods company, has operated from the same premises in Bond Street since 1846, its shopfront immediately identifiable by its delicate two-storey cast-iron structure and tall panes of glass. The Asprey name, applied in gold lettering to the black fascia, is a distinctive signature in an area where jewellers, fine art and antiques dealers, and auction rooms are largely concentrated.

Unlike other luxury goods companies, which have premises around the world, in 2001 Asprey had only its Bond Street base, which over time had become cramped and 'tired'. Giles Robinson, the project architect observes 'Because Asprey had discreetly conducted 80 per cent of its business with just a handful of clients, its shop had not had serious attention for decades.'

Over the years, Asprey had expanded its premises to occupy five adjoining properties on Albemarle and Grafton Streets, all of which are Grade II listed, and numerous alterations had been carried out to link them, including a roof over the rear yards at first floor level to expand the ground-floor retail space.

Remarkably, the architects found that this agglomeration of buildings encompassed sixty-four different floor levels. In addition to the shop, the basement and upper floors contained a maze of storage spaces and offices, together with the workshops where many of Asprey's silver and leather goods are made. Consequently, much of the design team's effort was directed towards rationalising the back-of-house areas and clarifying circulation, which was accomplished through a series of focused, but highly productive moves.

The shop originally occupied the ground floor with storage on a mezzanine that blanked out the upper half of the windows. The removal of this entresol has created a double-height retail space on Bond Street. As Foster notes, 'For the first time in its long history, the scale of Asprey's interior relates to the facade.' The office of Mr Asprey, an elaborate piece of joinery known as the 'boathouse' which was formerly buried within the block, now overlooks this double-height space and is, in turn, visible from the street.

Additionally, the first floor across the entire site – formerly a back-of-house area – is now devoted to retail space. On both the ground and first floors, new openings have been made, with ramps and stairs to connect the different levels and enable customers to move freely from room to room.

For the first time in its long history, the scale of Asprey's interior relates to the facade.

The generous Bond Street space connects directly to a roofed courtyard that has been created by removing earlier additions and restoring the rear facades. This strategy of revealing undiscovered or inaccessible space has been explored by Foster many times before, first with the Sackler Galleries at the Royal Academy and ultimately in the Great Court at the British Museum. At Asprey, the buildings frame an irregular light well – a space that is compressed in plan but expansive in section.

3

1, 2. The refurbished Asprey shopfront on Bond Street; and a corresponding sketch by Norman Foster, in which he articulates a strategy for the renewal of the store.

3. Entering the Bond Street shop – newly revealed as a double-height volume.

4. An early study of the Bond Street shopfront. The entrance has been reinstated in its original position and Mr Asprey's relocated 'boathouse' is visible from the street.

4

The design of the display cases was a real challenge. The breakthrough came with the discovery of an original Asprey case from the 1930s, which was beautifully made in bronze. That gave us our 'spark'. Then the problem was finding someone to make them. Most people we spoke to wanted to thicken up the framing. But Molteni was able to fabricate framing members that are both strong and slender. The finished thing looks very elegant, both modern and classic. Graham Phillips, formerly of Foster + Partners, in conversation with the editor, 2009
Right: A view of the London shop as it existed before the project began, with Mr Asprey's 'boathouse' seen centre.

Bond Street has had a colourful history of elaborate heists, so safety concerns informed the detail. We wanted to create an open, light environment, while at the same time ensuring security. Internally, some of the original Victorian and early twentieth-century cabinets had survived, which drove how we treated and created new elements in the store. Mostly these appear as displays with fine mahogany frames and curved glass but we also needed to incorporate state-of-the-art lighting and burglar-proof measures. As far as Asprey were concerned, these internal display elements were seen as an important part of its identity. Kevin Carrucan, formerly of Foster + Partners, in conversation with the editor, 2008

1. One of the new first-floor rooms, with display cabinets designed by the Foster team and fabricated by Molteni in Italy.

2. Looking from the double-height Bond Street store into the new courtyard.

3. A sketch cross-section through the courtyard, drawn by Norman Foster. The effect of the courtyard is to provide a central orientation and focus and to open up multiple possible routes through the shop.

A lift, tucked into one corner of the courtyard, provides access to the majority of floor levels. Within the void, an elliptical spiral stair connects two levels in the Albemarle Street buildings, its apparent lightness creating an air of generosity in the small courtyard – an effect amplified by the delicate steel and fritted glass roof, which brings daylight into the heart of the block. Looking up, what appears to be a simple diamond-grid roof structure is in fact more complex, with an irregular pattern enabling the steel frame to 'meet' particular points around the perimeter. This adjustment, not obvious to the casual observer, gives the space a sense of composure.

The cumulative result of this new circulation system is to make what was once a maze of rooms immediately legible and easy to navigate. These interventions are augmented by the creation of two new entrances on Grafton Street and Albemarle Street, which reinstate the original domestic front doors. In addition, the staircases of what were originally separate houses have been retained and restored, allowing customers to create shortcuts. The workshops, renewed and relocated to the top floor, continue to provide the bespoke service for which Asprey is renowned.

In the same way that the original cast-iron shopfront frame appeared magically to support the three storeys of brickwork above, so the creation of the double-height retail space on Bond Street and the large opening to the courtyard demanded great structural ingenuity. Similarly, to make the spiral stair hover seemingly effortlessly required the structural sleight of hand of a steel picture-frame structure embedded in the walls, which supports the stair at each landing.

Though the reconstruction has doubled the retail space, the old atmosphere of domestic intimacy has been preserved.

Within the rooms, cornices have been meticulously restored and services are threaded through the floor joists to dropped raft ceilings at the centre of each room. These house air grilles, lighting, and emergency and security systems as well as concealed uplighting for the cornices. This carefully judged juxtaposition of new and old is carried throughout the interiors. Traditional wooden architraves coexist comfortably with bronze-framed limestone panels; and sleek new bronze and glass display cases mix comfortably with antique bookcases and cabinets.

Though the reconstruction has doubled the retail space, Asprey's old atmosphere of domestic intimacy has been preserved. The quirky details of the historic interiors form the perfect stage set for Asprey's luxury goods and accessories. 'Much of what we have done here', notes Giles Robinson, 'is unglamorous work – removing accretions, inserting new structure, upgrading services and restoring period details.' This modest approach has paid dividends though, producing an understated elegance that reinforces Asprey's brand image, both acknowledging its traditions and projecting it forward into a new century.

Annette LeCuyer

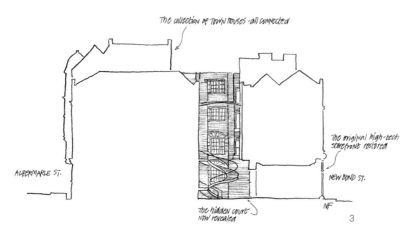

The collection of Town houses all connected

The original high-tech shopfront restored

ALBEMARLE ST.

NEW BOND ST.

The hidden court now revealed

NF

3

The real achievement of this project was to find a way of unifying the circulation in the five old buildings that Asprey occupied. It was a planning tour de force. The key to that was the discovery of the courtyard as the central focus. It is a space that never really existed at ground level before. But by clearing away all the outbuildings and roofing the space in glass, we were able to create a sort of mini Great Court, which ties everything together. Graham Phillips, formerly of Foster + Partners, in conversation with the editor, 2009

Right: Norman Foster, Graham Phillips and Giles Robinson explore the roofscape at Asprey London during an early site visit.

One of our first moves was to establish the relationship between the spiral staircase and the courtyard. There are echoes of our approach at the Royal Academy and again at the Great Court in the British Museum, albeit at a smaller scale. One of the main challenges it answered was to signal movement up through the shop and draw people in. The stair provides such a natural focus – and evokes such a strong sense of theatre – that the courtyard became the obvious venue for Asprey to launch its ready-to-wear range. Norman Foster, in conversation with the editor, 2012

5

6

4. The spiral stair is a welded steel, spiral box beam structure with limestone treads, glass balustrades and bronze handrails wrapped in leather.

5. Looking up at the glazed roof over the courtyard. To avoid a visually heavy connection detail between roof and walls, the roof is supported on a steel ring beam which is recessed into the brickwork.

6. Entering the courtyard from the original Bond Street shop.

4

Asprey
New York, USA 2002–2004

The location is spectacular, but the challenge was to identify the shop as a discrete entity within the context of what is really a very assertive landmark. With its strongly delineated white verticals and unifying black signboard, the London shopfront offered visual clues. The scale is larger, but we tried to evoke the delicacy and refinement of the London facade. The verticals are painted glossy white and their profile is quite deep so that they form recesses behind the glass. A horizontal black band with the company's sign runs at the midpoint to tie the composition together, and the windows are set on a granite base. The result is modern in spirit but rooted in the Asprey tradition. Norman Foster, in conversation with the editor, 2012

It was felt that the New York store should somehow acknowledge the Victorian facade of the Bond Street shop but the difficulty was sitting this within Trump Tower, one of New York's iconic buildings. We needed to bring the two elements together without losing the identity of either. Armstrong Yakubu of Foster + Partners, in conversation with the editor, 2009
Left: The original New York storefront, in the base of Trump Tower on 5th Avenue.

Modernism's theoretical basis in industrialised mass production and the idealism of Classicism may stand worlds apart philosophically, but they share common ground in notions of regularity, measure and repetition. In 2003, these two philosophies converged in surprising agreement at the corner of 5th Avenue and 56th Street in Manhattan in the design of a new flagship store for Asprey, within the corner of the landmark Trump Tower. As Asprey's flagship store in the United States, the design had to make a statement on 5th Avenue that would represent Asprey as an institution and a brand in New York and the country at large. It would also serve as a prototype for subsequent stores to be built in other cities around the world, with the ability to achieve a comparable profile and resonance in other cultures.

Foster decided to abstract the iconic London facade as a visual motif to identify the New York store.

Norman Foster understood that the history of Asprey represented a second context, after 5th Avenue itself. Foster and his team were at the time involved in redesigning the mother store on Bond Street in London, which has a distinctive arched, cast-iron Victorian facade beneath a glossy black signboard. Foster decided to abstract the iconic London facade as a visual motif to identify the New York store, and to translate it in a modern constructional idiom that could be applied in New York and elsewhere. The shop would be simultaneously modern and traditional, looking both to its nineteenth-century roots and twenty-first century future.

Although the corner site offered high visibility on 5th Avenue, the facade required a negotiated relationship between the assertion of Asprey's presence on the street, and its insertion within the body of Trump Tower, itself a strong but volumetrically sensitive composition sheathed in dark glass. The challenge was to create a cohabitation of equals.

Using a repetitive columnar motif distilled from the Bond Street store, the architects created a sequence of bays, each a double storey, framed in white gloss-finished aluminium, and glazed in low-iron glass. The horizontal spandrel dividing the two storeys does not coincide with the floors inside, but instead divides the bays into a taller lower level and a shorter upper storey. Together the two facades along 5th and 56th define what seems to be a discrete independent volume – a virtual pavilion. The effect is to re-establish the townhouse scale of 5th Avenue, still a vestigial presence expressed in other nearby structures.

The domestic scale and finiteness of the 'pavilion' presages the spatial quality of Asprey's interior, its layout recalling the townhouse and its related building type, the gentlemen's club. A broad staircase with wide, furnished landings rises through three generously scaled floors that could in another context be considered grand salons. On the second and third floors, these salons lead to smaller rooms to the side and rear that recall the drawing rooms of a townhouse. The scale of the staircase and the major front rooms is stately, and the promenade up and through the spaces seems both processional and ceremonial.

1

Opposite: A detail of the Asprey entrance on 5th Avenue. In an echo of the Bond Street shop, the double- height window bays are framed in white gloss-finished aluminium panels, with a black lacquer spandrel panel.

1. The Asprey shop commands the corner of 5th Avenue and 56th Street, establishing a strong individual identity – almost a pavilion in its own right – within the base of the Trump Tower.

2. An early sketch of the 5th Avenue facade by Norman Foster.

2

As part of our design research we found some of the original nineteenth-century mahogany display cases used in the London shop. We convinced the client to restore one of them so we could use it as a starting point for our design. They loved the finished result and that kick-started the development of the new cabinets which were very delicately done using mahogany, bronze, mirror and glass. However, while the materials we used were traditional the technology contained within them, like the LED lighting and non-reflective glass, was state-of-the-art. Armstrong Yakubu of Foster + Partners, in conversation with the editor, 2012

Asprey demanded incredible attention to detail. Just one example: in the New York store there was one column on the 5th Avenue facade that was slightly out of alignment; but for the elevation to work as we wanted, it had to be exact. And so we moved it, despite the costs involved. That level of concern filtered right down to the smallest cabinetry details – and it showed. Norman Foster, in conversation with the editor, 2012

A major breakthrough in terms of the Asprey identity was the reference to gentlemen's clubs. The Reform Club as an environment was bang on target. It has a central courtyard and a series of functional rooms off that – a morning area, library, breakfast room, reading room – effectively meeting places where people can negotiate business or pleasure. Internally it's quite a muted space with mahogany and a slightly lived-in feel. There's no polished brass or glare – no bling! This approach was a great counterpoint to all the polished silverware and diamonds on display at Asprey. Kevin Carrucan, formerly of Foster + Partners, in conversation with the editor, 2008

1

2

3

| 0 | | 10m |
| 0 | | 30ft |

4

As the major spatial feature in the 'house', the staircase provides organisational clarity, plus a sense of animation and understated spectacle. The goods in the vitrines, and even those historical Asprey articles on display, seem to be in their element.

The interior of the London store suggested the design approach that Foster would take for the development of the interiors using Asprey's trademark materials – bronze, curved glass and mahogany – as the basic palette. The design team also looked at traditional cabinetry from London silverware shops, which was built with an elegantly slender wooden structure.

It was on Foster's initiative that the design team worked with interior designer David Mlinaric, who selected antique English furnishings and Oriental carpets to reinforce the sense of visiting a comfortable club. Mezzanines between floors showcase carpets, walnut furniture and mahogany bookcases. Cold, white metals – aluminium, stainless steel and chrome – rather than warm, yellow metals once signalled the sea change from traditional to Modernist architecture, but here the architects edge the curved-glass balustrades with bronze handrails, and score expansion joints in the Venetian stucco walls with elegantly thin bronze strips. The bronze divides the walls into squares that break down what would otherwise read as a Modernist field of planes into discrete parts. A creamy limestone is used to pave the staircase, which gives way to light, luxurious Wilton carpets in the showrooms; pale leather lines the backs of wall vitrines and closets in the smaller rooms.

The coexistence of the traditional and the modern establishes an intriguing tension, but without the least trace of opposition. The commission is one of the few recent, large-scale commercial opportunities in America in which the design baton was not passed from the architect who designed the shell to another who created the interiors. As a result there is a seamless transition between outside and inside in what turns out to be, in a commercial context, a rare *gesamtkunstwerk.* Ernesto Rogers advocated the continuity and integrity of design 'from the spoon to the city', and Foster has achieved just that, from the facade to the display cases.

In some ways, the design is deeply resonant, representing, simply, the largest Asprey object, and it introduces clients to that world through its own architectural attributes: precision, invention, tradition and authenticity. No material in the store is painted. All colours are integral to natural materials left untreated. The store embodies the Asprey idea of quality and integrity through its very construction, as if store and contents were cut from the same exquisite cloth.

As a sad coda, in March 2006 it was announced that Asprey's parent company Asprey & Garrard, then recently emerged from 'technical administration', which is a restructuring that offers bankruptcy protection for British companies, would close its New York flagship store.

Joseph Giovannini

One factor that was integral to the success of the project in terms of getting the right identity was the involvement of an Italian company, Unifor/Molteni and Co. It's a family business and is probably one of the best furniture makers in the world. Led by Piero Molteni, they made all the new cabinetry for both the New York and London stores and the quality of work in all different materials – timber, glass and metal – was essential in creating the refined atmosphere we were trying to achieve. Graham Phillips, formerly of Foster + Partners, in conversation with the editor, 2009

Asprey's clients have included people like Queen Victoria – Asprey silversmiths even made the America's Cup. They've been around such a long time and have an extraordinary legacy. The different specialist departments that still exist, and the characters involved in them, such as in the gun room, were absolutely amazing. You'd be measured up for a pair of handmade shotguns like you would be for a suit; you'd get to select the timber and that would be carved to suit your ergonomics. These specialist facilities are an important part of the Asprey mix and they were keen on maintaining an amazing array of crafted accoutrements. Kevin Carrucan, formerly of Foster + Partners, in conversation with the editor, 2008

Despite the shop being arranged on three levels we wanted the space to flow, to give the impression that it was one continuous volume. We wanted the stairs to be very gracious so we created a grand staircase, clad in English Cadeby limestone and made in a very traditional way using big blocks of stone to try and create a seamless finish. Armstrong Yakubu of Foster + Partners, in conversation with the editor, 2012

6

5

1. Display cases are integrated within the window mullions on the upper levels.

2, 3. Moving around the shop at ground floor level; all the display cases and all the individual fittings were custom-designed – part of a conscious attempt to create a completely integrated visual environment for Asprey.

4. A plan of the shop at ground floor level showing its relationship with the base of the Trump Tower.

5, 6. The stairs, which are wide and relatively shallow, are designed for ease of movement. The drama of the staircase is enough to draw customers, who seldom take the lift.

Lighting Systems

2000–2007

I think our interest in light, and the qualities of modelling light, whether natural or artificial, is a major theme in our work. That theme extends to the design of the light fittings themselves.

Norman Foster

With the Louis Poulsen 550 range of lighting we wanted to avoid expressing the LED technology and instead concentrate on how the light was distributed through the fitting. To achieve this we designed a main structural ring containing thirty LEDs together with a set of reflectors which meant that we got three levels of light from it: the direct reflected light, the light which comes out through the little light shafts built into the castings and the light distributed through the glass piece. John Small, formerly of Foster + Partners, in conversation with the editor, 2010

Left: Norman Foster presents the RA panel lighting system to Artemide proprietor Ernesto Gismondi (far left). The panel was designed to fit into ceilings and is capable of housing multiple functions such as fluorescent lighting, track lights, smoke detectors and loud speakers.

Architects and designers have long been fascinated by the power of artificial light – how to engineer it, filter it, deflect and diffuse it; how to pull light into space and how that introduces change and unpredictability into a static environment. Beyond that lies the design of light fittings themselves. From track lighting systems to personal desk lamps, the Foster product design team has crafted a number of sculptural lighting solutions, some for the practice's architectural projects, but also an increasing number of stand-alone products and systems.

The Foster 550 pendant range for Louis Poulsen falls into both categories, having been commissioned independently but subsequently adapted for use in Foster's Winspear Opera House in Dallas. Louis Poulsen approached the Foster team to help develop the use of LED lighting. However, instead of designing a light that used exposed LEDs – as was the norm – the team wanted to create a fitting in which the lamps remained hidden and the light was distributed across multiple planes. A reference point was Poul Henningsen's artichoke lamp, designed for Louis Poulsen forty years earlier. Its multilayered structure means that the light source cannot be seen from any angle. The Foster solution was to arrange thirty LEDs within a cast aluminium ring topped by a larger glass outer shell. The end result is a luminous disc which appears to hover in space, its outer edge emitting a soft glow.

Multi-purpose functionality is at the heart of many of the lighting design solutions devised by the Foster team. The OTO system of adjustable and rotatable spotlights with inbuilt transformers for track mounting, manufactured by Artemide, is an advanced lighting product adaptable to a great range of demands and activities. The components are made from injected, pressure-moulded aluminium, which renders the spot unit highly robust and increases its capacity to disperse the heat given off by the source, guaranteeing high reliability for the components and easy maintenance.

Like OTO, the iGuzzini Radial system, with its minimalist contemporary aesthetic and versatility, was also devised to suit a diverse range of environments – from airports, to railway stations and large public spaces. Its origins lie in the development of a lighting system for the North Greenwich Transport Interchange, realised in 2000 as part of the millennium celebrations. The Greenwich luminaire, developed in consultation with lighting designer Claude Engle, merged the possibility of having both direct and indirect lighting in a single lighting fixture.

Seeking a similar solution for mass-market appeal, the iGuzzini Radial, made of die-cast aluminium, is not only lightweight but also capable of uplight, downlight, direct and indirect light emissions. Its 100mm-thick illuminated body can be suspended and wall-mounted while special attention was paid to its energy-saving features – the use of metal-halide, halogen and compact fluorescent lamps allows high-quality light output, but low emissions and maintenance costs.

Originally conceived by Foster for the Post Haus restaurant in St Moritz, the Illium light concept has now been extended to a family of lights for the Italian lighting manufacturer Nemo. The design of the standing, reading, table and pendant lamps is derived from the very material they are made from: Conturax – a ribbed Pyrex glass tube. The elegant tube of glass is lined with a frosted polycarbonate, so that the light is diffused, and the fluting of the glass creates a delicate play of light.

Nemo approached Foster to manufacture the light after seeing images of the restaurant's interiors in a magazine. For them, the lighting concept represented a perfect synergy as the Illium encapsulated not only an aesthetic quality championed by Nemo but also respect for the environment, with special attention given to fluorescent lights, which allow high light output with low energy consumption.

Libby Sellers

3

1, 2. The Foster 550 pendant range uses multiple LEDs arranged between a cast aluminium ring and an outer glass shell. A one-off version was developed for the foyer of the Winspear Opera House in Dallas. At 1.2 metres in diameter it is almost twice the size of the original fitting and includes a transformer because of the great length from ceiling to light.

3. A suspended iGuzzini Radial light with top diffusing screen, this model emits direct, indirect and reflected light. The range also includes wall mounted uplights and pendant downlights.

The Three-Sixty lamp is a good example of Foster's design philosophy. If architecture is also the relationship of volumes to the cityscape, then objects can exist in relation to the home-scape, constantly coming to terms with the issues of the materials utilised, the ergonomics of their use, the surrounding space, the relationship between light and shadow ... 'Good architecture', in Foster's view, 'happens when you are able to bring into synthesis all the elements that, one by one, characterise a building.' In keeping with this rule, good design happens in the moment of perfect fusion of the parts that compose the object, with its functional, ergonomic, aesthetic and tactile aspects. Danilo Premoli, *Interni*, April 2005

The Illium light was originally designed for the Post Haus Restaurant in St Moritz. The lights were made in the Foster studio by Werner Sigg who put all the various components together by hand before travelling to Switzerland to install the finished items. The light was eventually put into commercial production after Nemo saw images of the restaurant in a magazine. John Small, formerly of Foster + Partners, in conversation with the editor, 2010

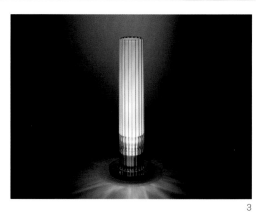

1

2

3

1. The Three-Sixty table lamp's head is adjustable through 360°. This, combined with novel hinges on both the shaft and arm, allows light to be channelled in all directions.

2, 3. First developed for the Post Haus restaurant in St Moritz, the Illium light has grown into a family of lighting options, which includes standing, reading, table and pendant lamps.

4. The Greenwich luminaire combines both direct and indirect lighting in one unit.

5. The Focus bollard, designed for DZ Licht, can accept a variety of fittings, from a compact fluorescent light to a high-intensity lamp.

6-8. Norman Foster's sketch studies for a high-level exterior light with a dished reflector – 'Moonlight' – designed to complement the Focus range. It was intended that the stem would use the same ribbed cast-aluminium profile as the bollard.

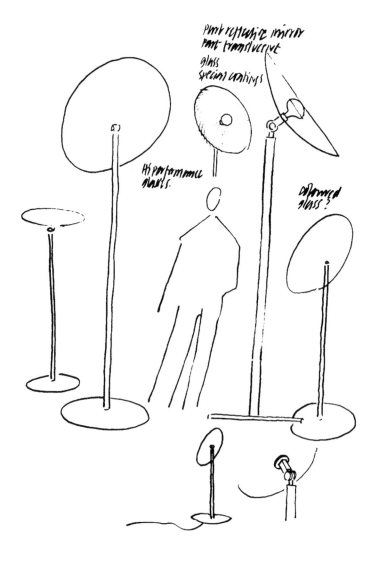

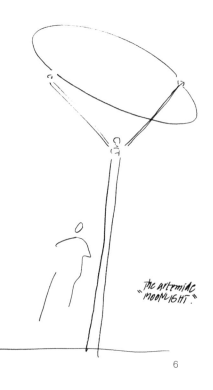

6

At the Greenwich Transport Interchange we wanted to light both the ceiling plane and the concourse but because it was such a large space, and because the undulating form of the roof made fixing the lights problematic, we were unable to find anything suitable on the market. As a result we developed a new light which was both capable of spanning the ceiling plane and big enough to light the space – this was later turned into a production piece by iGuzzini. John Small, formerly of Foster + Partners, in conversation with the editor, 2010

4

I find that the greater the constraints, the stronger the anchors are for the designer. Perhaps it is the fact that if you increase the challenge then you also have the potential to achieve an extra creative dimension. Lighting design is a good example of that – the parameters are generally very strict.

Norman Foster

5

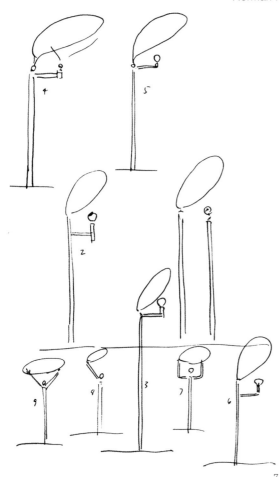

7

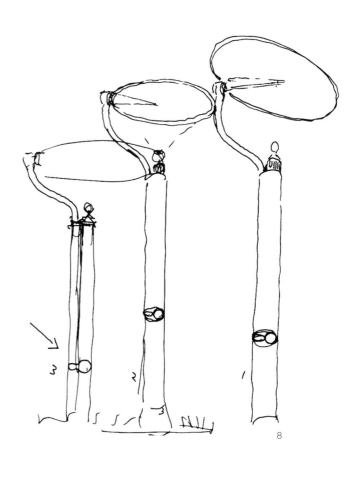

8

Sofa Systems

1999–2008

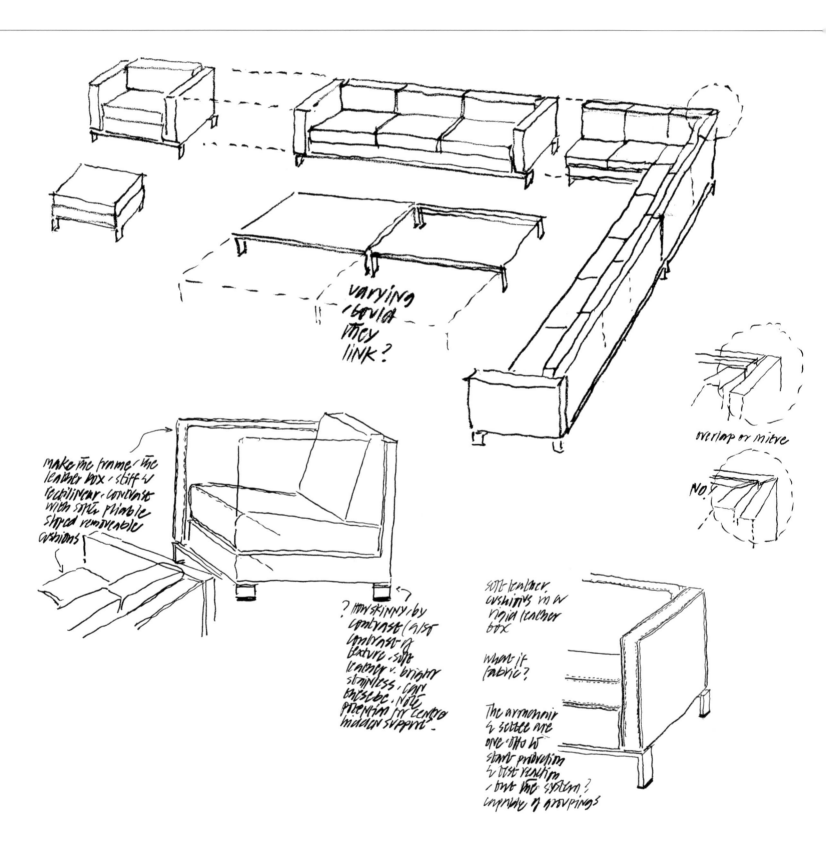

varying
!Gould
they
link?

make the frame the
leather box · stiff +
rectilinear, contrast
with soft pliable
shaped removeable
cushions!

? how skinny by
contrast (ist
contrast of
texture · soft
leather v. bright
stainless, can
enclose · Note
potential for centre
hidden support ·

overlap or mitre

NO!

soft leather
cushions in a
rigid leather
box

what if
fabric?

The armchair
& settle are
one · & to
start production
& test reaction
, but the system?
infinitely in groupings

The Reichstag sofas are very tall and deep, both because the public areas are large and because they were designed so that parliamentarians could sit and talk confidentially within them. It was while working on the Reichstag sofas that we began to discuss with Markus Benz, the owner of Walter Knoll, how we might develop other products. They are a great company to work with and have incredibly skilled craftsmen. We've added to the range starting with the 500 and 501, then developing the 503 and 505 and have just finished another range with them called the 510. John Small, formerly of Foster + Partners, in conversation with the editor, 2010
Right: The original sofas designed for the Reichstag.

The elements that you use, or sit on, or touch in a building, whether it is as large as a sofa or as small as a door handle, are a vital part of the total experience of that building – and in terms of our approach these aspects demand as much design rigour as all the larger elements. Norman Foster, in conversation with the editor, 2010

The route from design idea to finished product can take many different paths. A large proportion of the Foster product design team's work is derived from relationships and formal structures that are developed through the practice's architectural projects.

The design of the Walter Knoll Foster 500 series of sofas, ottomans and side tables was prompted by the interiors brief for Foster's transformation of the Reichstag in Berlin. As a building that sees high levels of footfall, noise and legislative commotion, the large public spaces surrounding the chamber and committee rooms needed buffer zones, or a more intimate spatial solution that offered places to sit and discuss the issues at hand. To furnish these areas, the product design team devised a series of high-backed sofas that offered both privacy and comfort. The German firm of Walter Knoll had been awarded the contract for the manufacture of the Reichstag furniture and a conversation was initiated for future design collaborations.

As the oldest upholstery company in Germany, the Walter Knoll brand has become almost a monument of German cultural history, creating new standards in the furniture market since it was founded in 1865. However, like most established companies faced with increasing competition and shifting consumer habits, it had started to lose its stronghold. When the Rolf Benz family took control in 1993, a much-needed injection of fresh thinking initiated new collaborations with designers and architects.

By commissioning Foster to design a new range, Markus Benz – managing director of Walter Knoll – was specifically looking for something architectural in its form and precision, but also sought a range that would feel approachable in its scale and proportion. The original 500 range of club chair, sofa and side table was expressly intended for the corporate market – and as such conforms to an established genre of corporate culture furnishings that include Le Corbusier's LC2 range and Mies van der Rohe's Barcelona series. Designed for reception areas, lobbies and breakout spaces, the Foster 500 range was, according to John Small, 'an exercise in proportion'. Once the decision had been made to focus the range on a cube, a detailed dimensional analysis was applied so that, when seen in the round, all angles and aspects conformed to the required precision.

1

Opposite: Norman Foster's sketches explore the adaptability of the Knoll Foster 500 series of sofas and ottomans. The system is based on a dimensional module which can be configured to create a variety of spatial arrangements.

1. The Foster 500 range has a leather-upholstered box frame, removable cushions and stainless-steel feet.

2, 3. The 501 series chairs have a fixed back and are smaller than the 500 range.

4. The Knoll 503 sofa range is characterised by a thicker arm profile and a higher back, lending it a more luxurious, softer form.

2

4

3

We had this rather odd phenomenon with the Foster 500 range in that it was designed specifically for the contract market but Walter Knoll later found out they were getting a lot of domestic sales, particularly in Germany, Austria and Switzerland, so they asked us to go back into the design. From this reappraisal we developed the 505 which has big proportions and is very deep; more recently we designed an even softer version, the 503. Interestingly this hasn't corrupted the sales of the original, although oddly the 503 is now also being used for contracts. John Small, formerly of Foster + Partners, in conversation with the editor, 2010

If you are involved in the design process it is very difficult to separate yourself from it, to stand back and take stock. If I were to try to define how the design process works, I would say that it has a lot to do with listening in order to be able to ask the right questions about the needs generating the design – whether that's a building or a piece of furniture. I think it also requires a certain naïveté – the ability to try each time to look at it as if it was the first project you had ever done and to start essentially with a clean sheet of paper and an open mind. Norman Foster, in conversation with the editor, 2012

1. The shell of the Molteni Still range is made from a single sheet of formed plywood, covered in the same fabric as the sofa upholstery.

2. Molteni Still sofa; the sofas are available in either a straight configuration or a gently curved format. The arms and feet are made from a continuous loop of stainless steel.

Yet when consumers started purchasing the Foster 500 range for domestic interiors, the company realised a new market potential and the more relaxed Foster 503 and 505 were subsequently introduced. As befitting domestic pieces, the main amendments to the original 500 range were a luxurious increase in dimensions and a softening of form. The body of the chair and sofa seems to float on a streamlined metallic base while the generous upholstered seating and occasional cushions temper the austerity of the armrests and strict angles. For both the design team and Walter Knoll, the extended range represents a logical development of their reinvigorated casual living designs but remains true to the clean lines of the original series.

The working relationship between Foster + Partners and Molteni SpA had been initiated through the Italian manufacturer's sister company Dada, for whom the product design team had designed the Place Kitchen. Although Foster was commissioned to design a product range similar to that for Walter Knoll, from the outset the Molteni 'Still' range of upholstered furnishings was intended for the domestic market.

John Small attributes many of the design decisions behind the Still series as being 'directly informed by the changes in Molteni's manufacturing process'. As a market leader in upholstered furnishings for the domestic market, Molteni had introduced a component orientated manufacturing system whereby, as with just-in-time production models, the individual elements of each piece were made in semi-industrial batch production, which were then stored and only assembled and hand-finished once an order was placed. To accommodate such an advanced production and distribution process, the Foster team designed a series of precise sofa and chair elements which could be brought together in a number of interchangeable configurations while still offering an identifiable 'family'.

At the heart of the Still system's success is the shell, or platform, of the sofa or seat – usually the least 'designed' of all seating components. Yet by giving the shell as much attention as the more visible elements of the range, a systematic formula was initiated for the rest of the range to be built around. The results – a growing family of streamlined and elegant soft furnishings – emphasise the innate beauty of the materials, while belying the ingenuity and labour applied to each piece.

Libby Sellers

Somebody once said to me there are two kinds of pilots: those who take off and are surprised if their engines fail them on take off, and those who are surprised if they actually keep going. I would like to think that we fit into the latter category as designers: we always expect things to fail and try to work forward from that through sketching and prototyping. We try, as far as possible, not to use the production line as a testing ground to discover whether something is going to work or not.
Norman Foster, in conversation with the editor, 2012

Carlo Molteni was interested in developing a range of furniture with us which was capable of being pre-manufactured so it could then be customised according to demand. We wanted the resulting pieces to have some visual relationship but not necessarily to look the same. We are now developing a table and dining chair as part of the Still range but which will be unlike any of the pieces we have previously designed. John Small, formerly of Foster + Partners, in conversation with the editor, 2010
Left: Norman Foster with John Small and James Milne of the product design team.

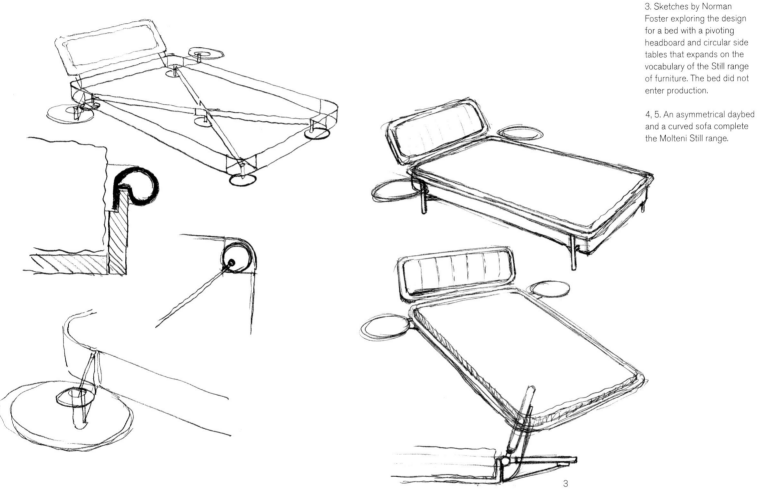

3. Sketches by Norman Foster exploring the design for a bed with a pivoting headboard and circular side tables that expands on the vocabulary of the Still range of furniture. The bed did not enter production.

4, 5. An asymmetrical daybed and a curved sofa complete the Molteni Still range.

3

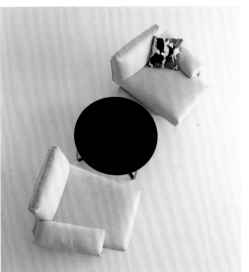

4

5

Stacking Chairs
2004–2006

1, 2. The 20-06 Chair continues a tradition that dates back to 1944 and Emeco's commission to supply lightweight, durable furniture to the US Navy.

3, 4. Norman Foster's sketches of the 20-06 Chair, with a detail of the riveted option for the seat.

5, 6. The R Randers RF1 Chair is designed for maximum flexibility. The seat and back can be specified in high-strength nylon or upholstered in a variety of fabrics. The seat can be tilted with a simple movement to facilitate access to rows and allow a higher density of seating.

7. Norman Foster's sketch study of the R Randers seat profile, designed for maximum ergonomic support..

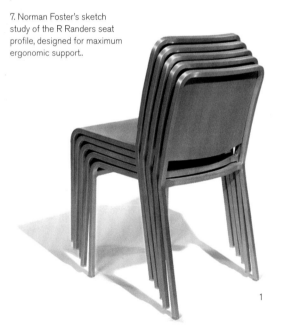

1

2

Emeco + rivets

3

4

For me the Navy Chair is one of the benchmarks of great industrial design, so it was a thrill to work with Emeco on the design of a new, even lighter chair.

Norman Foster

We have used furniture from R Randers many times before and they have a tradition of producing furniture of a very high quality, so it was natural for us to approach them when we wanted to put our RF1 chair into production. Randers' great insight into and experience with furniture production meant that we never had to compromise on the design; that's quite rare in our world and helped to make the process very rewarding. John Small, formerly of Foster + Partners, in conversation with the editor, 2010

Few objects tell the history of modern design as eloquently as the chair. Aesthetic trends, the emergence of new technologies, ergonomics, social and cultural developments are all reflected in the evolution of chair design. For many designers it is a challenge to which they are constantly drawn, intrigued by the problem of combining modern materials, new technology, comfort and good looks.

Stackable chairs have become central to the Modernist's lexicon: an egalitarian, utilitarian and often anonymous solution for temporary seating, and some of the best-known examples are among the most famous designs of the twentieth century: from Alvar Aalto's Model 60 Stacking Stool of 1932 to Robin Day's Polyprop chair, thirty years later. Iconography aside, the technical specificity of a stacking chair is an appealing starting point. With the R Randers RF1 and Emeco 20-06 chairs – both stacking chairs that were to be universal in appeal and lightweight for ease of use – the Foster design team was tasked with very similar concerns that resulted in two very different projects.

John Small, who led the product design team at the time, says: 'RF1 began its life as a question: is it possible to design a simple, elegant and comfortable chair with multiple functions?' From these speculative beginnings came a series of 1:5 models in plastic and cardboard that sought to reduce a standard stacking chair to its very essence, while maintaining ergonomic support.

R Randers is a Danish company, founded in 1940, specialising in furniture for classrooms, conference rooms and canteens. It seemed the perfect partner for manufacturing the stacking chair and the design team joined forces to answer the question initially posed by the RF1.

The resulting chair has a slender steel frame with a nylon or upholstered seat and backrest that imbues the chair with both a physical and visual lightness but also allows for constant aeration through the choice of fabric materials. The seat can be tilted up, allowing easy access to rows and a higher density of seating.

Collaborations are, for the product design team, an essential part of realising their designs as commercially viable products. Unlike the speculative origins of the RF1, the Emeco collaboration was initiated in 2004 when John Small met Gregg Buchbinder, Emeco's chairman, who was keen to expand the company's range of architect-designed chairs.

For Foster, the allure of Emeco's proposition was enhanced by the way they minimise materials and reduce weight, while employing a finely tuned balance of handcraftsmanship and industrial processes in their chairs – characteristics in tune with Foster's own design ethos. It was Emeco's alchemist-like ability to transform a pliable material like aluminium into a compound stronger than steel that also particularly appealed to Norman Foster.

Here, the Foster design team was tasked with very similar concerns that resulted in two very different projects.

Much of the dialogue with Emeco's craftsmen involved seeing how light and slender the chair could be (it weighs just over five pounds in comparison to the Navy Chair's seven) and still maintain its strength. The tubular structure was narrowed to its absolute limit while the walls were thickened for durability. Perhaps the most significant discussion centred on how to attach the seat and backrest to the frame. An early proposal for aircraft-inspired riveting was too costly and instead the ergonomically shaped aluminium forms are hand-welded and ground to achieve a seamless result. Remarkably, it uses 15 per cent less aluminium than the original Navy Chair, and of that metal 80 per cent is recycled, qualifying it as an environmentally sound product.

Libby Sellers

5

6

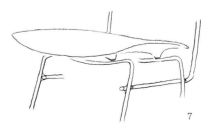

RANDERS/NF

7

Dada Place Kitchen

2003–2004

1. The kitchen comprises a complete range of flexible furniture, with a variety of height-adjustable surfaces, designed to create a multi-purpose, adaptable space – from functional kitchen to formal dining area or workspace.

2. An early sketch of the island unit by Norman Foster.

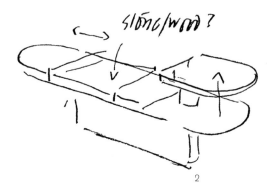

Numerous designers over the years have attempted to reinterpret the kitchen from a stylistic viewpoint. What we tried to do was to look at it from a functional standpoint – to start from first principles. In a way, we were aiming at what the Frankfurt Kitchen did in the 1920s – to create an efficient working environment, but keeping in mind the fact that the modern kitchen is also very much a social space. And there is the added component of flexibility – not just as it applies from kitchen to kitchen, but within the system itself. Norman Foster, in conversation with the editor, 2012

The Modernist kitchen was scientific and purely functional. However, the role of the kitchen has changed over the last fifty years. Now there is also a social function. You see the food being prepared – it's a display and an entertainment. These things reflect a cultural shift in the consumption and preparation of food, which is reflected in the Dada Place Kitchen. John Small, formerly of Foster + Partners, in conversation with the editor, 2010
Left: The pioneering modern kitchen, the Frankfurt Kitchen was developed in 1926 by Margarete Schütte-Lihotzky for the Römerstadt social housing project in Frankfurt, designed by Ernst May. Intended to enable efficient work and to be built at low cost, some 10,000 units were built.

The idea of the kitchen exerts a powerful hold on the imagination – evoking images and thoughts of hearth and home, family and domesticity. Yet, the social role of the kitchen often outweighs the importance placed on helping people undertake the various tasks for which it formally exists. This imbalance owes much to the development of the kitchen as more than just a site for food preparation. The disjunction between the idealised and real has been further exaggerated by outmoded kitchen designs that overlook a twenty-first century take on functionality. If form does follow function – what happens when that function becomes increasingly intangible or constantly evolves?

It was this question that led the Foster team to the genesis of the Dada Place Kitchen. The concept was developed during the renovation of a house by Norman Foster, when discussions about the design of a kitchen table led to a redefinition of the room as a whole and subsequently to the design of a range of flexible kitchen furniture.

If form follows function, what happens when that function becomes increasingly intangible or constantly evolves?

The Place Kitchen came from a collaboration between the Foster team and Dada SpA and coincided with the construction of Albion Riverside. Dada won the contract to supply the Albion kitchens, and that allowed the design team to refine the functional aspects of their original kitchen design. The primary objective was to introduce a system of responsive kitchen components, new technologies and functional devices, better to support the user. With research into freestanding industrial and galley kitchens, adaptable workbenches and a wealth of different mechanisms the team explored all possibilities for a highly efficient and versatile working solution.

Yet as this kitchen needed to be easily adjusted to suit different room sizes they also sought to challenge notions of the 'fitted' kitchen so as to minimise on-site installation time and cost. The cornerstone of the design is the use of ergonomic, height-adjustable surfaces, which promote multi-purpose, flexible spaces. The idea was to allow the room to be altered from kitchen to dining area or workspace, using simple gliding mechanisms. The dining table adjusts in height and docks to the kitchen worktop providing a breakfast bar, an extra preparation area or a work table. A 'work wall', which operates as a frame for all the fixed services, incorporates storage and houses a media tablet for TV, radio and internet access, highlighting the kitchen's increasing role as a space for relaxation as well as work.

Perhaps the most telling element is the inclusion of an integrated worktop lighting strip, which through subtle colour shifts, imbues the space with warmth and light as required. In the broader scope of contemporary design, function is relegated to being a hackneyed concept if it doesn't acknowledge the importance of creating an emotional connection with the end user. By emphasising such personalised design solutions the design team has devised a kitchen that allows for a constantly evolving dialogue between technology, design and the people who will ultimately use it.

Libby Sellers

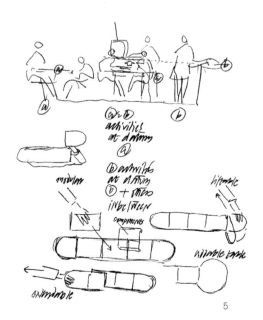

4

3. A 'work wall' incorporates storage and fixed mechanical equipment, including a retractable extract unit. The dining table adjusts in height and can dock with the kitchen worktop to create a breakfast bar, a preparation area or work table. Key elements include an integrated lighting strip that can be used to set the mood of the room by subtle colour shifts.

4. Detail of the cupboard doors; colours and finishes can be specified from a broad palette.

5. Sketches by Norman Foster exploring the kitchen's ergonomic criteria.

5

Lessons from Skiing
Norman Foster 1998

1. Chairlifts take downhill skiers up the slopes. The energy-consuming, visually intrusive infrastructure and heavy apparatus of downhill skiing contrast strongly with the ultra-lightweight equipment and seasonal trails of the cross-country sport.

As an architect I spend my life travelling the world working on projects, which because of their size or complexity are about pushing the limits. It is perhaps ironic that my private passions – cross-country skiing and the annual Engadin Valley Marathon – are also, in different ways, about pushing the limits. Downhill skiing is well publicised, and almost everyone knows about the Engadin Valley in Switzerland and its associations with the sport. But cross-country skiing – *langlauf* – is probably one of the best kept secrets in the world, or one of the most misunderstood pleasures – depending on who you talk to. Otherwise I would not be able to assail so many strangers to the sport with my wildly enthusiastic descriptions.

The Engadin Valley has hundreds of kilometres of ski trails, which traverse frozen lakes and climb up and down through forests and across fields. In all kinds of weather throughout the winter months, the valley is alive with two kinds of cross-country skiers, those who will glide along grooved tracks 'classic' style and those who will ski 'freestyle' on the smoother strip next to the tracks.

I find it impossible to separate aesthetics from any other aspect of my life – and *langlauf*, whether classic or skating, can be beautiful to behold, like a ballet. But when the theatre for this winter activity is a valley on the heroic scale of the Engadin, with its special quality of light, forever changing, then the combination is pure bliss.

The Engadin and the sport itself are full of contradictions. It is a paradox that a traditional playground for the rich and famous should also be a setting that has enabled some of the greatest minds to find creative inspiration – Hesse, Mann, Giacometti, Nietzsche and others. What mixture of sport and setting in the world could be at the same time so accessible, so intensely physical and yet so spiritual? It is a unique place, which can embrace such polarities.

On most days in the year – whether jogging in a London park, California desert, Hong Kong Mid-Levels or streets in Sydney and Shanghai – the cross-country Engadin Marathon is in my mind as a point of reference. After long hours in jets with time changes that can turn nights into days, I have to push myself to jog on arrival. I know that it is the only way to ensure that once a year, in the freezing cold of a March Sunday morning in Maloja, I will join up with 13,000 other souls who come together to celebrate their sport.

We start at nine in the morning from the southern end of the valley and travel for 42 kilometres, climbing and descending some 150 metres over the course. The race, like the activity itself, embraces all generations – from Olympic-level athletes at the front to the retired grandparents and less serious addicts who will follow behind.

There is a very satisfying equation between the ends and means of cross-country skiing.

Consider the range of age and background of the participants and try to imagine their widely differing priorities. The leaders will complete the course in about one hour and twenty minutes, and success or failure will be measured in split seconds. But many, like myself, will be competing for a different kind of pleasure – skiing against their own clocks. For me there is always time to be touched by the humanity of the spectacle: children anxious to pass on refreshment, strangers who cheer from the sidelines. It is difficult to describe the atmosphere – a mixture of celebration, tolerance and vivid colours. Regardless of their finishing times, for the vast majority of participants the event is a celebration.

One has a heightened sense of awareness on a long run. At the last marathon I developed a rhythm on the stretch alongside Samedan Airport, even though I only had one stick at the time, and I remember thinking that it felt close to flying (there are parallels to sailplanes and cross-country soaring). Then there is the way in which the mind can roam freely – from the most profound thoughts to the most prosaic, such as the promise of a beer and sausage at the end; and for those like me who enjoy food and drink, an even greater appetite afterwards!

1

Then there are other dimensions to the event – the precision of the organisation is awesome. The warm outer clothing that the competitors strip off at the start will be moved to the finish line by trucks, which average about the same speed as the skiers. The flow and separation of vehicles and pedestrians in this operation has many lessons for big cities; and the way in which your clothes always turn up just at the point where you believe they are lost somewhere in the system is uncanny! And how is it that among so many thousands you always manage to meet friends at the finish?

There is a very satisfying equation between the ends and means of cross-country skiing. You only get out of it what you personally put in, like life itself. Incidentally, it still surprises me that just a relatively short time ago I could never have imagined doing what I can now do on skis – a testimony to the patience and professionalism of my instructors! But there is always a long way to go – like chasing the end of the rainbow.

In the relatively brief history of this race, the speeds have increased dramatically – partly through technique and partly through the development of higher–technology equipment. I find a tactile and visual delight in the equipment of cross-country skiing; not only the skis and sticks but also the clothing – the best kinds of high technology. The contrast between the dead weight of downhill equipment and the featherweight equivalent of *langlauf* is dramatic. My downhill skis, sticks, and boots, which are agony to walk in, weigh much more than my cross-country gear. Because there is no waiting around in queues or sitting on open chairlifts, the equipment for the cross-country skier is lighter and very much more comfortable. Despite being able to cope with extreme conditions of winter chill, air and body temperature, perspiration, and freedom of movement, the clothing is only a fraction of the weight of those bulky parkas and ski suits.

Furthermore, when you have to power yourself uphill every gram counts and it shows in the refinement of design. The differences between these two kinds of skiing may be partly philosophical, but there is no escaping the fact that the performance of the independent cross-country skier is directly linked to the advanced technology of the equipment and clothing. On a typical Engadin winter day, it is interesting to compare the activities of those traversing the cross-country trails at the bottom of the valley and those skiing down the slopes. Aside from the outlay for equipment, the downhill group pays a high price for those facilities that lift them continuously to the top, unlike the cross-country group whose sport costs them virtually nothing. But how do you quantify the poetic difference between queuing for a ski lift and taking a stroll through the woods? The cross-country skier is liberated from the need for an all-consuming infrastructure. Even the ski trail itself is ephemeral. Almost invisible in winter, by spring it has disappeared into lakes and routes for walkers and mountain bikers.

Although I am privileged to share the pleasures of downhill skiing, I cannot help contemplating, as I ride an elegantly functional chairlift, that it consumes a huge amount of energy. For nearly every kilometre that we swish down the slopes with the force of gravity, our quilted bodies, heavy boots, skis, and poles are hauled back up the mountain for a similar distance by a mixture of cable cars, gondolas and lifts. It is hardly surprising that those ski passes cost so much money when we consider the outlay and running costs to power systems that for most of the year will lie idle. And although the scale of the mountains in the Engadin Valley dwarfs everything man-made, the urbanisation that relentlessly follows the pursuit of leisure is everywhere apparent and leaves permanent scars on the landscape.

2. Norman Foster photographed at the end of the cross-country Engadin Ski Marathon, which takes place in the Engadin Valley in Switzerland each March. Every year, the marathon attracts some 13,000 skiers, drawn from a wide range of ages and abilities. The 42km race starts in Maloja – 1,820 metres above sea level – and finishes in S-chanf – 1,670 metres above sea level.

3. Foster has been competing in the Engadin Ski Marathon since 1993 and has participated every year since, with the sole exception of 2003. This graph charts his times over that twenty-year span. His fastest ever time – 2:29:21.3 – was achieved in 2001. The fastest male competitor that year finished in 1:24:22.7.

2

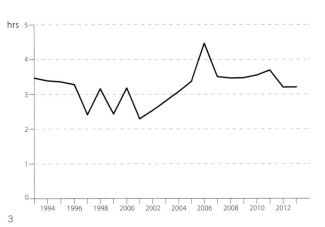

3

The noises of a stream or the wind in a tree, the light filtering through a tree top are complex sources for human stimulation, oscillating in the most pleasant ways. Our senses were developed for outdoor life, the set-up of our senses has not changed. There is no better light than daylight, no better air than fresh air. We should use these external qualities as much as we possibly can in order to gain comfort. Natural stimulation and comfort conditions are not only better for our health and wellbeing; they are also energy conserving, as we do not have to produce them artificially. Sophia and Stefan Behling, *Sol Power: The Evolution of Solar Architecture*, 2000

Don't fight forces, use them.
Richard Buckminster Fuller, *Shelter* 5, 1932

1. *Engadin II* by Andreas Gursky (2006). Gursky captures from above the spectacular passage of hundreds of skiers in the Engadin Valley. The Engadin Ski Marathon began in 1969 and in the early years only around 1,000 sportsmen considered themselves tough enough to master the distance. The event has grown from an exclusive gathering of cross-country athletes to a large, colourful and multinational competition. The fastest male skiers will complete the 42km run in approximately one-and-a-half hours.

1

It was Buckminster Fuller who drew attention to the revolution in the world of communication, which has some parallels with my skiing example. He compared the inefficiency of all those tons and tons of copper cable – the infrastructure which not so long ago rested on the sea-bed to connect continents – with the electronic freedom that lightweight satellites and invisible airwaves now offer. Fuller never lived to see the tiny mobile telephones that are a logical extension of his many optimistic predictions about society's ability to achieve 'more with less', but in an article written in 1969 Fuller makes the point thus:

'To demonstrate this fantastic improvement in performance, we witness that one communications-relaying satellite of only one quarter of one ton of material is now outperforming the transoceanic communications message capacity and fidelity capability of 175,000 tons of copper cable. This constitutes a seven-hundred-thousand-fold step-up in communications performance per pound of invested resources.'

In his book Critical Path, Fuller wrote about the first flight by a man-powered craft, demonstrating that improved technology would produce more effective results with fewer materials and less energy, and in less time. Some years ago, I met the designer of that aircraft, Paul MacCready, at a conference in Aspen. He talked about how he had achieved the seemingly impossible by going back to the basics of early flying machines and using advanced materials from other technologies. When congratulated, MacCready did not think that he was the most creative force in the equation – he believed that the truly creative act was that of a man called Kremer, who set the challenge and offered a significant prize for the first flight to be powered by human energy. I believe that MacCready's understatement is due partly to modesty, but his point is significant. In any arena, the designer, whether architect or engineer, can only act on the initiatives of those who set the priorities, environmental, political or otherwise.

In Sol Power: the Evolution of Solar Architecture Stefan and Sophia Behling similarly emphasise the importance of reference points from the contemporary worlds of communication and recreation. In one chapter they chart indigenous buildings from the past. I am reminded of Bernard Rudofsky's observation in Architecture without Architects that 'the philosophy and know-how of the anonymous builders presents the largest untapped source of architectural inspiration for industrial man'.

The performance of the cross-country skier is directly linked to the advanced technology of the equipment and clothing.

The true vernacular architecture of its time was often on the cutting edge of available technology far removed from the romantic associations that might follow in a later age. It is easy to forget, for example, that the concept of an acceptable level of thermal comfort has changed over time. Many instances can be found from the past of solutions that control summer overheating, but there are few that successfully confront the difficulties of heating in winter: the environment for a king in the Middle Ages would be unacceptable to those in many of today's societies who are classed as the poorest. It is surely an irony that the threat of global warming, corrosive pollution and depleted resources of non-renewable fuels should coincide with a rising demand for thermal comfort.

So what is it that connects the non-building references of our time, such as the cross-country skier, or the mobile telephone, with those indigenous structures of the past? Surely they were all pushing the frontiers of technology by showing ways in which the maximum benefits could be obtained from minimal resources. In the case of those earlier builders, they were, in the best examples, creating synergies between climate, resources and place. They are reminders that current building technology lags behind other sectors and could benefit from greater cross-fertilisation and long-overdue research.

2. The Caproni Vizzola A-21S sailplane in flight. Its natural economy, superior aerodynamic characteristics and elegant profile have been a constant source of inspiration for Norman Foster. A high-performance aircraft, weighing just 450 kilograms, its unique combination of metal frame and fibreglass fuselage make it both very light and extremely strong. It is also fast, capable of speeds of up to 65 miles per hour. There are natural affinities between a ski and the wing of a glider, both having to combine flexibility with lightness and strength.

2

One of the images I've used in lectures over the years is of the *Gossamer Albatross*, a man-powered aircraft designed and built by Paul MacCready, which allows a man to fly using only his own strength. It relies partly on the use of super-lightweight structural and cladding materials, but also on abandoning preconceptions about how a plane should look. I think we have a very similar approach to architecture. We start from first principles and make the most of new materials to reduce a building's need for high energy input. Norman Foster, in conversation with the editor, 2012

Left: *Gossamer Albatross* in flight.

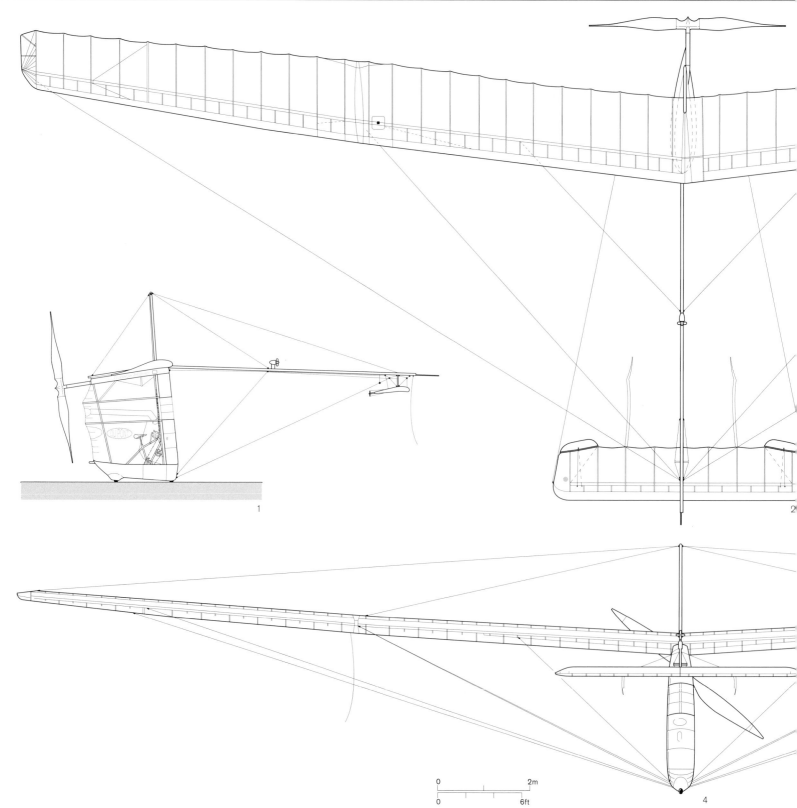

0   2m

0   6ft

The human-powered *Gossamer Albatross* was able to fly across the English Channel because the structural materials of which it was built were many time tensilely stronger than an equal weight of the highest-strength aircraft aluminium. The tensile strengths of the *Albatross*'s structural materials were sixty times stronger per equivalent weight than the strongest structural materials available to Leonardo da Vinci for realising the design of his proposed human-powered flying machine. Richard Buckminster Fuller, *Critical Path*, 1982
Left: The cover of *Critical Path*, 1982. Fuller's masterwork – and the summation of a lifetime's reflections on the life of the planet and the limits of its resources – the book is as relevant today as it was upon publication.

Left: The American aeronautical engineer Paul B MacCready (1925-2007) was the 'father of human-powered flight'. He trained as a US Navy pilot at the end of the Second World War. He started gliding after the war and in 1956 was the first American pilot to become the World Soaring Champion. He devised the MacCready Theory on the correct speed to fly a glider depending on conditions and based on the glider's rate of sink at different air-speeds. Glider pilots still use the 'MacCready speed ring'. With Dr Peter Lissaman he created the first practical human-powered aircraft, the *Gossamer Condor*, which was constructed from piano wire, bicycle parts, and mylar. In 1979, he built its successor, the *Gossamer Albatross*, which won the Kremer Prize for successfully flying from England to France.

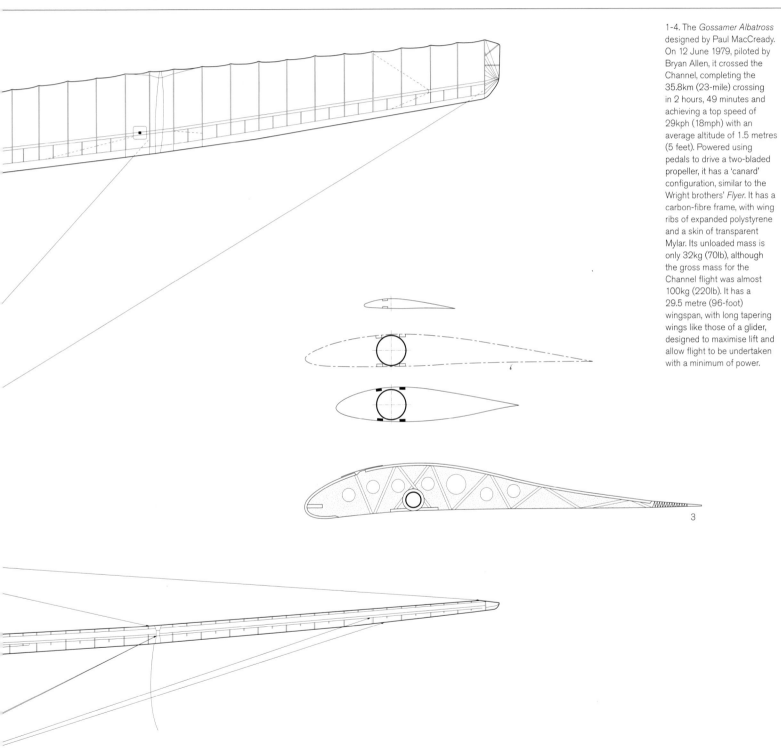

1-4. The *Gossamer Albatross* designed by Paul MacCready. On 12 June 1979, piloted by Bryan Allen, it crossed the Channel, completing the 35.8km (23-mile) crossing in 2 hours, 49 minutes and achieving a top speed of 29kph (18mph) with an average altitude of 1.5 metres (5 feet). Powered using pedals to drive a two-bladed propeller, it has a 'canard' configuration, similar to the Wright brothers' *Flyer*. It has a carbon-fibre frame, with wing ribs of expanded polystyrene and a skin of transparent Mylar. Its unloaded mass is only 32kg (70lb), although the gross mass for the Channel flight was almost 100kg (220lb). It has a 29.5 metre (96-foot) wingspan, with long tapering wings like those of a glider, designed to maximise lift and allow flight to be undertaken with a minimum of power.

3

Chesa Futura

St Moritz, Switzerland 2000–2004

The Engadin Valley is fascinating in many ways. The traditional buildings are arranged in clusters, perhaps originally for security, and to present a more comfortable microclimate. The buildings themselves are big – under one roof they will encompass what in other societies might have been separate buildings: storage, stabling for animals and rooms for people. The dramatic changes that occurred at the turn of the century with the explosion of tourism, produced in the same spirit very large but quite compact hotels. Chesa Futura extends that tradition – a compact building in the heart of the town versus the proliferation of suburban sprawl. Norman Foster, in conversation with the editor, 2012

It is a big building on a small site, three storeys of apartments and parking below, and even this is part of the agenda. This is an almost urban intervention into a sensitive site of great beauty but it has avoided a bunch of disparate chalets spread in a kind of Alpine suburbia. Its form certainly made waves when it was proposed. But ... as soon as it was completed it became a pivotal and indispensable part of its immediate landscape. Its presence will influence everything that comes in its wake. Edwin Heathcote, *Financial Times*, 28 January 2006
Left: St Moritz photographed for *Life* magazine by Alfred Eisenstaedt in January 1947; the original village form of the town is still discernible.

St Moritz is the largest town in the upper Engadin Valley, and at 1,800 metres above sea level, it is not a place you stumble on by accident, even if the legendary efficiency of Switzerland's railway system makes getting there a painless, even an exhilarating journey through some of Europe's most spectacular mountain landscapes. It's not quite where Alpine tourism was born, but it is a place whose natural beauty has made it one of the world's most famous mountain resorts. Its permanent population is less than 6,000 people, with another 3,000 in residence at peak times in the skiing season. Every year it attracts more than 250,000 tourists, enough to fuel its economy, without overwhelming it; and if St Moritz's visitors are outstandingly cosmopolitan, it is a place that still retains a distinctive flavour. It is far removed from the sites of the usual debates about the direction of contemporary architecture.

Most new construction here attempts to reinforce existing preconceptions about St Moritz's attractions to visitors. They like it as it is, and new development does its best to blend in. Chesa Futura presents another way of building in the town. Located on an elevated site overlooking the centre of St Moritz, within a cluster of conventional apartment buildings and houses, Chesa Futura ('house of the future' in Romansch) is not so much an apartment building as an attempt to create a limited number of homes for people who want a base in the town that is private and discreet, and which feels like a genuine part of its setting.

When the project was unveiled, Chesa Futura surprised some critics who regarded it as a departure for Foster. This was not the work of Foster + Partners as the world had come to expect it. It was more organic, more of a 'blob' or a 'pumpkin' or a 'bubble' than anything that the office had built before, and of course, it was faced in a hand-crafted material – larch shingles – that seemed to reflect attitudes very different from Foster's earlier work. In these critics' minds a Foster building relied on certain modern technologies, on an economy of means, on a spare, lightweight character; a Foster building, if not necessarily rectangular with a flat roof, would at least have a certain High-tech materiality.

With its voluptuous form, Chesa Futura is a striking addition to the architecture of St Moritz.

Chesa Futura epitomises none of these things. It is fluid in its form, and clearly a tactile, solid, material object. Its largest windows look south across St Moritz and its lake, the openings seemingly carved out of an apparently thick wall, as if they were caves eroded into a cliff face, or a snow drift. These openings frame deep south-facing balconies concealed within the sweep of the curved wall.

1

Opposite: Chesa Futura ('house of the future') fuses state-of-the-art computer design tools with centuries-old construction techniques to create an environmentally sensitive apartment building.

1. Looking down from the mountain on to Chesa Futura and the St Moritz Lake.

2, 3. In these sketches, Norman Foster highlights the strategy that led to the Chesa's form. Working within the permitted planning envelope it was possible to create a fluid-form building in which every apartment enjoys views and sunlight.

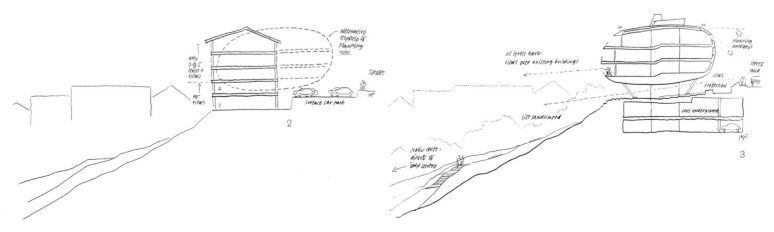

2

3

There was a finite amount of permitted building volume, so the first step was to ask what was the best way to reposition it. The first reason for the building's shape was, from a sustainability point of view, that a sphere has the best minimum wall-to-volume area ratio. Shaping that sphere in a way to optimise its shape and views was the next step, and then to try to create the illusion of it hovering, so that it would allow people walking past to look beneath it to the valley. Stefan Behling, in conversation with the editor, 2012

We look to vernacular traditions that are specific to the area in which we are working. Very often there are rich architectural traditions that work with and not against nature, which have been forgotten over time. Chesa Futura uses timber construction, which makes environmental sense for a number of reasons. It is culturally sympathetic, reflecting local architectural traditions, and it contributes to the established ecology of felling older trees to facilitate forest regeneration. Furthermore, wood is an entirely renewable resource; it absorbs carbon dioxide during its growth cycle; and if local timber is used, little energy is expended in its transportation. Norman Foster, in conversation with the editor, 2012

In this sequence of sketches, Norman Foster explores the building's response to place and its ability to 'touch the ground lightly'. The shape is an organic but nonetheless very precise and rigorous reaction to the sun, climate and views.

CONTEXT edge of town ... valley ... lake ... mountains ... views ... sun terraces

A RESPONSE TO PLACE

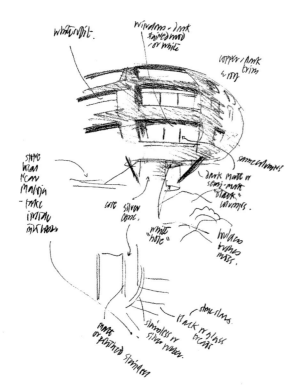

lightly touching down .... perched on the slope ...

There used to be a building on the site and by coincidence my family owned an apartment there, so I spent lots of time in St Moritz as a child. From my knowledge of both the landscape and the site we came up with the idea of lifting the building off the ground so that all the apartments would have a view of the valley. Matteo Fantoni, formerly of Foster + Partners, in conversation with the editor, 2009
Right: Norman Foster with project architect Matteo Fantoni in an impromptu design meeting on the flight to St Moritz.
Far right: Norman Foster with local architect Arnd Küchel and the design team in Küchel's St Moritz studio.

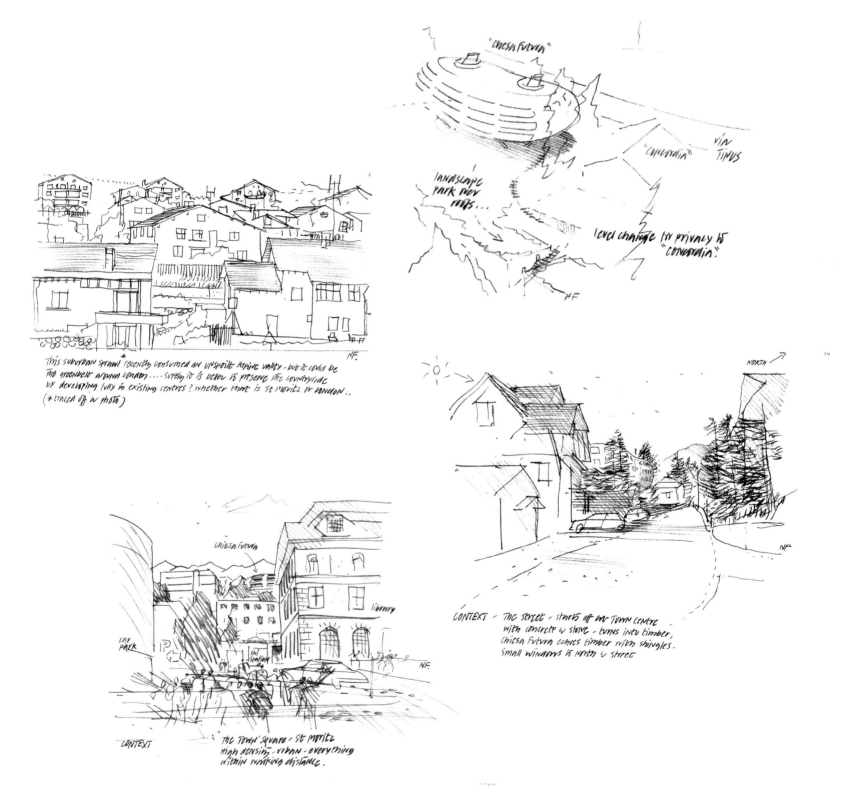

If you close your hand and put it on a table vertically, you get the shape of the original building. If you then turn your hand and put it horizontally – which is still the same volume – you get the shape of the new building. Basically we lifted the whole thing off the surface and turned it horizontally so that the ground and first floors could have lake views. Matteo Fantoni, formerly of Foster + Partners, in conversation with the editor, 2009
Right: Matteo Fantoni and Stefan Behling in a design review in the London studio.
Far right: Norman Foster sketches over a plan of the upper floor during a design review.

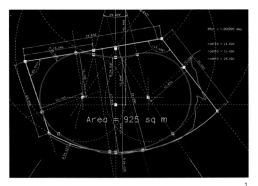 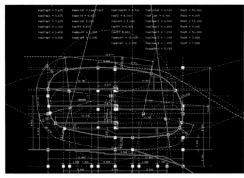 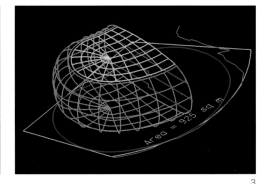

1

2

3

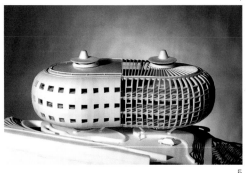

4

5

1-3. The free-form shape was controlled only by a schematic plan and section, which were rationalised as tangential arcs and then linked to act as parametric templates. This provided a control mechanism that allowed interactions between internal and external relationships to be resolved.

4, 5. Computer models were complemented by physical models at every stage of design development. The first detailed model was built using the same CNC data that would be used to construct the building itself.

On the more climatically exposed north elevation, where the view is quite limited, the windows are very different, reminiscent of the traditional deep-set Engadin farmhouse window, which is kept small to prevent excessive heat loss. Internally, each floor slab is split into two zones, marked by a step in section, with living areas opening on to balconies to the south and cellular bedrooms, kitchens and bathrooms to the north.

With its voluptuous form, Chesa Futura is a striking addition to the architecture of St Moritz. It explores new definitions of appropriate and modern in a setting shaped by vernacular architecture. Backed by a wall of Alpine peaks whose unfolding alignments have the effect of allowing it to be seen in silhouette against the sky only from very close up, its shape makes it immediately recognisable, but the timber from which it is built helps it to blend into long views across the town.

In spite of the surprise which Chesa Futura initially provoked, it has turned out not to be an anomalous one-off; instead it reflects a fresh direction in the practice's work. It is the smallest, but also one of the most successful of a group of contemporary Foster projects from the post-millennial decade that explored new forms, particularly the Albion Riverside housing development on the Thames, The Sage Gateshead, London's City Hall, the library at the Free University of Berlin and not least the tower for Swiss Re at 30 St Mary Axe. Like all these buildings, Chesa Futura's unique form was made possible by a new generation of analytical computer software that facilitates the use of complex geometries.

Right: Modelmaker Robert Turner at work on the detailed
structural model seen below.
Far right: Norman Foster and project architect Matteo
Fantoni discuss revisions to a large-scale model of part
of the upper floor.

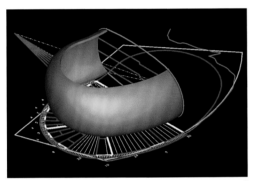
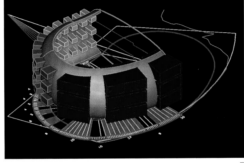
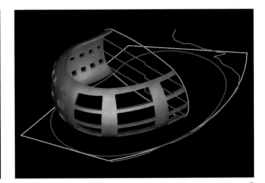

6　　　　　　　　　　　　7　　　　　　　　　　　　8

9

In comparison with some of Foster's earlier landmark projects, Chesa Futura is conceived on a relatively modest scale. It has just three floors of apartments, with two basement levels for parking and storage; and there is a discreet entrance lobby sheltered beneath the boulder-like form of the apartments. Yet this project has served to signal a significant new stage in Foster's evolving career that, in its own way, has had an impact as emphatic as the Hongkong and Shanghai Bank had in the 1980s, or Stansted Airport had in the 1990s.

Like those projects, it represents a departure in technical, formal and planning terms, bringing together a cluster of architectural innovations in a convincing synthesis. For example, it is unlikely that Chesa Futura would have arrived at the formal solution it has, without making use of the materials that Foster chose. It was specifically tailored for its site – optimising the permitted planning volume – and both form and materials serve to underpin the delivery of the structure's environmental performance.

Yet Chesa Futura is much more than a pragmatic response to a particular commission: it is a reflection of Foster's long-term personal relationship with a place that has come to have a special meaning for him, and the way that it has affected his own thinking. A dedicated cross-country skier, Foster has been coming to St Moritz for two decades, drawn by its winter sports, its architecture and the beauty of its natural setting. (Every year he takes part in the Engadin cross-country marathon; and he is an enthusiastic downhill skier too – a member of the Corviglia Club, with its mountain-top club room.)

He talks about the jagged mountains and how they are seemingly flattened against deep blue skies, and the essential qualities of life in a high Alpine valley community that has managed to retain much of its character even in the face of global tourism and the paradox of the luxury shops that have sprung up its narrow streets. St Moritz is a place in which traditional methods of building that evolved through centuries, when mountain life was far harsher than it is now, have survived as living practices. One example of this is the way in which timber buildings here are raised off the ground to protect the wooden skin from rot caused by the snow that lies deep on the ground for months at a time. In the case of Chesa Futura, this move has the added benefit of allowing the inhabited parts of the building to make the best of the spectacular views.

Foster arrived in Switzerland with an over-arching belief in the potential of technology and modernity, that shaped his attitudes to design, and he found a very strong, powerful local tradition, based on technique and natural materials. He explored the way that the traditional farms of the Engadin were made with the same analytical eye that he first brought to bear in his measured drawings of timber barns in Wales, and windmills in East Anglia, which he produced as an architecture student at Manchester University. The Engadin may have changed Foster's view of the world, but he was still determined to use what he found there in ways that reflected his experiences and beliefs.

6-8. The building's sculptural form was refined using a specially written computer program. The computer model acts like a conventional spreadsheet, enabling any part of the building to be altered and instantly generating a new overall form. This allowed numerous design studies to be tested within a fraction of the time required for conventional modelling techniques.

9. Cutaway visualisation; the building is a timber shell, shaped like a kidney bean but raised above the ground on raking steel supports.

Due to the climate in St Moritz you have a very limited window when you can actually build. Prefabrication is was our only real option. And here it is really cutting edge. Above the base, which is a mixture of concrete and steel, this is essentially a timber building. It was prefabricated in sections, shipped to site and assembled and then covered with what is for me the most logical of materials – the shingle. There are a quarter of a million of them, each one hand cut and applied individually. Norman Foster, in conversation with the editor, 2012

Because of the climate in the area you only have an eight month slot in which to build. We worked from April to December 1999 on the basement, cores and steel cabling, and then stopped until May 2000, when we began to erect the structure. Matteo Fantoni, formerly of Foster + Partners, in conversation with the editor, 2009

The curved prefabricated beams were slotted together on site like a three-dimensional jigsaw puzzle – there isn't a single straight line in the entire frame. What's interesting is that we talk about mating traditional materials with high-technology design tools, but the manufacturing process was equally high-tech. Thin pinewood planks, measuring 25 x 250mm by 12 metres long were chemically treated and bonded together in the factory; and the various geometric shapes were cut using the latest computer-controlled machines. These machines are so accurate that they were able to cut huge pieces with just 3mm tolerance. Matteo Fantoni, formerly of Foster + Partners, in conversation with the editor, 2009

1

2

3

1. Two concrete cores, 2 metres in diameter, house lift shafts and stairwells and provide lateral stability.

2, 3. The timber frame and wall panels were prefabricated in Germany using advanced CNC machinery. Each glue-laminated beam is made up of 12-metre-long thin pinewood planks bonded together to obtain the various geometric shapes. Using CNC machines it was possible to obtain very precisely sized elements with 3mm tolerances.

4, 5. Because of the winter holiday season, construction was restricted to less than eight months of the year, so a high degree of prefabrication was essential.

6. Looking down on the site from a vantage point above the town.

7. The tight site, which could only be approached via narrow winding roads, coupled with the length and width of the truck, meant that considerable thought had to go into the sizing of each building component.

4

5

6

7

We cloaked the building in hand-cut larch shingles – a centuries-old method of cladding in this part of Switzerland. Durable and maintenance free, they will last up to eighty years. Norman Foster

The larch shingles were cut by hand by a local family that has practised the craft for generations. They cut the trunk both laterally and radially to make the most efficient use of the wood. The two different cuts combine the water-draining characteristics of one cut and structural strength of the other. When you put them together you get a very interesting variegated visual appearance. It's a very efficient system – there's almost no waste. Norman Foster, in conversation with the editor, 2012
Left: Norman Foster with shingle-maker Patrick Staeger, whose family firm spans three generations.
Right, far right: Patrick Staeger still cuts the shingles by hand, using centuries-old techniques.

8

9

10

13

8-10. The larch shingles were cut by hand and nailed into position. To make the most efficient use of the material the timber is cut laterally and radially, thus combining the water-draining characteristics of one cut and the structural strength of the other.

11, 12. The double-curved timber frame shell is highly insulated. The roof is clad in copper, which has a long local tradition because it is sufficiently malleable to be formed on site at a temperature that may drop below 12 degrees.

13. Above ground the building is supported on a lightweight steel 'table', measuring approximately 20x40 metres, with eight tubular steel legs. The timber frame reduces the dead load of the building by as much as 40 per cent.

14. The north elevation under scaffolding.

11

12

14

Right: The traditional Engadin house is characterised by a solid, stone construction with a wide gabled roof, small windows deeply embedded in the walls, and large arched door. The embrasure-like windows are typical – the smaller the window, the lower the heat loss. The whitewashed reveals splay outwards like a funnel to draw as much light into the rooms as possible.

In this context we wanted to look at the historical vernacular and to build it with the least amount of embodied energy. That meant it had to be a very efficient, extremely lightweight structure that could be completely recycled. It is built entirely in timber and it works around a very complex frame, which at the time was pioneering. The shingle facade creates a very different dialogue with nature than a material that doesn't weather. Now it's got a nice silvery texture with a red belly – almost like the breast of a robin. Stefan Behling, in conversation with the editor, 2011

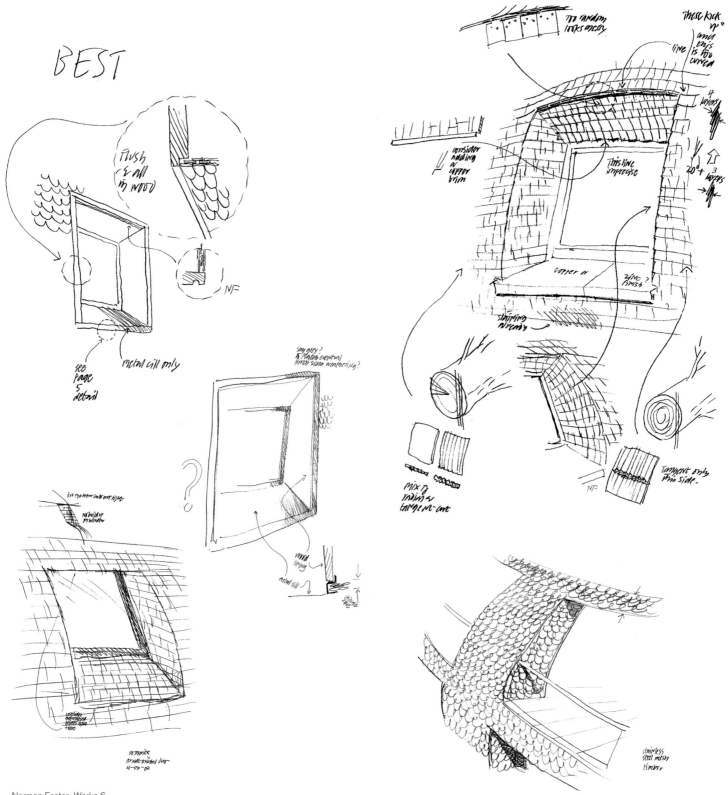

There are many examples of shingles being used in the Engadin Valley and they proved the ideal material to follow the geometry of our building. They're small, flexible and natural which fitted perfectly with the idea of having a very ecological building. The structure is made from glue-laminated beams which are then covered by a waterproof membrane which has a series of vertical and horizontal battens attached to it. The 250,000 shingles are then nailed by hand to the battens so that they work like a rain screen. Matteo Fantoni, formerly of Foster + Partners, in conversation with the editor, 2009

With Chesa Futura, Foster has built on the Engadin traditions, but at the same time, he has transformed them. The project depends on more than deploying the techniques and replicating the forms of the past. It is true that in certain aspects, it does evoke the *Berghütten* (mountain huts) or the ancient churches in the Engadin Valley, with their rounded forms. But it is also very much a design of its own time, one which demanded a lot from its makers. Foster has also described it as a building which can serve as a kind of manifesto about architecture that has relevance beyond the particular circumstances of its setting, in its concern for reducing energy usage, and advocacy for low-impact, high-density planning.

With Chesa Futura, Foster has built on the Engadin traditions, but at the same time he has transformed them.

Chesa Futura is Foster's mark on a place in which he has come to feel at home. It is the most distinctive new building in St Moritz, a passionate attempt by an architect who is in love with a very particular environment, to make something that is the product of its special character, and yet at the same time, reflects something of his own preoccupations about design and its responses to climate and place.

The project is shaped by the urban grain of St Moritz, the raw materials to hand, the sheer complexities of building at such a height and the constraints of the seasons, where labour can be in short supply and the frost makes construction all but impossible. By building to a higher density than is commonly adopted, Chesa Futura is also an attempt to make optimum use of the restricted sites available for building within St Moritz proper. For Foster, it echoes the Alpine vernacular of clusters of farmhouses, or the concentrated forms of the nineteenth-century Engadin hotels, showing how denser developments can be slotted into existing centres.

In doing so, it offers an alternative to eating up yet more precious land on the perimeter and the tendency to sprawl out into the landscape. It is also the first, and perhaps the most conspicuous of the projects that he has designed for St Moritz. Taken together, these can be understood as a respectful attempt to inject new life and energy into a place which, much as many people would want to maintain it exactly as it is now, must adapt and change if it is not to atrophy slowly.

Chesa Futura may not have been quite what some people expected from Foster, but it is the kind of building that was always a possibility in his mind. Even in the early days of the practice, a non-orthogonal form was used for Willis Faber & Dumas in Ipswich, in the shape of an undulating glass skin. At the time, serious consideration was also given to taking Willis Faber further in the direction of a free-form 'bubble'. In some of his sketches Foster explored the idea of a much more fluid building envelope with a complex curvature: 'Great possibilities!' he wrote on one sketch, 'But we lack the time and immediate expertise at technical level.'

The Willis Faber scheme was based in part on the Climatroffice concept that Foster investigated with Buckminster Fuller in 1971, after their joint project for the Samuel Beckett Theatre, which they planned to sink beneath the quadrangle of St Peter's College, Oxford. Climatroffice was rooted in concerns about sustainability that have preoccupied Foster from the earliest days of his practice, an attempt to make use of low-energy techniques in building and climate control. Chesa Futura can be seen to share many of the same concerns, even if appears to stand apart stylistically from much of Foster's built work.

Chesa Futura relies on the traditional materials and craft techniques of the Engadin Valley not because local planning controls demanded them, but because Foster had become as fascinated by these skills as he had once been intrigued by the engineering vernacular of the aircraft industry. Foster collaborated on the project with the St Moritz architect Arnd Küchel, and with a local craftsman, Patrick Staeger, whose family firm spans three generations.

1

2

Opposite: Norman Foster's sketches exploring the detailing of the deep-set windows on the north facade, and their counterparts to the south.

1. The larch shingles were cut from eighty local trees, producing 240 cubic metres of timber. Trees were sourced from the same altitude as the building, at 1,800 metres above sea level, and felled during the winter, when the wood contains no sap. The shingles change colour over time to a silver-grey.

2. Looking up at the north facade. The windows, with their deep reveals, reinterpret the Engadin tradition.

The idea was to allow the landscape to flow beneath the belly of the building so that there would be a very gentle connection between its base and the contours of the land. In Switzerland there is clearly a tradition of buildings which are lifted off the ground so it also works on a vernacular level. The building, rather than being horizontal, is tilted towards the valley to increase the area as much as possible while still remaining within the 15.5-metre datum set by the planning regulations. Matteo Fantoni, formerly of Foster + Partners, in conversation with the editor, 2009

By lifting the building up, and working within the invisible envelope of the restrictive lines imposed by the planners, we were able to design a building where everybody has a view. The landscape flows underneath – in the summer it's a rare patch of green. Norman Foster, in conversation with the editor, 2012

1

1. The Engadin tradition of elevating buildings to avoid the danger of wood decaying due to exposure to moisture, is reinterpreted here – a move that has the added advantage of allowing the apartments to enjoy views that would otherwise be denied.

2. The approach from the north-east.

3. The building is raised on pilotis, allowing the ground plane to continue unbroken beneath it.

2

3

When I was out one morning training for the Engadin marathon, I stopped in a little place for a drink in a village about 10km from St Moritz. The owner was talking and he said 'I had a local farmer who came in and he had been to St Moritz and seen your building. He said it is very logical because on the sunny side where the lake is, it is all terraces and on the back where the mountain is, and it's very cold, it has little windows like the traditional architecture in this area.' I thought that this was a much better description than I could give of the project – it was very interesting how this farmer had recognised the forces that had generated the form of the building. Norman Foster, in conversation with the editor, 2012

Chesa Futura is a play on Chesa Veglia, the old farmhouse saved from demolition in the 1930s by the owners of St Moritz's legendary Palace Hotel and turned into a fashionable restaurant and nightclub. It is a counterblast to the over-scaled, flat-roofed blocks of flats that have robbed the centre of the resort of its old-world charm. Foster's rounded forms make an intriguing contrast with the exotic 1901 Victorian Villa Concordia next to it. Like the Gherkin, the shape invites analogies from nature, as well as illustrations in children's stories. At night, when the windows gleam through the large balconies cut into the smooth skin it will be the Hallowe'en pumpkin. Marcus Binney, *The Times*, 22 March 2003

Chesa Futura is one of the most extraordinary buildings seen in the mountains in recent years. It resembles a spaceship landed among the spires and peaks of the village, yet it is an extremely sophisticated building intended to make a minimal impact on its environment. Clad in larch shingles small enough to follow the complex curves, its rich brown colour is already fading to a soft silver grey like so many other timber surfaces around it. Edwin Heathcote, *Financial Times*, 28 January 2006

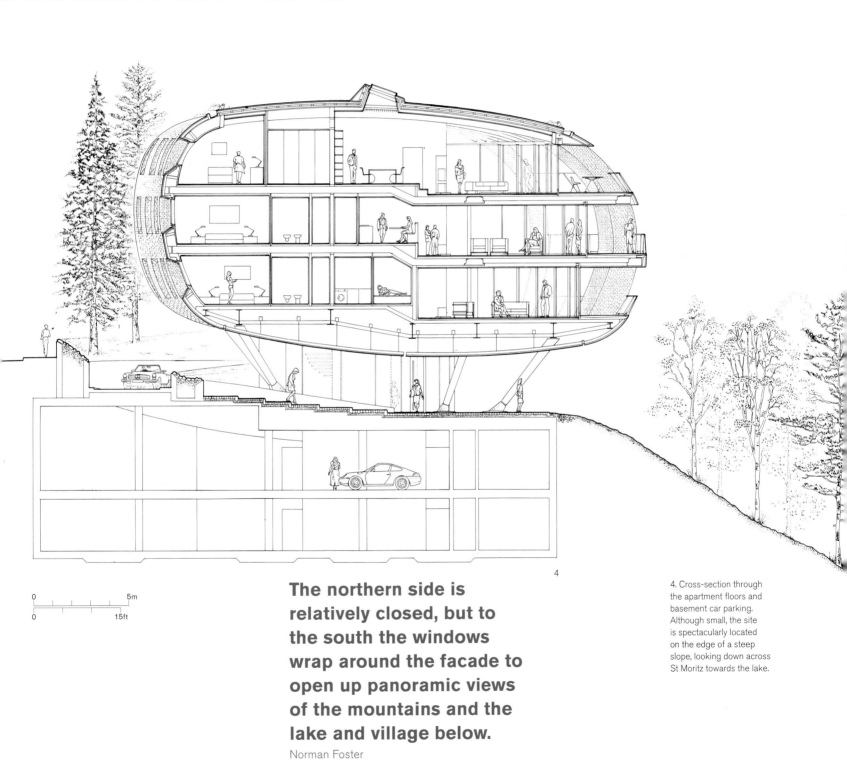

0 ————— 5m
0 ————— 15ft

4

The northern side is relatively closed, but to the south the windows wrap around the facade to open up panoramic views of the mountains and the lake and village below.

Norman Foster

4. Cross-section through the apartment floors and basement car parking. Although small, the site is spectacularly located on the edge of a steep slope, looking down across St Moritz towards the lake.

The building is like a boat. I had the opportunity to work with Germán Frers, one of the masters of boat design, on the yacht *Dark Shadow* and learnt from him that one of the most beautiful things about the shape of a boat is its hull. However, the sense of this is often lost once inside because of the storage arrangements – you never see the whole volume. So for me, the intention with Chesa Futura was to be able to read the shape of the building internally. All of the outer walls are left untouched with the storage arranged radially to the outer wall. It gives you a sense of orientation and you also get to see the beautiful double-curved spaces. Matteo Fantoni, formerly of Foster + Partners, in conversation with the editor, 2009

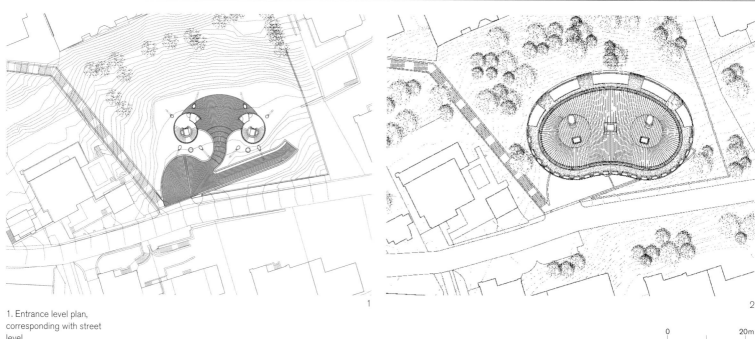

1

2

1. Entrance level plan, corresponding with street level.

2. Roof plan.

3. A typical apartment floor. Each floor has the flexibility to be divided into two or four, or configured as a single apartment, as shown here. Bedrooms line the northern facade, which is highly insulated, and the living areas are arranged to the south with broad terraces to take advantage of sunlight and views. Bathrooms and kitchens are located in the middle of the plan. The interior design is an organic extension of the overall architectural concept. Because the facades curve in two directions, the design of the interior elements is similar to boat design. To maintain the curved walls there is no storage against the outside walls, only on the internal partitions, which radiate from the cores.

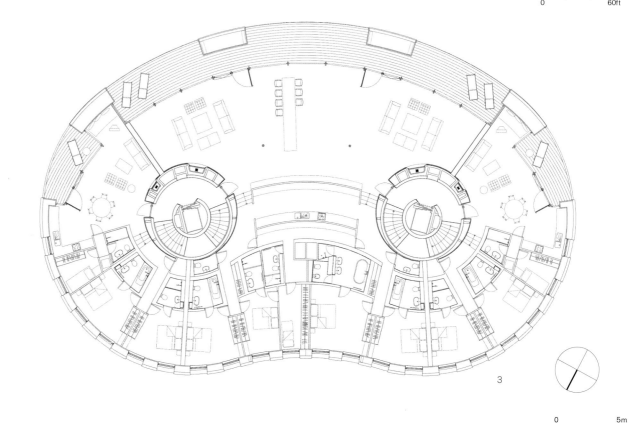

3

As soon as one does work on walls, the idea of
using the whole wall follows. It means that the
art is intimately involved with the architecture.
It is available to be seen by everyone. It avoids the
preciousness of gallery or museum installations.
Also, since art is a vehicle for the transmission of
ideas through form, the reproduction of the form
only reinforces the concept. It is the idea that is
being reproduced. Anyone who understands the
work of art owns it. We all own the *Mona Lisa*.
Sol LeWitt, interviewed by Saul Ostrow, *Bomb* 85, 2003
Right: Norman Foster commissioned Sol LeWitt to create
a wall piece that lines the staircase, rising from the car
park to the top floor.

It was Staeger, the shingle-maker, who gave
Foster the same sense of engagement with the
material world beyond architecture that he had
once had from his time spent with pilots, boat
builders and cyclists. Staeger spoke little English,
Foster not much German, but they were able to
work together in an instinctive, intuitive way
based on shared assumptions.

The 250,000 larch shingles were individually
cut by hand from eighty trees, producing 240
cubic metres of timber. The trees were sourced
from the same altitude as the building and felled
during the winter, when the wood contains no
sap. By choosing a material that grew and was
processed so close to the site, the energy used
in transporting it was reduced to a minimum;
and, as Foster points out, it contributes to the
established ecology of felling older trees to
facilitate forest regeneration.

Chesa Futura is clearly a modern building, using materials and techniques that are indigenous to the place, but in a way that is unfamiliar.

Shingles cover the walls and roof, and if you
walk beneath the building, you discover that it has
a shingle underbelly too. Nailing the shingles in
place by hand involved two months of painstaking
work. While it is a cladding material that makes
any form possible, the craftsmen who realised it
had to find some new and entirely untraditional
ways of getting to grips with their task – fixing
the shingles as they curve towards the horizontal
involved lying flat under the belly of the building,
rather like Michelangelo on his back, painting
the ceiling of the Sistine Chapel. Look beneath
the shingles though and you find that this is a
project based on the kind of accuracy, planning
and factory production that have always been
an essential underpinning to Foster's work.

The 12-metre-long curved glue-laminated
timber beams that radiate to form the
superstructure were prefabricated in sections
– cut to a tolerance of only 3mm using state-
of-the-art CNC machines – then shipped to site
and slotted together like a three-dimensional
jigsaw puzzle. There isn't a single straight line
in the entire frame. The superstructure sits on
a base formed from a mixture of concrete and
steel. Two circular concrete cores, each 2 metres
in diameter, house lifts and stairs and provide
lateral stability, allied with a lightweight steel
'table' with eight tubular steel legs that provides
additional support.

The larch shingle is a material with many
of the qualities that more modern building
components lack. It is robust enough to have a
design life of at least 100 years. Turn one over,
and you find the other side still looks as good as
new years after it was first installed. Larch also
has the ability to mellow and weather gracefully
with age, gradually gaining a silvery tint. It is this
that gives Chesa Futura a quality lacked by so
many contemporary buildings.

Modernity has come to be associated with an
initial gloss that rapidly tarnishes. Metal and glass
aspire to the quality of perfection; and once they
lose their sheen of newness they have little else
to offer. An aluminium-skinned building left in the
rain all too often starts to look like an abandoned
refrigerator, its surface compromised by weather
and wear. Wood, on the other hand, used in the
way that it is in the Engadin, exhibits a kind of
tolerance that gives it a margin of latitude; it is
far more forgiving. And yet Chesa Futura remains
a clearly modern building, using materials and
techniques that are indigenous to the place, but
in a way that is unfamiliar. In the years since it
was completed, Chesa Futura has aged gently,
receding into the background. It is no longer
a striking newcomer, but a familiar part of the
fabric of St Moritz, and a pointer to the way in
which contemporary architecture can aspire
to traditional architectural qualities.

Deyan Sudjic

4

4. Closed to the north, to the
south the building opens up
expansively with terraces that
embrace the spectacular view.

Overleaf: The building nestles
into the mountainside above
St Moritz. Taken overall,
Chesa Futura might be
regarded as a mini manifesto
for architecture, not just in
the Engadin Valley, but in
other parts of the world too.
Contrary to the pattern of
sprawl that disfigures the
edges of so many expanding
communities, it shows how
new buildings can be inserted
into the existing grain at
increased densities, while
sustaining indigenous
building techniques.

The Murezzan
St Moritz, Switzerland 2003–2007

1

The project's theme and its solution were suggested above all by the area's trading connections. The building takes its curved lines from the site and the slope of the land, forming a well-defined and fluid shape in an organic whole. On the street side, pedestrians are protected from traffic by an arcade, which also lets them browse the boutiques and galleries without being disturbed by bad weather. By contrast, on the side open to the lake and the mountains, we have tried to establish an almost osmotic relationship with the landscape and the sun. Norman Foster, in conversation with the editor, 2012
Right: The site of the Chesa, photographed in 2003.

The pattern of residential migration in St Moritz has been subtle and sophisticated. The first step was from hotels to private homes. The next step is from private villas to private apartments where you have the service but not the hassle and you can give the keys to friends and everything is taken care of. We have a concierge on site, so if they want a doctor or ski teacher, or want to book a flight, they can do so with one call. Our aim is to restore these old hotels and bring them into the twenty-first century – very much like the Plaza development in New York. Giorgio Laurenti, client for the Murezzan project, quoted in *Ultra*, Winter 2007

San Murezzan is the Romansch language name for the town that most of the world knows as St Moritz. The Murezzan development, on the lower slopes of the town, looking out over the Murezzan lake, forms a segment of the outer rampart of the complex of buildings that constitute St Moritz's urban core. It is a mix of refurbishment, restoration and new construction.

Significantly, it is a project that reflects the town's steady social transformation, from the winter of 1864 when the hotelier Johannes Badrutt introduced the town to the idea of winter tourism, to today when it has some 250,000 visitors every year. In the late nineteenth century, grand hotels such as Badrutt's Palace attracted entire families, supported by their own domestic staff, while smaller hotels catering for the middle classes sprang up in the town.

In The Murezzan, Foster's customary polished restraint is combined with the best of vernacular tradition

More recently, regular visitors have sought to acquire houses: a reflection of their longer stays, made possible by modern communications and different customs. Latterly, such visitors have favoured edge-of-town locations, fuelling the unsightly sprawl of villas and increased levels of traffic that are threatening the character of the town. Located within a two-minute walk of the ski slopes, restaurants and all the other amenities of St Moritz, The Murezzan represents a step change, reinterpreting the traditional resort hotel to provide sixty fully-serviced apartments for residents or visitors.

Apartments in the development may be bought or rented, which makes it attractive to a wide range of people, and it is situated in the heart of the town, which means that even if you arrive by car you don't have to drive while you are there. It is a model for Alpine urban living.

As Foster himself emphasises, the project is not about one distinct building, or a collection of individual buildings; it is, properly speaking, a piece of place-making that sets out to reintegrate the fraying edges of St Moritz's centre with its historic core, socially, physically, and in the way that it encourages people to move in and through it. The starting point was the updating of two neighbouring hotels on the fashionable via Serlas: the Albana and the Posthotel.

Completed in 1907 and 1908 respectively, in a Jugendstil take on the Engadin vernacular, both had reached a point in their history where they needed either to be refurbished or 'reinvented'. Recognising the need for a new type of destination in St Moritz – which would combine the convenience of an apartment with the amenities of a hotel – the developer bought the hotels and acquired the vacant site across the street, which had hitherto been used as a car park.

2

1. A detail of the aerofoil-section timber cladding that forms the facade of the Chesa.

2. The Murezzan project, which spans via Serlas in St Moritz, involved the conversion of two former hotels – the Albana and Posthotel – and the creation of a new block, the Chesa, seen here. Boutiques and galleries line the street front, with apartments taking advantage of the magnificent view behind.

3. Early sketch studies of the Chesa by Norman Foster.

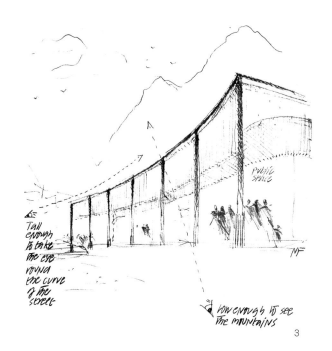

3

The conversion of the Posthotel, the first part to be completed, demonstrates the potential of such schemes. Careful renovation has brought historic features back to life in a central building that risked falling into disrepair. Haig Simonian, *Financial Times*, 1 December 2007
Right: The Posthotel, completed in 1908, photographed in its heyday.
Far right: The Albana Hotel, completed in 1907, which stands next to the Posthotel.

1

1. A model showing how the new Chesa relates to the two historic hotels: the Posthotel (left) and Albana Hotel (right).

2, 3. Ground and first-floor plans of the Chesa.

4. Cross-section through the Posthotel and the Chesa. Each of the apartments in the old hotel building is unique, reflecting the diversity of the original structure. An underground passageway leads to residents' car parking beneath the Chesa.

5. Sketch by Norman Foster, exploring the detailing of the Posthotel facade, which is inspired by Engadin tradition.

6. Details of the remodelled Posthotel facade. Bay windows have been added to capture lake views.

7. The Albana Hotel (right) now provides apartments above shops at street level.

The latter is the site for the Chesa, a building that provides a mix of apartments and shops. Dug into the sloping site and kept low in section to preserve the marvellous views from the two hotels, the Chesa is modestly scaled and finely detailed in timber to provide a sense of continuity with its context. Overlooking the valley, the apartment terraces have unrivalled views of the lake and the mountains beyond, while on its street front the Chesa forms part of the bustling life of St Moritz. In the past this was a forlorn spot, which people would cross the street to avoid. Now it is fully integrated with the town, both sides of the street are lined with shops, and it has changed the ebb and flow of pedestrian circulation.

It was Foster himself, in a series of preliminary studies, who identified the strategy for piecing together the various elements of this complex urban puzzle. Like many Alpine towns, St Moritz is reached by a single road that snakes up from a valley floor, through a series of S-shaped turns. Over time the town has grown by following the road as it climbs, but the resulting urban blocks are consistently sliced through by staircases and paths that provide shortcuts up and down the slope, cutting across the twists in the road and drawing views of the landscape into the heart of the town.

Foster's reading of this distinctive urban form guided the scheme. His observations and informal soundings provided the strategy that on a larger scale might have come from the kind of detailed surveys and stopwatch timings of the Space Syntax team that mapped Trafalgar Square before it was transformed.

He treated the huge hotels in effect as permeable city blocks, cutting routes through and forging connections between them. There are sky bridges and a multiplicity of entrances that respond to the changes of level on the steeply sloping site. A key aspect of the project is the link that runs beneath the street to connect the Chesa with the cliff-like older buildings. It also provides a connection from the apartment suites to five underground parking levels beneath the Chesa.

The Murezzan was designed working with a local associated firm. During the design process, Foster explored in detail a number of cladding options for the Chesa, in particular the screen that shelters the arcade. He had a full-size mock-up made of a version carved in traditional fashion and looked at other possibilities, before adopting the eventual solution.

In the context of the hotels, Foster's customary polished restraint is combined with the best of vernacular tradition – contemporary architecture is only hinted at in the treatment of the new bay windows and the rooftops. Both hotels had suffered a series of ill-conceived alterations over time, so the starting point was to research the original drawings in order to be able to renovate the existing fabric sympathetically. Each of the apartments is unique, reflecting the legacy of the original buildings and the demands of different lifestyles. There are fireplaces and timber floors – familiar icons of an Alpine lifestyle – and bay windows and vaulted ceilings that refer to what the buildings once were, and the era that created them.

```
0          10m
0          30ft
```

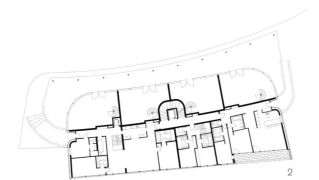

2

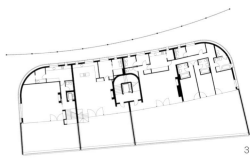

3

In the Posthotel and Albana we used a modern reinterpretation of Sgrafitto rendering for the facades. While it is a cleaner, crisper and more geometric pattern than that used in older buildings, it still uses the same traditional technique which gives it a real Swiss presence. Armstrong Yakubu, of Foster + Partners, in conversation with the editor, 2011

The existing hotels had been extended and added to over the years and were very 'tired'. At their heart they were Art Nouveau but for the most part they looked as if they were from the 1970s, particularly the Albana which had changed quite drastically. I felt very strongly that where possible our interventions should aim to restore their original grandeur and detail without resorting to pastiche. Norman Foster, in conversation with the editor, 2012
Right: A sketch of the arcaded base of the Posthotel by Norman Foster.

5

6

7

For the Post Haus bar and restaurant the big idea was to have a relaxed place to meet and eat and also a place which would be open all seasons rather than just in winter. Norman wanted it to feel as if anyone could just walk in there with their skis and feel totally at home. During the day it is very informal but it becomes transformed at night. Armstrong Yakubu, of Foster + Partners, in conversation with the editor, 2011

The Posthotel used to be the post office for St Moritz and the whole of the Engadin Valley. When we went through the archives in Zurich we found the original plans and discovered that it contained a large lobby space which had since been lost. We reinstated that space. We wanted the street level to be very active and accessible to the public, so the ground floor of the Albana became a bank, while the corresponding floor of the Posthotel became shops. It is in the tradition of European buildings where the ground floor is related to the public and the floors above are private. Matteo Fantoni, formerly of Foster + Partners, in conversation with the editor, 2009

I didn't want to create just another luxury restaurant, but something that St Moritz didn't have: a meeting point that would always be open, popular in its own way but with the fascination of St Moritz's old traditional venues, where people can relax, have a drink, a meal or just read the newspapers and soak up the magical view. Norman Foster, in conversation with the editor, 2012

1

2

Previous pages: looking east along Via Serlas, which has been revived as one of St Moritz's premier shopping streets.

1-3. The Post Haus restaurant is located at first-floor level in the former Posthotel. The original neo-gothic window openings create a landscape effect that Norman Foster describes as 'vaguely medieval'. The light fittings were custom designed for the space.

3

The facades of the old Posthotel and the Albana have been preserved, the Posthotel's neo-gothic stone arches forming a colonnade at street level, which is echoed across the street in the slender timber columns of the Chesa. Key elements of the original buildings have been restored and new bay windows of elegantly minimal design have been inserted discreetly into the street facade of the Posthotel to capitalise on the spectacular view. Above the stone base, the Alpine decorative technique of Sgraffito has been used to render the walls, giving the composition a certain formal unity.

Without making stylistic gestures to suggest a period piece, the Post Haus restaurant has the flavour of well-ordered Swiss simplicity.

Hotels by their nature demand a rather more theatrical approach than many building types, their interiors providing the scenery for the performances that unfold in them. An Alpine resort hotel, or the apartments that The Murezzan offers, belong not to the world of work, but of family, of celebration, of relaxation. The balance between the reassurance that a hotel has conventionally tried to offer to travellers in unfamiliar places, and the sense of being rooted in the specificity of place that we look for as we travel, has shifted. Increasingly we look for character, personality and the sense of regionalism, which The Murezzan provides.

These themes come together eloquently in the design of the Post Haus restaurant, located in the Posthotel, which Foster treated as a special project, designing every aspect of the interior, from the furniture to the wood-burning grill that forms its centrepiece. With seating for 180 diners, the Post Haus has two main areas, a casual bar with leather sofas, and a more formal restaurant.

It echoes Harry's Bar in Venice, which for part of the day is characterised by plain wooden tables, and at other times brings out the linen and a more elaborate menu. In the morning the Post Haus is a place to take coffee and read the newspapers, or lunch at a simple table in front the fire. In the evening the tablecloths come out.

Foster made extensive use of local craftsmen to fabricate the fixtures such as the grill and the fireplaces. The family of specially designed glass light fittings was designed and made in the Foster studio in London. Pendant fittings hang from the ceiling, while a smaller version sits on some of the tables. Foster's approach has been to produce a comfortable interior which feels as if it has always been part of the place. The tone is set by the Posthotel's run of neo-gothic arches, which look out across the street to the lake. Without suggesting a period piece, the restaurant has the timeless flavour of well-ordered Swiss simplicity. Some walls are accented in earth-tone colour, and the principal decoration comes from a sequence of images of the Engadin Valley by the legendary St Moritz photographer Albert Steiner.

As an urban project, the Murezzan works both on the most intimate of scales, as well as at the larger level of urban infrastructure, reflecting and extending the close grain of St Moritz. Crucially, as one of a series of projects that Foster has devised in the course of his long relationship with the town, it is underpinned by an observation of how St Moritz's structure developed historically and offers a guide to the direction it might take in the future. A polished demonstration of gentle adaptive renewal, it has quietly helped to reinforce and reinvigorate the centre of St Moritz.

Deyan Sudjic

4

5

4. The photographic prints that line one wall of the restaurant are by Albert Steiner, the legendary Swiss photographer, who lived and worked in St Moritz.

5. The wood store provides fuel for the open fire and the grill on which Chef Reto Mathis prepares his signature Mediterranean fish and meat dishes – for which the Post Haus restaurant is famous. Contemporary design is allied with more traditional elements, such as fireplaces and wooden floors, which are familiar icons of an Alpine lifestyle.

Norman had the idea of cladding the building in timber slats. He'd gone through the process of building Chesa Futura, so was much more aware of how timber is used and formed in that part of the world. We looked at various options and they were modelled and mocked up and prototyped. The timber has given the new building a very clear identity and a definite presence in St Moritz. It fits in, but not necessarily using the material in a way that you might expect. David Nelson, in conversation with the editor, 2012

With the creation of the project we wanted to suggest the idea of the city, so we expanded the public-pedestrian area around the Chesa and the Murezzan to give the buildings a very strong public impact. There is a bank, a restaurant, offices, a spa, so it's quite an elaborate piece of architecture whose functions are quite mixed. The building gives something back to the city, something which is about quality and a new way of living which is very open. Matteo Fantoni, formerly of Foster + Partners, in conversation with the editor, 2009

The Chesa has two fronts: one very urban which looks on to the main street and is essentially a colonnade filled with shops; and one residential which has a lakeside presence characterised by terraces, balconies and sliding windows. Armstrong Yakubu, of Foster + Partners, in conversation with the editor, 2011

1-3. Large expanses of glazing and generous terraces orient the Chesa apartments towards the view of Lake St Moritz and the mountains to the south.

All the apartments are unique because the client sold them as we developed them so we were able to personalise things like the kitchens and bathrooms. The palette of materials and finishes we used throughout was very luxurious – there is a lot of stone, particularly marble and quite a lot of glass, especially in the bathrooms. There is a definite thread in the choice of materials between the three buildings, particularly in the window framing and flooring, so that when you pass from one building to another you know it's the hand of one architect – it's an ensemble. Armstrong Yakubu, of Foster + Partners, in conversation with the editor, 2011

The three buildings have a common language of materials, so even if their exteriors – especially the Chesa – look quite different, when you go inside you're immediately aware that they are all from the same family. The way we treated the stairs, the lifts, the handrails, means that everything is coordinated. Matteo Fantoni, formerly of Foster + Partners, in conversation with the editor, 2009

It was a very design-focused project that worked from the urban scale, right the way down to the smallest details. The light fittings, for example, were purpose designed and have since been developed further for production. David Nelson, in conversation with the editor, 2012

3

Modern GPS technology can give us our precise geographical position – a location in motion. This new form of portrait (of the landscape as much as the body) is, like snow, a metaphor for the ephemeral. 'Where Are You?' offered virtual portraits of the mountains of Sestriere, Norman's studio in London and mine in Barcelona, united as a tattoo on the snow, as a kiss on the landscape.
Jaume Plensa, in conversation with the editor, 2008
Left: Jaume Plensa with Norman Foster in Sestriere.
Right: 'Where Are You?' under construction. Individual letters and figures were cut precisely using plywood templates. The entire composition was lit at night using lamps attached to boards embedded within the depth of each cut in the snow.

Snow is the medium of a personal passion – cross-country skiing. It is something that takes me away from urbanity and into nature – a world of deserted valleys, glaciers and frozen lakes – over hills and along forest trails. Through changing light, terrain, weather and place, the sport, for me, is an indivisible blend of aesthetics and athletics. By the point of contact with the snow – a wax-coated ski – I am constantly aware of the fickle changes in the medium. The angle of the skis is influenced by the density, temperature and texture of the surface – hard or soft, rough or smooth. These and other variations, such as slope and wind, determine whether the experience has the liberation of flight, or a battle against the elements.

The circle, a symbolic and timeless motif, linked the snow-carved site, Jaume's studio in Barcelona and my own London workplace.

My annual ritual covers around 700 kilometres, starting in winter and carrying on into spring. It culminates in a marathon-length race in the Swiss Engadin Valley. Blue-tipped sticks mark out the route at intervals of 20 metres, while graphic displays every 2.5 kilometres count up the distance travelled and later start to tell you how few kilometres remain to the finishing line. Apart from the emotional buzz of the crowd of 13,000 skiers, it is a mental and visual experience that continuously relates the changes of space, time and place.

These three ingredients were central to the work that Jaume Plensa and I created together for the 2006 *Snow Show*. Instead of a linear route of many grooves through the places which define a Graubünden Valley, our work was a single circular groove in the mountains of Sestriere, near Turin. The circle, a symbolic and timeless motif, linked the snow-carved site, Jaume's studio in Barcelona and my own London workplace. These places were defined by the degrees, minutes and seconds of latitude and longitude, using the precision of global positioning satellites.

This ephemeral relief in the snow, like an imprint or seal, was also evocative of the circles of prehistory – except in snow rather than earth or stone. The distinction might suggest the transience of snow and the permanence of stone. But in truth everything that is man-made is ultimately temporary – the pace of snow change is simply faster – like the pace of change itself on our planet: also perhaps a metaphor for global warming? The interconnecting circles of the Olympics, a contemporaneous event, also establish another visual link. Appropriately both events are celebratory.

Norman Foster

1

Opposite: 'Where Are You?' – an installation by Norman Foster and the artist Jaume Plensa for *The Snow Show* in Sestriere, 2006, seen at night. Conceived in 2000 by independent curator Lance Fung, *The Snow Show* has constructed an ongoing series of structures using the ephemeral materials of snow and ice. Each one stems from a collaboration between an artist and an architect.

1. Placed within a circular groove in the snow are the GPS coordinates of three specific locations: the Foster studio in London, Jaume Plensa's studio in Barcelona and the site itself.

2. One of a series of sketches by Norman Foster which formed part of an exchange of ideas with Jaume Plensa.

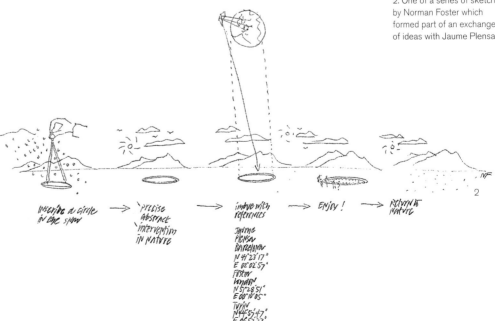

2

The Office in the Sky
Francis Duffy 2012

1. The Guaranty Building, Buffalo (1894-1895) by Louis Sullivan and Dankmar Adler. Sullivan wrote of the tall building: 'It must be every inch a proud and soaring thing, rising in sheer exultation that from bottom to top it is a unit without a single dissenting line.'

2. A drawing from Elisha Otis's elevator patent, 15 January 1861. On 23 March 1857, the first Otis safety elevator was installed at 488 Broadway in New York. The design is similar to one type still used today. A governor device engages knurled rollers that lock the elevator into its guides should it descend at excessive speed.

Of all architectural stories the genesis of the high-rise office building, particularly in Chicago in the last two decades of the nineteenth century, has achieved a mythic quality not least as a consequence of the autobiographical enthusiasms of Louis Sullivan and Frank Lloyd Wright. Given the originality of Norman Foster's contributions to the genre and his potential for yet more innovation it is quite possible that by the middle of this century, if not before, Foster's contribution to the reinvention of the high-rise office building may well have attained a similar canonical status.

This essay has three aims: first, to explore the social, technological and economic context of Foster + Partners' high-rise office buildings; second, to estimate as accurately as possible what exactly has been the significance of his contribution to this most glamorous of all building types, not just in the UK but in relation to other recent work on high-rise offices in Europe, North America and Asia Pacific; and third, to examine the possible longer-term significance of Foster's innovative work on the high-rise office in the context of the rapid and far reaching changes currently taking place in office technology, work processes and culture.

A brief word is necessary on the method that has been adopted in writing this essay as well as on the architectural and indeed philosophical position upon which this analysis depends. Important as the contributions of individual architects have always been to design innovation, attention should also to be given to the technological, economic and cultural contexts within which architects work and which act as powerful agents in stimulating the architectural imagination and thus making invention achievable.

That the development of the first wave of high-rise office building in the last decades of the nineteenth century and the early decades of the twentieth century did not happen by accident is well explained by Carol Willis in her book, *Form Follows Finance*. Financing and leasing arrangements as well planning and building regulations explain differences in the way the high-rise office building developed in New York and Chicago. Even more fundamentally, the vast and highly concentrated explosion of economic activity in the United States in the decades following the end of the Civil War created the conditions that were necessary for the invention of high-rise office buildings and largely determined their form.

Business processes relying on novel labour-saving devices such as the typewriter and on new communications devices such as the telegraph and later the telephone increased trading and administrative functions exponentially. The result was the huge burst of energy which quickly revolutionised building technology – the invention of the steel frame (for rapid construction), the lift (to conquer height), artificial lighting (to extend working hours), and eventually artificial environments (to make deep spaces habitable). Chicago, especially after the great fire in 1871, was the city that took maximum advantage of whatever technologies came to hand to forward the development of the high-rise commercial office building. The rebuilding of the city gave exceptional opportunities to a remarkable group of planners, architects and engineers – William Le Baron Jenney, Dankmar Adler, Daniel Burnham, Louis Sullivan and, of course, Frank Lloyd Wright – all of whom were able to extract maximum architectural advantage from new wealth and new technology.

1

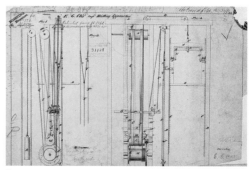

2

A century later somewhat different technological, economic and cultural circumstances have made possible but have also conditioned Foster's innovations in high-rise office building design. Of course, no one can deny the power of this architect's intensely individual vision. However, being in the right place (or rather, as will be seen in Foster's case, in multiple places) at the right time, having access to ambitious clients and the latest technology, as well as enjoying the stimulus of a manageable mix of economic pressures and resources are all external factors the importance of which must also be acknowledged.

Like Sullivan and Wright, Foster has been fortunate enough to have been able to address the design of the office building in a time of rapid change.

By the last two decades of the twentieth century the great North American tradition of high-rise building design had lost much of its youthful energy, despite brilliant contributions earlier in the century by architects of the calibre of Van Alen (the Chrysler Building, NYC), Raymond Hood (the McGraw Hill Building, NYC), Mies van der Rohe (the Seagram Building, NYC), Roche & Dinkeloo (the Ford Foundation, NYC) and SOM (Lever House, NYC, and the Inland Steel Building, Chicago). Office building and interior design gradually became more and more constrained by standardised constructional and environmental engineering practices and by the equally rigid protocols of investors, developers and real estate brokers.

Consequently, innovation in the design of high-rise office buildings became difficult. At every level and in every way – constructional techniques, floor plate and core design, environmental systems, external cladding, ceiling grids and lighting, workplace layouts, office furniture – North American office design, having started so propitiously, was eventually diminished by the narrowing vision of the powerful group of interests that finance, construct and manage office buildings. Unsurprisingly in a highly competitive industry lacking, for a variety of complex reasons, adequate feedback from consumers, the single and increasingly narrow focus of attention in high-rise building design became cost cutting. Only in the design of the exterior skin of high-rise office buildings have American architects been able to retain any latitude.

However, as Scott Adams' cartoon character Dilbert eloquently testifies, the vast majority of end users have been given very little say in determining the quality of their working environment. Most corporate clients now devolve such decisions to real estate executives and facilities managers who, rather than being advocates of strategic business purpose and end user values, are with rare exceptions practically impossible to distinguish from the supply side, i.e. from those whose rewards come from delivering office buildings as cheaply and quickly as possible and whose interest is more in the exchange value of real estate than in its contribution to business performance.

Late twentieth-century resistance to change in office design in North America is a paradox since nowhere else in the world over the same period has the development of office work and office technology been so ingenious, rapid, profound and widespread. The importance of the current revolution in work processes and work culture should not be underestimated – these technological and cultural advances will have even more impact on office design than the economic, technological and social changes that created the first high-rise buildings in Chicago over one hundred years ago.

3. Lever House, New York (1951-1952), designed by Gordon Bunshaft of Skidmore, Owings and Merrill. The quintessential and seminal glass box International Style skyscraper, it was also the pioneer curtain-wall skyscraper in New York. The external glass envelope was entirely sealed, the offices being fully air-conditioned.

4. The Seagram Building, New York (1954-1958) by Ludwig Mies van der Rohe. A masterpiece of corporate Modernism, it was designed as the headquarters for the Canadian distillers Joseph E Seagram & Sons. Its monumental form, of bronze and dark glass, is set back from Park Avenue to create a granite-paved plaza – a new public space whose creation was unprecedented in midtown Manhattan.

3

4

1. The atrium of the Larkin Building, Buffalo (1904) by Frank Lloyd Wright. Wright later wrote of the Larkin: 'It is interesting that I, an architect supposed to be concerned with the aesthetic sense of the building, should have invented the hung wall for the WC (easier to clean under), and adopted many other innovations like the glass door, steel furniture, air-conditioning and radiant or gravity heat. Nearly every technological innovation used today was suggested in the Larkin Building in 1904.'

2. The North American office environment of the 1920s – FW Taylor's vision of efficiency at work.

3, 4. The atrium, and cross-section, of the Hongkong and Shanghai Bank, Hong Kong (1979-1986). Following Wright's example at the Larkin Building, the stairs and lifts are pushed to the perimeter to free the heart of the plan as a light-filled atrium.

Today it is in Europe rather than North America that social and technological change is affecting office design most profoundly. This is doubly surprising. First, as noted above, developments in office technology continue to originate largely in North America. Second, European office buildings, certainly until the 1960s and 1970s, have generally been timid and provincial variants of North American models. The vast majority of European office buildings, even in dense city centres, continue to be low-rise. High-rise offices are a matter for anxious debate in planning circles rather than the accepted norm.

In mainland Europe, for a variety of historical reasons, office buildings have tended to be much more intimately integrated with the general fabric of cities in their physical form and, to some extent, even in their pattern of use. Older concepts of the integration of diverse urban activities persist. The sharp contrasts between high-rise downtown and low-rise suburbs, between office functions and other activities, and between working hours and the timetable of leisure activities that are so characteristic of North American cities, are far less clear. Nor until relatively recently has there been anything in Europe like the clear division of labour in the design professions, for example, between architects who work primarily for developers and interior designers and space planners who work primarily for corporate users of office space. In the UK especially, until the late 1970s, few serious architects regarded office design as an intellectual or artistic challenge.

However, during the period from 1980 onwards during which the decline of invention in the North American office design became so pronounced, the Northern European office began to develop a new and independent agenda of its own as much in its high-rise as in its low-rise manifestations. Foster has played a critically important part in this unexpected evolution. Like Sullivan and Wright, Foster has been fortunate enough to have been able to address the design of the office building in a time of rapid change and from a novel perspective and to have had his architectural imagination fired by the potential made evident, and indeed brightly illuminated, by rapidly changing circumstances.

The Hongkong Bank is one of the first high-rise buildings to have exploited at this scale the light projecting, interior space enhancing and place-making potential of the central atrium.

What are these circumstances and what are the forces that are re-shaping the Northern Europe office? Six specific factors come to mind, the social and cultural importance of which is sometimes hard to understand from the much more cost-driven North American perspective. The first and perhaps the most important factor is the social democratic legacy of the Second World War – a deeply rooted determination never to let the abrogation of individual human rights ever occur again. This has been manifested in office design in several countries by building regulations designed to give every office worker the right to aspect, daylight, privacy, amenities and, even more importantly, by the workers' rights to be consulted about any office design proposal that may affect the quality of their working lives. Consequently many Northern European businesses are much more collectively and socially responsible and much more aware of their culture, traditions, mutual dependency and shared responsibilities than their North American counterparts, who on the whole continue to conform to a much more mechanistic view of the relationship between employees and employers founded ultimately on Frederick Taylor's vision of 'Scientific Management'.

1

2

Taylor, who was an exact contemporary of Sullivan, developed managerial principles that made the modern office possible but at the same time, because of their very success, made it inevitable that American office architecture would be imbued, indelibly it seems, with features that were originally designed to emphasise division of labour, separation of functions, supervision, hierarchy and control. From a European perspective it is harder to forget that both Hitler and Stalin were numbered among Taylor's fans.

A second and closely related factor is the depth and widespread nature of the European sense of environmental responsibility, particularly with respect to the part that buildings play in determining, one way or another, the quality of humankind's collective future. The increasingly important part that the office plays in the knowledge economy has encouraged a great increase of interest in ways of designing working environments that are as efficient as possible in terms of energy consumption, not just as a centrally managed whole but also in terms of the control that individual office workers have over the environment of their own workplaces. Hence openable windows, cross ventilation, individual shading devices as well as the enormous attention given to the design of office building skins, solar energy systems, and healthier and more efficient environmental systems, even in very high office buildings.

The third factor that distinguishes recent European high-rise office architecture and sets it apart from most North American office buildings is the renaissance in structural engineering. There are now many examples of extremely inventive structural design applied to high-rise office buildings, many originating in Europe where the imaginary constraints taken for granted in much North American high-rise design have been dismissed as irrelevant compared with the delights and the rewards of ingenuity and daring.

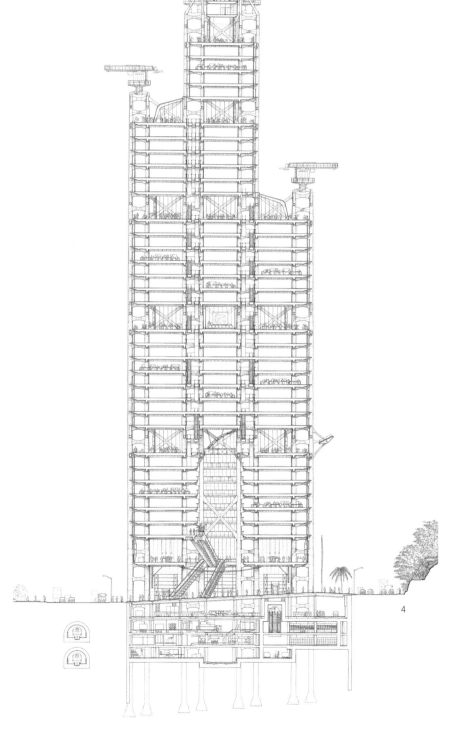

3

4

1. In recognition of the increasingly diverse nature of office work, in the 1950s in Germany the Quickborner team of management consultants developed the concept of *Bürolandschaft* – or 'office-landscape' – derived from organisational theory. Furniture is arranged in large, open office spaces with mechanically controlled environments. Low partitions and plants are used strategically to create a degree of differentiation and privacy.

2. The atrium and escalators of the Willis Faber & Dumas Headquarters, Ipswich (1971-1975). With its unprecedented range of staff facilities, banks of escalators, open office planning and cabled floor, Willis Faber represented a radical advance in workplace design in Britain at the time.

A fourth factor is the revival, since the austerity of the immediate post-war period, of the European love for its own sake of craftsmanship in building. Using good materials well assembled, while obviously not absent in North America, is by no means universal and has been in serious decline in the field of office building – as can be immediately ascertained by comparing the quality of detailing of the tautly constructed masterpieces mentioned earlier, such as the Seagram Building in New York and Inland Steel in Chicago, with the constructional arbitrariness of even such a highly regarded project as SOM's recently completed Time Warner Building at Columbus Circle in New York.

Fifth, already discussed, is the importance in European culture of the urban fabric, which has fostered a profound popular interest in the impact of high-rise offices on the fabric of cities. What is it besides a bold image that high-rise office buildings can contribute to cities, especially to cities that self-consciously see themselves as major players in a globalising and increasingly competitive knowledge economy?

The sixth and final factor, and by no means the least important, is the process by which large office buildings are procured. There are major differences between Northern Europe and North America in the nature of the relationships between landlord and tenant and between architect and client. In North America, developers have become stronger and corporate clients weaker because they have tended more and more to devolve responsibility for their office accommodation to lowly subordinates or even to outsource it altogether. In this commercial context, external professional advisors such as architects tend to be very much under the control of developers, while internal corporate real estate executives and particularly facilities managers have no real power base for insisting on excellence.

In Northern Europe, particularly in Germany, the opposite tends to be the case: developers are still relatively weak, corporate clients are stronger, often willing to think strategically about the ways in which office space can contribute to business. Consequently professional advisors, internal and external, have strategic business arguments to bolster their position. The practical consequence of these six differences is that neither reflex cost cutting nor habitual acceptance of formulaic solutions is as appealing to Northern European clients as it is to their North American counterparts.

Today it is in Europe rather than North America that social and technological change is affecting office design most profoundly.

Conversely, interest in, and appreciation of, the potential benefits of design innovation are much stronger. The benefits for Foster, as a European architect, in developing new ideas about the nature of the high-rise office and being able to put them into practice have been enormous. That he has also learned a great deal from North America is clearly evident, for example, in the enormous HSBC building in Canary Wharf. It is an extremely efficient, beautifully constructed exercise in the mode of the conventional, central core, American high-rise office, apart from one highly significant difference – the bold internal streets at every level and the common spaces at the three levels corresponding with the lift interchanges. Together, they represent an unconventional architectural device that engenders chance meetings and social interaction between the different departments of the bank.

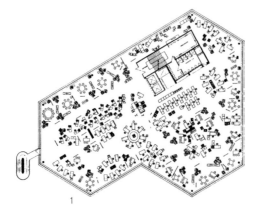

1

2

Other Foster high-rise projects are much more adventurous and innovative. However, Foster's career as a designer of high-rise office buildings began neither in Europe nor North America but in Asia with clients who were prepared to trust his judgement and who had the resources to allow him to experiment. It is important to remember that his first completed high-rise office building is in Hong Kong – also for the Hongkong and Shanghai Bank, but almost two decades earlier. This astonishingly original and accomplished building still holds its dominant place on the Hong Kong skyline, although surrounded today by larger, and much more assertive, buildings.

What is even more remarkable, however, about the Hongkong Bank is the uninhibited freedom of its internal planning: the bold use of the atrium, very rare at that time in high-rise buildings, the asymmetrical position of the cores, the importance and transparency given to vertical movement both by escalators and lifts. The last feature is in complete contrast to the inevitable consequence of conventional tightly planned and highly economical central cores which is that they proclaim, unintentionally but fatally in architectural terms, that circulation in high-rise buildings is treated as an unimportant and regrettable necessity.

Foster's other early Asian high-rise office, Century Tower in central Tokyo, is equally bold but externally so. Foster displays his structural imagination in a highly orthogonal city by making a strong architectural feature of the usually hidden diagonal structural cross bracing necessary in high-rise buildings in a seismic zone. It now seems obvious that Foster needed the freedom given him in these two Asian projects to allow him to reject and escape from what could have been the overpowering influence of conventional North American high-rise office building norms, and thus giving free rein to his European sensibility and imagination.

Foster's contribution to the design of the high-rise office building is best understood, first, in contrast to this building type's North American origins and, second, in the context of the values that have shaped post-Second-World-War Northern European office architecture. The term 'Northern European', although it is historically and sociologically accurate, is by no means intended to be a strictly geographical or an exclusive expression.

The values in question are nothing more and nothing less than the three universal architectural qualities: responsiveness to user criteria, inventiveness in technique, and love of creating what pleases. In other words: commodity, firmness and delight.

Foster's contribution to the development of office design is evident with different emphases, in very different ways and at different scales in the high-rise office buildings that are discussed below. The most interesting features of this chronology of development are not just the persistence and variety of Foster's attempts to rethink office design but, astonishingly, how all these innovations can be traced back to one of his earliest, most original and seminal office buildings, the low-rise, site filling, glassy, curvilinear Willis Faber & Dumas office building in Ipswich (1971-1975).

This building can be positioned historically within the line of European open plan offices initiated by the Schnelle brothers' invention of *Bürolandschaft*, a form of space planning based upon the then radical notion that a quasi cybernetic understanding of patterns of communication within office organisations would lead inevitably not just to the open plan but to a freer, more fluid notion of the overall form of the office building. The fundamental question that had been raised by the Schnelles' Quickborner consulting team in the 1950s was, 'What place is there for cellular and orthogonal office planning in a cybernetic world?'

3. Looking down into the atrium of the Hongkong and Shanghai Bank; transparency – both physical and social – is an overarching theme.

4. The atrium of Century Tower, Tokyo (1987-1991). Although it advances ideas explored in the Hongkong Bank, Century Tower is not a corporate headquarters but a prestige office block with a wide range of amenities, including a health club and museum. It grew from the conviction that the commercial realities of speculative offices could be reconciled with an architecture of distinction.

3

4

1. The atrium of the Citibank Headquarters, London (1996-2000). Located alongside the new Jubilee Line station at Canary Wharf, the Citibank headquarters occupies a key position in this emerging financial quarter of London.

2. HSBC World Headquarters, London (1997-2002). As the owner-occupier of its Hong Kong building, HSBC was able to encourage formal and technical experimentation to an unprecedented degree. At Canary Wharf, however, the bank decided to follow a commercially led solution that had to work within tight cost limits and meet market expectations for high-quality, flexible office space. That meant providing an air-conditioned building with a central core, to maximise the development potential of the site and optimise net to gross floor ratios. The challenge was not simply to meet market expectations, but to raise values in every area, from materials to ecological performance, thereby setting new standards.

The influence of this powerful argument on subsequent high-rise office projects is amply illustrated by Foster's continuing interest in achieving big, simple, open-plan floor plates from, for example, the Hongkong Bank in Hong Kong right through to the HSBC building in Canary Wharf. Of course, as the influence of North American office planning practices increased from the 1980s onwards such huge, largely open-plan floor plates became very common in the UK if not quite to the same extent in Continental Europe. More particular to Foster's work is the realisation of the potential of curvilinear forms, in both plan and section, which became increasingly feasible as a result of the increasing use of CAD and particularly what is now known as computational design.

Foster has succeeded in creating an unrivalled series of formally sophisticated and technically advanced high-rise office buildings that enhance the quality of the urban fabric.

Such forms are realised with triumphal effect in the Swiss Re building (1997-2004) as well as in several contemporary, low-rise Foster office buildings such as Moor House (2005), also in the City of London. Willis Faber's strongest architectural feature is the immense confidence, indeed brio, with which entrance and circulation have been handled throughout the whole building, with long and highly visible escalator flights leading through the office floors up to the social facilities and roof gardens – transforming the discipline of the route into a tour de force.

The Hongkong Bank developed this theme on a colossal scale by emphasising escalator movement within a huge atrium topped by an ingenious light scoop designed to be a great reflector. This massively magnified version of the Willis Faber prototype established the pattern of innovative rethinking of the high-rise office as a building type within the Foster studio that has persisted until today. A vitally important feature is that the entire building is experienced as a route – strategically located escalators emphasise movement through the building as a whole.

Breaking with the conventional North American central core plan, the Hongkong Bank is one of the first high-rise buildings to have exploited at this scale the light projecting, interior space enhancing and place-making potential of the big central atrium. Lifts and other core elements are located prominently but unconventionally on either side of the big office floors, keeping them clear and uninterrupted. Big diagonal braces and other robust structural elements are used internally and externally to create a series of intermediate scales between the building as a whole and individual floors.

Atria and banks of exposed and transparent lifts are used to celebrate the importance of vertical circulation in the Canary Wharf building now occupied by Citibank (1998) with its magnificent ten-storey-high art work by Bridget Riley. Citibank also demonstrates Foster's continuing sensitivity to achieving a humane ratio between size of floor plate and proximity of as many workplaces as possible to windows – achieved in this case by secondary atria which are stepped to allow light and air to penetrate deep into the building. The far bolder and higher atrium in the Deutsche Bank Place building in Sydney (1997-2005) and the relatively small floor plates (by New York standards) and the elaborate entrance sequence of the Hearst Tower in New York (2000-2006) achieve the same effects for the same reasons.

In the case of the Hongkong Bank, Citibank and Deutsche Bank Place, the central core is completely displaced. This idea was pioneered in SOM's magnificent Inland Steel Building in Chicago (1957) but would now be considered a wasteful heresy in contemporary conventional North American office design, the principal objective of which is to increase planning efficiency by ever more tightly compacted central cores.

1   2

Disintegrating the central core into separate elements,
as has been done at Deutsche Bank Place, takes Foster's
benign heresy one step further. However, the three great
benefits of stripping out the core from the floors and giving
it an architectural identity of its own are: first, that vertical
and horizontal access is emphasised in the grandest possible
way; second, the office floors themselves are completely
clear and uninterrupted; and third, views are maximised
for all occupants all the way up these very high buildings
with their breathtaking views.

At a more intimate scale, achieving transparency and
interconnectedness between office floors is becoming more
important as office organisations seek more continuous and
intense interdepartmental communications – an idea latent in
the open configuration of Willis Faber. Achieving this in
high-rise buildings became an important and highly original
feature of the floor plates of the Commerzbank in Frankfurt
(1991-1997). This purpose-built office building is strongly
influenced by German environmental and social regulations,
which emphasise the environmental, the local, and the
personal rather than cost cutting and operational efficiency.

The Commerzbank has, most ingeniously, a triangular
plan, within which a series of eight-storey, mini office
buildings appear to be suspended between the cores
occupying the three corners of the building. This pattern
occurs, *en echelon*, on all three facades. These units of
office space, which serve to break down the scale of this
huge building, are also separated vertically by micro-atria,
generously landscaped, which provide a series of
environmentally friendly, inside-outside, transitional
environments linking activities, processes and departments.
While they may not be efficient in conventional office design
terms, they create a tissue of connectivity, of interactive,
social spaces that draw together not just the building but
much more importantly the operational and the social
fabric of the bank.

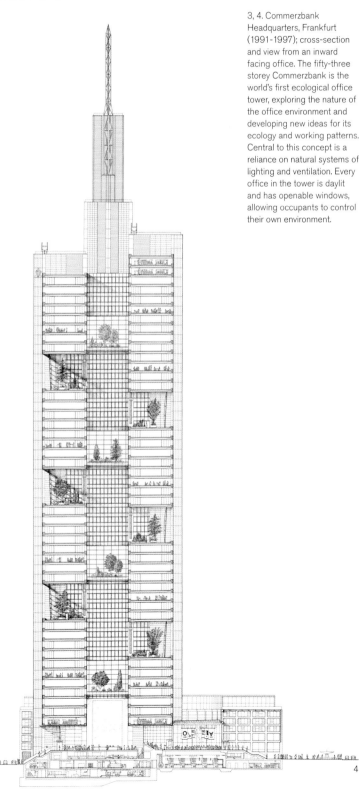

3, 4. Commerzbank
Headquarters, Frankfurt
(1991-1997); cross-section
and view from an inward
facing office. The fifty-three
storey Commerzbank is the
world's first ecological office
tower, exploring the nature of
the office environment and
developing new ideas for its
ecology and working patterns.
Central to this concept is a
reliance on natural systems of
lighting and ventilation. Every
office in the tower is daylit
and has openable windows,
allowing occupants to control
their own environment.

3

4

There are many points of convergence between the design of Swiss Re and some of the thinking we explored with Bucky in the 1970s in the Climatroffice project. In both cases ovoid forms enclose the maximum volume with the minimum surface skin – there are analogies with the naturally efficient forms of birds' eggs – and walls and roof dissolve into a continuous triangulated skin. This energy-conscious enclosure regulates the internal microclimate. Norman Foster, in conversation with the editor, 2012
Right: Cross-section for the Climatroffice project (1971).

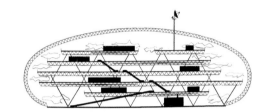

1. Swiss Re Headquarters, London (1997-2004); sketch by Norman Foster showing air movement and light penetration through the building's spiralling atria.

2. Conceptually the Swiss Re building develops ideas explored in the Commerzbank and before that in the Climatroffice, a theoretical project with Buckminster Fuller that suggested a new rapport between nature and the workplace. The atria that spiral up the building function as the building's 'lungs', distributing fresh air drawn in through opening panels in the facade.

However, by far Foster's most highly developed and sophisticated version of such innovations is the Swiss Re tower. Here the entire form of the building is circular (recalling in three dimensions the fluidity of the Willis Faber plan), the cladding is fractal, and the entire building is encased in a metre-deep double skin designed to enhance sustainability. Spiralling mini-atria, skewed to follow the building's curved skin, provide a flow of linkages between floors. Since this device occurs six times on every floor the cumulative impact is amazing, providing not just an extremely attractive sense of three-dimensional transparency but, for business purposes, the full interaction-enhancing potential of highly integrated and interconnected space. There has never before been anything quite like this in high-rise office design. So novel is this idea and so unclassifiable in terms of ordinary office design practice that so far internal layouts (not by the Foster office) have failed to take complete space planning advantage of what is inherently a highly practical idea. Instead, letting agents seem to be nervous of the novelty of the building's form.

Letting brochures studiously avoid acknowledging the special nature of innovations which are clearly regarded as eccentricities rather than as powerful devices that could be used to support interaction and sociability among office workers, enhancing the collaborative work processes that are so important for the knowledge economy. Such is the entropic power of conventional thinking. Less controversially the occupiers of the Swiss Re building also enjoy access to the completely glazed dome at the top of the building which provides 360 degrees of visibility of the whole of London and is perhaps the most beautiful modern room in the City.

The Swiss Re building has instantly become a much-loved addition to the London skyline. From a distance its subtle form has the magical capacity to close and complete not just one vista but many throughout the whole of central London, north and south of the River, and from Holborn to Whitechapel. Equally deft is the way in which its circular form slips into the complex streetscape of the City at ground level. Architectural insiders may know that the building has a genetic continuity, key feature by key feature, with its great predecessor, the Willis Faber building. More importantly, the radical discontinuity of this great building from all conventional office design is clear for the whole of London, and indeed the whole world to see.

What may be less obvious is that by emphasising the importance of interior circulation and by the spatial integration of floors by devices such as the mini-atria, Foster has taken an important step in the design of these huge high-rise buildings towards treating their interiors not just as so much office space to be subdivided and sublet but as miniature cities in their own right, with an increasingly legible structure of interior 'streets', 'squares' and 'places'. Foster has always aimed at another kind of integration – linking not just the building and its context but also making structural and environmental design complement one another as well as, at an operational level, weaving together interior space planning and circulation. Achieving interdependence between all these levels of design is as crucial in architecture as in aeronautical design.

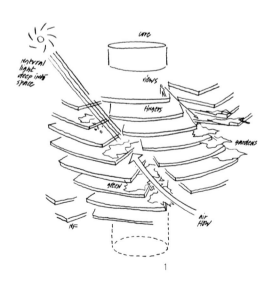

1

2

There is a complex relationship between function and cultural aspiration. The medieval towers of San Gimignano were defensive but they were also symbols of power – each family building higher to demonstrate its wealth and prestige. Interestingly, if one tower was under threat, a temporary bridge was used to evacuate to the neighbouring tower. There are clues there for us today – it would be interesting to see in future projects if we could link the sky lobbies or refuge areas with bridges in the sky. The movies have long since played with such ideas – Fritz Lang's *Metropolis* featured bridges linking skyscrapers. Norman Foster, in conversation with the editor, 2010
Right: The medieval towers of San Gimignano, Italy.

This integrative aspect of Foster's work is also magnificently evident in the bold external structure of the Hearst Tower, on 8th Avenue in Manhattan. Here is a reprise of the external structural display of the Hongkong Bank and Century Tower, but even bolder. An offset core suggested a diagonally-braced structure for the office floors, which gives the new building scale and determines its energetic profile while at the same time acting as part of what is intended to be an intelligent and environmentally responsive skin. Moreover, the new building, the novelty and integrity of which is already clear on the Manhattan skyline, does two things that are very unusual in New York.

In a time of rapidly accelerating technological change the imaginative challenge of inventing what new kinds of offices will need to be like is immense.

First, the building rises above a base which is a landmark building, the former Hearst offices, and which internally has been totally transformed into a magnificent sequence of entry into the new building above. Second, as discussed above, the Hearst floor plates are relatively small, partly to accommodate the smaller business divisions but also, of course, to allow more access to daylight and views. It was very satisfactory to observe from the vantage point of DEGW's twenty-third floor offices on 8th Avenue in New York the construction of not only Renzo Piano's building for The New York Times but also, several blocks further north, the more advanced construction of Foster's tower for the Hearst Corporation. They offer evidence of movement and improvement even in the highly conservative world of real estate in New York – which is not surprisingly dependent upon outside influences.

Foster's unconventional approach to high-rise office design is now acceptable and achievable in the country where the high-rise office building was invented. More importantly, his studio's well-structured ideas about the changing nature of the high-rise office building are already influencing, redirecting and transforming that context. He and his team have succeeded in creating an unrivalled series of formally sophisticated, ingeniously planned and technically advanced high-rise office buildings that enhance the quality of the urban fabric. They are designed to be highly legible internally in ways that are stimulating and pleasant for people to enter, to find their way round and to always know where they are. Better than anyone Foster has designed high-rise office floor plates that are big and efficient while simultaneously maximising views for everyone to enjoy.

Clients are discovering how to use these floor plates in ways that make them interesting and memorable places, supporting concentrated work at the same time as facilitating and encouraging social networking between, as well as across, floors.

By the simplicity of these designs, Foster has safeguarded future space-planning options. Far more inventively than any other high-rise office architect, he has experimented with ways of escaping from the tyranny of the two-dimensional floor plate by opening up vertical connections, thus enhancing interaction between people and departments and creating an enhanced sense of community. Fascinated by precise and elegant construction, he has risen to the challenge of designing the high-rise office building as an environmentally sustainable device.

3. Since the design of the Hongkong and Shanghai Bank, Foster has continued to redefine the nature of the office tower and to explore how it can respond to the context and the spirit of the city in which it stands. The thirty-one-storey Deutsche Bank Place, located on a prominent site close to the harbour, explores new strategies for flexible, column-free office space and creates a new 'urban room' in Sydney's dense central business district.

3

1. Hearst Tower, New York (2000-2006). The project revives a dream from the 1920s, when publishing magnate William Randolph Hearst envisaged Columbus Circle as a new media quarter in Manhattan. Hearst commissioned a six-storey Art Deco block on 8th Avenue, anticipating that it might eventually be reconfigured as the base for a tower. The design of the tower echoes an approach developed in the Reichstag and the Great Court at the British Museum, where the new is offered as a harmonic counterpoint to the old.

Well over one hundred years ago a tiny group of talented architects made Chicago the prototype of the cities of the twentieth century. Foster, more than any other high-rise architect, has broken free of the unthinking and obsolescent conventions to which their great legacy has been reduced. However, there is much more to be done. In a time of accelerating technological change, the imaginative challenge of inventing what new kinds of offices will need to be like is immense. Office buildings, and particularly high-rise offices, are no longer the relatively stable entity they have been for a century. The boundary is shifting fast between the growing convenience of virtuality and the more subtle benefits that can be derived from face-to-face ways of working. Co-location and synchrony are no longer necessary conditions for the conduct of the greater part of office work. In fact the more we come to depend upon virtuality, the more we will need serendipitous and unplanned face-to-face contacts, the more we will need place. To explore what kinds of places we shall need is a grand quest that is best embarked upon by systematic and imaginative exploration of what architecture can do to enhance the quality of working life and business performance.

There are three ways in which office architecture can support new ways of working and three corresponding ways in which the contribution of office space to business performance can be measured. The first is to enhance the efficiency with which space is used, not just by square metres per person, but by the intensity of its use over time. Distributed work means that office space will be used more intensively, more communally and more diversely. For office design this means finding ways of accommodating a much more mobile, certainly more demanding and possibly in aggregate smaller office population which, however, will use office space more intensively over time and thus more economically. Another consequence is that the workplace will have to become more agile to accommodate accelerating organisational and technological change.

Hearst Tower is a reprise of the external structural display of the Hongkong Bank and Century Tower, but even bolder.

The second way is to create working environments that will help people to work more effectively, in ways that demonstrably add value to business. Office buildings that support communities of practice and stimulate interaction and creativity will be most highly valued. People in the knowledge economy will see offices less as arrays of individual workstations and more as places equipped to enrich collective intellectual discourse. For office design this means finding ways (some of which Foster has already explored) of using office space to encourage interaction especially serendipitous encounters.

The office will support more elaborate use of technology including pervasive computing, i.e. architecture itself in effect taking a much more important part of the dissemination and development of ideas. Office environments will have to become more appealing places to attract and retain talent. Because of more mobile ways of working a wider range of environments will be needed, probably leading to mixed use and a much more fluid and permeable boundary between office use and other kinds of urban activity.

1

The third and perhaps most important way in which the office will contribute to business is that it will be recognised as a powerful medium for expressing social, business and cultural values. In the knowledge economy let us hope that office architecture will no longer be used to express opacity, division and hoarding but rather the exact opposites: transparency, accessibility and sharing. For office design this means the office environment becoming more and more of a means of expressive corporate branding. Conversely the office will also have to be designed in ways which allow office workers to express their own individual and shared values.

Foster has already gone a long way to show how the high-rise office building can be rescued from the deficiencies of the outmoded conventions of developers and corporate real estate practitioners, particularly of the North American kind who have contributed so much to the decline of what was once a great tradition of office design. Measurement is the key to the reversal of that decline because measuring office design systematically against business targets will create the feedback that is essential to justify investment in improving the quality of the working environment.

This vision is creating a fresh and marvellous moment in office design. The opportunity is to invent the architecture and the urban structures, including densely occupied high-rise structures in the centres of great cities, designed to accommodate multiple and ever changing uses and new patterns of working culture, in fact nothing less than the infrastructure of the knowledge economy, the twenty-first-century city. That is why Foster's iconoclastic contributions to the development of high-rise office design are so important – they demonstrate that change is possible as well as desirable and that, when accomplished, it works for people and business too.

2. The main spatial event of Hearst Tower is the lobby, which occupies the entire floor plate of the old building and rises up through six floors. Like a bustling town square, this space provides access to all parts of the building. It incorporates the Hearst cafeteria and auditorium and mezzanine levels for meetings and special functions.

3. The forty-four-storey Hearst Tower rises above the old Art Deco building, linked on the outside by a skirt of glazing that encourages an impression of the tower floating weightlessly above the base.

2

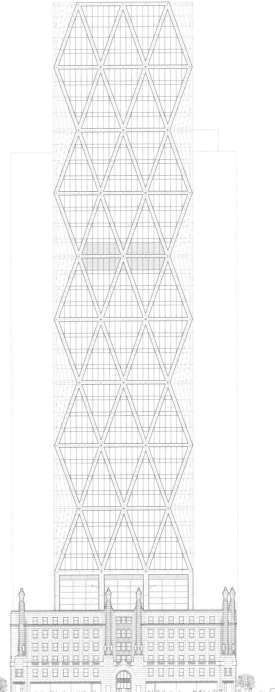

3

New York Times Tower

New York, USA 2000

1. Winter gardens are located at every seventh floor on the eastern facade; these communal spaces also function as the building's green lungs.

2. Within the distinctive wedge-shaped enclosure, the building is configured as a series of stepped back volumes, which when viewed in profile give the impression of a traditional New York set-back. The western facade evokes the billboards that line Times Square, animated by the exposed glass lift cars that constantly run up and down.

Foster thinks holistically. He gets his mind around structure, space-programme and image, making of them an integrated system. He turns problem-solving into an art. And he is acutely responsive to the well being of those who inhabit his buildings. His proposal for the Times didn't work for the clients, who saw it as not sufficiently flexible to accommodate the building's lease tenants. The design is a space frame in the shape of a right triangle. Along the hypotenuse winter gardens were planned at intervals of seven storeys. Each seven-storey segment was conceived as a village in a vertical urban stack. The effect was an apotheosis of the New York set-back. Herbert Muschamp, *New York Times*, 22 October 2000

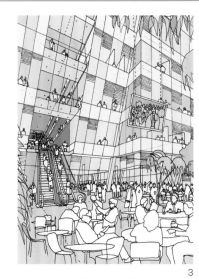

The client wanted the first ecological building in Manhattan. We used a diagrid structure, which gives huge savings in steel, and the building was triple glazed and naturally ventilated, allowing it to breathe during the day and shut itself down at night. It really pushed the energy efficient building beyond what we had achieved with the Commerzbank. Armstrong Yakubu, of Foster + Partners, in conversation with the editor, 2009
Left: The site was in the 42nd Street Development Project area. Design guidelines were drawn up by Robert Stern in the 1990s and focused on the area's history as an entertainment centre, encouraging the use of signage, lighting and billboards. Stern described it as: 'the first plan in history that took as its mandate legislative vulgarity.'

The New York Times invited four of the world's leading architects to enter a competition to design its new headquarters in 2000. The brief was for a forty-five-storey, environmentally advanced, landmark building to be situated on the east side of 8th Avenue between 40th and 41st Streets. Half of the available space was to be dedicated to the New York Times with the remainder given over to speculative office accommodation.

The Foster proposal reinvents the classic New York setback for the twenty-first century, sheathing the staggered blocks of the tower in a crystalline skin. In section, the building is a right-angled triangle, the opposite side of which faces west while the hypotenuse faces east and is home to a series of winter gardens. These are located every seven floors and are stepped back within the triangular glass envelope, creating a ziggurat effect when viewed in profile. The office accommodation is arranged in three distinct bays which open out on to the gardens. Office workers are never more than three floors away from the communal green spaces, which – much like the Commerzbank – function as the lungs of the building. Fresh air and natural light are let in during the day while at night the building shuts down to conserve the environment, acting like a giant thermos flask.

Both structurally and environmentally, the building prefigures Hearst Tower by more than a year. Like Hearst, the New York Times Tower has an offset core, and similarly, it makes use of a diagrid steel frame which is clearly expressed on the north and south facades. Together these elements create large, column-free floor plates in a structure which, despite being inherently rigid, uses far less steel than a conventional skyscraper. The largest floors, which measure 7,000 square metres, are reserved for the newsrooms. Here, circulation is via a series of zig-zagging escalators which rise up through a central atrium, animating the space and encouraging movement and collaboration between the floors.

At ground level, shops and cafés weave between the columns of the diagrid creating a dynamic, colourful ribbon along the north and south elevations. This motif is continued on the western aspect where two curved billboards mark the boundary between the building and the edge of the plaza. The lifts in the main core are open to the street, their glass cars moving up and down the facade like one of the animated billboards in the nearby Times Square, simultaneously reinforcing the dynamism of the building and acknowledging the heritage of the area.

Gavin Blyth

3. Access to the newsrooms, which occupy the five largest floors of the building, is via a series of escalators to help encourage movement and collaboration between the teams.

4, 5. Norman Foster's sketches imagine the activity at ground level. The drawing on the left shows one of the two large curved billboards that mark the boundary between the building and the edge of the plaza on 8th Avenue. The plaza faces the distinctive, X-framed Port Authority Building – the biggest bus station in New York, and the busiest in the world. The drawing on the right shows how the columns of the diagrid extend down to pavement level along the north and south elevations, providing space for shops and cafés.

4

5

Hyatt Tower

Chicago, USA 2000

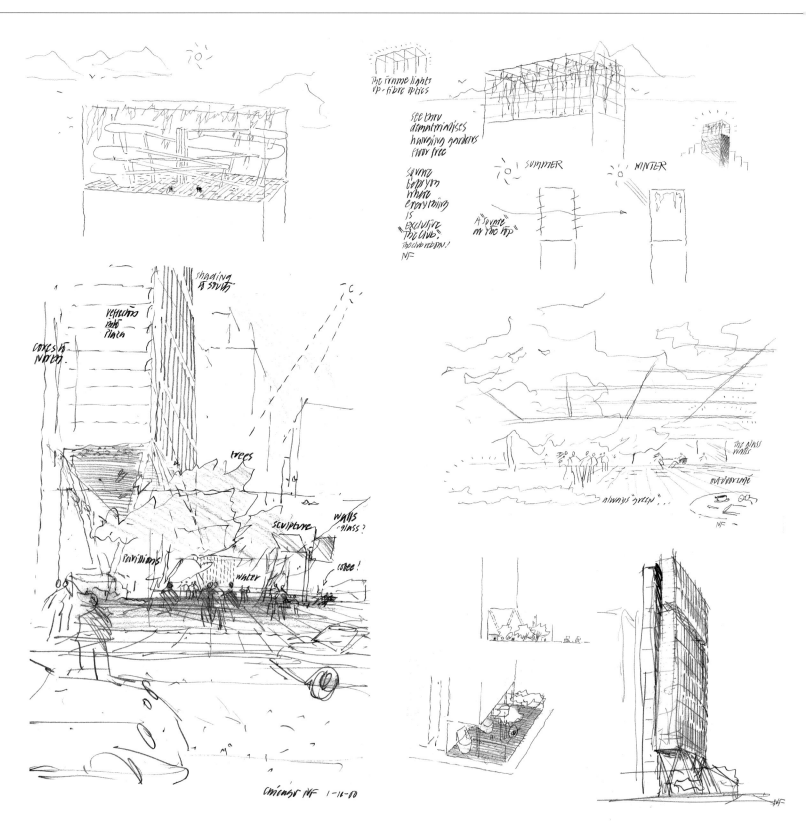

The effects of the offset core, combined with the height of the building, meant that the structure would have twisted. The only way to counter this was to stitch it. We then discovered, in conjunction with the engineers, that by cross-bracing the whole building we didn't need columns at the corners, a realisation which prefigured the Hearst building by three years. During a charrette in Chicago, Norman came up with the idea that the building and its base should reach out to the plaza, so we raised it up eight storeys to give it its presence and designed the entrances as a series of small pavilions. Armstrong Yakubu, of Foster + Partners, in conversation with the editor, 2012

With work progressing on the New York Times competition, the practice began designing another US high-rise building, this time in Chicago. The Pritzker Corporation – best known for its patronage of the Pritzker Prize – wanted a new headquarters for its Hyatt Hotel business and associated Pritzker companies. Like the New York Times, the brief was for a signature green building which retained 50 per cent of the space for itself while letting the remainder.

Instead of creating a plaza with a tower pushed back within it, Foster wanted the building to reach out to the city.

The proposed site was a car park, bounded to the south, east and west by major roads and to the north by an existing building. To optimise the available views and to bring as much light in as possible, the building's core is situated on the northern boundary of the site. To compensate for the loss of rigidity caused by moving the core away from the centre, the design team once again developed an elegant diagrid structure, which in this instance frames a sixty-storey block. The diagrid is a clearly articulated exoskeleton in which each triangular section frames an eight-storey-high module.

Access from the core to the main office accommodation is via a series of bridges which span a full-height atrium creating a dynamic, naturally lit circulation hub. The tower is capped by a transparent box containing a hanging garden which cascades down the open-plan, ramped floors within.

Chicago planning rules demand large setbacks for high-rise buildings. However, instead of creating a plaza with a tower pushed back within it, Foster wanted the building to reach out to the city. To achieve this the tower is elevated eight storeys above ground by a series of super columns which rake out on the southern side of the building, spanning the full width of the landscaped plaza below and mirroring the diagrid pattern of the facade. Here, trees meander in and out of the columns, humanising their heroic scale and serving as a windbreak to the plaza beyond. Triangular reflective pools located at the intersection of the columns add to the effect, helping to carve out a civic space beneath the structure – a restatement of a theme first explored in the Hongkong Bank. The public and private elements of the development are clearly demarcated by the use of a series of sculptural pavilions which serve as entrances to the building.

Despite neither the Hyatt nor New York Times buildings being realised, the systems and structures developed through their design would later find full expression in the Hearst Tower. The diagrid geometry and optimum dimensions to achieve column-free floor space were all worked out through these projects, providing the Hearst design team with invaluable research material.

Gavin Blyth

Opposite: Design sketches by Norman Foster. Clockwise from top left: the top of the tower is capped by a transparent, naturally ventilated volume containing a hanging garden which cascades down through the ramped floors within; the plaza is a year-round green oasis; the main office accommodation is connected to the lift core by a series of bridges; entry to the building is through a series of sculptural pavilions; and planting, water features and sculpture combine with cafés and shops to create a bustling public plaza.

1. The slim profile of the tower with its distinctive diamond-patterned facade, contrasts with the heavier, more traditional forms of Chicago's commercial building stock.

2, 3. Alternative approaches to the base of the tower. On the left, a series of super columns rake out from the building, spanning the full width of the plaza; the drawing on the right shows an earlier treatment.

2

3

Connections Hearst Tower

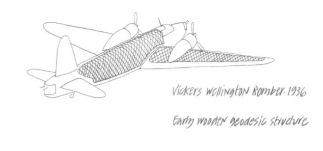

Vickers Wellington Bomber. 1936

Early wooden geodesic structure

Hearst Tower continues themes that have been explored separately in the context of historic buildings, and in the practice's exploration and reinvention of the high-rise as a building type, which Norman Foster began as a student in the 1960s. However, Hearst is unique in combining these concerns within the context of an office tower. The juxtaposition of old and new on this scale is a guiding theme in projects such as the Reichstag and the Great Court at the British Museum – projects that have also introduced within their precincts public spaces that can be thought of as 'urban rooms'. The structural 'diagrid' has its own developmental timeline, with roots in the lightweight airframe of the Wellington, developed by Barnes Wallis, the geodesic structures of Buckminster Fuller and more recent investigations into structurally efficient high-rise forms in projects such as the Millennium Tower and the headquarters for Swiss Re.

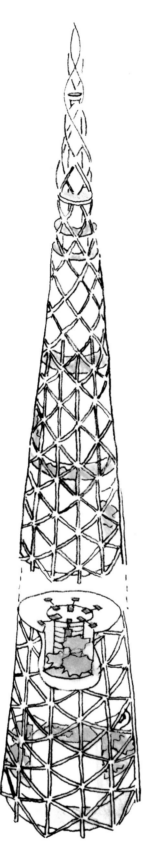

Humana Headquarters - St Louis · 1982

Triangulated structural facade enables a tower free of internal structure.

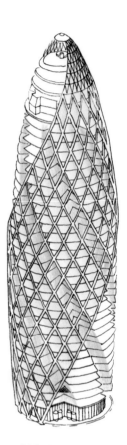

Swiss Re Tower · London · 1997-2004

Highly efficient diagrid structure also defines the atria which spiral up the tower and act as green lungs, an important part of its sustainable

Millennium Tower - Tokyo Bay · 1989

A research project to establish the feasibility of a tower (840 m. high, 170 levels) as a self sufficient mini city. Both wind and deadloads are carried by the geodesic outerframe.

Autonomous Solar House 1982-3

A collaboration with Buckminster Fuller to create family dwellings for the Fullers and the Fosters.

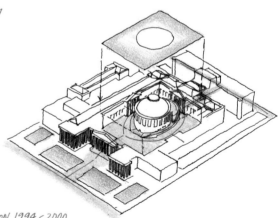

Great Court British Museum London 1994 - 2000

Each of the modern interventions into the historic fabric of these three important public buildings uses the technology of today, but is informed by the heritage of the original structure.

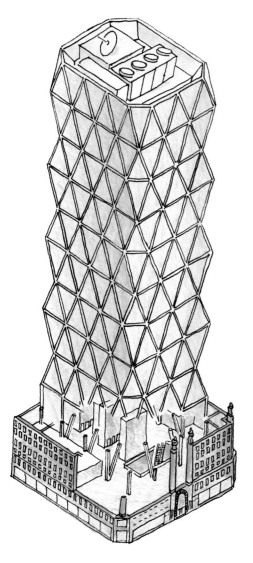

Hearst Tower - New York 2000-6

The Hearst tower draws on all the themes developed over time in the projects shown here
- Integration of a historic landmark building, recycled and transformed as as a social heart for Hearst.
- Insertion of a tower with the economies of a diagrid structure and a sustainable agenda
- sensitivity to encourage urban life at the sidewalk level by preserving the shopping areas.
- a clear ascending route through the base via cafés and meeting areas to the tower circulation
- a new and identifiable symbol of the Hearst organisation

Office Tower - Yale 1961

It has been suggested that this student project has all the seeds of the later HSBC Bank in Hong Kong. The planning principles of an offset core serving open flexible office space continues in the Hearst tower.

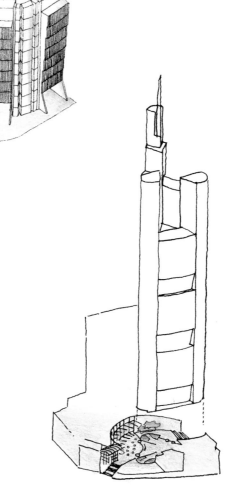

Commerzbank Tower - Frankfurt · 1991-97

This headquarter tower grows out of a base - part historic and new - which is sympathetic to the tight urban scale of the city quarter. An internal pedestrian arcade crosses the site and relates to a popular restaurant located within the new part of the podium.

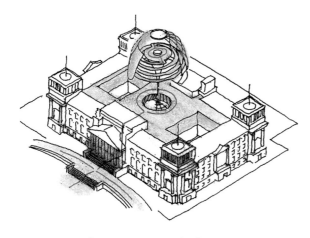

New German Parliament - Reichstag · Berlin 1992-99

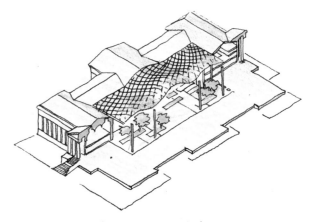

Courtyard Smithsonian Institute Washington 2004-7

NF 2012

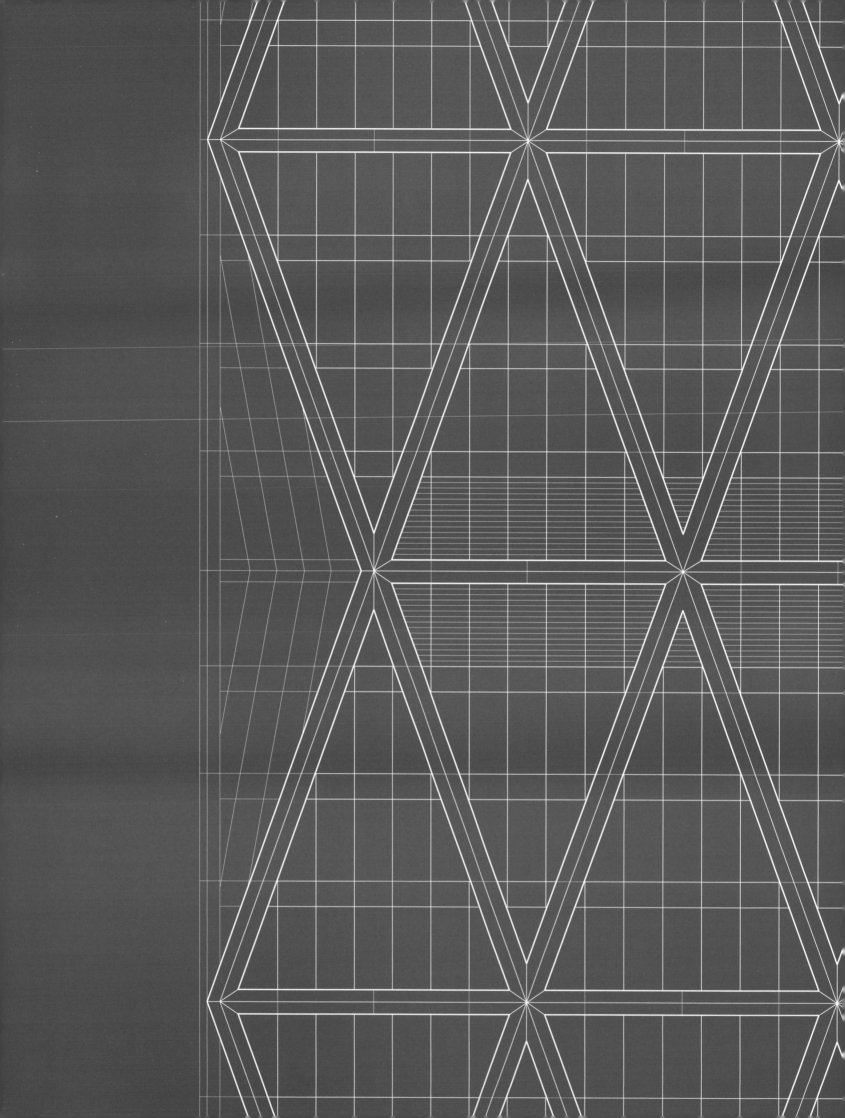

Hearst Tower
New York, USA 2000–2006

In the 1920s, when William Randolph Hearst built his Art Deco headquarters on 8th Avenue, he intended that it would one day form the podium for a tower. The challenge in designing such a building at seventy years remove was to establish a dialogue between old and new. The glassy tower rises above the stone base, linked by a skirt of glazing that encourages an impression of it floating weightlessly, and the entire footprint of the old building has become a lobby on the scale of a busy town square. Structurally, the tower has a distinctive diagrid form, a solution that uses 20 per cent less steel than a conventional structure – and 85 per cent of that steel is recycled. The building is also significant in environmental terms – the first Manhattan tower to achieve a gold rating under the US Green Building Council's Leadership in Energy and Environmental Design Program (LEED) A herald perhaps of greener buildings to come in the city.

Norman Foster

Left: William Randolph Hearst (1863-1951) on the cover of *Time* magazine, 15 August 1927. Hearst ran his first newspaper, *The San Francisco Examiner*, while still a student at Harvard. By the 1930s, 'The Chief', as he was known throughout his company, commanded the largest newspaper and magazine business in the world. Twice elected to the US House of Representatives, his life story was a source of inspiration for the lead character in Orson Welles' classic film, *Citizen Kane*.

Right: Hearst realised the symbolic power of architecture and was a noted architectural patron. His extravagant 'castle' at San Simeon, California (1919-1947), was designed by the San Francisco architect Julia Morgan, who also designed the Los Angeles Examiner building for Hearst.

1

Previous pages: Hearst Tower seen from the corner of 8th Avenue and 57th Street.

1. Commissioned by publishing magnate William Randolph Hearst and designed by Joseph Urban, the International Magazine Building was completed in 1928. It was designated an 'important monument in the architectural heritage of New York' by the New York City Landmarks Preservation Commission in 1988.

2. Five stages in the development of the project: the Joseph Urban building of 1928; George B Post & Sons' unrealised tower of 1946; the new tower placed directly above the base; introducing the separation between old and new; and the creation of the 'piazza'.

New York, like nature, abhors a vacuum. For all the grandeur of its skyline, there are very few great public rooms in Manhattan. The city so defined by verticality remains, inside all those towers, spatially horizontal, organised in section like stacks of pancakes. That is because all the main forces that typically drive the building ecosystem – real estate maximisation, design assumptions, architectural typologies, construction convention, engineering practice and banking expectations – conspire to restrict if not eliminate their existence. There are, occasionally, buildings that vary the pancake stack enough to accommodate atria in their upper reaches, but such spaces are few and only rarely rooted in the building's fundamental concept. In this respect, as in many others, the Hearst Tower is an exception.

Walk past the original building's meticulously restored facade between 56th and 57th Streets, and through the lobby at 959 8th Avenue, and a bank of escalators rises through sheets of cascading water to deliver you into a cavernous, six-storey volume beneath the new tower. It is a revelation of space, light and openness.

The original Hearst building, at the base of the tower, which occupies half a Manhattan block, masks the 3,600-square-metre lobby space on the third floor. So for the first-time visitor its expansive presence at the top of the escalators comes as a complete surprise. V-shaped super columns at the corners and edges hold the tower 21 metres above the floor, which is otherwise free-span and column free. The lift core serving this generous space lies off centre, toward the western end of the building. For New Yorkers used to feeling spatially compressed inside towers as they pass from the lobby into lifts through corridors to their offices, the space is a major event, and an unexpected gift, in a city where majesty of space seems to be losing the battle against the bottom line.

When the corporation decided to consolidate its New York operations under one roof, Hearst's vision of a tower above the building was resurrected.

The origins of this space can be traced back many years. The existing structure, grandly called the International Magazine Building, was commissioned by the media baron William Randolph Hearst who, by the late 1920s, had long put architecture to use to manifest his journalistic empire. Newspapers were local institutions, and Hearst appreciated how architecture could shape the perception of the newspapers in the communities they served, reinforcing their status and credibility.

For a publisher whose enterprises thrived on declamatory headlines, architecture was rhetoric made permanent. In California, he commissioned Julia Morgan – who also designed his eclectic estate at San Simeon – to create the Los Angeles Examiner building, where the tiled dome and reaching arms still bear impressive witness to the power of a newspaper that no longer exists.

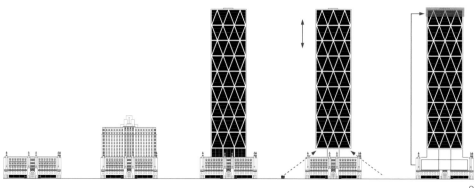

2

3   4   5   6

For Hearst, who saw the International Magazine Building as the company's spiritual home, the building was the flagship structure in his empire. Hearst was always at the cutting edge of journalistic expansion, and with the emergence of national magazines early in the century, he wanted to build in Manhattan a structure that would not only house his growing stable of titles – he owned twelve magazines at the time – but also advertise their collective presence and the momentum of his journalistic power.

A theatrical personality know to his colleagues as 'The Chief' (memorably portrayed by Orson Welles in *Citizen Kane*), Hearst commissioned the expatriate Austrian architect and set designer Joseph Urban to design the new headquarters building in collaboration with George B Post & Sons. Urban, who was art director of Hearst's film-making studio, had remodelled the Criterion and Cosmopolitan theatres for Hearst, and designed the Ziegfeld Theatre, which Hearst financed. Post had significant experience designing office towers. Hearst cabled Urban that he wanted a building of 'conspicuous architectural character'.

The structure that resulted from their collaboration was a six-storey Art Deco building, U-shaped in plan, that was envisaged as the base of a nine-storey office tower to be built in a second phase. The base was an office block traditional in its massing and eclectic in its surface decoration.

Allegorical figures representing music, commerce, art and industry sat atop pylons set around the centre and corner entrances. The base was organised so that the tower would be fitted in place at a later date, with building systems, such as vertical circulation, already aligned in the base structure, simply awaiting extension into the upper reaches.

From the early years of the twentieth century, Hearst had acquired several large parcels of land around 57th Street and 8th Avenue, near Columbus Circle, anticipating that the area would become an extension of the city's burgeoning theatre district. He secured the site for the International Magazine Building in 1921. Its location meant that the new building would form a pivot between the theatre district and the site of the nearby Metropolitan Opera House, for which Joseph Urban was also preparing designs at the time. It would be another important element in a swathe of the city devoted to the arts and entertainment.

3-6. The design team explored many different massing options for the tower, some of which are shown here. The tower had to conform to a strictly enforced Manhattan zoning envelope and sit comfortably above the Art Deco base building.

7. An early concept sketch exploring the relationship between the Hearst Tower and The Sheffield apartment building (to the left). Moving the lift core to the western edge of the tower, abutting the blind wall of The Sheffield, had the effect of opening up the office floors and allowing uninterrupted views from window wall to window wall.

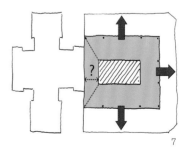

7

I know the tower doesn't have a conventional flourish on top. But the building is unconventional in many ways – and for that I make no apology.
Norman Foster, in conversation with the editor, 2012
Far left: David Nelson and Brandon Haw in an impromptu design crit.
Centre: Modelmaker Damien Flallo puts the finishing touches to a cladding study used to examine the intersection of beams and location of floor plates.
Left: Mark Henderson and Gareth Verbiest analyse CAD data relating to the 1:200 presentation model under construction.

In these sketches, Norman Foster begins to explore the relationship between the base of the new tower and the existing Hearst building and alternative treatments for the top of the tower.

We were originally scheduled to present the design on the morning of 9/11. By coincidence, Frank Bennack, the chairman of Hearst, and I were staying in the same hotel and we bumped into each other over breakfast. We exchanged pleasantries and said we'd see each other later. But, of course, other events unfolded. When we finally came to present the scheme around three weeks later the mood in the room was both positive and defiant. There was a sense that this sort of event shouldn't make things stop and that life must go on. Brandon Haw, of Foster + Partners, in conversation with the editor, 2011
Left: Brandon Haw and Norman Foster present the final schematic design to the Hearst design board.

After 9/11 Hearst had to reassure its employees that moving to a high-rise building was a safe option. Both Frank Bennack and Victor Ganzi made a point of talking to every one of their 2,000 employees to explain why they were keeping the tower scheme and to detail what measures had been taken to enhance the structure's security. Michael Wurzel, of Foster + Partners, in conversation with the editor, 2011

When planning began in 2000, the consensus held that sustainable design is priced out of Manhattan, but the Hearst team's discoveries (if early measurements and projections are realistic) refute that assumption and set a proof-of-concept precedent. Efficiencies over the building's life cycle will more than offset initial 'green premium' costs, establishing a business incentive to choose greener features, at least for buildings with long-term owner occupancy. Bill Millard, *Icon*, May 2006

As the project progressed, Norman was instrumental in us getting the Gold LEED rating. He persuaded us it that it was an important thing to pursue. We had always wanted the best for the city and our employees but I don't think we had understood the full significance of sustainability. Norman helped us to see that. Frank A Bennack Jr, Hearst Corporation Vice Chairman and CEO, in conversation with the editor, 2011

1. The roof collects 25 per cent of rainwater, which is used to irrigate landscaping and in *Icefall* in the lobby.

2. Summer cooling. Warm air is drawn in at plant level, cooled and distributed via a heat exchanger to all office floors. The lobby is primarily cooled by the radiant floor, which absorbs heat gain from solar exposure. Further cooling is provided by spilled air from the offices and by *Icefall*. Solar radiation is reduced by the high-performance glazing.

3. Winter heating. Cool air is taken in at plant level and is dehumidified and cleaned before passing through a heat exchanger. Warmed air is distributed to office floors through ceiling supply ducts, which also extract used air. At lobby level, the radiant floor system provides heating while *Icefall* humidifies the air.

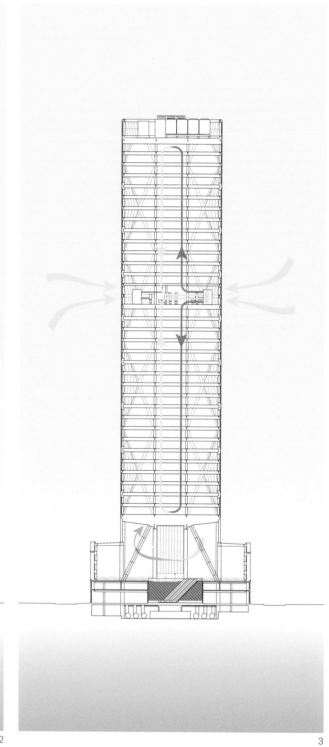

1

2

3

Hearst is both a product for a corporate client and a broader experiment attempting to confront global ecological problems through design. The tension between these identities helps generate its interest and its influence Bill Millard, *Icon*, May 2006

The design avoids the two most obvious approaches: imitating the design of the base or erecting a neutral glass box. Joseph Urban's goal in the original Hearst building was to create a respectable form of flamboyance, and Foster has figured out how to do the same thing with his tower, but in unquestionably modern terms, and without compromising his commitment to structural innovation. Paul Goldberger, *The New Yorker*, 19 December 2005

When we presented the diagrid system to the client Norman did a fantastic demonstration using the Bucky Fuller principles of how a triangle is stronger than a rectangle. We also argued that it would become a classic silhouette in Manhattan because although it wasn't the tallest building the diagrid would signal its uniqueness. Brandon Haw, of Foster + Partners, in conversation with the editor, 2011

4

4. An early 1:200-scale presentation model of the final scheme.

5, 6. Diagrams illustrating alternative structural treatments: diagrid versus post and beam. The inherent efficiency of the diagrid system means that the building uses only 8,453 tonnes of steel, as against 10,756 tonnes to achieve the same area using a conventional frame.

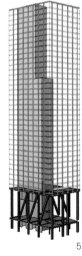

5

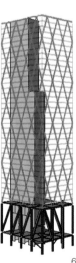

6

I remember standing with Norman across the street from the building for the first time and thinking: how do you put an office tower on top of that? But gradually, like all the best projects, through careful analysis and the unpicking of various strands of thought it started to dawn on us that the base of the building was no longer useful. The first two levels were good for retail but the four above, with their low ceiling heights and deep plan, were not ideal for office space. So we began to formulate the idea of creating a more collegiate space at the base of the tower. Brandon Haw, of Foster + Partners, in conversation with the editor, 2011
Right: Brandon Haw with a model of the Hearst atrium.

We seized the opportunity to create a generous lobby space by using the entire four-storey volume of the Urban building and moving the offices to the upper floors. The concept was to create an 'urban room' – a piazza that mediates between the private spaces of the building and the public realm of the city. There is the impression of being in a bustling town square rather than a conventional office lobby. Norman Foster, in conversation with the editor, 2012

1-3. In this early model, built to study the base of the tower and the arrangement of the lobby, the escalators rise from entrance level through an oval cut in the lobby floor. This was later changed to a rectangular cut, with the escalators rising diagonally. The V-shaped super columns carry the tower 21 metres above the lobby floor.

1

2

3

Hearst's instincts proved prescient. The 'media mile' he predicted was finally consolidated with the construction of the Time Warner Center at Columbus Circle, and the Hearst Tower is now the keystone he intended in that cultural arch through the city.

Designed during 1926-1927, the International Magazine Building was completed in 1928, but the Depression cut short ambitions for the tower. Still, the Hearst Corporation maintained the right to build a tower and Post returned to make proposals in 1945-1947 and file plans for a scheme, which was not built. (There are no drawings extant of the first tower, and no proof in fact that it was ever designed.)

Throughout the following decades, the Hearst Corporation continued to expand and diversify. By 2000, some 1,800 employees were scattered in nine office buildings in the area. The company owned some of the properties, and rented others. When the corporation decided to consolidate its New York operations under one roof, Hearst's vision of a tower above the Hearst building was resurrected. The new tower would be an expression of a newly invigorated phase in the corporation's development as it headed into the twenty-first century – architecture could do once more what it had done for Hearst before.

However, by that time the International Magazine Building was designated as an 'important monument in the architectural heritage of New York' and the preservation laws in the city, put in place after the demolition of Penn Station, were highly protective. The issue of adding to a historic monument was obviously sensitive, and required approval by the Landmarks Preservation Commission. According to New York preservation standards, a new structure in this context should express its own time yet respect and strengthen the original historic building, although any intervention should also be 'appropriate' to the original.

The lobby is a major event, and an unexpected gift, in a city where majesty of space seems to be losing the battle against the bottom line.

Interestingly, the notion of 'appropriateness', a highly subjective issue, has stalled or defeated many proposals in the fiercely contested space of Manhattan, where New Yorkers are famously territorial, and resistant to change. Hearst was advised to search for an architect who could think outside conventional New York practice.

We brought all our people together from diverse places around the city. In New York, two blocks away can be a massive chasm as deep as the Grand Canyon … people tend to stay where their offices are. The new building created a wonderful interchange and an aggregation of people. The café and atrium created a wonderful space where people meet and have lunch – and it is very popular. As well as that, the people who work for Hearst are extremely proud of their building. Victor Ganzi, former Hearst President and CEO, in conversation with the editor, 2011

Hearst Tower is premised on a core Modernist principle: a faith that architectural innovation can catalyse broader social improvements. Even if its fusion of a sleekly faceted tower with an Art Deco-ish base suggests a postmodern hybrid, its programme and philosophy are unapologetically Modernist; it is spearheading an effort to reanimate Modernism under the rubric of sustainable design. The critical difference is that this isn't an optimist's futurism, eyes lifted towards Utopia. It's a futurism for staving off dystopia, a green Neomodernism for the infinite emergency dead ahead. Bill Millard, *Icon*, May 2006

The interventions which we made with the Great Court at the British Museum and the Reichstag – while obviously significant – were relatively small when considered in relation to the scale of the existing fabric. Conversely, the Hearst tower forms by far the largest part of the complete structure. Therefore, the interesting question became: how can one still respect a historic structure when adding a volume whose scale effectively renders it subordinate? Michael Wurzel, of Foster + Partners, in conversation with the editor, 2011

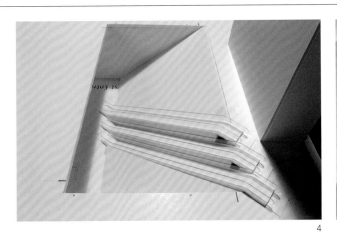

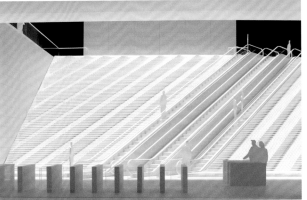

4-5. Two of the many sketch models made by the design team to explore the diagonal configuration of the escalators leading up to the lobby. The model on the right shows an early incarnation of *Icefall*.

6. Perspective section showing the entrance sequence from 8th Avenue. The International Magazine Building's original vaulted entrance hall has been maintained. From there visitors and staff ascend to lobby level via banks of escalators.

4

5

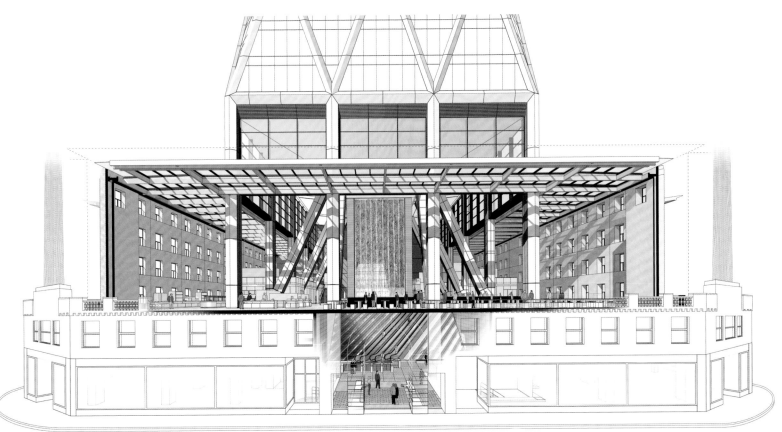

6

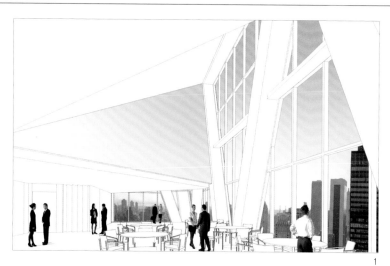

1-2. Perspective studies of a double-height executive area and a corner editorial office on the upper levels of the tower, with the view across New York as a backdrop.

Hearst approached Foster + Partners because of the practice's considerable experience of making sympathetic interventions within historic structures. In the Reichstag in Berlin, for example, Foster renovated the historic shell and incorporated a glass dome that has become a major landmark in the city. In London, the practice created the Great Court at the British Museum, throwing a carapace of glass over an outdoor space to create an elegant atrium. But beyond the architects' successes at operating with almost surgical precision on historic buildings, the Foster team had cultivated specialties that would serve the Hearst project well.

Structure has emerged in Foster's practice not just as a metaphor for architectural order, but also as a salient feature of his systems-oriented designs. Rather than assuming conventional structural systems, Foster frequently reinvents them, and in association with other innovations, such as removing lift cores from central positions in the plan, innovative structural engineering has in his hands proved spatially liberating.

In the Hongkong and Shanghai Bank Headquarters, for example, Foster built a bridge-like structure, with trusses spanning between the corner towers. By doing so, he was able to open up the ground level as a sheltered piazza and create a soaring atrium and double-height floors within the building itself. The structure cracked open a section that would otherwise have been tightly closed, allowing space and light to flow freely through the building.

It is hard to overestimate the importance of the Hongkong Bank in the history of high-rise design. Foster's tutor at Yale, Paul Rudolph, was interested in porous sections, and Rudolph himself was influenced by the spatial porosity of sections designed by Frank Lloyd Wright – for example, at the Larkin Building in Buffalo. But Rudolph basically sculpted interior space, and Wright used conventional structure. For Foster, structure has been the enabling instrument that opens form to volume.

Foster has never taken established typologies as fixes; instead he likes to look at a problem from first principles.

In subsequent commissions, with different programmes in different climates and cultural circumstances, Foster pursued the idea of carving out significant interior spaces, and the porous sections became increasingly open, taking on an environmental role. The Commerzbank in Frankfurt, for example, has garden atria within a structure triangulated around a light-well that runs through the full height of the tower. The gardens provide the key to the building's natural ventilation system as well as forming social foci for groups of office floors – places to stop for a coffee or meet during breaks in the daily routine.

One of the defining characteristics of Foster's design method is the way the team develops a scheme through a systematic analysis of the problem. They do not approach a project with a priori solutions and geometries, but try to understand the commission in terms that will define its own design trajectory. The necessity of keeping the historic structure played a major role in determining the Hearst design, but it was but one factor in a larger physical and commercial system of interrelated concerns.

The historical outer wall, which the architects were required to preserve, was the first of several issues to be resolved. Compositionally, it was determined that the old Hearst building would act as a 'plinth' to the tower on top – as originally envisaged by Urban and Post. However, the existing U-shaped building was configured around an offset courtyard whose fourth side was formed by the service core of an adjacent residential tower, the Sheffield Building. Thus the six-storey plinth threatened to overwhelm the lower storeys of a tower planted in the hollow of the 'U', severely restricting daylight penetration. On the other hand, had the lower floors been reconfigured to fill in the courtyard, the resulting floor plates would have had an impracticable depth ratio from window to core.

There was a further complication. The usual assumption of a tower is that it is four-sided, with perimeters open to the view on all sides in a pattern of rising desirability: the higher the floor, the longer the view, the greater the prestige. However, the Sheffield Building was built to the common north-south property line, and therefore would have blocked the view of any west-facing facade for most of the height of the building.

The solution was to let the Sheffield lift core exert a magnetic pull on the Hearst core. The architects moved the core to the extreme west of the site, in effect laminating it to the Sheffield Building. This displacement had a liberating effect on the eastern part of the tower. The office floors, which no longer had to circle the core, could be completely open from window wall to window wall, giving considerable planning flexibility.

There were further forces acting on the placement of the tower. Because the floor heights of the Art Deco building were unsuited to contemporary office space, and because the lower floors of the tower would lose light if nested within the existing courtyard, the height of the 'plinth' building tended to push the base of the tower up to a height where it would not only clear the top of the plinth, but also float above it. Articulating the plinth and the tower from each other had the potential for creating a very tall, light-filled space within the plinth that could be ringed by clerestory windows.

Separating the old building from the new tower with a horizontal spatial reveal also solved the issue of how to design the transition from the 'heavy' masonry base to the 'light' glass-and-steel superstructure. The two elements represented a change of era and a different attitude to materials and structure. It was therefore a difficult but important transition to resolve.

3. Study model of a typical office floor. The offset core generates a U-shaped floor plate, with a large open area to the east. Glass-walled cellular offices are arranged around the perimeter of each floor, with support areas inboard. Each floor of the tower has a gross area of 20,000 square feet (1,900 square metres) and is typically occupied by a single magazine.

4, 5. Some of the many space-planning models made to show proposals for office layouts.

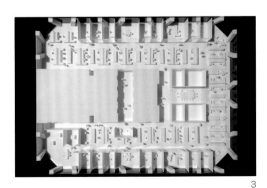

3

4

5

Far left: The New York skyline, looking north across Central Park, c1920. Midtown Manhattan is still occupied by low- to medium-rise buildings, with terraces of brownstones surviving on what would later become the site of the Rockefeller Center. This is the city with which William Randolph Hearst and Joseph Urban would have been familiar.

Left: The corresponding view, c2000; commercial and residential high-rises have marched up from Downtown to stand at the very edge of the park.

1. Site plan. Located just below Columbus Circle in the heart of Midtown Manhattan, Hearst Tower has frontages on to 8th Avenue, 56th Street and 57th Street. Abutting it to the immediate west is The Sheffield, a high-rise apartment building.

2. Plan at Level 41.

3. Plan at Level 40.

4. Plan at lobby level.

5. The Good Housekeeping Institute on Level 28.

6. Typical lower-level office floor plan.

7. Plan at street level.

 1 lobby
 2 subway entrance
 3 retail spaces
 4 stairs to exhibition space
 5 Café 57
 6 servery
 7 kitchen
 8 Joseph Urban
   Auditorium
 9 high-rise lifts
10 low-rise lifts
11 cellular offices
12 open-plan offices
13 meeting room
14 executive suite

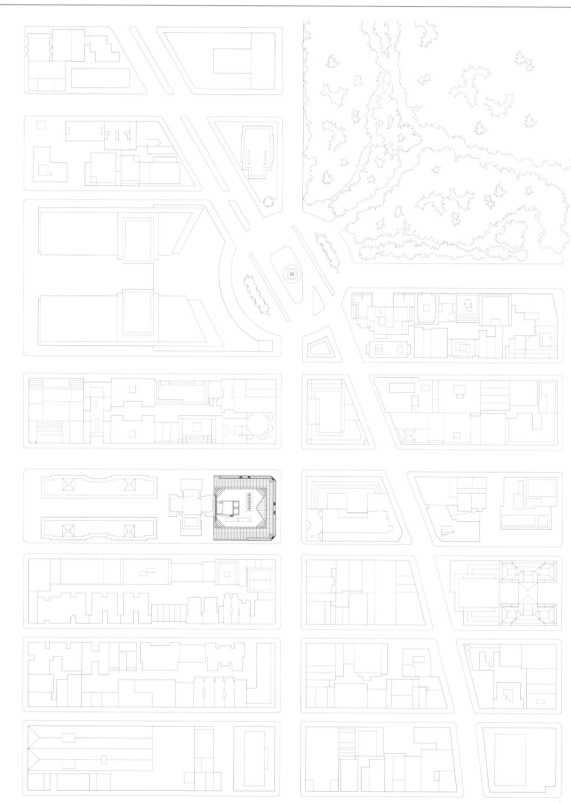

0   100m

0   300ft

1

The enthusiasm for the project was a unique blend. After 9/11 America became very patriotic and focused on Americans getting along with Americans. We built up a very, very good working collaboration with everyone we dealt with. You have to go through the local community board and also city planning … we didn't get one negative vote at any of the agencies. In fact, the head of the community board showed up at city planning and supported the project. She said: 'I'm here to support the Hearst Tower project, and you need to remember – we're not in favour of anything!' Victor Ganzi, former Hearst President and CEO, in conversation with the editor, 2011

We initially had trepidations about whether we could get the project through planning given that there had never been an overbuild to a landmark building in New York City … but it was clear at the first and subsequent meetings that the city authorities were sold on the project; they were behind it and were absolutely of the opinion that it was a great thing for New York. Frank A Bennack Jr, Hearst Corporation Vice Chairman and CEO, in conversation with the editor, 2011

It was testing, it was trying, it was massively time-consuming but building Hearst Tower is an accomplishment I will be proud of for the rest of my life. We built something very special from the user's standpoint, from the viewer's standpoint, and from the architectural standpoint. People have told me they think it's the most significant piece of architecture in New York City since the Seagram Building in 1958. Victor Ganzi, former Hearst President and CEO, in conversation with the editor, 2011

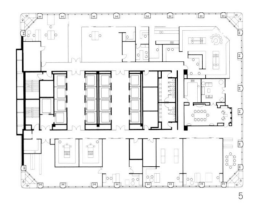

Overleaf: Cutaway drawing. The tower rises above the shell of the original International Magazine Building, held aloft by a series of V-shaped super columns. From the entrance hall on 8th Avenue escalators rise to the four-storey-high sky-lit lobby which occupies the entire footprint of the old building. Within, or accessed from this space are the staff restaurant – Café 57 – an exhibition space and auditorium. The glass roof above the lobby spans between the tower and the external walls of the old building. Within the tower, each floor typically houses a single magazine or publication. One exception is the Good Housekeeping Institute, whose specialist facilities are located immediately below the mid-level plant area. The upper three floors contain executive offices, with double-height meeting spaces. Additional plant is located on the roof.

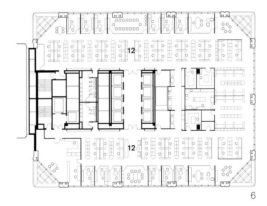

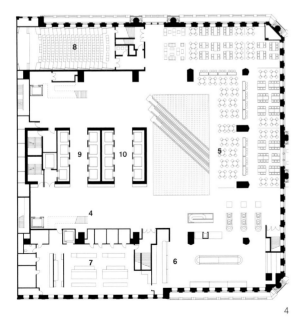

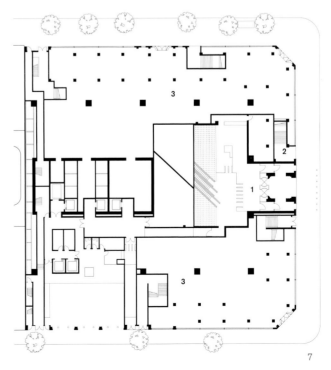

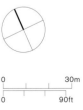

0   30m
0   90ft

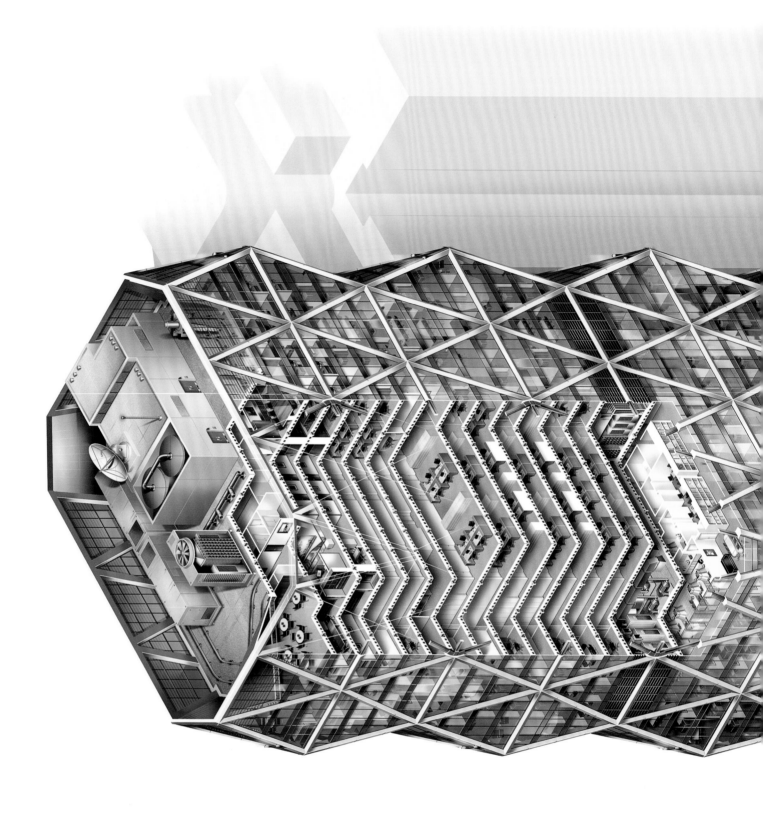

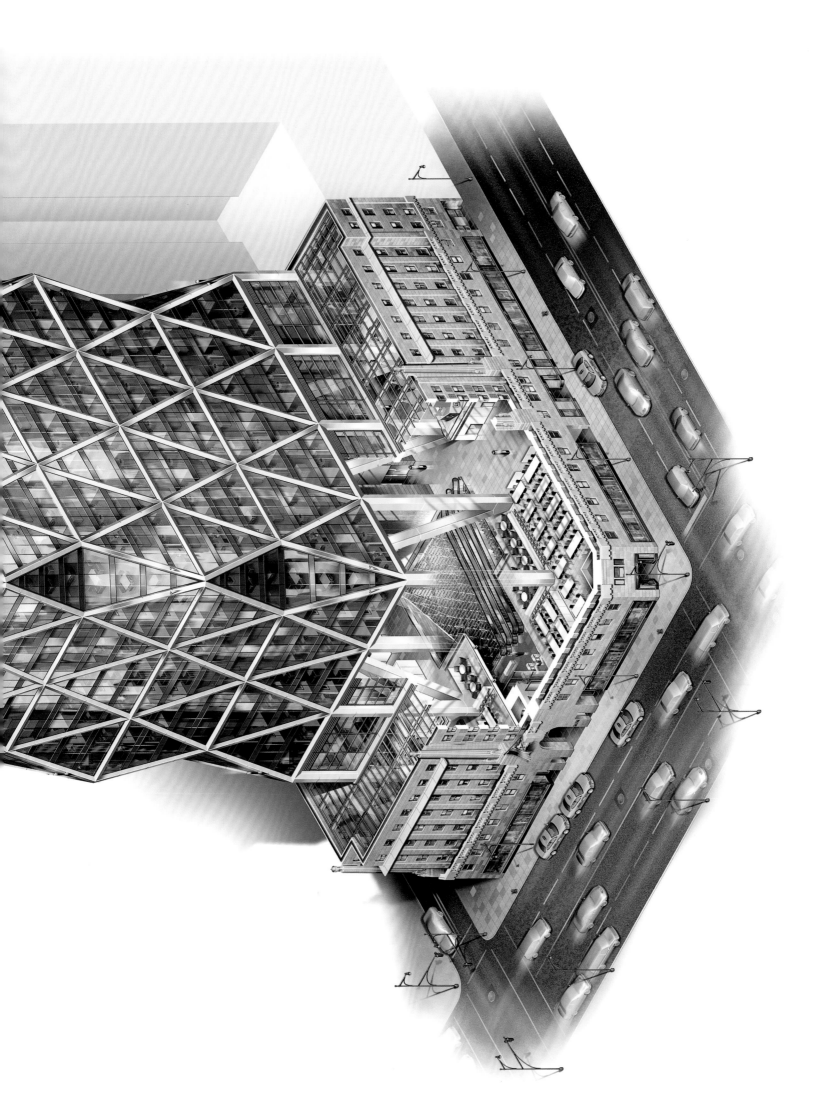

The new Hearst Tower makes a bold statement, not only in terms of its sophisticated and dynamic design, but also in the confidence it expresses in our city. In moving forward with this project so shortly after 9/11, Hearst sent a message to the world that the business community remains committed to and positive about New York City's future prosperity. Jerry I Speyer, President and CEO of Tishman Speyer Properties, speaking at the groundbreaking ceremony, 30 April 2003

One of New York City's most valuable assets and one of its most defining character traits is its unrivalled intellectual and creative capacity. I believe that is why Hearst is making such a major commitment to the city and why corporations such as Hearst, which is driven by its human assets, are one of the city's greatest selling points. Michael R Bloomberg, Mayor of New York City, speaking at the groundbreaking ceremony, 30 April 2003
Right: Michael R Bloomberg, Norman Foster, Jerry I Speyer, President and CEO of Tishman Speyer Properties, and Victor F Ganzi, President and CEO of the Hearst Corporation break ground for the construction of the Hearst building.

1

1, 2. Construction workers install one of the Y-nodes, which form the connecting pieces within the diagrid structural frame.

3. The profiled stainless-steel frames for the 'bird's mouth' sections were manufactured in Italy and assembled in Montreal, before being transported to the site in separate sections.

4. A section of the 'bird's mouth' framing is hoisted into place.

2

Far left: To mark the placement of the highest steel beam, 597 feet above the six-storey Art Deco base, the building was 'topped out' on 11 February 2005; the ceremony was attended by Norman Foster, Hearst Corporation President and CEO Victor F Ganzi, Vice Chairman Frank Bennack, the Governor of New York State, George E Pataki, and New York City Mayor, Michael R Bloomberg.
Left: Norman Foster joined invited guests and the contractors in signing the final steel beam before it was secured in place.

5

6

3

4

7

5. Only the facade of the old International Magazine Building remains, the rest of the structure was demolished and excavated down to the bedrock. The outer wall is shown here with its temporary supporting structure.

6. Looking down into the lobby space from the lower deck of the tower – corresponding with the tenth floor of the finished building. The V-shaped super columns that support the tower are of steel, filled with concrete for reinforcement.

7. Looking up at the tower as the frame nears completion; the cladding and glazing are progressing in sequence. Structurally, the tower comprises a steel core with a diagonal perimeter system forming four-storey-high triangular frames. Each triangle is 54 feet (16.6 metres) high; and 85 per cent of the steel used is recycled. The diagrid cladding is of profiled stainless steel. The floor-to-floor glazing uses high-performance low-emission glass, which is highly energy efficient.

Initially, the contractors who were hired to erect the steelwork said the diagrid design could not be built. But after we'd sat down with them for a couple of hours and explained thoroughly how it was going to work they got very excited about the job. Ultimately the steel workers were so proud of what they had achieved that they invited their families along to the site one weekend to look at their work. Michael Wurzel, of Foster + Partners, in conversation with the editor, 2010

Only a few diagrid structures have ever been built, so the construction crew didn't really know how to put it together. But one of the interesting things we found was that they loved working on the job because it was different and they got to do something they hadn't done before – it was all very intriguing. Victor Ganzi, former Hearst President and CEO, in conversation with the editor, 2011

Foster animates the tower not just by exposing its triangulated structure – an arrangement that is strong enough to reduce the cost of the steel by 20 per cent compared with a conventional design – but by crumpling the facade, pushing each corner in and out to follow the geometry of the building, giving it a massive, craggy quality very different from the curtain-like nature of most glass towers. But this is not just a convincing piece of sculpture and structural logic: it is equally a piece of contextualism, and of historic preservation, that makes a strong contribution to the vitality of the city. Deyan Sudjic, *The Observer*, 8 January 2006

1   2   3   4

1-8. Construction was rapid: ground was broken on 30 April 2003; the steel frame was topped out on 11 February 2005; the building was finished by March 2006; and staff began to move in during May. On completion it was recognised as the first 'green' commercial building in Manhattan, awarded a Gold LEED rating from the US Green Building Council.

The decision to align the core with that of the Sheffield Building, presented an engineering challenge, because the decentred core could not stabilise the entire tower as it would in a conventional structure. To compensate for the displaced core, the architects needed to devise a structural system that could provide the neccessary bracing on the eastern side of the tower.

Foster + Partners actively pursues research and development programmes through its commissions. This manifests itself in different ways. For example, the diagrid (a conflation of 'diagonal' and 'grid') structure developed for Hearst emerged as a very practical solution because it provides greater strength and greater structural redundancy, using 20 per cent less steel than a conventional post-and-beam structure – a saving of approximately 2,000 tonnes of steel. It could also be deployed as an exoskeleton, thus keeping the interiors relatively free of columns. Additionally, the frame was constructed using 85 per cent recycled steel, which has a considerable impact in terms of the building's embodied energy.

Foster has never taken established building typologies as fixes; instead he likes to look at a problem from first principles, allowing the physical givens of a particular programme or site to suggest a process of inquiry. As Foster says: 'Over time, we've accumulated a body of knowledge and a continued thirst to explore what makes a building – and that has a very strong research component.

'That curiosity extends to every aspect of the building – how it's constructed, how it's assembled, the materials used, the potential those materials might have to adapt to new uses, and so on. It's really a series of parallel explorations in terms of what generates the need for the building and how that building is in turn realised.' The unique characteristics of the site in this case acted as determinants in a process that was, by its physical logic, self-organising if not self-designing. Interestingly, Foster's scheme sailed through the approvals process, aided by the fact that Urban's structure was always intended as the base for a tower (and the fact that there was no record of any of his design intentions).

As with all Foster designs, the Hearst Tower is sleek, refined and filled with new technology. It looks nothing like the Jazz Age confection on which it sits. The addition is sheathed in glass and stainless steel – a shiny missile shooting out of Joseph Urban's stone launching pad. Paul Goldberger, *The New Yorker*, 19 December 2005

The Hearst Tower presents us with a curious paradox. In this work built by a refined British architect in one of the most European of all American cities, it seems we can see something of the spirit that characterised over a century ago the design and constructive practice of the 'Chicago School' a peculiar mixture of barbarism – seen here in the brutal grafting of the new tower on to the existing edifice – and the daring pursuit of a form capable of expressing the character of a tall office building. Marco Mulazzani, *Casabella*, November 2006

5

6

7

8

The architects were encouraged in their open-minded search by the desire of the Hearst Corporation to stake out creative ground on the New York skyline with a tower whose profile would characterise the company itself as progressive and forward thinking, ready to take on a new century. Hearst enjoys great corporate independence, because it is privately held rather than publicly traded, and can therefore venture beyond conventional real-estate wisdom without having to account to shareholders.

The tower that New Yorkers see today is a unique diamond-gridded web whose stainless-steel members form a thirty-four storey structural tube arranged in a diagrid eight tiers high: each tier is composed of sequentially paired triangles four storeys high. Where the grid turns the corners at a 45 degree angle, the structure opens up to form what the architects call a 'bird's mouth' (each corner has four bird's mouths), which together have the effect of creating a change of rhythm at each corner of the tower.

The glazing on the upper half of each bird's mouth leans forwards and that on the lower half inwards. Consequently, floor plates vary, both in the distance across the breadth of the 'mouth', and in the inclination of the glass. Inside, the architects dedicate each corner to a public use, and the corners allow unobstructed, panoramic views that are diagonal to the city, a view that is all the more dramatic in the upper part of the cut, which positions viewers as though they were in the gondola of an airship, or the bubble of a helicopter, looking down.

Individual floors range from 1,580 to 1,860 square metres (17,000 to 20,000 square feet), and each is occupied by a magazine or a corporate department. On the top floor – reserved for meetings and receptions – there is a triple-height space in each corner plus one in the centre, which opens eastwards to offer a sweeping panorama of the city.

Overleaf: North-south cross-section through the lobby and tower, looking west towards the lift core.

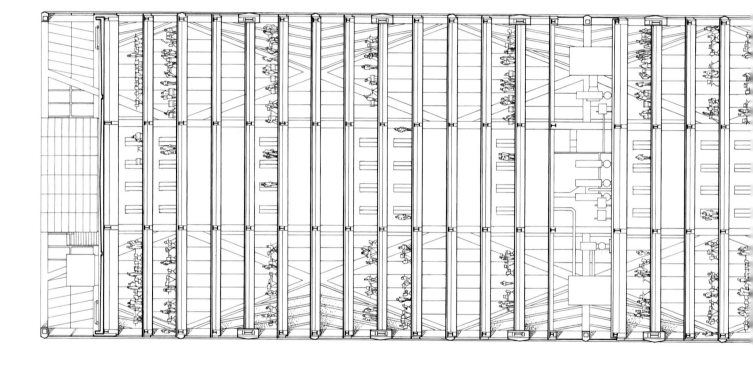

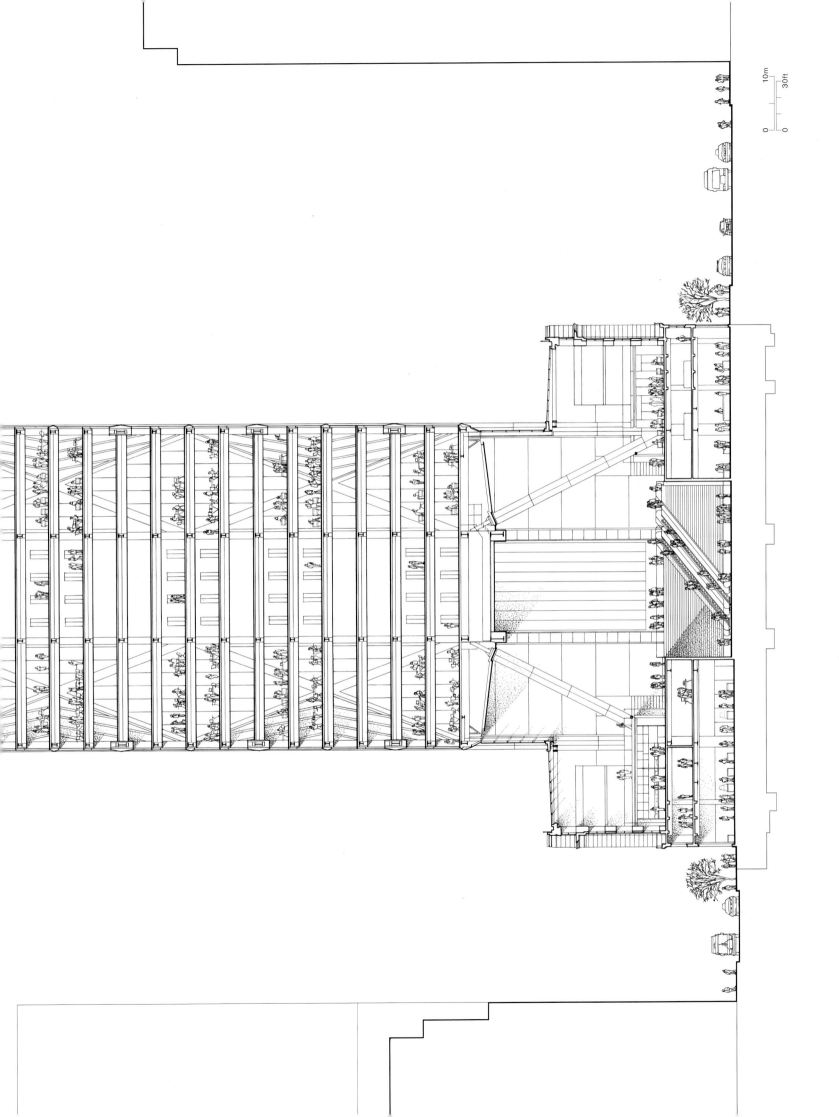

10m
30ft

0
0

In general, my work is about leaving or making my mark, with wide variations of permanence or visibility, like footprints or handprints. In *Riverlines* the raw materials of mud and water are directly mediated by my own hand and energy. Each line is roughly the width of my reach without the mud drying, so I could keep a continuous surface of wet mud as I came down each line, working with the ease of gravity, like a river falls from source to mouth. Richard Long, *Riverlines*, 2006

Right: Richard Long at work on *Riverlines*; although it was many months in the planning, the piece was completed in just three days, from 26 to 28 April 2006.

In a sense, Richard Long has brought nature inside the building. Like a cave painting for the twenty-first century, *Riverlines* is made from mud 'harvested' from the banks of the Avon and Hudson rivers and celebrates the metaphor of the river as a symbol of journey, movement and life. Richard is an artist whose work I admire deeply – it is based in a profound understanding of nature and inspired by natural forms and materials. His 'mud works' convey an incredible sense of physical energy. They are literally 'hands on'. Norman Foster, in conversation with the editor, 2012

Left: Norman Foster, on a site visit to the Hearst lobby, waves to Richard Long.

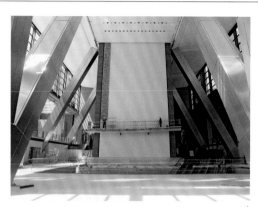

1

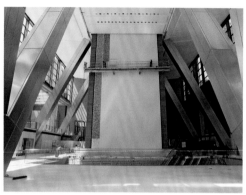

2

3

4

1-7. The artist Richard Long was commissioned to create a site-specific art work for the lobby. The result – *Riverlines* – is made from mud 'harvested' from the Avon and Hudson rivers and is described by the artist as a 'cave painting for the twenty-first century'. The 20-metre high piece was months in the planning, but took Long just three days to complete. It was made entirely by hand. The vertical sections correspond roughly with the width of Long's reach without the mud drying, to allow him to keep a continuous surface of wet mud as he came down each line.

8. Looking north across the lobby. *Riverlines*, seen to the left, is a commanding presence in the space.

The architects evolved the structural design in association with structural engineer Ahmad Rahimian, of the US engineering firm Cantor Seinuk. The tower as a shaft is structurally unique within New York, and while it is by no means the first exoskeletal steel structure, it represents – after Swiss Re – one of the first applications of the diagrid at large scale. (Foster subsequently proposed a similar system for his twin towers in the competition to rebuild the World Trade Center.) The uniqueness of the diagrid translates in New York into an iconic image for Hearst, within a skyline that is highly competitive.

What distinguishes the Hearst Tower is that the iconic quality is not achieved through the crown but the shaft, along its entire length, and even then the shaft is not figural but systematically triangulated and regular. The triangulation, which creates a self-bracing structure, eliminates the need for the diagonal bracing that can often be seen threaded through conventional structural frames. Additionally, the efficiency of the exoskeleton eliminates almost entirely the need for internal columns (there are only two on each floor, required because the displaced lift core lengthened the open floor plates significantly in the east-west direction).

Another significant strand in the development of the building is that it was one of the first in the United States to integrate energy efficient design and concerns about sustainability in a large-scale environment. As a company, Hearst places a high value on the concept of a healthy workplace – a factor that it believes will become increasingly important to its staff in the future. Indeed, Hearst's experience with the green building process may herald the more widespread construction of environmentally sensitive buildings in the city.

The Hearst Tower lobby is an interior urbanism on a daring scale.

Hearst Tower has been designed to use 25 per cent less energy than it would had it minimally complied with the respective state and city energy codes. This has earned it a gold certification under the US Green Building Council's Leadership in Energy and Environmental Design (LEED). It was the first occupied building in New York to receive this certification and it reinforces Foster's observation that it is owner-occupiers – of the likes of Willis Faber, the Hongkong and Shanghai Bank and the Commerzbank – who can be relied upon to pioneer innovation, often setting new standards that will later be adopted by the market.

We worked with glass specialist Jamie Carpenter and Jim Garland of Fluidity in the creation of *Icefall*. The escalators from the lobby rise diagonally through a cascade of chilled water, which plays a significant environmental role, reusing collected rainwater to cool the atrium in summer and humidify the space in winter. Jamie Carpenter devised a system of cast-glass prisms that capture and refract light. They make the water sparkle with sunlight, just as it would in nature. Norman Foster, in conversation with the editor, 2012

In summertime, you walk into the building and the moment you get close to the waterfall you have the calming influence of the sound of water falling down a slope. Plus you have the cooling effect it gives. So as soon as you come in you get away from the hustle and bustle of the street and into a more relaxed, more refined atmosphere. Victor Ganzi, former Hearst President and CEO, in conversation with the editor, 2011

The pleasure of the Hearst Tower doesn't end with the exterior. It has one of the most dramatic entrances of any tower in New York. You go in through Urban's original arch – which along with the rest of the base's exterior, has been meticulously restored – and up a set of escalators. What comes next is an explosive surprise such has not been seen in the city since Frank Lloyd Wright led people through a low, tight lobby into the rotunda of the Guggenheim. Paul Goldberger, *The New Yorker*, 19 December 2005

5

6

7

8

Previous pages: Escalators rise diagonally across a two-storey cascade of chilled water, *Icefall*, designed by glass specialist Jamie Carpenter and water designer Jim Garland. The water plays an environmental role, reusing collected rainwater to cool the atrium in summer and humidify the space in winter.

1. Looking down towards the street entrance from the mezzanine level in the lobby.

2. The self-service food-counter in the staff restaurant, Café 57.

3-4. The Joseph Urban Auditorium, located in the lobby, can be used as a cinema or as a venue for lectures and talks.

This effort required not only intelligent structural and environmental engineering but the introduction of high-performance materials and integrated systems that achieve a very high degree of operational efficiency. For example, the tower's glazing incorporates a low-emissivity glass that allows the offices to be flooded with light while blocking solar radiation; sensors on each floor control artificial lighting levels, and switch off lights when a room is vacant; and the building's heating and air-conditioning equipment utilises outside air for cooling and ventilation for approximately 75 per cent of the year, a move that not only saves energy but improves air quality considerably.

The reduction in electrical energy use that these systems bring is estimated at 2 million kWh, which will save 900 tonnes of carbon dioxide annually – the equivalent, the engineers say, of taking 180 cars off New York's streets.

Efforts are also made to conserve water. The roof harvests rainfall, which is stored in basement reclamation tanks. This 'grey' water replaces water lost to evaporation in the air-conditioning systems and irrigates planting inside and outside the building, and supplies the water feature in the lobby. The lay audience may not understand and appreciate the building's environmental science or engineering per se, but the tower's daring structure piques curiosity, and an involvement with its architecture through questioning. Looking up, you have to ask yourself: 'if corners stabilise a structure, how does a building without corners stand?'

At ground level, the perception is more settled. Foster affirms the traditional New York urbanism by restoring the existing perimeter wall and maintaining its intimate relationship with the street. The old arched entrance and lobby to the Hearst building remains where it always was, on 8th Avenue, and shops occupy the rest of the street frontage. The architects kept only the facade of the old structure, one bay in and two storeys tall for retail, with the remainder of the floor plate dedicated to back-of-house services. The third through to the sixth floors have been removed, and the perimeter wall, stuccoed on the inside, now defines a new space starting on the third floor, which forms the building's lobby.

For Foster, structure has been the enabling instrument that opens form to volume.

The steel frame that originally supported the six-storey building has been entirely removed, except for a bay that stabilises the limestone facade. By cutting a new subway entrance through the building and otherwise improving the subway station itself, Hearst earned the right to add an additional six floors to the tower.

The Hearst lobby is an interior urbanism of a daring scale. A building with 79,500 square metres in forty-four storeys houses roughly 2,000 people – the equivalent of a small town – all of whom have business in common. New York skyscrapers are notorious for isolating workers within lift cars, in corridors and in cubicles. With Hearst, in contrast, by separating the tower from the base, Foster creates a huge volume of 'found' space that he dedicates to public use in order to socialise the building. It is the equivalent of a campus quad, or watering hole, or as Foster says, 'a town square', an urban room designed to encourage a sense of identity and community.

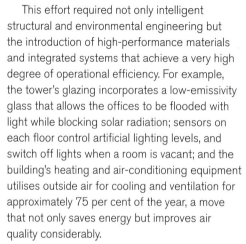

Our managers contend that in the new building our people arrive earlier, stay later and dress better – that's a great combination. There's huge pride involved and the staff see it as a great symbol for the company. Frank A Bennack Jr, Hearst Corporation Vice Chairman and CEO, in conversation with the editor, 2011

Right: On 9 October 2006, Hearst celebrated the opening of the building with a grand gala party, which culminated in acrobatic displays and a guest performance by Stevie Wonder.

The Hearst Tower scored decisive points because it is more than a refinement of an existing type. It is really a prototype. Michaela Busenkell, curator at the Deutsches Architekturmuseum, describing the conclusions of the jury for the 2008 International Highrise Award, which was won by Hearst Tower, *Architectural Record*, November 2008

6

5. The view up through the glass skirt that occupies the space between the old building and the tower and forms the roof of the lobby.

6. The space is conceived as an 'urban room' – a piazza that mediates between the private spaces in the building and the public realm of the city. There is the impression of being in a bustling town square rather than a conventional office lobby. The walls are finished in stucco that reflects, in tone and colour, the cast stone of the facade.

5

I visited the building on a May afternoon, just as the first 'Hearsties' were moving in. A storm front came in just as we reached the top, and I felt like Zeus. Water poured on to the roof shelves of the atrium. It seemed as though we were on a ship in a storm and I felt like Ahab – or would it be Andrea Doria. It was thrilling. Joseph Giovannini, in conversation with the editor, 2011

When we first showed the client the corner offices they had two questions: how do you clean the glass, and how do the blinds work? While we were able to outline a solution straight away it took a long time to resolve fully because of the complex geometry involved. The system of blinds turned out to be far more intricate than the glazing because they needed to go up like sails due to the angles involved. Likewise, the cleaning boom needed to be capable of getting into the corners rather than being a standard system which just drops down, the end result is a system which is as intricate as that used on Swiss Re. Michael Wurzel, of Foster + Partners, in conversation with the editor, 2011

Despite the Hearst Corporation being a very traditional company with a long history, they were keen to embrace new ways of working. They wanted a series of spaces that could function flexibly. For these we came up with a ceiling system, a wall system and an office pod system which were all relatively simple so that the different magazines could each stamp their own personality on it. We were trying to cater for everything from *Cosmopolitan* to *Popular Mechanics* so it was important to come up with a simple kit of parts. Mike Jelliffe, of Foster + Partners, in conversation with the editor, 2011

1

2

3

4

1-4. The Good Housekeeping Research Institute on the twenty-eighth floor provides state-of-the-art kitchen and food preparation spaces, together with archive and product display areas.

5. Editorial meeting spaces are located in the corners of each floor – in the 'bird's mouths'.

6. An editorial conference taking place in one of the glass-walled offices.

5

6

We worked with Hearst to achieve a building that not only consumes far less energy than a conventional tower, but also provides a light-filled and naturally ventilated working environment for all.

Norman Foster

I spent seven years working on Hearst Tower, from the first pencil sketch in London, to seeing the project through on site, to now working in the building. Foster + Partners is the only non-Hearst entity to have office space in the tower, which is testament to the great relationship we've built up with the client over the years. It is a very special experience for an architect to get to know a building post-construction and really understand how it works. Michael Wurzel, of Foster + Partners, in conversation with the editor, 2011
Right: Norman Foster and Spencer de Grey in discussion with the team in Foster + Partners' New York studio, located on Level 26 of Hearst Tower.

Almost five years after 9/11, skyscrapers are popping up all over Manhattan. Emerging business realities have trumped terror-attack risk. Managers have learned that putting together an enormous range of human talent is more valuable than ever in a globally connected workplace. By tuning its tower to the collaborative workplace norms of the future, Hearst sets the bar compellingly higher. James S Russell, *Bloomberg*, 6 July 2006

7

8

9

In designing this space, the architects have taken great care to create an environment where people meet casually, linger, chat, and perhaps transact a little business. The lobby contains the Joseph Urban Auditorium and the building's primary restaurant, Café 57, so that it acts as a powerful social magnet. The space is also configured so that it forms an essential part of the route into the building, through which people disembarking from the escalators walk to the lift banks that will take them to the upper floors.

Sitting in the cafeteria, employees look up through the perimeter skylights and see the exterior of the tower on one side and the wall of the original building by Urban on the other. At night, the clerestory windows are lit, creating a band of light on which the tower seems magically to rest. Illuminated from within at night, the tower, with its basket weave, looks like a lantern.

The lobby is also the scene of two significant collaborations with artists. The first of these, with the glass specialist Jamie Carpenter and Jim Garland of Fluidity, has resulted in the creation of *Icefall*. The escalators rise diagonally between a three-storey cascade of water, which plays over a series of cast-glass prisms that capture and refract light. 'The water sparkles with sunlight, just as it would in nature', says Foster. *Icefall* also has an environmental function, circulating harvested water to humidify the atrium in winter and cool it in summer.

Reaching the top of the escalator visitors are confronted with a second work – Richard Long's *Riverlines* – a tall mural set against the grey stone of the elevator core. Long brings nature inside the building in another sense. Like 'a cave painting for the twenty-first century', it is made from mud 'harvested' from the banks of the Avon and Hudson rivers and celebrates the metaphor of the river as a symbol of journey, movement and life.

Impressive as these two pieces are, by far the most striking feature of the space is the volume itself. It is the latest in a long line of social spaces that Foster has conceived in tall office buildings, from the Hongkong Bank and the Commerzbank to Swiss Re. In each case he rejects the notion of collecting workers at the same address only to disperse them within the isolating layers of the usual pancake office floors. Surely, he argues, that defeats the potential of creating a community of co-workers, and developing the networking and synergies possible across a large corporation.

With Hearst Tower, Foster has designed a plan and section that gather people under the same roof in the same space: this is an arena of collaboration, and perhaps the best argument against balkanising workers in home offices linked by the computer. Hearst's corporate agora is designed to make the experience of the city and the office simultaneously far more liveable, enjoyable and productive.

Joseph Giovannini

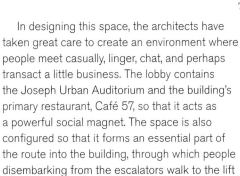

7. Looking into the offices of *Seventeen* magazine.

8. An executive office on the forty-second floor; each person was encouraged to choose his or her own furnishings.

9. A double-height executive break-out space on the forty-second floor.

The best work of corporate architecture to grace New York in decades, Norman Foster's Hearst Tower negotiates deftly between its crystalline exoskeleton and the fanciful 1928 base by Joseph Urban. Turns out one era's version of modernity can always talk to another's. Justin Davidson, *New York Magazine*, 7 September 2008

The Hearst tower is the most beautiful skyscraper to go up in New York since 1967, when Skidmore, Owings & Merrill completed the stunningly serene 140 Broadway in lower Manhattan. After all the inchoate, collage-like skyscrapers that have been built around Times Square in the past decade, it's refreshing to see a tall building that clearly emerges from rational thought. Paul Goldberger, *The New Yorker*, 19 December 2005

The tower's presence on the skyline is magnificent. The triangular forms of the diagrid provide an interesting pattern, the angled stainless steel columns give it a delicate sense of depth, and the corners with indented triangular wedges enhance its sculptural form and relate to the chamfered corners on the base building below. Jayne Merkel, *Architectural Design*, 1 September 2007

1

1, 2. Old and new combined. The original building, by Joseph Urban, is in an eclectic mixture of styles, combining elements of Classicism with Art Deco themes of the day. The facade incorporates allegorical figures representing music, art, commerce and industry.

3, 4. The tower glimpsed on 8th Avenue and from Central Park. It has become an instantly recognisable landmark in the city.

5. A detail of the facade; each triangle in the diagrid is four storeys high and measures 54 feet (16.6 metres).

Overleaf: Looking north up 8th Avenue towards Central Park; The Sheffield apartment building abuts the Hearst Tower immediately to the west; SOM's Time Warner building is just visible to the north.

2

It's a small skyscraper by Manhattan standards, just forty-four storeys. But it peeps out on to Eighth Avenue between 56th and 57th Streets, pale, silvery, white, confident with its distinctive bevelled corners, but not belligerently so. It's gentlemanly, courteous. **An Englishman in New York.** Tom Dyckhoff, *The Times*, 4 January 2006

Architecture is so important to the life of cities and participating in this project has been a pleasure for me … and in the case of Hearst it's made us a better company. It has made us better known in a city that we've been in for over 100 years – in a way that wouldn't have happened if our people were all over town as they once were. Frank A Bennack Jr, Hearst Corporation Vice Chairman and CEO, in conversation with the editor, 2011

Foster started off with a box, then sliced off the corners and ran triangles up and down the sides, pulling them in and out – a gargantuan exercise in nip and tuck. The result resembles a many-faceted diamond. The corners of the shaft slant in and out as the tower rises, and the whole form shimmers. Paul Goldberger, *The New Yorker*, 19 December 2005

3

4

5

Hearst is very important in terms of its sustainable credentials. It was the first office tower in Manhattan to apply for a LEED Gold standard. In that sense it has been a groundbreaking project for the city.

Norman Foster

World Trade Center

New York, USA 2002

I was in New York, for a meeting with Hearst, on 11 September 2001. When I returned the following weekend I sat down with my partners and resolved that we would do our own studies into safety in tall buildings. We established a cross-disciplinary discussion forum with our colleagues from Arup Structures, Arup Fire, Lerch Bates, Roger Preston and Allegiance, a company with which we have worked on airports and railway stations, but which had never been involved in high-rise buildings. We felt that we should avoid discussing the matter as an abstraction, and that it would be sensible to design a hypothetical fifty-storey building, which is what we did. Norman Foster, in conversation with the editor, 2012

Building on the site of the World Trade Center was a challenge that went far beyond questions of architectural style. We had to reconstruct the fabric of the city, to heal the scars, both physically and spiritually, and look forward to the future. We also had to try to commemorate the tragic events that unfolded there and the lives of those who died. I think that for all of us involved it was an extraordinary competition. It demanded our attention at many different levels – strategically, architecturally and spiritually. It was emotionally and physically demanding. Norman Foster, in conversation with the editor, 2012
Left: Before the storm – the iconic twin towers celebrated in a picture-postcard view of New York.

The tragic felling of the World Trade Center towers in New York, on 11 September 2001, needs no introduction here. Their destruction left a void, which architects from around the world sought to fill – both physically and symbolically. In his presentation in the Winter Garden of the World Financial Center in New York, in December 2002, Norman Foster – who had been in Manhattan on 9/11 – said: 'Architecture is a response to needs: this project starts with the needs of the local community – the neighbourhood – and it extends out to embrace the City; but it also has a global dimension … How do you give physical presence to such intangibles as "loss" and "emptiness"? And if you can, how do you balance that against life and regeneration?'

He went on to describe his World Trade Center towers as 'the tallest, the greenest and the safest in the world.' But beyond that, the towers were firmly conceived as part of a three-dimensional urban composition. If there is a single drawing of the project that contains its essential DNA, in this regard, it is a memorable sketch by Foster in which he depicts the site as a whole, focusing on points of view. From the towers, you can see for ever, past even the adjacent towers because of the triangulated geometries. From the voids of the memorial gardens you can see clouds and sky, but not the surrounding buildings – not even the trees in the park.

It is a remarkably complete scheme in every respect, but its complexity is even more astonishing considering that it was achieved in a period of just three months. Foster's proposals incorporate everything from an integrated transport infrastructure and 'Ground Zero' memorial to a pair of crystalline towers that both reinterpreted Minoru Yamasaki's originals and might even be considered to have reinvented the skyscraper form itself.

Foster may have developed the proposals quickly, but it is tempting to view his entire professional life to that point as a preparation for such a moment: forty years in which he had developed an architectural philosophy, honed a systems-based methodology, expanded his office's expertise to include issues such as safety and sustainability, and not least amassed a body of work at an increasing scale so that he could draw from his own experience and precedent.

The scheme was entirely commensurate with a commission uniquely charged with strong emotions and high expectations. It did not win the competition, but it was significant among those presented by the seven teams in that it garnered overwhelming support in the polls conducted among New Yorkers at that time, drawing both popular and critical acclaim. In the final analysis, it was also among the few that merited being built.

How do you give physical presence to intangibles such as as 'loss' and 'emptiness'?

Foster's buildings not only matched in stature Yamasaki's elegantly minimal towers, but also improved on the originals. The 500-metre (1,600-feet) towers reclaimed the Lower Manhattan skyline, re-establishing the very right of New York to build to its ceiling and preside over its own air space. They emerged as iconic equals of the beloved Empire State and Chrysler buildings, though of a more advanced conceptual order.

In a bold move, the proposal promised to heal psychic wounds that many felt would remain if at least the equivalents of the World Trade Center towers were not rebuilt. Foster's towers rejoiced in their skyward reach. With their shifting, angular silhouettes they had unusual charisma. The sides of each three-sided tower creased in triangular folds and each facet angled forward and back up the shafts to the top so that with changing points of view they became kinetic. At two points along their height, they touched, or 'kissed'. Activated by the motion of the viewer, they almost seemed to dance together in a fluid pas de deux.

1

Opposite: An aerial view of Lower Manhattan taken in the wake of the terrorist events of 11 September 2001. The rebuilding of the World Trade Center site was one of the most significant urban and architectural challenges of recent times.

1. Designed by Minoru Yamasaki Associates, with Emery Roth & Sons the 110-storey twin towers of the World Trade Center (1966-1977) commanded the Lower Manhattan skyline. When completed, the 416-metre (1,353-feet) towers were the tallest in the world. The structural system for the facades was lightweight and economical: in effect, a prefabricated steel lattice, with columns on 1-metre (39-inch) centres. The office floors had no interior columns; and the upper levels each provided as much as 3,700 square metres (40,000 square feet) of space. 'Economy is not in the sparseness of materials that we use', said Yamasaki of the $350 million cost, 'but in the advancement of technology, which is the real challenge.'

Immediately following the events of 9/11 –
and quite independently – we brought together
a team of architects, structural engineers, vertical
transport consultants and fire experts to conduct
in-depth research into the optimal design of
future tall buildings to ensure that such a terrible
disaster could never happen again. We gained a
huge amount of knowledge from that exercise –
and the lessons we learned informed the design
of our new tower. Norman Foster, in conversation
with the editor, 2012

From the outside, the building envelope was
designed to be blast-resistant and special
fixtures prevented injury from falling debris. Extra
strength, redundancy and resilient connections
were designed into the primary structure. The
central core incorporated blast-proof walls and
wider staircases, as well as a dedicated emergency
lift. Escape and access measures included
additional escape stairs at the perimeter – above
and beyond code requirements – terrace-level
helicopter rescue points, and specially protected
refuge floors. Brandon Haw, of Foster + Partners,
in conversation with the editor, 2011

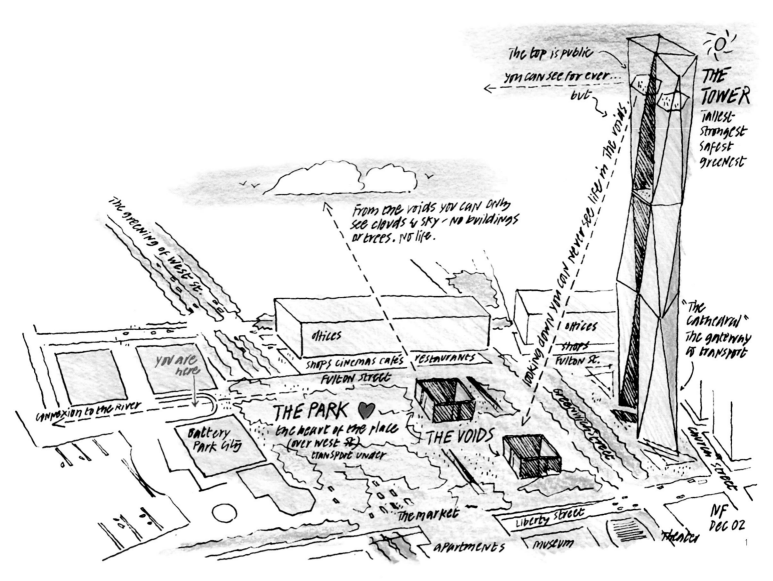

1. Norman Foster's concept
sketch describes how the
98-storey 'twinned' towers
are integrated into the fabric
of Lower Manhattan. The
scheme is about memory,
but equally it is about rebirth,
demonstrating to the world
the continuing strength and
faith in the future that has
traditionally shaped the
New York skyline.

We proposed crystalline
twinned towers – the
tallest, safest, and
the most socially and
ecologically progressive
in the world – rising as
symbols of rebirth.

Norman Foster

The towers were, however, only the most visible components of a scheme that was deeply rooted in Lower Manhattan's urban strata. Beneath their feet was a transport node, where subways, PATH trains and a proposed air train to Kennedy Airport converged. The transportation fed underground shopping areas, next to bus and car parking zones. Poignantly forming voids in this complex mix were the footprints of the original towers. Screened by high, isolating walls that remained mute, they formed opaque objects within a vast new park at street level that extended from the base of the new towers towards West Street. The park and towers, along with adjacent smaller office, apartment and cultural buildings, were organised within a street plan that meshed the site back into the urban fabric of Lower Manhattan, remedying the contextual damage wrought by Yamasaki in his tabula rasa approach in the 1960s.

The logic that produced the towers combined an assessment of the complex programmatic requirements of the project with an instinctive understanding of the need to create a defining image. Norman Foster and senior partner Brandon Haw were in New York on the day the planes struck and they experienced at first-hand the deep sense of loss felt throughout the city. Coming to the project nearly a year later, they believed that the skyline had to be restored – and with its full iconic power. The city, and architecture itself, could not retreat in the face of terrorist threat: as Haw says, 'tall buildings are part of our civilisation.'

In creating equivalent towers, Foster was not proposing a mimetic response but one that resonated with the originals in a transformative way. Although the exact poetics of form would emerge organically, as it always does in Foster's projects – the result of exacting structural, economic and organisational analysis – Foster and his team shared the intuition that rather than rebuilding towers which were static, closed and inexpressive, like the originals, the design in some way would have to speak in subjective terms that would be understood in the context of tragedy and rebirth.

The urban agenda for the competition was set by the Lower Manhattan Development Corporation (LMDC). Technically, the goal was to establish a masterplan, and the emphasis of the LMDC was that through streets, severed in the Yamasaki plan, should be reconnected to knit the site back into the larger urban context. The LMDC was especially concerned that Vesey and Fulton streets should be restored to carry east-west connections to Battery Park City, and that Greenwich Street should re-establish a north-south route. Given the integrative nature of the brief, the Foster team began by analysing the site's boundaries, which presented quite different edge conditions. There was, for example, an existing street pattern to the east, where Fulton and Vesey streets bordered the site, but not to the west, where Battery Park City creates quite a hard frontage – an alien urban form in Manhattan.

The geometry of the re-emergent street grid helped determine the placement of the buildings. To define the northern boundary, Foster placed a set of mid-rise office blocks between Vesey and Fulton streets, affirming the east-west axis. He also identified locations to the south of the site where he proposed more mid-rise structures, to accommodate housing, offices and cultural amenities. Allowing Greenwich Street to penetrate through the site isolated the footprints of Yamasaki's original towers in an area west of Greenwich that could be made into a park large enough for further cultural uses. Extending Greenwich also created a wedge of land to the east that could accommodate the bases of two new towers.

2

3

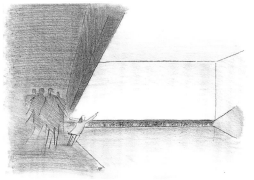

4

2-4. Sketch studies by Norman Foster of the Memorial to those who lost their lives on 9/11. The footprints of the destroyed towers are preserved as sanctuaries for remembrance and reflection. Ramps lead down into an ambulatory lining an open volume where each tower once stood. Here, the city is hidden from view, the sky above empty.

In a sense the 'twinned tower' carried an echo of those that were lost. It was offered as a tribute to the spirit of New York and the optimism of the American people. Norman Foster, in conversation with the editor, 2012
Right: Some of the many dozens of sketch models made by the design team during the course of the project.

1. Proposals for the World Trade Center site being developed in the Foster studio in September 2002.

2. A sketch model, showing the Memorial sites at the base of the new tower.

3, 4. The tower is articulated vertically as village-like clusters, each with its own tree-filled atrium – effectively a 'park in the sky'. The building is naturally ventilated through its multi-layered, 'breathing' facade, and the atria play an environmental role, performing as its 'lungs'.

Symbolically, it was an opportunity to create an enduring icon for New York, whose skyline has been shaped by the urge to build tall.

Norman Foster

However, this planimetric 'inevitability' is deceptive, because 'ground' in Manhattan is relative, and the streetscape at the WTC site was several storeys removed from bedrock. Foster solved one of the most difficult aspects of the site, the edge along West Street – which at street level is a wide, high-speed traffic artery – by using the fall across the site to his advantage. In an elegant move, he extrapolated west the level of Greenwich Street, so that as the site naturally sloped down towards the Hudson River the level of the park remained constant, becoming a deck that could be extended over West Street as a landscaped bridge. Cesar Pelli had designed the World Financial Center for this eventuality, so the deck with its memorial park created a seamless connection into Pelli's complex.

Along the northern edge of the site, shops in the bases of the mid-rise buildings lining Liberty Street resolved the height differential between the park and Vesey Street. On Liberty Street, the southern boundary of the site, shops fronted the pavement, providing the base for the park on the roof above. All the edges of the park plane were protected from traffic, yet urbanistically they were activated with shops and cafés, thereby connecting the scheme with the surrounding streets. At the base of the towers, the plaza parted, revealing the underground concourse of shopping and transport: natural light flooded into an area that had been covered in Yamasaki's closed scheme.

Foster orchestrated the flows from the various tributaries into this vast multi-level space, so that people would rise through the concourse and into the plaza beneath the towers.

The exigencies of the site and the demands of the brief determined one context, but the project must also be seen in the context of Foster's own oeuvre, in which many different precedents are drawn together. For example, the Hongkong Bank exercised an influence in New York, with its escalators, its expressed truss structure and observation decks. So too did the Commerzbank, where garden spaces act as 'lungs' within the building and define social 'villages'. But with each successive project, Foster and his colleagues bring new thinking to bear, so the design response at the WTC was the result of compounded research, past and present, done around the world.

In the context of the attacks on the WTC, structural strength and security were paramount considerations, and Foster's team drew on tall building safety studies that they had begun long before 9/11, while researching bomb-resistant structures. The Foster studio also pioneered the use of double- and triple-skin technologies in facades to temper the effects of heat gain in towers. Going into the competition, then, they were already expert in safety and sustainability, and in the ecological and social benefits of developing complex building sections.

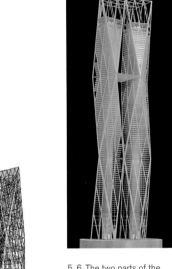

6

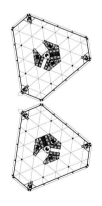

5

5, 6. The two parts of the tower 'kiss' at three intervals over its 500-metre height, creating strategic links – escape routes in case of emergency – which correspond with public levels containing observation decks, exhibition spaces and cafés.

7. The triangulated geometry generates plan forms that range from equilateral triangles to pure hexagons, with hybrid forms in between.

3

4

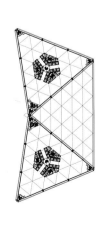

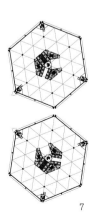

7

Within the park is the site of the Memorial. Pure, elegant, tranquil, the rectangular forms of the original twin towers are framed by monumental walls of stone and glass. Below is a sanctuary for remembrance and quiet reflection. Families and loved ones are provided with a sanctum with individual shrines for commemoration and tribute. Visitors follow a separate path. From within these spaces only the sky is visible, no buildings or trees. They are reflective spaces where sky and shadow create quiet and calm in the heart of the city – places for remembrance, reconciliation and renaissance, a lasting reminder of the value of human life. Norman Foster, in conversation with the editor, 2012

Architecture is a response to needs. This project starts with the needs of the local community – the neighbourhood. It extends to embrace the city, but it also has a global dimension. How do you give physical presence to such intangibles as 'loss' and 'emptiness'? And if you can, how do you balance that against life and regeneration? We propose three memorials, the empty voids, the footprints of the twin towers, a 20-acre park, with transport hub and parking below, and two towers that kiss and become one – the tallest, strongest, and greenest in the world. Norman Foster, speaking in New York, 18 December 2002
Left: Norman Foster presenting the scheme in the Winter Garden of the World Financial Center, 18 December 2002

From a structural point of view, research yielded the diagrid as a solution that would achieve maximum strength with minimum use of materials. Strong, and highly efficient, this triangulated system not only maximises structural strength and stiffness, but also creates a 'skin' of robust structural elements that provide multiple back-up load paths ready to be engaged in case of an emergency. Additional strength in this case was provided by the service and circulation cores, which were constructed from reinforced concrete (a structural element fatally missing from the Yamasaki towers). Along with passenger lifts, fire-fighting lifts and freight shafts, each core contained four emergency escape stairs. As a further measure, each tower incorporated three additional fire escape stairs in the corners of the floor plates, where they were physically protected by the substantial corner diagrid structure.

Foster's claim for the towers as 'the tallest, greenest and strongest' is surely no exaggeration.

The 'diagonalised' exoskeleton that gave the towers their iconic profile appears more abstract than it is. The architects simply manipulated a basic triangular floor plate in a systematic rotation, the equilateral triangles shifting by 120 degrees to each other at forty-two-storey intervals. The triangulation of the structure in this way produces a regularly changing prismatic external form with predominantly six-sided floor plates whose dimensions change each storey in rotation. At Level 42 and Level 84 the floor plates are triangular; at Levels 21, 63 and 105 they are pure hexagons. The geometry allows each structure to capture lateral views that would be blocked in buildings with a rectilinear geometry. At the two points where the two towers touch – Levels 42 and 84 – the floors open up to become observation decks and refuge points. Here, restaurants and sky gardens led out on to observation decks with spectacular views across Manhattan.

As in many Foster projects, the building was conceived to be gregarious. As with the Commerzbank, and the projected Tokyo and London Millennium towers, Foster envisaged buildings with an interior urban life – effectively 'cities in the sky'.

In the eye of international attention, the new towers had to be principled in many ways, and not just as a response to terrorism and a reassertion of New York's right to height. Foster built on the practice's expertise in sustainability, proposing numerous linked environmental strategies in what amounted to an orchestrated ecosystem.

A ventilated double-skin facade was designed to minimise heating and cooling requirements, while heat gain from computer terminals, lighting and so on would be recycled. Like the Commerzbank, the sky gardens provided the building's 'lungs', allowing natural ventilation to take over from mechanical systems during certain periods. Photovoltaics in the facades generated electricity to supplement energy produced by the project's own tri-generation energy plant – an integrated energy circulation system designed to minimise the building's fuel consumption and carbon emissions, while producing power for the whole site. There was the potential too for wind turbines at the top of the towers, while the diagrid structure, by providing greater strength with less material, reduced embodied energy.

Foster's claim for the towers as 'the tallest, greenest and strongest' is surely no exaggeration. Yet, what truly distinguishes the towers is that – like the scheme as a whole – they are multi-perspectival, yielding more than one experience. Unlike most skyscrapers, the design embodies multiple narratives, rather than a single absolutist idea. Foster's towers are structurally lithe and acrobatic, triumphantly tall and emotionally powerful. What makes them unusual within Foster's opus is that they move beyond the purely rational into highly expressive territory. In their dance, their changing silhouette, their elusive geometries and their crisp, crystalline beauty, the towers verge on wonder.

Joseph Giovannini

1

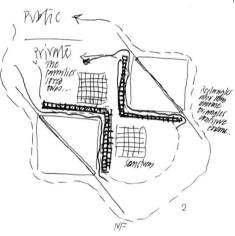

2

Opposite: The redevelopment was seen as a catalyst for the regeneration of Lower Manhattan, an opportunity to repair the street pattern that was eradicated in the 1960s and to bring new life to an area suffering economic decline.

1. A model of the memorial. The footprints of the original towers are framed by walls of stone and glass. Below is a sanctuary for remembrance and reflection.

2. Sketch by Norman Foster exploring how a sanctuary for the families of the victims of 9/11 might be created in the public garden.

We planned to repair the street pattern that was eradicated by Yamasaki's World Trade Center development, reconnecting the site with Battery Park City, TriBeCa and the surrounding districts. Instead of a barren plaza, we envisaged streets lined with shops, cafés, theatres, cinemas and bars. New York is the 'city that never sleeps' – but that was never true of the area around the World Trade Center. It was a commercial hub by day and a ghost town by night. We saw this as an opportunity to bring the area to life around the clock. Norman Foster, in conversation with the editor, 2012

1. Directly below the tower is a new mass transit interchange linking the PATH train, subway lines, AirTrain links to JFK and Newark Liberty airports, a bus station and parking. This new gateway into Manhattan is celebrated by a soaring glass canopy. Above ground, the original street pattern is restored, reconnecting the surrounding neighbourhoods.

2

3

1

We reinstated the original street pattern, with spaces lined with shops, theatres and restaurants. Below, a multi-transportation hub provided links to the city's airports – a new gateway to Manhattan.

Norman Foster

4

2, 3. The public park at the base of the tower.

4. A public viewing deck at one of the intermediate 'kissing points' part-way up the height of the tower.

Overleaf: Looking south from Midtown Manhattan and the Empire State Building to the 538-metre (1,764-foot) twinned tower.

Pacific Currents
Chris Abel 2011

1. Arata Isozaki, 'Clusters in the Air' (1962). Massive pylons support elevated housing and office systems as well as parks and walkways, suspended above the existing city. This and other projects produced during the course of the 1960s echo the Metabolist manifesto, with its dynamic solutions for Tokyo's rapid post-war growth.

2. Kenzo Tange, Yamanashi Press and Broadcasting Centre, Kofu (1961-1967). The project develops in microcosm ideas first propounded in Isozaki's Joint Core System project of 1962, in which the new multi-layered vertical city hovers over the traditional streetscape. Tange described his urban work in Metabolist terms: 'By incorporating elements of space, speed, and drastic change in the physical environment, we created a method of structuring having elasticity and changeability.'

The expansion of Foster + Partners into Asia Pacific over the past quarter century has coincided with a period of the most dramatic and far-reaching economic and cultural transformations in the region, the consequences of which are being felt around the world. From the iconic Hongkong and Shanghai Bank, through the Century Tower in Japan and the various airport designs, both built and unbuilt, around the region, to the studio's most recent projects in Malaysia, Singapore and China, Foster's architecture reflects the deeper currents underlying what has come to be known as the Pacific Century, or the Pacific Age.

Heralded by the BBC in a 1982 radio programme, the new era was principally identified at the outset with a resurgent Japanese economy and the smaller but flourishing 'Tiger' states of Hong Kong, Taiwan, South Korea and Singapore. Placing events within a broader historical context, in his book, *Pacific Shift*, published in 1985, William Irwin Thompson argued that the growth of global trade between the countries bordering the Pacific Rim marked a fundamental change from a global civilisation and culture originally based on printed media and maritime communications and centred around the Atlantic, to one based on electronic and airborne systems of communication, the main poles of which were the high-tech industries of Japan and California.

Being rooted in the new technologies of communication, the cultures underpinning this new civilisation, like the cultures underlying the major world civilisations that preceded it, which were based on other modes of communication and geographical centres, would also be fundamentally different from anything that had gone before.

Amongst other defining changes of the new age, Thompson posits the decline of independent nation states and ideological thinking, or 'us and them', against the generation of a planetary wide culture in mirror response to the perceived dangers to the planetary ecosystem. Underpinning this movement, he argues, is the 'Gaia politique', an emergent political culture, the chief characteristic of which is non-ideological thinking, or the ability, as Thompson puts it, 'to entertain opposites in consciousness'.

Most observers accept that a major shift of economic power in favour of the Pacific Rim is under way and is probably irreversible.

Most observers now accept that a major shift of economic power in favour of the Pacific Rim is well under way, and is probably irreversible. However, not all of Thompson's analysis has withstood the passage of time. Along with the anticipated displacement of printed media – still very much with us – by electronic media, Thompson also forecast the erosion of free-market capitalism by socialism, neither of which has been borne out by subsequent events. His division of the world into four major power blocks – the USA, Europe, Russia and China, each with its own distinct economic and social systems – also looks shaky in the light of the dramatic changes in Russia and China over the past twenty years. Globalisation has also greatly extended liberal capitalism during the same period, creating its own controversial planetary culture. Other aspects of Thompson's thesis, however, have struck a more enduring chord. Partly inspired by James Lovelock's Gaia theory, and partly by Chinese Buddhist philosophy and its stress on the interconnectedness of all things, the conjunction of advanced communication technologies, reverence for nature, and holistic ways of thinking, is closer in spirit to Eastern than to Western traditions of thought.

1

2

The vision of a cultural shift towards Eastern values and modes of thought dovetails neatly with Fritjof Capra's arguments in *The Tao of Physics*, published ten years earlier. Capra drew striking parallels between developments in theoretical physics over the previous half century and Eastern mysticism. Relativity theory and quantum theory together represented, he argued, a fundamental movement from the kind of mechanistic or atomistic thinking underpinning classic physics, where everything is broken down into the smallest possible constituent parts, towards holistic models and ways of thinking. In this new world view, all things are interrelated, sometimes in bizarre ways, and 'opposites are complementary', a principle closely similar to the dynamic unity of opposites represented by the ancient Chinese T'ai-chi T'u symbol.

Significant aspects of the new paradigm derived from related sources, were also finding their way into architectural theory and practice within the region. In 1960, the Japanese Metabolist group made their first public appearance at the World Design Conference in Tokyo, effectively burying the already defunct CIAM as an international forum for Modernists. Partly inspired, as the name suggests, by biological processes involving the transformation and recycling of energy and matter, the Metabolist vision was also founded in an Eastern world view dominated by the flux and change of events, where stability is regarded as only a brief illusion.

The translation of this ephemeral vision into built practice, however, proved difficult, and was hampered by technological limitations. Partial solutions were sought, and found, in familiar techniques and inspirational figures. A year before the Tokyo conference, Le Corbusier completed his National Museum of Western Art in the same city, the spiralling square plan of which was based on his 1939 project for a 'museum of unlimited extension'. Constructed in reinforced concrete, Le Corbusier's building demonstrated that a dynamic concept might still be expressed in relatively static materials. Louis Kahn's logical and structural separation of 'served' from 'servant' spaces in his Richards Medical Research Building, completed at the same time, was another essential reference, and helped Metabolists to articulate different levels of change, which they represented in their characteristic 'megastructure' designs.

The few fragments of these ambitious schemes that were actually completed, however, such as Kenzo Tange's Press and Broadcasting Centre (1967), at Yamanashi, only hint at a larger urban framework, and look strangely out of place among the urban sprawl. The most successful products of the movement, such as Kisho Kurokawa's Sony Tower (1976), in Osaka, with its prefabricated 'pods' suspended on the outside, were designed as relatively modest experiments in flexible structures and prefabrication techniques, and fit relatively easily into their surroundings.

Foster's Hongkong and Shanghai Bank, with its flexible steel frame and suspended open floors, service modules hanging at the side and dynamic aesthetic, slips comfortably into this broader picture. Moreover, it achieves what Japanese architects themselves had not: a no-holds-barred, full-scale working example of Metabolist principles, that both looked and performed as it should, dynamic control systems and all. That is surely no accident. Underscoring any personal empathy between the designers and the Japanese group, Foster's holistic 'system's approach' has its roots in the same biological analogies and dynamic process models underlying both Metabolist theory and Capra's new paradigm.

Synonymous with the studio's integrated design methods, the approach has long been recognised as a defining characteristic of Foster's architecture. It was already clearly apparent in the early works, from the close integration of structure, mechanical services and functional programme of the Reliance Controls factory, when Foster was with Team 4, through to the tailor-made components and environmental-control systems of Willis Faber & Dumas, closely followed by those of the Sainsbury Centre, to the first use of computer-controlled production techniques in the Renault Centre.

3. Louis Kahn, Richards Medical Research Laboratories, University of Pennsylvania (1957-1961). Service towers are articulated from three stacks of laboratories, creating a distinction between 'served' and 'servant' spaces.

4. Hongkong and Shanghai Bank Headquarters, Hong Kong (1979-1986). The building draws together Kahnian and Metabolist themes, creating a highly flexible structural armature to which service modules, lift and stair towers can be attached.

3

4

It is perhaps when one is in motion, when one becomes a part of the ongoing pageant, that one appreciates Hong Kong best. In that sense, Foster – with his vertical circulation systems and his atrium over a plaza that affords a view of the passing populace – has captured the spirit of the city. Hiroshi Watanabe, *Architecture*, September 1985

I think it is something of a reflex that when we start to work on a project we are always thinking about ways in which you can re-examine a building to see how it can contribute to the city around it, or add a dimension of public space to improve the quality of life within that city. I have always been fascinated by public space – the way in which, for example, the Milan Galleria creates a very generous public realm even though it is essentially a private building. You see that in the Hongkong Bank, where we lifted the banking floors off the ground to create public space – a very precious commodity in a high-density city like Hong Kong. Norman Foster, in conversation with the editor, 2012

1. Hongkong and Shanghai Bank Headquarters, Hong Kong (1979-1986). Designed for complete flexibility, the building has purpose-designed raised floors and suspended ceiling systems. This drawing shows a single-bay floor close to the top of the building.

2. Century Tower, Tokyo (1987-1991). The building advances themes first explored in the Hongkong Bank, the structure in this case articulated as a series of eccentrically braced frames, which respond to seismic engineering requirements in a city where earthquakes and typhoons are a constant threat.

All of these buildings, most of which were conceived as free-standing 'pavilions', were also designed with the potential for future growth and change, both externally and internally. These more dynamic aspects, however, were sometimes subverted, as with the Sainsbury Centre, by a Classical aesthetic – partly tied up with the pavilion type – and Foster and his growing team of innovative designers often seemed uncertain as how best to express such qualities.

The Hongkong Bank blew away all such questions in a bravura display of dynamic architecture and integrated design, topping anything the Metabolists themselves had accomplished. 'Godzilla and Madam Butterfly' rolled into one, the Yin-Yang marriage of transparent spaces and fragile fenestration with brute megastructure, perfectly captures the dynamic unity of opposites expressed in the T'ai-chi T'u symbol. And just in case anyone might miss the connection, there are the removable floor panels fitting neatly into the planning grid just like tatami mats, and the shoji-like translucent partitions on the upper floors, both features borrowed directly from traditional Japanese architecture.

In hindsight, given the historical exchanges between Japan and the West in the formative years of Modernism, the connection between Foster's architecture and Japanese traditions is less surprising than it might first appear. But what Foster and his team were able to bring to these cultural exchanges, in addition to their systems approach and renowned ways with flexible spaces, was a mastery of advanced technology of which the pioneers only dreamt and which contemporary Japanese architects, hampered by a more limited professional role, could not match.

Where Japanese Modernists, including prominent Metabolists, had been most successful, was in reinterpreting traditional timber post-and-beam construction techniques in a contemporary idiom of reinforced concrete. Thus, while Tange's Communication Centre, like many similar works of the same period, left much to be desired as far as any actual potential for growth and change was concerned, the massive 'beams' and supporting 'columns' bear a clear if exaggerated resemblance to those earlier building forms.

This itself was no mean achievement, the credit for which lay as much, if not more with Japanese architects' deep appreciation of their own building traditions and forms, as with any outside influences. For all Le Corbusier's and Kahn's undoubted impact on post-war generations, it cannot explain the intuitive skills with which so many accomplished designers were able to translate a formal and technical vocabulary which had evolved for a relatively limited range of building types and purposes, into a completely different technology, better suited to broader and more complex needs. Even when the architects departed from obvious structural precedents, as with Kiyonori Kikutake's Sky House, 1958, with its slab columns and cantilevers, Tange's National Indoor Stadiums for the 1964 Olympics, with their sweeping cable hung roofs, or Sachio Otani's Kyoto International Conference Hall, 1966, with its sloping walls, awe-struck Western observers knew beyond doubt that they were looking at a specifically Japanese design.

Seen in this light, Foster's Century Tower in Tokyo is more than just the follow-up to its immediate predecessor in Hong Kong it is often taken for. As convincing as any exercise in regional Modernism produced by native architects, Century Tower offers a unique insight into the transformative process by which others achieved similar results. Exhibiting the same contrasts between strength and lightness as that of its Hong Kong parent, the building also shares many other characteristic features: a division into separate structural volumes of different height; column-free floors; soaring atrium and exposed vertical movement systems and services. But it is the eccentrically braced frame, with its stacks of two-storey-high segments and splayed pairs of columns, which first catches the attention. Likened by local critics to the massive timber gateways typical of Japanese temples and palaces, it is tempting to think that the Foster team might have been similarly inspired.

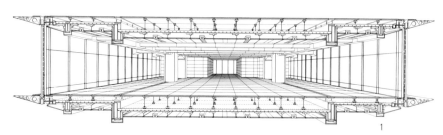

1

2

I like to think that our Japanese work has its own identity – its own inherent Japaneseness. The influence of place is immediately apparent in any consideration of Century Tower – it is as much steeped in the context of Tokyo and its client as the Hongkong Bank is grounded in Hong Kong, or Beijing Airport is inspired by Chinese tradition and the dynamism and poetry of flight. A sense of place and an understanding of the personality and culture of the client have always been guiding principles. Norman Foster, in conversation with the editor, 2012

Right, far right: Norman Foster sketching in the gardens of the Imperial Villa of Katsura on his first visit to Japan in 1987; and one of his sketches made on that visit.

However, this is not the way Foster and his partners, and their engineers, Arup, actually work. Designed to withstand the most severe shocks in one of the world's most dangerous earthquake zones, the splayed legs reduce the floor spans on each segment, at the same time as spreading their loads towards the building's extremities, where they help to brace the whole structure. What direct visual connection there is with Japanese traditions derives from the decision to expose the frame on the outside as well as the inside, together with the beefed-up proportions necessitated by the two-storey segments and layers of fireproofing and cladding. In other words, the resemblance originates more in a shared feeling for space and structure and their expression than in any effort to echo a specific form or motif from the past. Outdoing even the Hongkong Bank, it is this derivation from shared principles that lends Century Tower its special character and authenticity and which provides the metaphorical bridges between contemporary and historical works.

All too often, the glittering new CBDs contrast with vast areas of urban poverty and distress in sprawling megacities.

Both the Hongkong Bank and Century Tower were designed and built at a time of growing debate concerning the principles and merits of a Modern architecture for our time, which might successfully fuse elements of international and regional cultures, so combining the best of both worlds: the local and the global. The debate struck a special chord among committed architects, both local and foreign, working in Asia Pacific, which, like Africa and South America, has a long history of cultural exchange and exposure to Western influence, both through trade and colonisation, the balance of which invariably favoured the West.

The architectural legacy of this exchange was far from being one-sided, however, and colonial builders were compelled to adapt to the tropical climate in most parts of the region, often with impressive results, well into the latter half of the twentieth century, when air conditioning saved them the trouble. As in Africa, many excellent works, including well shaded and naturally ventilated schools, universities and hospitals, were designed by government agencies, as well as by expatriate firms such as James Cubitt, Wells and Joyce, Raglan Squire & Partners (RSP), and Palmer & Turner.

Swamped by endless numbers of air-conditioned offices and other identical building forms cloned from Western models, these early cultural hybrids were largely forgotten until the closing decades of the last century, when a small but vocal number of architects and critics began to question the increasing sameness of the built environment around the world, and the consequent loss of cultural identity. The completion of the advanced-technology Hongkong Bank and Century Tower within a few years of each other therefore had a special meaning for Asia Pacific architects, stretching the boundaries of what had hitherto seemed acceptable, or even possible, within regional movements.

The same period also saw a great surge in high-rise building around the Pacific Rim, reflecting the growing prosperity of its cities and the impact of globalisation. Few of the new structures, however, realised the potential for the future held out by Foster's two buildings. The benefits of economic growth were also far from being evenly distributed. All too often, the glittering new CBDs contrasted with vast areas of urban poverty and distress in sprawling megacities, the social and physical infrastructures of which struggled to keep pace with their fast growing populations. By the end of the last century, having scraped through a near disastrous financial crisis, during which growth rates and confidence in the region plummeted, Thompson's bright vision of a homogeneous new world culture was looking overly optimistic, if not naïve.

3. The demolition of the Old Quarter in the Pudong district of Shanghai. The pace of development in Shanghai is breathtaking, but it echoes the pattern of emerging megacities around the world, in which traditional, low-rise forms of urban development are being swept away.

4. Kuala Lumpur, Malaysia: the Petronas Twin Towers and the luxury Radisson Hotel rise behind slum housing in the centre of the city.

3

4

1, 2. Contrasting snapshots of the Shanghai skyline, taken forty years apart in 1960 and 2000, looking across the Huangpu River towards Pudong. Shanghai is mainland China's premier centre for commerce and finance, and has been described as the 'showpiece' of the world's fastest-growing economy. The city's population has more than doubled in the last twenty years. In 2007 Shanghai had 18.58 million permanent residents, making it the most densely populated city on the Chinese mainland.

It is not as though the faith shown by Thompson and others in the potential of the region was unfounded. In 1985, aside from Japan, only Malaysia and Singapore had nominally democratic governments, and even those were led by autocratic personalities, and were intolerant of genuine opposition or a free press. Much of this has now changed, not only in those countries, but all around Asia Pacific. Since 1986, following the 'people power' revolution in the Philippines, the countries of South Korea, Taiwan, Thailand, Indonesia and East Timor have all seen the emergence of fledgling democracies. Praising the 'democratic transformation' in the region, Francis Fukuyama, the author of 'The End of History?', 1989, attributes these changes partly to a shift in American foreign policy, which had previously backed the former regimes. However, according to Anand Panyarachun, former prime minister of Thailand, the main pressure for change came directly from economic development: 'A modern society and the management of the economy needed people with different qualifications from generals and air marshals'.

Despite impressive strides, however, the transition from closed to open forms of government and society, generally remains far from being complete. Social and cultural tensions, usually left over from previous regimes and exacerbated by yawning gaps between the 'haves' and 'have-nots', continue to hinder development in the region. New governments, led in many cases by deeply conservative and often corrupted political factions – including a few former generals – continue to favour privileged groups and special interests, creating further tensions. Deforestation and other environmental abuses, openly tolerated and even encouraged in many cases by local authorities, are also familiar elements of the political and economic equation.

Thompson foresaw the dangers posed by such abuses very clearly. In his account of the impact of the four great stages of human development on regional ecologies – Riverine (Middle East), Mediterranean, Atlantic and Pacific – he noted that, in addition to all the other symptoms which characterised each civilisation, each also produced its own typical forms of environmental abuse: from localised cases of salinisation and soil loss, through widespread deforestation, to industrial pollution and atmospheric changes on a planetary scale, culminating in the Greenhouse Effect, 'not one (of which) has been "solved" since 3500BC'. In a prophetic passage, he warns: 'Although this new culture is focused on the Pacific Basin, the global quality of the fourth cultural ecology is expressed in the fact that there is not simply one crisis, but an accumulation of all the preceding crises'.

Many of China's coastal conurbations are made up of clusters of smaller cities, which have grown together in a haphazard way to form one continuous megalopolis.

In the same way, it may be argued that, rather than each civilisation completely displacing the other, as Thompson's linear model of succeeding cultural ecologies suggests, what history presents is an accumulation of different civilisations, none of which ever entirely disappears. Much like Fukuyama's own deterministic and much disputed world view of the complete and final victory of liberal capitalism and democracy over competing economic systems and ideologies, Thompson's theory of displaced cultures sits uncomfortably with the evidence of history and the complexity of events.

1

2

It is estimated that by 2030 two-thirds of the world's population will be urbanised. While the established giants such as London continue to expand we are already beginning to see the growth of a new generation of mega-cities of unprecedented size and urban conurbations in excess of twenty-five million people are predicted in the next fifteen years. The challenge in such cities is to accommodate more and more people, at greater densities than before, while seeking to create a higher quality of urban life. The tall building may not be the only key, but with finite resources, and with less and less land on which to build, it is a vital component of the future city. Norman Foster, *Sky High: Vertical Architecture*, 2003

One of the things I find remarkable about Japan is that it has a very strong sense of tradition. Yet it also embraces progress and has a mastery of advanced technology. These contrasting themes coexist in a powerful way. Tokyo is interesting in that it is a liberated, dynamic city, undergoing a continuous process of change. It is the polar opposite of the city as museum that you sometimes encounter in the West, where you cannot pull anything down, simply because it is old. Norman Foster, in conversation with the editor, 2012

Like the unfortunate accumulation of environmental effects, what is happening throughout the region is more like an addition of new culture forms 'on top of' existing forms, which still persist, albeit sometimes in an altered state, creating a kind of cultural and technological 'layer cake'. In this model, different forms of life coexist in 'parallel worlds' – not always in complete harmony or even full awareness of each other, but not independently either. More prosaic than the infinite number of simultaneously existing universes, or 'multiverse', envisaged by quantum theorists and science-fiction writers, the picture of multi-layered development presented by these quasi-independent systems can nevertheless be equally unsettling; conflicts and tensions are normal and nothing quite seems to fit together as neatly as it should – or used to.

China's late entry upon the scene and its rapid development following Deng Xiaoping's economic reforms in 1978, epitomises this model, presenting many of the contradictions and problems dogging the region's transformation. China's phenomenal economic growth and expanding global influence has been gained at considerable social and environmental cost. Most of the new development – and the primary source of the success stories – is concentrated in the main centres of urban growth along the coastal states in the so-called Special Economic Zones, or SEZs, where new industries and businesses enjoy tax breaks and other incentives intended to encourage foreign as well as local investment.

The result is a growing economic and social imbalance between different parts of the country, the winners being the largest coastal cities like Shanghai and Guangzhou, and the losers being the farmers and workers in the interior states, where average wages are one tenth of those on the coast. (Reality check: as of 2007, the annual GDP per capita in China was just $5,300; this compares with Japan's $33,800.) As in other parts of the developing world where similar stories are being played out, the general effect is a steady flow of the population from the country into the major cities and urban areas, which offer the prospect, if not always the actuality, of more gainful employment.

Spreading over vast areas, many of China's coastal conurbations are made up of clusters of smaller cities, which have grown together in a haphazard way to form one continuous megalopolis. The newest and largest of these, like the Pearl River Delta conurbation, which runs from Guangzhou through to Hong Kong, have little apparent spatial or formal urban structure, aside from what remains of former city centres and the nodes and connections created by the main elements of the infrastructure.

As the Metabolists and other Japanese architects discovered for themselves decades ago in the sprawling chaos of the Tokyo-Yokohama megalopolis, the scope for any significant architectural intervention in these circumstances is severely limited, and is generally focused upon the design of those same infrastructural elements, or isolated gestures of other kinds. Paradoxically, the role these infrastructural elements play in national and regional development, as well as in the economic life of local cities, infuses them with an importance far beyond that of any ordinary building.

The Foster studio's airport designs in Hong Kong and China have consequently had a considerable impact on perceptions of development in the region, over and above their individual architectural merits. Since the Hong Kong airport at Chek Lap Kok, which was conceived and built to serve as a principal transport hub for the whole of Asia Pacific, the Foster practice has progressively elaborated upon the model of airport design it first established at Stansted. In the process, it has transformed the idea of the terminal type itself into something far broader and more urban in scope, reflecting the changing nature of the twenty-first century metropolis.

The pattern was already firmly set in the unprecedented scale of the Hong Kong airport – equivalent in area to that of a small city – with its integrated railway and bus terminals and adjacent new town, which was built to serve the airport and house its thousands of employees. However, for all that airport's considerable functional and structural innovations, the architects were constrained from exploring alternative planning solutions by the airport authority's masterplan, which was drawn up by independent consultants.

3. The vast urban sprawl of metropolitan Tokyo, looking towards Mount Fuji. Greater Tokyo is the world's largest megacity, with a population of 33.6 million – larger than the entire population of Canada.

3

I strongly believe that the quality of the routes, connections and public spaces – the 'urban glue' that holds our cities together – is as important as the design of the individual buildings. Collectively, they comprise what I call the 'architecture of infrastructure'. When I am asked to concentrate on the urban design aspect of our work I realise that I cannot separate out individual buildings we have designed and the cities or towns of which these buildings form a part. For me, the edges are totally blurred. Norman Foster, interviewed in *Corriere della Sera*, 10 January 2005

It's a commonplace that airports are becoming like cities. Usually this is a result of their scale and complexity rather than any sense of civic ambition. However, with Shanghai and Guangzhou airports in China we proposed something new – a fully integrated 'airport city', with housing, shops, hotels, offices and a whole range of other facilities – for which the terminal building was the catalyst. Just as in the nineteenth century new towns grew up around railway stations, in the twenty-first century emerging cities will surely coalesce around airports, with the advantage that they are connected as much with the world at large as with their neighbouring town or region. Norman Foster, in conversation with the editor, 2012

1. Shanghai Pudong Airport (1996). This competition scheme – one of a series of such projects undertaken for Pacific Rim cities in the late 1990s – sets out a vision of the international terminal as a fully integrated 'airport city' – a place in its own right. Commercial and retail buildings are gathered in a linear development extending north along the metro line and the approach roads into the terminal buildings.

2. Guangzhou Airport (1998). Guangzhou expanded on ideas explored in Shanghai Pudong, proposing an 'airport city' that could be constructed in phases, eventually handling 80 million passengers per annum.

Designed under different conditions, the competition schemes for Shanghai Pudong and Guangzhou airports, together offer a more accurate insight into the partnership's vision of the airport of the future. Up until this point, all of the practice's airport terminal designs, from Stansted onwards, have included generous provision within the main structure for shops and other commercial outlets, which, aside from distracting passengers from the tedium of waiting to board their aircraft, are an essential feature of airport economics. However, while making ample room for such facilities, which at Hong Kong are the size of a town shopping centre, the Foster strategy has always been to never let them overwhelm the experience of flight – a common failing of most terminals – so that passengers are always aware of the main flow of movement towards the aircraft, and of the majestic space and structure all around them.

In the competition scheme for Shanghai Pudong Airport, Foster and his team departed from the consultant's brief (a move which probably cost them the competition but which characteristically opened up the whole design process), arguing that it failed to make adequate provision for the commercial facilities that would be needed to help the airport pay its way. They proposed instead a radical plan, which, in addition to providing commercial outlets within the structure, created an entire commercial centre situated across the approach roads between the two terminal buildings. Including a World Trade Center with hotels, offices, conference and exhibition facilities, the commercial centre would stretch out alongside the planned metro line like a small linear city.

A similar linear plan was proposed for Guangzhou, the brief for which was relatively open-ended. Coupled with a dynamic terminal design to match the twenty-first century vision, the self-contained 'airport city' suggests an entirely new world of air travel and commerce, where time-challenged executives would dock in, catch some sleep, freshen up and do business, before returning to base, or flying onward; all within hundreds of yards of the aircraft. They would be joined, not only by tourists and other air-travellers with time to kill, but also by city-dwellers feeling like a bit of out-of-town shopping and/or entertainment in a glamorous setting.

To some extent, all of these facilities and activities are accommodated at least in part at many of the world's major airports, including hotels and conference centres. The Shanghai and Guangzhou airport schemes differ radically, however, in bringing these amenities together and giving them a positive urban form and identity – something airport developments with their scattered buildings and facilities generally lack. In many respects, these ambitious visions also symbolise the layer-cake model of development, with all its contradictions, which typifies so much of recent developments in China, as it does of developments in other parts of the region. Looked at from one angle, Foster's airport cities comprise an important part of the more prosperous tip of the Chinese economic and political iceberg, the less prosperous but far greater part of which gets relatively little coverage, either in the popular or professional media.

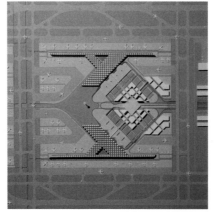

1

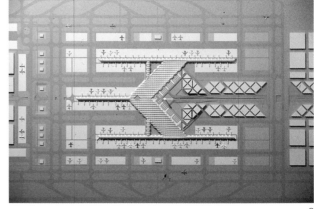

2

One huge advantage we enjoy in China is that we have offices in different time zones, so we can effectively work a twenty-four-hour day between Beijing or Hong Kong and London. That means a client presentation can finish at 6.00pm in China, and we can have all the revisions and alterations worked through and ready for them by 9.00am the following day. That efficient turnaround means we can always match, or be ahead of, our Chinese clients – and that's hugely important. Luke Fox, of Foster + Partners, in conversation with the editor, 2011

The way in which projects are built in China is shifting very quickly. For Beijing Airport we had around 30,000 workers on site, all producing work that was hand-finished but had the appearance of machine quality. Now what's happening is that new systems are being adopted by contractors and they're able to create export-quality materials – making the transition from having many low-paid workers to having many high-quality machines to produce with. And because the work ethic is extremely strong, the turnaround is much faster than anywhere else in the world. Luke Fox, of Foster + Partners, in conversation with the editor, 2011

Situated away from established city centres, the concept of the airport city might also seem at variance with the Foster studio's principles of high-density, mixed-use urban design, which are generally aimed at intensifying the urban experience. Serving the global as much as the local community, the vision of jet-lagged executives flitting from one airport city to another without ever going any further or getting to know the territory and people beyond, also conjures up a more troubling picture of 'parallel worlds', where globetrotters rarely encounter the inhabitants of any world but their own.

That, it may be countered, is what already happens everywhere anyway, and if creating a sufficiently interesting and diverse built environment around an airport terminal is going to make the experience, for passengers and airport workers alike, a more pleasurable one, then the concept deserves to be tested. Much, it may be speculated, may also depend upon the detailed design of these small cities, and on the transport links that tie them to the mother city and hinterland, which would help to draw people out to them. At their best, such places may function effectively more like self-contained new towns with runways, rather than runways with shops, which is more often the present case.

Foster's airport cities comprise an important part of the more prosperous tip of the Chinese economic and political iceberg.

Foster's building at Beijing Airport, raises many similar issues. Planned to serve the city during the 2008 Olympic Games and thereafter, the symbolic and functional importance of the terminal in the wider context of that event, and the development of the capital, can hardly be overestimated. Together with other major works designed by leading foreign architects, either for the Olympics or for other prestigious commissions, Foster's Beijing terminal presents an image of a progressive Chinese architectural culture barely conceivable even ten years earlier. Part of an ambitious plan for the transformation of Beijing into a 'world' city, the airport is one of a list of impressive projects, representing the cutting edge of advanced design, engineering and production technology. Comprising a veritable urban laboratory of experimental architecture, these include: the Central Chinese Television (CCTV) building by Rem Koolhaas/OMA; the Beijing National Stadium by Herzog & de Meuron; and the National Swimming Centre by Australian architects PTW.

In addition to these and many other construction projects, the masterplan included drastic (but only partially successful) measures to reduce the city's notoriously high levels of air pollution in time for the Games. By 2008, most of the city's buses and taxis had been switched from diesel to natural gas, while extensions and improvements to the light-rail and metro systems helped to reduce traffic. The supply of natural gas into the city was increased fourfold, helping to wean the remaining 15 per cent of residents still using coal-burning stoves, away from another major source of pollution. Over 100 factories were also relocated from inner-city locations to the outskirts, reducing the amount of inner-city industrial land by half.

Serious as they are, traffic and industrial pollution are not the worst of Beijing's environmental problems. Like many of China's other major cities, particularly those in the coastal states and SEZs, Beijing is suffering the environmental backlash resulting from years of over-farming and over-grazing in the surrounding country, which have turned much of the hinterland into a wind-blown desert. To help control the dust storms that now regularly plague Beijing and its inhabitants, the city is planting hundreds of thousands of trees in a 125km belt around the city.

Together, both individual projects and environmental measures mark a turning point in the history of the capital, the legacy of which will undoubtedly last for many years. At the same time, it should be apparent to even the most optimistic observer, that the day for easy and verifiable correlations between the nature and form of a country's architecture and its political and social constitution, let alone its economic health, is long gone.

3. Dense smog hangs over the Olympic Park in Beijing – conceived as virtually a second capital within the city. It was the Americans, with the Los Angeles Games, who invented the concept of the Olympic economy. But with Beijing the Chinese took that idea to a new level. The amount spent on the Olympics is estimated at US$40 billion, of which only US$8 billion was directed toward facilities built exclusively for the Games. The balance was invested in Beijing's permanent transport infrastructure – an essential factor for any city aiming to establish a post-Games urban 'legacy'.

3

1. Beijing International Airport (2003-2008). Completed as the gateway to the city for the twenty-ninth Olympiad, Beijing's international terminal is the world's largest and most advanced airport building. A symbol of place, its soaring aerodynamic roof and dragon-like form consciously evoke traditional Chinese colours and symbols.

Prior to 1978, contemporary architecture in China could almost be divided into two kinds, public monuments and mass-produced state housing, both of which were designed according to rigidly imposed aesthetic and social criteria. Like the Stalinist-era architecture in the Soviet Union, upon which post-war Chinese architecture was closely modelled, both forms reflected the autocratic regime that built them.

State housing is still turned out at even greater rates, only slightly modified by improvements in layout and construction. However, since 1978, the repetitive blocks have been joined by a bewildering mixture of private apartments, office towers – including some of the tallest and most advanced in the world – and shopping malls (among other benchmarks, China now lays claim to the largest mall in the world), which have no conventional place in a tightly controlled socialist state. As Mihai Craciun writes in *Great Leap Forward* (2001), Rem Koolhaas's study of China's Special Economic Zones with the Harvard School of Design: 'The SEZs are the cradles of a culture of contradictions'. Deng Xiaoping's creation of a hybrid 'socialist market economy', Craciun argues, not only threw Chinese socialism into crisis, it undermined the Communist state's hitherto relatively stable modes of architectural and urban production, discarding 'the assumed correspondence between ideology and form'.

The most surprising aspect of this transformation, however, has been the change in approach towards major public buildings, of which Foster's Beijing Airport, Andreu's National Theatre, and the Olympics buildings are conspicuous examples. Where public architecture was once perceived as the ultimate bastion of conservatism and orthodoxy, it is now presented as the progressive face of a new China, open to untried concepts and technologies, and even ready and eager to embrace a green environmental agenda when the opportunity arises.

Olympics or no Olympics, Beijing was in any case due for a new airport terminal, the timing of which has as much to do with China's entry into the World Trade Organization and the increased volume of trade resulting from that event, as with any temporary increase of air traffic due to the sporting occasion. Like Hong Kong's Chek Lap Kok in its own time, the new building is the largest of its kind in the world. Built entirely by Chinese owned construction companies, the project is a showcase for local industry, as well as advanced design. Astonishingly, the entire airport was designed and built within just four years, an extraordinary timetable which Foster tellingly compares with the twenty years required for Heathrow's Terminal 5, which is just half the size. Decked-out 'dragon-like' in Chinese red and yellow livery and connected to the city by dedicated new rail and road links, the airport provides travellers with an entrance to the capital fit for the Pacific Age.

Foster's Beijing terminal presents an image of a progressive Chinese architectural culture which was barely conceivable even ten years earlier.

In the long run, however, Singapore, though vastly different from China in its history and development as well as its minute size, may offer a more reliable and positive political and social model for the region. Not without its own contradictions, as the wealthiest and most advanced economy per capita in Asia Pacific after Japan, the tiny island state has had a regional and global import far beyond its area or the number of its population (currently 4.6 million). Castigated by Western architectural critics for its dull public housing and destruction of much of the colonial city, and by the press for its restrictive culture, Singapore's achievements are often overlooked. In terms of the distribution of its wealth alone, however, Singaporeans can rightly lay claim to enjoying one of the most equitable as well as prosperous societies on earth. The state's infrastructure-led approach to urban planning, with its decentralised network of compact new towns, combination of efficient public transport systems, and restrictions on traffic, also presents a model of sustainable urban growth scarcely matched anywhere else in the world.

1

Interestingly, the value of Singapore's experience has not been lost on China's urban planners, who, in one of the more hopeful signs for the future, have been picking the country's brains in recent years in the search for solutions to their own problems.

Behind the carefully controlled facade there lies a more complex reality and a typically Asian layer-cake of different but overlapping economic and cultural systems. Similar to the 'dual economies' of other, less developed countries, alongside the large-scale, corporate headquarters and other modern firms, Singapore boasts a thriving small-scale, bazaar economy based upon traditional family ties and personal connections. Colourfully visible in the busy ground-floor eating places and small shops and services spilling out from under most apartment blocks, they comprise as much as 25 per cent of Singapore's economy, including small family businesses and cottage industries of every kind.

Hitherto suppressed, the richer and more diverse side of Singaporean cultural life has also recently been allowed freer rein as the country's leaders have come to realise that competing in the global economy requires an innovative society as well as efficient management, which in turn requires freedom and diversity of expression. Characteristically, the government has responded with carefully targeted and well-funded projects aimed at turning Singapore into a major focus for the arts in the region, as well as a business centre. Public architecture, as the most visible expression of the new policy, is one of the main beneficiaries, of which the Singapore Performing Arts Centre, 2003, by Stirling Wilford, was the first and most direct result. Similarly, Foster's Expo Station and more recently the Singapore Supreme Court take their place in a government-sponsored programme of high-profile buildings, intended to raise architectural and creative standards as well as to fulfil their specific functions.

As the first station on the metro line taking passengers from the airport into the city, and the main stop for the Singapore International Expo, Foster's sleek structure with its cantilevered, titanium roof, provides a stunning gateway. Partly inspired by vernacular architecture and techniques of climate control, the naturally ventilated building is also one of the studio's most successful attempts to date to fuse traditional principles of regional design with advanced technology.

The Supreme Court, situated in the heart of the old colonial city just behind the former Neo-classical courthouse, also has an eye-catching feature in the form of a large, disc-shaped element housing the chamber of the Court of Appeal, not unlike the stainless steel 'flying saucer' poised over the entrance to the Expo Station. Hovering above the main body of the building, the streamlined chamber symbolises both the role of the Court of Appeal as the highest judicial body in the land, and Singapore's broader aspirations as a fast modernising country, punching far above its weight and about to take off in yet another stage of its carefully planned programme of advancement.

Other, more subtle features in the design of the Court signify major changes in the way the country runs its affairs, and wants to be seen. In line with the government's well established policy of greening the city, the programme required that the building use as much natural light and as little energy as possible. However, instead of following conventional practice with large, medium-rise buildings of this sort and opening up the middle with one or more atria or courtyards – the Willis Faber & Dumas building and many other examples come to mind – Foster and his team instead chose to slice open the eight-storey structure with broad internal 'streets' running in both directions right across the site. The effect is to break up the facade of the building as well as the interior, opening it up, not only to the sky, but also to the surrounding streets, symbolically as well as literally exposing the internal workings of the Court to the city at large.

2. Supreme Court, Singapore (2000-2005). Located within the Colonial District, on the north bank of the Singapore River, the building takes its cue from the scale of the neighbouring civic buildings, offering a modern reinterpretation of their colonial vernacular to convey an image of dignity, transparency and openness.

2

1. Expo Station, Singapore (1997-2000). The first Mass Rapid Transport station that visitors to the city encounter when travelling along the new Changi Airport Line, Expo Station serves the Singapore Expo Centre. Its design is both a celebration of arrival and an appropriate response to one of the warmest climates in the world. Two highly sculptural roof canopies overlap to dynamic visual effect; the platforms are otherwise left open to encourage a cooling flow of air through the station.

Other features of a contextual as well as a practical nature help to tie the building firmly into its place and climate. The prominent, right-angled sunshades on the external walls nod towards vernacular architecture, while the exposed slender columns along the same facades echo the Neo-classical colonnades of the earlier building and similar edifices from the same period. Not unlike the slim columns along the front of the Carré d'Art in Nîmes, which mirror the portico of the Roman temple opposite, they respectfully acknowledge the older buildings without recourse to mimicry. Similarly, the circular 'floating' chamber presents a twenty-first-century reinterpretation of the old Court's own crowning dome.

However, if any of Foster's recent works in the region captures the full spirit – as well as the ambiguities – of the Pacific era, it is the new campus for Malaysia's Petronas University of Technology. With over half the population made up of Chinese and Indian descendants of immigrants who settled in the country during British rule, education is seen by the Malay-dominated government as the indispensable foundation, not only for economic success, but also for a secular society open to all races and religions: Muslims, Buddhists and Christians alike. Named after its principal sponsor, the partly state-owned Petronas Corporation – the same oil company that commissioned Cesar Pelli's Petronas Towers in Kuala Lumpur – the university campus is a textbook exercise in sustainable design and modern regionalism. As the region's largest academic centre for all forms of engineering, like the Petronas Towers, it also symbolises the country's rapid growth and status as one of the second wave of so-called newly industrialised countries, or NICs.

The design of the campus draws a large part of its strength and character from its hilly jungle setting. Following the contours of the site, the academic blocks are strung necklace-like around a central park. At the eastern end of the park, terminating the access road, the main buildings are gathered together on either side of a large open-air piazza under a vast, circular roof canopy. A similar broad canopy runs around the campus, sheltering the linked walkways that run around the edge of the park.

In plan, the crescent-shaped canopies trace the outline and legs of a sea turtle, one of Southeast Asia's best-loved species, the park forming the shell and the main buildings the head – an accidental but endearing image which the architects exploited as the university logo. From ground level, however, like the Expo Station, the campus appears to be 'all roof' – a direct response to the need for protection from the tropical sun and heavy rainfall, while at the same time allowing the free passage of cooling breezes. While in the hot, humid climate most of the classrooms, laboratories and lecture halls are, by necessity, air-conditioned, the circulation areas in the academic blocks are predominantly naturally ventilated. Placed around the perimeter of each block and open to the outside in the fashion common to colonial-era buildings, the broad decks afford both shade and views. The combination of lush tropical vegetation and oversailing roof canopies, beneath which students and teachers move in all weathers, creates an extraordinary environment for learning.

One of Malaysia's largest new construction projects as well as one of the Foster studio's most important exercises in sustainable design, it is ironic that much of the research on this greenest of campuses should be devoted to the petroleum industry and related fields. For one of the region's most complex multi-racial and multi-cultural societies, however, such contradictions, as they are in China, Singapore and elsewhere, are commonplace, if not endemic to the country's economic and cultural evolution. The same learning and research institutions that are now engaged in Malaysia's petroleum industry will doubtless also be those – if not today, then tomorrow – researching and developing alternative sources of energy, probably funded at least in part, as they already are elsewhere, by those same petroleum companies striving to keep ahead of the game.

1

In concluding his thesis, William Irwin Thompson clearly struggles to deal with such ambiguities: 'Like an infant that knows what it needs and can point to food, even though it cannot define it, one can gesture and shake one's head in negation more easily than one can conceptually define a new cultural ecology when we have only just entered it.'

If any of Foster's recent works in the region captures the full spirit – as well as the ambiguities – of the Pacific era, it is the campus for Malaysia's Petronas University of Technology.

To a large extent, however, Thompson's difficulties, as are those of anyone looking for some kind of grand blueprint for the future, in Asia Pacific or anywhere else, are of his own making. Summarising the defining characteristics of the Atlantic and Pacific cultural ecologies, he lists: 'civilisation embodied in a world city', and 'technological clutter and gigantic buildings and machines' for the former, against 'planetary culture as participation in a moving process or network' and 'technological minimalism and miniaturisation; technologies that mimic organic processes' for the latter. As with all the other similar cases described here, rather than one cultural form simply displacing the other, what we now have in these instances is actually both forms of development, each overlaid and coexisting with the other.

Similarly, in promoting an irreversible shift of energies from the Atlantic to the Pacific, as a self-confessed 'European intellectual', anxious to offload his own intellectual baggage, or at least, not let it hinder his vision, Thompson may also be overstating the case. In creating the Alliance of Southeast Asian Nations, or ASEAN, an economic and trading organisation comprising all the countries of Southeast Asia, together with China and Japan as affiliate members, the institutional model that inspired their leaders to club together was the European Union (EU). Notwithstanding the usual diplomatic hiccups, as the international body that finally put aside traditional concepts of the independent nation state, or 'us and them', turning former enemies into business partners, there is also no better example anywhere else of an emergent political culture where non-ideological thinking rules.

As the main instigators and defenders of the Kyoto Protocol, the international agreement setting limits on greenhouse gas emissions, it is also the member countries of the EU, together with individual committed nations like Singapore, rather than any of the other major economic and political blocks, who are setting the global environmental agenda. Should the member nations of ASEAN eventually progress to the same advanced state of integration as the EU, which at this point in time remains a distant goal, then they would owe the transformation of cultures at least in part to those earlier Atlantic and Mediterranean civilisations from whence the European ideal arose.

Not least, as the present regional guardians of that more open tradition of Islamic thought and culture which once helped to lay the foundations of the European Renaissance (it was Muslim scholars who first translated the ancient texts of Greek scientists and thinkers and so brought their knowledge back to life) and held sway in Spain for hundreds of years, Malaysian Muslims, and to a lesser extent, Muslims all around Asia Pacific, are also the distant recipients of both earlier Mediterranean and Middle Eastern civilisations, no less than they are recipients of their own local cultures.

In summary, a true planetary cultural ecology, even one centred around the Pacific Rim, will most likely be composed of at least some of the positive as well as negative elements generated by all four civilisations interacting together: Middle Eastern, Mediterranean, Atlantic and Pacific, rather than just the latter. We should not be unduly surprised, therefore, to find that some of the most significant and representative architecture of the emergent era was created by an international team of designers and engineers, led by an architect hailing from Manchester.

2. Petronas University of Technology, Malaysia (1998-2004). The design responds to the physical landscape of the site and to the weather patterns particular to this part of the world. While it can be intensely hot in the sun, in the monsoon season the skies open every afternoon to bring torrential rain. To allow students to move around the campus while shaded from the sun or protected from downpours, elevated roof canopies protect the pedestrian routes that wind around the edge of the site.

2

Supreme Court
Singapore 2000 – 2005

The new Supreme Court in Singapore was the second Foster project to be completed in the city-state, and the first building of its type the practice has undertaken anywhere in the world. The building combines the functions of civil and criminal courts, together with the Court of Appeal, and presented quite specific programmatic challenges, aside from its situation in a tropical climate zone. However, as David Nelson – who led the project – explains, while the commission prompted research into the design of law courts, the design team's approach arose as much from the history and character of its unique urban and cultural setting as from any other factors.

The site cried out for a building that would not only respect its historical role and situation, but would play an equally important part in the life of the modern city.

The site lies in the government precinct close to the mouth of the Singapore River. Its location follows a pattern of placing key civic buildings together in the centre of the city going back to the earliest years of colonisation. The precinct laid out by Stamford Raffles in 1822 was part of a larger urban plan in which different areas of the city were segregated by both race and function. The government precinct formed the heart of the 'European city', surrounded by neatly laid out suburbs of detached villas, while the 'native city' of Chinese shop-houses and Malay 'kampongs' occupied separate but adjacent areas, parts of which still survive.

A prominent feature of the colonial city was a large public open space, or 'Padang', used for military parades and sporting events around which key civic buildings would be arranged. The former Singapore Supreme Court building – designed by the architects of the colonial Public Works Department (PWD), which was responsible for most such buildings – epitomises the imperial architecture of the period.

Completed in 1939, the Supreme Court marked the twilight of the colonial era. Its facilities being since then long overstretched, in the latter part of its life the functions of the Court had spilled over into the adjacent City Hall, eventually compelling the government to commission a new building.

The quality of Singapore's architecture since the Second World War is mixed, reflecting the pressures arising from the rush to modernise in the face of regional and global competition, often at the expense of the historical fabric of the city. Liu Thai Ker, the former chief planner of Singapore's Urban Redevelopment Authority (URA) and one of the leading consultants for the Supreme Court project, describes the buildings of the CBD and elsewhere in the city as the 'first wave' of international architecture, mostly indifferent to place and climate. What was needed now, he argued, was a 'second wave' more suited to, and expressive of, the tropical climate and character of Singapore. The new Supreme Court was to be among the first fruits of a conscious effort by the government to upgrade the architecture of the city.

Under Liu's guidance, a small number of practices was selected for what Nelson describes as a series of 'dialogues' between client and prospective architect, rather than the usual contest between competing schemes. Following the conclusion of the selection process, Liu continued to mediate between architect and client as consultant to the Design Advisory Committee. Consisting of judges as well as government representatives, the latter was to have a considerable impact on the development of the project.

Opposite: Located immediately behind the original Neoclassical court building and City Hall, the new Supreme Court is situated at the heart of the historic government precinct close to the mouth of the Singapore River.

1. An early concept sketch by Norman Foster showing how the old courthouse's dome might be reinterpreted for a new century.

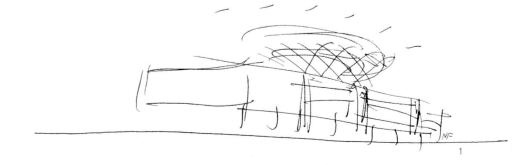

We were very impressed by the client team who had prepared an incredibly detailed brief. In many projects you don't get much of a brief so you have to draw it out of the client and develop it with them. At Singapore it was very advanced – they knew what they wanted. Edson Yabiku, of Foster + Partners, in discussion with the editor, 2011

There were a number of planning conditions in place, including a building envelope which we had to adhere to, so we had to mass the building in relation to what was there already. The site is at the historic heart of Singapore and while we were inevitably going to do a modern building we felt that it should sit comfortably with the existing historic buildings. David Nelson, in conversation with the editor, 2012
Right: Some of the many dozens of sketch models made to study massing options in the early design stages.

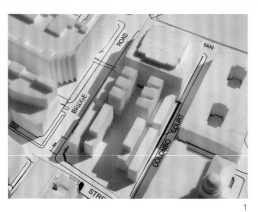 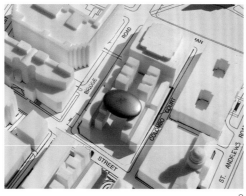
1   2   3

1-3. Examples of a series of early massing studies. A number of different configurations were considered: the first two models show the courtrooms arranged in two blocks at the front of the building; the third model is a closer approximation of the finished building.

4-8. Norman Foster's sketches show the 'flying saucer' as a reference for the design of the Court of Appeal at the top of the building – the 'light' disc floating impartially above the 'heavy' stone base of the courthouse. Further sketches show the plan form with its clearly defined axes and how they correspond to the sight lines and routes which lead to the Padang, the large open public space in front of the building, which is used for civic ceremonies – or more usually, cricket matches.

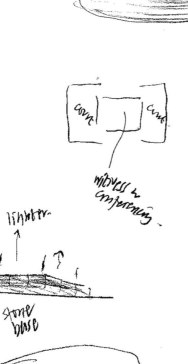
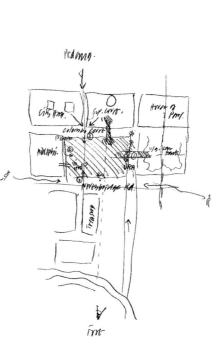
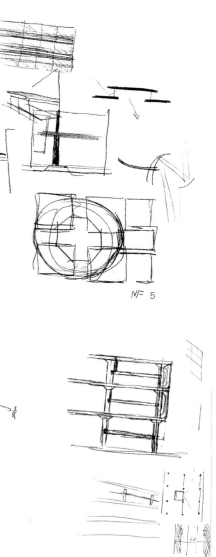

4

5

6

7

8

Transparency and public accessibility were key considerations for us – we wanted to establish the new Supreme Court as a representative symbol of justice in Singapore. Robert McFarlane, formerly of Foster + Partners, in conversation with the editor, 2008
Left: Robert McFarlane, Marilu Sicoli, Peter Stück and Edson Yabiku, discuss an early sketch model. Resolving the circulation of the court was a very three-dimensional puzzle: the difference in ceiling height between offices and courtrooms, together with the complex segregation required, meant that models such as these were the fastest and most efficient way of developing the scheme.

There was a lot of discussion about how a court should be and Norman and I visited a number, but the one I remember most was Jean Nouvel's in Nantes. It's all black and very dramatic so he clearly has a particular view about how justice should be represented. However, both we and the client felt that the courtrooms should somehow have a friendlier appearance so rather than being threatening it was trying to be something softer and warmer with a better ambience for the whole theatre of the court to play out in. David Nelson, in conversation with the editor, 2012

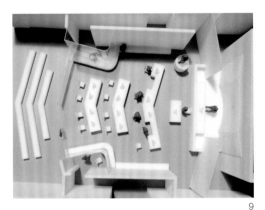

9

10

11

9-11. The initial brief called for a technologically advanced, paper-free courtroom. Several different layouts of the courtrooms were mocked-up, all of which included a sizeable AV screen to allow remote testimony to be given.

12. Norman Foster's sketches, exploring the form of the Court of Appeal at the top of the building.

Most people will associate the idea of a Supreme Court with the US version, which confines itself to cases of a far-reaching federal or constitutional nature. In Singapore, in contrast, it includes the High Courts – civil and criminal, dealing with the most serious cases of each kind – and the Court of Appeal, which is the final legal resort for both types of cases. Relatively minor offences are dealt with by a system of Subordinate Courts located elsewhere. Unlike most Western models, the Singapore legal system does not include juries, the judgment in all cases being the sole responsibility of a judge. Both in legal and organisational respects, therefore, the Supreme Court building embodies a clearly defined hierarchical structure.

The challenge for the architects was thus somewhat paradoxical: how to meet and express the resulting set of inflexible programmatic needs, while at the same time opening the building up to the public and integrating it as far as possible into the surrounding city, visually and functionally?

The key to the Foster team's solution lies in their approach to the site. Situated behind the old courthouse, it occupies a whole block on the edge of the government precinct next to the Padang. On its southern boundary the site looks across to a smaller green space terminating at the edge of the Singapore River. Facing into the same space to the south-east stands the New Parliament, and behind that is the Old Parliament, a Neoclassical building originally designed for residential use in 1827 by GD Colman, a noted British expatriate architect, on the very spot that Raffles is reputed to have landed just eight years earlier.

To the west, the site is bounded by North Bridge Road, the main route through the centre of the city. A short distance further west is Fort Canning Park, as important to Singapore's history as the Padang. Immediately to the north, the site is closed by the Adelphi building, a large retail centre, while beyond that is St Andrew's Cathedral, completed in 1857.

The strategy the design team followed was as much an exercise in urban design as architecture.

To Foster and David Nelson the site cried out for a public building that would not only respect its historical role and situation, but would play an equally important part in the life of the modern city. As such, it should reflect the urban pattern of Singapore, in density, texture and character – not so much a building in the city, as a microcosm of the city itself.

The strategy the design team subsequently followed was as much an exercise in urban design as architecture. The scale of the programme itself called for nothing less. The Court of Appeal alone includes three separate courtrooms together with adjacent hearing chambers and conference rooms, plus offices and facilities for the judges and supporting staff. In addition, there are as many as twenty separate civil and criminal courts, each of which has its own hearing chambers or conference rooms and other essential facilities.

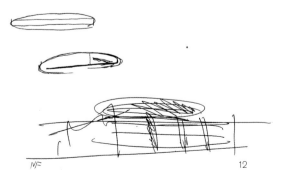

The design of the new courthouse will be flexible enough to allow for future advances in the administration of justice as well as growing workloads. Ultimately, the architectural vocabulary of the new Supreme Court building seeks to convey the image of dignity, incorruptibility, transparency and efficiency – qualities representative of Singapore's judicial system.
Chief Justice Yong Pung How, speaking at the foundation stone laying ceremony, 29 November 2002

It's probably one of the most complex programmatic arrangements that you could imagine: you have the public who want to go into the courtrooms; you have the lawyers who are also using the courts. There may be press who use a certain section of them and you also have judiciary who need to enter the space entirely independent of everyone else. And then there are the defendants entering from holding cells downstairs, who cannot interact with anyone but somehow have to enter the space. They may see each other but they certainly can't contact each other … the complexity of all that was incredibly three-dimensional. Andy Miller, formerly of Foster + Partners, in conversation with the editor, 2010

The Supreme Court was our first court building, which was great because we're always keen to develop new building types, but this was particularly difficult because of the many different types of people who would be coming and going there. It had to be both integrated and segregated and that had to be done vertically as well as in plan. This led to a highly intricate planning of the spaces and in particular of the circulation, because the judges wanted to be able to go from their offices to the courtrooms independently of the public coming to sit in the galleries.
David Nelson, in conversation with the editor, 2012

1. A 1:200 model, showing the Court of Appeal. The main courtroom is located in the centre with two further courts fanning out on either side of the foyer. Meeting rooms and offices wrap around the main courtroom.

2. Model view of the east facade. The maximum allowable height around the perimeter was five storeys. This was relaxed towards the centre of the building, which steps up to culminate in the Court of Appeal.

3. Sketches by Norman Foster exploring routes through the building – direct versus offset.

4. Ground floor plan.

5. First floor plan.

6. Second floor plan.

7. Fifth floor plan.

8. Eighth floor plan.

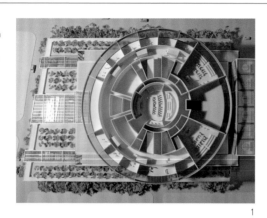

1

2

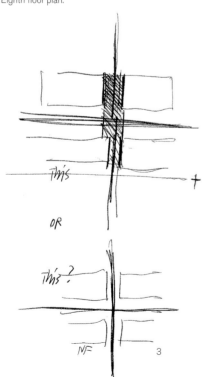

3

Each High Court judge in turn has his own office, and is supported by staff in the general office spaces, which take up a large part of the building volume, some of which can be changed to add more courtrooms at a later date.

Then there are the shared and semi-public spaces and facilities, including a 600-seat auditorium, a legal library and facilities for the Singapore Academy of Law, a permanent exhibition of the history of the Court, a canteen and bistro, a fitness centre, a nursery, and separate administrative offices. Finally, ample parking spaces had to be provided below ground, together with holding cells and separate secure access for prisoners, judges and other groups.

The ground floor, with its broad central avenue and cross axis, was conceived as an open, public domain.

Compounding the complexity of the programme, a height limitation of five storeys around the edge of the site constrained the possible spatial permutations. However, this restriction was relaxed further into the site, creating the possibility of increasing the height of the building towards the centre. This solved any potential difficulties with squeezing in the required amount of usable space, but it left the problem of getting natural light into the building where it was needed.

Faced with similar large building programmes and deep sites, Foster has previously opted for a single large atrium in the centre, providing both natural toplight and a spatial focus, the classic example being the Carré d'Art. Here, however, the team adopted a very different strategy, opting for a spatial system comprised of parallel blocks of accommodation running through the length of the site from north to south, separated by internal 'streets' covered by shaded steel and glass roofs.

Emulating the surrounding urban pattern of major and minor thoroughfares, the site is bisected along the main axis by a broad 'avenue' leading all the way from the main entrance facing the river, to the service and parking access at the far end down the side of the Adelphi. Two narrow streets slice through both sides of the site along the same axis, creating four parallel blocks. These are sliced up again from east to west, picking up a second visual axis towards Fort Canning Park and forming a broad cross-axis in the centre from one side of the site to the other, and again by two minor 'lanes' towards each end, linking up with the narrow side streets.

A dense urban pattern of 'blocks', 'streets' and 'lanes' is thus established within the boundaries of the site, creating something more like a sheltered pedestrian precinct than a conventional building. Within this framework, the blocks vary in width, height and transparency according to function and location.

We used to attend design panel committees on a regular basis and make presentations in the old City Hall with a young judge and an old judge present. That was part of the sophistication of the client – they wanted a balance in the design panel and there was always a lot of discussion about the project. Most of the people in the room were from the legal profession and would remember exactly what had been said. Andy Miller, formerly of Foster + Partners, in conversation with the editor, 2010 Right: David Nelson, Andy Miller and Marilu Sicoli discuss the design of the courtrooms.

We spent a lot of time trying to resolve the complexity of the circulation and trying different diagrams to achieve the segregation that was required. Courts are similar to football stadiums: the players have their own room, as do the media, the public and VIPs, but they should never meet apart from a certain slot where the media talks to the players. Edson Yabiku, of Foster + Partners, in discussion with the editor, 2011

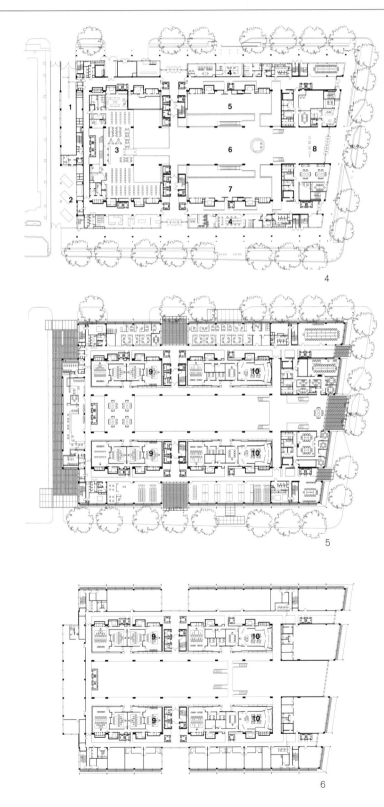

4

5

6

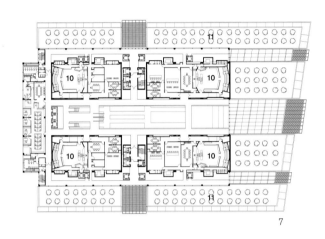

7

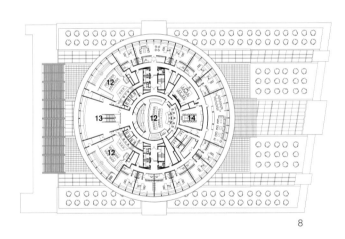

8

1 ramp to basement car park
2 prisoner drop-off area
3 library
4 offices
5 restaurant
6 atrium
7 exhibition space
8 main entrance
9 hearing chambers
10 High Court
11 roof terrace
12 Appeal Courts
13 lobby
14 meeting rooms

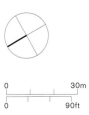

0   30m
0   90ft

Previous pages: The Supreme Court seen from the Padang.

1. Long section looking west from the Adelphi; the primary circulation route through the building is via a series of escalators. They culminate in one of the longest single-span escalators in the world, which leads up into the 'belly' of the disc that contains the Court of Appeal.

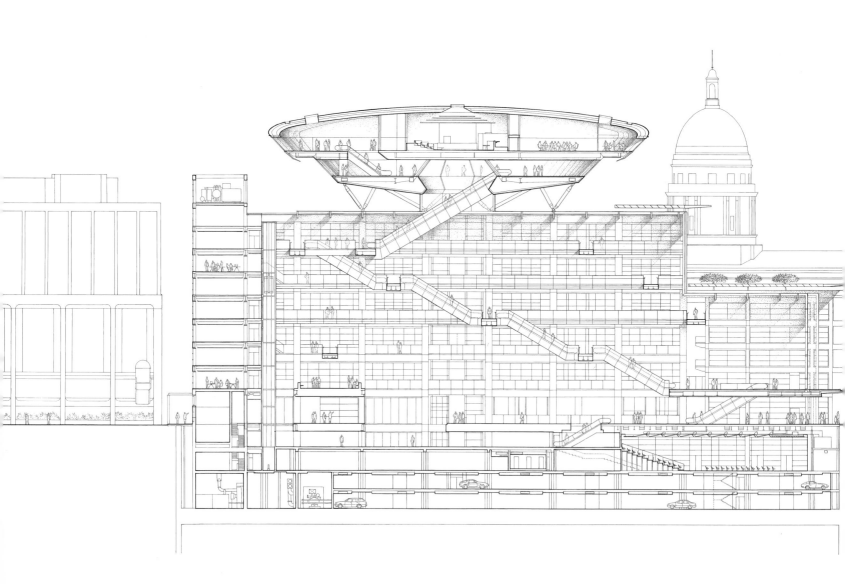

For Singaporeans of my generation, the old Supreme Court building stood out as an icon of the exemplary city in which we lived and worked. I can imagine what emotions it must stir for those who practised the Law and were familiar with its corridors, chambers and courtrooms. Today, I am delighted to be here to officially open the new Supreme Court building, which in many ways, reflects its very modern surroundings and the progress of our judiciary. The atmosphere of the new courtroom and the building is less daunting than the old Supreme Court building. It is more open and approachable. At the same time, it retains the air of dignity and solemnity that is associated with a Supreme Court. SR Nathan, President of the Republic of Singapore, speaking at the opening of the Supreme Court building, 7 January 2006 Left: The old Supreme Court building, seen here in the background, was the last of the great colonial-era Neoclassical buildings in Singapore. It was designed by Frank Dorrington Ward of the Public Works Department and constructed in 1937-1939.

Singapore has regulations to monitor building heights and setbacks etc. On first appearance they appear to be very rigid. But if you present an argument for doing things differently, they will listen. At the Supreme Court, the Appeals Court disc is actually outside the original height limitation, the shoulder of the courts is on the limitation, parallel to the neighbouring parapets, and the shoulder of the judges' offices is below the regulation to tie in with the Adelphi. If we'd just followed the rules, we would have ended up with a box, but we looked at the urban context and drew on that – and they could see the reason for the variation. Andy Miller, formerly of Foster + Partners, in conversation with the editor, 2010

The Court of Appeal, the highest court in Singapore, is raised symbolically in a disc-like form at the top of the building – a contemporary iteration of the old courthouse's dome.
Norman Foster

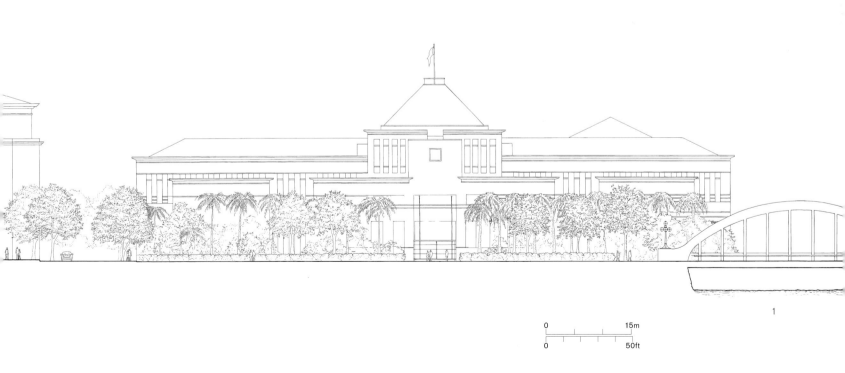

0   15m
0   50ft

1

The public atrium, the main interior space, with its carefully placed circulation elements such as escalators, walkways and bridges, is a vast animated space flushed with diffused daylight. It also forms a vista that opens out and connects the interior of the building to the city, framing the green space in front of the new parliament house and beyond. *Singapore Architect*, October 2005

The building is sited in the civic district of Singapore and when we first had conversations with the authorities, there was reference to the National Library up the road, but it was made clear that the new building was not to be of steel and glass – it needed to have an appropriate 'gravitas'. We decided to use marble laminated into glass so that during the day from the outside the building looks quite solid and grounded but inside it's very animated from the light passing through the panels; at night when the lights go on, it's the complete reverse and acts as a lantern. Andy Miller, formerly of Foster + Partners, in conversation with the editor, 2010

In the old Courthouse, the circulation was hidden, just as it was in most colonial-era buildings. It was a maze of corridors and relied on signage to tell people where to go. We wanted to make the circulation in the new building as intuitive as possible so that when you enter, you know straight away where things are – it's very simple. Emily Phang, of Foster + Partners, in conversation with the editor, 2011

1

1. Looking down on to the floor of the atrium from the first-floor balcony. Translucent marble panels correspond with meeting rooms on each level; the solid cladding denotes plant rooms, WCs and other service areas.

2. Standing on the first floor, looking up at the banks of escalators that cascade down through the the atrium.

3. Cross-section through the atrium and lower courts. The five-storey perimeter blocks contain offices; the inner blocks rise up another two storeys and house courtrooms. An auditorium and other semi-public functions are located on the two levels immediately below ground, with the remaining two floors below that given over to car parking.

2

When we were designing the appeal courts we had to decide whether to follow the internal shape of the other courts or express them externally and make three bubbles or boxes, but it was just getting too visually heavy so the disc seemed an obvious solution. This proved particularly effective because the underside is quite reflective yet also acted as a form of shading, so it had the dual benefit of preventing the atrium from overheating and bouncing diffuse light into the space at the same time. Edson Yabiku, of Foster + Partners, in discussion with the editor, 2011

The disc-like volume sitting on top of the public atrium is an ode to the dome of the old Supreme Court. However, unlike the dome of the old court, which is all exterior, as the dome is hidden away from view in the interior and houses no programme, the disc in the new Supreme Court houses the highest authorities in Singapore's judicial system – the Court of Appeal and offices of the judges. *Singapore Architect*, October 2005

We wanted to accommodate the three appeal courts on one level. This turned into an exercise about thinking how big a footprint we were going to need, and the most economical way of containing a large footprint is in a circle, so the circular form came fairly early on in the process. The difficulty then was how you entered it and how you connected and organised the space inside. David Nelson, in conversation with the editor, 2012

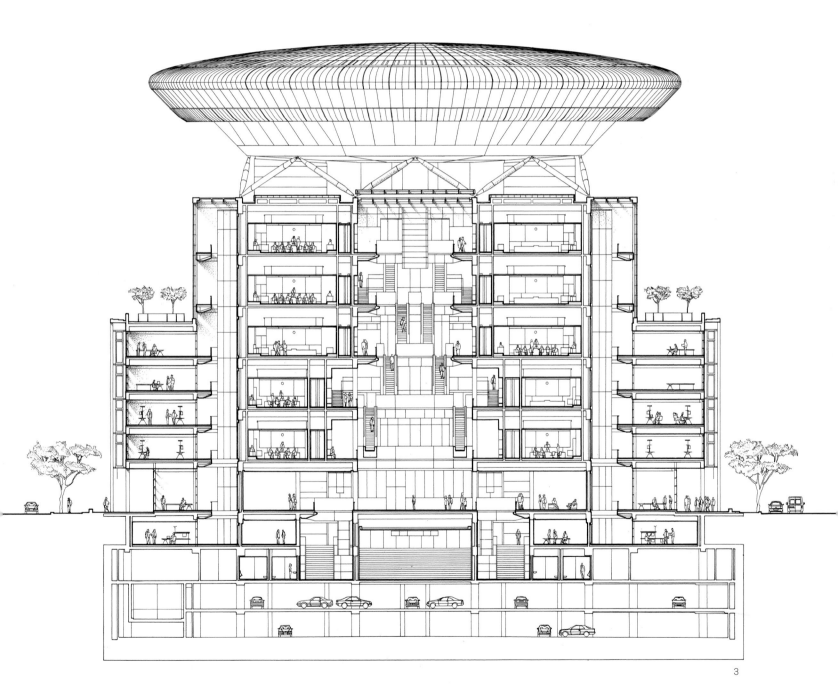

3

0 ——— 10m
0 ——— 30ft

We developed a prototype of a typical courtroom which we used as a proving ground for the actual detail of what the courtroom interiors were going to be – their materials and finishes. It was set up in the old courthouse, and was used for a number of court cases, so it was really tested before we made the final commitment to the design. It was a fascinating exercise in ergonomics and theatre. David Nelson, in conversation with the editor, 2012

When the judges visited the courtroom mock-ups they gave us feedback on issues such as lines of sight, whether or not they were comfortable with the position of the witness box, or where they would like the lawyers to be placed. It was a very interactive process. Eye contact is important, because the judges need to be able to run the whole court. That means being able to see the expressions of the witnesses, the lawyers and the defendant. This is especially critical in Singapore because there is no jury system – the judge makes the final decision. Emily Phang, of Foster + Partners, in conversation with the editor, 2011

1 2 3

1. A full-scale prototype of a typical courtroom was set up in the old court building prior to construction. Here, judges and officials were encouraged to participate and offer comments, allowing subtle refinements to be made before the design was finalised.

2. One of the twenty civil and criminal courtrooms on the lower levels, as seen from the judge's bench.

3. Looking into one of the side Appeal Courts on the upper level.

The blocks lining the main avenue, which house the law courts and have closed walls, are both wider and taller than the glazed perimeter blocks, which contain office spaces and require natural light. Reflecting their different functions, they also have different but related floor heights, so that two courtroom floors of 6 metres each equal three office floors of 4 metres.

Keeping within the height limitations, the perimeter blocks on three sides, which are covered by roof gardens, are just five storeys high, while the inner blocks, together with their enclosed side streets, rise in the middle of the site to provide another two floors of courtrooms. The largest and deepest courtrooms are also gathered together here on the uppermost floors. A further four floors are provided below ground level, covering the entire site. The lower two floors are taken up with parking, while those above house the auditorium, library and other semi-public functions, where they can be easily accessed from the entrance level.

Aside from the special urban qualities of the interior, the spatial geometry and block planning of the building is thus far perfectly consistent with planning and structural conventions. In keeping with the pattern of the former Supreme Court and its neighbours, the layout is also symmetrical around the main north-south axis – one of many such gestures towards its predecessor that run through the scheme. The handling of the Court of Appeal, however, appears at first glance to take the project into an altogether different realm.

The designers have gathered the three appellate courts into a circular element mounted a full storey above the central body of the building. Both in three dimensions and in section, the metal-clad disc, with its curved edges and spacecraft imagery, looks quite alien to the rest of the structure. In plan, however, the structure reveals a different side to its character, as regular and symmetrical as the rest of the building and rooted in the same tradition. The offices and other spaces on the main level are laid out in concentric rings around the chief courtroom, which is positioned centrally under the apex of the roof.

A smaller, octagonal, floor beneath the main level transfers structural loads to the steel support frame, which in turn rests on the building frame below. Indented in the centre, seen from underneath it visually mirrors both the circular shape of the courtroom above and the point where the two horizontal axes meet below. A circular skylight in the centre of the shallow dome over the courtrooms terminates the vertical axis with a familiar Classical flourish.

However, it is not until one stands in the open space to the south, well in front of the building, from where the dome of the old courthouse can also be seen, that the whole grand design clicks into place. The 'flying saucer' now appears as it was meant to be seen – no more nor less than a reinterpretation of the same Classical feature, the crowning glory of the Supreme Court, as carefully positioned at the peak of a hierarchical composition as is its predecessor, but recast as a horizontal element, introducing another set of possible meanings.

4

5

The same complex hierarchies and spatial relationships are built into the intricate pattern of circulation through the building. The ground floor, with its broad central avenue, was conceived as an open, public domain with entrances from the street on all three sides. Pedestrians could pause at the bistro, visit the public exhibition, or else simply pass through from one side to the other, as one would through any city arcade. Large areas of the ground floor slab are also opened up with stairways and light-wells revealing the lower floor and the way down to the auditorium and other facilities immediately below, reinforcing the general open ambience.

As originally conceived, security checks separating the visitor from the business of the courts would kick in on the first floor, where airport-style gates were to be installed. This floor is reached from the entrance level by escalators which afford visitors an unrivalled view of the river as they ascend. From thereon the escalators change direction, ramping up either side of the central void, all the way to the floor beneath the Court of Appeal. There they change direction again to lead up through the glazed neck into the belly of the disc, where there is a viewing gallery. Those who have business in the appellate courts take a final escalator to the topmost floor.

The intention was for the entire complex to be open to the public eye from the ground upwards. However, following 9/11, as has happened in so many parts of the world, security was tightened in Singapore. As a result, the two side entrances are now kept closed, while the security checkpoint has been moved to the ground level.

Happily, this change has had little effect on the principal users of the building, including the public attending the courts – once past the checkpoint they are free to circulate as high as they wish – and none at all on the spatial qualities of the interior, which unveils itself as a series of layered vertical spaces that create a varied and refined experience. Ascending the escalators towards the Court of Appeal, you are left in no doubt as to the legal pecking order. The final escalator journey up into the disc is appropriately awe inspiring, as the rest of the building drops away below, almost as though you are preparing for take-off.

Closer to earth, the narrow spaces of the side streets have their own special character. The quality of natural light, as it filters through the shaded glass roof and cross axis, is especially enticing, and highlights the layers of passageways and glazed lifts.

Theoretically, given their exposure on two sides the courtrooms could be naturally ventilated as well as naturally lit, employing the passive stack effect of air movement through the voids on either side. However, the high levels of humidity in the tropical climate rule out natural ventilation in most modern buildings, especially office spaces with all their paperwork, or crowded spaces such as courtrooms. Similarly, the need for security and maximum flexibility in the layout of the courtroom blocks took priority over introducing natural light.

4. The circular, central Appeal Court on the upper level.

5. A meeting room located alongside the Appeal Court; these and other rooms around the perimeter have spectacular views across Singapore.

At the time we were working with the marble, there weren't any examples where the laminated panels had been used as a weather wall. So technically, it was quite pioneering. We had to find the stone from Portugal and make sure it matched then we needed to work out how to laminate it to the glass and achieve longevity. Andy Miller, formerly of Foster + Partners, in conversation with the editor, 2010

Singapore can have a very strong, powerful sunlight. But it can also have a lot of grey days, so we thought very carefully about where we should use clear glass for views and connections and where we could have a translucent material to maintain a level of privacy. To achieve this we worked with a very thin Portuguese marble which was laminated on to the inside of the glass. The stone we picked had a strong veining and this seemed appropriate for the drama of the court. The veining of the panels, which are book-matched to achieve a symmetrical finish, always faces upwards because we thought this would be more optimistic and provide a stronger composition. David Nelson, in conversation with the editor, 2012

All the stone panels were cut and then dry laid at source before being photographed to illustrate how they would look and where they should be placed on the building. It was all predetermined before they got to site, so in the end it was like a giant jigsaw puzzle. Emily Phang, of Foster + Partners, in conversation with the editor, 2011

1, 2. Translucent marble panels allow subtly coloured, diffused daylight into the interiors. The panels have a unique laminated construction, consisting of two 6mm skins of glass with a 12mm sheet of Portuguese rosa extremos marble sandwiched in between, and bonded to the inner pane of glass. Manufacturing limitations dictated that the marble could not be supplied in widths greater than 1.8 metres, so each sheet was sliced in two and book-matched to create large panels, 3.6-metres wide.

1

2

We spent a long time studying the traditional Chinese shop-house. There you have a two or three-foot setback before the glazed elevation and a series of shutters sit in front of it. In many respects, the Supreme Court facade responds in the same way as the traditional Chinese shop – letting light into the building but stopping sunlight from entering and also protecting people at the lower levels. At the Court you have a series of layers. First there is a skin of fritted glass that stops the sun but allows light in, and behind that are the panels of stone and glass viewing panels that define the judges' office spaces. Andy Miller, formerly of Foster + Partners, in conversation with the editor, 2010

In addition to the layering of vertical voids through the building from outside to inside, and from narrow to broad and vice versa, there is another visual layering from transparent to solid, as the glass-walled offices give way to the blocks of courtrooms.

In keeping with traditional building techniques in the region, the layering begins just outside the enclosed structure, with a screen of metal shades. These are supported by slim columns placed 2 metres out from the glass walls, forming a colonnade on three sides of the building. The shades are relatively restricted on the south face, which receives the least sunlight, allowing the occupants to make the most of those splendid views across the river.

Not so much a building in the city, the Supreme Court is a microcosm of the city itself.

The east and west facades are lined by a sheltered colonnade, not unlike the 'five-foot way' Raffles legislated for in his building codes to protect Singaporeans from the tropical sun and rains. On the south face, the exposed columns strike another historical note, similar to the slender columns on the front of the Carré d'Art, facing towards the Roman temple. Here they acknowledge the colonnaded facades of the old Supreme Court and its colonial-era neighbours, while lending the new building a suitable dignity.

A similar layering of elements animates the choice of materials and finishes for the different enclosures. The windows to the outer offices have three equal frames comprised of a middle vision panel with integrated blinds, and a top and bottom translucent panel (the middle vision panel is omitted for greater privacy where a similar system is used internally). The translucent panels have a laminated construction, consisting of two skins of glass with a small air gap and a thin sheet of Portuguese 'rosa extremos' marble bonded to the inner sheet of glass.

During the day, the colourful fluid patterns of the marble are illuminated by sunlight to enrich the office interiors. At night, Singaporeans get to enjoy the same warm colours and patterns, which lend an extra touch of gravitas to the exterior of the courthouse.

Since its completion, the Supreme Court has met with mixed reactions. Most of the debate has revolved around the perceived relationship between the disc of the Appeal Court and the rest of the structure. Speaking for the defence, Koh Juat Jong, former registrar for the Supreme Court, sees the disc as its designers intended people should, as a contemporary reinterpretation of the old building's dome.

It may also be noted that, as the architects were very much aware, just as many people in Singapore will see the landmark structure every day from the vantage points of the numerous tall buildings in the area – from where the circular disc clearly signals the central authority of the Court – as will see it from below, where its form is more ambiguous. Nevertheless, while the logic of the design may be crystal clear, as it generally is with the work of the Foster studio, this in itself does not necessarily guarantee a soft landing, especially, perhaps, if the object in question looks as though it is ready to take off at any moment.

However, to this writer's mind, the perceived disjunctions and tensions between the two main elements of the Supreme Court may also be interpreted as an accurate, if unintended reflection of the wider disjunctions and tensions which characterise a small and multi-cultural Asian country, that has transformed itself from a British colony ruled from afar, to a self-governing, modern city-state with a global reach in less than half a century. Perhaps, when Singaporeans have resolved some of those inner struggles, they will read the building differently. In the meantime, the more Singapore's citizens get to take the impressive journey upwards to enjoy the view from their new, twenty-first century spacecraft, the more they are likely to take it to their hearts.

Chris Abel

3

4

3, 4. The influence of local colonial architecture and Raffles' 'five-foot way' can be found in the external covered walkways on the east and west facades, which provide shelter from Singapore's tropical sun and rains.

Overleaf: The main 'avenue' forms a natural extension of the public realm, reinforcing the concept of 'a city within the building', rather than 'a building within the city'.

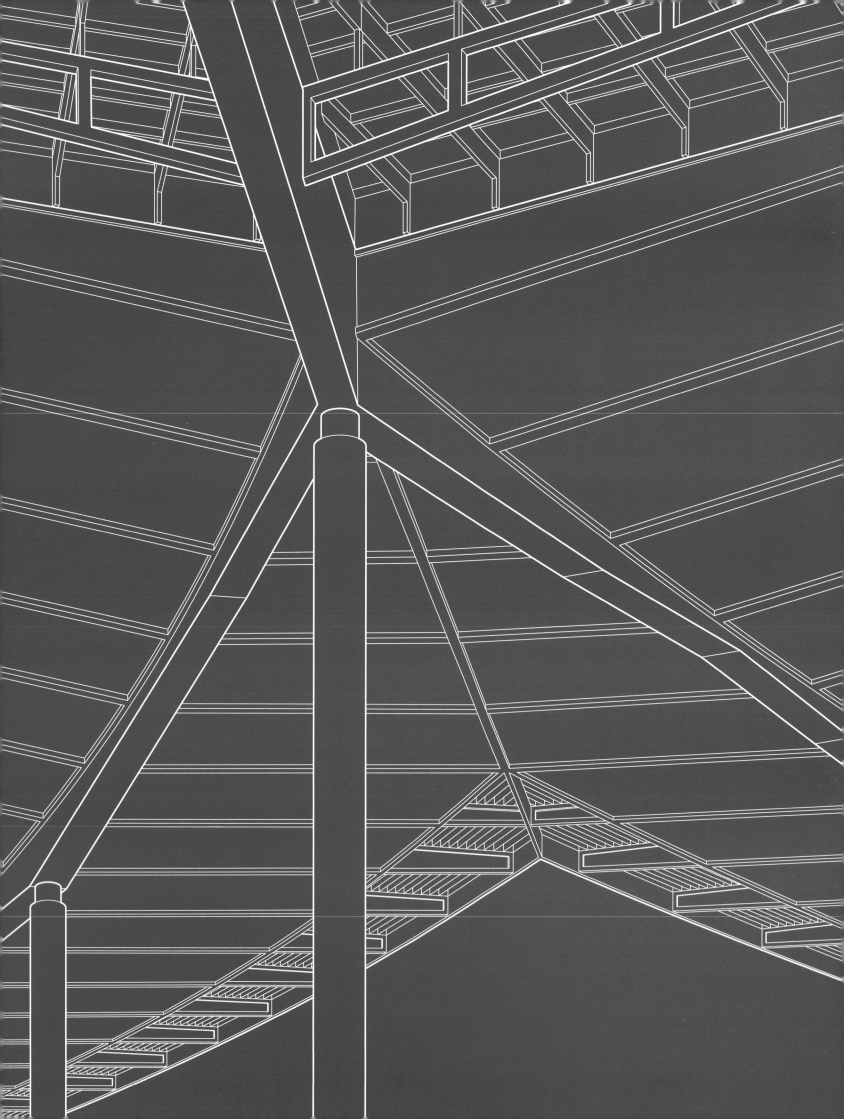

Petronas University of Technology

Bandar Seri Iskandar, Malaysia 1998–2004

The design of this university campus
evolved in response to both climate and
natural terrain. Intensely hot in the sun,
in the monsoon season the skies open
every afternoon to bring torrential rain,
creating a cycle in which the ground
is alternately scorched and soaked.
To allow students to move around
comfortably, whatever the weather,
elevated canopies protect the paths
that wind around the site to encircle a
landscaped park. Buildings for teaching
and research line the edge of the park,
forming four-storey blocks that tuck
beneath the canopies. Where possible,
the dense surrounding planting has
been left untouched. Cafés and other
communal facilities are located at
the canopy intersections, which also
correspond to the entrances to the
housing blocks. Marking the main
entrance is the drum-like form of the
resource centre, which with its library
and theatre, forms a social hub.

Norman Foster

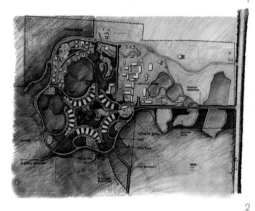

Previous pages: 'Tropical umbrella' canopies provide shelter from the harsh sun and monsoon rain.

1. Located 300 kilometres north of Kuala Lumpur, the site is a former tin-mine in a zone identified for regeneration. The University is poised to generate growth in the region as companies build close to the highly qualified labour market, as has happened at other universities, notably Stanford in California.

2. An early site plan. The 450-hectare site is characterised by shallow hills with lakes formed by flooded mine workings. The layout is prompted by this terrain and a desire to conserve as much of the natural landscape as possible.

Sponsored by the partly state-owned oil company Petroliam Nasional Bhd (Petronas), that built the Petronas Towers in Kuala Lumpur, the Petronas University of Technology in Malaysia is the largest educational and research centre for engineering in the region. It is also one of the Foster studio's most successful exercises to date in combining advanced building technologies with a sensitive response to place, climate and culture. Winner in 2007 of an Aga Khan Award for Architecture – a prestigious international award noted for the importance it attaches to cultural and regional factors – the project skilfully melds a large complex of educational buildings into a verdant tropical landscape, creating a model for sustainable design in the Southern Hemisphere.

For all the acclaim for the Petronas University as an individual work, it is best approached and understood as one of a series of experiments the Foster practice has undertaken outside the West in creating a modern regionalism for our times. Commencing with the Hongkong Bank, with its Japanese inspired fusion of transparency and structural expressionism, Foster and his colleagues have tackled a broad range of building types and designs in an equally wide range of cultural and climatic conditions, in the Middle East and Far East.

For the Al Faisaliah mixed-use complex in Riyadh, Saudi Arabia, for example, in addition to the more predictable but essential sunscreens and other passive measures of climate control, the designers configured the metal and glass-roofed link connecting the central office tower with the adjacent buildings after geometric patterns common to Islamic ornamental design. Crowning the whole complex, a blue-glass, spherical clubhouse atop the pointed tower adds an exotic flourish, creating a powerful landmark in the urban landscape.

Apart from the regional spirit of these and other elements, the general layout of the Al Faisaliah complex nevertheless follows familiar Western spatial typologies, with the main elements grouped around a large public open space (actually a green roof covering semi-underground conference and banquet halls). More recently, however, the Foster studio has embarked on a series of large-scale projects along the Gulf Coast embodying the characteristic design principles and historical typologies of Arab cities.

From the earliest design stage, significant parallels were emerging between the open configuration of the Petronas campus plan and the kampong, examples of which dot the surrounding countryside.

For example, the narrow pedestrian streets of the Central Market in Abu Dhabi, are modelled on the typical marketplace, or souk, of Arabia and other parts of the Middle East. As with the indigenous model, the strong sunlight is filtered down into the closely packed streets through various kinds of overhead screens, producing subtle effects of light and shade. Similarly, buildings are partially hidden behind intricate lattice screens affording both shade and privacy to the inhabitants.

The Foster studio's most ambitious project of this kind to date, however, is the city of Masdar, also in Abu Dhabi. Designed as a sustainable alternative to the car-dependent, sprawling urban pattern now typical of all major cities in the region, Masdar marks a decisive return to the clear demarcation between the open desert country and the dense, compact form of the historical city model.

We were originally commissioned to make a gentle readjustment of an existing masterplan to see how we could design buildings to fit within that framework. However, in a very short space of time we decided that wasn't the best way to proceed. We felt that the original masterplan could have been built anywhere in the world and as such didn't feel special to the site. We felt that there was an opportunity to create something that was more deeply rooted. Jonathan Parr, of Foster + Partners, in conversation with the editor, 2011

When you establish a university you embark on a process that is bigger than the university itself. The knowledge that flows from a university attracts businesses and employers who like to be close to centres of excellence. One of the reasons Petronas was planned away from the centre of Kuala Lumpur was to create another nucleus in the country, which could tap into the groundswell of activities based around the university. David Nelson, in conversation with the editor, 2012

Comprised of a labyrinthine complex of low-rise blocks, narrowly separated by shaded pedestrian streets and alleyways, in stark contrast to the typical Western model of dispersed urban form, Masdar presents itself as a largely contiguous building mass punctuated by open courts providing light and ventilation.

In the Far East, the Century Tower in Tokyo refined the oriental qualities first expressed in the Hongkong Bank, opposing a 'masculine', earthquake proof structure against a 'feminine' transparent skin and luminous interior spaces. On a more intimate scale, two houses in Japan designed by Foster for the same client also offer modern reinterpretations of Japanese traditions of architecture and landscape art, seamlessly blending layered sequences of interior and exterior spaces. At an altogether different scale again, as with Foster's previously completed airport terminals at Stansted and Chek Lap Kok, the dominant feature of Beijing International Airport is an all-encompassing, steel-framed roof.

However, while the roof structure at Stansted, with its square grid, has distinctly Classical overtones in the Western tradition, the sweeping canopies at Hong Kong and Beijing echo oriental building traditions, in which the roof is invariably the dominant element. At Beijing, in addition to unifying the whole immense structure, the curved roof with its long, hump-backed spine, sharply pointed skylights and richly coloured cladding and columns, conjures up metaphorical associations with Chinese dragons and suchlike. While explicitly designed to meet the demanding performance criteria of the world's largest modern airport, the references to Chinese traditions help to localise and humanise the enormous structure.

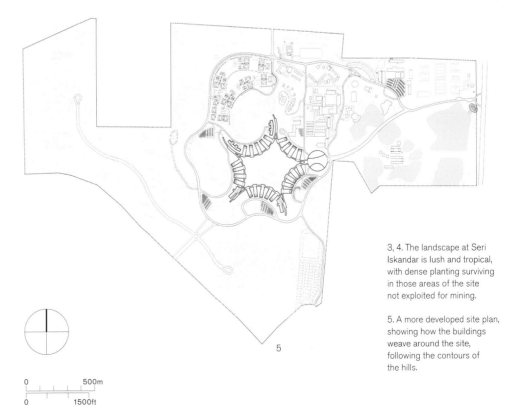

3, 4. The landscape at Seri Iskandar is lush and tropical, with dense planting surviving in those areas of the site not exploited for mining.

5. A more developed site plan, showing how the buildings weave around the site, following the contours of the hills.

0   500m

0   1500ft

What's interesting about a project like this is that universities are not just buildings when they're developed on this scale – they're actually part of a big eco-system. They introduce housing, schools, research, hospitals, roads, shops and so on. You can see that at Petronas; the difference in travelling there now, compared with our first journey is incredible. Now, off the main highway, another highway leads right to the campus … and all the way along it, what were abandoned developments have come alive. It has had a huge regenerative effect in the region. Andy Miller, formerly of Foster + Partners, in conversation with the editor, 2010

The canopy is the same height as the British Museum canopy – 20 metres – and is around 54 metres at its widest point. We spent a lot of time trying to minimise the structure, so it's quite cleverly braced at the ends to make it look as if it's hovering over a series of skinny legs. Jonathan Parr, of Foster + Partners, in conversation with the editor, 2011

We wanted the circulation between all the buildings to be external so that we wouldn't have to air-condition long corridors and also because we liked the idea of moving from building to building externally in order to feel part of the natural tropical experience. However, solar radiation is particularly strong in that climate, so much so that even on a cloudy day you can get sunburnt. In addition, the rain is obviously very heavy so we wanted to protect the circulation route. Out of this grew the idea of having a very large canopy that would link the buildings and allow people to move around in comfort. David Nelson, in conversation with the editor, 2012

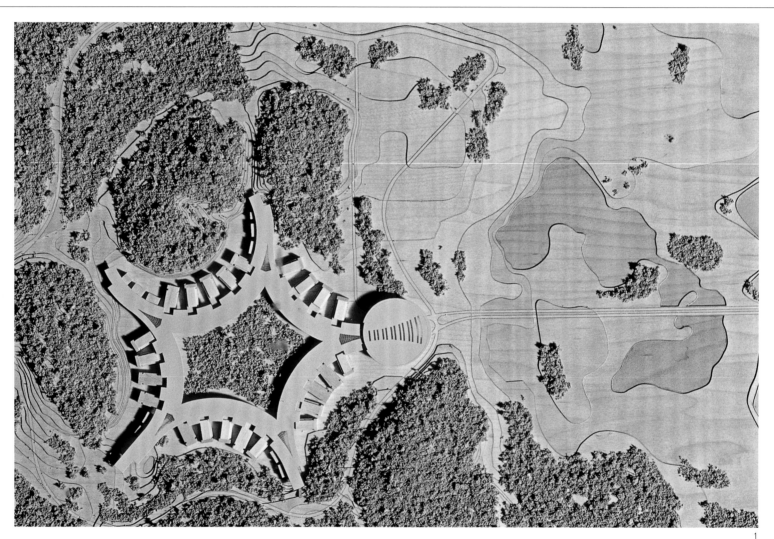

1

1, 2. A site model of the developed scheme, together with a corresponding planning diagram. Teaching and research accommodation is arranged around the edge of a central park. Cafés and communal student facilities are placed at the canopy intersections, which also correspond to the entrances of the housing blocks. Marking the entrance to the campus is the drum-like form of the resource centre.

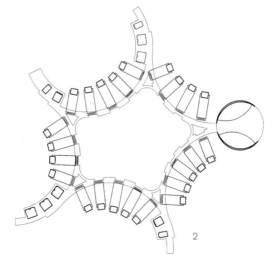

2

Soaring canopies protect the paths that weave around the edge of the site, allowing students to move around the campus while shaded from the sun or sheltered from the rain.

Norman Foster

Because it was based in a jungle, our driving force was to try to build something into the forest and move away from a conventional quadrangle model with a library and a great hall at one end and classrooms around the periphery. Instead, the scheme responds to the site directly. The reasons it's curved the way it is, is that inside each curve is a hill, so the site itself created the form of the main buildings. Andy Miller, formerly of Foster + Partners, in conversation with the editor, 2010

The nearest precedent for the design of the Petronas University, however, also lies closer to home, in Singapore, on the southern tip of the Malay Peninsula. Looking much like a giant beetle, the Expo Station was designed for the same hot, humid tropical climate as Petronas University. Though it was built to meet an entirely different and much smaller programme, it embodies many of the same essential principles and features. Once again, as with the terminals at Hong Kong and Beijing, the dominant element of the Expo Station is the cantilevered elliptical roof covering the raised platforms, together with a smaller, disc-shaped roof over the entrance hall and lift below. In this case, however, there is no substantial enclosed space to speak of at either level. As with the vernacular architecture of the region, the impression is of a structure that is 'all roof', the purpose of which is to shelter the inhabitants from the tropical sun and heavy rains, while leaving the space below open to the slightest movement of air.

In all of these cases, unlike the facile imitation of historical forms common to Postmodern architecture, the success of the design largely depends upon a subtle process of abstraction, whereby the underlying principles shaping regional building traditions are reinterpreted for our times and applied to modern building types and programmes. The problem is that, by definition, not all regional building traditions are the same, or are equally readily translated into modern building programmes, which by their own nature often cross regional and cultural boundaries. The existence and continuing relevance of indigenous urban models in Arabia, for example, has been a powerful stimulus for the Foster team in shaping the Masdar project – which includes a full-size university and research centre among its components – just as it has guided other large-scale Foster projects in the same region.

By contrast, no such lasting tradition of urban form, with all its related diverse building types, evolved on the Malay Peninsula prior to the colonial era. Aside from the isolated example of Malacca on the west coast, a small port-city built by Chinese settlers and subsequently occupied by Portuguese colonists, the primary form of local settlement on the Peninsula remained the Malay kampong, or rural village, well into the twentieth century. Comprised of a loose cluster of detached 'houses-on-stilts', the timber-framed architecture of the kampong, with its steeply pitched, overhanging roofs, permeable walls and well-ventilated spaces, has inspired countless contemporary residential designs. However, with a few notable exceptions, for most architects, indigenous Malay architecture has had limited relevance to the design of other building types and larger-scale programmes.

Faced with similar problems, the British colonists who eventually ousted their European rivals from Malacca and other coastal settlements, borrowed freely from indigenous architecture for the design of their own, well-ventilated detached dwellings, but sought inspiration elsewhere when it came to building schools, hospitals, government buildings and other imported types. The result was an eclectic mixture of motifs drawn from Mughal architecture in India and other parts of the British Empire, as well as the Italian Renaissance and other more familiar sources.

3

3. Detail of the 1:200-scale model, showing how the four-storey blocks for teaching and research are tucked beneath the edges of the canopies.

4. Concept sketch by Norman Foster, exploring the idea of the protective canopies as 'tropical umbrellas'.

4

When we first presented the scheme we were clear that it was to be very much of Malaysia. One of the ideas behind the plan form of the long teaching blocks were the Indonesian longhouses. These were communal family village houses shaped like an extruded upside-down V – like a Toblerone bar shape – with big overhangs at the short ends. You can sit outside but under cover from the torrential rain and sun, and air is drawn through – and it's raised on stilts to prevent snakes getting up. Jonathan Parr, of Foster + Partners, in conversation with the editor, 2011

The canopy connects the individual laboratory and teaching buildings, and each individual building is spaced apart and extended back into the jungle to create green courtyards. The promenade facing the park becomes a social space for students moving between laboratories and lectures. Cafés, restaurants and lecture theatres are concentrated at the ends of the promenades to provide social reference points. David Nelson, in conversation with the editor, 2009

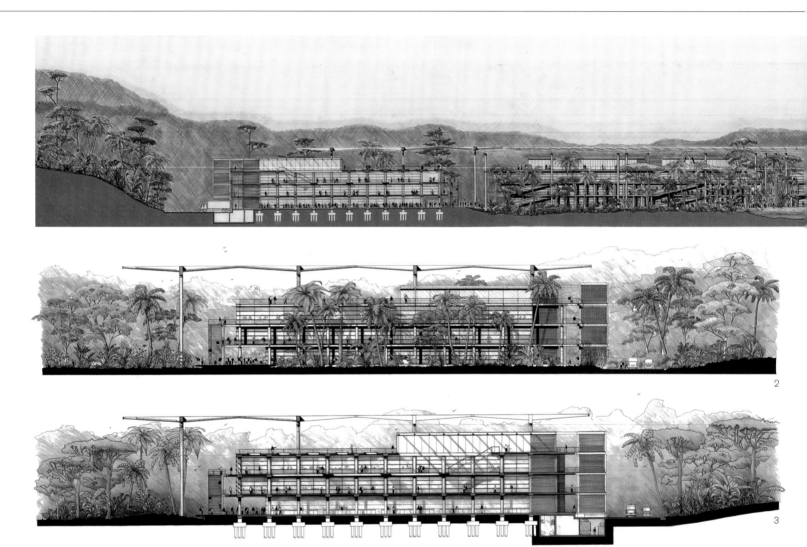

2

3

1-3. These presentation sections – hand-coloured by Tom Politowicz – give a real sense of light and shade and how the campus will 'feel' as the planting matures. Great care was taken to respond to the scale of the landscape; the level of the canopy, for example, corresponds with the height of the existing trees.

The design responds to the physical landscape of the site, with its dense planting, gentle hills and lakes, and to the weather patterns unique to this part of the world.

Norman Foster

The diagram is very simple: the middle and the deck are for pedestrians with a service road around the perimeter for vehicles. The services are on the outside and the people on the inside, so the two never meet. There is also a ring main of primary services connecting the back of the buildings so it becomes one big service route. Jonathan Parr, of Foster + Partners, in conversation with the editor, 2009

There were tall trees both on the site and around the edges of it where it met the jungle so the top of the canopy relates to the tree line and helps keep that connectivity with the landscape which we felt was very important. David Nelson, in conversation with the editor, 2009

1

Thus the characteristic colonial government building in British Malaya, as it was then called, comprised a simple, multi-storey box of cross-ventilated spaces wrapped around by external corridors and stairways and an ornate arched screen of stone. As well as partly disguising the true nature of the building, the richly decorated screens effectively shelter the surrounding corridors and interior from the sun and rain, splendid examples of which can still be seen today in the historic centres of Kuala Lumpur and other Malaysian cities. All of which may go some way to explaining the extraordinary complex of buildings that rose out of the virgin tropical jungle in the opening years of this century.

The site of the new campus is at Bandar Seri Iskandar, 300 kilometres north of Kuala Lumpur, close to the west coast of Malaysia near Highway 5, a principal north-south route through the country. In recognition of the university's potential as a catalyst for further development, the area was also identified as a prime location for regeneration, with the creation of a new town similar to other new developments in Malaysia, such as Cyberjaya and Putrajaya. Together with other supporting amenities, this will create a viable, self-contained community alongside the university. This phenomenon, of companies building close to an emerging, highly qualified labour market, has been observed close to universities in other parts of the world, most notably at Stanford in California.

In searching for an appropriate regional solution for the Petronas University, the size of which is comparable to a whole town in itself, the Foster team drew on British colonial architecture as well as indigenous traditions for inspiration. Overriding the design team's approach and driving the fusion between regional traditions and modern requirements and technologies, however, was the nature of the jungle site itself and the densely covered hills with their rich foliage, large parts of which remain untouched, which are typical of the Malaysian landscape.

Dissatisfied with the baroque masterplan superimposed on the landscape by their previous consultants, Petronas commissioned Foster + Partners to draw up an alternative scheme. Rejecting the previous inflexible layout, the Foster team instead proposed a loose necklace of buildings laid around a section of the jungle where the ground levels out between the hills. A covered pedestrian street links all the teaching blocks around the enclosed forest park, while vehicular access is restricted to a service road running close to the outer edge of the complex. The main auditorium, or Great Hall, and the library plus the central administration, are grouped in a drum-like Resource Centre building on the eastern side of the loop where the access road leads to the highway and this drum frames the entrance to the campus. Outside this complex, student and staff housing is dispersed between the surrounding hills.

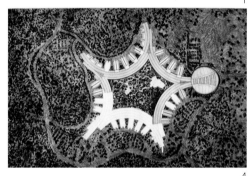

4

4. This coloured site plan illustrates just how much of the surrounding landscape was preserved in a natural state, although some marshy land has been activated to form a natural water installation. The planning geometry is not apparent from the ground, but in plan the site contours prompted the adoption of a star shape, which resonates with geometric patterns in traditional Islamic architecture and art.

The idea of the canopy was to bring the buildings together but for them not to touch, except where they reach the walkway. We wanted to let the students be in a natural environment, both underneath the buildings and in the laboratories. The labs are not air conditioned, just the teaching space itself. Underneath the canopy we tried to encourage as much greenery as we could and in fact, to regenerate growth after construction. There are also little pockets created there where students can sit and talk and so on. Andy Miller, formerly of Foster + Partners, in conversation with the editor, 2010

The university was the vision of Tan Sri Azizan, the former President and Chairman of Petronas, and he wanted something which felt as if it belonged to Malaysia. He wanted the students to be taught in an environment which always reminded them – because they were going to be in it – of the natural world which is why the jungle encroaches between the teaching blocks and why we tried to preserve the forest in the middle as much as possible. Jonathan Parr, of Foster + Partners, in conversation with the editor, 2011

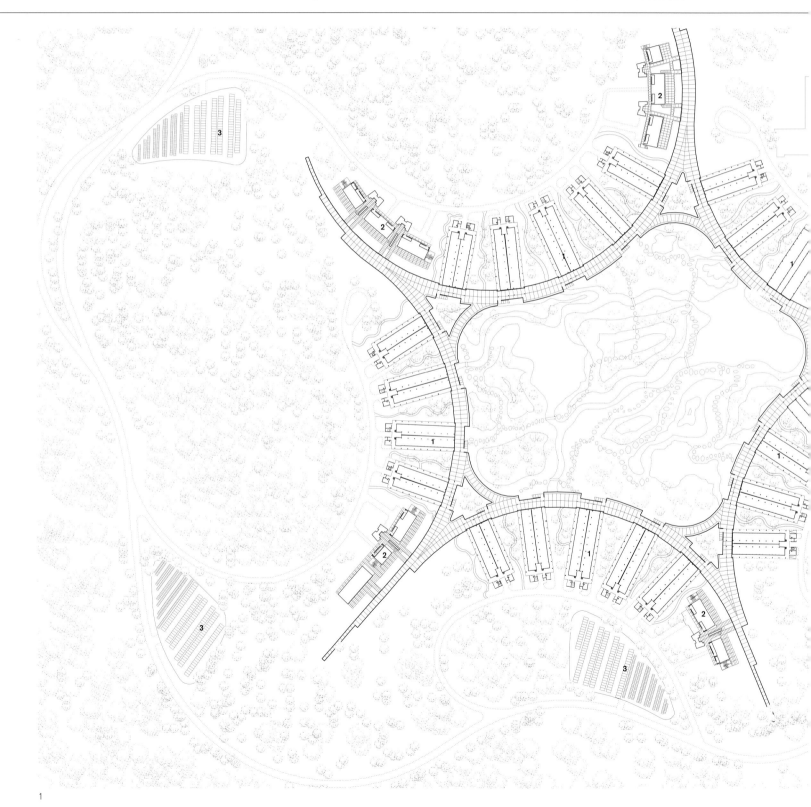

1

The university was very much Tan Sri Azizan's project and he understood what we were trying to do and encouraged us and gave us great support. He was very passionate about Petronas in all its forms and also very passionate about Malaysia. Tragically he died, and it was a great shame that he wasn't able to be there when the first convocations took place. David Nelson, in conversation with the editor, 2009
Left: Petronas president Tan Sri Azizan with project team leader Andy Miller.

Tan Sri Azizan had the passion for this project. He came from a kampong originally and had worked his way up to become chairman of Petronas. With his humble background came a vision to make a difference, which was this university. He wanted the students to be in a natural environment so that they would respond to it and remember it once they'd graduated and were building petro-chemical plants elsewhere in the world. From his point of view, the environment was very important and you shouldn't destroy it. Andy Miller, formerly of Foster + Partners, in conversation with the editor, 2010

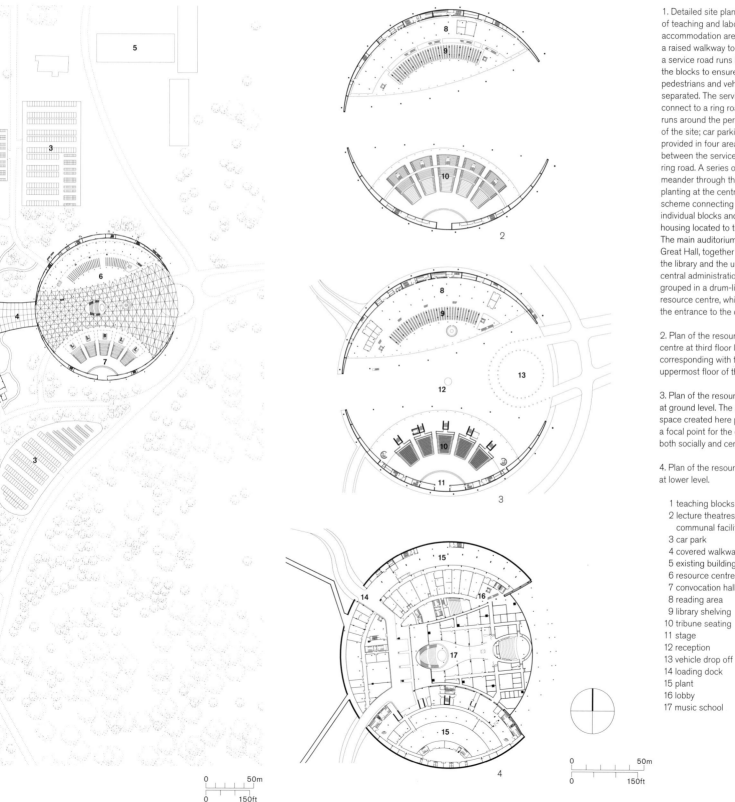

1. Detailed site plan. Blocks of teaching and laboratory accommodation are linked by a raised walkway to the front; a service road runs behind the blocks to ensure that pedestrians and vehicles are separated. The service roads connect to a ring road which runs around the perimeter of the site; car parking is provided in four areas located between the service road and ring road. A series of paths meander through the dense planting at the centre of the scheme connecting the individual blocks and the housing located to the north. The main auditorium or Great Hall, together with the library and the university's central administration, are grouped in a drum-like resource centre, which frames the entrance to the campus.

2. Plan of the resource centre at third floor level, corresponding with the uppermost floor of the library.

3. Plan of the resource centre at ground level. The sheltered space created here provides a focal point for the campus, both socially and ceremonially.

4. Plan of the resource centre at lower level.

1 teaching blocks
2 lecture theatres and
   communal facilities
3 car park
4 covered walkway
5 existing buildings
6 resource centre
7 convocation hall
8 reading area
9 library shelving
10 tribune seating
11 stage
12 reception
13 vehicle drop off
14 loading dock
15 plant
16 lobby
17 music school

Historically, the majority of universities throughout the world have formed and evolved over a long period of time. At Petronas, the decision was to build the whole thing in one go because they had identified a need which meant they wanted it to be established and running as soon as possible. It was one of the fastest projects we have ever done and we had to release drawings very quickly in order to get it built. David Nelson, in conversation with the editor, 2012

This was one of the first times we delivered a proper collaborative, split-service project. We had an excellent relationship with the local architect, GDP, and we've now worked with them on 70 per cent of our subsequent work in Kuala Lumpur. There was a real chemistry between the two companies and we just got on very well. Jonathan Parr, of Foster + Partners, in conversation with the editor, 2011

1-6. The scale of the undertaking, in creating a new university campus from scratch, and its logistical complexity, are best appreciated in construction photographs. These images chart progress on the teaching blocks and canopies during the course of a year and a half, from September 2001 to March 2003.

The canopy and large entrance steelwork were all manufactured in Malaysia using quite basic techniques. Some of the steelwork for the entrance drum and roof contained three-dimensional curves meaning they bent in both plan and section. To achieve the correct geometry the manufacturers used a system of jigs and bent the steel to fit. Using this method they managed to achieve tolerances of between plus and minus 5mm which is interesting because in the UK we work to plus or minus 20mm. Andy Miller, formerly of Foster + Partners, in conversation with the editor, 2010
Left: Andy Miller photographed on site, 2002.

5

6

The site was on a scale more consistent with urban planning than conventional building – it was almost like seeing a new town emerge from a jungle setting.
David Nelson

1. A visualisation of the completed campus.

2. Cross-section through the centre of the campus, looking towards the resource centre, showing the relationship between the academic blocks and the oversailing roof canopies.

1

While the basic features of the scheme remained mostly unchanged, the design was much refined as the project progressed. The first concept diagram shows an irregular, amoeba- like plan form, with some buildings radiating out from the centre, while others are arranged parallel to the outer edge. This soon changed as the architects worked to fit the plan more closely to the contours of the neighbouring hills. The final masterplan consists of five semi-circular segments of varying length joined at their ends and linked by covered streets following the same geometry. Each crescent-shaped segment fits snugly around the base of the adjacent hill, its centre of radius fixed firmly in the same landscape. The form and distribution of the teaching blocks is also regularised in keeping with the semi-circular geometry.

Classrooms and laboratories are housed in rectangular fingers positioned at equal intervals around each segment on the outer edge of the pathway, and point towards the same centre of radius. Blocks of lecture halls, canteens and other amenities are also evenly distributed around the campus at the junctions between adjacent segments, save for the junction on the eastern side of the complex, where the library, auditorium and other key functions are positioned, much as they were in the first scheme.

At basement level, a walk-through service tunnel situated directly beneath the plant rooms at the rear of each teaching block runs right around the campus, providing ready access to all the main piped and cabled services.

Aside from being tailored more closely to the contours of the site, the final scheme has marked advantages over the first, irregular concept plan. The semi-circular geometry greatly simplified the layout of the whole campus, each component of which could be precisely located around the circumference of the relevant segment, and back to the centre of radius. The radial orientation of the teaching blocks also opened up wide gaps between each building, offering clear views from the covered pathway out towards the surrounding landscape. Vice versa, drivers using the external access road can see straight into the enclosed park. As intended, these gaps are gradually becoming filled with lush vegetation, so that the forest outside seems to penetrate right through the linked buildings to merge with the park inside. Where possible, the jungle forming the park was been left in a natural state, although some marshy land was activated to form a natural water installation.

From the earliest design stage, significant parallels were emerging between the open configuration of the Petronas campus plan and key features of the rural kampong, examples of which dot the surrounding countryside. Like the kampong with its detached houses loosely sprinkled on the ground – far enough apart from each other so as not to obstruct any movement of air through the village – the loose necklace of separate buildings presents the minimum obstruction to air movement across the campus.

The open circulation system brings students into constant contact with the surrounding landscape as they move from class to class.

However, it is in the imaginative handling of the covered street linking the buildings that the architects achieve their most striking reinterpretation of regional traditions, and which ultimately gives the whole campus its distinctive tropical character and identity. Covered walkways snaking between buildings are commonplace on campuses in the tropics, where torrential monsoon rains are daily features of life for much of the year. Yet, as at the National University of Singapore (NUS), they are invariably designed as an afterthought when the buildings have already been laid out, and are barely wide enough to shelter a narrow footpath.

Conceived from the outset as an integral part of the masterplan, the sweeping canopy of the Petronas University is something else altogether. More like the great unifying canopy roofs of the terminals at Hong Kong and Beijing airports, or the streamlined open roof of the Expo Station in Singapore, the series of crescent-shaped roofs and radiating spurs dominate the whole campus, sheltering the teaching blocks as well as the broad walkway.

Branching out from tall, slender steel columns, they invite comparisons with the surrounding forest canopy itself, as well as with vernacular Malaysian architecture, with its prominent overhanging roofs. Pierced by dart-shaped roof-lights at the broadest sections where paired segments merge and edged with glazed panels, the canopy roof is both tall and wide enough to provide effective shelter against the strong sun and driving rains, without depriving any adjacent buildings of natural light. Lastly, as with the layout of the buildings themselves, while the roof canopy looks anything but standardised, the precise, semi-circular geometry of each segment also greatly simplified the design and fabrication of the steel and glass components, all of which were produced and erected, as with every other structure on the campus, by Malaysian contractors.

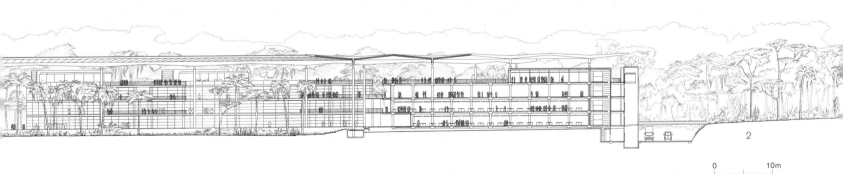

2

| 0 | | 10m |
| 0 | | 30ft |

Wherever possible the design has taken a holistic approach to using low-energy concepts. Whilst maintaining a harmony with the site, the blocks are separated by central passages that encourage air-flow. Hanif Kara, *Intervention Architecture*, 2007

There are big areas under cover with places for seating because the culture in this part of the world is such that people like to sit and talk. Jonathan Parr, of Foster + Partners, in conversation with the editor, 2011

The orangey-red colour of the deck was inspired by the colour of the region's soil. It was important to us that it should be of the place, so that it felt as though you were walking on the earth, even though the deck is at a constant datum above ground throughout the scheme. Jonathan Parr, of Foster + Partners, in conversation with the editor, 2009

1

We incorporated external circulation into the laboratory blocks which meant that we could induce airflow through corridor spaces which would normally have been closed and air-conditioned. The effect is similar to the local vernacular architecture. We had already noticed with our station in Singapore that there was a drop in temperature between the sheltered area and the fully open space, and a lot of traditional architecture in the region had exploited that effect over the years. It was only with the invention of air conditioning that such empirical knowledge vanished. It's been our job to reinvestigate such techniques. David Nelson, in conversation with the editor, 2009

As with the design of the canopy roof, the detailed design of the teaching blocks – in particular the circulation within and between each block – is strongly shaped by regional models, though from a different source. As well as regular classrooms and lecture halls, the brief for the academic programme, which covers a wide range of engineering subjects from chemical to IT engineering, called for a large number of laboratories. Given the hot, humid climate, it was therefore decided at an early stage that all the concrete-framed teaching blocks, most of which also include faculty offices on the top floors, would be air-conditioned.

Pierced by dart-shaped rooflights at the broadest sections, where paired segments merge, the canopies are tall and wide enough to provide shelter against the strong sun and driving rains.

To reduce the energy requirements, the designers adopted an open-air circulation strategy similar to the model of colonial architecture described above. Thus, while the top two floors of the four-storey blocks are served by an internal, double-loaded corridor, the lower two floors are wrapped around by external covered passageways (in some cases, all three lower floors have a similar arrangement). In addition, aside from a single internal flight of stairs connecting the faculty offices on the top floor with the floor below, all the main stairways, which are situated at the rear of each block between the plant rooms and washrooms, are fully exposed to the fresh air, further reducing the energy load.

Two open, raised passageways with scissor stairways at each end also connect adjacent teaching blocks directly to each other at the opposite end, on the far side of the main street beneath the canopy roof. Each block is also recessed on the ground floor where the street runs through so that students pass through a series of broad colonnades as they walk from building to building, similar to the colonnaded pathways in Malaysia's historic urban centres.

As well as reducing the energy load, the open circulation system brings students into constant contact with the surrounding landscape, providing them with views both within and beyond the campus as they move from class to class, creating a powerful sense of place. The same open-air, tropical ambience is carried through in the design of the pair of structures housing the Great Hall and combined Resource and Administration Centres, at the eastern end of the campus. The design of these buildings evolved rapidly from the two circular buildings in the very first concept plan, through a pair of elliptical structures of unequal size but similar curved shape, to the final unified design gathering both buildings in a drum under one great roof.

Comprised of two structures of different proportions but similar convex geometry, facing each other across a vast open space under the umbrella roof, the circular complex provides a stunning centrepiece and social focus for the whole campus, as well as an impressive gateway. Running east-west from the main access road, the cavernous space is only partly closed by wing walls at both ends, so that it is possible to see right through the drum in either direction.

Rows of skylights between the steel trusses of the dome flood the space below and the glass-walled enclosures either side with natural light, enhancing the open ambience. Both the steel trusses and the skylights also follow progressively curved lines in plan from west to east, so that they appear to ripple outwards towards the main entrance.

2

3

1. Looking across the park to the canopies that protect the pedestrian routes which wind around the edge of the site.

2, 3. The canopies are pierced with rooflights that allow sunlight to filter down into the buildings and they incorporate water collectors to allow rainwater to be reused in the gardens; they also play an important role in encouraging the natural flow of air through the individual buildings.

The university was still working on the brief while rushing to build, so we developed a basic grid system that would optimise the teaching spaces and allow us to create laboratories that were either side-loaded, or centrally-loaded modules. This means that the facilities are very flexible and can accommodate many different sorts of teaching and laboratory arrangements. By the time the building frames were going up, we knew what would be inside the spaces and that allowed us to implement a glazing system that worked with what happens within. Andy Miller, formerly of Foster + Partners, in conversation with the editor, 2010

1

2

3

1. Students working in one of the sun-protected 'pocket' spaces created at the intersections of the roof canopies.

2, 3. Laboratory spaces in one of the academic blocks. The region's largest academic centre for the study of civil, mechanical, chemical and electrical engineering, the university's approach is geared to applied sciences rather than to research. It aims to blend the best academic training with hands-on industrial experience to produce a new generation of graduates who can contribute to Malaysia's industrial development. In order to provide state-of-the-art laboratories, the practice worked with Research Facility Design laboratory consultants, who also collaborated on the projects at Stanford University.

Two rows of slender steel columns matching the outer ring help to support the shallow dome internally and reduce the outward thrust. Following the curved lines of the glass walls either side of the space, the columns add a further touch of grandeur, while two lines of freestanding pillars of light illuminate the same space at night. A circular void in the centre of the great space provides a focal point and leads down into the basement connecting the two main enclosures below ground level. The whole grand ensemble is capped by a cantilevered roof brim of aluminium louvres increasing in depth from west to east, providing maximum shade where it is most needed over the wider entrance on the east side.

The interior spaces of the Great Hall and Resource Centre offer spectacles of their own to match the open space between. Both structures are enclosed on their outer faces by service walls, which taper in depth towards their extremities, where they frame the entranceways at each end of the open central space. The Great Hall itself is designed as a multi-purpose theatre, equally capable of seating the entire population of the campus on ceremonial occasions, or housing conferences, together with musical and theatrical performances of all kinds. The freestanding concrete tiers of cantilevered seating present a robust image, more like an open football stadium than a theatre interior.

In the opposite building, Central Administration occupies the entire top floor while the Resource Centre is spread through the lower floors and basement. The library is split both vertically and horizontally into three tall floors of study spaces at the rear and six shallow floors of bookstacks at the front, facing into the central space. All floors in turn are cut back in an arc from the curved glass wall to form an elliptical void, exposing the metal-framed bookstacks radiating outwards from behind a row of slender concrete columns.

More than a model of modern regionalism and sustainable design, the Petronas University is a concrete expression of the high value placed upon education by Malaysia.

A second, narrow void between the study spaces and books divides each stack of floors into two crescent-shaped spans, repeating the geometry of the masterplan. Light steel bridges link the two segments while curved stairways cascade down through the void, opening up views in all directions between every floor. The combined effect of the elliptical and crescent-shaped voids, together with the views through the glass wall to the great open space beyond, and beyond that to the surrounding landscape, creates a memorable impact.

Because of the nature of Petronas's business the curriculum of the university is centred on oil. It is predominantly a science-based institution with tie-ins to the automotive business, including a link with Lotus as well as a lot of work based around exploration due to their expertise in drilling, mining and geotechnical techniques. In addition there is a very broad spectrum of research and teaching to do with the earth's resources and looking to the future with renewables. David Nelson, in conversation with the editor, 2012

4

5

6

Equal care and attention has been lavished on the details. The lush, patterned silk panels covering the walls of the Great Hall and the Senate Room in Central Administration are woven to give a rich pattern using a traditional process that integrates gold and silver threads. These panels subtly reflect light in a way that recalls the inspiring light of a mosque. As David Nelson, who led the project, observes: 'We tried to connect science to a more spiritual realm, as well as to link the university to local traditions and beliefs.'

The diagonal pattern of the ceramic tiles covering the outer walls of the drum is based on indigenous Malaysian designs, using locally sourced ceramic tiles, on precast panels, which form an iridescent pattern by varying matt and shiny finishes. The overall effect is not unlike the tiled shells of Utzon's Sydney Opera House. The paving also seems to belong to the earth, as the unified colours blur the boundary between the landscape and the campus, and interior and exterior, with warm earth-tones pervading the interior spaces. More familiar in the Foster oeuvre, the curved glass walls facing into the centre of the drum are a craftsman-like exercise in minimalism. Save for the bottom row of glass panes, which rest on the floor, the entire wall is hung by fine wires suspended from a beam running round the top of a row of ultra-slim steel columns, set just behind the glass.

The nearly invisible wires themselves are attached to thin metal transoms, in line with the butt-jointed panes. Both walls are held in place by minuscule stainless-steel distance pieces attached to the same row of steel columns (since the tall walls are sheltered, there is no need for stronger mullions to counter wind forces, as there is, for example, at Beijing Airport). Notably, for all the refinement, the project came in on time and at a cost comparable with similar programmes – as much a tribute to the local contractors as to the Foster practice.

More than a model of modern regionalism and sustainable design, Petronas University is a concrete expression of the high value placed upon education by Malaysia, as well as other newly industrialised countries in the region – a key factor in the growing shift of economic power and cultural energy towards Asia Pacific. It also provides a wake-up call to the increasing numbers of cash-starved Western universities that depend upon top fee-paying foreign students from the same region to keep afloat. With campuses such as this to tempt local students to stay in their own countries, it is doubtful that their overseas competitors will be able to rely much longer upon the same source of funds.

Chris Abel

4. One of the large-scale, double-height laboratories containing specialist heavy equipment; the laboratory spaces are planned around a fixed module so that a flexible structural grid could be developed to enable both single- and double-height volumes and small- and large-scale labs.

5. The computer centre, located at the deck level of the library.

6. The lecture theatre located in the undercroft beneath the library; each desk has its own integrated computer module.

The client, Tan Sri Azizan, wanted to make sure that this building was not a project that could just go anywhere in the world. He'd ask: where are the Malaysian elements? On special occasions people there wear a small wraparound skirt with a diamond-shaped pattern on it called a songket. We picked up on that: the inner and outer walls of the two main buildings carry that motif. The concrete panels are inlaid with glazed and matt ceramic tiles that reveal themselves in a diamond pattern when the sun shines. On the inside, we used woven silk panels with the same pattern, so the songket runs all the way through the building. Andy Miller, formerly of Foster + Partners, in conversation with the editor, 2010

It's a very large library – half a million books – and it's all about openness and being able to see the collections. From here you can look out through the great glass wall across the public **piazza to the convocation hall.** Jonathan Parr, of Foster + Partners, in conversation with the editor, 2011

We wanted to try to find a way of touching the culture of Malaysia for the big entrance enclosure. We'd become fascinated by the songket, a beautiful traditional fabric which has a metallic thread running through it. From that we developed a geometry which worked very well with the curved walls of the interior. They're diamond-shaped panels made from two different types of silk and the overall effect evokes the songket while the curve of the wall means the fabric catches the light. We used two different types of silk, one quite tight and the other more open, **which were woven locally.** David Nelson, in conversation with the editor, 2012

1. Looking down to the floor of the library from the fourth-floor balcony.

2. The enquiries desk in the library.

3. Students gather on the steps and piazza of the resource centre. The building is clad in locally sourced ceramic tiles which are arranged to form an iridescent pattern, using matt and gloss finishes.

4. A convocation in the assembly hall. The cladding in the hall is formed from silk panels woven using a traditional process that integrates gold and silver threads. These panels subtly reflect light in a curve that recalls the inspiring light of a mosque, so science is linked to a more spiritual realm.

1

2

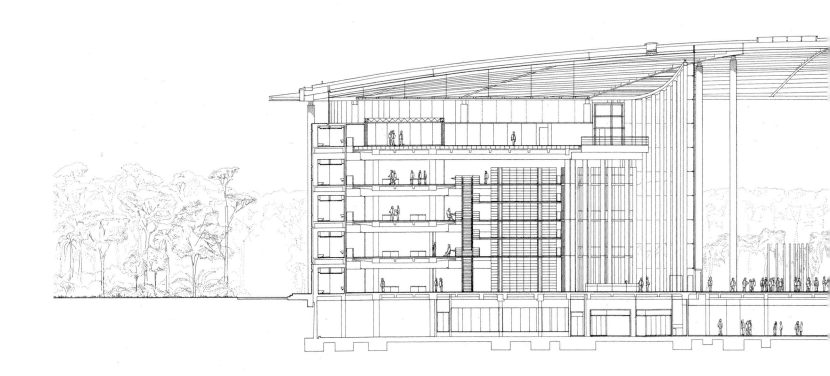

The project's significance lies in a number of aspects. First, its prototypical built configuration, consisting of an all-encompassing shaped canopy with functional boxes inserted underneath, is a contemporary reinterpretation of the classic metaphor for tropical architecture – an umbrella that offers protection from the sun and rain. Second, the building provides a defined shaded zone for social interaction and circulation under an overhead enclosure. This is a high-tech, emblematic architecture appropriate for a scientific university in a rapidly developing nation.

Third, the careful physical integration of a complex educational structure with the existing landscape is achieved in an ingenious way, by wrapping the built forms around the base of a series of knolls. And fourthly, this is an exemplary use of a performance-based approach to architectural design that goes beyond the diagram. The design has been carried through to completion with meticulous detail, rigour and persistence. It sets new standards in the quality of construction without significant cost premiums. In aggregate, the Jury found the design to be instructive, aesthetically satisfying and technologically novel. Jury Citation, the Aga Khan Award for Architecture, 2007

The Aga Khan Award was a great thing to get and I think what they liked about this project was the marriage between international global thinking and local climatic conditions and processes. We tried to get the best of both worlds coming together, if we were building it in Europe it would have looked and felt very different. David Nelson, in conversation with the editor, 2012

3

4

5. Cross-section through the resource centre. The building is both a gateway to the campus and its main architectural and social focus, containing a library, with half a million volumes, and a 3,000-seat multi-purpose assembly hall.

Overleaf: Looking from the library across the public piazza into the lobby of the convocation hall.

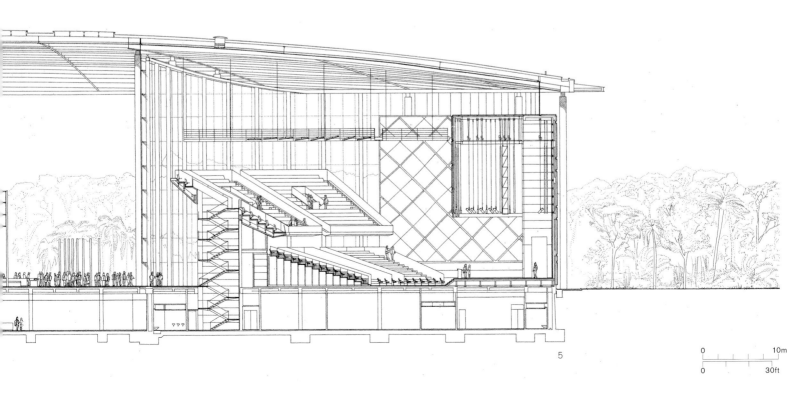

5

0   10m

0   30ft

Deutsche Bank Place

Sydney, Australia 1997–2005

1. Located in Sydney's dense central business district, the building's distinctive profile – with its setbacks and diagonal 'cage' – follows outlines dictated by city ordinances and right-of-light limits governed by its neighbours. The State Library of New South Wales is in the foreground.

2. The building at night, seen from the harbour.

3. Early design sketches by Norman Foster, exploring options for stepping the height of the building to protect daylight falling on two nearby public spaces.

1

In contrast to most of Foster's better known office buildings in other parts of the world, such as the Hongkong Bank and Commerzbank, which were designed for owner occupiers, Deutsche Bank Place is notable as one of the few tall office buildings completed by the Foster studio to be designed entirely as a speculative venture.

The difference between the two kinds of end users – whatever the size or shape of the building – is crucial to the design process, and to the outcome. A client that is committed to occupying a building, and with an eye on the long term, is far more likely to embrace innovation. In contrast, a client who is building to let will place a premium on keeping initial costs low and be less willing to invest in efficient operating systems. Of course, there are exceptions, as in the case of Foster's Century Tower in Tokyo, where a discriminating client clearly identified himself with the building, even though he occupied only part of it.

A major factor in the design was a desire to exploit views across the Botanic Gardens and the magnificent harbour.

Strategically placed within the heart of the central business district (CBD), the Phillip Street building joins several other distinguished office buildings in the area. These include towers by Harry Seidler and Renzo Piano, which – with the exception of Seidler's Capita Centre, whose site is hemmed in on three sides – are designed to open up parts of their sites to the public, creating breathing spaces in the dense city centre.

Foster has an established reputation for using high-rise projects as an opportunity to enhance the urban environment by creating open or covered public spaces at street level, as with the Hongkong Bank and Commerzbank buildings. However, constrained as they were by the restrictions of the Sydney site, David Nelson and the Foster team were compelled to cover the site from end to end, and to search for new ways to provide public access and amenity.

A major factor in the design was a desire to exploit the views towards the east and north-east across the Royal Botanic Gardens and the magnificent harbour. After much negotiation, a 32-metre wide view corridor was established between the building's southern edge and the Westpac tower next door, thus maintaining a view across the site from the buildings on the other side of Phillip Street. Partly filling the gap, Foster inserted a three-storey pavilion block aligned with the podium of the Westpac building. Containing shops on the ground floor, plant rooms above and a crèche on the top floor, this pavilion creates a link at street level between the two larger buildings. Other key dimensions of the building envelope – which is cut at the top at a 52-degree angle – were determined by the intersection of the primary sun-angles designed to protect the nearby public buildings and open spaces from overshadowing.

A series of design decisions followed, which, while logical in themselves, departed from conventional practice in several ways. Given its corner location and the long frontage along Phillip Street, the usual approach would be to position the offices facing into both streets while burying the service cores inside the building. Instead, seeing the tremendous views, the architects placed the office space along the eastern edge of the site, in the middle of the block, and gathered the lifts and service cores in a narrow structure facing west into Phillip Street where they shield the offices from the afternoon sun.

2

3

The original plans included a biosphere at the top which was designed to draw in air which could then be used to ventilate the atrium naturally. Because Sydney is humid, the biosphere would have contained a dehumidification system to treat the air before it dropped down into the atrium, so there wouldn't have been any processing of the air apart from the dehumidification. Because of the economic downturn this didn't come to fruition but we managed to retain the space and future proof the design so that the system could be retrofitted at a later date. Gerard Evenden, in conversation with the editor, 2009

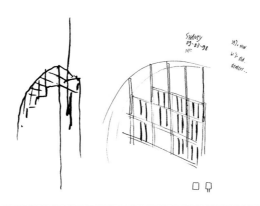

The biosphere was designed to aid cooling and provide fresh air to the office spaces. At the heart of the biosphere was a large-scale floating restaurant; essentially a transparent glazed box, it had a terrace on its roof so that visitors could be fully immersed within the green environment. Ross Palmer, of Foster + Partners, in conversation with the editor, 2010

Left: In these early sketches, Norman Foster envisaged that the top of the building would have a curved profile and culminate in a planted winter garden – or 'biosphere' – that would have naturally cleansed and recycled air within the building and provided an added amenity.

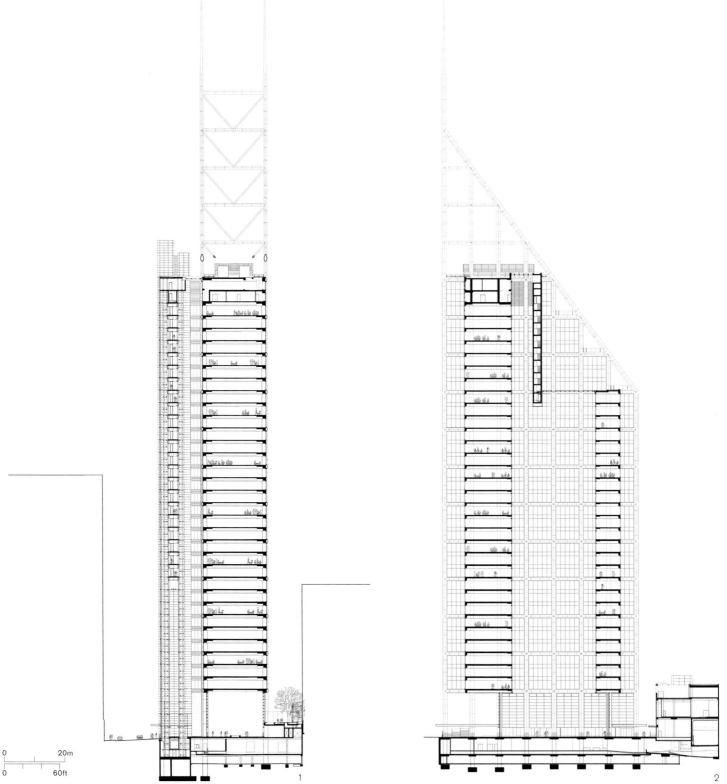

0   20m

0   60ft

1

2

 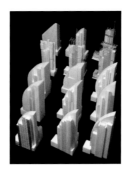

Given such a restrictive site, the challenge was to
turn constraints into benefits. The narrowness of
the plot ruled out a central core. That led us to a
remote offset core, which in turn generated highly
efficient, flexible, uninterrupted floor plates with
unparalleled views across Sydney. Then, by raising
the office floors we were able to create a very
special urban space at ground level. It's a similar
strategy to the Hongkong Bank. In return for
creating such a generous public space the
planners allowed us an increase in office floor
space, so it had a commercial component too.
David Nelson, in conversation with the editor, 2009

Keeping within the stipulated plot ratio, the
designers could then have fitted a rectangular
office slab with a conventional 4-metre-high
lobby on the ground floor and the maximum
allowable office space above. However, this
would have meant that the occupants of the
first fifteen floors would have been deprived of
those splendid eastern views. And so, instead of
calculating the height of the building by starting
at the ground level and totting up the floors
needed to provide the space allowed, Nelson and
his team started at the top of the envelope and
worked their way down. This left a 15-metre-high
void at ground level that would otherwise have
been occupied by viewless offices.

By creating a tall covered space at street level, the architects found an elegant way to provide public amenities on a cramped urban site.

By pushing the rentable volume of the building
upwards, the designers found that they could
greatly increase the number of floors with views,
thereby also increasing their economic value.
Stepped back on the top twelve floors in three
stages to accommodate the triangular shape of
the envelope, the building also gains a distinctive
profile – always an asset for an office tower –
which is accentuated by an open steel frame
that makes its own mark on the Sydney skyline.
In addition, the setback floors provide open
terraces with panoramic views.

No less important, by creating a tall covered
space at street level, the architects found an
elegant way to provide public amenities on a
cramped urban site. One is reminded of the
strategy deployed by Foster in opening up the
public space beneath the Hongkong Bank.
As in Hong Kong, in exchange for opening up
the ground plane in this manner, the Sydney
authorities granted a modest but useful
increase in the allowable floor space.

Bounded to the east and west by the giant
columns of the office tower, this cavernous,
granite-paved space adds a new and unexpected
dimension to the meaning of 'urban room'.
Measuring 65 by 21 metres, and open at its
northern end, the space serves as both anteroom
to the office building above and a sheltered
piazza. The centre of the floor is taken up by four
rectangular water features, which can be covered
over to provide display platforms. Glass walls
between the widely spaced columns on the
eastern side introduce shops and cafés.

On the opposite side, the glass walls are
punctured by a pair of revolving doors that lead
to the office entrance lobby – and the building's
other main surprise. Traversing the lobby, beams
of daylight draw the eye irresistibly upwards
through a forty-storey void between the two
banks of lifts and the office floors. Roofed in
glass and criss-crossed by glazed bridges, the
drama of the space is further enlivened by the
silent movement of the lifts, which sweep up
and down behind a full-height glass screen.
Passengers in the lifts that face into this void
have extraordinary views through the glass walls
of the offices opposite, and out to the city and
harbour beyond, each floor presenting a different
panoramic slice.

Only in the design of the fit-out of the office
floors is there any sign of the economics of
a speculative venture. Nelson and the Foster
team tried to persuade the client to adopt an
environmental control system with chilled ceilings
– silent as well as energy efficient – of the sort
used in the Commerzbank. However, unfamiliar
with such systems – which at the time had not
been used in Australia – and wary of the costs
involved, the client opted for a standard system.

Nevertheless, where users such as Deutsche
Bank have requested a non-standard fit-out, the
architects have ensured that the building can
accommodate it. The post-tensioned concrete
floor beams, for example, are designed so that,
should they be exposed, as on the Deutsche
Bank floors, they create a visually attractive
element as well as extra headroom.

3

4

1. Cross-section, showing
the offset core to the left,
the full-height atrium and
the column-free office floors.

2. Long section through the
atrium, looking towards the
office floors.

3. The office entrance lobby,
entered from Phillip Street.

4. Looking down to the floor
of the atrium from one of the
bridges that cross the space.

1, 2. A typical upper-level office plan and the plan at street level.

3. The four-storey Assembly – at the base of the tower, viewed from Hunter Street. The podium building can be seen through the glazing at the far end.

4. The entrance to the Assembly from Phillip Street.

5. Café tables spill out into the space.

| 0 | | 20m |
| 0 | | 60ft |

Similarly, staircases can be punched through between the main beams, connecting two floors occupied by the same company. The high level of daylight, together with other environmental measures, has also won the project a four-star rating – one below the highest – on the local official measure for energy efficient building.

Externally, the building makes its presence felt without calling undue attention to itself, as well-behaved neighbours should. The triangular steel frame, with its twin masts, adds extra height and brings the tower more into line with its taller neighbours to the north. The aluminium cladding is also designed so that every third floor beam has the same prominent profile as the main columns. This has the double effect of breaking down the facade into smaller sections and stressing the vertical over the horizontal proportions. On Phillip Street, the facade consists almost entirely of the transparent banks of lifts, bookended by the solid cores containing staircases, service lifts and toilets. This is best viewed at dusk, or on a late winter's afternoon, when the building is lit from within and the movement of the lifts is most visible, creating a constantly changing scene.

The main attraction for pedestrians, however, is to be found around the corner on Hunter Street, where the space under the offices opens out on to the pavement. Quite unlike any other public space in Sydney, this giant, open-air room – the Assembly – gives a new twist to urban place-making, providing a sheltered meeting and eating place that is simultaneously inside and outside. Though it is reminiscent of the space beneath the Hongkong Bank – a popular weekend picnic spot – it offers more amenities, coming closer in spirit to the great lobby beneath Hearst Tower in New York.

Like the Hearst lobby, the Assembly functions as both public square and anteroom, but has the advantage of being accessed directly from the street. Linked with the dramatic void over the lobby, the building delivers an impressive spatial double act. Lest there be any remaining doubt after Century Tower, Deutsche Bank Place should also finally quash the notion that speculative office construction under perfectly normal economic and commercial conditions, precludes good architecture or urban design.

Chris Abel

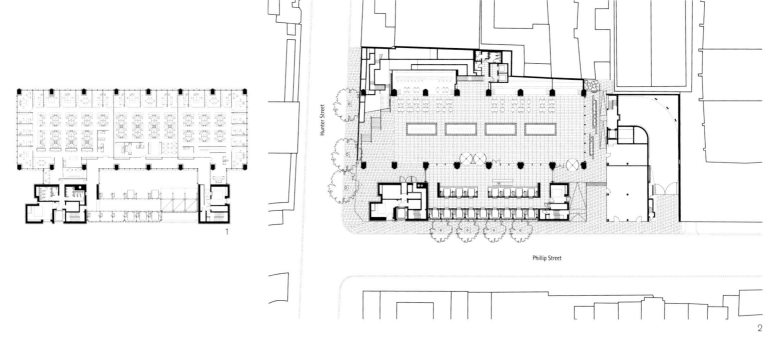

Deutsche Bank represented a sea change because at that time Sydney was heavily influenced by America and we were bringing in European ideas, particularly about sustainability. The actual form of the building – its floor plates, core and the space between – massively reduced its energy load. By putting the core on the western side we not only maximised the views of the harbour and made the floor plate super efficient, but it meant that the hot western sun hit the core while the cooler eastern facade was open to the view and only needed minimal solar shading. Gerard Evenden, of Foster + Partners, in conversation with the editor, 2011

At street level, the private world of the tower meets the public realm of the city in a four-storey-high covered piazza – the Assembly. A prelude to the office lobbies, it is lined with shops, cafés and a crèche and functions as a busy public square. Norman Foster, in conversation with the editor, 2012

When work began on the project there was a lot of empty office space in Sydney so there was a worry that the building might not be let because it was at the premium end of the market. However, once Deutsche Bank committed, everyone wanted to move in. Nine months before the building was completed it was fully let, which was unique for Sydney. Gerard Evenden, of Foster + Partners, in conversation with the editor, 2011

3

This giant, open-air room gives a new twist to urban place-making, providing a sheltered meeting and eating place that is simultaneously inside and outside.

Chris Abel

4

5

Regent Place
Sydney, Australia 2003–2007

1

1, 2. The development lies on George Street in the heart of Sydney's central business district, opposite St Andrew's Cathedral and close to the Town Hall. Two residential towers stand on a five-storey sandstone-faced podium that contains shops, restaurants and leisure facilities. The towers are set back to create a generous terrace on the roof of the podium; and the street elevations respond to the scale of the existing historic buildings, which have been integrated within the site.

3, 4. A study model of the developed scheme. The strategic importance of the site presented one of the key challenges for the project – the city planning authorities imposed very specific guidelines for the massing and the floor plates of the two towers, and the scheme reflects that.

5, 6. Early sketches by David Nelson, showing how the towers are articulated above their podium base.

2

Following the low-density pattern of most Australian cities, the greater part of Sydney's population lives in the city's outer suburbs, commuting to work by road or rail. However, population pressures and related changes in planning policies have recently combined to produce a marked shift towards higher residential densities and mixed-use developments. Built to meet the growing demand for high-quality apartments in the centre of the city, Regent Place is designed as a model of sustainable, high-density urban form combining home, work, commerce and leisure in the same location.

Though relatively conventional by comparison with some of the practice's other recent works, the design boasts a subtle and finely tuned response to context. Occupying the site of the former Regent Theatre at one end of a large block in the historic heart of the city, next to a conservation area, the plot comprises two interconnected parcels of land of unequal size, offering three street frontages. Both segments are joined by a narrow neck at the southern end of the site but are separated by several existing structures of varying size, age, character and function. The site is further complicated by a fall in level from the east towards the west side equivalent to a full storey in height.

Though the site is awkward, the location offers superb aspects and other advantages. Running along the eastern side of the block is George Street, the principal north-south artery through the city. Darling Harbour is a short distance to the west while the CBD lies within easy reach to the north. Across the street are St Andrew's Cathedral and the Town Hall, while the adjacent block is filled by the Queen Victoria Building shopping complex – the 'QVB'.

The main challenge, as David Nelson and the design team saw it, was to fit the programme of apartments, shops and cafés into the oddly shaped site, while capitalising on the three different street frontages and potential views across the city towards the Harbour from the upper levels.

The client also indicated a strong preference for an exterior with clean lines, as opposed to apartments with open balconies, with their inevitable accumulation of personal clutter. Local regulations also mandated a podium solution for the lower floors, conforming to the height of the existing street frontage, with setbacks for taller structures. The placement of the vertical elements was also largely determined by the split configuration of the site, together with the maximum allowable building envelope.

3

Regent Place is designed as a model of sustainable, high-density urban form combining home, work, commerce and leisure in the same location.

4

The completed design consists of a podium varying from four to five floors in height from east to west, with two towers of unequal volume but equal height positioned over the two main segments of the site. The larger tower contains a range of apartments and penthouses for sale while the smaller tower contains serviced apartments and is managed much like a hotel.

These two structures are joined at the lower levels by the podium, whose top floor and roof house recreational facilities for each tower; the lower floors contain a mixture of retail and cafés, together with separate entrance foyers for the towers. An additional lower floor of shops is also accessed directly from the west side, or by escalator from the upper street level. A further eight floors of parking are provided below.

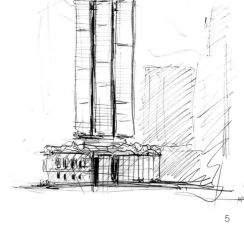

5

6

Right: Several different massing options were explored using simple block models. The challenge was to accommodate the required mix of apartments, shops and cafés into the irregularly shaped site while at the same time capitalising on the three separate street frontages, a problem compounded by the height restrictions imposed by local planning regulations.

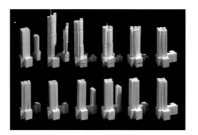

2

Designed with a fine eye for detail, most apartments have generous winter gardens with opening window sections and full-height folding glass doors separating them – or not – from the living spaces. An attractive alternative to conventional balconies, the winter gardens provide usable open-air spaces in all seasons and weathers, not to mention an extra acoustic and thermal barrier when needed.

Deep, narrow recesses in both blocks also separate individual apartments from each other and provide a source of natural ventilation to all rooms as well as acoustic privacy. Externally, the combination of deep recesses and clean facades stresses the vertical lines and slim proportions of both blocks, setting them apart from their mostly bulkier and fussier neighbours.

The sleek appearance is enhanced by the use of metal cladding with a fine vertical corrugation on the recessed walls, which is reminiscent of the cladding used on the Renault Centre, but also echoes the corrugated metal widely used on the roofs of vernacular Australian buildings. Each metal-clad wall terminates on the outer edge in a projecting curved nib, so that both towers read as a series of sharp, vertical lines reaching skywards.

The larger tower offers further attractions in the recreational and entrance spaces. It is here that the designers enjoyed the most creative freedom, to occasional dramatic effect.

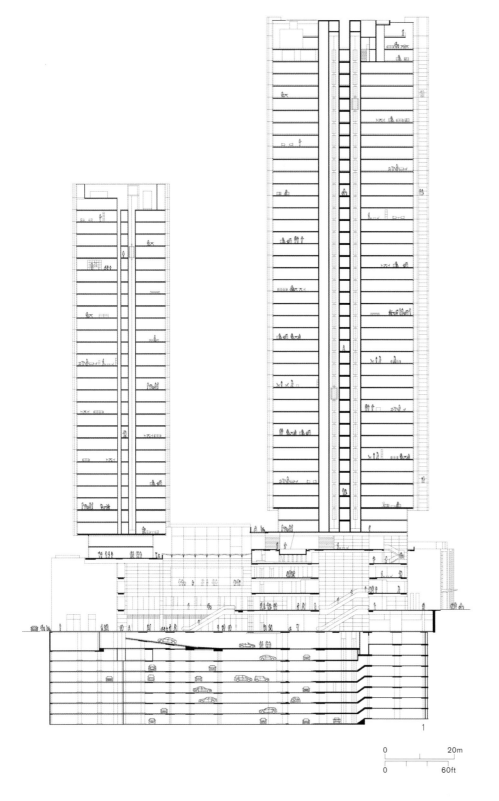

1

0   20m

0   60ft

Left: Three different local architects were commissioned by the client to do interior fit-out treatments for show apartments, one of which was former Foster + Partners architect William Smart, now of Smart Design Studio. His brief was to create a 'boys' toys' apartment. The resulting bachelor pad is finished in a bold black and white palette and furnished with design classics such as the Foster Nomos table and Fortuny lamp. Adding to the theme are a series of high-tech gadgets including an integrated sound system and a top-of-the-range mountain bike.

3

4

5

A 50-metre swimming pool runs almost the full depth of the tower from inside to outside under a glass curtain, terminating in the open air among the well-planted roof terraces. A glass section in the bottom of the pool over the entrance to the tower allows passers-by to glimpse the swimmers moving overhead. Inside, a row of massive, splayed concrete columns rises directly from the centre of the broad pool. The pool's appearance is made all the more striking by a dark colour scheme and subtle lighting, creating a cave-like atmosphere.

An attractive alternative to conventional balconies, the winter gardens provide usable open-air spaces in all seasons and weathers.

Immediately below the outer section of the pool, a cascading water feature leads you into the tall entrance foyer. Here the designers have created an equally dramatic black and red colour scheme, which they followed through in a circular mailroom lined with scarlet mail boxes that must easily rank as the most unusual space of its kind. This colour scheme only gives way around the corner at the rear of the foyer where the lifts are positioned. Here, the clever use of lighting and mirrored walls and ceilings gives the impression of a space illuminated by natural top light. This theatrical treatment highlights the transition from dark to light space and vice versa. Such details betoken a lightness of touch.

For the general public, the most important part of the Regent Place scheme will be found directly off the surrounding streets inside the lower levels of the podium. As well as being the main traffic artery though the city, George Street is by far the busiest pedestrian thoroughfare. In response, Nelson and his team have created a seductive labyrinth of internal lanes, shops and cafés with entrances on all three sides of the block. The podium is opened up vertically as well as horizontally, with a narrow glazed void slicing all the way up into the lower floor of the apartment block above, so that residents can peek at the shoppers below. A glass roof at the rear of the podium also brings daylight down into the heart of the block, further enlivening the whole place.

While there is no shortage of high-rise architecture in Sydney, with the notable exception of the work of Harry Seidler, well-designed tall buildings are few and far between. Together with Foster's Deutsche Bank Place office tower in the nearby CBD, which notably features a major public open space at street level, Regent Place creates a modest but highly attractive addition to the street life of the city, as well as to the skyline.

Chris Abel

1. Cross-section through the podium and residential towers. The larger of the two towers rises to forty-eight storeys and comprises private apartments; the smaller tower is thirty-three storeys tall and provides serviced apartments and recreational spaces. The podium is cut through by a sequence of glazed routes that recall Sydney's traditional toplit arcades.

2. In a predominantly commercial area, the city planners discouraged the use of balconies, with their tendency to accumulate domestic clutter. Instead of balconies, apartments have internal loggias. These are separated from the living spaces by means of full-height folding glass doors which are opaque when seen from outside but transparent from within.

3, 4. A 50-metre swimming pool stretches almost the entire width of the site. Running from inside to outside it terminates on the podium's roof terrace.

5. The tall entrance foyer with its rich use of colour provides a counterpoint to the restrained metal cladding of the exterior.

An existing planning application had set the basic building envelope. There had to be two towers but to keep within the permitted envelope we felt would produce quite a heavy, large-scale block so we needed a way in which we could break down the scale. We developed a cluster system which was almost like individual apartments stacked one on top of the other next to another stack with an expressed gap in between. This gave the illusion of a cluster of eight towers rather than just one big block and because the slots and gaps were cut quite deep it meant that we could bring ventilation and natural light deeper into the plan and give the towers a kind of natural elegance.
David Nelson, in conversation with the editor, 2012

1

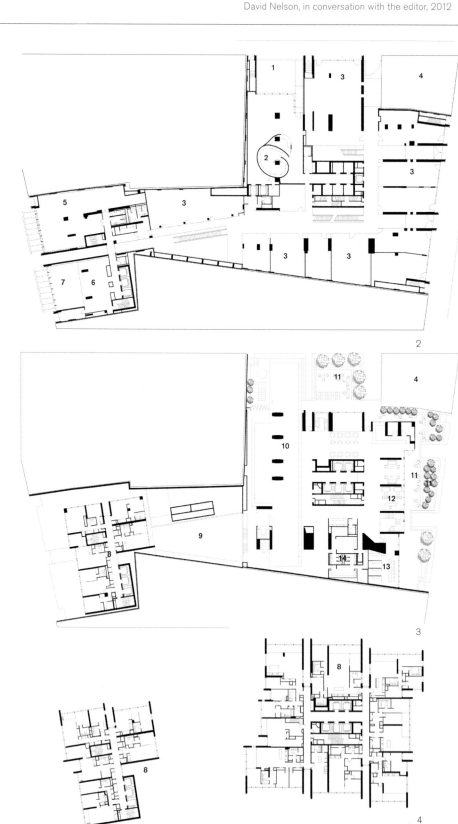

2

3

4

1. View from the main lobby to Bathurst Street – the water feature creates the illusion that it has eroded the pavement's edge.

2. Ground floor plan, corresponding with the datum of George Street.

3. Fourth floor podium plan.

4. Typical upper-level tower plans.

1 water feature
2 post room
3 retail
4 existing building
5 business suite
6 restaurant
7 void
8 apartments
9 atrium
10 swimming pool
11 terrace
12 lounge
13 dance studio
14 changing rooms

0   20m
0   60ft

For the water feature we wanted to develop something which contrasted strongly with its surroundings and which expressed the uncontrolled, wild character of water flow in its natural environment. We were influenced by the irregular forms of rice paddies and natural limestone pools and inspired by the sounds that are synonymous with mountain streams and wild landscapes. Phil Goodwin of Waterforms International, water feature designer, in conversation with the editor, 2009

When we developed the design we realised that if we used a very dark tint for the glass of the balconies, residents would be able to see out, but if they had a bike or a washing machine left there it wouldn't be visible from street level. It quietened the visual impact so that the curtains or objects wouldn't be seen, giving the building a more office-like elevation, so while it was always going to be a big, tall building it would still harmonise with its surroundings. David Nelson, in conversation with the editor, 2012

The water feature was great fun to work on. It was largely driven by the client's desire to create something amazing in the space. We kept coming back to him with ideas and he kept sending them away for being too boring until we eventually settled on this scheme, which was inspired by the Pamukkale pools in Turkey. Gerard Evenden, of Foster + Partners, in conversation with the editor, 2011

5. Planning regulations stipulate that every new development in the centre of Sydney must make provision for public art. To fulfil this requirement the team co-developed a water feature with local landscape architect Phil Goodwin. Taking its inspiration from the Pamukkale thermal pools in Turkey, the installation comprises a series of overflowing black granite pools which step down to pavement level, their irregular organic forms contrasting with the strong verticals of the entrance lobby. By night, when the water pressure is reduced to create a calming atmosphere, the pools are lit by a series of submerged LEDs which alternate in colour from red to blue to purple.

5

London: the World City?
Norman Foster 2012

Consider these statistics: the global population stands at 7 billion; by 2030 it is expected to reach 8 billion. In 2008, for the first time, more than half of the world's population lived in towns and cities; by 2030, if the current trend continues, that figure will have risen to 62.5 per cent – a total of 5 billion people. These projections pose entirely new social and technological challenges for cities and societies.

One result of this global population shift is the growth of cities of unprecedented size. Today there are twenty-seven 'megacities' – defined as continuous urban agglomerations with populations in excess of 10 million. Of these, seventeen are in developing nations. The top two – Tokyo and Guangzhou – have populations of 34.5 and 25.8 million respectively. The three cities in the next tier – Jakarta, Seoul and Shanghai – each have populations close to 23.5 million. All are on the Pacific Rim, which the World Bank predicts will be the fastest-growing region in the world over the next five years. New York City, the iconic New World metropolis – which in 1925 overtook London as the largest in the world – has slipped to eighth place, with a population of 21.5 million.

London as a conurbation stands far down the scale, at twenty-sixth, with a population of 12.6 million. It is interesting to look at the city's growth pattern, and see how that figure was reached. In 1801, at the time of the first official Census, the city's population stood at a little over one million. By 1825, London was by far the most populous city in the world, with 1.335 million inhabitants. With the advent of the Industrial Revolution, by 1841 its population had almost doubled to 2.23 million; and it would double again roughly every fifty years, the population of Greater London reaching 8.6 million in 1939. Since the Second World War, London's population has remained relatively stable, though it is expected to rise by 14 per cent in the next decade, driven by immigration and rising birthrates.

Contrast that evolutionary pattern with Mexico City, which in 1940 had a population of 1.6 million, and has since expanded fourteenfold; or with Seoul, which had a population of 1.14 million in 1940 and has exploded twentyfold. The pace of change in cities such as these is startling.

Looking at the list of megacities the immediate reaction is to note its diversity. Yet cities around the world have some common problems and can learn from one another. The key is to focus on what it is that makes a city sustainable. Let us begin by looking at energy consumption. Cities that sprawl are far less energy efficient than densely planned communities. Take a traditional European model, such as Copenhagen, and compare it with a car-dependent North American city such as Detroit. Urban Detroit covers an area of 359.4 square kilometres and has a population of 917,000. The municipality of Copenhagen covers 88.25 square kilometres and has 503,700 residents. With half the population density of Copenhagen, Detroit consumes seven times the energy per capita on transport, since people drive rather than walk or cycle, or take the bus or train.

We know that we must build more energy efficiently. But even if we could design every new building to run at a fraction of current energy levels and be carbon neutral, we will still have a significant problem if we encourage people to travel great distances by car between their home and workplace. To put this into perspective, in an industrialised society, buildings and the transport of people and goods between them account for 70 per cent of the energy total. It follows that if you reduce journey distances, by increasing densities, one result will be significant energy savings and carbon reductions. Car travel is a crucial factor. In densely planned cities, such as New York and London, less than half the population owns a car: in Manhattan, for example, 80 per cent of people using Grand Central Station arrive or depart on foot. Compare that with Detroit's traffic-choked freeways.

1

2

The history of cities is the history of change. Our cities continue to evolve as they are subject to the changing patterns in the way that we work, live, play, shop, communicate and travel. In the past cities were more balanced, with richer mixes of use and closer community ties. It was the American, Jane Jacobs, who identified the importance of a mixed-use urban culture to social well-being. In her seminal work of 1961, *The Death and Life of Great American Cities* she said, 'vital cities have marvellous innate abilities for understanding, communicating, contriving and inventing what is required to combat their difficulties … Dull, inert cities contain the seeds of their own destruction'. If there is a collective political will to challenge these destructive forces – to declare war on them – there are many available weapons. One must be the weapon of design skills, of architecture and planning. We must learn from the failures and successes of the past. We have to respond to the challenge of tackling the deprived areas and resist the easier pickings of fringe suburbia. We need to rediscover the culture of mixed-use and the integration of new cleaner industries into neighbourhoods. We must seek the potential of greener more ecologically sensitive structures and harness the economy and poetry of renewable energy. Norman Foster, AIA Gold Medal acceptance speech, Washington, 1 February 1994

Can cities transform themselves into self-regulating sustainable systems – not only in their internal function, but in their relationships to the outside world? An answer to this question may be critical to the future well-being of the planet, as well as of humanity. Herbert Girardet, *Creating Sustainable Cities*, 1999

Alarmingly, in most countries car usage is still increasing. China is the most extreme example. It is now the world's second largest car market after the United States, although car ownership is still only 80 per 1,000 of the population – a tenth of the figure in the US. In the past decade China has spent more on transport infrastructure than in the previous fifty years of Communist Party rule. In just four years, between 2006 and 2010, China constructed 639,000km of roads, including 28,700km of motorways, bringing its total motorway mileage to 74,000km, equalling the interstate highway network in the United States. Increased mobility between cities is likely to continue and that requires us to invest in higher-quality public transport systems.

Sustainability requires us to think holistically and that is as true of infrastructure – the 'urban glue' that holds a city together – as it is of architecture.

Interestingly, in China there are some hopeful signs amid the terrifying statistics. China now has the world's most extensive high-speed rail (HSR) network. More than 6,800km of HSR track was laid down between 2007 and 2012 and the system is used by almost one million people daily. The BRT (Bus Rapid Transit – the speed of a subway with the affordability of a bus) is another successful initiative. In the city of Kunming its launch resulted in car usage falling by 20 per cent.

Sustainability requires us to think holistically and that is as true of infrastructure – the 'urban glue' that holds a city together – as it is of architecture. Whether it is predominantly high-rise or lower with a mix of heights, the sustainable future city is likely to be high density with a high quality of urban lifestyle and a wide variety of choices. In this approach, buildings and infrastructure will be more closely integrated. I would argue further that the quality of a city's infrastructure impacts on the quality of life more directly than does the quality of its individual buildings.

If you visit any city, it is the sequence of spaces and connections – whether they are streets, squares, parks, bridges or transport systems – that shape your experience. If I was to take the many projects we have completed in London and try to rank them in terms of their social impact, I would probably elevate two of our infrastructure projects – Trafalgar Square and the Millennium Bridge – above the buildings.

In Trafalgar Square, we closed the northern side to traffic and reconnected the National Gallery with the heart of the space, through a generous flight of steps, to create a broad pedestrian piazza. This not only provides the National Gallery with an appropriate setting, but has transformed the square from an isolated traffic island into a truly grand urban space.

The change in the way the square is used – thronged with people in fine weather and during festivals – has been extraordinary. It is no exaggeration to say that it has helped to change the way people perceive and move around this part of the city. The Millennium Bridge has gone further still, opening up a new pedestrian connection between the 'rich' City of London in the north and 'poor' Southwark in the south. The ripple effect has helped to drive the economic regeneration of that part of the capital.

3. The Millennium Bridge (1996-2000), looking north. The bridge spans 320 metres between the City of London, close to St Paul's Cathedral, and Bankside alongside Tate Modern. Structurally, it pushes the boundaries of technology. A very shallow suspension bridge, its cables never rise more than 2.3 metres above the deck, allowing those crossing the bridge to enjoy panoramic views and preserving sightlines from the surrounding buildings.

4. Norman Foster's sketch of the Millennium Bridge made at the time of the competition in 1996. The bridge is conceived as a 'minimal intervention' and, like Bankside, as a symbol of regeneration.

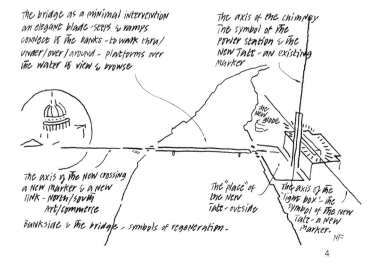

The bridge as a minimal intervention an elegant blade - steps & ramps connect to the banks - to walk thru/ under/over/around - platforms over the water to view & browse

The axis of the new crossing a new marker & a new link - north/south Art/commerce

Bankside & the bridge - symbols of regeneration.

The axis of the chimney the symbol of the power station & the new Tate - an existing marker

the new globe

The "place" of the new Tate - outside

The axis of the light box - the symbol of the new Tate - a new marker.

3

4

Nineteenth-century architects and engineers put in place much of the infrastructure that we now take for granted – new thoroughfares, parks, bridges, great railway stations. Look at some of those structures – such as Brunel's Paddington Station – and you find that allied with a deep understanding of structural and functional principles they had a great sense of theatre – a sense of occasion and celebration of travel. The journey started not when you got on the train but within the station itself. It brings some humanity into it. Norman Foster, in conversation with the editor, 2012

To persuade people to give up suburbs and their quasi-rural existence, they have to be offered urban qualities that are absent in sprawling cities: vitality, diversity, options for a wide mix of activities, social amenities and cultural facilities. In this context we have much to learn from historical cities and their lively pedestrian culture of markets, public squares and convivial meeting places. Herbert Girardet, *Creating Sustainable Cities*, 1999

The attraction, the appeal, the vitality, the richness of any city hasn't been created all in one flash – it came out of different periods of time, and surely the thing that is most enjoyable about it is its multiplicity of styles, each of its own time and age. I think that you can add to this life and vitality by making interventions in a modest way within it – keeping some facades or buildings and in other places where there is a hole, or a building just about to fall down, having the courage to do something distinctly of today, which will have the good manners to complement and respond to its surroundings. Norman Foster, in conversation with the editor, 2012

1. Two clusters of tall office buildings in London. In the foreground is the City cluster, congregated around Bishopsgate and Leadenhall Street to the east of the Bank of England. In the distance is Canary Wharf, built on the site of the former West India Docks on the Isle of Dogs. Since its foundation in 1988, Canary Wharf has grown to rival the financial dominance of the Square Mile and is the site of Britain's three tallest buildings: One Canada Square, which rises 235 metres (770 feet); the Citigroup Centre; and the HSBC Headquarters at 8 Canada Square (1997-2002), both of which measure 200 metres (656 feet).

It is worth noting at this point that one of the great achievements in London over the last twenty years has been to open the Thames waterfront on the South Bank as a public realm – an initiative that the Millennium Bridge has helped to galvanise. Yet the Thames is still under-utilised. As well as being a visual and social amenity, the river has the potential to become a vital transport artery, with its piers and river boats integrated with London's wider public transport network.

Alongside the Millennium Bridge and Trafalgar Square, I would rank the Great Court at the British Museum very highly as a project for the way in which it has created a new kind of city space – an 'urban room' generated by a cultural institution. It is both a destination in its own right and an urban shortcut: a link in the cultural route from the British Library and Bloomsbury, in the north, to Covent Garden, the river and the South Bank.

Although there is an echo in the Great Court of Bucky Fuller's Manhattan dome, its urban roots lie elsewhere: in the winter gardens and grand arcades of the nineteenth century. Examples that immediately spring to mind are the Barton and Lancaster Arcades, which I recall from the Manchester of my youth, and the Galleria Vittorio Emanuele in Milan – another enduring influence. More recently, it evokes the arcade we created beneath the Commerzbank Tower in Frankfurt which, with its bars and restaurants, has become a popular rendezvous in the city.

The restoration of the British Museum's forecourt – one of a series of related interventions within the museum – has connections with another central London initiative: the restoration of Horse Guards Parade, which lies between Whitehall and St James Park. That proposal stemmed from a series of seminars I held over breakfast in the studio in Battersea to generate ideas for enhancing the capital's public realm. We proposed clearing parked cars from the space and reclaiming it as a civic and ceremonial focus. Our cause was championed by the *Evening Standard*, London's evening newspaper, and Horse Guards was transformed.

London offers a very good potential model for sustainable future development in that it is a compact and relatively well-managed humanistic city, built to a relatively high density.

The sustainable city is a liveable city. The clean nature of much post-industrial work means that workplaces can be combined with housing, and localised mixed-use communities can be sustained when transport connections, businesses, schools, shops are all within walking or cycling distance of home. An example from my own experience is Duisburg, a city of half-a-million people in Germany's former steel-belt, where we have developed plans for urban renewal in several different areas.

In the first of these, in the derelict Inner Harbour, we introduced housing to industry, integrating apartment buildings and workplaces with new watercourses, parks and art galleries to create a thriving urban quarter. Significantly, the first steps involved building the infrastructure, creating the public spaces, digging canals and planting trees, to make the area attractive to new development.

1

With the second masterplan we made the equation work the other way. Buildings for the microelectronics industry were inserted within a dense residential quarter, focused on a new public park. Most recently, we developed a masterplan for the inner city, which aimed to strengthen Duisburg's civic identity by reinforcing its infrastructure and promoting higher-density development, with a mix of commercial, residential and cultural activity at its heart.

The critics of higher densities may denigrate this advocacy with slogans like 'town cramming' and the myth that it leads to something that is poorer – literally and also in terms of quality. Examine the evidence and you find the opposite is true. Macao and Monaco – with 20,800 and 16,500 people per square kilometre respectively – are among the densest communities on earth, yet their roots lie at opposite ends of the economic spectrum. Paradoxically, greater densities in a city often combine a desirable lifestyle with higher property values. In most examples, proximity to a park or green space is a major factor. Mayfair and Belgravia in London, for example, pair with Hyde Park, just as the Upper East and West Sides of Manhattan relate to Central Park; and significantly, in the recent competition for a cultural district in West Kowloon, the people of Hong Kong voted for our solution, which features a new waterfront park.

Building densely does not necessarily mean building tall – though in most cities there are places where tall buildings have a significant role to play – but it does mean building more intelligently. London is not a high-rise city, nor is it generally envisaged as one, but the city's organic nature does not preclude a coherent skyline. There are areas where clusters of tall buildings should be developed. Few people would seriously question the appropriateness of the existing clusters in the City, Docklands and Croydon.

There is also a case for encouraging greater population concentrations in places where public transport networks come together. In one sense, this is a 'chicken and egg' phenomenon, since in many instances they have grown together. However, if one looks at an area such as King's Cross in London, one finds that although it is incredibly well served in transport terms, it is underdeveloped in terms of density.

Our masterplan for King's Cross set out a vision for a high-density community with a green space at its heart. Predominantly low-rise, it also included two mixed-use towers – or 'spires' – which might have been the first of an eventual cluster. Why build tall in King's Cross, one might ask, but precedents abound. The Empire State Building, for example, was an isolated tall building when it was completed. It was off the beaten track in terms of where high-rise buildings in New York were at that time.

I would argue that along with their location, it is the quality of tall buildings that we must be vigilant about; that and how they function at street level, where they can create new urban spaces or play a part in tying one area of the city to another. These were guiding principles for us in the design of the Swiss Re building at 30 St Mary Axe, where we created a new public piazza and opened up pedestrian connections in this closely packed part of the City.

Another popular argument, widely used by the anti-tall-building lobby, is that they are socially alienating, not as friendly as the traditional low-rise street. Interestingly, however, if you care to look you find examples where this is far from the case. Our experience in developing a masterplan for Elephant and Castle in south London was enlightening. At the beginning of the consultation process we assumed that the residents of two towers – the twenty-four-storey Draper House and the twelve-storey Pyramid House – would welcome the opportunity to be rehoused in lower buildings, but this was not the case.

2. An aerial view of Notting Hill in west London. The garden squares around Ladbroke Grove in Notting Hill contain some of London's most desirable residential property. Yet the area is also one of the city's highest density districts, with some 13,000 residents per square kilometre. Laid out in the mid-nineteenth century, streets such as Lansdowne Crescent have elegant terraces backing on to generous communal gardens. Most of the originally large single-family houses have been converted into flats – proving their worth as popular and adaptable models of high-density housing.

3. The masterplan for King's Cross (1987-1990) in central London addressed a swathe of derelict railway land behind King's Cross and St Pancras Stations. The aim was to create an authentic, densely planned urban quarter. Mixed-use development was arranged around a new public park – the first to be proposed in the city for more than a century. The new buildings were predominantly low- or medium-rise, with the exception of two towers – or 'spires' – at the north-east corner of the site.

2

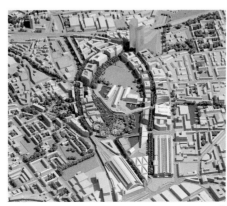

3

1. Milan Santa Giulia (2003).
Like many large cities, Milan
is bordered by former
industrial areas that can
be reclaimed and brought
to life as sustainable urban
communities. The Santa
Giulia site is blessed by a
combination of size, location
and excellent transport
connections. It lies close to
the heart of the city, yet near
to leafy suburbs. The question
was: is it possible to have
the advantages of the city
and suburbia without the
problems of either? The
answer is a series of
balancing acts – urbanity with
parks, pedestrians with traffic,
old with new, public transport
with private cars – to create
a 'city within a city'.

The residents expressed a strong sense of community
within the towers. All they wanted was new lifts and improved
communal areas. Similarly, they wanted the external public
spaces to be improved, the encircling traffic reduced and
transport connections enhanced – all of which was possible.

London offers a very good potential model for sustainable
future development in that it is a compact and relatively
well-managed humanistic city, built to a relatively high
density. In fact, some of the areas of highest density – such
as Kensington and Chelsea – are associated with the most
desirable lifestyle, with good public spaces, convenient
public transport connections, parks and communal gardens.
Kensington, for example, has 13,200 residents per square
kilometre: up to two-and-a-half times higher than some of
the capital's poorest boroughs, such as Hackney which has
9,000 people per square kilometre, or Brent, which has 5,000.

Significantly, a traditional medium-rise London community
like Notting Hill has 200 housing units per hectare. Before
the most recent UK planning legislation, much residential
development in London was typically being built at twenty to
thirty units per hectare. In other words, a typical sought-after
historic area of the city is up to ten times more densely
developed than its modern equivalents.

I am not suggesting that one fixates on a single model
– when you are creating new communities you need a high
degree of choice – but I think it is important to recognise
some of the core issues that affect design strategy. Perhaps
one of the main differences between London and a relatively
high-density European city such as Milan, where we planned
the new quarter of Santa Giulia, is that the latter has been
spared many of the planning mistakes of the 1960s, which
often resulted in a loss of traditional urban grain, and instead
has benefited from a slower pace of development. Visit Milan
and you notice how easy it is to walk to a restaurant, a bar
or a gallery and to enjoy that sense of closeness.

Of course, it would be better if the city were less congested
with traffic, if parking were easier and if there were more green
spaces. These are the things that make the suburbs desirable,
particularly for those people with young families, despite the
inconvenience of the commute. With Santa Giulia we aimed
to provide all the amenities of the suburbs, but at the density
of the city. The headline was 'quality of life', which is in itself
another key ingredient in terms of sustainability.

It is self-evident that if we are to reverse the flight to the
suburbs we have to create desirable urban communities where
people want to live. But how do you measure that? Of course,
you see polls that rank one city against another. Interestingly,
higher-density, lower-energy-consumption cities habitually
score higher in terms of quality of life. Copenhagen, for
example, consistently comes out close to top in worldwide
'liveability' surveys. European cities such as Munich, Vienna,
Zurich and Geneva also score very high. In North America,
Boston and New York are very desirable, so too is San
Francisco. London is a more complex case, and its appeal
is linked to the diversity of its different neighbourhoods.

It is self-evident that if we are to reverse the flight to the suburbs we have to create desirable urban communities where people want to live.

Each city has its own special characteristics – its own DNA.
There are contributing strands in this DNA such as climate,
scale and other physical attributes. Over time I have explored
what it is that distinguishes London from other cities around
the world, and tried to define what makes it so desirable and
liveable. Initially these explorations were ad hoc, but over time
they have become more systematic. If you look at a map of
London, it is obvious how graphically different it is from, say,
Paris or New York. There may be a number of reasons for
this, but I find it helpful to consider the example of a clock:
to me London is an analogue rather than a digital city. On
an analogue watch you read the time without reference to
numbers. It communicates the information more immediately
than its digital equivalent because you skip the conversion
process. The position of the hands on the dial is enough.

1

So, how does this relate to cities? Perhaps it is thus: to get an airport taxi driver to take you to, for example, the Carlyle Hotel in New York City, you must specify its location precisely: Manhattan, at East 76th and Madison. Similarly, if I want to be taken to a particular restaurant in Paris the immediate questions are: 'Which arrondissement? What number?' London is very different. To describe a hotel's location, you might say: 'between Berkeley Square and Grosvenor Square', or 'on the edge of Hyde Park, near Marble Arch'. The structure of London, with its absence of grids and numerical references, is more organic, having evolved from individual centres that have developed and coalesced over time. Each place has its own green space or, occasionally in the metropolitan centre, its own urban space, such as a square, to define it.

This emphasis on green spaces is reflected in London's extraordinary public transport network. Destinations on the front of buses give clues: Putney Common, Parson's Green, Shepherd's Bush, Hampstead Heath and Primrose Hill, to name just a few. The intensity of public open space, and the network of links between, is at the heart of the excellent quality of life you can experience in London, notwithstanding the social problems that are inevitable in any large city.

A walk in Battersea, where our studio is based, highlights the density of a London neighbourhood, the open spaces, the rich mix of uses, and the way in which a river bridge can signal a route and give a visual clue. The essence of a city is thus communication. Individuals come together in close proximity, and their movement to and from those denser areas is dependent on the routes between, say, a square and a park. Wherever we go, we are guided by symbols and signals indicating, for example, metro and railway stations.

Flaws in this system emerge where open spaces are not fully accessible. Sloane Square, for example, is an attractive place, but when you are there, navigating a route between passing cars and hugging its perimeter, you question whether such important spaces should function as traffic roundabouts. Some such spaces have to be partly geared towards traffic, but one cannot help remembering Leicester Square before it was pedestrianised. You could fight the traffic to cross it from one side to the other, but it took you nowhere. Now everyone takes Leicester Square's open, friendly form for granted.

It is worth noting, however, that the evolution of Leicester Square took nearly twenty years to unfold from the first idea to its eventual realisation – a not untypical London planning story. In contrast, our masterplanning studies for central London, which encompassed Trafalgar Square, Parliament Square, and the surrounding area in central London, unfolded relatively quickly. We began our work in 1996 and by 2003 the first major phase – the improvement of Trafalgar Square – had been completed.

In this case we were fortunate to have had the support of London's newly elected mayor, Ken Livingstone. I have seen first-hand how city mayors can be powerful catalysts for change. I witnessed Mayor Pasqual Maragall's transformation of Barcelona in the 1980s and '90s, and saw how he improved communications, created new public spaces, controlled traffic, replaced slums and embarked on a bold programme of modern public buildings while respecting the city's history and culture. In 1988, when Barcelona's skyline was threatened by the impact of hundreds of unregulated masts and antennae, I saw how he averted an environmental disaster and fought the three communication giants, persuading them to build a single unified structure, which we designed. The Torre de Collserola has become a symbol of civic pride. No committee or commercial group, however well intentioned, could have achieved that. It needed the right person to operate the right system.

2. Comparative plans of London, Paris, Barcelona and New York City at the same scale. From left: the Maida Vale district of London; the Avenue des Champs Elysées and Place Charles de Gaulle in Paris; the intersection of Passeig de Saint Joan and Avinguda Diagonal in Barcelona; and 5th Avenue in Midtown Manhattan. The urban grain of London, which has emerged ad-hoc over centuries, is quite different from the surveyor's grid of the North American city, or those European models that have had an overarching urban order imposed upon them.

2

1, 2. These images of Trafalgar Square were taken by members of the project team in 1996. The central area of the square had effectively become an island, encircled by vehicles. The pavements were generally very narrow, which increased the risk of stepping out into the path of traffic and access to the central area involved running the gauntlet of speeding cars and buses.

Similarly, in Nîmes, the support of an inspirational mayor, Jean Bousquet, allowed us to expand our project for the Carré d'Art to address the public space in front of it. The new square – which embraces the Roman Maison Carrée – has become in effect an outdoor room, lined with café tables and full of life. Railings, advertising boards and parking spaces were removed and the square transformed as a pedestrian realm. It shows how a building project, backed by an enlightened political initiative, can spark the reinvigoration of a city's social and physical fabric.

After I graduated from Yale I worked as a planner in New Haven, Connecticut, and I was involved in a number of urban renewal projects in the region. Interestingly, we found that if you did something in a district that had some distinction, that brought a new dimension or life to that particular spot, then there was a ripple effect into the surrounding area, which over time could be measured in a tangible way.

We have seen exactly that happen in Nîmes, and with the help of sophisticated surveying and modelling techniques, we have also been able to track real changes in and around Trafalgar Square following our interventions there.

One of the key tools we utilised in developing our masterplan for central London was the mathematical model and plan of the capital developed by Space Syntax at University College, London. We first worked with this study group on our King's Cross masterplan, in 1987, and as a result of my encouragement they set up their consultancy. Their London model can demonstrate with great clarity the potential for connectivity and easy pedestrian access at street level. It reveals a network of routes ranging from major arteries with the greatest potential for flow and accessibility, down to those that are cul-de-sac-like in their dysfunctional relationship with their surroundings.

Our initial research involved consultations with 180 public bodies and thousands of individuals. With all these interests to account for, we had to be analytical, examining traffic flows and accident reports as well as how exactly pedestrians moved, or tried to move, around the area. The results of this process of study and consultation confirmed the need to reduce the conflict between people and cars. The variety of techniques used also reflected the many facets of the modern city. The consultant group we brought together for the project included traffic engineers, urban designers and academics; and it was the range of perspectives offered by these different disciplines that allowed us to explore the discrepancy between the picture postcard image of London and the reality on the ground.

Above all, we concluded that any change would involve a balancing act. Improving access had to be reconciled with maintaining security; private cars with public transport; the needs of the tourist with those of the Londoner; ceremonial function with the everyday; culture with government business; and the old with the new. Additionally, local needs had to be measured against those of London as a whole; visual clutter and spontaneity had to be set against legibility and order; and design had to be supported by management. Among the most significant findings, we discovered that Londoners rarely used the centre of Trafalgar Square and few people walked the entire ceremonial route down Whitehall, from Trafalgar Square to Parliament Square; visitors could not stand back in safety and admire Big Ben, Westminster Abbey or the National Gallery from the most desirable viewpoints; Londoners could not negotiate with ease the heart of their city by any mode of transport; and London could not breathe.

1

2

This central London area has all the potential to be an appropriate urban setting for the civic heart of the nation. Yet when we began our study it failed on almost every count. Despite the grandeur of its buildings and the significance of its heritage, it offered a dirty, dangerous and unfriendly environment, dominated by asphalt and the car. It provided no facilities for the millions of tourists who visit each year; it was hard to find your way around; and while it contained the vocabulary of city spaces, it lacked the grammar to make sense of those spaces and facilitate communication.

The contribution that design can make in renewing a city's physical and social infrastructure is profound and far-reaching.

In an area of London that has both great variety and opportunities for grace and cohesion, a further challenge existed: to strengthen connections, both between its different parts and with the rest of the city. By this I mean making its public spaces understandable to pedestrians, including first-time visitors; making accessible the best vantage points for its spectacular views; presenting its buildings and monuments in the most flattering way; and drawing attention both to its centre and to its boundaries along the banks of the Thames and the Royal Parks. Our starting point was the belief that the heart of London should not simply be an impressive part of our heritage, but a delightful and comfortable place for everyone to inhabit – citizens and visitors alike.

The need to revitalise our cities by improving their urban fabric and achieving a far better balance between people and traffic is one of the keys to the future. In the last three decades, the cities of Barcelona, Berlin, Paris and Amsterdam have shown how the containment of traffic can lead to a better quality of urban life. As with all such bold initiatives, they met with some initial resistance, but it is now widely agreed that these schemes have contributed to the economic and cultural vitality of each of those city centres.

Historically, the city as a construct has represented the highest form of man's creative drive. But what of the city of the future: how do we continue to build, to create inspirational urban environments, but do so in a sustainable way? Before the age of oil, the traditional city was compact, walkable and mixed living with working. It had a strong sense of place and a messy vitality – the opposite of the car-dependent, zoned and sprawling metropolis.

The contribution that design can make in renewing a city's physical and social infrastructure is profound and far-reaching. But design is not static: it is evolutionary. Design solutions must be re-evaluated and updated as technology allows or circumstances demand. Many of the problems we face today – such as global warming – are exacerbated by irresponsible design strategies from the past. Let us learn from those mistakes and pursue sustainable strategies for the future. Small changes can have a significant impact; and as cities evolve over time there is a need for continual rebalancing.

Moving beyond our masterplan for the central area, London still requires a bold vision – one that gives priority to people yet recognises the need for movement and access. It is a vision for a higher order of civic environment. Over a century ago, the Victorians transformed a city of slums, pollution and congestion into a model of civilised urban life. London became the paradigm for cities around the world. Ours and many other urban initiatives offer London a similar opportunity to set an international standard for city-living once more. We should be ready to take up that challenge.

3. Trafalgar Square transformed. As part of a comprehensive programme of detailed improvements, the northern side of the square in front of the National Gallery was closed to traffic and a wide pedestrian terrace created; this connects via a new flight of steps to the central part of the square. Although in architectural terms it is a fairly discreet intervention, its effect has been radical, changing completely the visitor's experience of the square and the way it is used.

3

A map showing the location of key Foster + Partners' buildings in London.

1 Wembley Stadium
  (1996-2007)
2 Imperial College Buildings
  (1994-2004)
3 The Great Court at the
  British Museum
  (1994-2000)
4 Trafalgar Square Central
  London Masterplan
  (1996-2003)

5 Her Majesty's Treasury
  (1996-2002)
6 Albion Riverside
  (1998-2003)
7 Riverside Apartments
  and Studio
  (1986-1990)
8 ME London Hotel
  (2004-2012)
9 British Library of Political
  and Economic Science
  (1993-2001)

10 ITN Headquarters
   (1988-1990)
11 33 Holborn
   (1993-2000)
12 Millennium Bridge
   (1996-2000)
13 One London Wall
   (1992-2003)
14 10 Gresham Street
   (1996-2003)
15 100 Wood Street
   (1997-2000)
16 21 Moorfields
   (1995-)
17 Moor House
   (1997-2005)
18 Bloomberg Square
   (2011-2014)
19 The Walbrook
   (2005-2010)
20 50 Finsbury Square
   (1997-2000)
21 Principal Place
   (2004-)
22 Swiss Re Headquarters,
   30 St Mary Axe
   (1997-2004)
23 51 Lime Street
   (2001-2007)
24 Tower Place
   (1992-2002)
25 More London Riverside
   (2000-2010)
26 City Hall
   (1998-2002)
27 Bishops Square
   (2001-2005)
28 Citibank Headquarters
   (1996-2000)
29 Canary Wharf
   Underground Station
   (1991-1999)
30 HSBC World
   Headquarters (1997-
   2002)

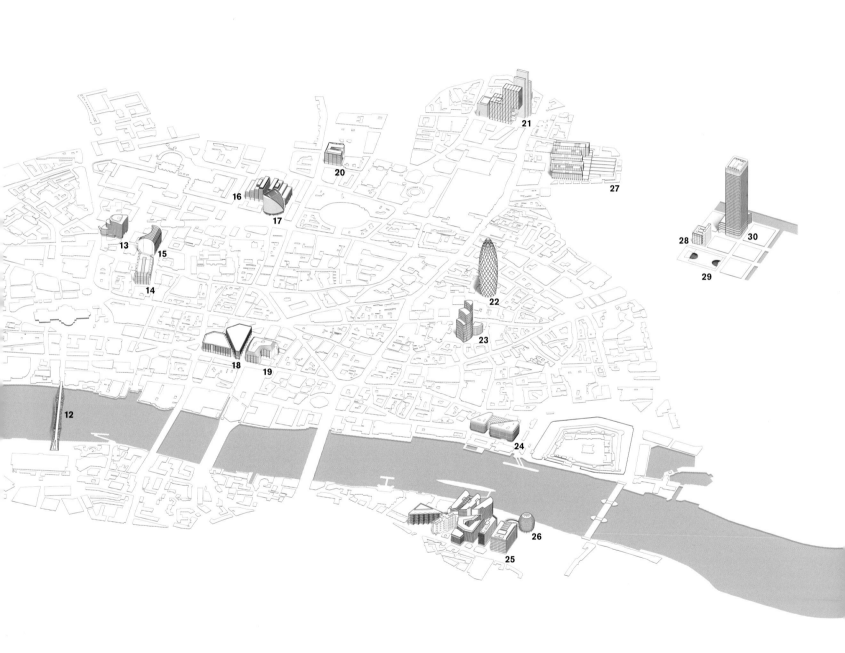

Her Majesty's Treasury

London, England 1996–2002

The refurbishment of the Treasury building, fronting on to Parliament Square, forms part of an ongoing process of restoration and renewal embracing the whole run of government buildings in the Whitehall area. It also represents another step in the practice's engagement with historic structures and their creative 'reinvention' to suit changing needs and times.

The Treasury building was designed in the 'English Renaissance' style and constructed between 1906 and 1915, initially to house a number of government departments. Its architect, JM Brydon, died in 1901 and the project was completed and somewhat modified by Sir Henry Tanner of the Office of Works. Its plan focuses on a central circular courtyard – inspired by that planned by Inigo Jones for Whitehall Palace – with two other large courtyards and a series of lesser courts and light-wells channelling natural light into the heart of the building.

By the end of the twentieth century random additions, alterations and general neglect had made the Treasury a depressing workplace, while the space within the building was inefficiently used. The challenge to the design team, led by Spencer de Grey, was to reorganise and upgrade the building in line with modern workplace practice, creating scope for team-working, greatly improving facilities for staff and visitors and modernising building services in line with a low-energy strategy. The £148 million project was undertaken on the basis of a private finance initiative (PFI) agreement, with a consortium formed by Stanhope and Bovis Lend Lease.

The project was far from straightforward. The building was listed Grade II and English Heritage as well as Westminster Council's planners took a keen interest in the proposals. To complicate matters, the building could not be entirely vacated. That meant that staff had to be decanted into one part while the first half was refurbished. Above all, the sheer scale of the complex was daunting: 500 rooms, 3.3km of corridors, 1,400 windows. As Spencer de Grey observes, at over 80,000 square metres, its area is virtually the same as that of the Commerzbank tower in Frankfurt.

Work began with the western half of the building, facing St James's Park, which was built in 1911-1915 and is architecturally somewhat inferior to the earlier phase on Whitehall. On completion, the accommodation there was occupied by the Treasury, with the remainder of the building eventually housing Inland Revenue and Customs & Excise staff. The fact that around 1,200 Treasury staff could be accommodated in around half the space they previously occupied demonstrates the rationale of the project.

The Treasury is one of a growing 'family' of Foster projects to involve the transformation of historic buildings and spaces.

Internally, the most impressive spaces were in the eastern block, and included a marble main staircase and some handsome conference rooms and offices. Much of the building, however, was given over to corridors lined with offices, their size reflecting the strict hierarchy of the organisations they housed, from ministers down to humble clerks. Net curtains, designed to contain bomb blast, made the offices gloomy and blocked views. Restaurant and other facilities were very poor; the central courtyard was choked with parked cars; and the subsidiary courts and light-wells were inaccessible. In short, the building offered a generally miserable working environment.

2

1. Located along the northern side of Parliament Square the Treasury building dates from 1906 to 1916 and is Grade II listed. The challenge was to transform a formerly labyrinthine and frequently under-utilised set of spaces into an efficient and enjoyable working environment.

2. The building has an approximately symmetrical plan, with two parts linked by a drum-like courtyard. The courtyard was freed from cars and repaved to recapture its original dignity.

3. Norman Foster's sketches explaining proposals for the central courtyard.

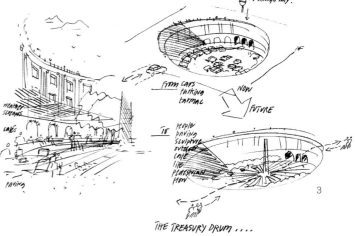

3

THE TREASURY DRUM . . . .

In the covered courtyards, with their ever-changing light, we hung a rainbow of banners. The system is quite simple. The banners hang five at a time. Four red and one joker – an orange – in one of the courtyards. In the next space the orange takes over and the joker is a yellow. Then four yellow and one bright blue; and so it goes on until eventually the full circle ends in the static 'sum' of the colours – three reds, three yellows and three blues – in a wall piece in the tall lobby. Per Arnoldi, in conversation with the editor, 2011

The interior was a confusing labyrinth of corridors leading on to hundreds of virtually identical cellular offices, laid out around three large courtyards and sixteen smaller light-wells. All architectural means of orientation within the interior were obscured. The courtyards and light wells were inaccessible and provided only light and air rather than being focal points. Only the circular courtyard in the centre of the building was accessible from the street – and that had been asphalted over as a car park. Philipp Eichstädt, formerly of Foster + Partners, in conversation with the editor, 2011
Left: Looking down into one of the Treasury building's light-wells, before renovation.

1, 2. The building is punctuated by courtyards and lightwells, which were hitherto unused. The lightwells have been capped with translucent ETFE pillows to create spaces that variously house a library, a café, training rooms and an entrance atrium. These lightwells also help to ventilate the building naturally.

3. Banners, designed by Danish artist Per Arnoldi, hang in the lightwells.

3

Before the renovation, visitors to the building entered through a small and rather mean entrance on Parliament Street, from where there were steps up into a gloomy reception hall. From there, more steps led up to the raised ground floor – some 2 metres above street level. Anyone with a disability was directed to the goods entrance, where a steep ramp – cluttered with pallets of paper and office supplies – let you in through the back-of-house areas. It was appalling. Resolving the issue of disabled access was obviously a high priority. Spencer de Grey, in conversation with the editor, 2012

The design challenge was to transform a 100-year-old building, with its deep plan punctuated by light-wells and courtyards, into an energy efficient, contemporary and accessible workplace. One of our main priorities was to improve accessibility by bringing as much transparency to the building as possible. The cellular working layout needed to be abandoned in favour of an open plan that would use the space more efficiently and promote a modern, communicative working environment. Philipp Eichstädt, formerly of Foster + Partners, in conversation with the editor, 2011
Left: One of hundreds of gloomy cellular offices in the Treasury building, before renovation.

Central to the project was the creation of substantial areas of open-plan offices in tune with modern workplace practice – where productive teamwork matters more than the preservation of hierarchy. Four staircases, partitions and chimney breasts were removed to create the open-plan spaces. Elsewhere in the building, particularly in the eastern half, the large cellular offices have been retained and adapted for the use of specialist teams or as meeting rooms. Informal meeting areas are distributed around the building, close to coffee points.

Equally fundamental to the project was the transformation of the courtyards and light-wells. The great central court was repaved and most of the car parking spaces relocated elsewhere. The two large internal courts were completely transformed. Raised by a storey to ground level, they have been turned into delightful gardens (to designs by Gustafson Porter), contrasting in style. Landscaped with trees and water gardens, they form calm oases where staff can sit and relax on fine days, and they provide the surrounding offices with an attractive outlook. (The sky gardens at the Commerzbank had proved a huge success with staff and provided something of a model, albeit in a very different context.)

The smaller courts, really just light-wells, were roofed with ETFE pillows – a method that Foster had originally considered for the roof of the British Museum Great Court. These tall narrow spaces, once unusable, are now full of light and colour and house staff restaurant and café facilities, a library and training rooms. One contains the main reception area for the Treasury offices. Art works by Per Arnoldi and good modern furniture add to their appeal.

In the case of the Treasury building, using ETFE to enclose the small courtyard spaces had advantages over glass beyond that of cost. The possibility of terrorist attack is now a serious consideration in the design of government buildings. In the event of a bomb blast, the air-filled pillows would simply deflate.

To provide the windows with protection against blast, the architects replaced the old sashes with fixtures that incorporate two layers of toughened, laminated glass. From the street, the fenestration appears unchanged, the only difference being the absence of the grimy net curtains.

Externally, there was little opportunity for alterations to the building, apart from the cleaning of the stonework. The only area where there was scope for extending it upwards was around the central courtyard. Here, an additional attic floor was cleverly inserted, with a terrace that provides fine views of the Westminster skyline. From ground level, it is all but invisible and cannot, of course, be seen from the surrounding streets.

Treasury ministers and civil servants now enjoy working conditions to rival any found in the private sector.

The restoration of the major interior spaces (including the Churchill Room, with the balcony from where the Prime Minister announced the end of the Second World War) was an important part of the project. Where possible, the original light fittings were restored and rewired. A contemporary note was introduced with the insertion of a colourful light sculpture by David Batchelor above the main stair and a carpet by Per Arnoldi for the Churchill Room.

In environmental terms, the project is exemplary. Existing components – for example, window frames and timber floors – were retained and refurbished; and 90 per cent of construction waste was recycled. The building is also naturally ventilated, with opening windows. The light-wells operate as thermal chimneys, exhausting air through vents at high level; and 'windcatchers' on the roof assist the natural ventilation cycle.

The Treasury refurbishment is one of a growing 'family' of Foster projects to involve the transformation of historic buildings and spaces, among them the Sackler Galleries at the Royal Academy, the Great Court at the British Museum, the Smithsonian Institution in Washington and, most spectacularly, the Reichstag in Berlin.

4

5

6

4. The entrance hall on Whitehall was meticulously restored. To aid accessibility, a doorway was cut at street level leading to a platform lift that allows access to the reception area.

5. Partitions were removed to create open-plan offices. This reorganisation enabled the entire Treasury staff to be accommodated in the western half of the building, allowing the remainder to be used by other departments.

6. A ring of offices was constructed at roof level around the courtyard. Set back from the parapet, they are invisible from street level.

The brief was to create a modern office space that could be utilised in the most effective way. Before, there were enclosed offices, with windows covered by curtains, and the accommodation was outdated. A lot of the project was about recreating from the inside, removing structure and staircases to make large open rooms. There are now 3,000 people working in the building, whereas only 1,500 or so were here before. Agnieszka Claveau of HM Treasury, in conversation with the editor, 2011

We are not like a conventional practice, which might specialise in the restoration of historical buildings, acting in an entirely passive role. I think it's fair to say that we bring something far more radical to that task. Spencer de Grey, in conversation with the editor, 2012

1

2

3

1-6. The building's two large external courtyards were originally sunk at basement level. They have been raised and landscaped with planting and pools to form recreation spaces for staff. Accessed from all sides, the courtyards have opened up new routes through the building, connecting the original Whitehall entrance to the new enlarged entrance on Horse Guards.

7. Plan at entrance level.

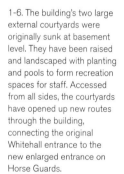

0   30m
0   90ft

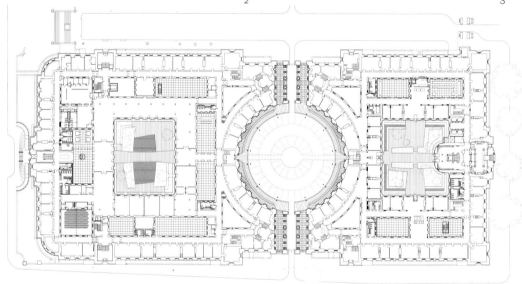
7

Left: The eastern courtyard as found. Simply asphalted over at basement level, the courtyards were permanently damp and extremely uninviting.

All these projects, including the Reichstag, include substantial areas of public space and, in the case of the museum schemes, new public forums that have transformed the ways in which those institutions operate. Similarly, one of the key ideas behind the Treasury project was the extension of the public realm into the heart of the building. Foster's involvement with the Central London Masterplan began around the time that the Treasury project was first considered – a public exhibition of the initial ideas was held late in 1997. The masterplan area embraced the civic and ceremonial heart of Westminster, including Parliament Square, Whitehall and Trafalgar Square. The highly successful reconfiguration of the latter was completed in 2003, but plans for Parliament Square, ultimately developed by another practice, were cancelled in 2008.

Foster had envisaged that the central court of the Treasury would be opened as part of a new public route, but security considerations make it unlikely that this ambition will be achieved in the near future. The beneficiaries of the project are the ministers and civil servants who now enjoy working conditions to rival any found in the private sector.

The project demonstrated the potential for providing highly efficient modern office space within a listed historic building, with an added element of joie de vivre provided by the imaginative use of colour and landscape in the new courts and atria. Delivered on time and to budget, it equally provides evidence that, in the right circumstances, the PFI system can deliver outstanding results.

Kenneth Powell

8. Cross-section from the entrance on Horse Guards to the formal entrance hall on Whitehall, showing the two landscaped courtyards and the formal central 'drum'.

Overleaf: A detail of the western courtyard. In warm weather, the courtyards are used for informal meetings throughout the day as well as by staff during breaks.

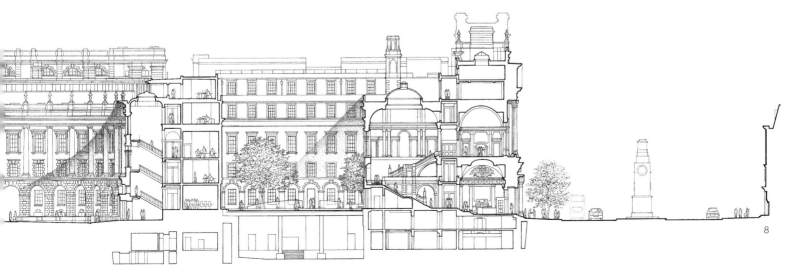

Knowing where the energy is coming from, monitoring how much is being used and where is very important in this building ... there are louvres installed on the upper levels that are connected to weather stations so depending on weather conditions and temperatures, they adjust to regulate air flow. Overall, 70 per cent of the building is naturally ventilated and we have 11,000 low-energy lights installed that supplement the ETFE roofs, which allow daylight in without the need for much extra lighting. Agnieszka Claveau of HM Treasury, in conversation with the editor, 2011

The true challenge of renewal is to continue the historical tradition of change but with a sensitivity to the spirit of the past. It is almost a cliché to say that this is about architectural good manners. There is no contradiction in suggesting that this approach to the new is informed by scholarly research of the past and a keen interest in the layering of history. True tradition is all about creative continuity. Norman Foster, lecture in Singapore, 15 February 2000

English Heritage had very strict requirements for the building as it's Grade II* listed. Things like underfloor heating are used, so that no radiators are fixed to the walls. Other heritage aspects also have a strong sustainable agenda, such as the original timber window frames … 92 per cent of which were reused. Similarly, 70 per cent of floor timber was recycled and all other timber was sourced from accredited suppliers. Agnieszka Claveau of HM Treasury, in conversation with the editor, 2011

I think people sometimes miss the point about modern extensions to or interventions in existing buildings. They're not simply there to show off modern architecture. They're actually there to facilitate access – to allow more people to use and appreciate the old building in a way that never would have been possible previously. In that sense, they are the ultimate compliment because they are precisely about recognising and preserving the value of a building and ensuring it is viable and accessible for future generations. Norman Foster, in conversation with the editor, 2012

Sustainability has not only been considered in terms of energy consumption, but also in terms of the ability of the building to adapt to lots of different requests and uses in the future. There is constant movement within government and the refurbishment has meant that we have been able to keep up to date with new technology and other internal changes without a lot of structural change. Agnieszka Claveau of HM Treasury, in conversation with the editor, 2011

Central London Masterplan

London, England 1996–2002

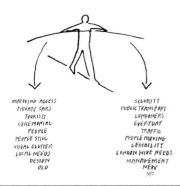

The bold and imaginative plans produced by Norman Foster to remodel Trafalgar Square and Parliament Square deserve full credit. The idea of transforming the historic heart of London into an accessible area which can be enjoyed by people on foot is vastly attractive. Leader, *Evening Standard*, 6 November 1997

A project of this kind is inevitably a balancing act, which has to promote genuinely integrated solutions. We began by listening to people – something like 180 separate institutions and thousands of individuals. What emerged was an obvious need and support for change.
Norman Foster, in conversation with the editor, 2012
Right: Norman Foster's sketch: the masterplan as a complex balancing act.

Central London's richly varied public realm – its streets and squares, parks and public buildings – is a legacy of its long history, throughout which many of these elements have undergone successive modification. Although the twentieth century added infrastructure such as the many Underground lines and stations, and cultural complexes on the South Bank and at the Barbican, arguably it contributed little else of major consequence or quality.

The goal was to better adapt this symbolically charged area of central London for the use and enjoyment of everyone.

However, in the 1990s, optimism in the run up to the Millennium, and the introduction of Lottery largesse, led to several additions and improvements to London's public realm. The architect privileged to contribute most to this transformation was Norman Foster, whose office was responsible for the Great Court of the British Museum, the Millennium Bridge across the Thames, the Central London Masterplan – originally called 'World Squares for All' – and its partial implementation in Whitehall and Trafalgar Square.

World Squares began as a study of how to transform the swathe of Westminster that forms the civic and ceremonial heart of London and beyond that, the country as a whole. Embracing Trafalgar Square to the north and Parliament Square to the south, the area involved extends from St James's Park on the west to the Thames to the east. Full of history and fine architecture, the area incorporates all the major institutions of government and Parliament, together with Westminster Abbey, St Martin in the Fields and other churches, numerous national monuments, the National Gallery and the high commissions of many Commonwealth countries.

As the project title indicates, the goal was to better adapt this symbolically charged area of central London for the use and enjoyment of everyone. This required synthesising, through detailed urban and architectural design, the inputs of many sorts of consultants, including traffic engineers and analysts of pedestrian movement, and designers of hard and soft landscaping. It also entailed consultation with the many landowners and bodies involved with the area. It was thus a fiendishly complex project, the final understated product of which reveals little of the diversity of considerations synthesised in shaping it – one hallmark of skilled urban design.

1. The masterplan area of Central London is familiar the world over. It contains a World Heritage Site – the Palace of Westminster and Westminster Abbey – and such national emblems as Nelson's Column and the Cenotaph. Yet when this exercise began, its two major civic spaces, Trafalgar Square and Parliament Square, were effectively reduced to traffic gyratories and the area as a whole was largely hostile to pedestrians. The aim was to improve visitor facilities and pedestrian access while enhancing the settings of the buildings, monuments and spaces.

2. Norman Foster's sketch map of the masterplan area, highlighting its landmarks and thoroughfares.

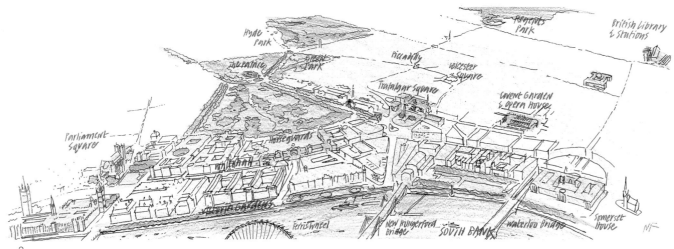

2

1, 2. Norman Foster's 'before' and 'after' sketches of Horse Guards Parade. In 1996, when not in use for a grand ceremony, the parade ground was one of the largest car parks in London. Foster argued that by removing the cars and linking the parade ground to St James's Park (2), Horse Guards could once again become one of London's great public spaces.

Horse Guards Parade is one of London's finest civic spaces, but like many of the city's squares and courtyards it had fallen into neglect and become clogged by cars. These sketches set out a strategy for its renewal.

Norman Foster

Although Foster refurbished the Treasury and built the National Police Memorial – both within the World Squares area – the most significant proposal from the original masterplan to be executed is the remodelling of Trafalgar Square. The success of the square indicates what might have been achieved had more been implemented, particularly in refurbishing the rest of what was to have been the central armature of the scheme: Trafalgar Square, Parliament Square and Whitehall – the ceremonial route that links them. A key theme, which emerged relatively late in the process, was to have been the contrasting treatment of the two major squares and the areas around them, a contrast that would have enriched their separate identities and meaning.

World Squares marked a confluence of the personal influence of Norman Foster with larger forces then in play, not least the increasing awareness in London of the transformations being undertaken in other European cities and of the relative failings of parts of central London, particularly in continuing to prioritise vehicles over pedestrians. The refurbishment of the Sackler Galleries at the Royal Academy, Foster's first involvement in a historic building, followed by the Albertopolis proposal to rework the public realm in the cultural enclave of South Kensington (which though unrealised paved the way for subsequent improvements), left Foster aware of the power of design to enhance the historic settings of other areas of the capital.

To help generate ideas, Foster convened a regular series of breakfast meetings in his Battersea studio, starting in 1995. Besides Foster and Spencer de Grey, the group included Bill Hillier and Tim Stonor of Space Syntax, whose input had been crucial to the seminal but unexecuted King's Cross masterplan. Other regular attendees were: Ricky Burdett, then of the Architecture Foundation and later to launch the first, very successful series of *Evening Standard* debates on the future of London; Peter Heath of Civic Design Partnership, an urban design consultant with a particular interest in working in historic contexts; David Kerr of Halcrow Fox; and Erica Bolton, who was to help publicise the emerging proposals.

Because Foster had then recently been commissioned to refurbish Her Majesty's Treasury, it was perhaps inevitable that attention would initially focus on the area of Westminster around that building. The first proposal to emerge from these meetings was for Horse Guards Parade, a little north of the Treasury, on the edge of what later became the World Squares site. The aim was to purge the space of the civil servants' cars that clogged it daily and to restore it to its former grandeur.

Opening on to St James's Park to the west and edged by the Horse Guards buildings by William Kent (probably London's finest example of Palladian architecture), Foster argued that the parade ground should be opened up to form part of the pedestrian public realm, which might even be expanded by closing Horse Guards Road to vehicular traffic. The proposal to recapture the square as part of the capital's public realm was campaigned for vigorously by the *Evening Standard,* and was subsequently implemented very successfully.

Foster's first major opportunity to enhance London's historic public realm came when the practice gained, through competitive interview, the World Squares commission, in 1996. Over the decades prior to this, many proposals had been made for transforming Trafalgar Square and elements of its immediate surroundings (such as the connections to the South Bank, the major cultural centre on the opposite bank of the Thames), better integrating them with each other and into London.

One well publicised scheme, for instance, was the Richard Rogers competition entry for an extension to the National Gallery that was to join with Trafalgar Square via a tunnel under the road at its northern edge. Again all such proposals had come to nothing, not least because there was no clear single or collective client with the power or will to execute them. However, activity nearby, such as the sequence of proposals by different architects to improve and extend the South Bank complex, as well as widespread awareness of how other European cities, notably Barcelona and Paris, were upgrading their public realm, increased the pressure for concerted action.

Eventually the Government Office for London (GOL), the body which administered London for the then Conservative government (which had disbanded the Greater London Council) announced the World Squares commission and, moreover, was prepared to undertake the role of convincing and coordinating all the different bodies, some 180 of them, with interests and responsibilities of various sorts in the area.

The Foster team won the commission not by offering a design solution but rather a commitment to a particular approach. This was to be based on rigorous analysis of the existing pedestrian and traffic movements in the area – by Space Syntax and traffic engineers in Halcrow Fox – which would generate equally rigorously tested proposals to ameliorate the problems found. These proposals would then be presented for discussion and negotiation with all the interested parties.

3. Horse Guards Parade transformed. Horse Guards has been used as a venue for royal events since 1540 when Henry VIII held the first Royal Tournament there. Completed in 1755, Horse Guards was built to designs by William Kent. The central archway is the formal entrance to St James's Palace via St James's Park, though this role is entirely symbolic.

4. Horse Guards Parade in 1996 – full of cars and unwelcoming to visitors.

I had a very personal experience in that when we had completed the masterplan design, but before we had begun the work, my uncle was knocked over by a double-decker bus on the north side of the square. Fortunately he survived despite being in a coma for six weeks. The Trafalgar Square project was a very serious matter, it wasn't just about making London a better place to live, it was about addressing one of the worst pedestrian accident hotspots in the capital. David Rosenberg, formerly of Foster + Partners, in conversation with the editor, 2011

We identified key areas that we would address with proposals to enhance the setting for buildings; provide better access to public spaces, with new facilities, including places to sit down; extend pavements and reduce the space for cars where it was appropriate; and improve the access for buses and taxis and cycles. We wanted to bring the spaces to life and improve the quality of life for people in the city. Spencer de Grey, in conversation with the editor, 2012

We did not set out to be radical. Instead we recognised that we had to find a balance between a series of competing interests: access and security, private cars and public transport, tourists and Londoners, the ceremonial and the everyday, the old against the new and so on. It was based in an understanding that at any point in time a city is like an organism, continually adapting to changing circumstances. Somewhere that was designed for the horse and carriage, not surprisingly does not survive that well with the daily onslaught – in Trafalgar Square, for example – of something like 17,500 goods vehicles, 35,000 taxis and 50,000 cars. Norman Foster, in conversation with the editor, 2012

1

Among the things specifically asked for in the brief were improvements to the pedestrian experience, which at the time was subordinated to the flow of traffic. The brief even suggested investigating closing to traffic one side of each of the two main squares. Also sought were improved pedestrian access to public transport and, where possible, improvements to the routes and times taken by buses. (All of this, it should be noted, was prior to the introduction of the central London congestion charge.) To undertake such a complex study and prepare a detailed masterplan required a multidisciplinary team. To the group that had attended the breakfast meetings were added Peter Walker & Partners as landscape architects and Davis Langdon & Everest as quantity surveyors.

The Foster team won the commission not by offering a design solution but rather a commitment to a particular approach, based on research.

Equally important to the success of both the original study and the remodelling of Trafalgar Square was the contribution made by leading members of GOL, particularly those people who chaired the client meetings, which included representatives from English Heritage, the Royal Parks, the City of Westminster, the Houses of Parliament and London Transport. Especially important in this regard were the roles played by Liz Meek and subsequently Joyce Bridges, who helped progressively to win over all the relevant bodies, and had the ear and confidence of everyone involved and were able to report directly to the Department of the Environment (under Secretary of State John Prescott following the 1997 General Election).

Another factor that proved to be immensely important in ensuring success was that once the team had analysed the existing situation – using the convincingly rigorous computer modelling of Space Syntax and Halcrow Fox – no single design solution was proposed. Instead, a series of eight 'opportunities for improvement' were offered, ranging from minor interventions – such as improved pedestrian crossings – up to the more radical solutions involving road closures, the banning of all but essential traffic, and changes to listed historic fabric.

After two months of detailed consultation these eight options were brought together to form four conceptual approaches, again of increasing levels of intervention. This clearly conveyed the openness of the team to the input of others and the readiness to seek a solution not through imposition but by seeking consensus. In retrospect, this approach seems exemplary. Spencer de Grey is convinced that, without it, it would not have been possible to implement such a radical approach as was eventually agreed for the whole site; nor would the remodelling of Trafalgar Square have been achieved.

The study started with Norman Foster, Spencer de Grey, Bill Hillier and members of their respective teams spending the best part of a day exploring the area in some depth. They observed patterns of movement and use, and the reasons for some parts not being better used, and made initial suggestions as to their remedy, as well as for other possible improvements. Almost all these observations and proposed solutions were confirmed with more rigorous measured observation and improved upon with further work.

Crucial to the functioning of the area would be the improvements made to the three components that constitute its central armature, Trafalgar Square, Parliament Square and Whitehall. Trafalgar Square was visually splendid and pivotally positioned where Whitehall and the Mall – ceremonial routes to the Palace of Westminster and Buckingham Palace, respectively – meet the Strand, leading to the City of London. But although used for political rallies and celebrations, and visited by tourists, the central square had little day-to-day use by Londoners.

1. A model of the masterplan area. The study area is entirely covered by four Conservation Areas and includes a World Heritage Site that embraces Westminster Abbey and the Houses of Parliament. The area contains in excess of 170 listed structures, of which more than thirty are listed Grade 1. The townscape is rich and varied, with features as diverse as the monumental, axial planning of the Mall and the intimate, discreet residential streets north of Smith Square. Green space adds a further dimension, the picturesque landscape of St James's Park complementing the urban mass of Whitehall. Architecturally, the area has retained a predominantly eighteenth- and nineteenth-century Classical character, with the exception of Parliament Square, where the Gothic and Gothic Revival styles dominate. For the most part, contemporary interventions have done little to alter this historic fabric.

Our studies of Trafalgar Square revealed some interesting insights. We charted the numbers of pedestrians and their movement patterns. We found that the heart of the space was typically deserted – most people moved around the edges. But there was a gravitational pull towards the southern edge of the square. We couldn't understand why, so we went to see for ourselves. We found that from a little triangle of pavement at the base of the King Charles statue you had the most fantastic views in all directions. But you had to risk life and limb to get there. Norman Foster, in conversation with the editor, 2012
Right: Norman Foster, Spencer de Grey and members of the project team on a site visit to Trafalgar Square.

Once, the National Gallery had its metaphorical legs sawn off by the road in front, and the serene pleasures of the art inside contrasted with the mini-motorway outside. Now the gallery has the setting it deserves and, with its portico at your back, you feel like a duke on the terrace of his stately home. Rowan Moore, *Evening Standard*, 3 July 2003

1

2

3

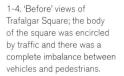

1-4. 'Before' views of Trafalgar Square; the body of the square was encircled by traffic and there was a complete imbalance between vehicles and pedestrians.

5. A diagram illustrating how pedestrian routes might be opened up diagonally across the square and directly from the Charles I statue to the National Gallery.

6, 7. One of the main research tools was a plan model of London developed by Space Syntax at University College London, which demonstrated the potential for pedestrian access and connectivity. These two diagrams show the views afforded from the centre of the square (6) and the King Charles island (7).

8. Surveys found that the square was used mainly by tourists (red dots) and that Londoners (yellow dots) hardly went there at all. The green lines represent uncontrolled road crossings.

9. Here, each green line represents one of 226 people followed by a member of the survey team. There is virtually no pedestrian movement into or across the square.

The reasons were obvious: it was isolated in a swirling maelstrom of heavy traffic; and it was impossible to traverse on a direct diagonal. The stairs down in the two northern corners followed a convoluted route and oriented those descending them to proceed along the sides of the square. It was obvious that a broad stair directly in front of the central portico of the National Gallery would facilitate the diagonal crossing of the square and so also open up its use for other purposes.

It was also apparent that the broad pavement overlooking the northern edge of the square was little used, while that on the other side of the heavily trafficked roadway outside the National Gallery was dangerously narrow, particularly with people queuing at the bus stops along it. These problems would vanish and access to the square be further improved if this roadway were closed to traffic and pedestrianised. Also observed was the considerable number of tourists who risked life and limb to reach the triangular traffic island on which stood the equestrian statue of Charles I. Crossing to it, the reason became obvious: this island commanded much the best panoramic view in the area, not only of the National Gallery, and the square and Nelson's Column in front of it, but also vistas down Whitehall and the Strand and through Admiralty Arch to the Mall. It was the ideal place from which to take photographs.

Also noticed on this initial reconnoitre was that although Whitehall links the two squares, few tourists walk its length. Instead they tend to walk from Parliament Square to see Lutyens' Cenotaph and Downing Street, and return, and walk down from Trafalgar Square to see the Horse Guards and Inigo Jones' Banqueting House, and return. To those who know about Space Syntax the reason for this is clear: Whitehall's gently curved alignment prevents one square from being seen from the other, so removing the incentive to walk between them. To back up the masterplanning study, more rigorous and exhaustive analysis was undertaken by the Space Syntax team.

Axial analysis was undertaken, plotting on a map the long axes of all spaces and assessing the average number of turns required to access each of them from anywhere else in the area – what Space Syntax refers to as its 'integration value'. This confirmed that the centres of both squares were poorly integrated into local pedestrian movement patterns. The next step was to track the movements of 10,000 people who lived, worked in or visited the area. As part of this process, pedestrian counts were taken at 306 locations (169 of them within the study area) at different times of day. This all served to confirm the initial observations. Only one person, for instance, was seen crossing Trafalgar Square on each of its diagonals during the study.

As well as informing the proposed changes, axial analysis was then applied to predict the consequences of changes such as the proposed road closures, improved pedestrian crossings and construction of the central stair on the north side of Trafalgar Square.

Right: The detailed observation of pedestrian activity and movement patterns was undertaken over a period of several months, commencing in November 1996; the movements of more than 10,000 people – Londoners and visitors – were recorded; 325 hours of observation were carried out at 306 locations, 169 of which were located in the study area.

Far right: A vehicle origin-destination survey of vehicles was conducted over a three-day period; 27,000 vehicles were stopped at all nine entry points to the study area and drivers asked to fill in a questionnaire about their existing and future travel patterns.

4

5

This showed clearly how much better integrated each square would be in the local movement network, and so how they would be brought alive by day-to-day public use. Also confirmed by this analysis was the viability of Space Syntax's proposed inducement to pedestrians to walk the length of Whitehall. Enhancing the existing Privy Garden, which is visible from both squares, as a public place, would make it an enticing destination and rest place midway along Whitehall. The rest of Whitehall was also to be remodelled, with narrowed traffic lanes, broadened pavements and an improved setting for the Cenotaph.

Equally important in confirming the aptness of proposals, and in convincing the various bodies concerned, were the numerous computer models studying the flows of traffic, particularly as a consequence of closing one side of each of the main squares. As well as distributing some traffic flows elsewhere in the area, this also entailed introducing two-directional traffic where previously there had been one-way flows, for instance on the south and west sides of Trafalgar Square. In turn this, and the proposed widening of many of the pavements, necessitated the subtle realignment of many traffic lanes. The whole southern part of Trafalgar Square was to have changed considerably, bisected by what would now be a broad two-directional roadway connecting Cockspur Street and the Strand.

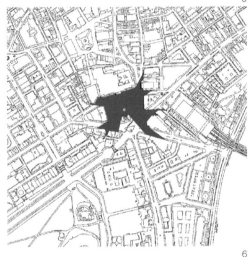
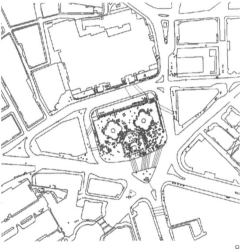

6

8

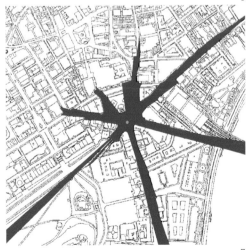

7

9

Ambitious plans to free the historic heart of London from choking traffic have won overwhelming public support … Foster's scheme to pedestrianise Trafalgar Square, Parliament Square and Whitehall for 2000 was backed by more than two thirds of all Londoners questioned. The results of the massive public consultation exercise conducted by Westminster City Council show that the ideas have the support of tourists, commuters, business, transport and even residents' groups. Perhaps surprisingly, the public has backed the more radical of the two alternative schemes. Paul Waugh, *Evening Standard*, 20 January 1998

1   2

1, 2. Early 'before' and 'after' models of Trafalgar Square, made for public exhibition. At this stage, many areas of the scheme, including the form of the terrace and staircase in front of the National Gallery were still in a state of flux.

3. A 'before' Space Syntax study of pedestrian accessibility levels within the masterplan area. Red is the most accessible; violet the least. The study indicates moderate to poor levels throughout, with overall levels in the south – in and around Parliament Square – being lower than in the north.

4. This predictive study indicates that improving access to the heart of Trafalgar Square has a ripple effect into Leicester Square and Haymarket to the north.

Adjacent to Nelson's Column, the central square was to have bulged southwards slightly; and much of the southern part of the square was to have been continuously paved with only single-lane routes cutting through the paving for turning traffic. (When it came to implementation, a more elegant arrangement was devised by WS Atkins, the new engineers for the project.)

Throughout the masterplan site, the architects proposed that pedestrians be given greater priority, with pavements widened along many streets, shade trees planted, street furniture rationalised and upgraded, and pedestrian crossings improved. This coincided with a more general concern of Foster's at that time, which also influenced the thinking behind projects such as the British Museum Great Court and the Millennium Bridge, and which he referred to as 'wayfinding'.

In addition to upgrading individual public spaces, Foster argued that it was as important to improve the connections between them.

This arose from the observation that London remained a collection of villages; although they had many fine buildings and institutions for tourists to visit, the pedestrian connections between them were often neither obvious nor pleasant. So, in addition to upgrading individual public spaces, Foster advocated that it was as important to improve the connections between them, as well as the legibility of pedestrian routes. All these ideas would be taken forward in great detail in the context of Trafalgar Square.

Just as Trafalgar Square once was, Parliament Square is a traffic roundabout that is not easily accessible to pedestrians. However, unlike Trafalgar Square, which is visually splendid, the central portion of Parliament Square is a visual nonentity lacking in identity and presence.

The square's significance comes from its location and the buildings that frame its outer edge, particularly those that constitute the Westminster World Heritage site: Westminster Abbey and St Margaret's Church and the Houses of Parliament – all in varieties of English Gothic.

The area's associations with Monarch, Church and Parliament are ancient. Like Trafalgar Square, Parliament Square settled into its present form slowly over the centuries. Its present format as a traffic roundabout dates only from soon after the Second World War when it was redesigned by Grey Wornum. This was never a satisfactory solution, not only because visually weak but also because difficult to access for pedestrians, who in any case have little reason to go there. Those who do so find the views of the surrounding Gothic and Neo-Gothic splendour spoiled by the constant whirl of traffic.

The World Squares study initially proposed closing the south side of the square to traffic so as to amalgamate the body of the square with the churchyards of St Margaret's and Westminster Abbey, and replacing the present grassed part with paving and a water feature. The trees along the western edge of the square were to be joined by a second row, to create an avenue extending from the north transept of the Abbey, which then folded around the north side of the square. The various other squares nearby – such as Broad Sanctuary forming an entry parvis at the western end of the Abbey and Old Palace Yard in front of Parliament, which are both diagonally bisected by major roads – were to be repaved so as to read as single spaces.

It was while developing the detailed scheme for Trafalgar Square that Foster and his team rethought the approach to Parliament Square and the spaces around and nearby. Having won the competition to develop a new concept for the area, they sought a theme that would both create some unity from the various spaces while also accenting, and rooting the design in, their historical significance. This would also invest the area with a character and identity very different to that of Trafalgar Square, so enriching London in terms of the kinds of places it has as well as in their symbolism and meaning.

Bill Hillier and Julienne Hanson, both of whom are professors at UCL and the founders of Space Syntax, worked on the project from the very beginning, so there was always an understanding that pedestrian movement analysis was going to be the key to making this work. Pedestrian movement versus traffic was really the crux of the whole project and that's where it began. David Rosenberg, formerly of Foster + Partners, in conversation with the editor, 2011

Space Syntax monitored the movements of 10,000 people, and that data led to a very interesting series of diagrams. Researchers from our team would follow people for ten minutes as they left the Underground stations, just to see where they would go, how long it would take them to negotiate the various sort of traffic intersections. Interestingly, we discovered that 60 per cent of the people in the area were Londoners and 40 per cent visitors. In the beginning everybody was absolutely convinced, even the people who wrote the brief, that it was the other way round. Spencer de Grey, in conversation with the editor, 2012

For years Trafalgar Square has been a sort of private joke for Londoners. Tourists felt obliged to brave torrents of traffic to reach its not-very-exciting middle, just because it was in their guidebooks. Londoners knew not to bother. Now everyone can enjoy it. Rowan Moore, *Evening Standard*, 3 July 2003

3

4

Walking through the cloisters and other spaces around Westminster Abbey is one of the great unknown experiences of London. It's an extraordinary sequence, and it culminates in a wonderful copy of the Wren Trinity Library. It stands in a fabulous garden, and then there's a wall and then you get College Green – the piece of grass on which all the TV interviews are done. Behind that wall is really wonderful – a real cathedral close. And very importantly, the Abbey and the Houses of Parliament form one World Heritage Site, not two. The challenge of Parliament Square is to unify all this visually. Spencer de Grey, in conversation with the editor, 2009

When we came to the detailed masterplan for Parliament Square we departed from our earlier strategy, which was essentially quite hard-edged, and came up with a much softer approach. Parliament Square is very different in character to Trafalgar Square, which is a big public space. It's not a tourist destination in the same way. It's much gentler – more like a collegiate English cathedral close. Instead of hard paving, we introduced a lot of greenery and I still think that's the right direction to move in. Spencer de Grey, in conversation with the editor, 2012
Left: An aerial view of Salisbury Cathedral, which has the largest cloister and the largest cathedral close in Britain.

1

2

3

4

Left: 'Westminster Regained', townscape proposals for Parliament Square and the Westminster precinct by Gordon Cullen, published in *The Architectural Review* in November 1947. Cullen argued for the expression of the area's natural character as a national enclave of collegiate pattern. Traffic would be removed entirely from three sides of the square, and strictly limited elsewhere; trees would be planted and railings realigned. Instead of a traffic circus, Parliament Square would become 'a very plain but very English courtyard, a place where those on business or pleasure may expand and breathe freely.'

Gradually, the concept crystallised of treating Parliament Square and the surrounding area as the equivalent of a traditional cathedral close, as one finds at Canterbury and Salisbury. This would enhance and extend the character of the churchyards to the north of the abbey and church, as well as that of Dean's Yard and other green spaces south of the abbey, throughout the whole area. The quiet and contemplative enclaves of the cathedral close and other ecclesiastical yards, with their lawns and trees, are a peculiarly English form of urbanity, an immensely satisfying mix of masonry and greenery, some echo of which is also found in the colleges of Oxford and Cambridge and London's Inns of Court.

In the interim, Foster had also been asked to investigate providing car parking and offices for members of the House of Lords. It was proposed that these be subterranean, with a vehicular ramp down in College Green and then a tunnel leading to a parking garage and offices, both sited under Victoria Tower Gardens. This is a large triangle of lawn sandwiched between Abingdon Street and the Thames. Huge plane trees edging both street and river make it a pleasant space, though its out-of-the-way location means that it is little used. Foster's proposals were only developed to sketch stage and investigated variants of the same solution. Set in a little from the nineteenth-century sewers that line the Thames, two levels of offices were ranged along either side of a linear light well, which was capped by roof-lights, sloped to catch some east light and set along the crest of grass-planted vaulted roof which would have afforded fine views of Parliament and the river.

By the time the selection process for commissioning a detailed scheme for Parliament Square unfolded, Mayor Livingstone had decided that the square would be merely one of the 100 London squares the GLA proposed to improve. This programme was inspired by a Barcelona initiative, by which the city first drew attention to itself in the 1980s and signalled its ongoing urban transformation.

However, the concept was neither particularly pertinent to London, nor the most urgent of undertakings for it, when issues such as socio-economic polarisation or the over dependence of London's economy on financial services deserved more urgent attention from planners.

Unfortunately, the enchanting aptness of Foster's proposals for Parliament Square, and the enrichment and intensification of symbolism and meaning it would have brought, seem not to have been properly appreciated, nor the relevance of such things to what should be the goals of urban design. This is not only about such things as the convenience of pedestrians and traffic, and aesthetic coherence, but also about shaping places of contrasting character and meaning, so contributing variety to a city.

Gradually, the concept crystallised of treating Parliament Square and the surrounding area as the equivalent of an English cathedral close.

Better yet is if this is done in a way that evokes or grounds the scheme in local history. Ultimately, the Parliament Square commission was given to another firm, and was treated as an independent scheme uninformed by the larger context that Foster's new ideas would have provided, so trivialising all further design initiatives for the square.

It transpired, along with some of the other schemes that were to be part of the 100 squares programme, that the remodelling of Parliament Square was among the first projects axed by Boris Johnson when he replaced Ken Livingstone as mayor. This could be a blessing as it leaves open the chance of implementing a far better, more considered and relevant scheme along the lines that Foster has proposed.

Peter Buchanan

5

1-5. Proposals for Parliament Square and environs were developed in some detail, though not implemented. Early proposals had focused on the square and its immediate relationship with Westminster Abbey, with the southern side of the square, nearest to the abbey, closed to traffic. As the scheme developed, however, the nature of the proposals changed. Here, the square and the wider area are considered together as an analogous cathedral close. Predominantly green, with a range of formal and informal spaces, its character contrasts strongly with the hard urban environment of Trafalgar Square. Along the water's edge, a raised terrace would have created a riverside walk edged by benches.

Some of our proposals were really quite modest. You have to look quite hard to see what we've done in Whitehall. But we found that we could easily widen the pavements and extend the space around the Cenotaph and calm down the traffic. We could make special provisions for this area in terms of signing. We could remove a lot of the civic vandalism that we take for granted: the yellow lines, bollards and so on. Individually these are quite subtle moves, but the cumulative effect is quite powerful. Spencer de Grey, in conversation with the editor, 2012

The masterplan area encompasses an interesting mix of the ceremonial and the everyday. I remember someone at one point saying, 'you know, Whitehall is a dead kind of space'. But perhaps the Covent Gardens and the Sohos of a city are only lively because they have their counterparts in the ceremonial spaces, the Whitehalls. It would be an incredibly boring city that was wall-to-wall Covent Garden or Soho, or wall-to-wall Whitehall. But I think that without the ceremonial you don't appreciate the spontaneous and vice versa. Norman Foster, in conversation with the editor, 2012

We'd got to the point where the study was finished and our final recommendation had been approved by the Government Office for London (GOL) and then we hit the whole upheaval with the advent of the GLA and the incoming mayor. When Ken Livingstone came to power he was handed World Squares on a plate as a proposal and enough money from GOL to complete Trafalgar Square, which was £25 million. It was obviously a quick and popular win for him because all the strategic work had been done. Spencer de Grey, in conversation with the editor, 2012

'Before' and 'after' images of strategic views throughout the masterplan area.

1, 2. Parliament Square; the southern side of the square is closed to traffic, linking the square with the Westminster Abbey grounds.

3, 4. Old Palace Yard.

5, 6. Whitehall and the Cenotaph.

1

2

3

4

5

6

Trafalgar Square is a national symbol and yet it was once horrible. The traffic would come to a standstill; the body of the square was uninhabitable – a sad scene. Now it is a kind of outside living room – an extraordinary place for spectacle, for events, for participation. It's brought a new level of urban civility to London. Norman Foster, lecture in Madrid, 17 April 2009

The pavement in front of the National Gallery used to be as dangerously crammed with pedestrians as the platform on the Northern Line at Leicester Square. Now it's an open space that stretches an expanse of York stone smoothly over the lip of the square, and cascades a vast set of granite steps down into the space below … The new steps also do some useful cosmetic surgery on the National Gallery's notoriously weak front facade, by giving its centre section the appearance of a thicker base, injecting some much-needed gravitas. Deyan Sudjic, *The Observer*, 29 June 2003

Trafalgar Square, the Great Court and the Millennium Bridge: with these three simple, obvious urban interventions, Norman Foster has changed not just the face, but also the character of London. Because of them London feels like a city at ease with itself, well balanced, obsessed with neither the past nor the future. Every moderately active tourist sees all three, and the locals are quietly proud of them. Colin Davies, *Architecture Today*, May 2007

7

8

7-10. Trafalgar Square; the northern side of the square is closed to traffic and a terrace and broad flight of steps created to link the square with the National Gallery.

9

10

These 'before' and 'after' images were intended as a visual summary of our Westminster proposals; they show how the symbolic and ceremonial heart of London could be transformed.
Norman Foster

Trafalgar Square
London, England 2002–2003

1

1, 2. The transformation of Trafalgar Square represents the culmination of almost a decade's work to improve the urban environment in the heart of London. The most significant move was to close the northern side of the square to traffic and create a new terrace in front of the National Gallery, which leads via a new flight of steps to the centre of the square. Below the terrace, a new café with outdoor seating provides a much-needed visitor amenity. Detailed improvements in the square and the neighbouring streets include new seating, better lighting and traffic signage and a paving strategy that utilises visual and textural contrasts. The cumulative effect has been to transform the life of the square.

2

The remodelling of Trafalgar Square is only the latest in a long series of changes it has undergone over time. John Nash first cleared the space in 1811 as part of his comprehensive London improvements and it started to take some of its present form when Charles Barry created the flat centre enclosed by retaining walls in 1840. Prior to this most recent intervention, the last major alteration had been Edwin Lutyens' remodelling of the fountains, as late as 1939. Whatever the square's functional problems identified in Foster's masterplan study, it had a visually potent identity immediately recognisable to many around the world.

This identity derives in part from the buildings that edge the square, which include the National Gallery and St Martin-in-the-Fields to the north (both Grade I-listed Historic Monuments), and South Africa House and Canada House (representing two of the ex-Empire's, and now the Commonwealth's, largest dominions) to the east and west respectively. Aptly enough, all these buildings are in some form of Classicism, the style of Empire since the days of Rome. Consistent with this, except for Landseer's lions at the base of Nelson's Column, all the sculptures are of military leaders or monarchs.

Crucial in giving the large and somewhat amorphous square its visual coherence and memorable form is the recessed flat centre, set within bounding walls of considerable presence. Then tying this in with the National Gallery are the visual alignments that Nelson's Column makes with the central portico and those the fountains seem to make with the flanking porticoes. By the time of the masterplan study, these had all become seemingly sacrosanct listed monuments. It says a lot for the determined negotiations of the Government Office for London (GOL), the compelling and readily communicated case made by Foster's scheme, Space Syntax's graphic analyses and the open-mindedness of English Heritage that considerable, if also very respectful, change was eventually permitted.

As a result, when democratically elected local government was returned to London in the form of the Greater London Authority (GLA) with Ken Livingstone as its first Mayor, Foster's scheme for the remodelling of Trafalgar Square was fully primed for implementation. All the agreements had been negotiated and the budget allocated. The GLA readily gave the go ahead, though it also, and quite correctly, asked for the inclusion of a lift for the disabled near the northern central stair and for public toilets and a coffee shop to be incorporated behind the retaining wall to either side of the stair.

3

3. A plan of the remodelled square, highlighting the new terrace and steps in front of the National Gallery and the enlarged setting for the King Charles I statue., to the south.

4. Norman Foster's panoramic drawing of the transformed square. Originally laid out in the 1840s by Charles Barry, it is dominated by Nelson's Column and lined by fine buildings, including the church of St Martin-in-the-Fields and South Africa House to the east, Canada House to the west, and the National Gallery.

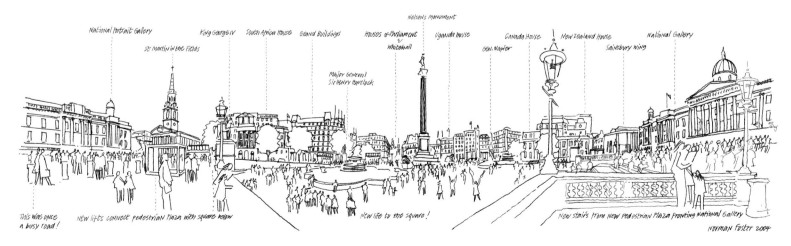

4

I remember feeling out of place when visiting the square – it is such a great symbol of London and yet few Londoners ventured there, only tourists. It was never a rendezvous; you would never say 'I'll meet you in Trafalgar Square' – now you can.

Norman Foster, in conversation with the editor, 2012
Left: An image of the square before work began; compare this with the photograph below.
Right: Norman Foster with Mayor Ken Livingstone at the opening ceremony.

AS IT WAS BEFORE
pedestrians forced around the edge
roads on all four sides

1

2

3

4

1. Norman Foster's sketch of the square as it was before – hemmed in by traffic on all sides.

2, 3 and 5, 6. Scenes from the square on a summer's day; it has become a venue for all kinds of formal and spontaneous public events.

The effect of our changes has been to transform the life of the square – a once hostile urban environment has been restored as a truly civic space.

Norman Foster

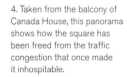

5

6

4. Taken from the balcony of Canada House, this panorama shows how the square has been freed from the traffic congestion that once made it inhospitable.

7. Cross-section through the Café, which was created beneath the terrace.

8. Two new platform lifts link the terrace with the body of the square.

9. The Café has become a popular destination for visitors and tourists.

Overleaf: An aerial view of the remodelled square.

Despite the agreements reached with English Heritage and others, Foster recognised that the proposed alterations to traffic routes, especially the closure of the north side of the square to traffic, could yet provoke sceptical reaction. He thus deemed it politic that the project be led by a traffic engineer rather than an architect, whom some might see as an impractical idealist. Atkins was chosen, both because the firm had recently remodelled part of the Strand, and was thus familiar with the area and had up-to-date computer models of traffic flow and so on, and because Peter Heath, who had been instrumental in developing the World Squares proposals, had recently joined its urban design team.

The Atkins team contributed a considerable improvement to the design of the square, and to traffic flows. Instead of extending the Charles I island into an elongated triangle at the head of Whitehall, it was enlarged into an oval roundabout. This solution works far better, not least in easing traffic flows in all directions. Additionally, the creation of a substantial island around the statue and safe pedestrian access to it, no longer required the southern edge of the main square to curve further out; instead it could remain as it was. Nevertheless, almost every other traffic lane around the square was subtly realigned, often to improve the pedestrian crossings.

Besides the closure to traffic of the roadway along the northern edge of the square, a section of road was closed to the east of the Edith Cavell statue and north of the steps of St Martin-in-the-Fields. Arriving from the north, this paved space now forms a kind of forecourt to the main square, which is partially visible from it.

From here it is now possible to walk on an only slightly curving diagonal route to the new broad stair and down it and across the square to exit to the south of Canada House. Similarly, it is also possible to take a diagonal route from the end of Pall Mall East, down to and across the square, and out to the south of South Africa House.

The stair that links the body of the square with the National Gallery is generous enough to allow a more or less diagonal route through the space. The stair has been designed with such care as to seem as if it had always been there, the original balusters being reused atop its side walls. Equal thought also went into the design of the bronze handrails, for which there was no immediate precedent. These are substantial enough to suit the scale of the stair and the space, and yet include side rails scaled to the human hand. Similar attention was given to the detail of the bronze and glass box of the lift on the upper level.

The success of the remodelling is now obvious from the throngs found on the square and upper terrace in front of the National Gallery on any sunny day, and by the numbers of people who now traverse it en route to elsewhere. Regular public events of various sorts are now organised on the square and these are consistently popular. Through the crucial concept of 'way finding', of making more pleasant, legible and convenient pedestrian connections between parts of London, that Foster intended, it is now possible to walk from Leicester Square, to the north of Trafalgar Square, to the South Bank cultural complex and cross only one major road – a remarkable achievement.

Peter Buchanan

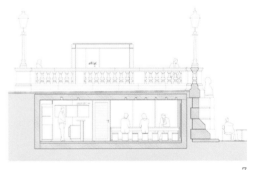

7

8

9

National Police Memorial

London, England 1996–2005

1. The Memorial takes the form of a black granite-clad tablet; set into its face is a vitrine containing a book that lists the names of every British police officer killed in the course of duty. Standing alongside it is a slender pillar of glass, which emerges from a reflecting pool. The two objects stand on a floor of Portland stone, together defining a sanctuary for quiet contemplation.

This memorial marks the personal sacrifice of officers murdered or killed during an arrest or performing a heroic act. Though divided by time, all are united by a common bond, service and courage, which led them to lay down their own lives for the protection of others. It is surely appropriate that this should be positioned in The Mall – an area of London so often associated with our national way of life. When people pass by the memorial, I hope they will pause and reflect on the proud traditions that it represents. The courage and personal sacrifice recorded here will, I am certain, serve as an inspiration to us all.
HM The Queen, unveiling the National Police Memorial, 26 April 2005

The purpose of this memorial is very, very simple – it is to say thank you to those police officers who have been killed in the service of their local community and in the service of their country. Thank you for your courage; thank you for your dedication; thank you for your commitment.
Prime Minister Tony Blair, speaking at the unveiling of the National Police Memorial, 26 April 2005
Left: The pages of the Book of Remembrance, listing the names of fallen police officers, are turned every two weeks. Officers who have recently been killed have their names presented on a page of their own.

To design a commemorative monument is among the most challenging of commissions for a modern architect, particularly one with a preference for an understated and abstract formal language rather than sculptural gestures. So when designing the National Police Memorial, for members of the force killed in the line of duty, the Foster team, led by Spencer de Grey, sought a quiet and reflective dignity rather than sculptural force or symbolic meanings.

The shock the British public felt at the very public death of WPC Yvonne Fletcher, killed by a shot from an upper window of the Libyan Embassy during a demonstration outside the building in 1984, provided the initial impulse for the monument. The late Michael Winner launched and sustained the campaign, founding the Police Memorial Trust to raise the funds to build it and to seek a suitable site. One was eventually allocated on the edge of the World Squares area.

At night the glass wall, lit from fibre-optic cables in its base, glows blue, the colour of the lamps once found outside police stations.

On a triangle of lawn just off the Mall, between a bunker behind the Admiralty and St James's Park, and close to Horse Guards Parade, the site is both central and yet seems slightly peripheral and residual. Worse, it was dominated by a rectilinear air vent that, with its cladding of exposed aggregate precast concrete panels, was almost aggressively ugly. But this air shaft serves the Underground and so was immovable.

Initial design studies investigated concealing the vent, for instance by wrapping it in walls that were part of the new monument; but no such solution was judged successful. Eventually it was decided to both civilise and camouflage the vent, cladding it with sober black granite panels that give it a sombre dignity, and softening and partially obscuring most of it with Virginia creeper supported on a trellis of wires so that it blends in with the bunker behind it, which is enveloped in the same creeper.

Across the narrow north end of the vent, projecting slightly forward of its long east side and kept free of creepers, is a wall of the same black panels, which is intrinsic to the monumental ensemble. Set flush within it, below an incised insignia of the Metropolitan Police and the name of the memorial, is a vitrine displaying the Book of Remembrance in which the names of fallen officers are recorded. Projecting forward from this wall into the grass is a rectangular patch of Portland stone paving that, together with the wall and the monument itself, defines a place of quiet contemplation. The actual monument is at the St James's Park end of the paving. A rectangular, solid glass monolith, layered up from sheets held together by five steel tension rods that form shadowy presences within it, it rises from a recessed slot into which water trickles from the shallow surrounding pool.

At night the glass wall, lit from blue fibre-optic cables in its base, glows blue, the colour of the lamps once found outside police stations. But it is perhaps most beautiful when irradiated by the low sun, particularly in the winter when this falls for a time on its bright-lit narrow southern end, from which the intensity of its seeming inner glow gradually declines towards the northern end. More subtle, but also satisfying, are the soft shadows of the plane trees lining the Mall cast by the direct sun in early morning and late evening.

Peter Buchanan

2

2. Water flows around the base of the glass wall, gently falling into a narrow weir.

Overleaf: At night the glass wall is lit by blue-filtered fibre-optic cables, which are incorporated in its base. This gives the glass a soft blue glow, evoking the lamps that once burned outside every police station.

There are memorials to soldiers, sailors and airmen who fight wars on our behalf. The police fight a war with no end. Why should they not be honoured publicly? Michael Winner, Founder of the Police Memorial Trust, *Sunday Times*, 1 May 2005
Right: The late Michael Winner founded the Police Memorial Trust after the death of WPC Yvonne Fletcher on 17 April 1984, while policing a demonstration outside the Libyan People's Bureau in St James's Square, London. WPC Fletcher was killed when shots were fired into the crowd from an upper window of the building. A memorial – the first ever to be erected in memory of a serving police officer – was dedicated to WPC Fletcher in the square.

It is a very sombre thing, and unlike some other monuments, which are simply used for memorials, this is much more immediate because the names of the officers are entered in the book in a ceremony which takes place straight after their death. One of the reasons the design is so restrained is that the services take place during a time of raw grief, much more so than something like the Cenotaph where the immediacy is removed by ceremony and time. Andrew Thomson, formerly of Foster + Partners, in conversation with the editor, 2011

Lutyens pointed the way with the design of the Cenotaph. He designed a quiet, civic memorial without swords, cannons or battle standards – a graceful, simple, timeless and remarkably unmilitary monument to those who died in the two world wars. It's very much a part of London. With the Police Memorial, we wanted to emulate that spirit, if on a much smaller scale. We hope too, that in some small way, the memorial might bring police and public closer together in a civilised and humane way, especially at a time when law and order is such a controversial part of the political agenda. Spencer de Grey, in conversation with the editor, 2012

Low beat, this nicely judged design is one of those minor landmarks that turns a corner in central London, pointing the way for visitors, as do much older nearby memorials such as those to the grand old Duke of York and Queen Victoria. Jonathan Glancey, *The Guardian*, 27 April 2005

The site was a small triangular lawn in front of the Admiralty building. The lawn was occupied by an uncommonly ugly, dominant and unbudgeable Underground air vent. The first ideas focused on sculptural camouflage – on how to conceal it. But with every attempt to hide it, it swelled like wet oats. Other tricks had to be tried. As all conjurors know, to draw attention away from an object, you have to shift attention to something else. So, to reduce the concrete block to B, we had to create an A – our shining, illuminated glass column. Something light to counter something heavy; something transparent against something solid – that was the exercise. Per Arnoldi, in conversation with the editor, 2011

City Hall and More London Riverside

London, England 1998–2010

Though seldom realised in the commercially focused culture of our times, major public buildings can articulate key social and political events in the history of the cities in which they stand in ways that no other culture-form can. While the specific nature and memory of those events might be diluted in the years following completion, they may leave their traces in the form and placement of the structure itself, the motivations for which cannot be fully understood without reference to their social and political origins.

More than just a landmark building, City Hall symbolises the rebirth of democratic local government in London.

City Hall, the building for the Greater London Authority (GLA), marks the resolution of a battle between central and local government in London. Angered by the contrary politics of the Greater London Council (GLC) in 1986, the Conservative government of Margaret Thatcher abolished the GLC. Thus it was that London became the only major capital in the world without an elected local body to oversee its affairs. When Labour, led by Tony Blair, came to power in 1997 it resolved to restore local government to London and to create a body with strategic planning responsibilities for the development of the city – the GLA.

A London referendum on the reinstatement of local government was held in the spring of 1998, the outcome being a resounding three to one in favour. Shortly afterwards, a competition was held to select the team that would design and build the GLA's new building.

Nick Raynsford, as both Minister for London and Construction at the time, drew up the Bill defining the GLA's organisation and powers – the longest such Bill since the Government of India Act of 1935. He also had the responsibility for organising the competition. Naturally, City Hall was intended to symbolise the rebirth of local government in London.

In accordance with the new authority's environmental commitments, it would be designed and built to the highest standards of energy efficiency and provide a model for future government projects. More than that, it would establish a new model of open government in the UK. Foster's design for the Reichstag, the New German Parliament in Berlin, which was nearing completion at the time of the City Hall competition, had established the benchmark for transparency and public accessibility for government buildings. Raynsford had visited the Reichstag when researching his own brief and expressed a desire for a similarly high level of openness in the new building.

The competition itself differed from most such exercises in several key respects. Normally, the client body will invite outline proposals for a site that it already owns or leases. However, in order to broaden the possible options and to engage developers as well as architects in the process, competitors were invited to submit proposals for the development of sites in London of their own choosing.

The winning team of CIT Group and Foster + Partners, who competed in a field of fifty other teams, proposed a mixed-use development, including City Hall, for the present site on the South Bank. The choice of site alone, with its exceptionally high exposure and other attractions, was therefore a crucial factor in the final decision.

Opposite: Standing on the floor of the assembly chamber looking up at the ramp that winds up through the building, creating a public route that runs from the entrance level up to 'London's Living Room' on the top floor.

1. City Hall at night, seen from the terrace in front of the Tower of London.

2, 3. Sketches by Norman Foster, showing the developing scheme; the earlier drawing shows the 'fencing mask' solution, which eventually gave way to a much more fluid form.

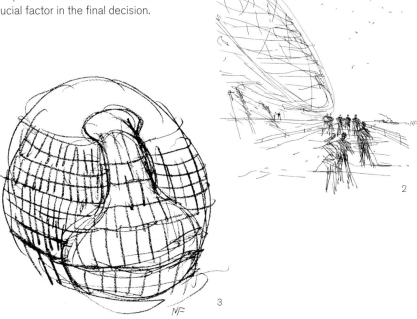

The flask-shaped form of the assembly chamber came out of a series of acoustic studies we did with Arup. The flask gave us the purest possible acoustic for the space and actually meant that you could speak in there without microphones. You can stand at the very top and still hear what is going on at the bottom of the chamber. Max Neal, formerly of Foster + Partners, in conversation with the editor, 2011
Right: Members of the City Hall team at work in the pavilion studio at Riverside.

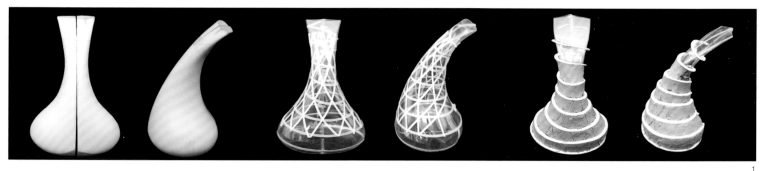

1

3

1, 2. The glazed 'flask' that forms a container for the ramp was a consistent feature throughout the scheme's development. Seen here are some of the many study models made to explore the form of the flask and its integration with the structure systems of the main body of the building.

3. One of the earliest proposals was for an abstract 'egg' form, supported on three raked legs, which would have cantilevered out over the river. This plasticine model was made during the course of a design meeting.

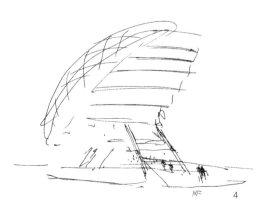

NF   4

Historically, the Thames has not only been the city's life-blood and main source of trade, it was and remains the traditional seat of power – the Palace of Westminster and the former Greater London Council building are both situated on its banks. Conversely, the Thames has also been a cause of geographical and social division.

Until the second half of the twentieth century, the main political, cultural and financial centres of the city, together with the wealthiest residential areas, remained concentrated to the north. By contrast, with the exception of Battersea Park, the south was mostly characterised by industrial sites and working-class housing. However, beginning in the 1950s with the building of the Royal Festival Hall, followed by the Queen Elizabeth Hall and the National Theatre, concerted efforts were made to shift the city's cultural focus southwards.

However, the concentration of so many cultural heavyweights in the newly designated Southbank was criticised for creating a 'cultural ghetto', unsupported by any of the other functions and activities which go to make up a vibrant city.

Since that early burst of construction, the Southbank has blossomed with new cultural interventions, both high- and low-brow. More London Riverside, for which City Hall provides a focal point, is located strategically on the cultural route that runs eastwards from the London Eye and the Southbank to Tate Modern, the Globe Theatre and on to HMS Belfast, Tower Bridge and the Design Museum. Thus More London and City Hall have played a key role in transforming the urban environment along this route and advancing the economic regeneration of the Borough of Southwark.

A political and cultural agenda of this order calls for something unusual. It is not difficult to imagine, for example, how the symbolic aspects of the project might easily have dominated other more programmatic considerations. However, while the final form of City Hall is appropriately charged with symbolic dimensions, the lens-like section could almost be described as a diagram of the effects on the design of the sun-path and orientation towards the best views.

Early drawings show a very different concept, however. The main components of the brief included an assembly chamber for the twenty-five elected members, the mayor's offices, committee rooms and offices for 500 staff, together with exhibition spaces and other public amenities.

Designed to fit into the pattern for the rest of the site, the architects' first proposal shows a block of offices, terminating in a glazed circular element containing the chamber. The only unusual part of the scheme is the flask-shaped atrium and winding publicly accessible ramp over the chamber, which penetrates the floors above all the way through to the roof. As well as bringing natural light down into the chamber and providing a passive system of ventilation, like the Reichstag's dome and ramp, the vertical void offered dramatic views into the chamber itself.

An additional attraction was the transparency of the chamber, which could be clearly viewed from outside. While the rest of the scheme did not survive beyond the first stage of design development, the flask-shaped void, public ramp and transparent chamber were retained as key elements in the final concept, though in a much modified and refined form.

We were told from the outset that the GLA just wanted a plain, ordinary building which looked like any other office block, so our first presentation to Nick Raynsford was literally a square building with a chamber at one end. However, he changed his mind and instead asked for a landmark building which would be state of the art in terms of sustainability and also highly accessible to the public. So we threw away the rectangular building and started again from **first principles.** Max Neal, formerly of Foster + Partners, in conversation with the editor, 2011

We played around with very organic forms at the beginning of the design process. It was when we arrived at a stage where we realised we were going to have to make a building and think about how the glass panels were going to look and how we were going to put it all together that we began to work closely with the **Specialist Modelling Group.** We then began to rationalise the structure, **the facades and the services.** David Kong, of Foster + Partners, in conversation with the editor, 2011

Because City Hall would act as the debating forum for the whole of London, the feeling was that the chamber should be the heart and soul of the building. That is its primary function, so all the offices wrap around it, and then we thought wouldn't it be wonderful for the staff if, instead of going down an escape stair or lift to get to another floor they would actually go via the chamber, which is when we introduced the **idea of a ramp.** Max Neal, formerly of Foster + Partners, in conversation with the editor, 2011

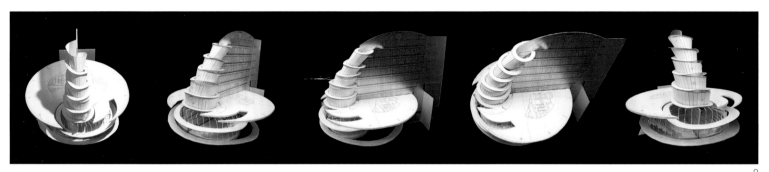

2

Meanwhile, the masterplan for the site was also evolving and with it, the need for a stronger focal point. The plan consists of several blocks of varying size, limited to ten storeys to preserve view corridors to St Paul's Cathedral from Greenwich and Blackheath. Their footprints radiate to address a new public space on the waterfront, and beyond that the Tower of London, thus rooting the development in the history of the city. A strong diagonal boulevard, intersected by smaller alleyways, slices through the blocks to open up a pedestrian route from the waterfront to Tooley Street, which forms the southern boundary of the site, and thence to London Bridge Station. The landscaping includes mature trees and fountains and extends to the design of paving and street furniture. Along with offices, there are shops and cafés, a hotel, health club and the Unicorn Children's Theatre. It is a lively and congenial working community.

Prominently located on the riverfront, City Hall stands apart from the densely planned buildings to the south. Immediately to the east is Potter's Fields Park and to the west the new piazza. City Hall is thus differentiated both geometrically and spatially from the rest of the development. In the process, the distinction between civic building and commercial development has also become formally translated into that between monument and urban commercial vernacular.

The architects' first alternative concept, following the rejected conventional scheme, took the shape of an egg, hovering over the river's edge on its own 'legs'. This abstract geometry was subsequently greatly modified in response to the orientation and sun-path – a process that only enhanced the design's cosmic character.

5

Like the Reichstag, City Hall is transparent and accessible – a place where Londoners can come to see their representatives at work. There are none of the barriers that normally surround such buildings.

Norman Foster

4. Another early Norman Foster sketch of the 'fencing mask' solution. The stepping southern elevation was another consistent feature – a way of providing natural shading to those parts of the building most exposed to sunlight.

5. This 1:200-scale model shows the building approaching its final form; the riverside elevation, and the position of the assembly chamber relative to the ground plane, are two significant issues still to be resolved.

There is, and always has been, an immense difference between the arbitrary aesthetic expressionism of architects like Frank Gehry, Zaha Hadid and Daniel Libeskind, and the complex scientific structure and envelope design that is embodied in the shape of City Hall. To treat the haphazard forms that emerge from the so-called avant-garde as though they possessed the same validity as advanced computer-modelling techniques – which have made possible the geometrically modified sphere and backward-inclined shading of the Foster building – is to minimise the achievement it represents. This is a structure that will, over time, come to be seen as a redirection of the spirit of Modernism, from the arid meaninglessness into which it has sunk in recent years towards a rich and complex importance not seen since the 1950s. Martin Pawley, *The Architects' Journal*, 1/8 August 2002

City Hall was an exercise rationalising a free-form double-curved skin to achieve the panelisation of the surface. The challenge was to find a geometric rationale that would not compromise the design concept. Whereas any curved surface can be easily subdivided into a triangular mesh, a quadrilateral mesh may result in panels that are twisted and therefore difficult to fabricate. However, designers tend to prefer quad rather than triangular panels in terms of visual appearance and there are also compelling economic considerations that result from simpler node connections, fewer framing members and less material wastage. Hugh Whitehead, formerly of Foster + Partners, in conversation with the editor, 2011

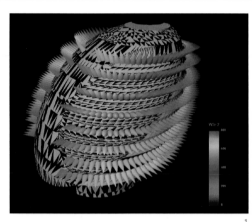

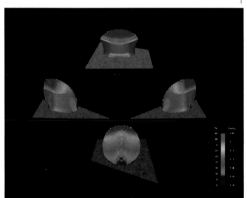

1. Computer-generated model showing the impact of solar radiation on the building's external envelope. The cones represent the direction from which each of the facade panels receives sunlight, while the colours indicate the level of energy received; red being the maximum and blue the minimum.

2. A solar impact analysis model, based on an early iteration of the building, showing average annual heat gain. This information enabled the building's various elements to be positioned accordingly. For example, the chamber is located behind the 'coldest' part of the facade to allow maximum glazing, while the photovoltaics are placed on the 'hottest' part.

The tilted, lens-shaped design shown in the first detailed proposal is close in outline to the completed building. Unlike the directionless geometry of the 'egg', the orientation of the built design can be clearly read from its asymmetrical section. The northern half of the building where the assembly chamber is located is covered by a shallow, glazed dome tilted to align with the sun-path, so that the sun never strikes the glass surface directly. The occupants of the chamber and adjacent offices are thus treated to unrestricted views of the Tower of London, while the public can likewise see into the chamber from outside. Conversely, each floor on the southern face is stepped outwards so that it shades the one below. The flask-shaped atrium over the chamber also steps backwards at each level, opening up views down into the chamber and across the river from every floor.

Complementing the advantages of the building's orientation and unique geometry for passive energy design is a comprehensive strategy for energy efficiency.

Following the precedent of the Reichstag, where the roof level and dome are accessible by the public, the top floor of City Hall is also given over to public use. Named 'London's Living Room', the designation is a pointed reminder of who is meant to serve whom.

Complementing the advantages of the building's orientation and unique geometry for passive energy design, the Foster team devised a comprehensive strategy for energy efficiency. Passive measures include natural lighting and ventilation for all the office spaces, which are fitted with opening windows for personal comfort. The low external surface-to-floor area ratio of the compressed spherical structure also reduces solar gain and heat losses.

However, since the building plan is too deep to be ventilated entirely by passive means, a mixed mode strategy was recommended. A form of low-energy air-conditioning, or 'displacement ventilation', is employed in which cool air is introduced at floor level and rises as it warms, to be extracted through the ceiling. The natural stack effect inside the void above the chamber is also utilised to help ventilate the chamber and surrounding spaces. Active systems include chilled ceilings fed by cold ground water pumped up from deep below the building, energy recovery devices, sophisticated lighting controls, and the use of photovoltaic panels on the roof.

Overall, it is calculated that City Hall uses only half the energy consumed by a conventional, fully air-conditioned office building. The same energy-conscious approach informs the design of the surrounding buildings; the last to be completed, 7 More London Riverside, having the distinction of a BREEAM 'Outstanding' rating.

As the design progressed it was clear that the building's unusual shape called for equally unusual technologies of design and production. Any exterior surface composed, as the surface of the City Hall is, of double curves, creates special problems in the design and fabrication of the cladding. The office's Specialist Modelling Group (SMG) has its own software for rationalising complex curves geometrically into a series of flat planes suitable for cladding panels. For example, conceived in its early 'lens' shape, it was possible to rationalise the northern face of the building as a 'torus patch' – a geometric form resembling a slice through a tyre – with the advantage that the whole area can be divided into identical separate rings, each made up of the same flat panels.

As the design progressed, the 'lens' with its separate 'skirt' of overlapping floors behind gave way to a more integrated form, known as the 'pebble'. This initiated an extraordinary creative process involving a mixture of cutting-edge software with hands-on model-making techniques, including the use of plasticine and other materials.

The borehole is one of the biggest energy-saving devices. It pumps water up from the aquifer and takes it into the chilled ceiling system. Chilled ceilings are far superior to traditional fan coolers because there's less maintenance and you don't need a big chiller plant on the roof, where it was always our intention to fit solar panels. When that was rejected because of cost we made sure that the structure was capable of being fitted with a solar array at a later date, which is what happened. We attached posts to the roof so that the solar panels are lifted off the surface to act like a rainscreen. The cavity below the panels also means there's no issue with heat soak. David Kong, of Foster + Partners, in conversation with the editor, 2011

Left: A large-scale model of the north facade of City Hall was made to show the client how light would penetrate. In order to get as close an approximation to reality as possible this was presented in the on-site marketing suite.

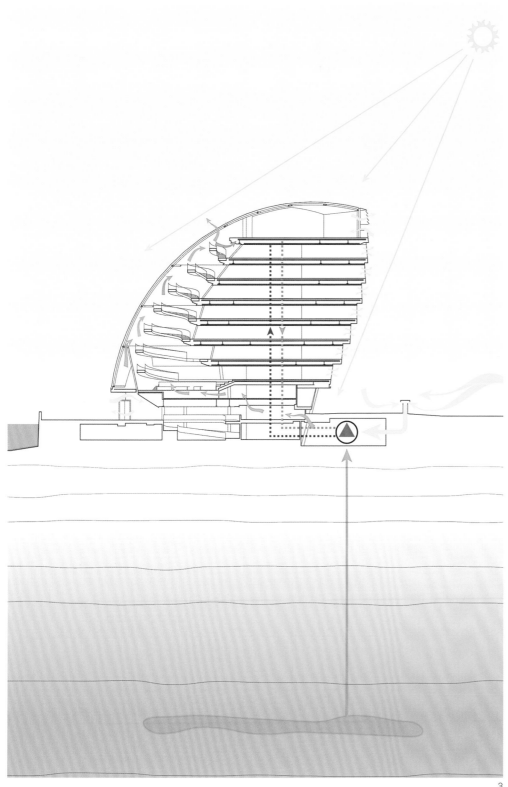

4

3. Environmental section, showing the many passive environmental systems deployed to reduce energy consumption. For most of the year the building requires very little active heating – the major potential energy demand comes from cooling. To assist passive or low-energy cooling, the building is naturally ventilated for most of the year, with openable windows in all the office spaces; heat generated by people, computers and lights is recycled; and cold ground water is pumped up to supply chilled ceilings.

4. Looking down on the roof of City Hall, with its array of photovoltaic panels, which were proposed from the outset but not finally fitted until 2007.

Heat changer

Natural ventilation

Ceilings chilled by ground water

Warm air extracted via ceiling is recycled

Cold water from underground aquifer

3

The form began as a sphere, which provided minimal surface area for a given volume. This was transformed into an egg shape with its axis inclined towards the sun. Slicing this form with a set of horizontal planes produced floor plates that were close to elliptical. We found that the proportions changed progressively up the building, with the long and short axes becoming transposed through a circular floor plate at the mid height. This could have provided a way to rationalise the geometry, but the problem remained that twist in the cladding surface could only be resolved by triangulation, which would make it difficult to accommodate office partitions. However, by making all the floor plates circular, the complex surface became a family of 'sheared cones'. While it is obvious that a cone with a vertical axis will have a simple flat panel solution, it was not widely known that when the cone axis is inclined the facets become trapezoidal, but they remain planar. Circular floor plates also allowed the space planning to be coordinated with a radial grid, while the partitions could be connected to inclined mullions with triangular closer pieces, each cranked to the required angle. Hugh Whitehead, formerly of Foster + Partners, in conversation with the editor, 2011

1

2

3

1. The riverside terrace outside London's Living Room on the ninth floor of City Hall.

2. There is a strong visual connection between the offices on the upper floors and the winding public route of the ramp.

3. Visitors climb the stepped ramp up to London's Living Room. The building is open to the public every day from 8.00am to 8.00pm, and special events are frequently held at weekends.

4. Looking into the assembly chamber, with the London Assembly in session.

5. The public levels beneath the assembly chamber form a venue for exhibitions and other events. On the lower ground floor the London Photomat shows an aerial view of the whole of Greater London, at a detail precise enough to pinpoint individual houses and buildings.

6. An event for schoolchildren in London's Living Room

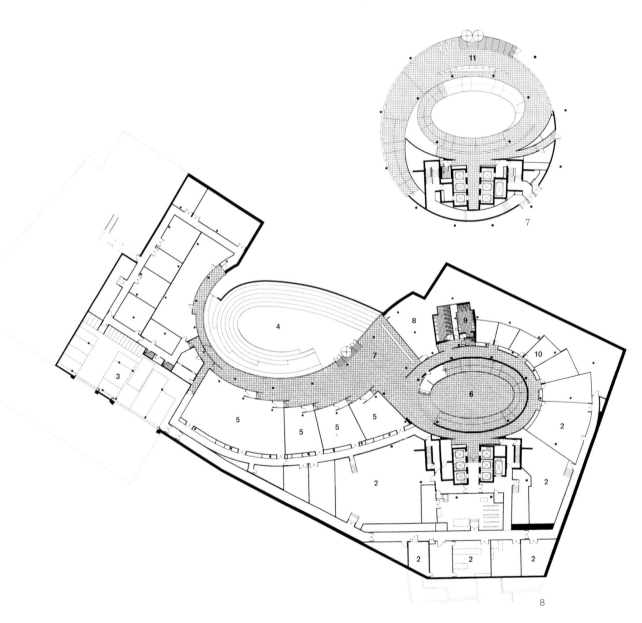

0   20m
0   60ft

City Hall is a landmark for the capital. For fourteen years London had no city-wide government ... it is appropriate then, that our permanent home should be a dramatic new building which will become a distinctive addition to London's landscape. Ken Livingstone, former Mayor of London, opening City Hall, 23 July 2002
Left: The twenty-five-member London Assembly held its first meeting in the chamber in May 2002.
Right: City Hall was officially opened by HM the Queen on 23 July 2002. The Queen and Prince Philip were given a tour of the building by the Mayor of London, Ken Livingstone, and the Chair of the London Assembly, Trevor Phillips. The celebrations included a performance by a local children's brass band.

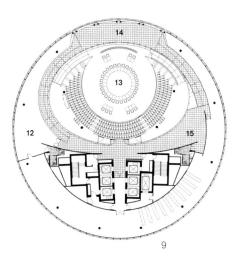
4

5

6

9

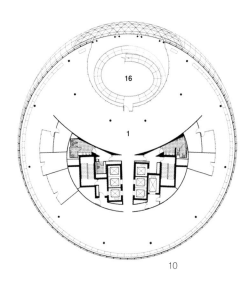
10

7. Lower ground floor plan, corresponding with the floor of 'The Scoop'.

8. Ground floor plan, corresponding with the riverside terrace.

9. Second floor plan.

10. Fourth floor plan.

11. Sixth floor plan.

12. Ninth floor plan.

1 offices
2 plant
3 loading bay and disabled parking
4 The Scoop
5 committee rooms
6 exhibition space
7 café
8 kitchen
9 public toilets
10 meeting rooms
11 entrance/reception
12 library
13 assembly chamber
14 viewing gallery
15 press/exhibition area
16 ramps
17 London's Living Room
18 external viewing gallery

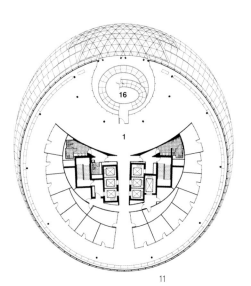
11

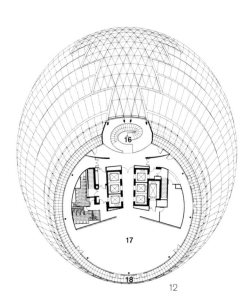
12

The public space around City Hall, replete with amphitheatre, must be one of the best-used new spaces in Central London and enjoys a fabulous City panorama … These spaces are bustling, even before the population reaches its full complement of 20,000 next year (equivalent to the working population of Canterbury). Keith Priest, *Architecture Today*, May 2010
Right: City Hall was the first of several London landmarks to be used as a canvas for the work of American artist Jenny Holzer as part of her project *For London,* in which xenon light projections of poems by Samuel Beckett and other writers flowed over the city at night, April 2006.

The orientation of the building was a key factor from the beginning. It faces north-south and leans back in order to present a minimal surface to the sun. It steps back at the rear to provide self-shading and is clear at the front because there is no direct heat-gain. There is a common misconception that heat loss is the biggest problem in buildings but in commercial buildings it's cooling rather than heating which causes the biggest problem. David Kong, of Foster + Partners, in conversation with the editor, 2011

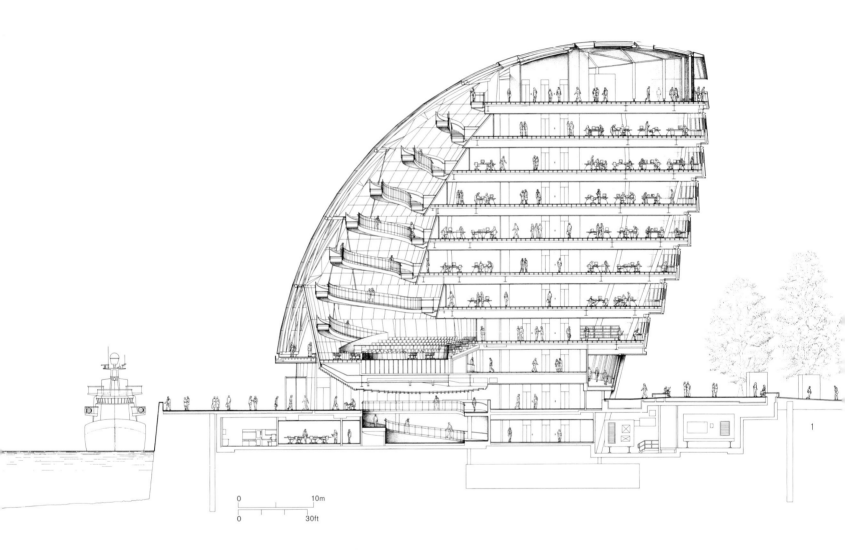

0   10m

0   30ft

1. Cross-section through the assembly chamber and spiralling ramp, showing the relationship with the riverside.

2, 3. 'The Scoop' at the base of the building is a popular venue for summer concerts, or just a good place to relax during lunch breaks.

2

3

As a student I got completely carried away by studying a whole range of spaces – Georgian towns like Bath, Shepherd Market in Mayfair, London, the Campo in Siena, the Milan Galleria – and I measured them and drew cross-sections and observed them and tried to pin point exactly why they were so successful and so popular – why they were meeting points, why they brought life to their respective cities. And I think that this concern with routes and spaces in the city is one which has stayed with me all my life, and has certainly underpinned a lot of our work. Norman Foster, in conversation with the editor, 2012

In thinking about the design of the public spaces, we tried to eliminate superfluous details and to minimise visual clutter. Grant Brooker, in conversation with the editor, 2011

We quite enjoy the fact that the pedestrian route wraps around The Scoop. As you walk through the site you're forced to go past The Scoop so you're able to look down on the activities taking place there. You're also pushed close to City Hall so you get an interaction with that as well. I think it works very well because part of the joy of the city is the odd surprise you get or the odd quirky bit you encounter. Max Neal, formerly of Foster + Partners, in conversation with the editor, 2011

4

4. City Hall and the sunken amphitheatre of The Scoop seen from the west, looking towards Tower Bridge.

City Hall is a building of great symbolic importance in London – a combination of public platform, accessible democratic assembly and responsible environmental design.

Norman Foster

Although the site is a stone's throw from the City's financial district, it remained undeveloped for decades. Despite numerous attempts, no one could make anything happen because it was south of the river. It was only with the advent of the new Jubilee Line station at London Bridge, just a few minutes walk from the site, that development finally became feasible. Yet, even then, psychologically, it was still very far from being a sure deal. Grant Brooker, of Foster + Partners, in conversation with the editor, 2011

The landscape design is all about knitting-in with the existing and predicted pedestrian patterns. In addition to the continuation of the riverside walk there was a very strong demand for people walking from London Bridge Station to Tower Bridge to cross into the City. Until then it had been a tortuous route through Hay's Galleria, so we created a route down Tooley Street which cut diagonally through the development and on to Tower Bridge. Max Neal, formerly of Foster + Partners, in conversation with the editor, 2011
Left: The masterplan site as found. In development terms it was a blank canvas, but one with a very strong frame, formed by Tooley Street to the south and the River Thames to the north.

1   2   3

1-3. At the western end of the diagonal route where it meets Tooley Street, a new public square creates a gateway into More London from London Bridge Station and Bermondsey. This south-facing piazza is delineated by trees and stone water benches which – like the water wall in Manhattan's Paley Park – mask traffic noise to provide a visual and acoustic threshold to the site. A rill of water and views of Tower Bridge draw people along the diagonal route to a second public space at the river's edge.

Taking a pure sphere as a starting point, the primary software model was constructed as a 'parametric pebble' using proportional relationships and controls that could be manipulated by the design team. The designers were thus able to adjust both surface and volume to their satisfaction while accurately recording each new dimension. Solid models were also frequently generated from the same software using rapid-prototyping machinery in the studio's own model shop, providing a visual and tactile test-bed for further development. Experimenting with different cladding patterns, designers would sometimes even draw or tape the lines of the cladding frames directly on to the solid models.

In parallel with these experiments, Arup's engineers were exploring alternative structural concepts and refining the environmental performance of the design, based on their own computer models. The ring of inclined columns around the outer floor edges that characterised the earlier scheme was retained, but they now continue down to the ground level, where they are exposed externally; and the twin circulation cores were replaced in the final design by a single, moon-shaped, reinforced-concrete core in the heart of the building, providing both lateral and vertical support.

Similarly, Arup's dynamic 3D models, showing the varying patterns of solar gain on different parts of the structure, had a considerable impact on the final design, shaping the optimum tilt and form for energy efficiency.

By converting the resulting form into a stack of sheared cones, one for each floor plate, the SMG team found that the entire surface could be translated into a series of flat panels suitable for glazing and fabrication. Raking back progressively, the trapezoidal panels add a suitably streamlined finish to the building.

As the focal point of More London Riverside, City Hall has played a major part in the redevelopment of the city along the South Bank.

Similar ingenuity was applied to designing the glazing separating the assembly chamber and atrium from the offices. A digital model was created enabling the architects to manipulate the shape of the void, with its long neck, until a fit was found between the geometry of both void and structure. Initially, the ramp was wrapped around the outside of the neck with the glazing located on the inside rim.

This arrangement had acoustic advantages over a smooth surface, effectively dispersing sound up through the void, but complicated the surrounding glazing, which followed the same twisting geometry as the ramp. In the process of adjusting the void to fit the internal volume of the structure, it had also morphed in plan from a circular shape into a more compact and graceful ellipse, further complicating the three-dimensional geometry.

A significant distinction between More London and earlier generations of mixed-use schemes is that there are no gates or doors. All the streets, alleys and squares are open air and accessible to everyone around the clock. More than half the site is public open space, and the two piazzas, instead of being cocooned within the private realm, are at the edges of the site, so helping to integrate the development within the grain of the city.
Norman Foster, in conversation with the editor, 2012
Right: An aerial view of the Southwark riverside and the More London site in the late 1980s.

More London is interesting in that cars are banished to create a pedestrian-friendly environment. The scheme has only minimal car parking; but we've found that building owners on sites with good public transport links no longer regard parking as essential or even desirable. Apart from emergency vehicles, which can enter the site along designated routes, a single vehicle access point on Tooley Street leads to a secure undercroft that services all the buildings. Eliminating vehicles from the precinct also addresses concerns about security in an increasingly volatile world. Grant Brooker, of Foster + Partners, in conversation with the editor, 2011

4   5   6

4-6. Opposite the Tower of London and laid out on the scale of Leicester Square, the riverside space forms the forecourt for City Hall. The site falls approximately 3 metres from Tooley Street to the Thames. Within the elongated diagonal route, this change of level is taken up by a barely perceptible ramp, which splits at the riverside to form a raised terrace with stone benches set in a grid of fountains, and the riverfront walkway below, where The Scoop – a sheltered-amphitheatre – hosts free theatrical and musical events. The detailing in the public spaces uses a restricted palette of dark grey Irish limestone paviours, deciduous trees and water.

7. Site plan, showing the ground-floor plan of City Hall and all the new buildings within the More London masterplan area.

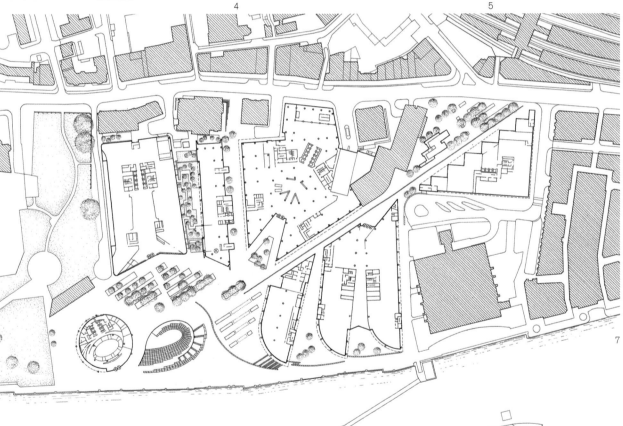

7

0   50m
0   150ft

All too often in developments of this kind, the temptation is to start by designing the buildings. Here we did the opposite. The three key physical generators are derived from the context: the River Thames, Tower Bridge and the Tower of London. The organisation of the site is defined by a network of public routes and spaces that focus on or respond to these landmarks. The most important of these is a new diagonal route linking Tower Bridge and City Hall to London Bridge Station. The buildings are slotted between the routes, arranged like the open fingers of a hand.
Norman Foster, in conversation with the editor, 2012

The site had lain empty for twenty years and had been cleared of its Victorian warehouses. But the developer had been unable to find a suitable masterplan, despite appointing several architects, including Philip Johnson. However, when a new developer came on board he appointed us and we devised a masterplan that could be reconciled with the commercial demands of the clients on one hand, and the aspirations of local groups on the other. Max Neal, formerly of Foster + Partners, in conversation with the editor, 2011
Left: An early masterplan model; a diagonal route was an early fix, though the forms of the buildings gradually evolved. The form of City Hall itself changed radically.

1-3. The final building within More London, 7 More London Riverside is the headquarters of PricewaterhouseCoopers LLP. The building's wings open towards the river and its serrated facades address a variety of diagonal perspectives. The facade also contributes to a highly progressive environmental strategy that has allowed the building to achieve a BREEAM 'Outstanding' rating. The landscaped approach to the main entrance mediates the transition between the building and the public space on the waterfront.

4. Looking south towards City Hall and More London from Tower Place. With City Hall acting as a magnet, More London provides 200,000 square metres of offices together with shops, cafés, a hotel and theatre. The buildings are limited to ten storeys to preserve view corridors to St Paul's Cathedral from Greenwich and Blackheath. More London's hard landscaping is complemented by Potters' Fields Park, next to Tower Bridge, designed by the Dutch architects and urbanists, West 8.

The designers solved the problem by moving the ramp inside the glazed void, allowing the inclined panels to be positioned separately between the edges of each floor. This retained the acoustic properties of the previous arrangement – enhanced by absorbent materials on the underside of the ramp – while displaying the full length of the suspended ramp itself in all its winding glory.

In its final built form, the spiral ramp, with its public accessibility and dynamic, constantly changing geometry, provides both a dramatic centrepiece and primary circulation route through the building. In this, the City Hall ramp follows a long line of related Foster projects in which a public pathway through the building has been created with both symbolic as well as practical intentions. Whether slicing through a whole block from street to street at one level, as with the Carré d'Art in Nîmes, and the Great Court of the British Museum, or opening up new kinds of vertical spaces, as with the suspended ramp in the Reichstag's dome, Foster has created new ways of merging public and private realms.

All these precedents are crystallised anew in the City Hall version, which is as much a ceremonial route as a public pathway. The complete journey begins outside the building, in the public piazza on the river's edge. An elliptical sunken area on the eastern side – The Scoop –resembling a stepped amphitheatre, echoes the open public space under the building in the earlier scheme, now replaced by a full basement floor of public functions and plant rooms.

The lower level of the amphitheatre leads inside the building to a second elliptical space directly beneath the assembly chamber, merging both external and internal public spaces into a unified, swirling plan-form containing public meeting rooms and exhibition spaces.

The internal elliptical space also marks the beginning of the dramatic route upwards, following the spiralling ramp all the way through the assembly chamber and the narrowing void above, till it reaches its final destination in 'London's Living Room'.

For all the conscious precedents, the experience of traversing slowly upwards or downwards through this changing void, pausing to soak in the extraordinary views inside and outside the building, is like none other. More intimate in scale than the Reichstag ramp, though lacking nothing in excitement, the City Hall route capitalises, as it was intended to do, on the spatial proximity between the members in the chamber and the public circulating overhead. To what degree that proximity will be translated into concrete social results depends, as it always will, on both the public and their elected representatives fulfilling their designated roles and promises. But neither party can complain that they do not have a suitable seat of government expressive of their highest aspirations.

Chris Abel

1

2

3

We wanted both a powerful reinstatement of the riverside walk and to announce the site on Tooley Street, so it was always very clear that the buildings should be pulled back to create something public around the edge. Unlike a lot of large masterplans, like Bishopsgate, for example, where the public spaces tend to be in the middle, we placed them at the two edges as we knew we had strong links running east to west on each side. Crucially, we then connected them diagonally across the site to make it very clear that when you move from the railway station you can orientate yourself very easily via Tower Bridge. Grant Brooker, of Foster + Partners, in conversation with the editor, 2011

The Foster masterplan is deceptively simple and has proved remarkably resilient, enduring the twists and turns of the planning and development process ... More London has undoubtedly made a major contribution to the transformation of the northern sector of Southwark, now confidently facing the river rather than backing away. Keith Priest, *Architecture Today*, May 2010

To achieve a sustainable way of being we must work at all levels and scales and with both traditional and new technology. At the smallest scale this might involve the use of solar components and systems, such as solar panels or solar thermal collectors. The next scale up from the design of individual components is the design of buildings as integrated energy systems and from there the next jump is to neighbourhoods and cities. From there we begin to look on a national and ultimately a global level. We need to work in parallel on all these fronts. Stefan Behling, of Foster + Partners, Ivorypress conference on sustainability, Madrid, 17 September 2009

4

The challenge of the Southwark riverside was to create a genuinely diverse, open and inviting environment that could mediate between the river and the hard urban edge of Tooley Street beyond.

Norman Foster

In Discussion with Peter Wynne Rees
Kenneth Powell 2011

In the eyes of some contemporary critics, the post-war rebuilding of the City of London was insufficiently radical. Substantial areas of the surviving street pattern were retained. It was only in areas laid flat by bombing – such as London Wall and Paternoster Square – that the Modernists were able to seize the day, embarking on comprehensive redevelopment which was to produce environments that most people found hostile. Even as the tide of aggressive reconstruction was running high, however, one planner had an alternative vision. Gordon Cullen, an assistant editor on *The Architectural Review* in the 1950s and author of the hugely influential *Townscape* (1961), promoted the idea of a gentler approach to new development, which respected historic context.

That philosophy has had a lasting influence on Norman Foster, who as a student discovered Cullen's townscape articles in the *Review*. Looking at the projects completed by Foster + Partners in the City over the last fifteen years, Peter Wynne Rees detects Cullen's influence at work. As City Planning Officer since 1987, Rees is widely credited with transforming attitudes towards new architecture there. Significantly, Rees began his career as Cullen's assistant. Cullen, he says, 'had no hard-and-fast set of rules – he taught you to observe, look, and learn, and that it was much easier to destroy than it was to create. That was the essence of his philosophy of townscape.'

'Foster has the ability to run with the spirit of the place.'

When Rees arrived in the City in 1985, initially as Controller of Planning, Richard Rogers' Lloyd's Building was nearing completion, a modern landmark created against all the odds. But in the previous half-century the City had been an architectural backwater – 'there had been nothing of real quality since Lutyens' Midland Bank', says Rees. In the post-war period, development in the City had been dominated by commercial practices whose principal attraction to clients, it seemed, was their ability to produce the conventional: 'nobody wanted to break ranks, or draw attention to themselves'. By the 1980s, however, with the transformation of the City economy following the so-called Big Bang, there was huge scope for renewing its building stock, with many poor-quality 1960s buildings ripe for replacement. But could developers be persuaded to invest in good architecture; and could redevelopment respect the special character of the City, which by the 1980s was seriously committed to protecting the best of its architectural heritage?

Rees believes that Foster's City projects provide a lesson in building in tune with context and, in particular, adding to the total of that precious City commodity: public space. The latter is a concern that has always figured strongly in Foster's work. 'Foster's buildings sit well on their sites and have a carefully considered relationship to them', says Rees; 'Foster has the ability to run with the spirit of the place.'

It was Cullen, says Rees, who opened his eyes to the qualities of the City townscape. 'It's like an Italian hill-town,' he argues, 'intricate, complex, a place that it takes a long time to get to know and appreciate, rarely spectacular, but, at its best, consistently intriguing.' The City's intimacy and variety, he believes, is part of its attraction as a place to do business. Its narrow streets and alleyways are a wonderful way of crossing the City – perfect places for chance encounters and the gossip and exchange of news that have been part of City life for centuries. Rees's aim has been not only to preserve but also to enhance the City's permeability. 'Spaces matter just as much as buildings,' he says, a lesson lost on many of those responsible for the post-war reconstruction programme.

A classic illustration of the deficiencies of much post-1945 development was the 1960s Tower Place: an office development built of grey concrete and planned around high-level walkways. As a neighbour for the Tower of London it was disastrously intrusive. When the prospect of its replacement arose Rees was convinced that a big name was needed to work so close to the Tower. The City's aim was to secure a scheme that enhanced the Tower's setting while creating a significant new public space around the church of All Hallows-by-the-Tower. Foster's scheme for Tower Place was the subject of extended dialogue with the City and other relevant bodies. It provides a publicly-accessible covered atrium and open piazza on a scale without precedent in the City.

Another early Foster City project, One London Wall, also had to address the failures of post-war planning. A key planning objective in discussions about replacing the existing slab office block was to create a more attractive pedestrian connection to the Museum of London, which was stranded on a high-level walkway. Much delayed by the recession of the early 1990s and completed in 2003, the scheme underwent radical redesign, assuming a distinctly organic look, with upper floors set back to reduce its perceived size. New bridge links provide a route to the museum, but the principal point of entry to the new building is at street level. For Rees, the scheme is 'a real success – it benefited from the delays in its realisation.' Further east along London Wall, another Foster project, the nineteen-storey Moor House, includes a new public square with shops and cafés animating the street level.

One of the characteristic City alleyways so prized by Peter Rees connects Wood Street with the ancient churchyard of St Mary Staining, a church lost in the Great Fire. The tiny churchyard is most notable today for a single magnificent plane tree. Foster's 100 Wood Street, which backs on to this space, might seem at first over-deferential to context, though its stone-clad street facade is clearly intended as a neighbourly gesture to the surviving Wren tower of St Alban's church and the 1960s Classical police station by McMorran & Whitby.

However, the key element of the scheme, Rees argues, is its response to the alleyway and churchyard – the building's rear elevation seems to pivot around the plane tree. It bridges across the alley by means of a slender, transparent glazed link, as beautiful as it is functional – 'a superb gesture,' says Rees; 'the relationship of the building to the ancient City route is the star feature of a project that has been critically undervalued.'

Close by, Foster's 10 Gresham Street has received its fair share of critical praise. Taking its cue from Mies van der Rohe, the project creates an elegant office pavilion using high-quality materials. In Peter Rees's view 'this is one of the best things achieved during my time in the City.' The site was restrictive, not least because the architecturally undistinguished 1950s Wax Chandlers' Hall had to be retained. But somehow the Foster team squeezed out of it a new alleyway and a small but attractive public space and café on Gutter Lane, which is a real asset in this densely built-up quarter of the City.

Alongside Gresham Street, the Swiss Re building at 30 St Mary Axe is, for Rees, Foster's supreme achievement in the City. It occupies a site initially envisaged for Foster's 385-metre Millennium Tower. That project was, says Rees, 'too much, too soon – it scared people.' In contrast, 30 St Mary Axe has, he believes, done a great deal to promote the cause of modern architecture in Britain. It is a genuinely popular high-rise, one of the buildings that have made the City a place of pilgrimage for tourists interested in modern architecture. 'For one practice to have designed the perfect twenty-first-century commercial palazzo and a building that is a symbol of London worldwide is an amazing achievement' he says.

A crucial aspect of 30 St Mary Axe was the creation of a piazza around the base of the tower. Again, the theme is permeability and movement: the building that formerly stood on the site filled the entire block. Foster opened up new pedestrian through routes and the base of the tower contains a popular café. A similar strategy was pursued at Lime Street, across the road from the Lloyd's Building, where Foster's project cuts new alleyways through the previously enclosed site. Public space is woven around the base of the new buildings and Lime Street itself has been partly pedestrianised.

Peter Rees's interest in London extends beyond his immediate fiefdom and he is pleased that the benefits of the recent development boom have spilled over into adjacent boroughs. Foster's Bishops Square has transformed Spitalfields, where the market area was in limbo for decades, and has created really generous areas of covered and open public space as well as a mix of offices, shops and housing.

Another project of crucial importance for Rees is Foster's Millennium Bridge, an embodiment of the City's historically close relationship with Southwark, itself developing a major business district around London Bridge, where Foster's More London has had a profoundly positive impact. The bridge exemplifies Rees's pursuit of connectivity and his belief that the City is not a self-contained 'island'. The City has changed immensely in the quarter-century that Rees has worked there – and for the better, he believes. It is no longer an architectural backwater, nor is it dead in the evening and at weekends; retail, restaurant and hotel projects have had a transformational effect. It is also increasingly a place for people, where architecture and public space work in harmony. Cumulatively, Foster's projects have had a huge impact in this respect, helping to re-establish a sense of place and to broaden the City's appeal as a place in which to live and do business.

1

City of London Office Buildings
London, England 1992–2010

The Swiss Re building at 30 St Mary Axe, the most distinctive of a new generation of tall buildings in the City of London, has become a symbol of the capital and that rare phenomenon in Britain, a genuinely popular new tower. Its dramatic form and prominent position have naturally made it a landmark; less immediately understood is its contribution to the public realm, with the creation of a generous piazza and new pedestrian routes across the previously landlocked site. It is a contribution shared by all Foster's projects completed in and around the City over the last decade. Each of the projects considered here, however reticent they might at first seem, reflects an ongoing quest for a modern commercial architecture rooted in contextual tradition.

The basis of this approach can be traced to Foster's student days in Manchester, where he saw the strengths of that city's Victorian heritage, not least its covered arcades and the majestic Town Hall, where he worked for a time. He witnessed the beginnings of the clearance campaign that was to destroy much of that heritage and simultaneously warmed to the critical approach of *The Architectural Review*, and the great apostle of 'townscape', Gordon Cullen, whose wholehearted rejection of banal Modernist planning orthodoxies was the starting point for a quiet, reflective approach to urban design.

When Foster first came to address the challenge of inserting a modern office building into a historical context, for Willis Faber & Dumas in Ipswich, he produced a solution that responded fluidly to the irregular street pattern, and created a new setting for the neighbouring historic meeting house. The project also pioneered other themes restated in some of the projects here: a low-rise solution where a high-rise might have been expected; an innovative approach to workplace design, with a roof garden and generous staff amenities; and an acute awareness of townscape.

Foster's skill at creating attractive new routes and public spaces is demonstrated in the City to excellent effect.

Appropriately, it is another project for the same client – now known as Willis – that introduces this group of City buildings. The development at 51 Lime Street brings the whole of Willis's London workforce together on one site. But whereas the Ipswich building was commissioned by and for the company, Lime Street is essentially a developer's building, though it has been tailored to meet Willis's needs.

Opposite: An aerial view of the City of London. In the foreground is 51 Lime Street (2001-2007); 30 St Mary Axe commands the skyline; and in the distance is Bishops Square in Spitalfields.

1. Approaching 51 Lime Street from St Mary Axe.

2. Ground floor plan; the eastern part of the tower and the entire ground floor of the six-storey podium building, are given over to shops and cafés.

3. Typical upper-level office floors of both buildings.

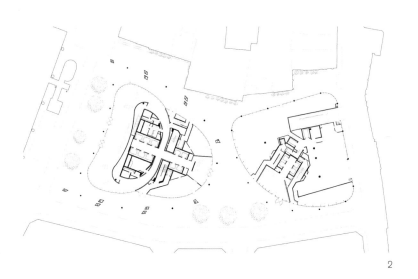

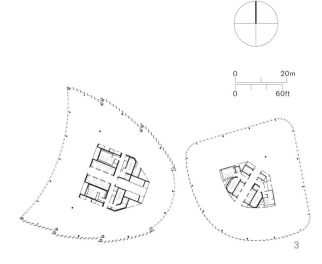

0   20m

0   60ft

Left: The site was occupied for nearly half a century by the distinctive 1950s classical extension to Lloyd's designed by Terence Heysham. In 1954-1957 the sculptor James Woodford created four panels, representing the Four Elements – both as the material and basis of prosperity and as threatening to it – which were raised high on the building's two south towers. They were saved and repositioned at street level, where their quality and detail can be better appreciated.

1. The entrance to the Willis offices on Lime Street faces that of the Lloyd's Building – now an established landmark in the City. In response, the facade of 51 Lime Street (2001-2007) is drawn back to create an elongated piazza.

2. The Willis entrance lobby on Lime Street. A glazed curtain wall encourages a sense of continuity with the life of the street beyond.

Narrow and curving, Lime Street is typical of the City's largely medieval street pattern. An ancient route, which has been largely pedestrianised, it leads to Leadenhall Market at the core of a Conservation Area, which lies just to the west. On one side of the street is Lloyd's London (housed in Richard Rogers' building of 1986). The wider context is extremely varied: to the north are the 1960s Aviva Tower and Manhattan-style plaza, and the Swiss Re building. To the east, on Fenchurch Avenue and Billiter Street, the urban scale is altogether more modest.

The scheme consists of two elements – a stepped tower, rising to twenty-nine storeys on the western side of the site, close to Lloyd's – and a ten-storey block abutting the smaller-scaled buildings on Fenchurch Avenue. Foster's tower is an ingenious design, consisting of three interlocking volumes, stepping back to the east in two stages. The resulting terraces form communal gardens that can be accessed directly from the offices – an echo of the roof garden in Ipswich. A key strategic move was to retain the deep basement of the 1950s Lloyd's extension, which formerly occupied the site. This now houses an auditorium that has quickly established itself as a popular venue for conferences and lunchtime concerts.

The tower's strongly modelled form, with a concave frontage to Lime Street, makes it an appropriate neighbour for Lloyd's, its stance respectful rather than deferential, and its sleekness contrasting with the almost obsessive articulation of Rogers' building. The new route created between Foster's two buildings is fundamental to the sense of permeability and represents a welcome move in this dense part of the City, extending its network of lanes and alleys. Foster's skill in creating welcoming public spaces is demonstrated here to excellent effect in the planting, paving and seating. The shops and restaurants are busy at lunchtime and the area is alive with activity, providing a vivid contrast with the bleak Aviva piazza nearby, which has not come to life in forty years.

Virtually all Foster's City buildings have replaced post-war structures, none of which reflected any sympathy for history or context – none more so than those on London Wall, where the practice has completed two projects: One London Wall and Moor House. This part of the City was at the epicentre of the wartime Blitz. When it was rebuilt in the 1960s, London Wall became effectively an urban motorway, lined with office slabs accessed via bleak pedestrian walkways.

Foster's project has succeeded in breaking down the urban block and introducing light, air and a sense of space into the heart of the city.

The site of One London Wall was complicated by the existence of the post-war Plaisterers' Hall, which had to be retained, and height limitations imposed by the St Paul's Heights policy; the City also wanted the scheme to provide improved access to the Museum of London.

The form of the building is curvaceous, even organic, reflecting a tendency found in a number of recent Foster projects. A bold riposte to the orthogonal geometry of neighbouring buildings, it can be read as three interlocking volumes, stepping down from the east, where the thirteen-storey height matches the buildings on Aldersgate Street. Open terraces provide fine views across the City. It might appear, for all its functional efficiency, a rather self-conscious exercise in the creation of memorable form. It is, however, a highly logical response to context.

The urban pattern was set in the 1960s, when the corner of London Wall and Aldersgate Street was shaved off and a roundabout created. Powell & Moya's Museum of London bastion reinforces this geometry. Foster's building completes the composition to provide a sensitive, but far from recessive, preface to the now highly variegated run of buildings along London Wall.

In the design of a new building there is a chance to create or add to a public realm that ideally already exists. You can do that with content – retail, cafés, restaurants – you can do it with space, with light – but the point is really that the front door is the face of an organisation. It's where its public credentials are located: is it a good citizen or a bad citizen? And I think that's something that fascinates us. David Nelson, in conversation with the editor, 2012

If you can create environments that people enjoy, and that bring life to the street, with shops and cafés – as we've done at Bishops Square and around Lime Street – you find that the landlords will appreciate it in commercial terms. If their building is in a location with a vibrant life, that becomes a magnet in its own right, then that is very attractive to potential tenants. The skill is to create a balance in planning terms. Grant Brooker, of Foster + Partners, in conversation with the editor, 2011

3

3. City neighbours: 30 St Mary Axe is seen behind the Lloyd's Building (left) and 51 Lime Street.

4. At street level, a pedestrian route that existed on the site historically has been reinstated and a small piazza created on Fenchurch Avenue. This new space is lined with shops and cafés and has quickly established itself as a popular lunch spot for City workers.

4

London Wall as rebuilt in the 1960s was an alien environment – quite inappropriate in this traditionally low-rise, dense part of the City. At ground level it was particularly disconnected – you had to climb up to one of the windswept raised walkways to gain access to the buildings. The fact that these office slabs very quickly became dinosaurs was an opportunity to repair some of the damage they had done, to reinforce the lost urban grain and reconnect the buildings with the experience at street level. Norman Foster, in conversation with the editor, 2012
Right: The former One London Wall, photographed shortly before demolition.

1

1. One London Wall (1992-2003) stands at the corner of London Wall and St Martin's Le Grand, occupying a site whose boundaries were established by the redevelopment of the area in the 1960s.

2. Looking north from a vantage point above St Paul's Cathedral down St Martin's Le Grand to the Barbican. Compositionally, One London Wall mediates between the traditional scale of St Martin's Le Grand and the high-rise development on London Wall, stepping up in three discrete stages.

3. The facade of 100 Wood Street (1997-2000) provides a visual foil to the tower of Wren's St Alban's – all that survives of this once grand City church.

4. In contrast to the Classical discipline of the Wood Street elevation, the rear facade – which looks on to the former churchyard of St Mary Staining – is more fluid.

5. Cross-section through One London Wall, with 100 Wood Street (seen on the right). The large volume seen lower right in the London Wall building is the existing Plaisterers' Hall, which was incorporated into the scheme.

2

The differences between our building and its neighbour, by Richard Rogers, reflect the planning constraints, which in turn relate to the different settings. Richard's building is in some ways like our building for ITN, which is very transparent. Perhaps this is down to the similarity of the sites, both of which are experienced as streets. But, in Wood Street, the planners were concerned that the prime views of our building would be oblique, from Love Lane, past the tower of St Alban's. They insisted that the facade should be mainly of stone. Individual architects inevitably have their own approaches, but here the planning constraints exaggerated the contrasts. Grant Brooker, of Foster + Partners, in conversation with the editor, 2011

Wood Street was a challenge to achieve a viable scheme on a tight site with many constraints. Ironically, the features that make the site attractive – such as the magnificent tree which is hard against the back of the site and the church tower by Wren – added to the constraints. Then of course St Paul's is also close by. We tried to turn the constraints into opportunities. For instance, the tree inspired a semi-circular garden, literally scooped out around the branches. In one sense the building is like a grand house – looking out through windows to the hard urbanity of the street at the front while the rear is like a great conservatory opening up to quiet and greenery. Norman Foster, in conversation with the editor, 2012

What you find is that space in the City is so valuable that you maximise all the small pockets of public space created. There are fragments – garden spaces that are the remains of churchyards wiped out by the Blitz – and those remnants have been reincorporated, such as at Wood Street or the Walbrook. They remain, they're precious and they get drawn into the scheme. Grant Brooker, of Foster + Partners, in conversation with the editor, 2011

A significant gain from this and other recent developments on London Wall has been the reinstatement of ground level as the main point of access to the buildings, which has brought life back to the street.

Moor House lies close to the junction of Moorgate and London Wall, an area still dominated by the high-rise Corbusian vision of the 1950s. To the south and east, however, the traditional grain of the City remains. A small group of Victorian buildings survives nearby, including Fox's umbrella shop with its Art Deco fascia. The challenge was to create a building that could mediate between these two scales. On its eastern elevation, the building sweeps back to create a ski slope that is part wall, part roof. It reflects the way in which this facade joins the curving elevation to the south and defers to the group of listed buildings nearby. The ground and first floors are given over to shops and cafés, set behind an arcade that edges a new piazza.

Immaculately detailed in the best Foster tradition, this is a building that responds confidently to a complex brief, producing an urban marker that reflects a specific moment in the history of the City's development. Little is left of the grim post-war vision of London Wall: unity and the supremacy of the overall plan have given way to a more appropriate diversity and a little self-expression.

Wood Street, which runs into London Wall, provides a microcosm of recent trends in British architecture. At the northern end, straddling two lanes of traffic, is Terry Farrell's bizarre Postmodern confection of Alban Gate. It is flanked to the south by Richard Rogers' refined 88 Wood Street and the more recent Aldermanbury Square development by Eric Parry, its masonry facades conducting a dialogue with the progressive Classicism of McMorran & Whitby's 1960s police station. The final element in this striking urban scenario is the St Alban's tower: the only element of Wren's church to survive the war.

Foster's building at 100 Wood Street articulates the transition between Gresham Street and London Wall, which represent the traditional and modern aspects of the City respectively. At first sight, it seems uncharacteristic. The proximity of Wren's tower prompted strict planning requirements: the eaves line could not be higher than the tower, and the street elevation had to be faced in stone and articulated as base, middle and attic. The resulting facade has an alternating pattern of glass and Portland stone panels, which aims to mediate between the stone facades on one side and glass on the other.

3

4

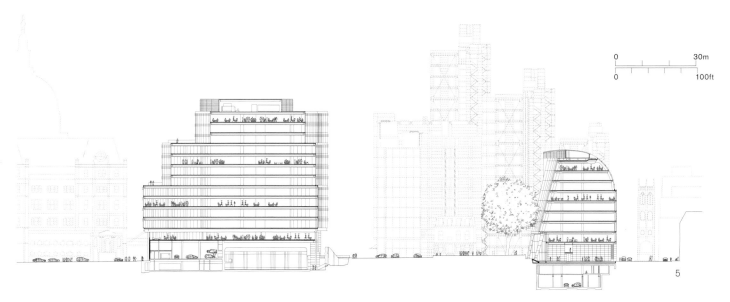

5

Each of the City buildings addresses a different condition. For instance, Moor House is a transitional building – you have the lower buildings around Finsbury Circus and then the project itself rises towards the London Wall towers. Physically it's a big swept curve in section, creating a generous two-storey space at ground floor – the prime part of which is retail and addresses the small Georgian houses. It also repairs disastrous 1960s walkway planning, which had killed any connection to the City. We changed all of that: it feels much grander and takes London Wall straight through to Moorfields, where the station sits. Grant Brooker, of Foster + Partners, in conversation with the editor, 2011

We set out to establish a reputation for good value commercial projects, to deliver quality and we achieved that. Along the way you could say that we've radicalised our clients, made hard-headed developers think innovatively and changed the workplace for the better. Brandon Haw, of Foster + Partners, quoted in *The Architects' Journal*, 6 May 2004

A lot of people cannot understand why, when we can do cultural projects, we would take on a tough commercial building. There are many reasons. One is that we've always been driven by understanding the economics of what we build. There is no greater training for an architect than to live through a tough, highly commercial project and to learn how you can save money and still maintain the design. It's a difficult fight. You might find that later you're working on a museum project and everyone wants different things and you've got to be in a position to value-engineer that. That skill is honed by an awareness of the commercial world. David Nelson, in conversation with the editor, 2011

1

1. The nineteen-storey Moor House (1997-2005) stands at the junction of London Wall and Moorgate. It occupies a pivotal point between the Barbican and other post-war developments to the north and west and the more varied historical street pattern to the south. At ground level, shops, restaurants and bars line a covered arcade

2. A long section through the atrium of 10 Gresham Street (1996-2003). The structural solution allows office floors unencumbered by columns.

The back of the building, however, is of a very different order. Tucked away behind Wood Street is the tiny churchyard of St Mary Staining with its ancient plane tree, a narrow alley – a typical 'secret' City route – providing access. The churchyard elevation is completely glazed, and set back at ground level to create a sheltered arcade. Thus Foster makes the churchyard the visual focus of the offices, in the process rediscovering a lost City space. Gordon Cullen, one imagines, would have approved of this deft exercise in urban drama.

Terminating the view south along Wood Street is Foster's building on Gresham Street, which despite wartime devastation remains palpably part of the City's historic core. The Guildhall and Corporation church of St Lawrence Jewry are close by, and the magnificent Goldsmiths' Hall stands immediately to the west, alongside the post-war Wax Chandlers' Hall.

Arguably the most assured of Foster's City schemes, it has an integrity that is rare in recent London office buildings. It makes full use of the irregular site, building up to the pavement edge and establishing the sense of enclosure that is a vital part of the City's character. The stepped atrium is one element in a highly efficient diagram that adapts easily to a variety of internal layouts.

Lifts and services are concentrated in two central cores with additional cores, set diagonally at the four corners, incorporating escape stairs. Clad in white limestone, the latter are expressed as towers framing the curtain-walled office elevations. The upper two office floors are set back behind canted elevations, allowing the corner towers to stand free as incidents in the townscape.

This is a building with an air of generosity – particularly in terms of its urban contribution.

Great care has been taken to give the Wax Chandlers' Hall an appropriate setting. A narrow passageway – characteristic of the City – leads between the two buildings to an intimately scaled court on Gutter Lane and a small restaurant with space for outdoor seating. Overall, this is a project that eschews display in favour of solid dignity – the rigorous discipline of the elevations is as frankly Miesian as any of Foster's buildings. It has an air of generosity and is rooted in City traditions – a worthy counterpart to the venerable institutions that form its neighbours.

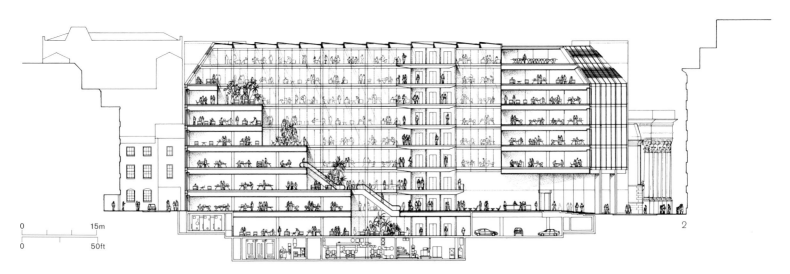

0   15m

0   50ft

2

Of course the City needs to generate business but what they're looking for is how buildings can also enhance the street life and be pleasant places to be in – they need to change the environment in a positive way. You've got to solve both those problems. The greater the density, the higher the demands and the more the public environment has to work. That is the hallmark of our buildings in the City. Grant Brooker, of Foster + Partners, in conversation with the editor, 2011

For centuries architects understood that a city must have good ordinary buildings to line its streets and squares and form a backdrop for its monuments. The pre-war commercial buildings in the City of London were founded on this principle, but somewhere in the 1960s that discipline was lost. Gresham Street was an opportunity to renew that tradition, to build discreetly in this quiet City backwater and to reinforce the street frontage. The counterpoint to that strategy is the atrium, whose dramatic potential is exploited to the full. Again though, that's very much in the tradition of the City and its splendid commercial halls. Norman Foster, in conversation with the editor, 2012

On the face of it, the Foster building is … as sensitive to the context as a glass-and-steel office building can be. It is restrained and elegant – it is the City at its most tasteful. Justin McGuirk, *Icon*, October 2005

3

3. No 10 Gresham Street glimpsed along Lawrence Lane, which is typical of the narrow lanes in this dense part of the City.

4. Limestone-clad stair towers anchor the building strongly in the streetscape. Immediately to the west is the Neo-Georgian Wax Chandlers' Hall, constructed in 1958.

4

Right: The slab form of the Daily Mirror Building, which once occupied the site on Holborn Circus, compared with the new building, which has a much lower profile. Credited to Sir Owen Williams (with Anderson, Forster and Wilcox), the Daily Mirror Building was designed and built between 1955 and 1961. Williams was a specialist in the design of this complex type of building. He was the structural engineer for the Daily Express Building in Fleet Street (1929-1931), and had designed many other such facilities for the newspaper industry. Early in his career he had worked as an engineer for the architects Simpson & Ayrton on the British Empire Exhibition buildings at Wembley, including the Empire Stadium.

Early in the morning, as the sun shines on your building, it reflects light on the church opposite. It does so in such a way as to appear to point arrows towards the church. It's quite beautiful and moving. I have no idea if you realised your design would do this. If you did, I wanted you to know someone noticed, and if you didn't, it's quite a hidden treasure of the new lighting up the old and weaving their worlds together … Kindest regards and congratulations on a beautiful building, the effects of which have quite inspired me. Extract from a letter to Norman Foster from Amanda Mackenzie, whose office in Holborn overlooks 33 Holborn, 8 July 2003

1. Office floors at 33 Holborn (1993-2000) look into a full-height glazed atrium that opens up to address Holborn Circus.

2. Site plan of 50 Finsbury Square (1997-2000). The building is located pivotally at the south-west corner of the square, just north of the Moorgate approach to the City.

3. 50 Finsbury Square seen at dusk. In line with a planning requirement for a stone facade, the building has a stone frame with fixed louvres that wrap and shade a transparent cube of offices. The required setback at roof level has been exploited to create a terrace with commanding views of the square.

The challenge in designing any new commercial project in the City is to create a building that can both acknowledge its immediate context and stand discreetly on its own terms, something that The Walbrook does with notable success. Standing next to Wren's Church of St Stephen Walbrook and close to St Paul's Cathedral, it replaces an undistinguished group of offices from the 1950s.

The facade is articulated as a series of bays, which evoke the domestic scale of the buildings that would have stood here originally, and the cornice line is determined by the facade of Wren's church. Horizontal bands of reflective brise-soleil offer a contemporary statement in an area where planning guidance has traditionally favoured the use of stone. The louvres wrap the entire building, unifying the main volume with the receding upper levels, so that from the street the facade reads as a continuous arc.

It is at ground level that Foster makes the most intricate moves. On The Walbrook the facade is drawn back behind a colonnade, lined with shops and cafés; and to the rear, the building curves around a newly landscaped church garden – a refuge from the noise and activity of the street – that is reached by a new flight of steps. A public route through the site to St Swithin's Lane has also been reinstated.

Moving further afield, the building at Holborn Circus marks the point of transition from the City to the West End. Foster's instinct was to create a grand internal space that would have an axial relationship to the Circus, much as the atrium in the unbuilt BBC Radio Centre addressed Nash's All Souls. The deep site adapted naturally to a move of this kind, the atrium bringing daylight into the heart of the plan. A key aim was to restore views of the dome of St Paul's from Primrose Hill and the building's profile is therefore some 20 metres lower than that of its predecessor, making it naturally more sympathetic to the prevailing scale of Holborn.

Foster addresses a similar 'gateway' condition at Finsbury Square, which lies just north of the City boundary. The square is lined by commercial palazzi of up to nine storeys, ranging in date from the 1900s to the late 1980s. The site at the south-west corner of the square was an opportunity to create a 'marker' on the approach to the City. The planning constraints were severe, yet Foster was able to produce a distinctive building that seems at one with its context. Foster describes the building's outer shell – a stone structural frame, incorporating fixed horizontal louvres – as an 'eco-skeleton'. This forms an eroded masonry cube that wraps around and shades the glass-fronted office building within. At sixth-floor level the glazing is scooped back to create a terrace that provides a social space with fine views of the square.

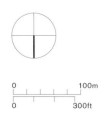

0   100m
0   300ft

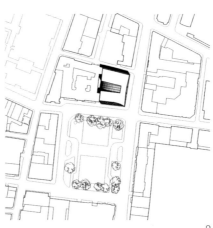

2

3

In the City of London, as in most places, design is subject to the democratic processes of consultation and discussion. That was the case with Finsbury Square – in a quite prescriptive way. One may not always agree with the limitations that often follow from such procedures, but one has to respect them and work within them. I once said that an architect complaining about planning regulations was like a sailor complaining about the weather. Norman Foster, in conversation with the editor, 2012

Extraordinary parts of the City exist and you have to look at the spirit of those environments and see how you can create something that is sympathetic to the space. Grant Brooker, of Foster + Partners, in conversation with the editor, 2011

5

4, 5. The Walbrook (2005-2010) occupies a compact City site close to the Mansion House and next to Wren's Church of St Stephen Walbrook. The facade is wrapped in a grid of highly reflective cast-aluminium brise-soleil. Shops animate the ground floor; and an ancient churchyard behind the building has been remodelled in the tradition of the City's intimate courts and gardens. The blades of the brise-soleil grow in density as they rise, responding to the increasing requirement for solar shading, and shimmering more intensively at the upper level. The break between the roof and the facade incorporates services systems and refers to the cornice line of Wren's church and the parapets of neighbouring buildings.

4

We had a million-square-foot building – the size of a tower in Canary Wharf – that had to fit within a medieval street pattern. The challenge was to get the human scale right. Because the building is designed in 'fingers' and is physically and visually permeable you hardly notice its size. We wanted to make sure that people who crossed from the City would stop, enjoy Spitalfields and maybe carry on to Brick Lane, so permeability was extremely important. We also tried to encourage more of a street culture, so we introduced wider pavements, cafés and entertainment – such as the musical events in the square. Michael Bear, Regeneration Director of Hammerson, in conversation with the editor, 2010

Spitalfields is probably our best example in London of public space because most of the ground plane is heavily populated with other activities. Yet it's very private above, as soon as you're beyond the first couple of storeys it could almost be residential. David Nelson, in conversation with the editor, 2012

The relationship between the Allen & Overy building, the existing buildings on Spitalfields, and the new covered marketplace, created an extraordinary change. It showed how the base of a building could be integrated with the community. Ironically, the new buildings with their cafés and restaurants are more active than the existing market building, which was restored. The space is very flexible and allows for a range of different tenants – from small units to bigger shops – all opening up to each other. The new tenants who came to work in the buildings were pleased to be there because it was already so alive and vibrant. That's very important. Grant Brooker, of Foster + Partners, in conversation with the editor, 2011

1. Looking towards the Allen & Overy headquarters building from Bishops Square (2001-2005). The development combines a mix of uses – offices, apartments, community facilities, cafés and restaurants – with a network of public spaces, including a square larger than the piazza at Covent Garden.

2. A plan of the development at street level, showing how public spaces and amenities are woven through it.

3. The roof of the Allen & Overy building is arranged as a series of terraces, with gardens overlooking the square below.

4. A shopping promenade runs behind the retained market buildings on Brushfield Street; the spire of Christ Church is visible through the roof canopy.

5, 6. The covered public space at Crispin Square forms a link between the new office development and the Victorian market buildings.

7. Among the amenities on Bishops Square is a tented structure that forms a venue for concerts and other events.

At the eastern boundary of the City is the area known as Spitalfields, which grew up in the early eighteenth century as a centre of the Huguenot silk weaving industry. However, as its fortunes changed over succeeding centuries Spitalfields gradually declined, its fine houses used as sweatshops or worse. Many were demolished, a tragedy that led to the formation of the Spitalfields Trust and the restoration campaign that has seen numerous houses rescued by a wave of affluent incomers, who rub shoulders with the Bengali community that grew up here from the 1970s.

The decision to close Spitalfields Market in 1986 generated a further crisis in the area. The market had occupied the site since the late seventeenth century but had been rebuilt in 1883-93 and much extended in the 1920s. With the City booming, and the Broadgate complex looming just across Bishopsgate, the obvious use for the site seemed to be as offices for the expanding financial services industry, an outcome opposed by the conservation lobby at the time.

When Foster was appointed to rethink the development, the existing masterplan allowed for the retention of the listed Victorian market buildings, while the 1920s extensions to the west were to be redeveloped. The scheme received a huge impetus when the legal practice of Allen & Overy agreed to pre-let the entire development to house some 4,000 staff.

The offices are arranged in four parallel stepped blocks, of five, nine, eleven and seven storeys respectively. The plan form results from the lawyers' requirement for a mix of open plan and cellular space. It also helps to break down the building's perceived scale (it is in fact 65 per cent larger than 30 St Mary Axe). The office floors are punctuated by three relatively narrow atria and service cores. By far the most striking feature is the provision of rooftop gardens on the lower blocks, beautifully landscaped and used by staff at lunchtimes and for summer parties.

What reads most positively from street level is the scheme's vital element of public space. Firstly, there is Bishops Square, with its raised gardens, mature trees and, an unexpected addition, the remains of an ancient charnel house, preserved as the centrepiece of a sunken piazza. Then there is the pedestrian arcade, the spire of Christ Church visible through its glazed roof – a classic townscape vista – which extends eastward from the square, hugging the offices to one side and the retained brick pavilions of the 1920s market to the other, the latter converted to provide flats above shops.

Beyond the arcade is Crispin Square, a lofty glass-roofed extension to the Victorian market, which is packed with stalls and lined along its southern side with restaurants and cafés. The bold, industrial structure enclosing it is in the spirit of nineteenth-century market halls: structures that Foster has long admired.

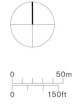

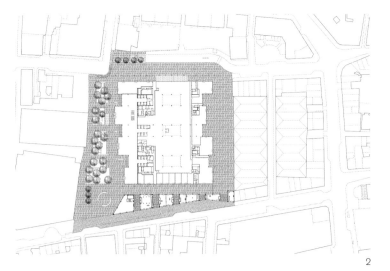

0 50m
0 150ft

2

3

Right: Charnel House, a fourteenth-century chapel, was discovered during archaeological excavations on the Bishops Square site and has been preserved below street level within a sunken courtyard. It is protected by glass paving, which also serves to light the space naturally.

The way that we engaged with the community was to give people cameras to document the sort of place that they would like to see. They wanted lawn, they wanted art that would be alive – so we have a six-month programme where the sculpture is changed. They were keen that the history of the site should not be lost, so we buried parts of the archaeology in light boxes. If you look around the hard landscaping you'll find every now and again a little box with a piece of pottery, or musket balls, or workers' pipes. They were also pleased that we preserved the Charnel House chapel and that you could go and look at it.
Michael Bear, Regeneration Director of Hammerson, in conversation with the editor, 2010

4

5

6

7

Sol LeWitt had an extraordinary ability to distil the multi-dimensional entities of space, context and culture into the language of painting. I saw first hand how he was able to intuit – and then express – the architectural 'spirit' of a building with energy and conceptual clarity. Our first collaboration was here at Tower Place, where he created two wall pieces. Magisterial in scale, they frame the piazza and establish a strong connection between inside and outside. Their vivid colour and strong geometry also combine to evoke the tradition of medieval heraldry, which is very appropriate in this ancient part of the City. Norman Foster, in conversation with the editor, 2012

1. The atrium of Tower Place (1992-2002) was conceived as very much an extension of the public realm – a continuation of the precinct of All Hallows by the Tower.

2. A detail of the limestone cladding and aluminium brise-soleil of the east building.

3. The glass wall of the atrium floats free of the ground, so that there is no threshold between atrium and piazza.

The atrium is in the spirit of the great nineteenth-century arcades, an urban route but also a place to pause and enjoy – a space of civic dignity.

Norman Foster

1

2

3

Willis Faber introduced the idea of the 'groundscraper' – a low-rise, deep-plan, energy-conscious office building. Then we could only consider such a revolution in office design because the client was an owner occupier. Thirty years later we are replacing obsolete 1960s office towers with lower-rise structures for progressive developers. What was once avant-garde has entered the mainstream. Norman Foster, in conversation with the editor, 2012
Far left, left: Willis Faber & Dumas (1971-1975); the building sits comfortably within its low-rise context.
Right: Norman Foster's early sketch for Willis Faber challenges the ubiquity of the office tower.

I would say that the Willis Faber building is one of the most successful urban interventions of the twentieth century. I think what Norman did there was a masterstroke. It showed that it is possible to put two very strong things together – a bold and striking building within a long established and dense urban presence. David Chipperfield, in conversation with the editor, 2005

The redevelopment of Spitalfields Market is inevitably the result of a compromise that will not please everyone. Yet the predicted transformation of the area into yet another office district has not happened. What remains in the memory are the public spaces and the commitment to mixed-use as part of the area's regeneration. It is a development from which the East End has genuinely profited.

Tower Place, completed in 2002 on a site close to the Tower of London – a World Heritage Site – is another project in which commercial development has produced real community benefits. It is significant not just for its distinction, but for its contribution to repairing the damage inflicted on the City by mundane post-war redevelopment. The site was formerly occupied by a depressing complex of aggregate-faced blocks linked by pedestrian decks ('remarkably grubby', commented *The Buildings of England*) that intruded into distant views of both the Tower and St Paul's and created a dismal context for the neighbouring church of All Hallows by the Tower.

Perhaps more than any of the projects considered here, Tower Place echoes themes introduced by Willis Faber and goes a step further, giving the City a new sheltered public space. By dividing the accommodation into two seven-storey blocks, a connection is re-established between the Tower and Great Tower Street, the riverside and All Hallows.

The two buildings are triangular in plan, with rounded corners, their fluid forms evoking the irregular grain of the City. Flowing between and around them is a piazza, which extends to embrace All Hallows. In fine weather, this new space is well used by City workers. However, given London's climate, the enclosure of part of the piazza within a glazed atrium is a welcome feature. The space is protected from the weather but is neither strictly external nor internal, the glazed wall that forms the enclosure being suspended a full storey height above pavement level. A remarkable feature are the slender glass struts or 'needles' that tie the glazing back to the columns.

With their sweeping roofs – kept free from visual clutter – the two office buildings make a positive contribution to the riverside scene, looking across to More London on the South Bank. Those working here enjoy some of the most attractive views from any City office building, but it is emphatically in terms of its public and urban dimension that Tower Place stands apart from most recent office projects. It exemplifies Foster's belief that commercial development must respond not only to the needs of its users but equally to the life of the city. This conviction extends throughout the Foster office's work worldwide, but is nowhere more clearly demonstrated than in the City of London.

Kenneth Powell

4. A view along the executive floor of the east building.

5. Sol LeWitt's mural in the lobby of the west building; there is a partner mural by LeWitt in the lobby of the east building.

6. Cross-section through the atrium; seven floors of offices sit above two levels of parking for cars and tourist buses.

Overleaf: Looking out through the suspended glass wall of the atrium towards the spire of All Hallows.

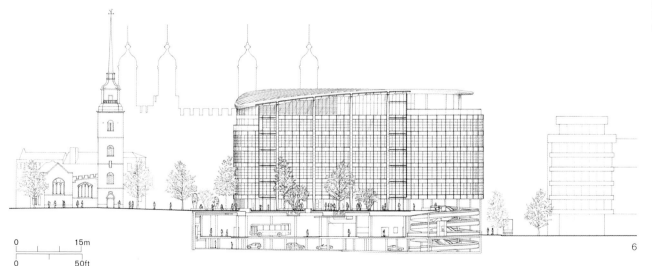

0   15m

0   50ft

6

Leslie L Dan Pharmacy Building

Toronto, Canada 2002–2006

1

During the past fifteen years, the University of Toronto has undertaken an extensive programme of renewal and development. Situated in the heart of a city that is booming, its urban campus is hemmed in on all sides, so significant lateral expansion has not been a viable option. Instead, the university has intensified the fabric of the existing campus by the insertion of new buildings and extensive reworking of the ground plane to create a varied, yet coherent network of spaces that knit buildings and landscape together.

The entrance atrium provides both a social centre for the pharmacy school and a major public space that connects this south-east corner of the campus to the city.

The Leslie L Dan Pharmacy Building transforms a key site at the corner of College Street, which is the boundary between the campus and a mix of commercial and residential areas to the south, and University Avenue, a major north-south boulevard, which leads to Ontario's Provincial Parliament, located east of the site. This pivotal piece of ground was formerly occupied by university glasshouses that turned their backs to the street. To free the site, the university negotiated with the authorities to move one glasshouse, designated as a heritage structure, to a nearby city park and to restore it for public use; the remainder were demolished.

In 2002, the university held an invited competition in which architects presented to a public audience an approach to the project rather than a scheme. When Foster + Partners was appointed at the conclusion of this process, the university's development plan included an approved five-storey building envelope on the site, scaled to be equal in height to adjacent historic buildings to the north and west and to the Parliament building across the street.

The university's aim for the new building – which includes laboratories, classrooms and faculty offices – was to consolidate the pharmacy faculty, previously dispersed across the campus, in a new and identifiable home and to enable it to more than double its enrolment. 'What quickly became clear,' notes senior partner David Nelson, 'was that the programme for the building would not fit within the approved envelope without extensive and costly basements, so we had to devise a different strategy for dealing with the historic context.'

The design team – led by David Nelson and Nigel Dancey – tackled the problem by analysing the brief and demonstrating that it naturally split into two parts. Research labs, the largest component in area, had only a small population of faculty and graduate students. In contrast, undergraduates, who comprise 90 per cent of the building's population, were concentrated in teaching labs and classrooms. The scheme therefore logically concentrates the densely populated undergraduate facilities near ground level and puts research labs on the upper floors.

Faced with such a large programme on a tight site, many architects would have sought to minimise or even omit public space. To the contrary, the Foster team's response was to dedicate half of the site footprint to a five-storey public atrium, with labs, offices and a mechanical floor compactly planned on eight levels above, and two lecture halls in basements below. These three, stacked programmatic zones are united by a 9-metre-wide east-west light slot that penetrates the full height and depth of the building. In addition to connecting all floors visually, this void provides a focus for the building's vertical circulation.

The laboratory floors are efficiently planned and flexible. The plan is zoned in east-west bands with faculty offices on the north face of the building, graduate student offices looking into the light slot, traditional wet labs, lab support spaces, and a mix of offices and lab support on the south face of the building.

2

3

1. Seen here illuminated at night, the five-storey colonnaded area that forms the lower part of the building. This transparent volume forms the hub of under-graduate activities and offers a window on to the campus. The space can be variously illuminated in red, green and blue, and reflections of the pods in the darkened glazing generate a striking image.

2, 3. The Pharmacy Building occupies a key position on Queen's Park, at the south-east corner of the University of Ontario campus, adjacent to the Ontario Legislature and the Royal Ontario Museum.

1

1. The five-storey colonnaded element provides the building with a public face and is configured to align with the 20-metre cornice heights of nearby university buildings.

2. Cutaway perspective. The building provides state-of-the-art facilities for more than 1,000 undergraduate and postgraduate students, creating the largest pharmacy faculty in Canada. There are fourteen floors – twelve above and two below ground. The colonnaded circulation space also houses a resource centre, study spaces and administrative offices, and provides access between the basement lecture theatres and the laboratories and the library above. The upper floors contain postgraduate student and faculty research facilities. An atrium slot runs up through the building, providing visual connections between all floors.

2

'We wanted a space that was really good for the researchers to work in, because we were hiring a lot of faculty. One of the new faculty members can't believe how successful she's been since working here because she's able to get people from the USA to come and do post-doctoral training. Once they see the building everyone says 'Oh, I'd love to work there!' K Wayne Hindmarsh, Professor and Dean Emeritus, Leslie L Dan Faculty of Pharmacy, in conversation with the editor, 2010

We inverted the standard diagram by putting the laboratory block at the higher level. By aligning the datum with the cornice of the existing block and putting the labs above we could achieve highly rationalised floors which filled the whole floor plate. These could then be stacked one above the other in a very sensible, logical manner. This allowed us to open up the space below to facilitate circulation and create the communal open spaces. David Nelson, in conversation with the editor, 2012

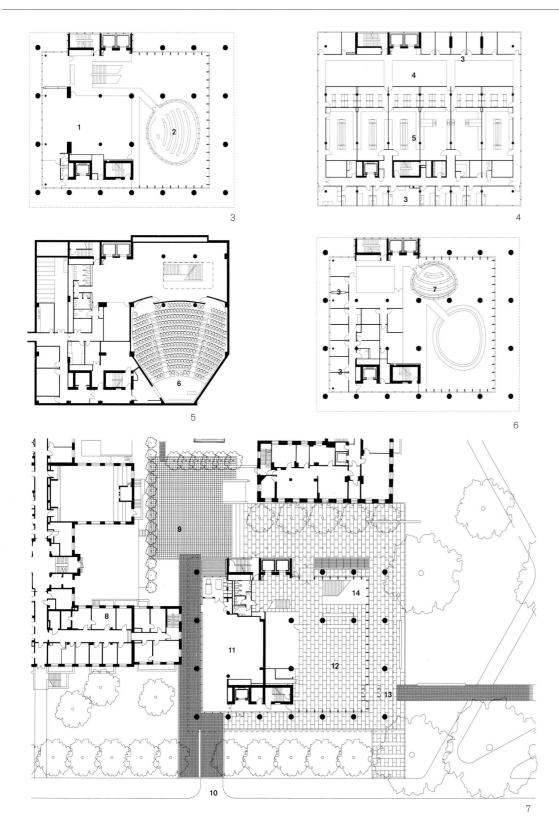

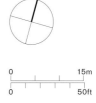

3. First floor plan.

4. Typical upper-level plan.

5. Lower ground floor plan.

6. Third floor plan.

7. Ground floor plan.

8. One of the postgraduate research labs on the upper floors.

9. There are two undergraduate lecture theatres, located below ground level.

1 learning resource centre
2 60-seat lecture theatre
3 offices
4 void
5 laboratories
6 300-seat lecture theatre
7 25-seat lecture theatre
8 Fitzgerald Building
9 external courtyard
10 pedestrian link
11 loading dock
12 seating/café area
13 entrance
14 stairs down to lecture
   theatre

0   15m
0   50ft

It's always interesting to trace connections between projects, but it's only recently that I realised the link between our building in Toronto and our scheme for the Hôtel du Département in Marseilles, a competition we entered in 1990. It was the first time we'd experimented with abstract forms, or 'eggs', as counterpoints to large atrium spaces – an idea we re-examined here. The Marseilles eggs were bigger, but their function is very similar – containing council chambers and auditoria. The Toronto eggs are lighter and seem more fragile – the product of a more delicate bird!
Norman Foster, in conversation with the editor, 2012
Left: Norman Foster's sketch of the cavernous Marseilles Hôtel du Département atrium with its twin ovoid auditoria.

1. Looking down through the atrium to the smaller of the two 'pods'.

2-4. Two silver-coloured pods are suspended within the colonnaded space. The larger, lower, of the two pods houses a sixty-seat lecture theatre and a reading room. The smaller one contains a twenty-five-seat classroom and the faculty lounge. The pods are suspended on 100mm-diameter steel rods; six rods support the large pod and four the small one.

Movement along the north side of the light slot provides access to faculty offices, with bridges across the void to graduate student offices and labs. On the east and west faces of the building, circulation routes gain panoramic views of the city. To the south, the double-loaded corridor provides direct connections between offices, laboratories and support spaces.

The central laboratory zone is planned in 6 x 10.5 metre modules. On the upper research levels, these are typically organised into six labs per floor, with the potential to join modules if larger labs are required. In contrast, on floors five through seven just above the atrium, the graduate student office zone and laboratory modules combine to create large undergraduate teaching labs capable of handling classes of 120 students. Laboratory services are exposed on slab soffits, providing easy access for maintenance and adaptation to particular research requirements.

As they move through the atrium, faculty, students and visitors help to animate the university's public presence at this key juncture in the city.

In addition to being the hub of undergraduate activities, the entrance atrium provides both a social centre for the pharmacy school and a major public space that connects this south-east corner of the campus to the city. Overlooked by student computer lounges and offices above, the atrium is activated by a café at ground level and two egg-shaped pods, which are suspended within the space on steel hangers. The larger pod houses a classroom with an open study lounge above. The smaller pod, which floats within the light slot, contains a computer classroom with a faculty lounge on top. The school's dean, who occupies a fully glazed office on the fourth floor, has sweeping views of the atrium and is highly visible within this public zone of the building.

The atrium is the product of lateral thinking, or what Nelson calls 'a different take' on the relationship to the neighbouring historic buildings. He recalls, 'We thought about Mies van der Rohe's Federal Center scheme in Chicago, particularly the way in which the positive volume of the two-storey post office combines with the double-height entrance lobbies of the towers to create a connecting datum across the site. In Toronto, the 20-metre high atrium matches the cornice heights of the historic buildings, allowing clear views through the site of these neighbouring buildings, while the new labs hover above.'

The taut skin of the building supports this contextual strategy. On upper floors, a sleek curtain wall forms a veil comprising transparent, finely fritted vision panels that offer sunshading, and opaque spandrel panels with a dot frit. By day, the simple volume of the tower has a unified but textured appearance, while by night it is punctuated by horizontal bands of light. In contrast, the glass envelope of the entrance atrium maximises views through the site. Set back behind the fair-faced concrete columns, the glazing here is wind braced internally by 400mm-deep steel-plate fins, which also carry theatre lights to illuminate the pods dynamically at night.

Both by day and by night, the pharmacy building creates a new threshold to the university that connects directly to the subway station at the corner of College and University streets, as well as serving the significant pedestrian population travelling between the teaching hospitals and the campus. Moving around and through the atrium, faculty, students, staff and visitors help to animate the university's public presence at this key juncture in the city. The strategic value of this location has not gone unnoticed by the Provincial legislature. Since the building's completion, many televised press conferences have been staged in the atrium, extending the public impact of this new building from its locus in the city to a regional and national constituency.

Annette LeCuyer

Because we wanted to create circulation at the lower level and allow people views through the space, adding a lot of floors there would have been inappropriate. However, we still wanted some contained accommodation so the logical progression was to create the pods. In order to gain the maximum amount of usable space from these we incorporated meeting areas and common rooms on their top surface. David Nelson, in conversation with the editor, 2012
Right, far right: the steel-framed hulls of the pods under construction.

2

The lower floors form a colonnaded study area – a generous daylit volume punctuated by the silvery forms of the 'pods' overhead. This space is the hub of undergraduate activities – a link between the lecture theatres, laboratories and library.

Norman Foster

3

4

Business Academy Bexley

Thamesmead, England 2001–2003

We liked the idea of a business academy because it might give a flavour of the sort of environment in which some of the children might work in their future lives. There is a suggestion of an office environment and that is intentional. We even have a mini dealing floor in the entrance hall, which relates to the City of London and ways of working there. It is filled with natural light and, importantly, wherever you are in the building you are aware of the total entity – everybody feels a part of the school community, not isolated in separate classrooms or buildings on their own. It is very much one building and one organisation. Spencer de Grey, in conversation with Susan Marling, 'Designs for Learning', BBC Radio 3, 26 March 2006

To those who fear radical change – and who claim we would be better off not tampering with the comprehensive schools we inherited from the 1960s – I say: come here to Thamesmead, visit the local community, hear about the failed school of the past, compare it with the Business Academy which is already becoming a beacon of hope and aspiration to the whole community, and see what a change for the better has taken place. Prime Minister Tony Blair, speaking at the opening of Business Academy Bexley, 18 September 2003
Left: Thamesmead Community College, which the Business Academy replaced.

The Business Academy Bexley was the first of a new series of UK secondary schools designed under the Academies programme, introduced in spring 2000. The programme promotes the building of schools to replace those that are underperforming, in some of the country's most economically deprived areas. Funding in each case comes directly from central government, in the form of the then DfES, as opposed to the local education authority, and supplements £2m capital from an individual or corporate sponsor. Architecturally, as well as educationally, this unusual funding arrangement has resulted in a significant breakthrough in school design, partly, says Spencer de Grey 'because the enthusiasm of the sponsors is reflected in the schools – and individuality is celebrated'.

In the case of the Business Academy Bexley, the sponsor, Sir David Garrard, approached Norman Foster directly. The two had an established professional relationship and Garrard was confident that the Foster studio would embrace his vision of an open-plan, light-filled building without corridors, reflecting a 'grown-up' environment more than a school. Little did he realise that for Foster this was a long-awaited opportunity to realise ideas he had put forward in the competition for Newport School as long ago as 1967. The school was never built, although some of the planning principles were realised at the Lycée Albert Camus in Fréjus (1991-1993), which has a large light-filled space at its heart. Here was an opportunity to develop the concept further.

The Newport School is a precursor to the studio's designs for the Academies programme in several significant ways. Firstly, one of the intentions of the DfES and in particular of Sir David Garrard at Bexley, is that the academies should prepare students for life after they have left school, both by way of the subjects offered, and by the nature of the built environment in which they learn. Like the Newport School, the Business Academy has been designed to foster a sense of community and aid orientation. In both schemes, students and teachers can see into partially open-plan teaching spaces.

The enthusiasm of the sponsors is reflected in the schools – and individuality is celebrated.

Senior partner Grant Brooker and his team developed the design together with the sponsor and the educationalist Valerie Bragg (formerly a head teacher at one of the City Technology Colleges). In her new role as one of the founders of the schools regeneration company 3Es, Bragg acted as the project manager with responsibility to the DfES. The collective desire was for a school that would be transparent, both physically and in its methods of working, and which would have a series of clearly defined focuses.

1

Opposite: The Business Academy Bexley represents a radical departure from educational norms – it was the first purpose-built, part-privately funded independent state school in Europe. Portraits of students and staff in the business court are intended to foster a sense of community.

1. Approaching the school's main entrance.

2. Cross-section through the art and technology courtyards. The building has a double-layered facade to minimise energy use; external louvres automatically track the sun's path to provide shade and reduce heat gain during the summer months.

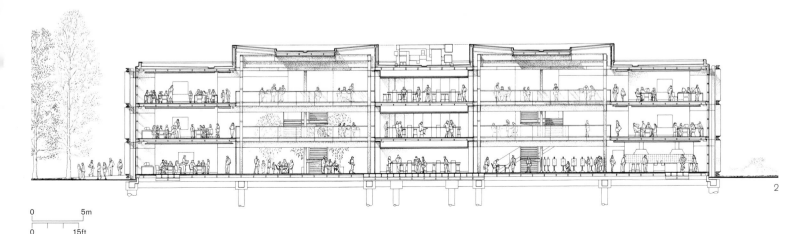

0   5m

0   15ft

2

In the late 1960s I was drawing visionary schools that would be open-planned, filled with light, democratic and flexible, with no corridors, no institutional barriers and with a philosophy of integration. Today, we have realised that school in Bexley. Norman Foster, speaking at the opening of the Business Academy Bexley, 18 September 2003
Far left, left: Drawing and model of Newport School, Wales (1967); a school without walls in the conventional sense, it was conceived in opposition to the prevailing conventional, closed and strongly hierarchical school model.

1. An early study model of the school. The design emphasises open, transparent and compact spaces to encourage integration, communication and cross-fertilisation between students of all age groups, students and teachers, students and visitors, and all the different educational disciplines in the curriculum. Teaching spaces are separated from each other by partitions – which are designed to be moved to change the sizes of teaching areas or adapt them for other uses – but are open to circulation space and courtyard space. There are no corridors and circulation occurs through the business court, art court and technology court at ground level or along the courtyards at levels one and two.

1

'We had to decide', explains Brooker, 'how we could make a model for this type of interaction and this kind of openness and visibility. In educational terms it's unusual, but in the workplace it's actually a very well investigated model.' The result is a school structured around three open, toplit courts, one each for business, art and technology. On the ground floor of these courts are open working areas, above which some classrooms open directly on to the circulation gallery and are separated from each other by partitions that can be moved to alter the sizes of teaching areas or to adapt them for other uses.

Like the Newport School, the Business Academy has been designed to foster a sense of community and aid orientation.

Other spaces, including the science labs, are environmentally sealed by means of a glazed wall, which still allows for uninterrupted visibility across the building. Acoustic insulation is provided by perforated metal panels in the soffit of each classroom space and carpets have been fitted wherever appropriate to help to absorb sound. Most importantly, there are no enclosed corridors, which helps to eliminate noisy pressure points at busy change-over periods in the day. 'The essence of the school', explains Brooker, 'is not so much that it is open plan, but that it is physically open. It is transparent and layered.'

Immediately to the left of the main entrance is the open-plan restaurant, which serves the pupils from as early as seven in the morning and acts as the social heart of the building. Opposite the entrance, in the business court, a mini stock exchange is set up beneath a dramatic photo wall depicting every pupil and member of staff.

The stock exchange is a physical reminder of the school's business emphasis, while the portraits above give the students a sense of ownership and community. A two-storey theatre and gymnasium also share this end of the building, but contrary to convention are elevated on the first floor in order to group all the social space together at ground level.

This clustering together of the larger facilities also means that the northern end of the building can be securely closed off when the school is being used for public events. The academies are seen by the government as the catalyst for much wider urban regeneration in particularly deprived areas, and this kind of integration with the community is encouraged wherever possible.

In order to ensure that the new building is safely linked to the surrounding residential estates the team demolished an existing foot bridge, which was a notorious black spot for physical assaults and therefore largely unused, and replaced it with a toucan crossing. For many of the children it is important that the building gives them a sense of security and wellbeing that might otherwise be missing from their lives. In some ways its external appearance provides a metaphor for the protective, necessarily inward-looking nature of the school, as well as expressing the low-energy environmental strategy. Most of the classrooms and all the court spaces are naturally ventilated; the soffits are exposed precast concrete slabs which provide thermal mass for cooling. The science labs, technology rooms, art rooms and music and media recording rooms are necessarily mechanically ventilated. The building's double-layered facade is designed to reduce heat loss in winter and heat gain during the summer; external shading louvres prevent glare.

As with many education projects, the timeframe for building the Business Academy was extremely tight. Planning permission was granted in December 2001 and the first phase had to be completed for the start of the school year in September 2002.

With Bexley we had many months talking with the DfES, with David Garrard and his team – the educationalists he brought in to advise him. There was a very healthy period I think in which the ideas for the school changed and developed as we came forward with design ideas and everybody else responded from their point of view. There was a very good dialogue in those early meetings and I think that shows in the final product. Spencer de Grey, in conversation with Susan Marling, 'Designs for Learning', BBC Radio 3, 26 March 2006

The Academies programme signalled a moment in the UK when people realised that we were going to start spending more on education. The programme was about replacing failing schools, not just changing an existing school's buildings. We were changing every aspect, so while this meant a new building it also meant a new approach and a completely new educational regime and because Bexley was the first we felt an almost overwhelming sense of responsibility. Grant Brooker, of Foster + Partners, in conversation with the editor, 2011
Left: A classroom in the old Thamesmead Community College, which the Business Academy replaced.

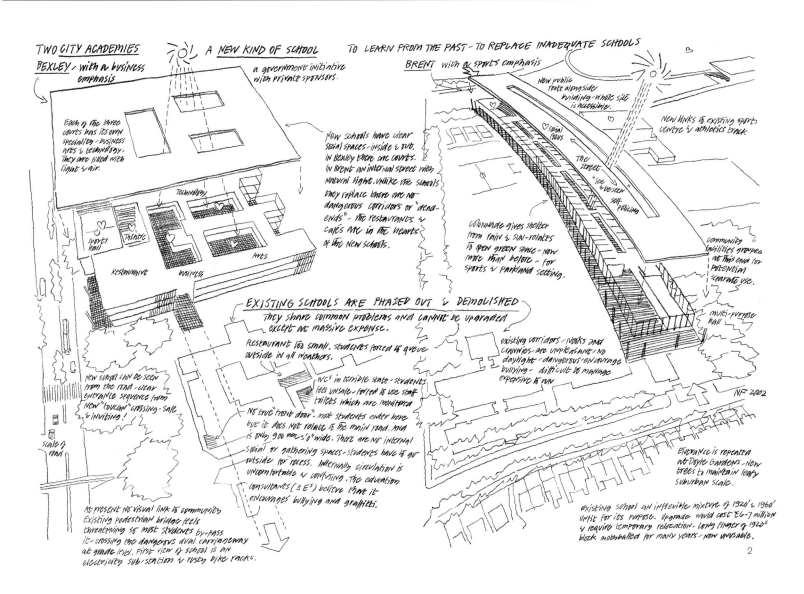

Bexley was the first new Academy. Even before it opened, over 200 parents had made it their first choice of school – a remarkable act of faith.

Norman Foster

2. In this drawing – which formed part of the narrative of an exhibition at the British Museum – Norman Foster outlines two different architectural strategies for the practice's first two academies: the courtyard scheme for Bexley, and the 'street' scheme for the Capital City Academy in Brent.

My aspiration for the Business Academy is that it will produce students whose academic achievements are consistent with the top schools in the UK; and, just as importantly, students with self-confidence and self esteem, a sense of responsibility for themselves, one another and the community as a whole – well adjusted young people of integrity and principle, who look forward to going out into the real world knowing that it is a place where the education, training and the guidance they have received makes that world welcoming as opposed to intimidating or frightening. David Garrard, sponsor of the Business Academy Bexley, in conversation with the editor, 2002

Left: David Garrard, the sponsor of the Business Academy Bexley, speaks to students. As chairman of the property investment and development group, Minerva plc, Garrard has over many years combined his commercial activities with an involvement in both charity and public service work. He is chairman of the trustees of the International Centre for Child Studies; patron of Handicapped Children's Aid; trustee of the Police Foundation; a patron of the Philip Green Memorial Trust; a director of the British Property Federation; and sits on the steering committee of the business expansion committee of the Prince's Trust.

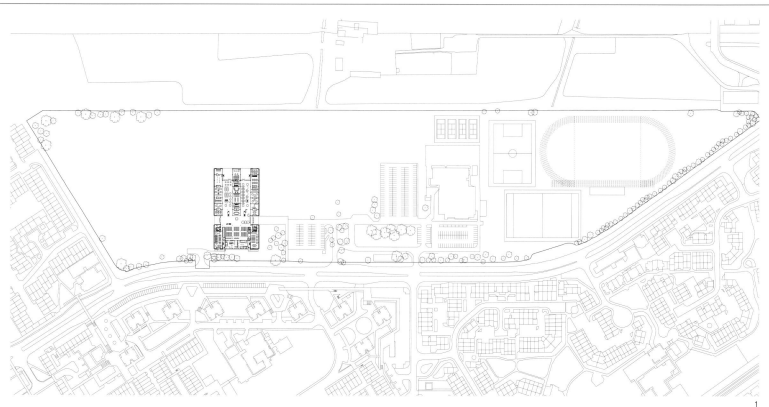

1

1. Site plan.

2. A colour-coded plan by Norman Foster: classrooms are blue; circulation yellow; theatre orange; sports hall green; and plant rooms grey.

3, 4. Ground floor and level one plans.

1 technology studio
2 cooking studio
3 classroom
4 staff room
5 laboratory
6 technology court
7 meeting room
8 business court
9 café
10 kitchen
11 plant room
12 art court
13 art room
14 administration
15 student centre
16 auditorium
17 sports hall

| 0 | | | | 100m |
| 0 | | | | 300ft |

Bexley 2003
– courtyard

2

3

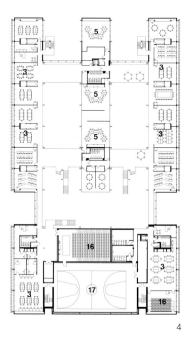

4

| 0 | | 20m |
| 0 | | 60ft |

The team agreed to build one complete section, approximately 10 per cent of the scheme, which would give all the users of the school an idea of what to expect when the building was opened in its entirety a year later, in September 2003. The aim of the design team was to give the academy a robust building that can withstand the wear and tear of school life. Both students and staff report feelings of initial disbelief and then pride when they saw the professional, polished appearance of the first phase, which included an internet café, a lecture theatre and various teaching areas.

In the year before its transformation as the Business Academy the school's predecessor, Thamesmead Community College, recorded the worst set of GCSE exam results in the country. There were no students interested in, or capable of, moving into the sixth form, and the majority of the school's external walls were covered in graffiti. Just one year later, in 2003, the GCSE results had improved elevenfold, the sixth form was reinstated with 86 students, and there were no incidents of graffiti on the campus.

The Foster team is quick to acknowledge that it takes an enormous shift in the management of a school to bring these changes about, but all, including the academy's head teacher, Tom Widdows, agree that the architecture has gone a long way towards realising the untapped potential of the students. The physical transparency and compact nature of the court structure has promoted integration and communication between departments and across different age groups. It has also increased the level of visibility throughout the school, resulting in a much calmer environment that is largely self-policing.

The students are proud of their school, and treat it accordingly. Many of them can't believe their luck and spend as many hours as possible in the building, only leaving when it is locked at seven in the evening. This turnaround in fortunes is reflected in the Business Academy's 'code': respect for self; respect for others; respect for your environment – all of which is becoming second nature to the young residents of Thamesmead.

Nicola Jackson

The courtyards form the essence – the heart – of the building with the teaching spaces related to them visually. As you enter, you orient yourself immediately.

Spencer de Grey

5. The business court is the social hub of the school, housing a café at ground level, with access to a theatre, television studio and gym above. It also houses a mini stock exchange, which offers students their first taste of City trading.

Overleaf: Courtyards link the teaching spaces visually and functionally on different levels. This is the art courtyard, viewed from the balcony on level one.

The children greeted the new school with a mixture of elation and disbelief. For most of them it was the most extraordinary building they had ever been in and they found it hard to believe that it was going to be their school. That pride gives the teachers a fantastic head start because people are genuinely excited to be there. Grant Brooker, of Foster + Partners, in conversation with the editor, 2011

If you look around it's just marvellous. I like it because everything is really open and light and it doesn't feel like a school. I like the boardroom on the ground floor. It's in the centre of everything. Everyone can see you, but no one can hear you. Year nine student, Business Academy Bexley, in conversation with the editor, 2003

We were so disillusioned by the schools in the area that we were considering moving away. However, when we attended an open evening about the academy, everything changed. Everybody was dedicated to encouraging the students to develop whatever talents they may have. David Garrard talked about the ethos of the academy, about teaching children to believe in themselves and giving them opportunities we never dreamed they would have here. I want to give my daughter the best and to know that she is in safe hands. Jennie McClymont, one of the first parents to send their child to the Business Academy, in conversation with the editor, 2003

In the English department we have noticed how the building and the structure of the open plan and the close proximity of the classrooms has really helped team dynamics within our department. Moving between classes during lessons, sharing resources and administratively the open-plan design works incredibly well. Learning Manager, English, Business Academy Bexley, in conversation with the editor, 2003

Students come into the theatre and they are just inspired by what they see. There is so much opportunity for them, and when it comes to exams they are going to be able to have the whole 'theatre experience' when they perform. They recognise that they are not just doing drama; they are really performing – it's real – and it's a really incredible opportunity for the students and for me as a teacher as well. To be able to come here, use these facilities and know that if I want to do something with the students nothing will stand in the way is a great feeling. Claire Faulkener, Learning Manager, drama, Business Academy Bexley, in conversation with the editor, 2003

As a designer it's inspirational to work in here. It's a really good opportunity for everyone who is here. I'd love to be in year seven now and just starting out. Sixth-form student, Business Academy Bexley, in conversation with the editor, 2003

Capital City Academy
London, England 2000–2003

1. The school has a gently curving, linear plan with a covered promenade lining the long elevation overlooking the sports field. The building assumes a local scale and is orientated to create a new public route, which allows access to the whole site.

2, 3. Stone benches create gathering points in the school's covered forecourt.

At the same time as the Business Academy Bexley was being designed, another team in the Foster studio, this time headed by Spencer de Grey and Simon Bowden, was working on a new academy to replace the notoriously underperforming Willesden High School, in Brent, north-west London. As with the Business Academy, the design for Capital City Academy promotes flexibility of use, with classrooms arranged either side of an internal street – a direct development of the plan of the Lycée Albert Camus at Fréjus. The linear plan form is also a response to the site and to a low-energy strategy that relies on natural ventilation, with the street providing a generous sized central circulation space in place of corridors.

At Capital, existing school buildings to the south had to remain open during construction, so one of the early proposals was to build to the north of the site, where it would also be possible to introduce a link to the Willesden Sports Centre. The disadvantage of this was that it moved the school away from its known address on Doyle Gardens; hence the solution to stretch the building along the site's eastern edge, from Doyle Gardens up to the sports centre. This resulted in the majority of the site to the west being freed up for sports fields.

The importance of an association with the local sports centre, which was to be refurbished by the council, and the quality and quantity of sports facilities relates to the sponsorship of Capital City Academy by Sir Frank Lowe. With a professional background in sports management, he was keen to sponsor an academy specialising in sport. As with the sponsors of other academies, he contributed to the design development, bringing experience from a wide variety of disciplines, including his involvement in the worlds of advertising and the arts.

The central street is entered via a lobby and reception, which leads into a large entrance hall with tables and chairs set out for cold lunches, designed to create an informal environment much like a village square. This space also doubles as a foyer for the main hall alongside it, a flexible space that can be used for assemblies, performances or exhibitions. The deeper classrooms – workshops and laboratories – are accommodated on the eastern side of the street, with shallower spaces for general teaching overlooking the playing fields to the west.

The design of the school consciously takes account of its role within the wider community.

From the entrance at Doyle Gardens, to the sports hall at the northern end of the building, the site rises by 3.5 metres. The architecture capitalises on this, turning the street, which starts with the generous triple-height entrance, into a gently sloping ramp. Unlike the straight street at Fréjus, Capital's street is curved, creating a more dynamic space. Approximately halfway along its length, after the first of a series of bridges which link the two wings of the building, one storey is lost and the volume at the furthest end of the building drops to two storeys. This has the advantage of creating some classroom and studio spaces that are one-and-a-half or two-storeys high, which can be used for music, dance and drama – disciplines that benefit from the increased volume. Beneath the bridges, the street widens to accommodate study areas for out-of-class research, and to allow additional circulation space during busy change-over periods.

The sports hall, which is sized in accordance with Sport England guidelines for national and county standards, and therefore requires a greatly increased volume, is sunk partially below ground, so that it can be accommodated at the higher end of the site, at the same time as reducing its mass visually.

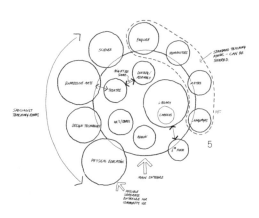

4. Approaching the school's entrance loggia.

5. With a tripartite client group consisting of the school, DfES and sponsor, bubble diagrams such as this proved a useful way of conveying information and stimulating discussion. This diagram looks at ways of organising the school's internal space: smaller, non-specialist teaching rooms are grouped together in one location while specialist functions requiring greater space are located on the opposite side. Spaces which can potentially be used for multiple functions are also highlighted, demonstrating the benefits of a flexible approach to space planning.

The Academies programme first attracted me because it provides a chance for schools in situations where the previous system has failed. It also provides opportunities for many children who come from the under-privileged part of our society. We hope it will be a great success for the children and their families, the teachers and for the wider community of Brent. Sir Frank Lowe speaking at the opening of Capital City Academy, 12 June 2003
Right: Norman Foster and Sir Frank Lowe at the school's opening ceremony.

Frank Lowe helped set up a very good relationship with the DfES and in the end what is so great about the Academies programme is you get someone from outside who has been successful in their own particular sphere and who has the direction, drive and enthusiasm to make things happen and I think this kind of fusion of private individuals and government organisation has the potential to be very successful. Simon Bowden, formerly of Foster + Partners, in conversation with the editor, 2011

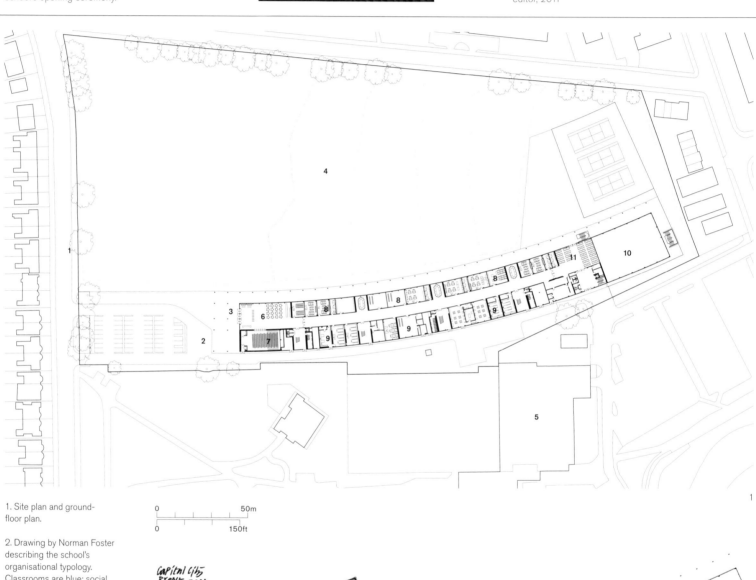

1. Site plan and ground-floor plan.

0   50m
0   150ft

2. Drawing by Norman Foster describing the school's organisational typology. Classrooms are blue; social spaces pink; circulation yellow; theatre orange; sports hall green; plant rooms grey.

3. First floor plan.

1 Doyle Gardens
2 car park and drop-off
3 entrance
4 playing fields
5 Willesden Sports Centre
6 informal dining area
7 theatre
8 general classrooms
9 specialist classrooms
10 sports hall
11 dining hall

0   30m
0   90ft

As we hadn't really done any schools in the UK before it was good for us to think afresh. Obviously the sponsors come from the outside as well, so the process was all about considering the specialism and thinking about the kids and what we could do for them. This was quite a troubled school so we were trying to give a level of hope. But there was also a level of ambition brought by the sponsor who said: 'look we just want to give these kids a chance.' Paul Kalkhoven, of Foster + Partners, in conversation with the editor, 2011

The sponsors I have worked with do not claim or wish to be educationalists. At Capital City Academy, we have benefited hugely from Sir Frank's passion for sport and the arts, which has helped us to develop links with top sports clubs and national arts organisations. He cares deeply that our building is clean and cared for and that our grounds become beautiful gardens. He wants the school to be happy as well as successful. In all these areas, his strong views are indisputably influential – just as one would hope is the case with all school governors but, sadly, is not, especially in the most troubled schools. Philip O'Hear, Principal of Capital City Academy, *The Daily Telegraph*, 11 May 2005

The environment inside is very different to that of the old school. It is all carpeted, it is a quieter space, but not oppressively so. It has some grand spaces, it has more intimate spaces. It has a good relationship to the playing fields and its speciality is sport. Our hope is that all of these things come together to give the children there a better start in life. The ambition of the Academies programme is to try to provide an environment that is optimistic, outward-looking and engaging. Spencer de Grey, in conversation with Susan Marling, 'Designs for Learning', BBC Radio 3, 26 March 2006

4

5.

Teachers report that the change in students coming into the school has been wonderful to witness – their self-esteem has grown and the better they feel about themselves the better they approach their studies.

Norman Foster

4. The academy specialises in sports and in particular basketball. To help foster this, the sports hall was designed to accommodate national level matches and is now home to London Capital, a professional team in the British Basketball League.

5. The academy also specialises in the visual and performing arts. This double-height dance studio is one of two within the school.

It was a brave new world for the DfES and I think they learned a lot from Capital City and the Business Academy Bexley and probably a few of the other projects such as Rogers' Mossbourne Community Academy. They used them as guinea pig projects to try and clarify what it was they were doing and in many ways that was very good because it prompted a fresh start. Spencer de Grey, in conversation with the editor, 2012

We are lucky to have been given a beautiful building. It has taken time for the school community to learn to use the building in the best possible way. The way the circulation is centralised is very different from what people have previously experienced in schools. What the building creates is an enormous degree of transparency and a great sense of community in the life of the school. Together with the excellent learning resources inside classrooms, the building as a whole has helped to support our development as a really good school. Philip O'Hear, Principal of Capital City Academy, in conversation with the editor, 2009

At the beginning of the design process the teachers' expectations were very low because they had a difficult enough job just trying to keep the existing school going. Because of this there was an element of training people, taking them on courses and out to other schools to make them realise they wouldn't be in this environment forever and to give them an idea of what could be possible in a twenty-first century school. Simon Bowden, formerly of Foster + Partners, in conversation with the editor, 2011

1. Restaurant facilities are located at the heart of the building to encourage social interaction, and the dining hall looks on to the activity of the sports hall.

2. The main entrance hall, with security gates.

```
0          15m
|___|___|___|
0          50ft
```

Unlike the separate blocks that house sports halls in most schools, the Foster team recognised the importance of integrating the facility within the academy, both physically and visually. A glass wall above the first storey allows students and staff in the restaurant, and those in the adjacent entrance area, to see what's going on in the sports hall, and those in the hall to feel connected to activities within the school.

Like Bexley, the school is naturally ventilated. Air is drawn through the classrooms from the outside into the street and out of the building through vents in the central rooflight. Fresh air is evenly distributed throughout, giving a direct benefit in educational terms by preventing the stuffy, sleepy atmosphere that is often associated with the backs of classrooms. By incorporating perforated panels in front of the vents in the facade system, windows can be left open to allow night-time air to cool the warmed exposed mass of the concrete soffit of the classroom ceilings, at no risk to security.

Like the Business Academy, the construction period was tight. The structure was therefore designed as a kit-of-parts that could be assembled quickly and economically. The structural steel frame and concrete floors are clearly expressed, as is the central concrete roof and the insulated metal roof. The roof extends out over the entrance and along the whole length of the west elevation to create a generous canopy that protects the classrooms from solar gain during the spring and summer. It also creates an all-weather route through the site, which has proved particularly beneficial at the beginning and end of the day when children are being dropped off or picked up.

The two long elevations are treated differently, in response to their outlook. The west elevation, of general classrooms facing the playing fields, is set back behind the colonnade and therefore entirely glazed, with a screen of louvres providing solar shading. In contrast, the east elevation, where there are facilities that require less natural light, is composed of strips of glazed and stainless-steel panels. Stainless steel was chosen in preference to timber or masonry partly because it is a durable material in this relatively harsh environment.

The change for students, which the academy represents, has been wonderful to witness.

Landscaping, although initially minimal, includes a drop-off area and car park in front of the school, so there is no longer any need for coaches or cars to park along Doyle Gardens. Children who arrive on foot approach the school via a pedestrian route to the side of the playing fields, and enter through a gated entrance, away from vehicles. In addition, a service spine runs along the eastern side of the building so that deliveries can be made directly into various departments instead of being taken through the central street. It can also be used for emergency vehicle access.

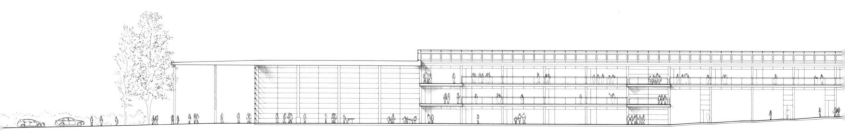

It will take several years before the impact of the new educational regime and the concept of city academies is fully felt. The idea that you can move into a new building and that overnight everybody will get 'A's, is a pipe dream. In terms of results, it is more important to get a feel for the atmosphere and the abilities that have been nurtured. Just to go by tables published every year is not enough. If there are detectable trends beginning to emerge at grass roots level, then I think that those should be fed back into the process and influence the design of the next set of academies. We shouldn't just stand still – it has to be an ongoing process. Spencer de Grey, in conversation with Susan Marling, 'Designs for Learning', BBC Radio 3, 26 March 2006

As soon as we thought we might design the school with an internal 'street' and tie that in with the natural ventilation strategy we took the sponsors, school and DfES to Fréjus to gauge their reaction – this turned out to be overwhelmingly positive. Simon Bowden, formerly of Foster + Partners, in conversation with the editor, 2011 Right: The internal 'street' of the Lycée Albert Camus, Fréjus (1991-1993).

The design of the school consciously takes account of its role within the wider community. By designing a 'dumbbell' with the main hall at one end, balanced by the sports hall at the other, both with independent entrances, the academy can be used by community groups outside school hours with minimum threat to security. An outreach programme is in place to allow children from other schools in the area, including primary schools, to use the sports, arts and performance facilities at designated times.

The contrast with Willesden High School is extreme. Before the opening of Capital some parents in the area were unwilling to send their children to the school. Now it is regarded a privilege to go to the academy. It is still a tough school, filled with children of numerous nationalities, speaking many languages, but the architecture has gone a long way to defuse old tensions, and inspire a new attitude towards learning. The decision to get rid of corridors and provide light, open circulation spaces has led – as teaching staff have noticed – to a marked improvement in the mood of the children at the start of lessons. 'Our job as architects', says Simon Bowden, 'was to design a building that was as good as possible, in order to enable the team of extremely dedicated staff to do their job, rather than as an end in itself.'

The school's first head teacher, Frank Thomas (who has since moved on), is enthusiastic in his praise: 'The building is exciting and innovative and offers an extraordinary opportunity for the staff and students … the change for students which the academy represents has been wonderful to witness. It has shown in their pride and self-esteem which has grown immeasurably.'

Nicola Jackson

3. Two bands of teaching accommodation are arranged on either side of a central galleria or 'street', which ramps gently along its length responding to changes of level on the site. This space is the social focus of the school and contains informal research and study areas. The partially glazed walls admit daylight and create visual links between classrooms and departments.

4. Long section through the school. The roofline follows a constant datum; the sports hall – the largest volume in the building – is dug into the rising contours of the site.

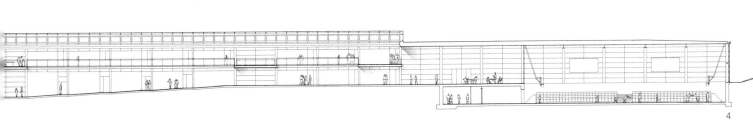

Djanogly City Academy

Nottingham, England 2002–2005

1, 2. A terrace forms an L-shape around the west and south facades of the school; shading to both the terrace and the south-facing classrooms is provided by a deep brise-soleil.

3. The southern side of the building looks out onto a densely planted area which acts as an environmental buffer between the school and the busy main road.

Shortly after beginning work on the Capital City Academy in Brent, Spencer de Grey's team turned its attention to the Business Academy in Bexley, and Nottingham's Djanogly City Academy. With 810 students in three year groups, accommodated in a building of 8,000 square metres, it is the smallest of this group of academies, but none the less impressive.

The academy is named after the sponsor, Sir Harry Djanogly, one of the founders of Coats Viyella and a prominent UK philanthropist. It is the first example of a City Technology College (CTC) with a proven track record converting to a City Academy; more often the academies replace failing secondary schools. Here, the Djanogly City Technology College, Forest School and Nottingham Local Education Authority, collaborated to allow Forest School pupils to be educated within a school that was already performing well. The academy is based on two sites, with this building housing the eleven to fourteen year olds.

From the start, the head teacher, Mike Butler, had a clear vision of the way in which he wanted to teach, including an emphasis on information and communication technologies (ICT). He wanted to revolutionise the way in which pupils could learn, and this had a direct impact on the design. Every student has a laptop, which they take with them as they move throughout the academy, using it in every lesson and emailing homework directly to staff. Talking to the team it is apparent that the clarity of Butler's approach informed and aided the design decisions, and the result is seen very much as a collaborative effort.

The external appearance of Djanogly is reminiscent of Capital, although here there is no curve to the linear plan. The south-facing entrance elevation faces on to the busy Gregory Boulevard, and the Forest Recreation Ground, site of the Nottingham Goose Fair. To make the most of its green setting, a wide external terrace runs the length of this elevation, with brise-soleil offering shade to the terrace and classrooms. All the classrooms maximise views of the park, with the playground and sports fields located to the north, safely away from the traffic.

The head teacher wanted to revolutionise the way in which pupils could learn, and this had a direct impact on the design.

An early scheme anticipated an entirely open plan, inspired by the client's first visit to the Foster studio in Battersea. (The client for the Business Academy Bexley had been similarly impressed with the studio.) However, an open solution ran contrary to the guidelines contained in the latest Building Bulletin and so a more conventional plan form, with enclosed classrooms, was explored. Although the classrooms are partitioned, the doors are glazed, and this at least provides the required transparency and helps to ensure legibility throughout the building, both of which were key motivations for the design team.

4

4. One of the double-height art studios. In common with the school's other specialist teaching spaces, these studios are located on the ground floor to take advantage of the deeper plan.

5. North-south cross section. The school is arranged around a central internal 'street' with home-base accommodation on the first floor and specialist teaching areas at ground level.

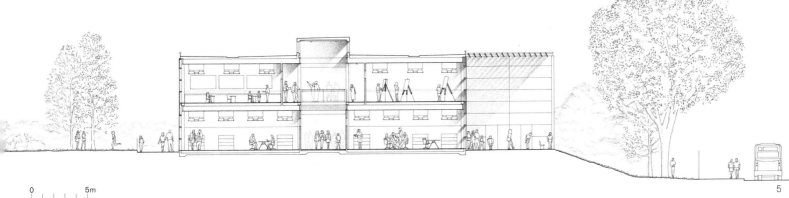

0 ___ 5m
0 ___ 15ft

5

The academies are procured in a different way from PFI projects. It is a far more traditional approach. Importantly, the process allows time at the beginning of the project to talk about the aims and aspirations of the building, and the educational brief, which of course is fundamental. That allows us to explore the options, in terms of strategic design, to discuss those with the client, the educationalists, the head teacher and the sponsor and develop the design together, which is very much how we like to work. Spencer de Grey, in conversation with Susan Marling, 'Designs for Learning', BBC Radio 3, 26 March 2006

We are not there to tell teachers how to teach, we're there to create effective spaces that facilitate teaching. Perhaps one of the errors architects made in the 1960s was that they became too cocky with the social determination of 'I know best'. We believe that it shouldn't be down to architects to decide the educational approach, that's down to the teachers. The whole concept was that we would work with teachers who had good ideas and could turn a school around and so naturally we listened to them. Paul Kalkhoven, of Foster + Partners, in conversation with the editor, 2011

Left: Education Secretary Charles Clarke lays the foundation stone for the Djanogly City Academy.

1. Drawing by Norman Foster showing the organisational layout of the school: teaching areas are coloured blue; social areas pink; sports green; the theatre orange; and circulation yellow.

2. Site plan.

3. Ground floor plan.

4. First floor plan.

1 entrance
2 cyber café
3 library
4 changing rooms
5 plant
6 kitchen
7 dining area
8 theatre
9 assembly hall
10 sports hall
11 specialist classrooms
12 Year 7 home-base
13 Year 8 home-base
14 Year 9 home-base

This engenders trust and respect among pupils and staff, and there is a sense, as with the other Foster-designed academies, that the building can be self-monitored, thanks to this inherent transparency.

Internally, the building is organised along a central 'street', a tall, light and airy space, which is made more dynamic by brightly coloured panels on each structural bay, by artist Sophie Smallhorn, and by the glazed balconies which link the seven individual classrooms of each of the three 'home bases' on the first floor. Each of the home bases, which are similar in idea to those at West London Academy, has its own resource area, staff facilities, stairs and toilets. Two pairs of classrooms in each home base are divided by moveable partitions to provide the flexibility of teaching in larger or smaller spaces.

Specialist spaces, such as laboratories and workshops, which require more fixed equipment, are located on the ground floor. The greater depth of the plan allows for larger classrooms, and materials can more easily be delivered at ground-floor level. Additionally, all the internal walls are non-loadbearing, which allows flexibility for future change. Double-height spaces accommodate the dining area, art room, sports hall and multi-purpose hall for assemblies, exhibitions and performances, as well as an impressive entrance hall and library.

These communal areas are organised around the entrance, to the east of the plan, allowing for out-of-hours use by students and the local community; the teaching areas are to the west.

In view of the noise pollution from the road, and the heat generated by computers, the whole of the south side is mechanically ventilated and the upper-level classrooms are cooled by chilled beams. The north of the building is naturally ventilated using a similar cross-ventilation system to the one employed in the Capital City Academy, with high-level vents in the facade and facing the internal street, allowing air to be exhausted through the rooflights in the street. This system allows for night-time cooling of the exposed precast concrete soffits.

There is no missing this high-profile, refined new building on the outskirts of Nottingham, and yet it sits within its urban landscape with a quiet confidence that would have most visitors believe it has been there for years. The very most has been made of views of the park so that students look out on to greenery from the majority of the classrooms and communal areas. In the street and the huge double-height communal spaces, order has been created out of potential chaos. The result is testimony to the teamwork of the Foster studio and to a client with an unusually clear vision.

Nicola Jackson

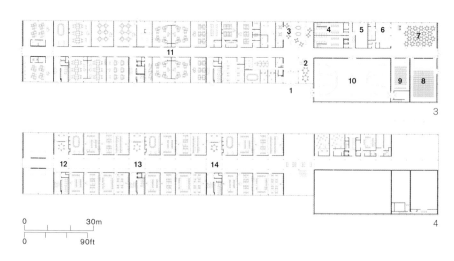

Swipe cards, electronic notebooks and pens, plasma screens and music CDs produced through desktop computers. These are just some of the state-of-the-art equipment being used by Nottingham teenagers at one school on a daily basis. Welcome to Djanogly City Academy, the future of education in Britain. It boasts facilities that schools, and many companies, can only dream of. Stephanie Bungay, *Nottingham Evening Post*, 1 October 2005

Right from the beginning we had a huge input into the design process, working closely with the architects. We abandoned the idea of traditional ICT suites at an early stage, because students in these environments spend most of their time looking at the wall, so the teacher can see over their shoulder what's on their screens. In many lessons we have every child's screen projected on to the main board – twenty-four mini-screens in effect – so that the teachers can see at a glance where to concentrate their attention and effort. Sanjesh Sharma, Assistant Principal of ICT and Core Services, quoted in *Schools for Life*, 18 July 2006

This was the first school where we specified shallow raised floors to accommodate the cabling and to provide future flexibility. It was quite an eye-opener for me how much technology there is in the modern school. By the time you add labs and kitchens, together with all the computers there's more technology than inside a lot of offices. Paul Kalkhoven, of Foster + Partners, in conversation with the editor, 2011

5

5. Looking down from one of the three home-base areas on to the internal street. Coloured panels by artist Sophie Smallhorn run the length of the school.

6, 7. Both the library and the dining area are housed in the eastern end of the school adjacent to the entrance and away from the classrooms, enabling the local community to use the facilities out of school hours.

6

7

West London Academy

London, England 2002–2006

1. The year bases comprise two cedar-clad boxes linked by an enterprise zone, these radiate out westwards from the main entrance and are separated from each other by planted courtyards.

2. Horizontal timber battens help with solar shading on the courtyard-facing elevations of the year base classrooms.

West London is the first 'all-age academy, incorporating a nursery, primary and secondary school, alongside the John Chilton School for children with special needs.

Spencer de Grey

Central to the success of the academies is the vision and commitment of the sponsor. Alec Reed, chairman and founder of Reed Executive plc, the recruitment and human resources agency, and the sponsor of the West London Academy, is no exception. His vision was for an academy that would specialise in two particular areas: sport and enterprise. This, he hoped, would encourage creativity, confidence and teamwork within a culture that accepts risk-taking as part of an individual's development and actively celebrates success, something that in recent years has become less fashionable in schools.

Once again, it fell to the Foster team to realise this vision, drawing on the team's experience of designing Capital City Academy, the Business Academy and Djanogly City Academy. Unlike its three predecessors, West London Academy is designed to serve students all the way from nursery age, through to the sixth form, and to nurture them in year groups, the divisions of which are clearly reflected by the building. The school is also significantly larger (though not as large as the Thomas Deacon Academy in Peterborough, designed a year later), accommodating some 1,720 students in a building of 15,520 square metres. It replaces Northolt Primary School and Compton High School and Sports College, as well as incorporating John Chilton School, a special needs school which remains independent, although it is physically integrated within the new building. It also provides facilities for adult education.

The form of the West London Academy was inspired, as at Capital, not only by the educational brief but also by the site. In this case, designing a building that is protected against the four-lane A40 road to the north and open to the south, with the associated environmental benefits, was pivotal to the design strategy. Surprisingly, despite its position alongside a busy road, the site falls within a Nature Conservation Area, a band of land along the northern boundary that cannot be built upon and which reduces the impact of noise and air pollution on the building. The topography of the site, which rises 4 metres from the south-east to the north-west, militated against building the academy anywhere along the bottom of the slope, because of poor drainage. This decision was compounded by the fact that for economic and strategic reasons the existing buildings to the south and south-west had to remain open during the construction period. By curving the linear plan the new building has a better relationship to the site entrance to the north-west, for the primary and John Chilton schools, and increases the distance between the academy and the housing estate to the south-east.

The two long elevations of the linear plan are treated quite differently, in response to their outlook. The 'soft' south elevation, with its timber-clad blocks pushing through a long glazed wall, takes advantage of the southerly aspect. In contrast, the opaque northern elevation is 'hard', clad in cedar to reflect its proximity to a Nature Conservation Area, but also to provide insulation from noise and air pollution; windows on this elevation are not designed to be opened.

3

3. Attenuated louvres draw in air to cool the year base classrooms; the south side of each enterprise zone – which is fully glazed – is shaded by a brise-soleil.

4. Cross-section. An internal street separates the year base accommodation located in the south of the school from the specialist classrooms to the north.

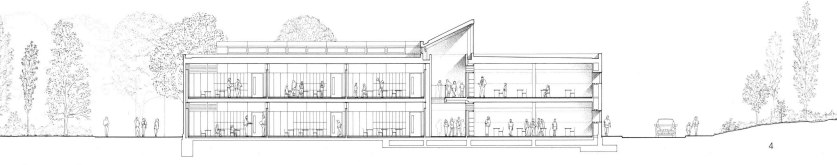

0   5m

0   15ft

4

All the academies in one way or another – particularly the early ones – were trying to get away from the image of a traditional school. They were trying to create something new which would inject enthusiasm into the local community and offer a new way of looking at schools which would hopefully avoid the problems inherent in the existing building stock. Spencer de Grey, in conversation with the editor, 2012

Before being turned into academies, the majority of the schools had spread and been extended over the years meaning they were physically very hard to teach in. The kids were everywhere so it was a very confusing set up which made it hard to keep control when things got out of hand. A tighter, clearer organisation is good for both pupils and teachers and that's what we tried to achieve architecturally. Paul Kalkhoven, of Foster + Partners, in conversation with the editor, 2011

1. A typical year base classroom; it was originally intended that children would remain in these classrooms for the majority of their lessons only moving to take part in specialist subjects.

2, 3. Environmental diagrams: summer day and night. Attenuated louvred panels on the home-base blocks provide natural cross ventilation to the classrooms, helping to prevent a stuffy, sleepy atmosphere. In the summer months deciduous pin oaks planted in the adjacent courtyards provide shading.

The design of the natural ventilation system is similar to that at Capital and the Business Academy, with attenuated louvred panels for cross-ventilation, although an undercroft is included beneath the north side of the building to draw fresh air from the south to ventilate the spaces to the north.

The contrast in the two main elevations and the use of materials reflects the organisation required by the educational brief, which was to incorporate a series of year bases. The emphasis on providing these self-contained bases had to be reconciled with creating flexible teaching spaces that can be adapted easily to changing teaching methods, technologies and philosophies. In order to create a safe, light-filled environment that can be controlled by the staff, and which inspires the students, some of the strategies employed at Capital City Academy and The Business Academy were embraced. These include the addition of open-plan informal teaching spaces (the Enterprise Zones in each year base), and a strong circulation spine which in this case is fully glazed along the south side only.

This central street also provides a physical link between the individual 'schools' within the academy, encourages integration and reduces intimidation. The specialist teaching rooms, for sport, drama and various workshops – as well as the plant rooms, kitchens and stair cores – demand large spaces and fixed equipment, but do not necessarily require the natural light and ventilation needed by the core teaching spaces. They are therefore arranged along the north of the circulation spine.

The south side, with its sunny aspect, houses the year bases within a series of clearly articulated boxes. These are the core interactive teaching spaces which are occupied all day. Each year base focuses on a courtyard or 'enterprise zone'. Years seven and eight, and years ten and eleven are grouped together around double-height courtyards with year nine (the transition year) occupying a zone on its own. To the east and west of the zones are twelve classrooms arranged over ground and first floors, forming fingers of more traditional cellular teaching accommodation in contrast to the open-plan spaces. There are six classrooms on each floor, for the individual year bases, connected to each other and to the central enterprise zone by the circulation spaces.

It was Reed's belief that this way of dividing the school physically would give pupils a sense of belonging and stability as well as encouraging teamwork and creativity, all of which he and the school regard as critical to pupils' academic success. Despite the original intention for the staff to move from base to base, with the children remaining in their classrooms, the Academy has reverted to the traditional system of pupils moving between lessons, for reasons of practicality, but this hasn't compromised the architectural design significantly, and pupils still appear to have a clear sense of belonging to a particular 'base'.

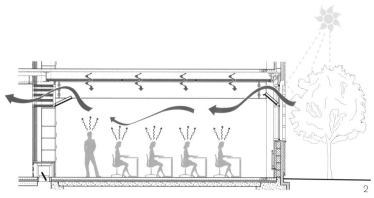

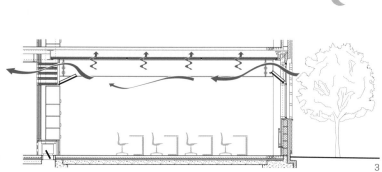

The administrative and main entrance areas follow the architectural form of the enterprise zones, for design consistency, and also to maximise flexibility and the creation of a bright and open working environment. The sixth form is located in the final year base above the main entrance space; the hope is that they will demonstrate the success of this system both to visitors and those within the academy, as they enter and exit the building.

The overall impression is one of an architectural lightness of touch and sensitivity to the complex needs of growing children.

The external courtyards are a valuable bonus, resulting from the box-like arrangement of the year bases. They provide intimate transition spaces between the inside of the building and the sports fields, and can even be used for teaching during the summer. They are also spaces that can easily and unobtrusively be monitored by staff from within the building, while allowing the children a sense of freedom and space during school hours. Planting has been carefully considered, with deciduous pin oaks providing shade to both external and internal spaces during the summer, and maximising light during the darker months.

For all the academies there is a government requirement to foster links with the local community. Here this is enabled by grouping together the sports hall and performing arts departments to the east of the building, close to the main entrance, so that both facilities can be accessed easily. Behind each year base block is a circulation core and a small plant room, which means that the school can be opened in individual sections during the school holidays, for example.

This sense of welcome and accessibility is immediately tangible when visiting the school. But perhaps what is most striking, particularly for a school building, is the quality and specification of the materials and the attention to detail. The use of organic materials, from the western red cedar cladding to the internal birch ply lacquered panels, as well as the curve of the plan, softens what might otherwise seem a large and overbearing building. The overall impression is one of an architectural lightness of touch and sensitivity to the complex needs of growing children. It is perhaps a high point in the long and successful run of school buildings by the practice; a building that looks very much more sophisticated and elegant than a typical school, but which is able to function efficiently and adapt to the increasingly complex and varied demands of contemporary education.

Nicola Jackson

6

4, 5. Environmental diagrams: winter day and night. In winter, the fenestration, shading and planting are configured to maximise daylight in the classrooms.

6. Each year base is arranged around a central enterprise zone which is used for informal teaching. Originally, these spaces each had their own distinct art works and interior design but now use the more conventional furniture used throughout the rest of the school.

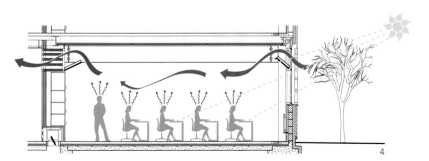

4

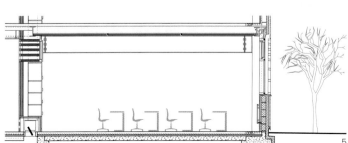

5

The use of wood in the West London Academy signalled a 'softening up' of the academies, a lot of the schools prior to this – Bexley in particular – wanted something that didn't look like a school. They wanted to be more business-like, which is not as appropriate for an academy which contains both a primary and a special-needs school, so we used wood to signal the more caring, greener, social nature of the school. Paul Kalkhoven, of Foster + Partners, in conversation with the editor, 2011

1. Site and ground floor plan.

2. First floor plan.

  1 primary school and
    nursery
  2 John Chilton School
  3 year base 7
  4 year base 9
  5 year base 10
  6 main entrance and office
    accommodation
  7 sports hall
  8 specialist teaching rooms
  9 year base 8
 10 year base 11
 11 sixth form

3. Drawing by Norman Foster showing the organisation of the school: teaching areas are blue; social areas pink; sports green; the theatre orange; and circulation yellow.

It is interesting to compare this country with Holland, for example. We have a reputation for shifting from one educational concept to another. In Holland it is much more stable – the strategy for the way they teach children there has gradually evolved. I would make a plea that we don't chop and change all the time. I think it is much better, having started a programme of city academies, that we have the confidence to continue them. But we must not be nervous about standing back and analysing the programme – not from league tables, but in a considered way and learning from that and moving forward on that basis.
Spencer de Grey, in conversation with Susan Marling, 'Designs for Learning', BBC Radio 3, 26 March 2006

When schools get to a certain size – 1,000 or more pupils – you need to start articulating that. You need to ensure that the pupils aren't just a number in a bigger space and that's where year bases come in. Here you typically have six or so classes arranged around the year base so pupils know where they are and who they belong to.
Paul Kalkhoven, of Foster + Partners, in conversation with the editor, 2011

4

The school specialises in enterprise and sport and aims to promote life-long learning by encouraging after-school use, providing a valuable resource for the wider community.

Spencer de Grey

5

4. One of the informal teaching areas or 'break out' zones which look out onto the planted courtyards, these are accessible from the specialist teaching areas to the north of the internal street.

5. High-level glazing to the northern edge of the street helps flood the space with natural light; birch ply lacquered panels are used to clad the interior.

London Academy
Edgware, England 2002-2006

1. Pupils returning to their home base via one of the two courtyard entrances at the rear of the building. As well as providing access to the school's hard play areas, the courtyards are used for teaching in the summer.

2. Shading to the southern elevation is provided by an overhanging roof which runs the full length of the building.

London Academy has a home-base system that combines the benefits of a more intimate learning environment with the sophisticated facilities and opportunities that only a larger school can offer.
Paul Kalkhoven

The brief for the London Academy, Edgware, which specialises in business, enterprise and ICT, was clear: 'to provide students and teachers with space built around a cluster of classrooms.' This year-base approach – where space is organised according to year groups rather than subjects or faculties – had already been tried and tested by the Foster team at Djanogly Academy and was part of their brief for West London Academy which was designed simultaneously with Edgware. At Edgware this effectively meant dividing the academy into an upper and lower school, each of which contains three year groups. For the most part, children remain in these areas and take the majority of their lessons in the same classroom, only travelling elsewhere to attend specialist lessons, eat or play sports.

The building has a sophistication and refinement not often seen in schools architecture.

In common with many academies, Edgware was built on the playing fields of the school it was designed to replace. However, unlike most schools created under the initiative it had been established as an academy for a full two years before it moved into its new building. Because of this the school was able to implement much of its new teaching and learning ethos before moving in, thus easing the impact of what was for both staff and students a radical change of direction. Central to this vision were the principal Phil Hearne and academy sponsor Peter Shalson, an entrepreneur who had grown up in the area.

Both the principal's brief and the relatively compact site – a footprint of just 5,425 square metres for 1,425 students – suggested designing the school around a courtyard plan rather than adopting the linear approach of Capital City or Djanogly.

The site itself is sandwiched between a main road to the north and the now demolished Edgware School to the south. While the former school was situated in the heart of a 1950s housing estate, most of its pupils were drawn from further afield so it was decided quite early on to orientate the academy away from there, in order to signal change. The most obvious location was facing Spur Road, a busy A-road to the north, both because it provides direct and easy access and because the land on the northern side of the road had been acquired for new playing fields.

In plan this has resulted in a three-storey structure arranged around a top-lit atrium. As well as acting as the school's main circulation spine, the atrium contains a café area at its western end and a demountable theatre space to the east. Twin cantilevered staircases run parallel to the space, their attendant bridges connecting the home bases to the specialist teaching areas. Specialist teaching rooms for subjects such as science, art and technology, are located on the northern side of the atrium while the two blocks of year-base accommodation are situated to the south and are each organised around their own mini atrium.

3

3. An elevated enclosed walkway connects the sports hall to the school's playing fields north of Spur Road. A small pavilion located at the northern end of the walkway houses changing facilities.

4. Long section through the top-lit atrium, which forms the main circulation focus.

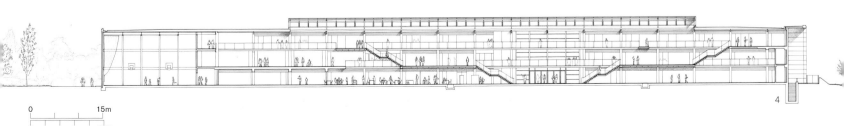

0 ———— 15m

0 ———— 50ft

4

1. Home bases are arranged around their own atrium. In addition to non-specialist classrooms and staff areas, each contains lockers and a social space for students.

2. Site plan.

3. Ground floor plan.

4. First floor plan.

5. Second floor plan.

1 pavilion
2 playing fields
3 Spur Road
4 entrance
5 changing rooms
6 sports hall
7 kitchens
8 dining area
9 staff room
10 library
11 school office
12 drama rooms
13 music room
14 assembly/theatre space
15 courtyard/outside teaching space
16 home base
17 gym
18 specialist teaching rooms
19 bridge link

The home bases contain an average of eight classrooms on each floor, together with a staff room and common facilities such as lockers and toilets. A separate block, containing a triple-height sports hall together with a double-height gym located directly above the ground-floor changing rooms, is located in the far west of the building. The playing fields to the north of Spur Road are also accessible from here via an enclosed elevated walkway.

With its aluminium and glass facade the academy's architectural language has more in common with the worlds of business or industry than that of education. This reflects both the school's specialism and a desire to address its pupils in a more grown-up and sophisticated manner. The rigorous horizontality of the north elevation – strips of monochrome cladding sandwiched between rows of fixed glazing and openable vents – is only broken by the deep incision that runs the full height of the facade to provide a striking, fully glazed entrance.

In contrast, the sports hall – which only requires minimal glazing – is clad in the same blue-glazed bricks as the base of the north-west facade, which is stepped back from the upper storeys. In common with the Capital, Bexley and West London academies, Edgware is largely naturally cooled, using a system of attenuated louvres for cross ventilation.

A further two incisions in the southern elevation – which is made up of a similar pattern of glazing and cladding as the north – provide tranquil outdoor spaces which can be used for social interaction or teaching in the summer months. Here, the roof overhangs the entire facade by 7 metres, providing a generous colonnade which both shades the classrooms on the upper floors and provides a transitional space between the teaching spaces and the hard play areas. Additional louvres attached to the slender columns provide further shading.

Edgware was the first of the Foster academies to be constructed using an in-situ concrete frame, and this together with the concrete soffit, is clearly expressed throughout the building, adding to its industrial aesthetic. The quality of the concrete finish is exemplary with no exposed conduit or trunking visible. The fact that more than 2,000 holes were drilled into the concrete soffit alone to hide the building's services is indicative of the team's painstaking approach to the entire project. The result is a building which has a sophistication and refinement not often seen in schools architecture, an achievement which is all the more remarkable given its relatively modest budget.

Gavin Blyth

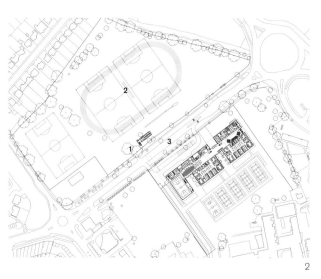

0 ____ 50m
0 ____ 150ft

2

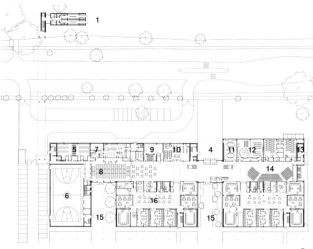

3

The home-base system involves a physical progression through the school. The pupils come in on the lower level in the first block and then move up through that before going on to the next block, so they're always progressing through the building. You can imagine that for a fourteen-year-old it's quite a big thing when you move into the upper school because you are suddenly with the senior pupils rather than the kids. Darron Haylock, of Foster + Partners, in conversation with the editor, 2011

The plan offers clarity, but in its resolute rationality there is perhaps too little room for the spatial idiosyncrasies around which traditions develop, and on which memories of school are founded. Equally though, one could argue that this is not an architecture that patronises children with jolly shapes and colours. Indeed, critics of Foster's academies have been discomfited by their resemblance to adult workplaces. This is muddled thinking that confuses the corruption of a liberal education with the proper function of schools in preparing pupils for life outside. Chris Foges, *Architecture Today*, October 2006

The galleries are about social control because you know if you can be seen – the staff rooms also have glass walls – then you are more likely to behave. The school only has gallery spaces, no corridors and no dead ends so that the main circulation is out in the open. That means you have a strong sense of direction and, in turn, people can see where you're going. Paul Kalkhoven, of Foster + Partners, in conversation with the editor, 2011

7

6. Drawing by Norman Foster showing the organisational layout of the school: teaching areas are blue; social areas pink; sports green; theatre orange; and circulation yellow.

7. On the first and second floors, access from the home bases to the specialist teaching areas and vice versa is via a series of bridges. These, like the galleries and stairs, are open and visible to the rest of the school, as are the fully glazed staff rooms located in the home bases.

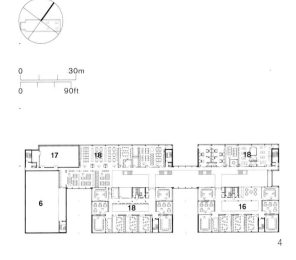

0   30m
0   90ft

4

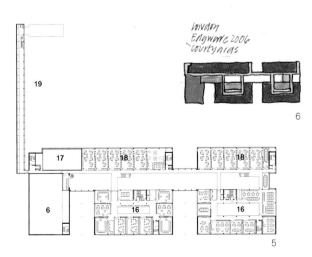

London Edgware 2006 courtyards

6

5

0   30m
0   100ft

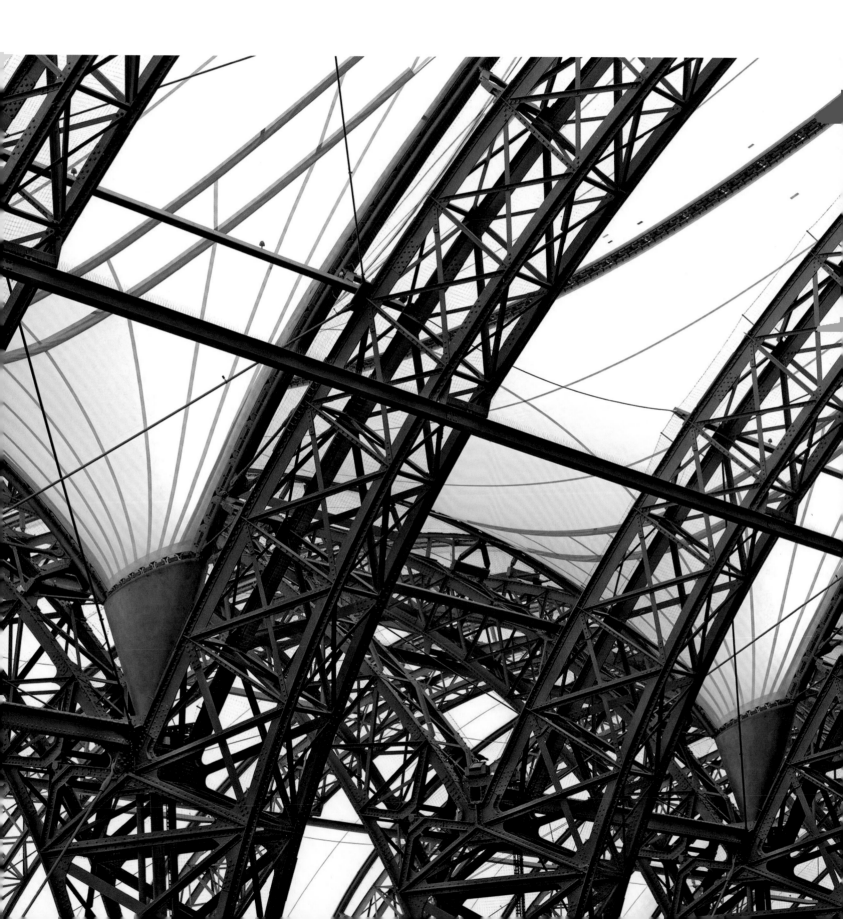

Completed in 1896, Dresden's central station (Hauptbahnhof) was one of many heroically scaled stations built throughout Europe in the late nineteenth century. Like most of its contemporaries, it combined a Neoclassical station building with a steel and glass train shed – the former housing offices, ticketing halls and ancillary facilities such as restaurants, the latter sheltering platforms and tracks. Dresden's station was, however, unique in its general arrangement.

The city's proximity to the Czech border meant that it was served by both German national trains, for which the Hauptbahnhof was the terminating station, and by international trains going on to Prague and Budapest, for which Dresden was a through stop. The design of the station therefore contained three sets of tracks – one on a central ground level serving national trains and terminating behind the station building, and two on flanking, raised structures serving international trains, which spanned the station's forecourt.

The flood of light through the new membrane roof and the way it outlines the skeletal structure below will be seen by some as engineering wrought with a sculptor's hand.

This configuration was emphasised by a shed roof supported by three interlocking ranks of wrought iron arches, a taller one in the centre over the national rails, and two smaller ones over the international. These arches merged at the vertical offset between tracks, coming together in pinned ankle joints at the lower platform level, delicate iron details that contrasted with the heavy Neo-classical composition of the surrounding station. The sheds covering the international rails extended to the front edge of the station building, bookending its stone mass with two fine iron arches.

The combination of subtly deployed engineering with the rather pompous formality of the station building was typical of the era, and was emphasised further at Dresden by the station's long side elevations, which because of the track arrangement actually provided its main frontages to the city. The north elevation formed the terminus to the Pragerstrasse, once Dresden's major shopping street and the station's connection to the historic, Baroque centre of the city. On the eastern side, the station building faced a trapezoidal forecourt, formed by the passing international rails and linked to the city's primary north-south street, St Petersburger-strasse. The station complex essentially offered two sides of a U-shaped ground plan to the city, with entrances beneath the international tracks at key locations – on the station building's central axis, across the front of the courtyards and through its domed space, and at its rear.

This arrangement served Dresden well for fifty years. However, the Allied bombing and subsequent firestorm of 13-14 February 1945 reduced the Hauptbahnhof to a burnt-out shell. Believing that the region's railways would be used by retreating German troops, the station was a particularly key target; in fact, it had been full of fleeing Polish and Czech refugees, hundreds of whom died of asphyxiation in the firestorm after seeking shelter in the station's basement.

1

Opposite: A detail of the fabric roof membrane. The membrane is fixed to a discreet system of secondary steelwork, which lifts the fabric above the top chords of the arches. The membrane is pulled down at every second arch position between the central and side halls, to create low points in the fabric structure. This both provides structural shaping of the fabric in the longitudinal direction and establishes rainwater drainage points.

1. Looking along the station's central hall.

2. An early sketch by Norman Foster, showing how the fabric canopy responds to the form of the structural arches below.

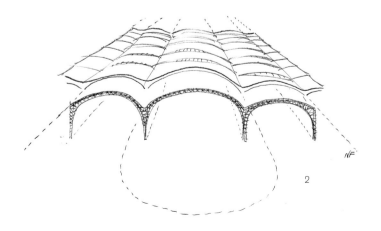

2

1-3. Dresden's Hauptbahnhof, photographed shortly after completion in 1898. Built to a design by Ernst Giese, Paul Weidner and Arwed Rosbach, it is the third largest station in the eastern part of Germany, after Leipzig and Berlin, and one of the most impressive late-nineteenth-century railway stations anywhere in Europe. Linking Dresden with Berlin and Prague, the railway played a significant role in the city's industrial and economic growth in the first half of the twentieth century.

4. The station was severely damaged in the Allied bombing raids that destroyed 80 per cent of the city on the night of 13-14 February 1945, though the majority of the basic structure survived intact.

While its roofs and interiors were destroyed, the vast volume of the Hauptbahnhof, and its solid construction, meant that much of its structure survived the war intact, the only building in the vicinity to remain even skeletally after the firestorm consumed the city around it.

History was doubly unkind to Dresden, as the city was 'rebuilt' by the East German government, eschewing its historic Baroque fabric for vast, cheaply constructed housing slabs and bureaucratic office blocks. While several major monuments in the cultural centre were rebuilt, the Pragerstrasse was reconfigured as a vacuous pedestrian commons surrounded by typically banal housing. The station itself, which had been put back into partial operation within days of the bombing, was covered in the postwar reconstruction with a metal deck roof, while the station building's spaces were lined with low plaster ceilings and standardised, Russian-designed canteen and office facilities. Most tellingly, the subtle iron decoration of the long north facade was hidden beneath a mute, stone exterior that deliberately buried the 'decadent' original ornament.

The station suffered from low maintenance and continued vandalism in the name of efficiency throughout the course of East Germany's history. Much wartime damage was never repaired, and the iron arches in particular deteriorated further over time.

Following the reunification of Germany in 1989 and the re-incorporation of the eastern network by Deutsche Bahn, Germany's national railway, Dresden was seen as a key link to other, recently liberated Eastern Bloc nations. The station and its rail infrastructure were scheduled for extensive upgrading to enable international high-speed trains (ICE) access from Berlin and western Germany to Prague and Budapest.

In 1996, as work on the Commerzbank neared completion in Frankfurt – the city where Deutsche Bahn has its headquarters – and in the midst of well-publicised work on the Reichstag, Foster + Partners was asked to present ideas for both a masterplan and a renovation plan for the station. At the time, though Foster's ability to create legible, user-friendly environments for transport was perhaps better known to Deutsche Bahn, the practice also had a growing track record of consistently sensitive interventions in historic settings. This combination was ideal for the task at Dresden, where the historic nature of the station was matched by the formidable requirements of a high-speed international rail network.

In the project's early phases, Foster and his team – led by Spencer de Grey – proposed opening the station up to the city, connecting it to the increasingly revitalised Pragerstrasse through a dense precinct of new office buildings along the lively urban setting of the Wienerplatz. Foster proposed to draw the life and activity of Wienerplatz into the fabric of the station itself by hollowing out new public areas beneath the train shed.

After the war, the East German authorities replaced the station roof and re-covered the facades. Initially we thought they had been rebuilt, but when we looked behind the rather grizzly post-war yellow plaster, we found that the original facades were still intact underneath. So in a way quite similar to the Reichstag, which like Dresden had in the 1950s been filled with all sorts of crude post-war accretions and over-layers, our approach was a process of stripping away to reveal the original details as much as possible. Spencer de Grey, in conversation with the editor, 2012

Right: Details from a series of murals, dating from the 1950s, which masked reduced window openings. These were stripped away and the original openings restored.

The idea that the past has become so sacred and precious that you have to imitate it must be questionable, but, by the same token, that does not mean we ignore it. Research into the history of site and building is critical to our method.
Norman Foster, in conversation with the editor, 2012

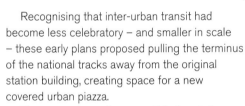

5   6   7

Recognising that inter-urban transit had become less celebratory – and smaller in scale – these early plans proposed pulling the terminus of the national tracks away from the original station building, creating space for a new covered urban piazza.

This carving out of space within the station was matched, in the initial plans, by new accommodation for ICE trains, which are nearly 400 metres in length. At nearly double the length of the station's original shed, these trains required extensive new sheltering structures, and Foster proposed that the nineteenth-century sheds be extended in front of the station by new canopies. While these were shown as shallow vaults with a much lower profile than the arches, their elevation across the forecourt entrance would clearly denote a continuation of the shed roof's logic, providing a legible contrast between old and new and emphasising the modern aura of the high-speed trains.

In keeping with Deutsche Bahn's optimistic assumptions about the new, synergetic economy of eastern and western Germany, Foster drew up plans for a hotel and office tower across the forecourt from the station building. This took advantage of a wedge of land between the flanking international tracks and offered a dramatic formal counterpoint, cantilevered out over the tracks, to the solidity of the station's stone facade.

8

There are no dramatic gestures here, no purple architectural prose. Rather, connections to the past are implied or simply revealed, and the result is both powerful and personal.

Thomas Leslie

5, 6. In the post-war period, the station lost much of its grandeur due to unsympathetic rebuilding and poor conversion. Much of the surviving historic detail was either concealed or destroyed, window openings were reduced, and a new – and quite alien – decorative scheme was introduced in the reception building.

7, 8 The original station roof was partially glazed, but after the war it was almost entirely replaced with timber, admitting very little daylight to the platforms.

Rather than a conventional solid roof, a translucent skin of Teflon-coated glass fibre has been stretched over the original steel arches spanning the platforms, and the effect is striking. Arriving at the station by rail, with the winter sun low in the sky, natural light floods into the vast curvaceous space, and every element of the three-arched structure is thrown into sharp relief; even if you had no interest in trains or architecture, you'd have to confess it's a thing of beauty, like pulling into an enormous Zeppelin. Steve Rose, *The Guardian*, 23 November 2006
Left: A key reference image for the design team – the Graf Zeppelin in its assembly hangar at Friedrichshafen, Germany 1928.

For me, juxtaposition is not about shock value or a forcible contrast – it is about dialogue, illumination, integrity, sensitivity to both past and present. It can be respectful and exciting at the same time. Norman Foster, in conversation with the editor, 2012

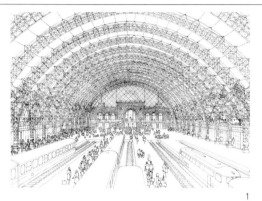

1. A perspective study by Helmut Jacoby of the central hall with its fabric canopy.

2, 3. Screen grabs of the computer-generated model, whose development allowed the design team to study and develop the form of the fabric roof canopy in great detail.

4. The computer model was complemented by numerous physical models; this one was built to study the roof detail at the junction of the central and southern arches.

However, as work on the masterplan progressed, the discontinuity between the older sheds and the newer canopies proved troublesome. Economically, there was no good way to continue the huge volumes of the flanking vaults for the extra 200 metres along the ICE platforms. Furthermore, structural analysis showed that reconstructing the original roof covering would add loading to the arches that would push them beyond allowable contemporary standards – despite the fact that they had borne these loads for their first fifty years.

Foster and his team were also keen to integrate the historic renovation of the station with elements that emphasised the contemporary state of the building arts, a dialogue that the pure reconstruction of the roofs would not have generated. In early 1998 they suggested treating the entire roof structure – over all three sets of arches and their extensions over the ICE platforms – as a continuous fabric membrane, an element that would 'hold its own' against the skeletal arches while providing a smooth transition to the extended platforms.

Such a suggestion was quite novel given that the practice had only rarely considered fabric structures in the past. While the roof of the unbuilt Hammersmith Centre (1977-1979) was shown as a stretched fabric membrane, and early work by the office had included the temporary Air-Supported Office for Computer Technology (1969-1970), more recent work had generally eschewed membrane solutions. In part, this reflected the difficulties of membrane design at the time.

While membrane structures necessarily adopt statically compelling forms, the difficulties of three-dimensional 'form finding' in their design had traditionally meant that their shapes were determined primarily by engineers; or more accurately by proprietary software developed by engineers. The nature of this software meant that the shapes of tent structures could only be fixed after their anchorage and edge conditions were established, and would rarely be subject to the sort of iterative process crucial to Foster's success at melding structural and formal design.

At nearly double the length of the station's original shed, the high-speed trains required extensive new sheltering structures.

Nonetheless, from the point of view of weight, light, form and cleanability, a membrane solution was an attractive one, as the parallels between their morphology and the existing skeleton were striking. Membranes carry roof loads by their shape, which must be calculated to ensure that the entire surface is always in tension, no matter what the loading pattern. To permit loads to 'flow' through the surface, they must be double curved – concave along one axis, convex along the other. In theory, any shape defined by three points not in the same plane creates a potential membrane structure, but forms with less curvature must be tensioned more in order to carry loads.

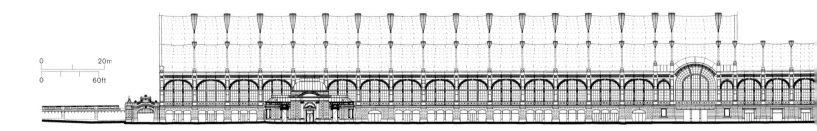

The Landesamt für Denkmalpflege Sachsen believes Foster + Partners' proposed membrane roof for the historic platform sheds to be a forward-looking element that builds symbolically on the achievements of the past. The roof covering on the side facade further signals a turn towards the city. The station will thus doubly become a significant gateway: to the world, and in particular to south-eastern Europe; and to the future. Extract from a letter from the Landesamt für Denkmalpflege Sachsen (Regional Saxony Office for the Protection of Historic Buildings) to Deutsche Bundesbahn AG, 6 September 1999

Dresden is the first time we've used a single-layer membrane roof. I don't think this is a reflection of any design nervousness about using them, but just a question of what is appropriate for the projects themselves. We had actually first proposed using a membrane roof back in 1978 for our Hammersmith project but of course it was never realised. Spencer de Grey, in conversation with the editor, 2012

In the past, these kinds of structures were developed using physical models – stocking material stretched over supports and then pinned and glued. Measurements would be taken from the models and fed into a computer programme as the first approximation. Parametric analysis allowed us to shortcut some of these physical studies. The work we did on Dresden happened at the same time as work we were doing for Swiss Re, The Sage and City Hall. It was really the start of the parametric modelling division of the office. Hugh Whitehead, formerly of Foster + Partners, in conversation with the editor, 2009

2

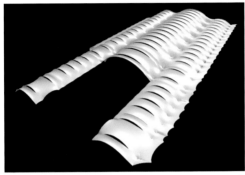

3

4

5. This aerial perspective by Helmut Jacoby shows how the roof canopy was originally intended to wrap around the station forecourt.

6. One of a series of sketch drawings illustrating the fabric installation sequence.

7. North elevation, as seen from Wienerplatz. At this early stage it was anticipated that the canopy would cover the through-train platforms, which were to be extended to twice their length to cater for the planned introduction of ICE high-speed trains. Although the introduction of the ICE trains was postponed, they may still be introduced at some future date.

5

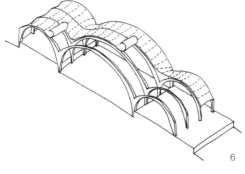

6

7

Dresden is one of the finest nineteenth-century stations in Europe and one of the very few major buildings to survive the tragic air raid of February 1945. It also survived the flood in 2002, which marked a milestone in its recent history. We had been commissioned in 1997 to create a masterplan for the station and the wider area, but the flood provided the catalyst for work to begin in earnest. The damage it caused left us with no option but to restore the reception building, which now forms the heart of the project. In a nice twist, the project was completed in time for Dresden's 800th anniversary celebrations. Norman Foster, in conversation with the editor, 2012
Left: The station under water, 16 August 2002.

The membrane material we installed had this slightly unnerving quality of starting off a kind of deep yellow colour. After about three months the yellow bleached out to a much nicer pale creamy white, but in those first few months we kept thinking that something had gone terribly wrong. We really didn't want to take any visitors around the site until it had settled down. Spencer de Grey, in conversation with the editor, 2012

1. To allow a full train service to be maintained while work to the roof progressed, moveable platforms were used with scaffolding on top.

2. The timber covering is stripped from the roof of the south hall.

3. Prompted by the flood of August 2002, work to the reception building began in October 2003. The roof and layers of plaster added after the war were stripped away to reveal the structure beneath; in the central aisle, GDR-era 'restoration' work was removed in order to restore the original scale of the window openings.

4. Work proceeds on the roof of the south hall. The first sections of membrane were installed in February 2001.

5. The tubular-steel secondary structure to which the membrane is secured is fixed in place.

We sought to celebrate the nineteenth-century structure using modern means. Light and translucent, the new roof covering reveals the fine historic detail and washes the platforms with daylight.

Norman Foster

A number of different studies were done for the roof, analysing factors such as maximum possible loads, work flow, sun radiation and shading, together with the logistics of covering such a big area. We wanted to regain the airy lightness of the original building but using glass would have been too heavy, so instead we began to think about tensile structures. This had the dual effect of letting in light while reducing the loads on the beautiful cast-iron structure. Christian Hallmann, formerly of Foster + Partners, in conversation with the editor, 2010
Left: Christian Hallmann with Spencer de Grey on a visit to the site.

The introduction of a loadbearing skin makes the use of secondary purlins unnecessary – the double-curved membrane surface creates the required stiffness to span the maximum distances between the arches without the need for additional intermediate supports between the new secondary steelwork. This offers advantages: as only pairs of arches are linked by rigid purlins, and the spaces in between are linked by the flexible membrane, the whole structure is able to flex slightly to accommodate elongation of steel structure due to temperature changes.
Michael Vitzthum, of Buro Happold, *Architecture Today*, January 2007

6

7

8

10

9

6-9. Details of the membrane installation. The tubular steel secondary structure to which the membrane is attached transfers loads from the membrane to the top chord of the arches. The arches were designed for vertical loading and have little resistance to horizontal forces. Therefore, longitudinal loads are transferred to the braced end bays of each hall, which act in effect as 10-metre wide trusses. Steel cables beneath the fabric allow for catastrophic loading due to membrane failure.

10. Looking down on the roof of the reception building as stripping out proceeds.

11. The north and central halls with their roofs partially complete.

11

The big decision was what to do with the roof. The elaborate structure, though quite fragile, was almost completely intact. Originally the roof covering had been partially glazed, but after the war it had been boarded over. We decided to remove that covering and to sheathe the frame in a more appropriate, lightweight material – in this case a skin of Teflon-coated glass fibre. This material transmits daylight, which reduces the need for artificial lighting; and if the decision is made to run an international high-speed rail service through Dresden, this canopy can be extended to provide cover for the trains, which are twice the length of the old platforms. Norman Foster, in conversation with the editor, 2012

What is so extraordinary is that a structure that was designed in the 1890s looks incredibly fresh with its new roof covering. The two marry very happily into quite a celebratory space. I like to think that if the nineteenth-century builders had had a membrane roof available to them, they might well have used it. Spencer de Grey, in conversation with the editor, 2012

1. Cross-section through the platforms, looking towards the reception building. The iron arches of the central hall span 59 metres; those of the north and south halls span 32 metres. The international platforms are raised a storey above those of the domestic trains, allowing direct connections between the central hall and the streets on either side.

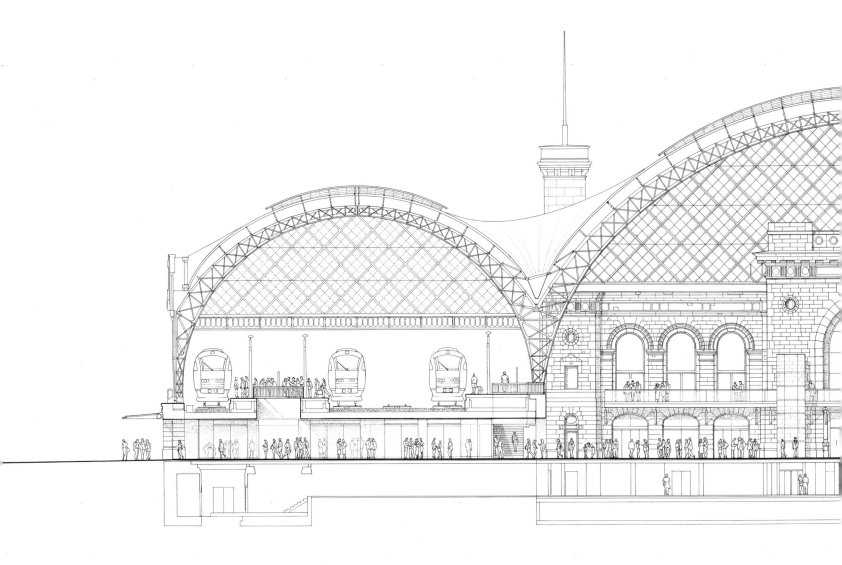

Dresden Station draws together several threads that run through earlier projects. The lightweight roof canopy, for example, can be traced back to Stansted or our project for Hammersmith in the 1970s; and the theme of new and old goes back to our work at the Royal Academy and more recently the Reichstag. There's a new theme too, which is the juxtaposition of technologies from different eras. It is tempting to think that the nineteenth-century architects would have been very excited to glimpse some of things that are possible today.
Norman Foster, in conversation with the editor, 2012
Left: The roof canopy of Stansted Airport (1981-1991).
Right: The Sackler Galleries at the Royal Academy of Arts (1985-1991).

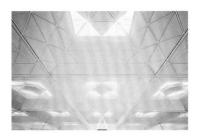

Overleaf: looking along the station's central vaulted hall; completed in 1898, to a design by Ernst Giese and Paul Wiedner, Dresden is the third largest station in the eastern part of Germany, after Leipzig and Berlin.

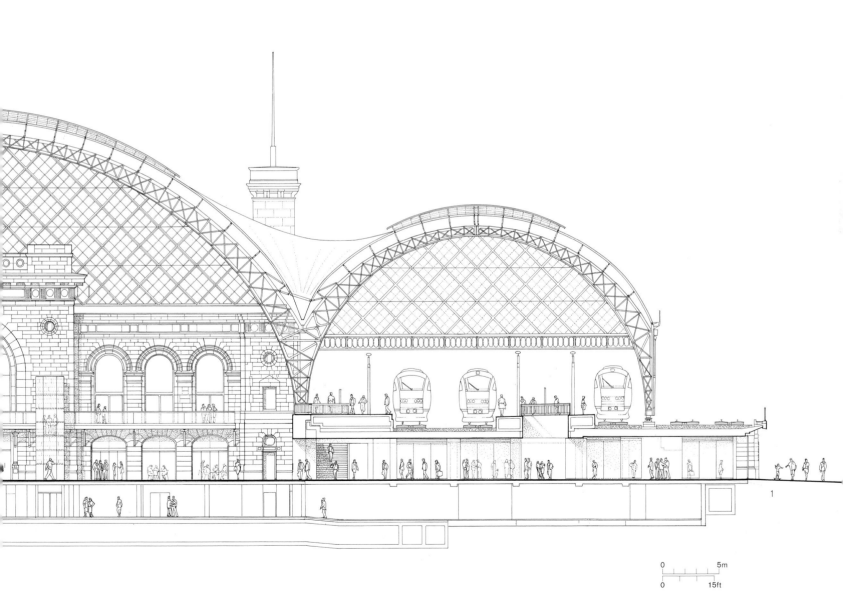

0   5m

0   15ft

Research was our constant companion throughout the whole project. We never stopped looking to history, continually comparing what we had found with what we had designed. We wanted to find out what the standard of the day was in order to pay tribute to the art of the engineers while at the same time adding our own contemporary interventions. Christian Hallmann, formerly of Foster + Partners, in conversation with the editor, 2012

Certainly one of the biggest challenges was the sheer size of the roof. It's difficult to appreciate just how big this station is. It's double the size of Paddington Station, for example. The individual spans are vast – 80 metres or so across the main platform. Also, the fabric was basically continuous over the full length – a 110-metre-long strip. There were a lot of issues about how you could build these massive fabric panels and get them to site and still create a dead fit. Because the roof was clamped to the steelwork, there was little room for post-tensioning and the panel patterns had to be very, very precise. Angus Palmer, of Buro Happold, in conversation with the editor, 2010

It is the aesthetic effect that is chiefly remarkable, both for the fine quality of the diffused light through the white fabric roof and for its formal qualities. Instead of the parallel linear roofs and gutters of the original, the new fabric is pulled tightly down into the springing points of the arches in alternate bays, forming a fan vault somewhat reminiscent of that of King's College Chapel. RIBA European Awards jury report, 2007

1

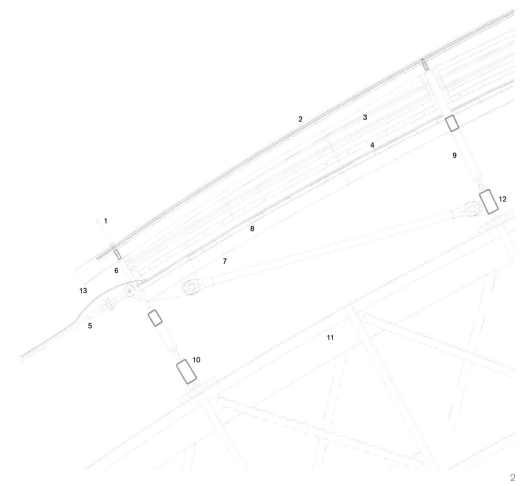

2

1. Looking up at the underside of the roof membrane and the roof-lights that correspond with the position of each arch.

2. Vertical section, showing the roof-light detail.

1 lightning rod
2 6mm laminated safety glass
3 perforated aluminium louvres
4 0.8mm thick PTFE-coated glass-fabric roof membrane
5 22mm diameter steel cable
6 50 x 50/4mm steel SHS
7 114.3/12.5mm steel CHS
8 membrane connection clamp
9 120 x 80/12.5mm steel RHS
10 200 x 100mm steel RHS purlin
11 upper chord of existing roof arch
12 purlin adaptor welded to upper chord
13 membrane lip, fabricated off-site

The shape of such a structure is therefore inevitably a trade-off between the tensile capacity of the fabric and the magnitude of the curvature. Excess tension requires strengthening, which is both expensive and very visible across the otherwise smooth fabric surface. In situations where membrane structures stand on their own, or are intentionally contrasted with surrounding structures, this process has proved adequate, and the resulting tents often form compelling foils to heavier structures. At Dresden, however, such a bold distinction was not desired. Instead, the design team wanted to explore the notion of an all-encompassing membrane structure as a fully integrated element. Initial physical studies with stretched silk stockings – a traditional method of initial form determination – proved the possibility of a fully responsive shape.

However, the coarseness of this method did not allow the fine-tuning that would ensure a consistent, smooth flow between the existing skeleton of arches and the surfaces of the membrane roof. The office at the time was developing extensive modifications to its CAD software that permitted parametric modelling, in which three-dimensional elements can be altered in relation to one another. Rather than defining each of the thousands of elements that make up a typical CAD model in isolation, parametric systems allow the user to change one variable – say, the height of a building – and the software models the consequences; for example, the height of curtain wall panels, or the relative positions of floor plates.

The fabric surface has a wonderful flow to it. We made several attempts to model membrane structures for this project, but it didn't matter what surfacing technique we used, we could never get a convincing or realistic curvature. This was because a realistic curve is not something that you can ever draw or model or sketch. If a curve hasn't been analysed and engineered structurally then the final surface will never look right. This was one of the reasons why the project was so important, because it gave us a way of running a form-found analysis on a surface so that the design team could get more precise input from the engineers. Previously, the engineers would say, 'tell us when you've decided on all the boundary conditions and we'll run an analysis on proprietary software that we've developed for ourselves. One run of that software would often cost you several thousand pounds, and we were trying to support a design team that wanted to run it several times a day over a period of weeks. By developing our own form-finding programs, we could offer much cheaper and closer support for the design team. And when the designers then went to the structural engineers, to run the proper analysis, they were able to have a much closer and more advanced level of dialogue. Hugh Whitehead, formerly of Foster + Partners, in conversation with the editor, 2009

The actual software behind the analysis wasn't new on the project; what was new was the addition of the fabric roof over the existing structure and the way the forces were tied to the existing arches. Normally you'd either use a whole new frame or else you'd isolate a new structure separately from the old; but we were trying to work in a more holistic way, to utilise as much of the existing structure and minimise new interventions. Angus Palmer, of Buro Happold, in conversation with the editor, 2010

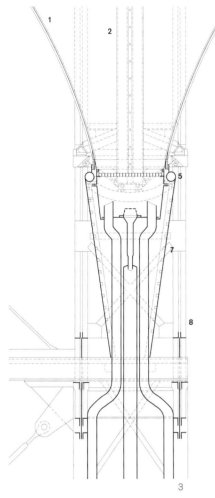

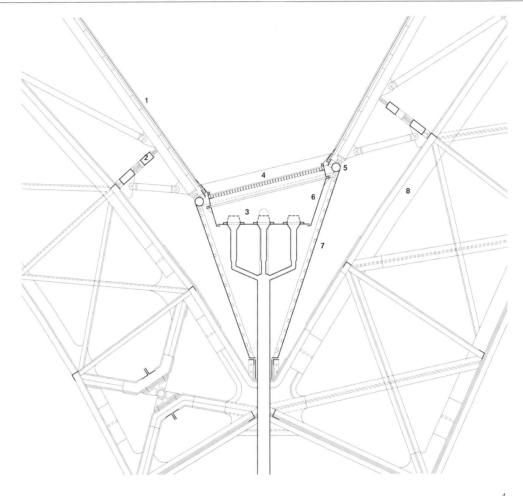

3

4

This concept came into its own with the complex curvatures of the Swiss Re tower and the roof of The Sage Gateshead, and it offered the perfect tool for the design of Dresden's roof. By using parametric software to 'tag' virtual elements with physical properties, the design team was able to create a three-dimensional model of the roof's structure. Using commercially available software from membrane specialists Birdair, this information then formed the basis for an iterative form-finding technique. The parametric model of the structure generated a virtual surface, which in turn was gradually refined by Birdair's program. The surface was broken up into hundreds of nodes and panels, which were analysed and adjusted in turn.

5

3-5. Between the central and side halls, the membrane is pulled at every second arch to create low points, which provide structural shaping and rainwater drainage points. The detailed sections show a typical low-point, looking east-west and north-south.

1 0.8mm thick PTFE-coated glass-fabric roof membrane
2 114.3/12.5mm steel CHS
3 rainwater intake
4 30 x 30/3mm grating
5 114.3/8mm CHS oval-shaped ring
6 intake funnel: 6mm stainless-steel sheet
7 funnel grommet: 3mm steel sheet
8 upper chord of existing roof arch

The original stonework behind the GDR facade was in poor condition. We were able to restore some of it but where the stonework was entirely missing or beyond repair we have replaced it with rendering. As with the rest of the station we have brought back the original proportions and shapes rather than reintroducing ornament where it no longer exists. Ulrich Hamann, of Foster + Partners, in conversation with the editor, 2010
Right, far right: One of the main entrances on the north facade before and after demolition work. As with the rest of the structure the facades had been clad in anonymous limestone during the GDR era masking the original ornament and geometry.

The north and south facades suffered direct hits during the war, so in parts they are both bomb and fire damaged. This was further exacerbated by the addition of cladding during the GDR era. Because the cladding was secured by a series of anchors, when we removed it in some cases the original stonework came away too. The original entrances to the station were made from cast iron and so luckily these survived both war damage and that caused by the application of the cladding. Tillmann Lenz, of Foster + Partners, in conversation with the editor, 2010

Previous pages: Looking from the central hall across to the south hall.

1. The 29,000-square-metre PTFE-coated glass-fabric roof that covers the platforms is translucent, transmitting 13 per cent of daylight. It gives a gentle, even light and has significantly reduced the energy demands of artificial lighting.

1

Once the edge parameters were established – a relatively lengthy process – the Birdair software was able to generate a shape solution in seconds. This was a very lightweight version, and it left the actual stress calculations and cutting patterns
for further work by engineers. But it allowed the Foster team to analyse geometric options very quickly, and to develop a shape that harmonised with the arches. The parametric model could be adjusted – for instance, the offset distance of the fabric from the arches could be changed and the tension at the pull down points could be tightened – and the resulting shape then calculated quickly.

Dresden's roof structure presented several viable alternative shapes. At its simplest, the three ranks of arches could have been covered with a monolithic (albeit seamed) covering pulled down tight against the structure by cables running the length of the station. This would not, of course, have had the desired relationship with the subtle geometry of the arches.

What began to develop was a unique tent shape that borrowed the positive curvature of the main arches while 'cupping' between each arch in the longitudinal direction, and likewise creating funnel shapes in the interstitial zone between the three vaults of arches. Thus, seen in cross-section, the fabric would be curved one way, while in long-section it would be curved in the opposite direction. This established efficient membrane shapes within every structural bay, allowing for very simple, lightly tensioned fabric panels instead of the cables and strengthening patches that larger-scale solutions would have required.

Buro Happold, the engineers for the roof, welcomed this advance. They were able to take the shapes produced by Foster's modelling and very quickly perform fundamental stress calculations on them. This information was then fed back to the architects. Eventually, a balance between a formal echo of the station's curved structure, the economics of fabric reinforcement, and the performance parameters of the arches themselves produced an extraordinarily refined membrane solution.

0   30m
0   90ft

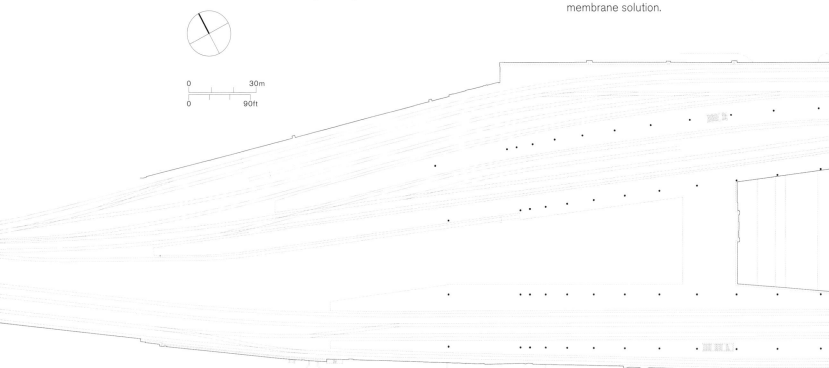

The GDR's changes to the station are an interesting mix of pragmatism – having little money or materials – and the will to change the architecture of the building. There was an attempt to make it look less Wilhelmine, to remove the Emperor's imprint from the structure. The evidence we found indicates that they intended to remove all decoration and create a modern building and had there been enough resources at the time this would probably have happened. Christian Hallmann, formerly of Foster + Partners, in conversation with the editor, 2010

There were very intensive discussions about whether we should replace the clock towers. We didn't replace stonework damaged by bullets and bombs in other parts of the building, but we though it was the right decision here because the damage was done intentionally. Still we wonder if it was the right thing to do. Maybe in another city we would have done something different. But it's important to many people in Dresden to have things back as they once were. Stanley Fuls, formerly of Foster + Partners, in conversation with the editor, 2010

2. A train driver's view of the approach into the station's central hall, which serves national trains. The flanking halls – to the north and south – serve international trains.

3. Plan at raised platform level. The scale of the original building is remarkable; the north and south elevations, flanking the city, are 240 metres long. The east and west elevations measure 122 metres; the reception building has a floor area of 4,500 square metres.

1 North Hall
2 South Hall
3 Central Hall
4 lobby
5 restaurant
6 tickets
7 lounge
8 meeting room
9 King's Pavilion
10 entrance plaza

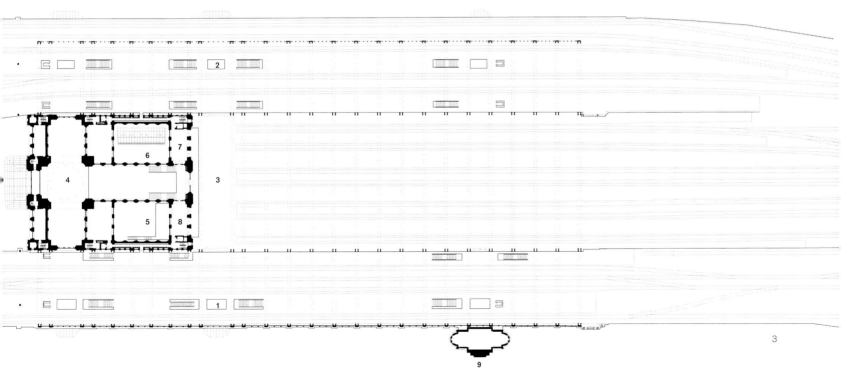

As much as for its technological and historical approach, Dresden also continues a tradition within this practice of the all-embracing social space or 'urban room'. Railway stations are not just about movement – they are also places of social interaction. Like airports, stations now are more than just about processing people: there is a renewed emphasis on lounges, club rooms and restaurants. So like the older, grander model of the Parisian stations in particular, stations I think will become known for their food and good living as well as their ability to get you from A to B.
Spencer de Grey, in conversation with the editor, 2012
Right: The gala evening to celebrate the station's opening, 10 November 2006.

1, 2. The reception building survived in essence but one of the principal rooms was totally destroyed, the other converted beyond recognition. The building now contains the travel centre, shops and restaurants. In this space, to the north of the central aisle, the brickwork has been left bare as a remembrance of the form and geometry of the original room, and the space enclosed with a simple, contemporary roof.

1

2

In addition to aligning drainage and floor connections with the existing arch supports, the final tent shape included openings over the arches themselves that brought in daylight and permitted the release of hot air during the summer. This concentration of light over the structure had the simultaneous effects of emphasising the rhythm of the arches while visually separating the twenty-first century technology of the roof surface from the nineteenth-century technology of the structure. This created a refined dialogue that would have been lost had the tent taken on a form less inflected by the shape and pattern of the original structure.

Deutsche Bahn's ongoing privatisation ran into harsh economic realities in the late 1990s. The merging of the two German economies had, more than anything, revealed the desperate financial state of the East and the turn of the century found Germany's economy suffering. As a result, Deutsche Bahn was forced to rein in plans for its eastern network, including the upgrading of lines between Dresden and Prague. By 2001, the Dresden masterplan was also scaled back, the development of the Wienerplatz was turned over to the city of Dresden, and the renovation of the Hauptbahnhof was reconsidered. With no ICE trains passing through, the canopies over the extended platforms became unnecessary. Likewise, Deutsche Bahn no longer had the funds, or the optimism, to turn over large portions of its station to civic space. The design team was asked to review the plans, and to divide the work into two contracts – one simply to re-clad the train shed, and one to renovate the historic fabric of the station head building.

This directive led the design team to a complete re-think. However, it quickly emerged that the membrane solution was adaptable to the new project constraints. The fabric could simply be terminated at the front arches, matching precisely the extent of the original roof, and still maintain both its structural validity and its architectural presence.

Once the design was fixed, Buro Happold used Foster's initial form-finding models to generate a calculable membrane shape and to produce a seaming pattern that could be laid out and cut – or 'lofted' – by the fabric subcontractor. To ensure proper stressing, these panels were generally cut 1 metre short and then stretched into position on the iron frame.

The restored and revitalised Hauptbahnhof presents the traveller with a remarkable sequence of spaces.

Construction proceeded while the station maintained a full service, meaning that work on the roof had to be rigorously segregated from activity on the platforms below. The first task was to clean and repaint the frame. Strengthening was added where required, although this was done carefully, to avoid distracting structural members interfering with the clean lines of the shed roof. Work proceeded on the sheds using travelling platforms, ensuring that a majority of the platforms were covered at any one time. In the event, a handful of arches needed to be dismantled and extensively repaired.

On the exterior, cladding added in the GDR-era was stripped away to reveal a wealth of ornament. This had been untouched in the station's earlier renovation, and as a natural complement to the purely structural ironwork on the interior it was left in place. The ornament thus serves as a foil to the smooth membrane roof.

Work to the station head building demanded a somewhat different approach. While the masonry structure remained largely intact, most of the original plaster decoration had been destroyed. Likewise, the original glass dome over the main crossing had been lost and replaced by a solid roof. In both cases, the decision was made to follow the strategy that Foster had employed at the Royal Academy of Arts in London and the Reichstag in Berlin.

The design solution would restore the geometry of the original spaces, and would expose original materials where possible, but it would not seek a literal reconstruction of period ornament. Spencer de Grey recalls being nervous about the possible reception of this strategy, but as at the Reichstag, the client was enthusiastic about the balanced approach to a historic, though long since compromised building fabric.

The restored and revitalised Hauptbahnhof presents the traveller with a remarkable sequence of spaces. Arriving from German locations, the rear elevation is briefly visible, giving a quick overview of the shed's tripartite logic. The membrane roof, however, only makes itself apparent once a train has pulled into the station, offering an explosive, light-drenched contrast to the heavy grey exterior of the end arches. Iron arches read in sharp contrast to the milky-white fabric, whose graceful curves add a subtle, resolutely modern balance to the regularity and simple geometry of the shed structure.

Unlike most membrane structures, the shape and seaming patterns of the roof flow with the surrounding architecture, testament to the validity of Foster's form-finding process. There is no divorce between bearing and tensile structure here, as in so many of the classic tent roofs in Germany and elsewhere. Rather, the membrane is both visually and structurally a refined participant in the arches' logic, establishing a dialogue of light and lightness with the historic structure.

Connections between the station and the Pragerstrasse will eventually be made through a combined transit and pedestrian piazza, the Wienerplatz. While undertaken by a different architectural team, the new piazza provides a pedestrian frontage to the station's flank, where the regular bays of the iron structure are now capped by the curves of the new roof membrane. This is an urban presence equal to the dramatic shed interior, all the more remarkable for Foster's willingness to play second fiddle to the historic elevation.

3

4

3, 4. The reception building is organised around a cruciform arcade, in the manner of a grand basilica. The crossing point was originally crowned by a 34-metre-high glass cupola and the space below it – Unter dem Strick – was a renowned meeting point in the city. After the war, the surviving frame of the cupola was shrouded in mock tiles, rendering it opaque, and the spirit of the original planning was lost. A key part of the renovation was to regain the building's original logic and clarify circulation. Flooded with daylight from above, the crossing point once again provides a central focus.

Dresden Station is a remarkable example of many of the practice's long-term interests, while serving as a testing ground for several new directions. Foster's careful, somewhat stoic approach to the tragic history of the station and its surroundings suggests a continuation of the inspired documentary approach at the Reichstag. In both cases, the building serves as both a functional container and a revelation and articulation of layers, exposing and preserving parts of the building in a careful balance of historical exposition.

There are no dramatic gestures here, no purple architectural prose. Rather, connections to the past are implied or simply revealed, and the result is both powerful and personal. Similarly, Dresden represents an ongoing engagement with the necessities of mass transit, and a discovery of architectural potential in its required efficiencies of circulation. Here, Dresden is reminiscent of Canary Wharf Station or, in its cross-section, of Stansted. The structure also continues Foster's search for social space within public or institutional buildings – the 'urban room' – which is most clearly elucidated in the extraordinary openness of The Sage Gateshead.

Dresden also represents remarkable departures in the firm's design work. The membrane roof is the most notable of these. Likewise, the Hauptbahnhof is the first major use in the office of CAD modelling to provide engineering feedback in-house, a transformation of the practice's long time leadership in digital visualisation. Here, as Hugh Whitehead, former leader of Foster's Specialist Modelling Group, points out, CAD is used as a system that models physics, not merely perspective, and this initial success has changed the way the practice views digital modelling. There is now a veritable battalion of computer programmers and experts working full-time in the office to model not only membrane structures, but also basic environmental strategies. The use of 'light' engineering in-house allows consultations with external engineers such as Buro Happold or Arup to begin from a highly informed position, in effect targeting their work more effectively.

1

1. Detailed section through the cupola. Beneath its post-war covering, the elegant structure was discovered intact. This has been restored and revealed behind the new glazing that encloses it. A 15-metre diameter, transparent ETFE foil cushion separates the volume of the dome internally from the concourse. It allows light to flood into the space and facilitates natural ventilation in summer; in winter, it rises to close off the volume so that heat is retained.

2. Looking up through the cupola glazing.

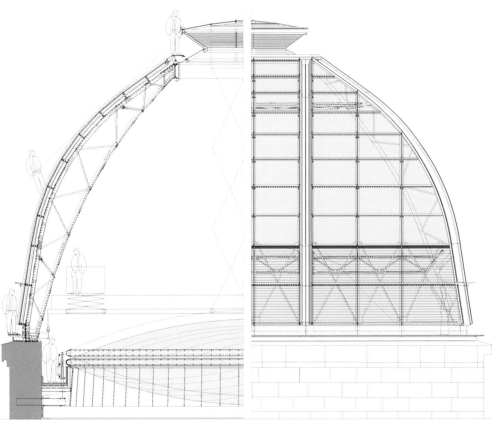

2

Our starting point was to strip away additions and alterations made to the building over the past sixty years in order to restore the integrity of the original design and to rationalise circulation within and through the station. Externally, the most striking new element is the glass dome above the main circulation crossing. The approach we followed here is similar to the one we explored at the Reichstag. Original surfaces have been exposed wherever possible, but there has been no attempt to recreate old forms or replace lost ornament: new and old are clearly articulated.
Norman Foster, in conversation with the editor, 2012
Left: The cupola of the New German Parliament
Reichstag, Berlin (1992-1999).

In its continuity with major themes in Foster's oeuvre and in its important departures from these, Dresden Station is a key project for its architects, its clients and its site. Deutsche Bahn and the city of Dresden both offered support for a solution that, de Grey believes, would not have been possible in the UK or the US, where a more dogmatic view is taken toward sites of compelling historic interest. Germany, however, has been willing to transform some of its most powerful, evocative relics of unhappier times into dramatic statements of optimism, and Dresden's Hauptbahnhof participates in this extraordinarily vital process through both restoration and metamorphosis.

Foster's careful, somewhat stoic approach to the tragic history of the station suggests a continuation of the inspired documentary approach at the Reichstag.

The flood of light through the new membrane roof and the way it outlines the skeletal structure below will be seen by some as engineering wrought with a sculptor's hand, by others as an intensely metaphorical evocation of the station's history and rebirth. De Grey will only go so far as to say that the space is 'celebratory', but the appropriateness of the fabric roof seems to reflect, as at the Reichstag, a deep awareness of architecture's emotional power even when deployed in so nuanced a fashion. De Grey is more willing to admit the appropriateness at Dresden of the Foster studio returning to its architectural birthright, the ferro-vitreous tradition in train shed design.

There is, without question, an unbroken line that flows from these structures through to the long spans of Nervi and Owen Williams, and into the post-war generation from which Foster can claim a direct inheritance. One can read in the tectonics of Dresden's shed – and many others – the quest for a light, efficient envelope that balances daylight with long spans and overwhelming scale with intricate detail.

3

Here, one thinks again of Stansted and comparisons with London's great nineteenth-century train sheds. In that sense, the membrane is a tribute and an acknowledgement of the practice's place in a long tradition of modern architecture based in structure and fabrication. But the train sheds of the late-nineteenth century also represent a nascent belief in the power of clearly conceived and developed functional diagrams to inform the essence of a large-scale architectural project.

It is possible to see in these structures the most compelling response to the compositional approach taken by the Beaux-Arts, one that would inspire generations of more empirically inclined architects to begin their designs from an understanding of the patterns of movement that would take place within them. Foster's work at Dresden draws all these threads together in a most compelling way.

Thomas Leslie

3. Externally, the glass dome above the main circulation crossing appears to be a striking new element. However, the form and structure of the cupola are original: only the glazing is new. The approach followed here is similar to that explored at the Reichstag. Original structure and surfaces have been exposed wherever possible, but there has been no attempt to recreate old forms or replace lost ornament: new and old are clearly articulated.

Overleaf: The station seen from the north-east, looking across Wienerplatz.

Smithsonian Institution Courtyard
Washington DC, USA 2004–2007

As we become increasingly urban in our way of living, the theme of spaces that are not over-specific, not totally prescribed, that are free and accessible, where people can go to meet friends, to eat and drink, to relax, is extremely important in a city. That was our starting point with the **Smithsonian.** Spencer de Grey, in conversation with the editor, 2012
Right: The courtyard of the United States Patent Office Building – now the Smithsonian Institution – seen at the end of the nineteenth century.

I go to the Smithsonian Courtyard for events and periodically I'll just go in during the day and sit down and be part of the space and enjoy it. It's both quiet and contemplative but also joyous because the kids can play with the water feature and people go there to meet – it's just a very inviting atmosphere. Robert Kogod, in conversation with the editor, 2009

The Robert and Arlene Kogod Courtyard, at the Smithsonian's Donald W Reynolds Center for American Art and Portraiture, makes a twenty-first-century statement at the historic heart of a meticulously preserved nineteenth-century landmark. The space has been wholly re-defined by Foster's sinuous canopy and the project demonstrates anew how Foster and his team, led here by Spencer de Grey, are able to balance respect for a historic structure with the contemporary requirements of a major institution.

The transformation of the courtyard within the old Patent Office Building – described by Walt Whitman as 'that noblest of Washington buildings' – was a project ideally suited to Foster. The practice's sensitive interventions within historical buildings – the Great Court at the British Museum and the Reichstag, among many others – provided an ideal point of departure for the reinvention of this hitherto under-used outdoor space as a year-round 'urban room'.

It is fitting that a building known as America's 'Temple of Invention' should be subject to such a degree of aesthetic and structural innovation.

While the general approach to the design may be analogous to other Foster projects, most notably the Great Court, important aspects of the Smithsonian programme are fundamentally different from anything that had come before. Most important, from the outset it was clear that any structural intervention could not impinge on the existing fabric of the building. Working closely with Washington's National Capital Planning Commission (NCPC) and the US Commission of Fine Arts (CFA), the Foster team devised a scheme that preserved the historical integrity of the building. Indeed, the structurally elegant solution that resulted might well have eluded a team less committed to the principles of architectural conservation.

Addressing an old building on this scale, Norman Foster has drawn the analogy with a city, in which layers of history exist side by side. Here, the courtyard canopy represents just the most recent layer of history in an evolutionary process that dates back to 1836, when Congress authorised a competition for a new Patent Office Building to store the growing number of models required to accompany each US patent application. When completed, it would be the largest office building in the United States.

The building's acknowledged architects are Robert Mills and Thomas U Walter, who oversaw the project during its thirty-two-year construction, from 1836 to 1868. However, it was the youthful William Parker Elliot – who had never had an architectural practice – who won the competition with a submission, in the Greek Revival style. Prompted by Elliot's inexperience, President Andrew Jackson appointed Mills to 'form plans and make proper changes', while respecting Elliot's general scheme. It was Mills who devised the dramatic interior detailing and circulation that characterised the early phases of building.

Congress had authorised funding for a structure that would serve for fifty years, not anticipating that it would take two-thirds of that time to build. Despite Elliot's manoeuvrings against him, under Mills' supervision, the south wing was completed and portions of the east and west wings were built. In 1850 Elliot complained to President Millard Fillmore that Mills was 'destroying the original plan'. The following year, he enlisted the help of the new commissioner of public buildings, William Easby, to oust Mills.

1

Opposite: The Smithsonian Institution occupies the Greek Revival former United States Patent Office Building (1836-1867), described by Walt Whitman as 'the noblest of Washington buildings'. It was transferred to the Smithsonian Institution for use as the National Portrait Gallery and the Smithsonian American Art Museum in 1958. The enclosure of the grand central courtyard was prompted by a desire to transform the public's experience of the galleries and, in the process, to create one of the largest event spaces in Washington.

1. An elevated view of the Smithsonian and the courtyard roof, seen from the corner of 7th and S Streets.

2. The defining design sketch by Norman Foster – the new roof is seen as a 'cloud' floating above the building.

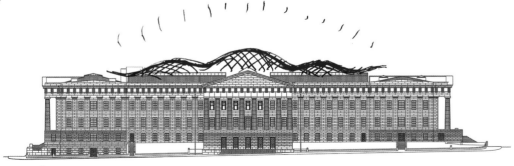

2

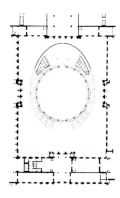

1, 2. An early 1:200-scale presentation model, shown with and without the courtyard roof. Structurally, the roof is a flattened tied-shell structure supported on eight 33-inch (850-mm) diameter columns, which take all loads and provide lateral stability. The columns also contain water downpipes. The roof shell is composed of three interconnected shallow domes. The primary spans measure 95 x 119 feet (29.1 x 36.35 metres), and the secondary spans 60 x 95 feet (18.17 x 29.1 metres).

3. An exploded drawing of the courtyard and its roof. This drawing shows the more developed scheme, in which the edge of the roof shell follows a constant line above the parapet, the only exception being where it swells in response to the portico of the South Wing.

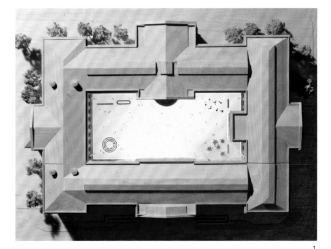

1

2

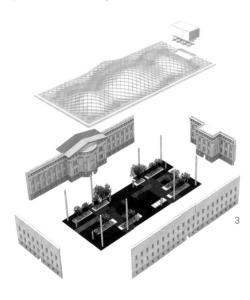

3

His replacement – Thomas U Walter, architect of the US Capitol – saw the project through to completion. Ironically, in the process, Elliot brought himself no closer to supervising the execution of his design. The monumental south wing, clad in brown Virginia sandstone, was completed in 1842. A graceful double stair led from the ground level to gallery spaces on the first and second floors. The staircase is expressed on the courtyard facade by a half-round bay that projects beneath a Classical pediment. The second storey featured an enormous vaulted exhibition space where the public could examine working patent models, like that of Eli Whitney's cotton gin. The Declaration of Independence was on display, as was a printing press used by Benjamin Franklin. In March 1865 the building hosted President Lincoln's second inaugural ball, just weeks before his assassination.

After a disastrous fire in 1877, the west and north wings were rebuilt, and other parts of the building remodelled, by the influential German-born Washington architect Adolf Cluss, his exuberant decorative scheme contrasting with the Classical austerity of the earlier work.

The Patent Office was based in the building until 1932, when the Civil Service Commission took it over. In 1953 its demolition was proposed, to make way for a parking lot. It was President Dwight D Eisenhower who signed legislation transferring the building to the Smithsonian in 1958 – an important victory for the historic preservation movement in the United States.

Ten years later, the Smithsonian reopened the building as the American Art Museum and National Portrait Gallery, restoring its historic focus on individual accomplishment, innovation and public exhibition.

By the late 1990s a full-scale renovation of the building was required – a painstaking exercise undertaken by the Washington firm of Hartman-Cox. In 2000 the Smithsonian closed to the public to allow the replacement of key mechanical and electrical systems and other improvements. By 2002 the scope of work had expanded to include the improvement of galleries and art storage spaces, the addition of a publicly viewable conservation laboratory and the introduction of an auditorium.

The most promising location for the auditorium was beneath the courtyard, which involved the removal of the garden. It was this that prompted the discussion of strategic new uses for the space and subsequently the design competition, which Foster won in 2004. The Smithsonian saw the benefits of an alfresco public space in fair weather, but recognised its limitations during the extremes of Washington's climate; they also needed a large events space. Accordingly, the competition brief called for the reinvention of the courtyard to retain its open feel while allowing year-round use.

We made a lot of study models – right up to full-size mock-ups. Working that way, we learned a lot about what was important and what wasn't. We made a sample section of the roof structure from painted plywood and suspended it 40 metres above the ground so that we could judge how it would look from below. It's a bit like designing for the theatre – if you're doing a piece that's up in the air, you don't need the elements to meet in a 1mm junction – you're quite happy for it to be a black line. Graham Collingridge, formerly of Foster + Partners, in conversation with the editor, 2011 Right: Members of the project team looking at a full-size mock-up of the roof structure at Josef Gartner's factory in Gundelfingen in Germany.

The Smithsonian team and Bob Kogod came together as fantastic clients. They were very hands on. We had many meetings in the London studio and they really put us on the spot – there was a real determination to get things right. We went into an enormous amount of detail on things like the choice of the stone for the floor; and they even came with us to Gartner's factory in Gundelfingen in Germany to see a mock-up of the roof structure. I wouldn't quite say that money was a secondary concern, but design quality was certainly paramount. Spencer de Grey, in conversation with the editor, 2012

4. Visually, the roof is raised above the walls of the existing building, clearly articulating the new from the old. The diagonal structure resulted from a number of studies, which analysed the proportions of the existing building and the spans required. The diagonal grid shell is a structurally efficient method, forming a lattice of fabricated steel members that allows the roof to 'flow' freely and appear animated as people move around below. In this early model the edges of the roof shell are not yet fully resolved.

4

5. Axonometric of a typical junction. The geometry of the glazing panels varies, the mid-point of the glass corresponding with the notional mid-point of the geometric surface, with its straight edges meeting those of the structural beam as a calculated 'best fit'. In total, there are 862 glass panels, of which ninety-two are triangular. All the glass sizes are different due to the varying geometry.

Initially, the Smithsonian had assumed that the courtyard would simply be paved in granite so that the space could be used for events and be as flexible as possible. However, conscious that a public amenity, in the form of the garden, had been lost, the NCPC encouraged a change of direction. Spencer de Grey regards the outcome as a very positive one: 'It prompted the discussion of how the garden could be reinstated and led us to commission Kathryn Gustafson as landscape architect. So in addition to a space that would accommodate museum circulation, a café, and provide a venue for every manner of ceremonial or social event, we were able to introduce a contemplative garden in the spirit of the original.'

The canopy's framing grid swells to form shallow domes in three places.

The solution to enclosing the space appeared to be a glass roof that would admit sufficient daylight to sustain planting, yet shut out the weather. Not surprisingly, the simplicity of this brief belied the depth of the implied challenges. As noted earlier, in contrast to the Great Court, the walls of the old Patent Office Building could bear no additional loads – an independent structure would be required to support the weight of any canopy; furthermore, the structure of the auditorium imposed several fixes in terms of the placement of supporting columns.

The ability to enjoy music, speeches, and regular conversation in the courtyard, was an equally critical acoustical requirement. That meant countering the long reverberation time that a glass roof and stone facades would normally induce. Innovative acoustic engineering would be essential. Heat gain beneath the canopy also needed to be managed, along with the trade-off with light reduction. Integrating and balancing the many technical demands would become the primary engineering focus of the project.

It has been the Foster studio's particular genius to be able to orchestrate the integration of complex engineering with the fine art of architecture, and it seems particularly fitting that the building known as America's 'Temple of Invention' would be subject to such a degree of aesthetic and structural innovation as resulted. Spencer de Grey emphasises the contribution of both client and patron in this process, 'combining as they did the Smithsonian's studious, civil-service ethos with Bob Kogod's spirited problem-solving approach'.

Buro Happold, the engineers for the roof for the Great Court, again contributed the engineering solution. Eight steel columns, subtly tapered and clad in anodised aluminium, support the undulating glass canopy. These slender posts are positioned around the perimeter of the space so as not to obstruct lines of sight within the courtyard; and their pale grey-gold colour blends harmoniously with the surrounding stonework.

5

A recurrent theme in Foster's oeuvre might be dubbed 'the urban room'. Typically this is a large, naturally lit space, an inward extension of the public realm into a corporate, cultural or institutional building ... it is an architectural type compensating for the loss of a conventional public realm and sometimes helping to regenerate this realm by forging new links within it. Peter Buchanan, *On Foster ... Foster On*, 2000
Left: The Galleria Vittorio Emanuele in Milan (1865-1877) – a constant point of reference for Norman Foster in any discussion of the 'urban room'.
Right: The Hammersmith Centre, London (1977-1979). An 'urban room' on the scale of Trafalgar Square, it explores ideas realised in the Smithsonian and the Great Court.

1. A cross-section through the courtyard, looking towards the North Wing. The space is capable of hosting everything from jazz concerts to grand balls. Services within the space are designed to be as flexible as possible. Eight pylons house the sound system and power sources for caterers and performers and supply conditioned air via handling systems in the basement. In winter, the space is warmed by radiant underfloor heating. The roof incorporates a number of environmental controls, including natural ventilation.

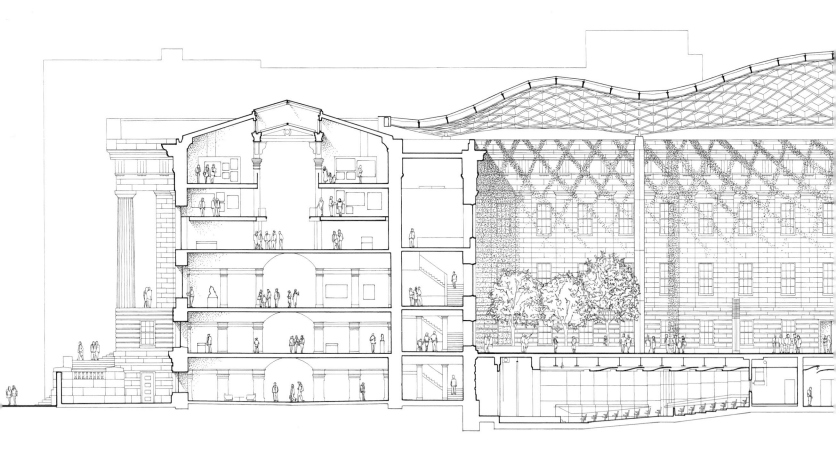

There are obvious parallels between the Smithsonian and the Great Court, but in truth they are conceptually quite different. Both spaces were originally built to introduce daylight and fresh air into big buildings. But the Great Court is essentially a focal point for circulation and facilities such as shops, lavatories, cafés and information. At the Smithsonian, however, the loos and information desks are cloaked within the main body of the building, leaving the courtyard free as a social space – a place to meet friends for a coffee, and a venue for everything from cocktail parties and concerts to grand balls.
Spencer de Grey, in conversation with the editor, 2012
Left: The Great Court at the British Museum (1994-2000).

With the canopy in place, and the courtyard resplendent with large ficus trees and a captivating water scrim – a fountain so shallow you can walk through it without mussing your shoes – the argument is over. Foster's canopy is distinguished, and it converts a courtyard that was once a spring-and-fall attraction into a year-round, compelling and peaceful mobile space. If you're meeting someone for dinner, a movie or theatre in Penn Quarter – the neighbourhood surrounding the Old Patent Office Building at Eight and F Streets NW – this is a good, free, sheltered place to do it. Philip Kennicott, *The Washington Post*, 19 November 2007

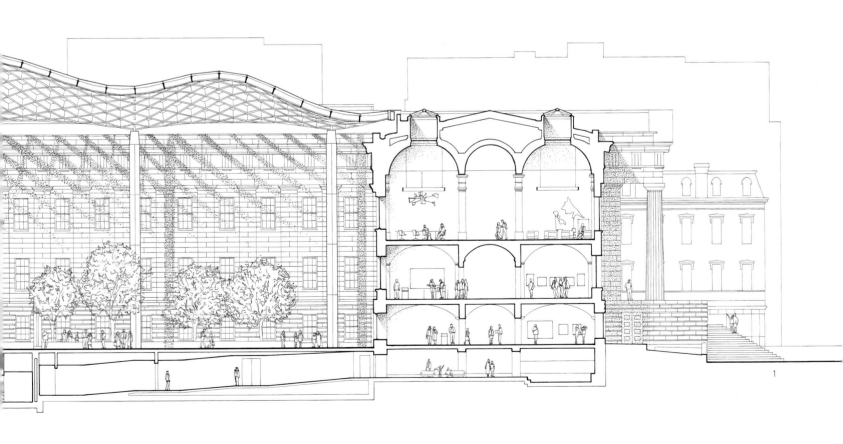

1

0   5m
0   15ft

I have described the roof as cloud-like – it billows on the skyline to announce the changed nature of the space beneath it. The shape itself is a fluid counterpoint to the Classical geometry of the old building. However, such a word picture belies the cutting-edge technology that made the structural poetry possible. Our sophisticated computer modelling software took half a year to develop. It enabled us to produce models of 120,000 different elements and explore variations rapidly. The outcome is 864 glass panels, mostly diamond shaped, and every one unique. Norman Foster, speaking at the opening of the Robert and Arlene Kogod Courtyard, 16 November 2007

The so-called hills and valleys of the canopy could not be overlit to compete with other Washington illuminations, so the coloured lights at night are directed downwards in a succession of blues, greens, pinks, purples, magentas, reds and yellows ... the trees stand out in this eerily beautiful light, with the planters appearing to float in rings of their own light. Paula Deitz, *New York Sun*, 27 November 2007

Left: The courtyard illuminated dramatically in celebration of its grand opening, 16 November 2007.

1

2

3

4

1-4. Changing scenes from the life of the courtyard; when used for major events, the space can accommodate up to 1,200 people.

5. The Courtyard Café, in the north-eastern corner of the courtyard, which is focal point throughout the day.

6, 7. The water scrim is very popular with younger visitors. The film of water is only a few millimetres deep, so there is no danger of getting too wet and feet are dry before people enter the galleries.

5

Water is a vital element of the design. When no function is being held in the space, the thinnest skein of water, about a quarter of an inch deep, runs virtually the full length of the courtyard, flowing from left to right and disappearing down a tiny slot in the stone floor. Children delight in splashing around in this wafer-thin river, which can flow at different speeds, thereby altering the clarity of the reflection. Ciar Byrne, *The Independent*, 7 February 2008

I wanted the water to reflect the beauty of the facade, so you would see the historic architecture and the Foster roof in the ground plane. Kathryn Gustafson, quoted in *Architectural Record*, March 2008

When you stare directly up at the grid of beams, it seems almost symmetrical; but as you move around the courtyard it begins to change form, undulating like a sheet in a gentle breeze. On sunny days the grid will cast a fishnet pattern of shadows over the old facades; at night its forms become more muscular and mysterious. Nicolai Ouroussoff, *The New York Times*, 19 November 2007

6

8

9

The roof has created a space that feels very much like an outside room in its ambience, volume and landscaping, but with all the benefits of an interior space – climate controlled and comfortable.

Spencer de Grey

7

8. The museum places great emphasis on encouraging younger generations to explore and enjoy its collections and organises supervised activities for children within the courtyard.

9. This juggler was one of many entertainers recruited to entertain visitors on the opening day.

If you go through the building into the courtyard you feel quite separate from the surrounding streets. That's what we and the Smithsonian liked so much about it. It is a place in which to escape from the city. Spencer de Grey, in conversation with the editor, 2012

Washington DC gets quite hot in the summer, but now you can go into the courtyard and it feels like a spring day. You don't feel as if there is an aggressive air conditioning system at work, it just feels very comfortable. You see people sitting around quietly, talking or having a coffee, which is exactly what they did before but now they are able to do it on 365 days a year. Dan Sibert, of Foster + Partners, in conversation with the editor, 2011

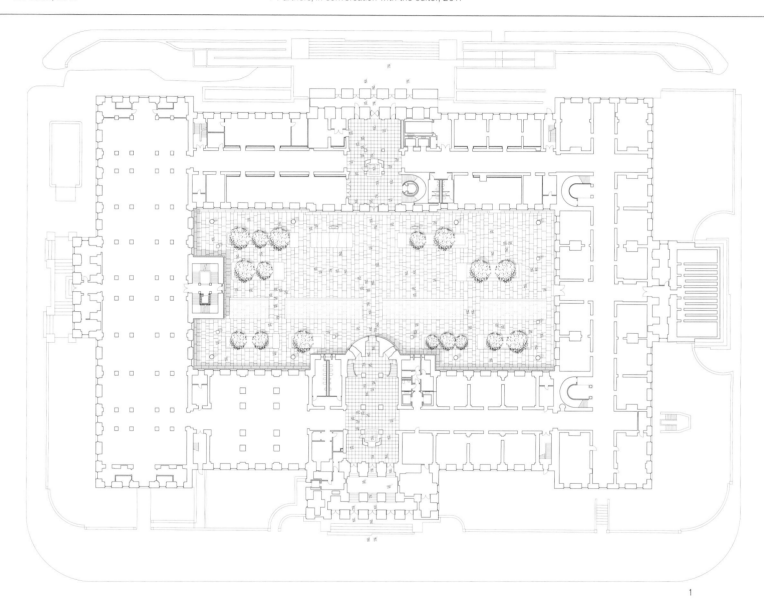

1

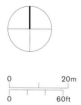

0   20m

0   60ft

With its trees and gardens, the old courtyard was an urban oasis. We have tried to preserve this quality, creating a space that can be used year round in a city whose climate spans extremes of hot and cold.

Norman Foster

Springing from the tops of the columns is the 900-tonne steel diagrid of square coffers containing 864 double-pane glass panels, each unit a unique size. The grid casts a soft web of shifting shadows that play obliquely across the stone facades. As in the British Museum, the surface of the low-iron glass carries a dot matrix of 'frits', imperceptible from below, which soften the shadows cast by the canopy. A reduction in solar gain is largely achieved through the high-performance coating on the glass, which reduces heat transmission by up to 70 per cent.

The canopy's framing grid swells to form shallow domes in three places, dispersing loads towards the eight pillars. A dome provides greater structural efficiency than a flat surface, and three domes, in this instance, are better than one. A single dome would have had to be significantly higher and therefore unacceptably obtrusive from the street. With three, even the central dome, which swells upwards to avoid cutting across the south portico, maintains a profile that is essentially invisible at street level. The three domes also acknowledge the subtle hierarchy of the courtyard's plan, with a dominant central area flanked by two subordinate zones.

Again, the design of the roof needed the approval of the NCPC and the CFA, but they required only very minor changes to the geometry, which had the effect of lowering the central peak slightly. The gentle undulation of the finished canopy captures faithfully the cloud-like character of Norman Foster's initial sketches.

Outward pressure exerted by the domes could not be absorbed by the surrounding structure, as it is at the British Museum. Interestingly, addressing this problem would solve another along the way. The Smithsonian canopy uses square panels, the primary motivation being to allow the sky to be as visible as possible. This differs from the Great Court's canopy, which comprises triangular glass panels that enjoy inherently greater rigidity than squares.

The square panel option requires the frame grid to be more rigid to keep the glass units from racking out of position and the domes needed to be braced; but if tie-bars had been used to brace the domes across the base of their arc, as they commonly are, they would have been visually intrusive. The solution provides strength to the columns and grid by paralleling the roof's valleys between the support posts, creating an unobtrusive subsidiary web.

The components of the roof's steel diagrid frame were manufactured in sections by Josef Gartner in Germany, shipped to Washington, then craned into position and welded together *in situ*. The computer precision needed to design and fabricate the frame was also required to install it, which meant frequent surveys of the roof's surface during the set-down.

The fritted glass panels were installed once the frame was complete, and each glass panel was bar-coded to ensure it was married to the correct coffer. The grid is fitted with aluminium seats, which accommodate the changing geometry of the glazing panels. In each case, the mid-point of the glass corresponds with the notional mid-point of the geometric surface, its straight edges meeting those of the structural beam as a calculated 'best fit'. This generates the stepped, iguana-skin appearance of the canopy's top surface.

1. A plan of the Smithsonian Institution, highlighting the new sequence of spaces created by the courtyard.

2. A plan of the courtyard showing the arrangement of planters and the water feature, in an arrangement devised by landscape architect Kathryn Gustafson. The planting comprises sixteen black olive trees, nicknamed 'shady ladies', and a pair of ficus trees, arranged on either side of the south portico; the trees are complemented with a mix of shade-tolerant ferns, Japanese pittosporum, sarcococca, boxwood and camellia to create a scented carpet of greenery.

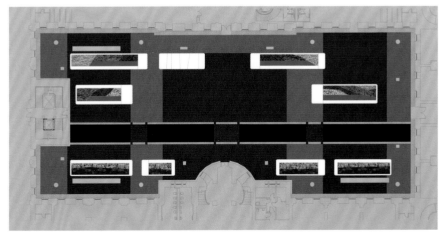

2

The roof members become wider as they meet the columns, which transfer the loads to the ground. It's partly a structural decision, but there's also an architectural component. Can you imagine a fragile roof meeting a big column and not responding to it? We felt that the junction should be acknowledged. Graham Collingridge, formerly of Foster + Partners, in conversation with the editor, 2011
Right to far right: The roof framework under construction. The framework was assembled in 8-tonne sections – the maximum lift by crane – and welded together on site. The glass panels were added from above as a separate process.
Opposite: Design sketches by the structural engineer, Mike Cook of Buro Happold.

1. A typical beam and roof detail. The primary structure is made from steel formed to create hollow beams 22 inches (555mm) deep. These are always perpendicular to the roof plane to minimise their appearance. The bottom member is a circular hollow section, which establishes a blade-like edge. Acoustic panels – made from recycled denim fibre – line the beams and are held in place by 15mm-diameter metal rods.

2. Reflected ceiling plan at a typical column head. The roof members widen as they meet the columns, both for structural reasons and to articulate the junction appropriately. Tie rods connect the column heads to prevent them from splaying.

Drainage is accomplished via channels at the top edge of the grid that direct rain and snow-melt to the tops of the hollow columns, which act as downpipes from the low points of the domes. The columns also bear lateral loads from the tie-bars and absorb wind forces.

At floor level, eight pylons, clad in the same anodised aluminium finish as the columns, deliver fresh air and contain electrical and sound systems. The lighting is designed to convert the space from a daytime external room into a night-time fantasy world. The roof is essentially kept dark – the canopy only contains task lighting and emergency lighting. Wallwasher lighting and projectors above the cornice are used to create dramatic effects for evening events; the trees are lit by spotlights to maintain their natural appearance against a multicoloured backdrop.

An integrated solution for the roof reduces what would normally have been about a ten-second reverberation time in the space to just three seconds. The surface of each beam in the steel frame is covered by a grille of horizontal 15mm-diameter rods. Behind these rods, a grey fabric lining conceals shredded denim jean material, which acts as an acoustically absorbent muffler immediately beneath the glass panels.

1

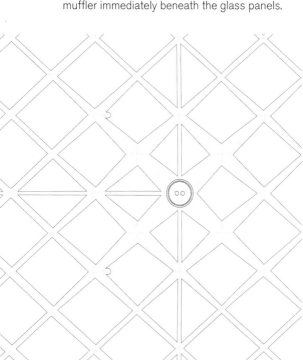

Working closely with Spencer de Grey and his team, Kathryn Gustafson created garden components that both refer to the building's past and invite visitors to pause and enjoy the space. Seven sleek, Vermont white-marble planters, each with bench-height edges, contain a variety of temperate-zone trees and plants that tolerate shade. An eighth platform, of the same Vermont marble, serves as a meeting point – 'like the clock in a train station' observes Gustafson. Most often used as a seat, it can also serve as a stage for performances.

Integrating and balancing the many technical demands would become the primary engineering focus of the project.

Contrasting with the white planters, the grey granite pavers underscore the outdoor feel of the space. The pavement's most novel attraction is a series of four water features running the length of the south side of the court: shallow 'scrims' of water emerge through narrow slots in the granite and run down an undetectable incline to a corresponding drainage channel. Visitors are invited to walk through the water, its depth calculated to allow shoes to dry before one re-enters the building. Unsurprisingly, school groups often spend at least as much time in the courtyard as they do looking at portraits.

The Smithsonian Institution courtyard, while not one of the Foster studio's larger projects, was nevertheless one of the most technologically complex and demanding to date, melding as it did, the stringent requirements of a historic preservation brief with the varied and sometimes conflicting requirements of the client's intended use of the space. Dedication, expertise and collegial collaboration have resulted in a space that brings refined aesthetics and leading-edge engineering to the service of a major museum's needs.

Edward R Bosley

2

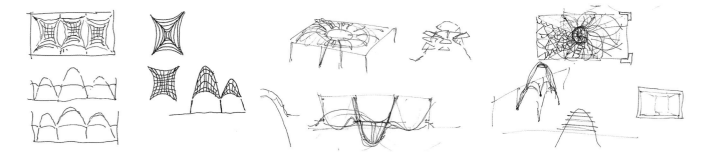

3. The glazing panels are made from low-iron glass to ensure that the colour of the light is as neutral as possible. To reduce solar gain, the glass is fritted, with a close matrix of 3mm-diameter dots covering 65 per cent of the surface area. Invisible to the naked eye from below, they soften the light and reinforce the impression of the 'cloud' above.

4. Early sketch studies by Norman Foster, exploring the junction between the column head and the roof shell.

Overleaf: The shifting geometry of the glazing panels generates a varied roofscape, the scale-like quality of the panels inviting comparisons to snakeskin.

4

3

Connections Beijing International Airport

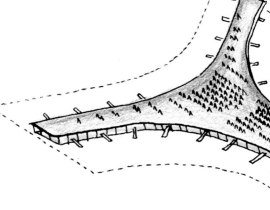

RENAULT DISTRIBUTION CENTRE SWINDON UK 1980-2

A roof umbrella covered a large warehouse, offices, canteen and showroom. The project explored the concepts of structural "trees" and natural top lighting.

Sainsbury Centre for Visual Arts - University of East Anglia - UK 1974-8

A flexible museum with natural top light capable of being adjusted to 'black-box' conditions for a wide range of exhibitions - from its permanent collection to visiting shows. Generous column-free space at ground level is serviced from an undercroft below. Although specific to the needs of galleries for paintings and sculpture plus a faculty of Fine Arts, the centre was also a later inspiration for Stansted Airport.

Beijing is the largest airport terminal building in the world, but it has its roots in the earliest buildings for aviation, in which organisational clarity and ease of navigation were givens. The search for clarity in the design of the modern airport terminal was brought to a new level of refinement by Stansted Airport, in which the quality of the passenger experience was paramount. The design of the Stansted concourse was also informed by a series of earlier projects, such as the Renault Distribution Centre and the Sainsbury Centre for Visual Arts, which introduced the concepts of the services undercroft and the lightweight roof canopy, with natural top-light. Stansted in turn informed the design of Chek Lap Kok in Hong Kong, though the scale is of a different order. In Beijing, as the scale increases yet again, the unifying roof canopy becomes virtually an 'artificial sky', evoking Buckminster Fuller's Manhattan Dome.

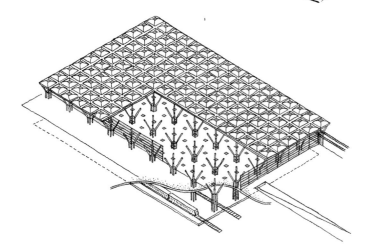

Stansted - Londons Third Airport 1981-91

Stansted literally turned the prevailing concept for a terminal upside-down. The network of pipes and ductwork normally in the ceiling were instead fed from an undercroft below the main concourse. The roof was then free to soar above and admit generous natural light - poetic, friendly and sustainable. This was a virtual reinvention of the building type and has subsequently been adopted by airport planners world-wide.

3.25 Km

0.3 Km

1.25 Km

COMPARISON - BEIJING, HONG KONG, STANSTED.

The earlier generation of airports started with a relatively small terminal which was expanded over the years by adding more terminals, this is typical of JFK in New York and Londons Heathrow, which now has five separate terminals. The single terminal of Beijing, which is the equivalent of all of Heathrows plus 17% is not only more sustainable, but avoids the complications of moving passengers and baggage over long distances between buildings. Arriving and departing under one roof is the ideal passenger experience and minimises transfer times. These diagrams show scale comparisons as well as the colouration of the Beijing terminal roof.

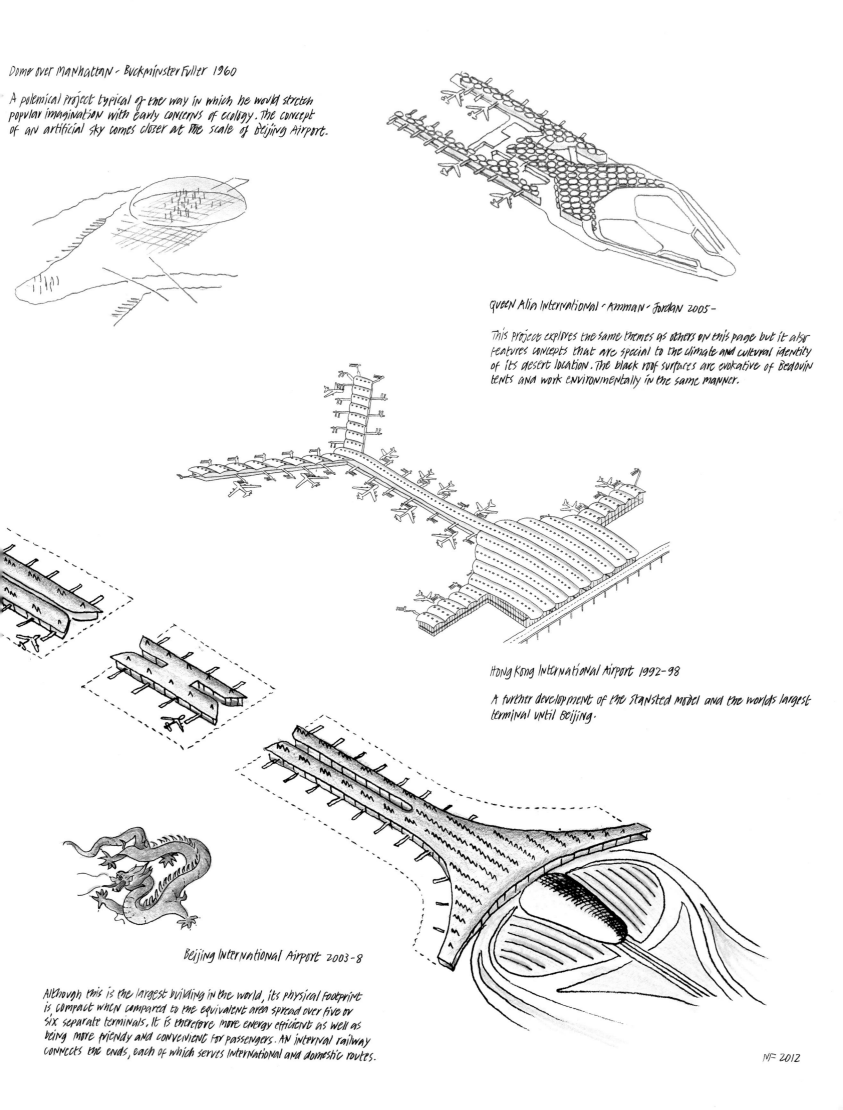

Dome over Manhattan - Buckminster Fuller 1960

A polemical project typical of the way in which he would stretch popular imagination with early concerns of ecology. The concept of an artificial sky comes closer at the scale of Beijing Airport.

Queen Alia International - Amman - Jordan 2005-

This project explores the same themes as others on this page but it also features concepts that are special to the climate and cultural identity of its desert location. The black roof surfaces are evokative of Bedouin tents and work environmentally in the same manner.

Hong Kong International Airport 1992-98

A further development of the Stansted model and the worlds largest terminal until Beijing.

Beijing International Airport 2003-8

Although this is the largest building in the world, its physical footprint is compact when compared to the equivalent area spread over five or six separate terminals. It is therefore more energy efficient as well as being more friendly and convenient for passengers. An internal railway connects the ends, each of which serves international and domestic routes.

NF 2012

Beijing International Airport

Beijing, China 2003–2008

Beijing's international terminal was conceived as the world's most advanced airport building – not only technologically, but also in terms of passenger experience, operational efficiency and sustainability. A symbol of place, its soaring aerodynamic roof and dragon-like form evoke traditional Chinese colours and symbols and celebrate the poetry of flight. Though it is the largest in the world, the terminal is designed to be human scaled and easy to navigate. Like Stansted and Chek Lap Kok before it, it is planned under a unifying roof canopy – the colour changing from red to yellow overhead as you progress to or from your gate. The design incorporates a range of passive environmental features, such as the skylights, which light the concourse and maximise heat gain from the early morning sun, and an integrated environment-control system that minimises energy consumption. Remarkably, it was designed and built in just over four years.

Norman Foster

We questioned at the most fundamental level the masterplan that the airport authority issued to the competitors in 2003. Instead of a series of individual terminals with the connections below ground, we proposed a linear building, similar in some respects to the Hong Kong diagram. The only problem with this is that the aircraft have to go a long way round to get from one side of the airport to the other. So, in the final version, we broke the building in two places, creating openings for the planes to go through, and pushed the connecting trains below the level of the runway. It works very well. Norman Foster, lecture at the Victoria & Albert Museum, London, 4 April 2008

The principal driver in determining the form of the building was that the client wanted a project that could be built in phases but would look as though it was completed in one. That led to the idea of phases one and two, with the third section – Terminal 3C – completed later. The dimension between the centre line of the two runways is quite small and the brief had a very unusual relationship between the number of contact stands and the building area, so the terminal is configured to maximise the length of the facade. It isn't an arbitrary whimsical, 'How about a curvy Y-shape?' It's derived from the requirements of the brief and for parking planes and so on. Martin Manning of Arup in conversation with the editor, 2010

I was part of the team that designed Chek Lap Kok and when we began work on Beijing – which was twice the size – we knew we had to produce something even better. That was a real challenge, not just because of its size but because Hong Kong had been voted airport of the year for several years in a row. Richard Hawkins, of Foster + Partners, in conversation with the editor, 2011

Previous pages: The outstretched form of Beijing Capital International Airport Terminal 3, the largest and most advanced airport building in the world.

1-4. Several different plan forms were considered for the terminal building before the final plan (4) was taken forward. Options 1 and 2 involved too many separate units and automated people mover (APM) stations; aircraft taxi routes would have been complex; so too would the passenger experience. Option 3 was too elongated and didn't allow for taxi cross routes. Option 4 comprises just three units, provides taxi cross routes; and has a manageable length and allows for phasing.

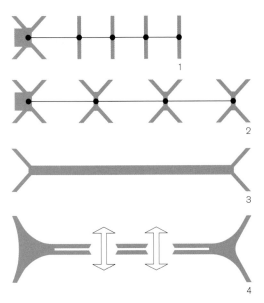

1

2

3

4

The opening of Beijing International Airport's Terminal 3 in advance of the 2008 Olympic Games, was an auspicious occasion, not only for China, but also for its designers. In 1986, working with Arup's engineers, Foster + Partners completed the Hongkong and Shanghai Bank Headquarters, their first venture into the Far East. Described at the time by this writer as 'a building for the Pacific Century', the Hongkong Bank symbolised the emergent shift of global power towards the East. Once again, more than two decades later, the same team has been responsible for another major landmark in the region's development.

In the intervening years, what was in the 1980s simply a projected, though well-founded scenario has become a global reality. The Pacific Century is now well and truly with us; and architecture in China, together with practically everything Chinese, has moved firmly from the 'periphery', as critics like to describe any building located outside the West, to centre stage. It is fair to ask, therefore, what this latest and most ambitious collaborative effort of the Foster and Arup practices in the Pacific Rim, tells us about how far both they and China have come since that earlier event.

The sheer magnitude and speed of execution alone set the project apart from all other recent and comparable endeavours. The terminal at Hong Kong's Chek Lap Kok airport, for example, completed ten years earlier by the Foster and Arup offices, was the largest single construction project of its time, involving the massive enlargement of the island site itself. Built as much in response to mainland China's rapid development as Hong Kong's, it was also the most advanced airport of its day.

No such manipulations of the land mass were required at Beijing, but at twice the size, with a million square metres of covered space – more if the adjacent Ground Transportation Centre (GTC) is included – and almost 3 kilometres long from end to end, Terminal 3 dwarfs its predecessor. Amazingly, it was also designed and built in a little over four years – half the time required for Chek Lap Kok and a fraction of the nineteen-odd years needed to complete Heathrow's Terminal 5, as Norman Foster himself pointedly observes.

The Beijing plan presents a perfectly symmetrical outline, equally balanced at each end of a lengthy twin spine with identical spreading 'wings'.

These and other astonishing facts are by now widely known; indeed Beijing airport must be one of the most publicised projects of our times. Much of this public interest stems from the new terminal's association with the XXIX Olympiad – a media-saturated event in itself. However, while the timing of the Olympics was crucial to the speed with which the project was completed, the expansion of the airport was conceived independently of that event, in line with China's breakneck pace of development. The admission of China to the World Trade Organization (WTO) in 2001 greatly accelerated that process, opening up markets and boosting international business activity. More than any of the structures built for the Games themselves, the terminal, like Chek Lap Kok before it, is therefore a direct outcome of the extraordinary economic expansion of the country since the liberalisation of the 1980s.

Aside from their respective scales, Chek Lap Kok provides other points of comparison. Ever since the practice's early industrial projects of the 1960s and '70s, Foster and his colleagues have been as much concerned with the development and refinement of selected building types as with more specific social or technological issues. London Stansted, Chek Lap Kok, and now Beijing Terminal 3, together with numerous uncompleted competition projects, comprise the evolution of the airport type. Though not necessarily a search for a Platonic ideal, this evolutionary process has resulted in a set of guiding design principles, of which many have since become standard airport practice around the world.

Thus, with appropriate variations, a unifying plan form and an umbrella roof, clarity of organisation – especially the flows of passenger movement from landside to airside and vice versa – and visibility of the aircraft at all times, minimal changes of level, abundant natural light, mechanical services contained within the podium or undercroft (rather than within the roof), and integrated ground transport systems, are all defining features of the terminal at Beijing, no less than they are of Foster's earlier airport designs.

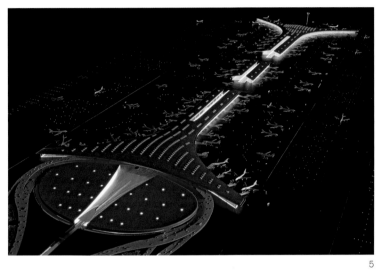

5. An early pilot's-eye visualisation of the terminal; at night the lighting reveals the gradated internal colour scheme.

6, 7. Concept sketches by Norman Foster, explaining the basic plan form of the building. It was originally intended that construction of the airport would be phased with the final, central element opening in 2030.

8. In this presentation sketch Norman Foster highlights the diverse group of people who will use the airport and the integrative process that brings them all together.

5

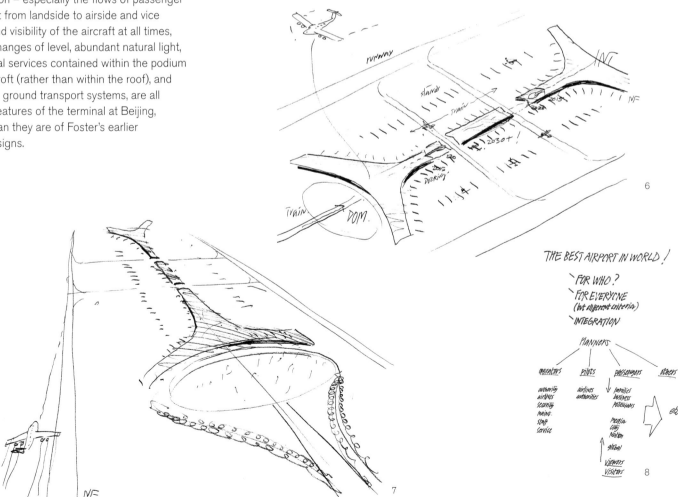

6

7

8

After we won the competition the clients said they wanted a team in Beijing immediately, so we were parachuted in from London. They gave us one of the old ballrooms from an airport hotel for an office – complete with disco balls – so we just put in some strong office lighting and desks and got on with the job. Once there, we were working in tandem with the London office so it was a twenty-four-hour operation. Luke Fox, of Foster + Partners, in conversation with the editor, 2011

China is a kind of testing ground, not only for architectural ideas, but for working on an unprecedented scale and that is what excites a lot of the people going out there now. They haven't had a chance to do stuff this big this fast before and it is very fast. They can just do it. Stuff that takes us a quarter of a century to think about, argue about and eventually do badly, they do in five years flat from start to finish. Hugh Pearman, *Front Row*, BBC Radio 4, 28 December 2007

In order to improve in design, you always have to reflect on your decisions and at Beijing the airside and aircraft movements are much more contained than in Hong Kong. This means that the aircraft have a greatly reduced taxi time and negotiating between aircraft taxiing on and off the runway is a large part of making an airport run efficiently. In Beijing you have two buildings facing each other with gaps in the spines through which the aircraft can more smoothly access the gates. Beijing has the potential to become the best airport, but it also depends on how it is run and I have great confidence that the Chinese will do that beautifully. Mouzhan Majidi, in conversation with the editor, 2012

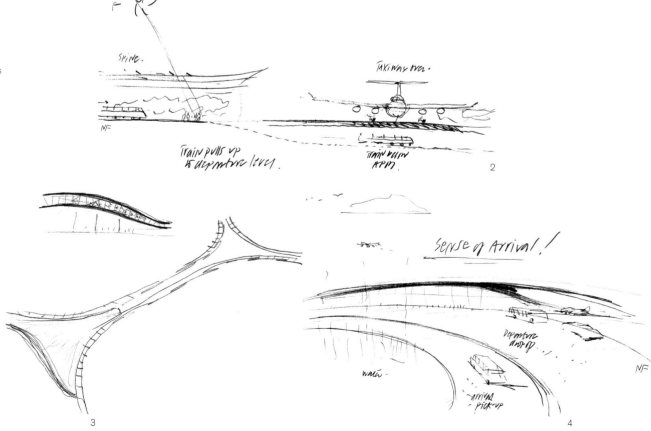

1. An aerial cutaway showing the airport arrival sequence. The Ground Transportation Centre (GTC) is in the foreground; the passenger drop-off point is accessed by the road that loops around the GTC. Domestic departures and arrivals are located in Terminal 3A adjacent to the GTC, together with check-in. International passengers progress to Terminal 3B via the automated people mover (APM).

2. Sketch by Norman Foster showing how the APM runs at ground level for the majority of its route, dropping below the surface where it meets an aircraft taxiway.

3, 4. The dramatic curve of the roof helps to create a sense of arrival and drama – as noted in these sketches by Norman Foster.

Into this mix Foster has injected a refreshingly romantic conception of air travel in the new millennium. Inspired at one end of the scale by the relatively uncomplicated buildings of the first airports, and at the other by the great railway terminals of an earlier age, all three completed Foster airport buildings have vast, luminous spaces under great roof canopies pierced by streams of natural light.

It is not widely known that the masterplan for Chek Lap Kok was drawn up by the Hong Kong Airport Authority's own consultants prior to the competition, and formed the basis for the brief and subsequent outline plan. However, such is the skill and thoroughness with which Foster and his team adapted this diagram to their own vision, and so successful is the Foster formula, it is hard to believe that it was based on anyone else's plan. In Beijing the design team had a freer hand.

The winning consortium included NACO, the Dutch airport consultants, who were able to work relatively fluidly with Foster and Arup on a joint masterplan. At first glance, the linear configuration of the Beijing terminal, with its distinctive 'Y'-shaped 'wings' at each end, looks in outline much like the Hong Kong scheme. However, closer inspection reveals significant differences in plan, operation and spatial character, indicative of the Beijing consortium's greater scope and ease of decision making.

At Chek Lap Kok, following the Airport Authority's organisational diagram, most of the main clearing functions for international travel (there are no domestic flights), including check-in counters, customs, immigration and baggage collection, together with the vast majority of retail outlets, are gathered together on several floors at the landside end, next to the GTC. The remainder of the building, including the central spine, outstretched 'arms' and 'wings', is basically comprised of passenger gates, adjacent lounges and aircraft docking spaces, or stands. The result is an oddly balanced scheme, only unified by the soaring, vaulted roof canopy the Foster team cleverly designed to pull it all together.

By contrast, the Beijing plan presents a perfectly symmetrical outline, equally balanced at either end of a long bifurcated spine, with identical spreading 'wings'. As in Hong Kong, the check-in counters for both domestic and international travel are by necessity positioned side-by-side at the southern landside end, where departing passengers arriving from the city can easily find them. However, everything else, excluding baggage collection, which likewise is necessarily positioned landside close to the exits and GTC, is distributed more or less evenly between the two forked ends of the terminal: domestic travel facilities south, and international travel facilities north.

While the timing of the Olympics was crucial to the speed with which the project was completed, the airport was conceived independently.

Departing from the Hong Kong pattern again, the twin spine is broken symmetrically in two places around the centre, creating a separate satellite terminal while allowing planes to cross from one side of the airport to the other, thus reducing aircraft taxiing distances. The satellite itself can be operated either independently – it was used exclusively for the athletes and officials during the Olympics – or as an extension of the domestic and international terminals on either side. A speedy automated people mover (APM), which runs down the length of the central spine, ties all three components together. Here too, the design breaks with precedent. Unlike the similar APM at Chek Lap Kok, which runs underground the full length of the terminal, the Beijing system runs on raised tracks level with the departure concourse, only ducking underground beneath the two roadways carrying the taxiing aircraft. The APM stations themselves are on the main floors, so if departing you do not have to change level – an innovation that represents a massive improvement in passenger convenience.

5

6

5. The transparency of the terminal building is communicated in this early model. The large expanse of glass around the perimeter, coupled with a roof studded with skylights, allows the rich Chinese-influenced colour palette to shine through at night.

6. A model detail of the Y-shaped wings that terminate each end of the building. The roof rises to its highest point at the crux of each 'Y', creating a dome-like effect.

Overleaf: Plan detailing the network of stands, runways and aircraft taxiways. There are a total of seventy-three contact stands and twenty-eight remote stands.

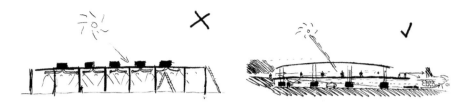

Far left, left: In these sketches, Norman Foster contrasts the conventional airport terminal cross-section, in which mechanical services installations are mounted on the roof, with the Stansted model, in which all the services are located in an undercroft, allowing the concourse to be naturally lit. This model is the basis of all subsequent Foster airport projects, at increasing scales.

Right to far right: Comparative plans of Stansted, Chek Lap Kok and Beijing International Airports – a series of leaps in scale. The Beijing terminal is the largest in the world, measuring 3.25km overall; Chek Lap Kok stretches to 1.25km. The Stansted terminal, at a modest 0.34km, would almost fit into Chek Lap Kok's baggage hall.

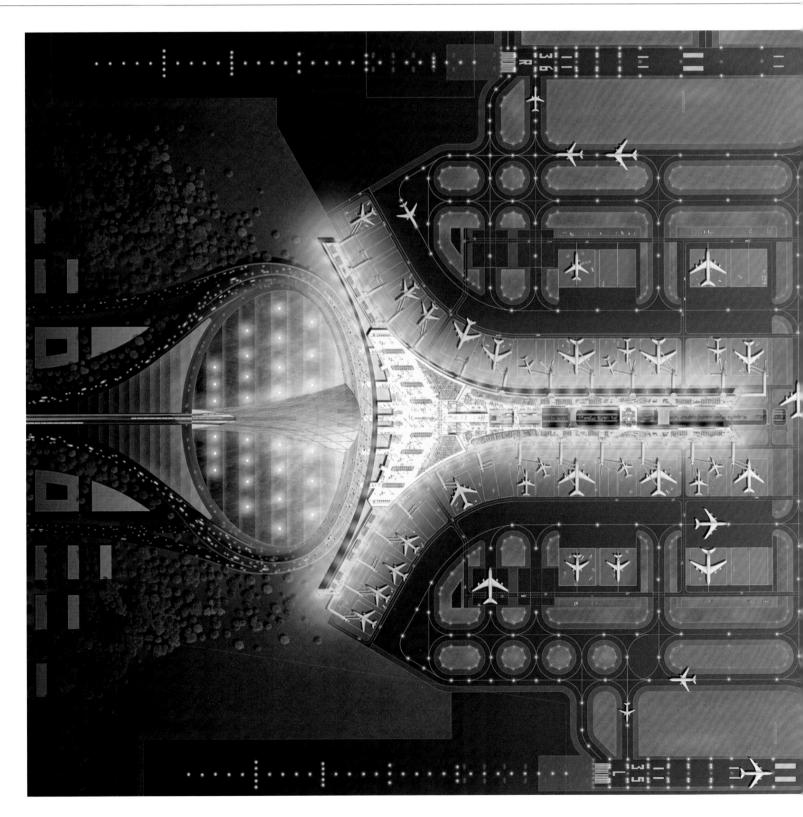

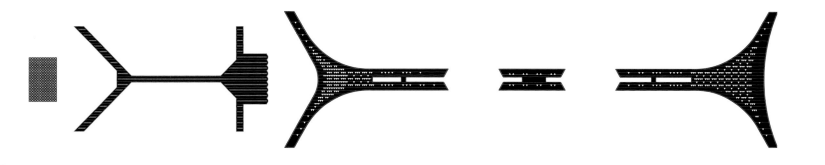

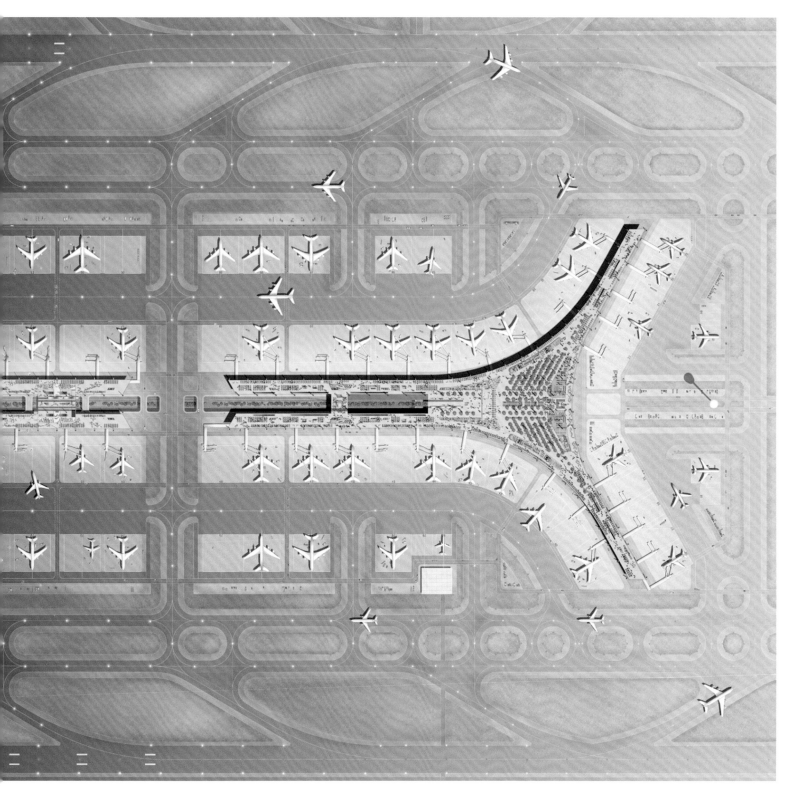

The building is laden with vital and lucky symbolism. The dragon shape is a sign of strength and a harbinger of luck in China. The terminal is shaped like the character for *ren*, which means 'people', an auspicious term and also a politically correct one in China, which is still Communist in theory. The colour scheme, running from yellow to orange to red is also in auspicious colours, and, of course, the hint of dragon scales serves only to underline its lucky aspects. Clifford Coonan, *The Independent*, 27 February 2008

The Beijing airport is very much of its place – it is designed in response to Chinese culture, especially in the way it uses colour. The idea of the vibrant ceiling and cladding system is referential to the traditional temples and architecture where colour gives richness. Beijing airport has great character – unlike so many airports in the world that are anonymous places – but we wanted to design something that would specifically draw on Chinese culture. Mouzhan Majidi, in conversation with the editor, 2012
Right: Mouzhan Majidi and Norman Foster discuss colour proposals for the airport's roof.

A gateway to Beijing, the building aims to communicate a unique sense of place, its dragon-like form evoking traditional Chinese colours and symbols.
Norman Foster

1. Study model of the space-frame roof, exploring detailed finishes and colour. The red colour of the structural steelwork glows through the 'veil' of white-painted louvres that form the soffit.

2. A detail of the same model, seen from above, looking at the angled skylights, which run the length of the building.

1

2

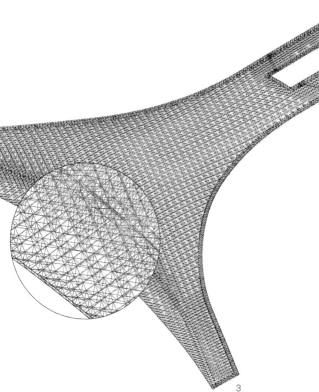

3

4

The swept curves and concave glass walls of the two 'Y'-shaped segments are also improvements over the straight walls and sharp inside corners of the Hong Kong plan, maximising the available space for aircraft stands externally and enlarging the interior volume between the wings and the spine. While only the airport operators and airlines might appreciate the extra number of aircraft stands this solution allows for, passengers can scarcely miss the visual and spatial results. It is within these larger volumes at each end of the terminal that Foster's vision of what the experience of air travel should be like comes fully into its own. As with the two earlier terminals at Stansted and Hong Kong, the insertion of all the mechanical services into the podium frees up the lightweight steel roof for its true purpose – to keep out the weather and let in light – and allows some spectacular engineering and spatial effects.

It might be thought that, given the far greater size of the enclosed spaces, the architects might have chosen to break up the roof form with a suitable large-span structural module, as they did at Stansted, with its square domes, and at Chek Lap Kok, with its parallel lines of vaults. Instead, they opted for a steel space frame made up of relatively small modules, with a triangulated geometry, which are welded or bolted together to follow the changing curves of the roof, creating a continuous surface plane top and bottom. This is clad on the underside with white painted, steel louvres, spaced apart to allow daylight to penetrate through from the triangular roof-lights above, while presenting an uninterrupted surface to the passengers below.

3. Drawing of the double-curved space-frame structure. The triangulated steel modules follow a variable geometry corresponding to the changing contours of the roof.

4. In this early visualisation the colour distinction between the international and domestic terminals reads very clearly. In the foreground are the GTC and the red glow of the domestic terminal; the international terminal, which has a yellow theme, is visible in the distance. The scale-like quality of the roof-lights and the dragon's-back form of the roof are also evoked in this image.

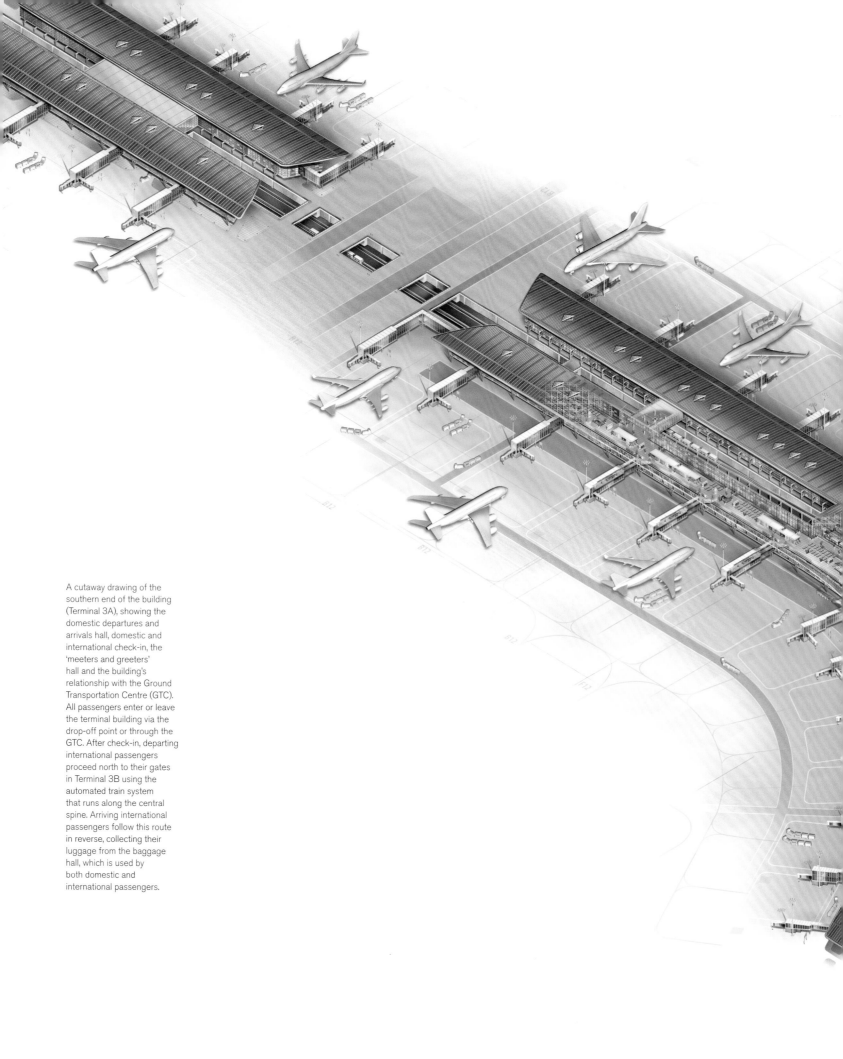

A cutaway drawing of the southern end of the building (Terminal 3A), showing the domestic departures and arrivals hall, domestic and international check-in, the 'meeters and greeters' hall and the building's relationship with the Ground Transportation Centre (GTC). All passengers enter or leave the terminal building via the drop-off point or through the GTC. After check-in, departing international passengers proceed north to their gates in Terminal 3B using the automated train system that runs along the central spine. Arriving international passengers follow this route in reverse, collecting their luggage from the baggage hall, which is used by both domestic and international passengers.

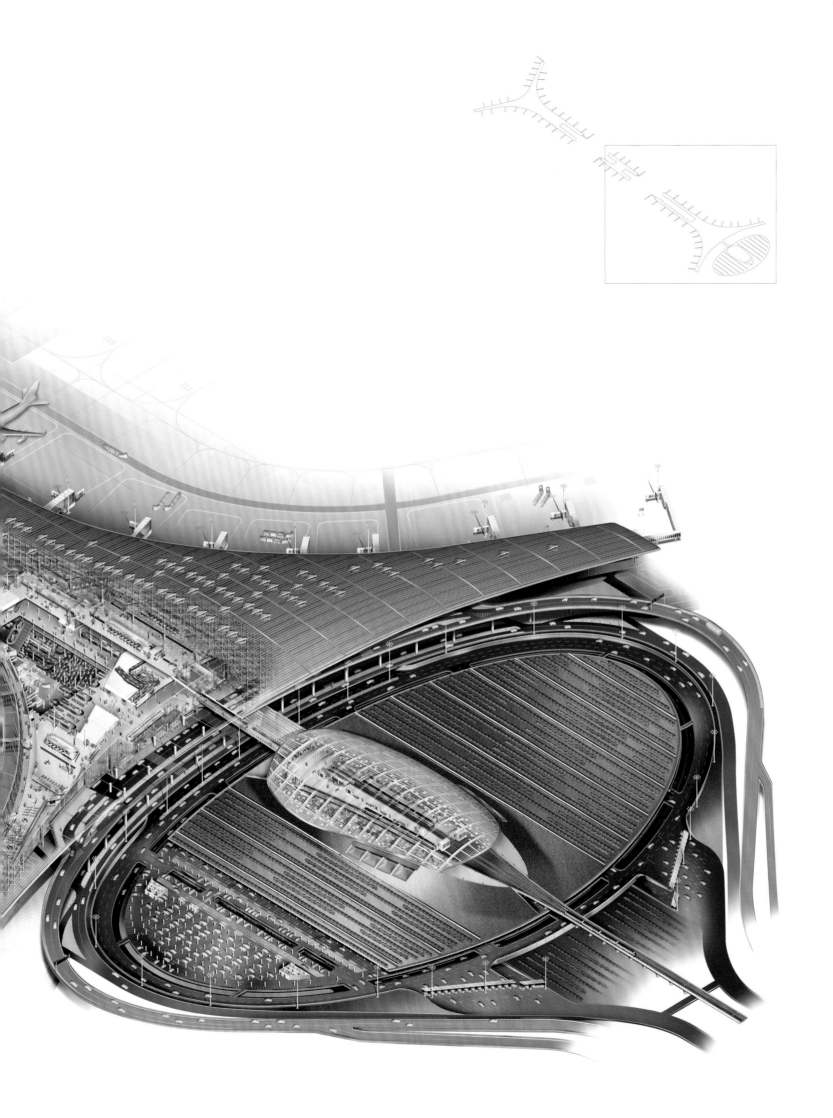

China is for me a very interesting society, full of contradictions at every turn. You look at the site and you say: 'Ah yes, it is all about manpower – hundreds and thousands of people.' But it is not really like that at all. It is not about throwing numbers at it. It is about a very high degree of intelligence and it is about every one of these people of a certain generation being raised as only children. They have been doted on by parents and grandparents. They are very special individuals. It defies every generalisation. Certainly, the quality and precision of the work is astonishing. There are things you can do in China that you could not do here. For example, the external columns are completely cigar shaped. They know how to make them because their steel industry is still related to a shipbuilding tradition, so they know how to work compound curves. It is a wider story than you'd imagine. Norman Foster, in conversation with the editor, 2012

Right: Airport workers gather for the groundbreaking ceremony for the new terminal, 28 March 2004.

1

2

3

5

4

1. Work began on site on 6 April 2004. Over the course of the next few months some 10.6 million cubic metres of earth was moved from the site and 19,488 piles sunk.

2, 3. Looking along the route of the APM system under construction; the tracks run for 2km along the central spine of the building, dipping underground beneath the two taxiways.

4. An average of 18,000 workers were on site at any given time with that number rising to 50,000 at peak periods. Work was carried out in twenty-four-hour shifts, seven days a week. In contrast to Chek Lap Kok airport in Hong Kong, built by British contractor Balfour Beatty, all construction in Beijing was carried out by Chinese contractors.

5. The elevated access road rises above the activity of the construction site.

6. Nets covered the underside of the space frame during construction to help prevent both workers and equipment from falling.

The project was built during an amazing period of change in China – the commitment it required will never be repeated. Fifty-thousand workers, in three shifts, laboured around the clock to complete the building on schedule.

Mouzhan Majidi

6

To undertake a project of this scale and quality was a once-in-a-lifetime opportunity: you'll never see that replicated anywhere else again in terms of its size and complexity. What we designed played to all the advantages of being in China at that particular moment. It pushed the boundaries of their technology and tested their manpower. They had to make things happen a lot faster so they put 50,000 workers on the construction site – it's unheard of. It was incredible to watch that many people coming together – it evoked what it must have been like to build the pyramids. Mouzhan Majidi, in conversation with the editor, 2012
Right, far right: Construction workers march at the groundbreaking ceremony, 28 March 2004.

The banners flying from flagpoles sunk into the mud everywhere carried the names of individual work gangs, each with their own territory. The gangs moved like disciplined cohorts of soldier ants, identifiable by the colour of their helmets, navigating the obstacles that littered the site. Some handling new deliveries, others preparing them for use, others shifting barrow loads of nuts and bolts across the site or, two at a time, carrying steel bars by hand. In the foreground, groups of men in crumpled suits stacked heaps of reinforcing steel, ready to be bent into the hooks that would keep them securely in place when they were finally buried in concrete. Deyan Sudjic, *The Architectural Review*, August 2008

7

8

9

7. At the peak of construction, 100 tower cranes occupied the site and up to 12,000 tonnes of steel reinforcement arrived each week. The structure was completed up to Level 1 by 13 April 2005.

8. An aerial view of the site, which covers an area of 1,480 hectares.

9. High-tech meets low-tech; traditional working methods still survive.

Despite its size and complexity, the quality and speed of construction was first rate. Any concerns that China lacked the skills or the technology to produce the level of finish we required were completely unfounded. Everything was manufactured in China, apart from the baggage handling system and APM, and all of it to a standard that matched or exceeded anything produced in the West. Brian Timmoney, of Foster + Partners, in conversation with the editor, 2011

Clearly, the designers of this building have been under immense pressure to build quickly and efficiently. Yet great panache has turned functional necessity to elegant advantage. There is something truly sustainable about this, meeting aspirations with every ounce of knowledge about how to build well. Structure and tectonics are used and applied with complete fluency. In the past, the encyclopaedic knowledge of architectural and engineering devices worked out by others ... has been applied by the Foster office with meticulous care. Now the firm's body of work is deep enough for a new generation to rework some of their own devices in the same way. Matthew Wells, *The Architectural Review*, August 2008

It is almost impossible to describe what it was like working in Beijing because you can't get across the scale of the project. You can look at the photographs now and be impressed by the size of holes in the ground, but unless you printed the photo the size of someone's living-room wall, you just can't convey how big it felt – it was absolutely gargantuan. And the sight of people digging with old-fashioned spades and using traditional wooden wheelbarrows in the bottom of an enormous hole, reminded you how much of a labour-intensive culture it is. Jonathan Parr, of Foster + Partners, in conversation with the editor, 2011

Logistically, the challenges were huge, but the project was given an unstoppable impetus by Beijing's hosting of the Olympics and China's modernising zeal, which is impelling the country forward at an unprecedented rate. Yet despite its vast size, T3 was designed and built in a mere four years – 'less time than it took to organise and conduct the public inquiry for Terminal 5', as Foster points out, putting British equivocation to shame in the face of rampant Chinese can-do. Some 2,500 design drawings were completed in four months by a team of thirty-eight in Foster's main London office and an eleven-strong satellite in Beijing set up expressly for the project. And though the building is an essentially repetitive, modular structure, it was constructed entirely in situ by a 50,000 strong workforce in a feat of manpower deployment that would have struck a chord with Egypt's pharaohs or, indeed, China's emperors. Catherine Slessor, *The Architectural Review*, August 2008

One of the most remarkable things about being there was going to the site and seeing twenty or thirty thousand workers. It was on a sort of *Ben Hur* scale and stretched as far as the eye could see – it was just amazing. Luke Fox, of Foster + Partners, in conversation with the editor, 2011

The quality of leadership was very strong, right the way through the project. Commander Chen Guo-Xing, the project manager, started his working day at 6am and would have his last meeting at 11pm. He lived on the site. He did not take time off even on Chinese holidays. And he entertained visitors in the works canteen, which was his dining room. Norman Foster, lecture at the Victoria & Albert Museum, London, 4 April 2008

When we started in November, I doubt if there were ten of us; by Christmas there were over 100, so we built a huge team very quickly of all the disciplines. We mobilised a lot of the offices in the UK, as well as in Hong Kong, Beijing, Shanghai and Shenzhen. The Chinese work from 8am to 8pm; that's 8am Hong Kong time to 8pm GMT – so they were working well over fifteen-hour days. Because it was moving so quickly and it involved so many people from different backgrounds there was a great feeling of commitment and excitement. It took us five months, 2,000 drawings and 10 million dollars to get the project to happen. Martin Manning of Arup in conversation with the editor, 2010

The Chinese architects we were working with were great, many of them sat alongside us in the Beijing office and watched how we would design and draw. Because they were using the same packages as us we were able to take them along with us. We all shared the same space: the project managers, engineers, planners and local architects all worked together. Luke Fox, of Foster + Partners, in conversation with the editor, 2011

1

2

3

Previous pages: Looking along the length of the terminal building as work progresses on the space-frame roof. A traditional bamboo scaffold provides access to the roof deck.

1, 2. The space-frame structure seen before the completion of the roof covering.

3. Looking towards the vaulted roof of the GTC.

4

4. A site entrance reminding workers that 'Quality is the life of a construction company' and that 'Safety is the guarantee of life'.

5. The vast open expanse of Terminal 3B before the completion of the roof.

6, 7. The roof of the GTC is a fabricated steel frame, clad with an aluminium panel system.

8. The space-frame roof structure is highly efficient – despite covering 70 per cent of the floor area it accounts for only 35 per cent of the building's weight.

9, 10. The roof is clad using an aluminium standing seam system; its terracotta colour was inspired by the roofs of the Forbidden City.

5

6

7

Airports are inherently complex, but this new Terminal had the added difficulty of also being the biggest building in the world. This was further compounded by the language barrier – everything had to be done through translators, which made trying to convey detailed technical information very difficult at times. However, we were very lucky to have a great team working on the project and eventually we finished two months ahead of schedule. Brian Timmoney, of Foster + Partners, in conversation with the editor, 2011

Left: Mouzhan Majidi, Brian Timmoney and Norman Foster on a site visit to the airport, shortly before it opened.

It was fundamental that we created on-site mock-ups and zones where we could have a look at prototypes and assess the quality of materials and finishes because the client wanted the project to be as good as, if not better than, Chek Lap Kok. Mock-ups helped us to achieve that, as did an incredible sense of pride on the part of the contractors who wanted to show the world how good they were. Luke Fox, of Foster + Partners, in conversation with the editor, 2011

8

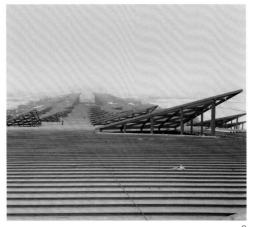

9

10

11

12

The skylights are both an aid to orientation and sources of daylight – the colour cast changing from red to yellow as you move through the building.

Norman Foster

11. Banners were used to encourage the workforce; the one on the left says: 'Build a good quality project – create a harmonious society'; that on the right: 'Always pay attention to safety to avoid accidents'.

12. Looking down into the 'meeters and greeters' hall as it approaches completion.

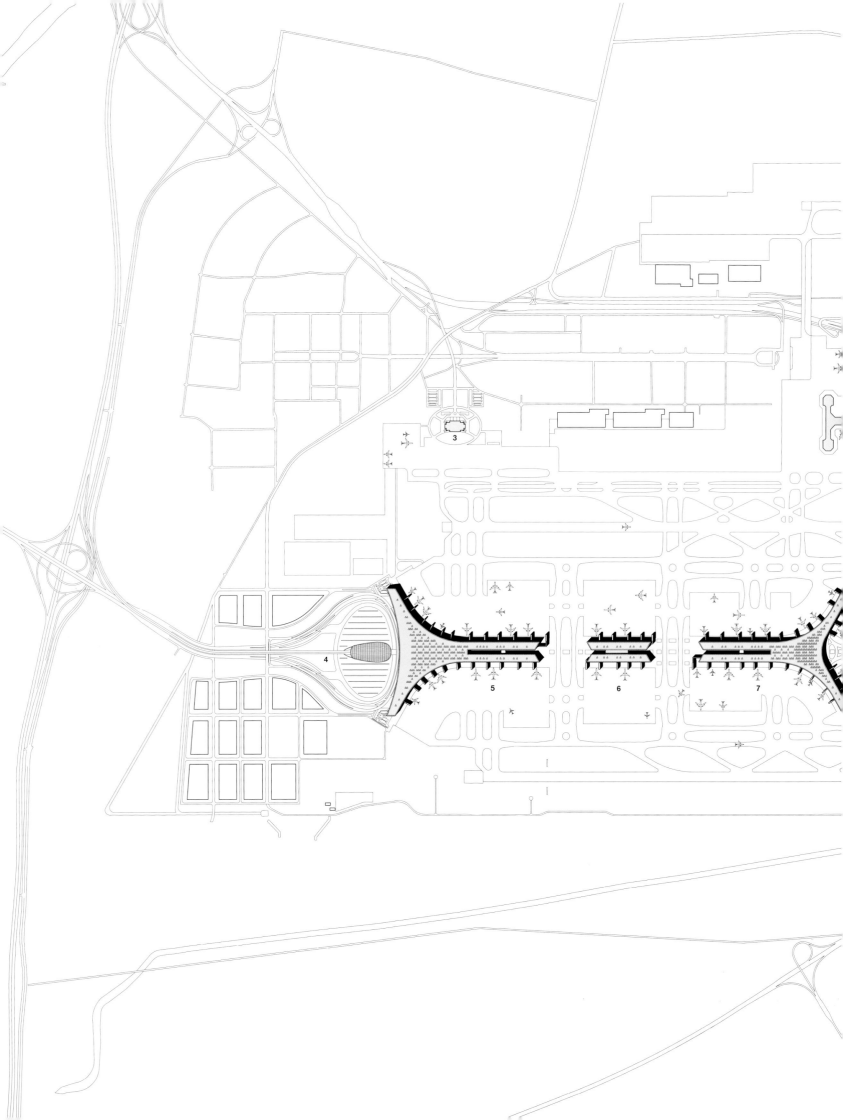

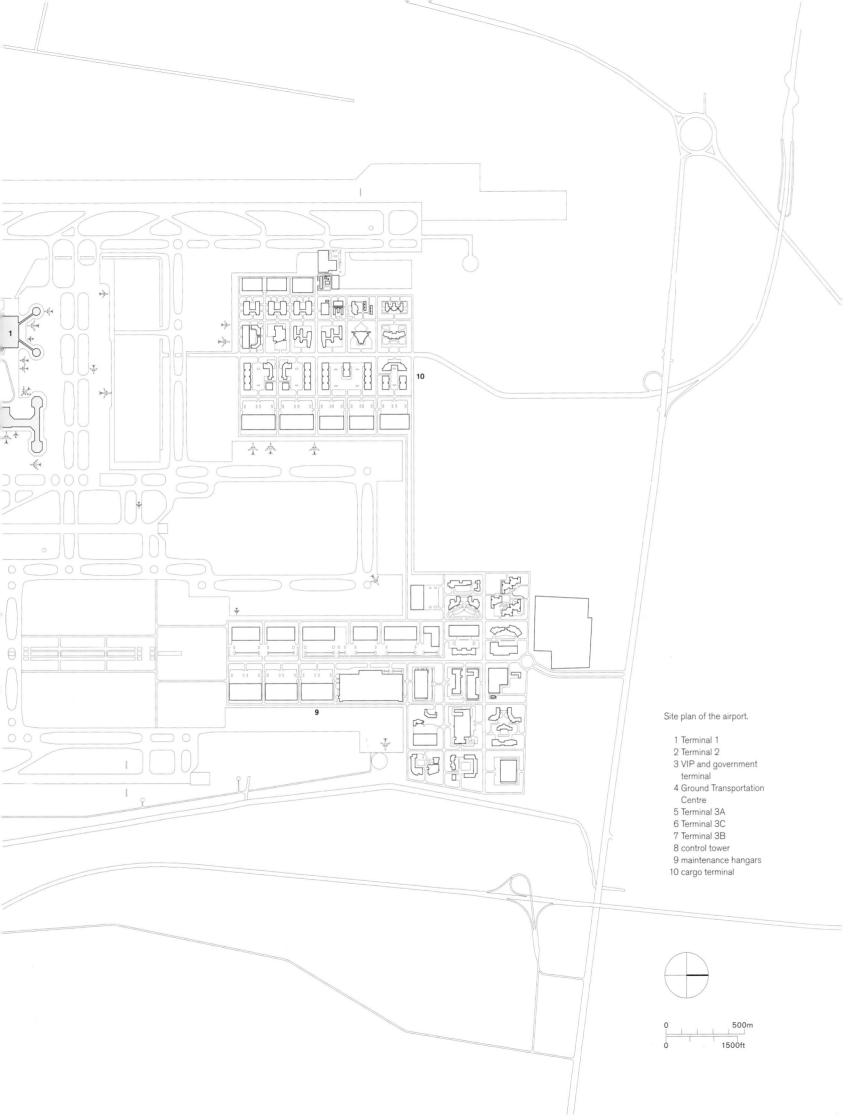

Site plan of the airport.

1 Terminal 1
2 Terminal 2
3 VIP and government
  terminal
4 Ground Transportation
  Centre
5 Terminal 3A
6 Terminal 3C
7 Terminal 3B
8 control tower
9 maintenance hangars
10 cargo terminal

0   500m

0   1500ft

Beijing airport is almost like two giant Concordes, nose to nose where you've got the delta wing at both ends forming this huge sheltering canopy. With Foster, there is nearly always aeronautical imagery in his airports. He cannot help himself and that is why you get the great wingspread, if you like, of these portals. For something that big to be that graceful, I think is a rare trick. It is red at one end and you can see through and it's yellow at the other end. There is this gradual colour shift as you move forward. Is it a leaping dragon or is it a crouching tiger? Who knows? **All the best imagery is multivalent.** Hugh Pearman, *Front Row*, BBC Radio 4, 28 December 2007

The Beijing terminal is the biggest building on earth. Compared with Heathrow Terminal 5, it's four times the size yet was built in one quarter of the time. It tells you a lot about China and how quickly everything is happening there. This building alone will cope with around 60 million passengers per annum. It took Heathrow forty years to reach that capacity, but China reached it in four years. So the rate at which growth and traffic flow is developing is ten times faster than the UK. It's astonishing to see. Mouzhan Majidi, in conversation with the editor, 2012

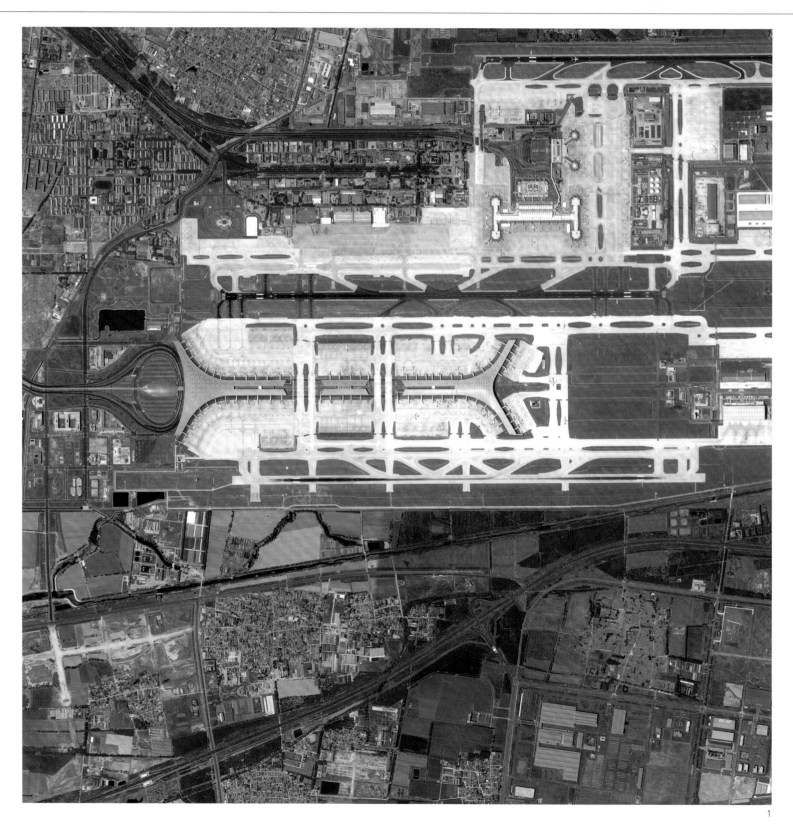

1

The trajectory from Heathrow Terminal 3 to Beijing Terminal 3 is one of those compelling studies in contrasts that neatly crystallises a wider zeitgeist. Completed in 1961, London's Terminal 3 is a broad but decidedly mongrel church, serving American, Asian and African long haul. Despite the recent addition of a new portico (part of a wider and much needed upgrading), it is still cramped, shabby and showing its age. If you fly Air China, the national carrier, this depressing milieu is your point of origin, but nine hours later you're blearily surveying the Gobi Desert and on approach to Beijing, where, in a Dantean transformation, airport purgatory morphs into airport paradise.
Catherine Slessor, *The Architectural Review*, August 2008

The effect of the continuous surface is to exaggerate the extent of what is already an enormous canopy. The space frame is supported on tapered, hollow steel columns of varying height and is curved in different ways, rising to its highest point at the centre of the 'Y' at each end of the terminal, where it forms a dome-like space. From there it falls gently towards the concave walls and further on down towards the spine and arms of the 'Y', where it flattens out into a shallow arch, finally arriving at its lowest point at the end of each arm.

The sheer magnitude and speed of execution of the project alone set it apart from all other recent and comparable endeavours.

Externally, the roof makes its presence felt in sweeping cantilevers shading the glass walls, the greatest projection – as much as 45 metres at its deepest point – being over the raised drop-off ramp at the southern end. The broad arc of the sharply tipped cantilever, which runs the full length of the two outstretched arms of the terminal, tapering off toward the horizon left and right, creates a breathtaking entrance.

Even that, however, hardly prepares passengers for what lies inside. The impact of this immense roof with its smooth, gently curved ceiling, which seems to dip and roll on for ever in all directions, has to be experienced to be believed. Only the parallel lines of downlights mounted in the roof break the continuous white surface, following the main flow of movement along the central axis and steering passengers along their way. The impression of limitless space is reinforced by the rows of giant, white-painted columns on their triangular grid, marching off into the distance at 36-metre intervals. The tapering of the round columns towards the top adds to the general effect, making both columns and space seem even taller than they actually are.

During the day, the whole of the vast interior is awash with daylight, pouring in through the tall glass walls with their beefy steel trusses, which are inclined outwards to reduce reflections, and through the rows of skylights above, which are clearly visible through the slatted ceiling. The natural light brings out the bold colours of the space frame itself, which is painted in subtly varying hues following traditional Chinese patterns: imperial red in the entry above the check-in counters, through shades of orange to yellow – or 'gold' – at the far end of the International terminal.

The graded colour scheme – a rare and welcome change from Foster monochrome – is continued internally on the wall trusses and externally within the cantilevered sections of the roof, matched by a ring of Imperial red columns located just outside the glazing. At night, artificially illuminated, the same boundless interior spaces take on a different, almost surreal character. Dotted with rows of tiny downlights stretching into what seems like infinity, the spectacle resembles nothing less than the night sky itself, or, at the very least, a mammoth planetarium simulating the same thing.

The celestial canopy helps to keep other more mundane distractions, such as the commercial outlets, firmly in their place. The visual pull and great height of the roof itself, combined with the huge volume of space contained below, has the effect of greatly reducing the impact of the densely packed outlets. What in most airports can be an exhausting jungle of competing cafés, shops and signage, is here mostly well contained, including the extravagant Chinese-style roofs and frontages. Only on the mezzanine levels beyond the check-in counters, where the roof of the terminal dips down towards the spine, do the highest outlets reach uncomfortably close to the structure itself.

1. The airport lies 27km north-east of Beijing in the Chaoyang Precinct, a largely suburban area which is also home to the city's diplomatic quarter. The first terminal, Terminal 1, which lies to the west of Terminal 3, was opened in 1958 and further expanded in 1980. However, by the mid-1990s a further expansion was needed so work began on a second terminal which was completed in 1999, in time to mark the fiftieth anniversary of the founding of the People's Republic of China. With the opening of Terminal 3 in 2008, Beijing is now the busiest airport in Asia.

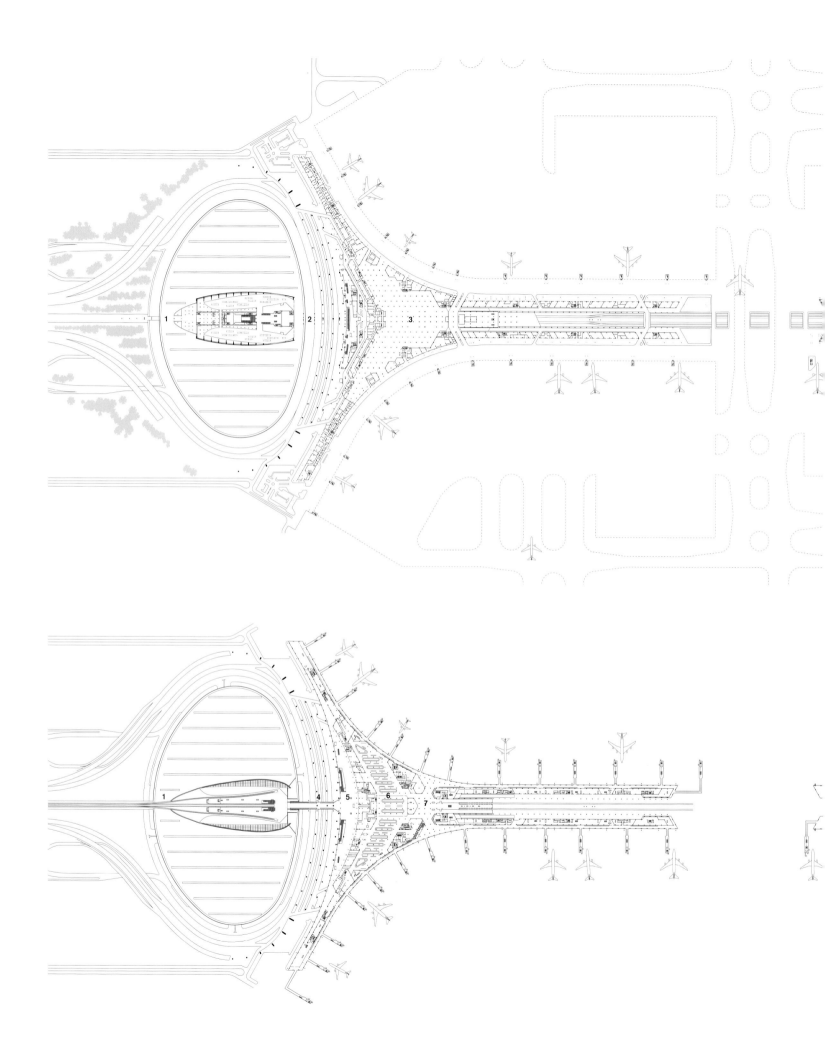

1. East elevation of the
Ground Transportation
Centre, the domestic,
intermediate and
international satellites.

2. Cross-section though
the intermediate satellite,
showing the route of
the APM.

3. Typical cross-section
through the concourse
and departure gates.

4. Cross-section through the
main processing terminal,
looking from the Ground
Transportation Centre

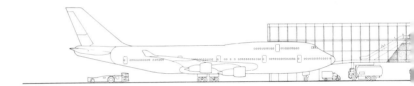

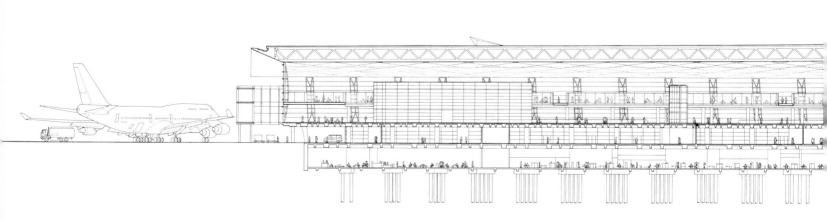

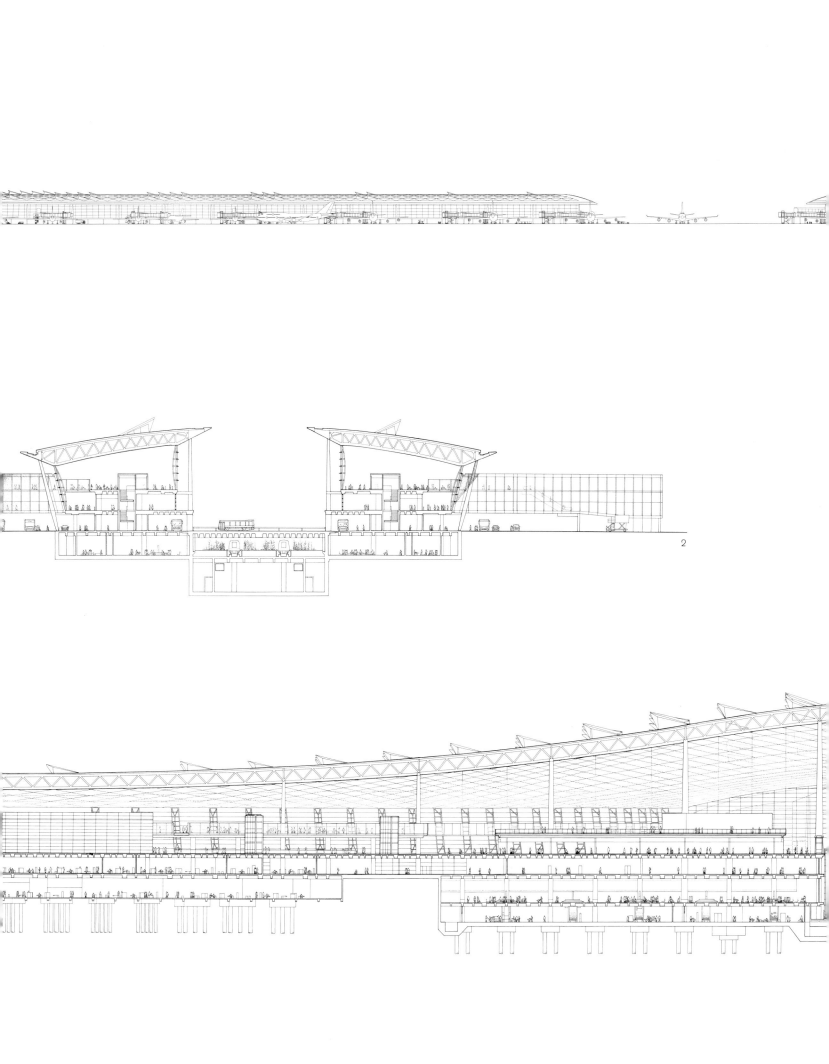

2

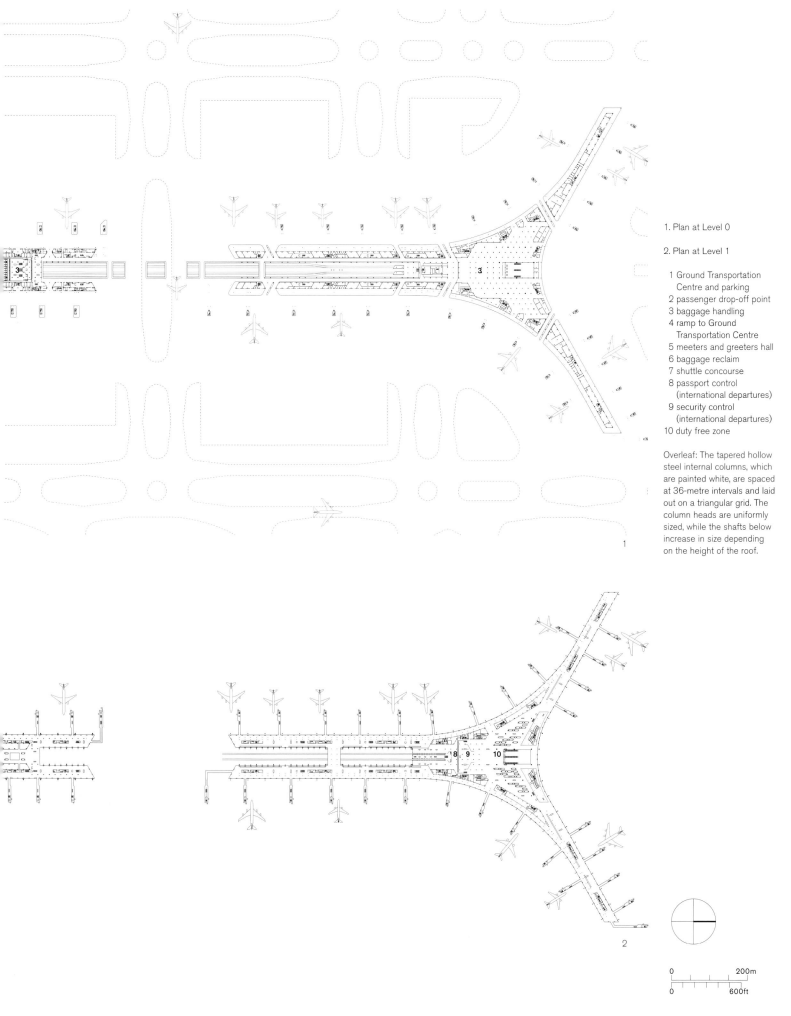

1. Plan at Level 0

2. Plan at Level 1

1 Ground Transportation
  Centre and parking
2 passenger drop-off point
3 baggage handling
4 ramp to Ground
  Transportation Centre
5 meeters and greeters hall
6 baggage reclaim
7 shuttle concourse
8 passport control
  (international departures)
9 security control
  (international departures)
10 duty free zone

Overleaf: The tapered hollow
steel internal columns, which
are painted white, are spaced
at 36-metre intervals and laid
out on a triangular grid. The
column heads are uniformly
sized, while the shafts below
increase in size depending
on the height of the roof.

0   200m
0   600ft

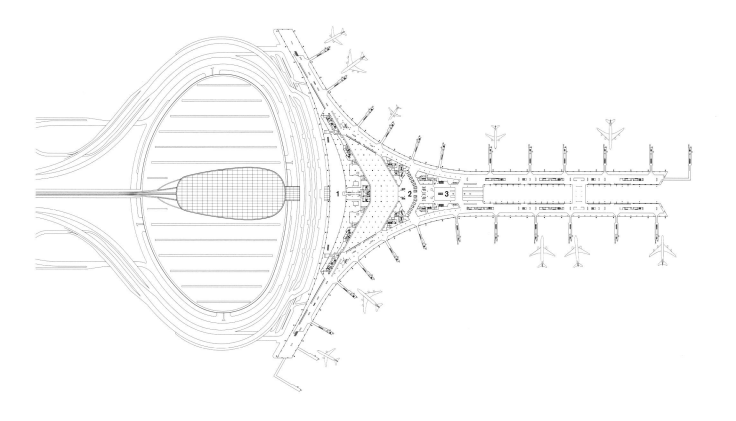

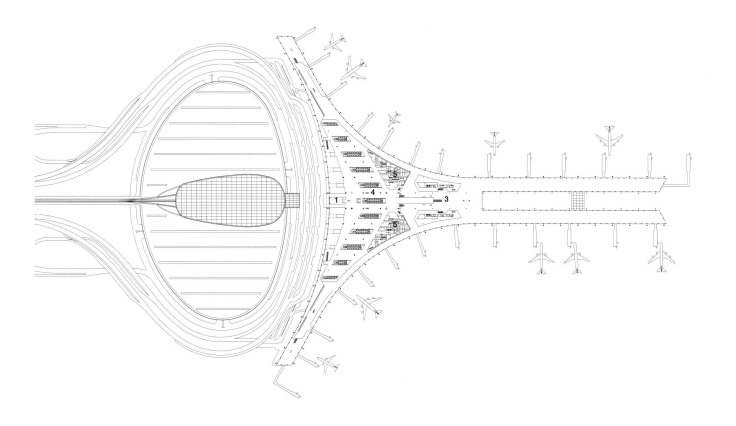

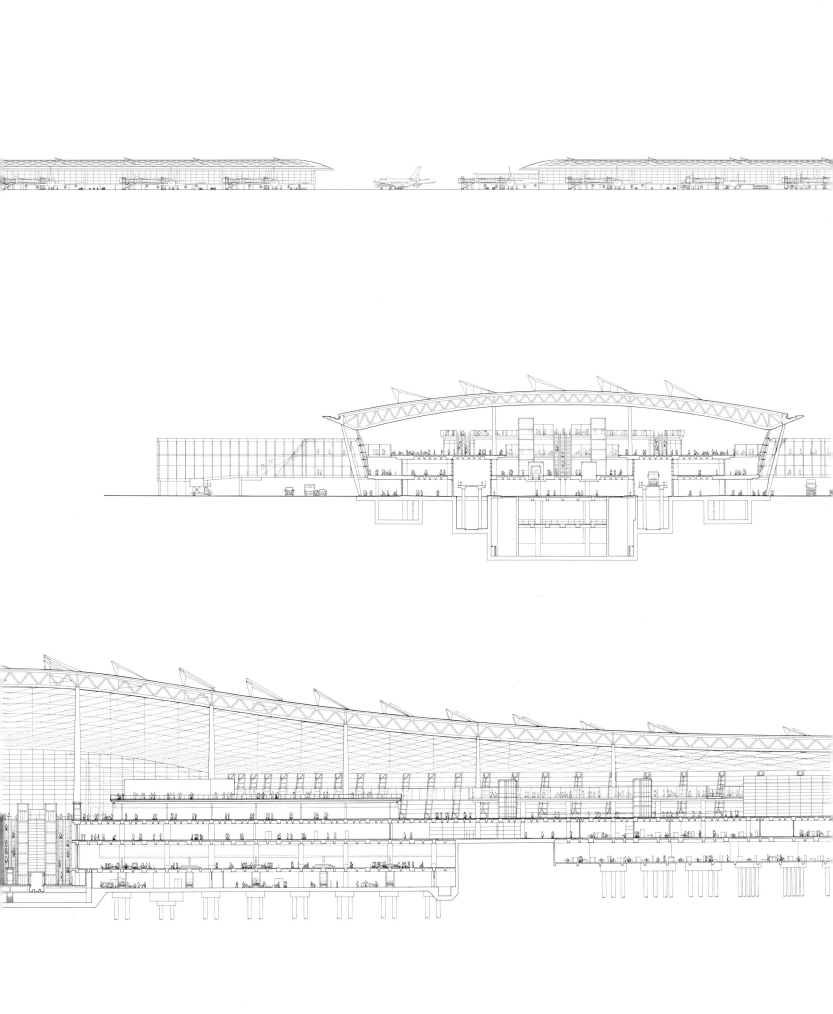

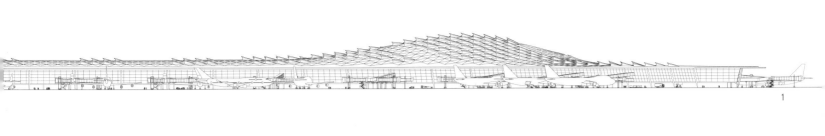

1

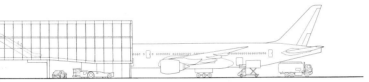

3

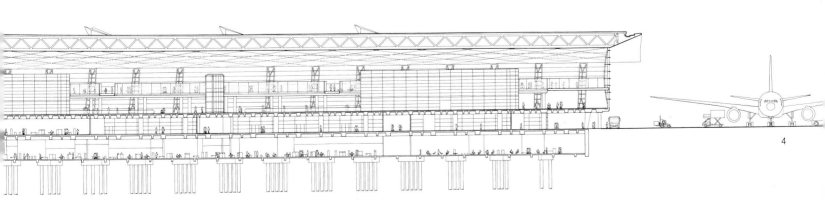

4

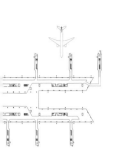
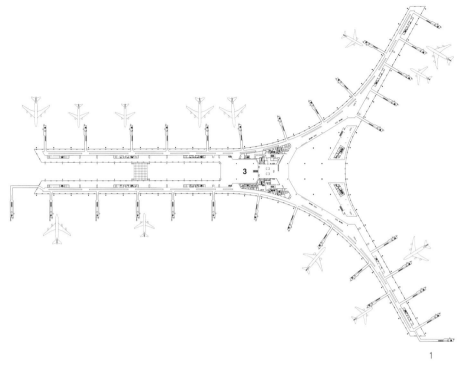

1. Plan at Level 2.

2. Plan at Level 3.

1 void over meeters and
  greeters hall
2 security control
3 entrance to APM shuttle
4 check-in hall
5 retail

Overleaf: Approaching the
airport after dark. In order
to maintain an uninterrupted
view from both the access
roads to the terminal and out
from the terminal itself, the
Ground Transportation Centre
is sunk below ground level.
During the day, the glazed
roof – which falls seamlessly
away on either side into the
surrounding gardens – floods
the station concourse with
natural light, while deep
cuts through the gardens at
regular intervals allow daylight
and fresh air into the car
parks below. At night, this
arrangement is clearly legible.

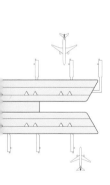
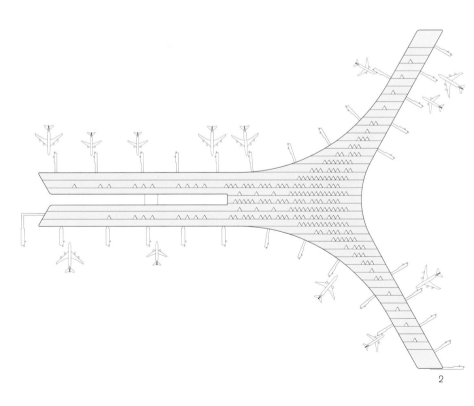

| 0 | | 200m |
| 0 | | 600ft |

As you approach the terminal, it seems to rise above the horizon, like another world. You struggle to grasp the scale; it must be half a mile across. Little peaks appear above the canopy like ridges on the back of a dragon. The arc dips below the departure level. You suppose that it is embedded in the foundations before rising again at the sides, but it stops short and seems to rest on the last of a slender enfilade of tapered red columns. These and the red trusses glimpsed through a soffit of aluminium strips (along with triangular skylights), pay tribute to a colour the Chinese hold dear, and there's even a hint of gold in the upturned knife-edge of the canopy. Michael Webb, *The Architectural Review*, August 2008

1. Walking towards the terminal from the station in the Ground Transportation Centre (GTC). A high-speed Airport Express train connects Terminal 3 to Dongzhimen Subway Station in central Beijing, the journey taking only twelve minutes.

Opposite: Looking across the GTC's light-filled concourse; at its widest point the glazed roof vault spans 100 metres.

At Stansted and Chek Lap Kok, departing passengers are privileged over arriving passengers and get to occupy the upper floor levels directly under the roof, where they enjoy the best views and spaces, while arrivals enter on the floor below. This arrangement is reversed at Beijing on the grounds that, as the primary gateway into China and the capital, the manner of entry counts for at least as much, if not more than the way people leave. Thus arriving international passengers experience the full visual and emotional impact of the great roof and surrounding spaces immediately they disembark.

What follows is an orchestrated sequence of almost operatic spatial events, from the full-blown opening chorus of the international hall with its endless roof, to the closing finale of the GTC, as arriving passengers pass through the terminal and of out the far end. After clearing passport control and diving down escalators or lifts one floor to catch the APM, the only change of level travellers have to negotiate after passport checks (departing passengers board the raised APM at concourse level), they emerge to walk directly into the baggage reclaim hall.

The baggage hall is an awesome space in itself. With its monumental arrays of concrete columns and triangular pattern of broad beams above, it is more like a colossal ancient temple than just a place to collect your luggage. The likeness to monumental precedents might have been even more pronounced, had the designers followed through on one of the many colour schemes they experimented with, including columns and beams painted in customary Chinese palettes. Eventually, however, both client and designers decided against the use of colour in this instance, opting instead for a calmer visual environment and a more reticent but maintenance-free exposed concrete finish.

After passing through customs, passengers finally spill out into the meeting and greeting hall. Drawing on the practice's own experience again, the designers clearly modelled the space on the multi-storey void and criss-crossing bridges at Chek Lap Kok, and it works no less successfully in the Beijing terminal. Thus, in one brief but memorable spatial moment, both arriving and departing passengers pass in full view of each other, as they journey in opposite directions at different levels. From there passengers either descend one floor to the lower access road to pick up a bus or taxi, or walk across a gently inclined ramp directly into the GTC, where they can catch a train into the city or pick up their own vehicle.

Bathed in natural light, whether arriving or leaving, passengers are treated to the same uplifting experience.

The integrated railway station and parking structure, with its arched glazed roof and acres of surrounding gardens covering the parking floors, provides a fitting coda to the main performance across the road. The entire complex is sunk below ground level in order not to obstruct views from the access roads or from inside the terminal. The railway station itself echoes other earlier Foster projects, most obviously the Canary Wharf Underground station in London, and more distantly the unbuilt design for the sunken National Indoor Athletics Stadium in Frankfurt. Bathed in natural light, passengers are treated to the same uplifting experience whether arriving or leaving. Even the two circular levels of parking beneath the gardens have parallel rows of deep cuts in their floors, which serve to ventilate the whole structure and bring natural light down into the lowest level – a great help in orientating jet-lagged passengers seeking their vehicles.

Architecture and building have many different facets; you could focus on flexibility for change, but equally you could focus on natural light, and describe buildings in terms of the quality of light and views they offer. It is, in the end, a balancing act of integrating and somehow responding to all those needs which are material and measurable, and those which are intangible and spiritual and quite subjective. Norman Foster, AIA Gold Medal acceptance speech, Washington, 1 February 1994

One of the main strengths of the building is that you're not really aware of its layout, even as it subtly directs you. But you are aware of the structure's sensuous curves, which all but embrace you as you approach on an entry road. It makes you think of movement, while still appearing serene. Paul Goldberger, *The New Yorker*, 21 April 2008

The roof cantilevers 45 metres at its deepest point. It's an echo of – or perhaps a tribute to – the roof of Tempelhof Airport in Berlin, which is really the mother of all modern airports. Norman Foster, lecture in Madrid, 17 April 2009
Right: Tempelhof Airport, Berlin (1934-1941), designed by Ernst Sagebiel. Tempelhof's generous roof canopy – which cantilevers 56.6 metres (170 feet) – was able to accommodate most airliners during its heyday, thereby protecting passengers from the elements. It was designed to last until 2000 and, remarkably, was in regular use until 2008 – the only major airport in the world to have remained virtually unchanged over more than sixty years.

1. The sweeping arc of the cantilevered roof at the southern end of the terminal. The cantilever runs the full width of the building, reaching 45 metres at its deepest point above the passenger drop-off area.

1

Don't let anyone tell you that size doesn't matter. At 1.3 million square metres, Beijing's new Terminal 3 is, according to its architects, the first building in the world to break the 1-million-square-metre barrier. 'Forget T5, here's T-Rex', declared architectural writer Martin Spring. From end to end T3 is 1.8 miles (3km) long and 16 per cent larger than all of London's Heathrow terminals combined (including the new T5) and nearly twice as big as Hong Kong's Chek Lap Kok.

By 2020 it will be capable of handling 50 million passengers annually, as air travel, formerly a perk of the party elite, becomes more widely available to the masses. In 2002 Beijing was ranked 26th in the global league of passenger handling; now it has risen to ninth and aims to go even higher. Without doubt, this is China's Year of the Airport.
Catherine Slessor, *The Architectural Review*, August 2008

As with the major buildings designed for the Olympics' events themselves, the entire construction was carried out by Chinese-owned contractors, to a level of quality comparable with current international practice. This simple fact alone signifies a major leap for the Chinese construction industry, some sections of which were already well advanced. The fabrication of the complex double curves of the terminal's roof structure provides a case in point. On plan, the triangular grid controlling both superstructure and podium is perfectly regular. However, projected upwards, where the grid strikes the curving surface of the roof, the three-dimensional geometry of the space-frame modules is distorted in small but significant increments, resulting in thousands of variations in both the length and thickness of the steel components.

Not only was the consortium able to find local fabricators prepared to do the job, they came ready equipped with the advanced, computer-controlled (CNC) machinery needed for the task. To put that into perspective, it should be remembered that none of the main contracts for the Hongkong Bank was awarded to a Chinese firm. Faced with similar daunting numbers of cladding variations for the Bank, the American firm that won the cladding contract, Cupples, was also compelled to re-equip itself for the job with state-of-the-art CNC machines – the first time that such machines had been used on a large scale in the construction industry.

The organisation and performance of the Foster consortium's local partners, the Beijing Institute of Architectural Design (BIAD), who supervised the tenders and construction, offers further insights into how much has changed in China in the past two decades. With a core staff of over 1,600 employees, including some 700 architects, BIAD, which provides a full range of building services, is the largest of several such institutions in the capital. Formerly operated as a branch of government, BIAD now functions independently in a competitive market. Following a 'masterclass' scenario, the BIAD team and designers from the various manufacturers worked alongside each other in the Foster office to develop the design and fabrication under the architects' supervision.

As the designers and builders of Beijing's Terminal 2 – still operating on the far side of the main runway – BIAD was the consortium's first choice to help bring the project to fruition. Such matters are too often overlooked in the critical search for visual and formal clues as to how well foreign architects have succeeded in 'localising' their designs. For all its burgeoning global scope, the Foster practice has a credible record in this respect. From the Hongkong Bank to the Petronas University in Malaysia, for which it won an Aga Khan Award in 2007, the practice consistently formulates designs that say as much about their region and locale as about their global genesis.

The broad arc of the sharply tipped cantilever, which runs the full length of the terminal's two outstretched arms, creates a breathtaking entrance.

However, an international airport is by its nature a global creature through and through, irrevocably linked by umbilical cord to some of the most technologically advanced products of human invention. There are limits therefore, as to how far such a building type can be fine-tuned to its location. Despite these inherent limitations, Terminal 3 resonates with some distinctly Chinese images. Much has been made, both by its architects and by the media, of the resemblance of the lengthy humped-back, winged terminal, with its protruding roof-lights, or 'scales', to a dragon's back and wings – metaphors given credence by the designers' evocative use of colour on the rooftop, as well as elsewhere. The two 'Y'-shaped terminals have just as readily been interpreted as outsized Chinese ideograms for 'human being', 'person', or variations thereof.

2. The passenger drop-off area, which is located at the upper level.

3. Looking down into the taxi and car pick-up area at the lower level. There are fifty-four pick-up bays, allowing for 2,400 taxis at peak hours. Additionally, there are thirty-one bays for buses and sixty-nine bays for cars.

There really is, on this planet, a huge international airport that is easy to navigate and a pleasure to use. Its architecture leads you through with little need for signage. Clean lines are suffused with light and a sense of limitless space. There [are …] smiling attendants offering information; uncrowded check-in desks and no waiting line for passport control. A clear division between domestic and international departures. A train to speed you to each group of gates, and people-movers to carry you to the point of departure. A dream? Will it be this good when it begins to reach capacity? Probably not, but it should still have the capacity to awe and delight its users.
Michael Webb, *The Architectural Review*, August 2008

Right: International athletes arrive at Beijing airport ahead of the Olympic Games, 24 July 2008. From left: members of Italy's synchronised swimming team; Croatia men's basketball team; members of the United States national women's soccer team; Britain's men's field hockey team.

1. Looking from the Ground Transportation Centre across the access road into the main terminal building.

2. At the narrowest sections of Terminal 3A – the points of the 'wings' – domestic passengers enjoy a dual aspect view as they wait to board their flight. The bustle of the drop-off zone can be seen to the south while the taxiing and preparation of aircraft takes place to the north.

3. The terminal's signage and wayfinding systems are a development of those first developed for Chek Lap Kok. A combination of hanging and floor-standing units, in a uniform blue, are used throughout the building to identify gates and check-in zones.

1

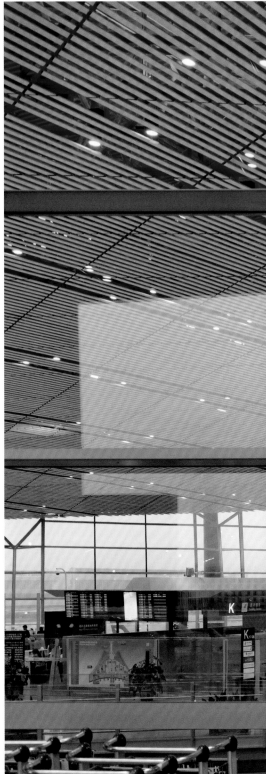

2

The terminal is the largest and most advanced airport building in the world – not only technologically, but also in terms of its operational efficiency and sustainability. Yet despite its size it is also friendly – from the traveller's point of view, spatial clarity and high service standards go hand-in-hand.

Norman Foster

If architecture is about the creation of spaces, both inside and out, then light is the medium that models and brings those spaces to life. There is a poetic and spiritual dimension to the ever-changing qualities of daylight, which many of our projects seek to capture. This passion for light can take many forms beyond merely reflecting or diffusing light into the heart of a building. It can inform the ways in which the building opens up to sun, to shade, or to views – enabling those who use the building to feel a natural sense of orientation, of ease and, where appropriate, a sense of theatre or celebration. Norman Foster, lecture in Singapore, 15 February 2000

Foster has done for airports what Reed & Stem did for train stations with their design for Grand Central, a building whose greatest achievement is not its sumptuous main concourse but its orchestration of an intricate web of people, trains, taxis and passing automobiles into a system that feels straightforward and logical, as if the building itself were guiding you from the entrance to your train. Foster, likewise, has established a pattern so clear that your natural instinct to walk straight ahead from the front door takes you where you need to go … Even more remarkable than this organizational feat is the fact that Terminal 3 is also an aesthetically exhilarating place to be. Paul Goldberger, *The New Yorker*, 21 April 2008

The red banners you see here are very interesting. The one on the left says 'In time of war if you are afraid of death you cannot be a member of the Communist party', and the one on the right says 'In time of peace if you are afraid of hardship you cannot be a member of the airport team'. That sums up the ethic of the project. Interestingly, as architects, I think that we have attitudes very much in common. It may explain why – of all the international consultants who came together on this project – we are the sole survivors. There's no doubt that it was a great team effort. Norman Foster, lecture at the Victoria & Albert Museum, London, 4 April 2008

The structure of Beijing's new terminal uses the minimum of means to achieve its effects. Though the basic format is familiar – a steel canopy over a concrete plinth, glass side screens and internal mezzanines – it is the rigour with which the structural decisions are carried through and the determination to extract from each element several levels of use that gives this building its **particular grace.** Matthew Wells, *The Architectural Review*, August 2008

The space frame wasn't made to the same high tolerances that a European version might be – packed and labelled with all components tagged and identified. Instead a huge array of similar sized pieces would arrive on site and they would just assemble them, weld them together on scaffolding, because they could find 200 people at the drop of a hat to do that. Arguably that was better than trying to do it our way – they knew how to engineer things to make it work for them. Jonathan Parr, of Foster + Partners, in conversation with the editor, 2011

A major breakthrough in the design came when Norman sketched out an idea of two planes, one showing the outer surface, the other the inner. Crucially, these weren't parallel, demonstrating how we could make the roof zone either thicker or thinner depending on the structural requirements. Richard Hawkins, of Foster + Partners, in conversation with the editor, 2011

Previous pages: The vast, light-filled space of the check-in area seen shortly after the airport opened. A column still carries a banner encouraging the team to: 'Build a harmonious airport to glorify the Olympic Games.' The tapered steel columns do 'double duty', supporting the roof and containing downpipes for the siphonic drainage system.

1. The 'meeters and greeters' area in Terminal 3A.

2. Looking from the balcony of the check-in hall on Level 3 into the arrivals area below.

Although it is conceived on an unprecedented scale, Beijing expands on the new airport model created by Stansted and developed at Chek Lap Kok. Welcoming and uplifting, it celebrates the thrill and poetry of flight.

Norman Foster

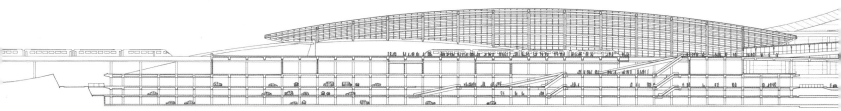

I suspect that the airport will be the true city of the twenty-first century. The great airports are already the suburbs of an invisible world capital, a virtual metropolis whose faubourgs are named Heathrow, Kennedy, Charles de Gaulle, Nagoya, a centripetal city whose population forever circles its notional centre, and will never need to gain access to its dark heart. JG Ballard, *Blueprint*, September 1997

3

4

3. The check-in islands in the main hall cater for both domestic and international flights. The desks are connected to a high-speed tub conveyor system, which is controlled by intelligent IT and automation systems.

4. A replica of a traditional Chinese temple offers a place of quiet retreat for passengers in Terminal 3B.

5. Long section through the Ground Transportation Centre and Terminal 3A at the southern end of the building.

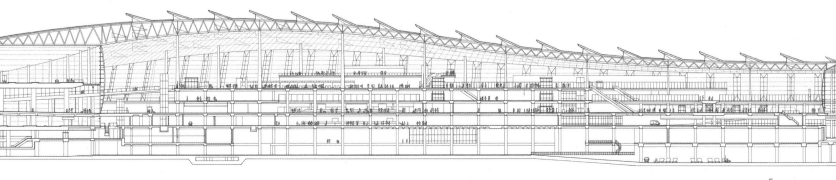

5

The main issue with Beijing that is different to Hong Kong is that you have two types of flights – international and domestic – and therefore you have different processes to manage and different passengers to accommodate. The challenge was to keep the differences very simple – you see this in the way the train moves between the two terminals; it comes into the building, collects passengers and runs to the other terminal. Passengers can see the train entering at the departure level and it then smoothly dips down under the taxiways – they don't have to look for the train or change levels which recalls the idea of minimising change originally explored at Stansted.
Mouzhan Majidi, in conversation with the editor, 2012

1

1. The automated people mover (APM) concourse in Terminal 3A.

2. Looking down into the APM station in Terminal 3B.

3. Full-height glass screens separate passengers from the trains ensuring a constant temperature is maintained within the terminal buildings.

4. The automated train services to Terminals 3B and 3C run at two to three minute intervals, the trains accelerating to a maximum speed of 80kph and taking just two minutes to travel the 2km between Terminals 3A and 3B.

5. Apart from briefly ducking under the two bridges that allow taxiing aircraft to cross from one side of the airport to the other, the APM trains run in 'green canyons' along the terminal's central spine.

Given the typically laborious research and known precedents that the Foster team have drawn upon for their design (the angled roofs of the south-east facing skylights, for example, are designed that way to catch the light and heat from the low morning sun and to shade the openings from the high midday sun), such readings tell us more perhaps about the human need for other levels of meaning, than about the origins of the relevant concepts and forms. Be that as it may, it suffices that the design is sufficiently rich in itself to generate such interpretations, coincidental or not.

Taking a more rational if less colourful line, a plausible case might also be made that both the great scale and symmetrical planning of Terminal 3 are in perfect accord with the monumental scale and classical planning typology of the historic capital itself. For instance, the principal highway that cuts across the centre of Beijing past the Forbidden City, known locally as the Ten Kilometre Avenue, could easily accommodate three such terminals down its arrow straight length, with ample room for another satellite.

We should be careful, though, of interpreting such achievements solely through Western eyes. The Sydney based author and academic Xing Ruan has observed (in conversation with the writer) that modern Chinese generally adopt an unsentimental approach to their past and cultural heritage, which Westerners can find unsettling. Keenly ambitious, they simply want the best of everything currently on offer, no matter where they find it. Consequently, they are in a constant state of flux, deciding what is or is not worth keeping within their own culture, as well as borrowing whatever they want from other cultures, including modern airports – decisions not always appreciated in the West, which often advises non-Western cultures against modernising too quickly, while speeding ahead itself.

Beyond such debates about form and meaning, however, the completion of Terminal 3 begs a much larger and more worrisome question, around which the future course of air travel hangs, and with it, much of modern development generally. Foster and Mouzhan Majidi – Foster's CEO and lead architect for the project – who also worked closely on Stansted and Chek Lap Kok, justly claim that, with all its energy efficient features, including plentiful natural light and low-level displacement air supply (note the characteristic Foster service 'pods'), Terminal 3 is one of the most sustainable buildings of its kind.

During the day, the whole of the vast interior is awash with natural light.

However, unlike the grand railway terminals that partly inspire the Foster model, the fact is that airport terminals are designed to support a far different form of transport – one that is only gradually coming to terms with notions of sustainability. This has long been a contentious point, but soaring fuel prices and levels of pollution – not least in Beijing itself – have brought the issue into sharp focus, as never before. Many years earlier, the Hongkong Bank faced a promising but uncertain future as Hong Kong prepared for the then colony's return to China. Conceived and designed on a suitably expansive scale for a transport industry serving the fastest growing and second largest economy in the world, Beijing's Terminal 3 and its users face an equally promising but suddenly uncertain future of a different kind. The Dragon has spread its wings, but how long it will be able to maintain its headlong flight, or what new directions it might take, remain to be seen.

Chris Abel

Formalities dispensed with, passengers descend one level to connect with the shuttle that speeds them on axis to baggage reclaim. Superimposing the terminal on a map of London, this is roughly the equivalent of going from the Victoria & Albert Museum to the Houses of Parliament in a dead straight line. Foster seems to relish the futuristic allure of shuttles (Stansted being an obvious example) and here they trundle through landscaped clefts before whooshing under the runway … One palpable advantage of the shuttle is that for departing international passengers (going in the opposite direction), it regulates the flow of people through customs and security, thus reducing queuing times and mitigating the general mayhem that has descended on airports worldwide since the War on Handcream was declared nearly two years ago. Catherine Slessor, *The Architectural Review*, August 2008

2

3

4

5

The geometry is based on functionality; all the other Beijing Olympic projects were kind of stand alone architectural pieces in which the function fits the idea. For the airport, the functionality drove the curvature and the heights of the roof. I think this is very important, geometry based on functionality will survive; everything else is fashion. What happens from the outside is also happening on the inside: it's optimised, it uses a clear language – the layman and the architect and the engineer can visit and immediately understand how it works. That is the technical beauty of the project. Dr Holger Falter of Arup in conversation with the editor, 2010

The roof is a simple diagrid, a space frame of triangulated trusses deep enough to walk in, and is notably efficient in its use of materials. Whereas once the regular grid would have set up an orthogonal space around itself, the application of generative component modelling by computer allows the covering to be lifted and shaped like a scarf spread across the ground. The standard components of Wachsmann's hanger system are abandoned in favour of automated manufacture, cutting and shaping each element for its allotted place. Matthew Wells, *The Architectural Review*, August 2008

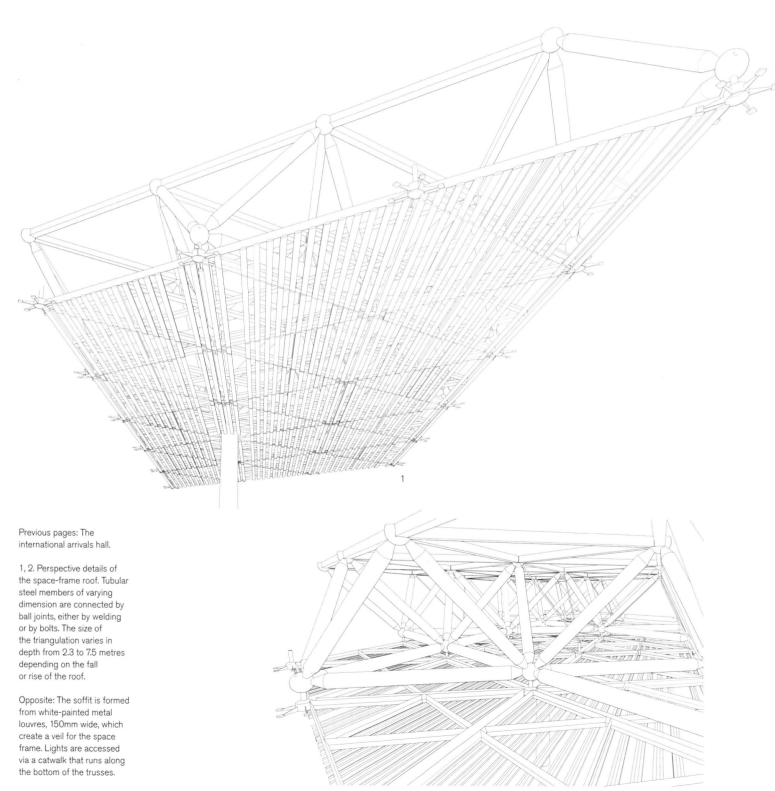

1

Previous pages: The international arrivals hall.

1, 2. Perspective details of the space-frame roof. Tubular steel members of varying dimension are connected by ball joints, either by welding or by bolts. The size of the triangulation varies in depth from 2.3 to 7.5 metres depending on the fall or rise of the roof.

Opposite: The soffit is formed from white-painted metal louvres, 150mm wide, which create a veil for the space frame. Lights are accessed via a catwalk that runs along the bottom of the trusses.

2

Because the building is so large, seismic performance was a particular issue. We knew the steelwork was going to be a double-curved element and I think the particularly smart thing was to decide to build a space truss. If we'd had a single member spanning in one direction it would have been much more difficult to find a solution. We had to bring the weight of the roof down and in order to achieve stability we had to minimise the mass. We could do that only by making a full model and optimising every single member. The computer model we made was one of the largest Arup had done and it would not have been possible fifteen years earlier. Martin Manning of Arup in conversation with the editor, 2010

Konrad Wachsman said, 'When production technology is changing, architecture is changing.' You could say that fifteen years earlier, Beijing Airport would have been very difficult to build. All the roof members are different, there's no rationalisation, and it makes full use of automated fabrication. Dr Holger Falter of Arup in conversation with the editor, 2010

The rooflights can be thought of in many different ways. They are highly scientific in the way that they are angled. The combination of sidelight and top-light ensures that, in terms of energy, you capture the low sun and its warming influence. The pattern of the roof-lights changes depending on their orientation on the roof. Externally, they evoke the scales of a dragon, and the body of this linear, sculptural building appears, in an organic way, to move through the landscape. It swells where it comes to the entrance and extends in a great cantilever to enhance and dramatise the sense of arrival. Norman Foster, lecture at the Victoria & Albert Museum, London, 4 April 2008

The really smart thing is the way in which natural light is allowed into the building. The idea of the roof-lights and their configuration is that you let direct low sunlight into the building in the winter so it warms up the slab and then you don't let direct light in at any other time; you let reflected light into the middle of the building because the plan is so deep. Dealing with the sunlight in this way brought a huge reduction in the energy load. It was a major breakthrough. Martin Manning of Arup in conversation with the editor, 2010

The curvatures of the roof are mild enough for simple profiled metal decking and shallow enough not to set up arching forces so that the tie rods of Chek Lap Kok are absent. Large and widely spaced rooflights punctuate the roof plane, becoming denser over the main pavilion halls. They are formed as extensions of the main roof, rather than heavily framed intrusions of it, and from inside, the pearlescent soffit carries the eye outwards. The delicate, submarine quality of light, traceable back through other projects to the Sainsbury Centre, is like being under lily pads. Truss elements act with the soffit baffles to modulate the light. Matthew Wells, *The Architectural Review*, August 2008

1

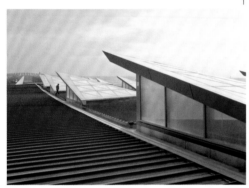

2

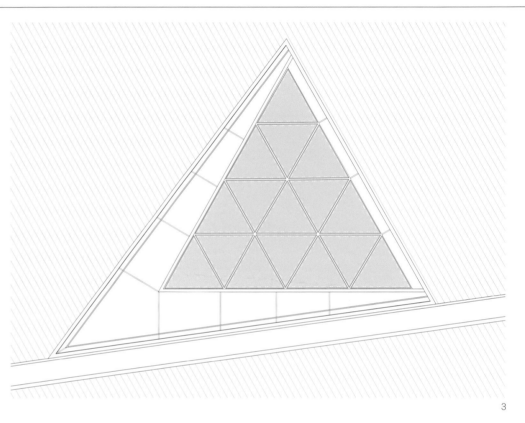

3

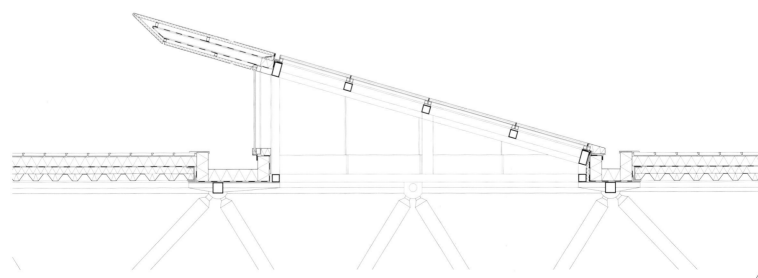

4

Beijing Airport is an unequivocal masterpiece: the culmination of everything this team has striven to achieve for forty years, in the lucidity of its plan, the boldness of its expression, and the audacity of its structure. The world's largest building seems ready to fly away. In the early 1990s, when Foster was asked to talk about his favourite piece of architecture for the BBC TV series *Building Sights*, he chose the Boeing 747. 'This machine blurs the distinction between technology and building, and what's more it flies', he remarked. 'I believe all modern architecture is capable of this intrinsic style and beauty without compromising its function.' Michael Webb, *The Architectural Review*, August 2008

One could make a lot of points about the relationship between flying, flying machines and architecture. The mainframe of a building and indeed the airframe of an aircraft have a certain life, whereas those elements that drive them – the avionics, the electronics, the turbines, the generators – have a limited life. They're subject to technological improvement and evolution. And the best sort of building or aircraft will respect and respond to and accommodate those changes. Norman Foster, in conversation with the editor, 2012

1. Looking south along the length of the terminal.

2. Rainwater gutters are placed at 36-metre intervals on an east-west orientation.

3. Plan of a typical skylight; the skylights are of a uniform size and constant orientation, opening up to the south-east to maximise heat gain from the early morning sun and enable a passive system of pre-warming.

4. Detailed section through a typical skylight.

  1 60mm-deep insulated aluminium panel
  2 160mm-deep steel I-beam
  3 58mm laminated safety glass
  4 175mm steel SHS
  5 double glazing: laminated safety glass
  6 roof construction: 1.5mm aluminium sheet standing-seam deck; 200mm thermal insulation; vapour barrier; 150mm acoustic insulation; 150mm steel deck
  7 stainless-steel composite gutter
  8 steel upper node of space truss
  9 300mm-diameter steel CHS

5. A Lufthansa Boeing 747 being readied for flight on a stand in the international terminal – Terminal 3B.

5

The raking perimeter columns are quite extraordinary sculptural elements and, undoubtedly, their creation has something to do with the fact that China still has very close connections, in terms of its steel fabrication, with the shipbuilding industry. They are very nautical in that sense. Norman Foster, lecture at the Victoria & Albert Museum, London, 4 April 2008

The structure of the glass enclosure is very simple. Supported by coloured tubular steel bowstrings with welded junctions, boxed mullions and transoms subdivide the main bays into threes. Gone are the fetishised joints of earlier steel frames, the coverplates and linkages of Stansted. Column feet simply submerge themselves into the all-encompassing ground plane. While Heathrow's Terminal 5 energetically celebrates springing points with castings and pins, here, just like the Hongkong Bank, an immensely sophisticated structure meets the ground with indifference and great sophistication. Matthew Wells, *The Architectural Review*, August 2008

1

1. Perimeter bow-string trusses are spaced at 13 to 13.5-metre intervals. External transoms span between the trusses to take the wind load and provide sun shading.

2. Detailed section through the external wall.

 1 roof construction: aluminium standing-seam deck; 200mm thermal insulation; vapour barrier; 150mm acoustic insulation; 150mm profiled steel deck
 2 250mm steel SHS
 3 flexible facade connection
 4 640-1130mm steel column with internal roof drainage
 5 steel bowstring truss: 200mm-diameter steel CHS
 6 140-200mm steel RHS transom
 7 double glazing: 10mm laminated safety glass +16mm cavity +15mm toughened glass with low-E coating
 8 facade rail, sun shading, fixed aluminium louvre
 9 connection of column to ceiling deck
10 3mm-thick aluminium 100 mm sandwich panel
11 column support detail with base plate and shear studs

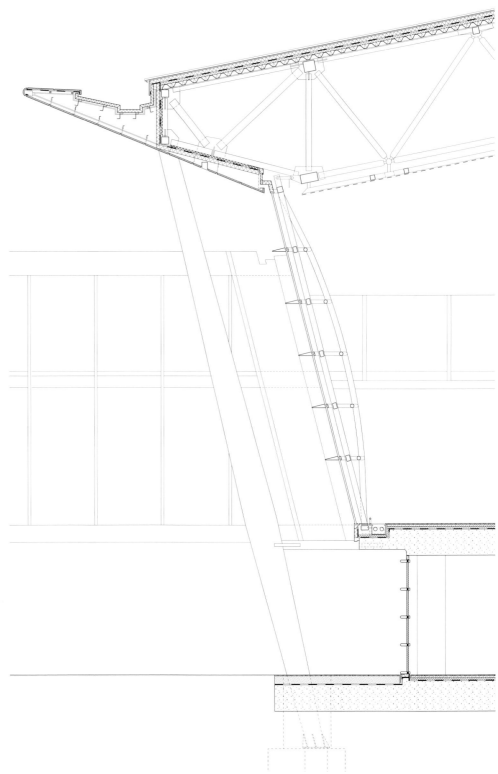

2

Distinct from Stansted or Chek Lap Kok, the structure of Beijing gives space direction through primary form and secondary linings instead of the principal grid. The allusion to organic form – the 'spine of the dragon' – is also more muted than the concrete wing spreads of Saarinen's TWA terminal at JFK, or Calatrava's ribbed structure at Bilbao. Yet without showiness, the engineering supports the 'single stroke of the pen' to achieve a beautifully straight cornice line along the vast building elevation. Matthew Wells, *The Architectural Review*, August 2008

As your 747 taxis to its stand, the hump and swell of the dragon's back hoves in and out of view through Beijing's omnipresent veil of smog, as if the creature actually breathes smoke. The saw-tooth scales of the triangular rooflights add a further, suitably scabrous touch. The only discordant notes in this seductively serpentine choreography are the double-decker air bridges (proportioned to accommodate the new generation of A380 double-decker planes) which protrude from the terminal's glazed flanks like a regiment of stubby umbilici. Catherine Slessor, *The Architectural Review*, August 2008

The angled glazing is particularly good from a shading point of view and it enabled us to have fully glazed elevations. It is part of the whole progression of light-filled airports which begins at Stansted and continues through to Hong Kong and Beijing. Richard Hawkins, of Foster + Partners, in conversation with the editor, 2011

3

The cigar-shaped steel columns were fabricated individually by highly skilled craftsmen – they are almost works of art in themselves, each unique to its time and place.

Mouzhan Majidi

4

3. The roof is supported at the perimeter by raking tubular steel columns that range in height from 13.5 to 40 metres. Painted in Imperial red, the columns taper asymmetrically and are pinned back to the building just below their widest point.

4. The double-decker air bridges were designed to accommodate the latest generation of Airbus A380 planes, the world's largest passenger aircraft.

Left: A special-edition can was issued by Coca-Cola to commemorate the completion of the airport. The limited production run of just 20,000 cases was only available to purchase within the terminal building.

1

1. The view down from the arrivals hall into the departures lounge in the international terminal: Terminal 3B.

2. Looking along one of the 122 travelators that help passengers to move swiftly through the airport.

2

Walking distances for passengers are short, with few level changes; transfer times between flights are minimised and public transport connections are fully integrated.

Norman Foster

Compared with the usual shuffling boredom of immigration halls, formal entry into China is now an extraordinarily dramatic, even transcendent experience. 'Modern cathedral' is an overused soubriquet, but here it is entirely apposite. The intricate, light-filled lattice of the lucky yellow roof (which changes to lucky red in the domestic part) soars munificently above the traveller pilgrims who cluster around the checkpoints, seeking state benefaction. Catherine Slessor, *The Architectural Review*, August 2008

The terminal concourses are the ramblas and agoras of the future city, time-free zones where all the clocks of the world are displayed, an atlas of arrivals and destinations forever updating itself, where briefly we become true world citizens. Air travel may well be the most important civic duty that we discharge today, erasing class and national distinctions and subsuming them within the unitary global culture of the departure lounge. JG Ballard, *Blueprint*, September 1997

3

4

5

3, 4. Transparency is a pervasive theme. As they wait to board their planes, departing passengers are afforded views of both the curve of the terminal itself and of the activity outside.

5. Departure gate E30 in Terminal 3B; the fixed boarding bridge for arriving passengers is visible above the concourse. There are 100 such boarding gates in the terminal as a whole.

The baggage delivery system is designed to be very fast – within a maximum of ten minutes of the aircraft docking, the first bags are in the baggage hall. I joined the crew who were doing the testing and commissioning in November 2007, several months before the building opened. The army came in, with huge numbers of bags to test all the systems. It all worked and they've had no major problems since then. Norman Foster, lecture in Madrid, 17 April 2009
Right: Norman Foster sitting in the baggage hall, November 2007.

Baggage reclaim takes place in the terminal's lowest public level, where the tapering columns from the check-in floor above flare and thicken into more substantial, tree trunk-like structures. The system aims to deliver your bags from hold to belt in 10 minutes, so it's not a place to linger, but even so, this functional transit zone is conceived as a kind of elegant cavern or … a hypostyle hall (shades of the Temple of Karnak). However, the real spatial punch is waiting to sock you on exiting into the scooped out void of the terminal frontage, with its Piranesian display of bridges, walkways and escalators that take you down and off to various modes of ground transportation. Catherine Slessor, *The Architectural Review*, August 2008

1

1. In contrast to the departures and arrivals areas, the cavernous baggage hall has a concrete ceiling supported by cylindrical concrete columns, which vary in diameter according to their position and the loads placed upon them. The ceiling follows a diagrid pattern which echoes that of the structure on the floor above.

2. The other end of the baggage experience: the luggage conveyor behind the check-in desks.

What you don't see in an airport are the systems that drive it behind the scenes. The baggage system in Beijing is an extraordinarily complex, state-of-the-art installation, with 50km of conveyor belt alone.
Norman Foster

2

Foster is one of a handful of architects around the world who can take a building type and move it on a level, take it to something else such that it becomes public property. Hugh Pearman, 'Front Row', BBC Radio 4, 28 December 2007

Following Beijing's successful Olympic bid, the city underwent a large-scale, high-speed period of development which was carried out by some of the world's most renowned architects. Beijing has since become a world architecture museum with the buildings constructed during this period helping to strengthen its influence and image as an international metropolis. Xunyong Li, Secretary General of the 'Top Ten Beijing Architectural Competition', 2009. Beijing International Airport came first in the competition, which was voted for by an astonishing nine million members of the Chinese public.

A bilingual poster, pitched to residents and visitors, exhorted: 'Welcome the Olympics! Improve Manners! Foster New Attitudes!' Norman has fulfilled his part of that injunction. Michael Webb, *The Architectural Review*, August 2008

3. A total of fifteen carousels are regularly spaced across the breadth of the baggage hall with special units at each end designed to handle oversized luggage. The baggage system is designed to deliver the first bag from the aircraft to the carousel in just ten minutes.

Overleaf: The terminal and control tower seen from the air. The first aircraft departed from the terminal in February 2008. By 2020 it is expected to handle 43 million passengers and 500,000 peak hour aircraft movements per annum.

3

Foster in Future
Deyan Sudjic 2012

1. The flat at 16 Hampstead Hill Gardens that became Foster Associates' first office in 1967. Before that, it had been home to Team 4.

2. Foster Associates' first London studio in Bedford Street, Covent Garden: a floor leased from engineer Tony Hunt, from 1968 to 1971. The move to Bedford Street, which happened 'virtually overnight', was prompted by an imminent visit from a new client – IBM. By that time, the Hampstead Hill Gardens flat was virtually bursting at the seams.

3. The entrance to Foster Associates' Fitzroy Street studio, London's 'first storefront design studio', where the practice was based from 1971 to 1981. The full-height glazing had to be built twice. The first installation, which employed aluminium mullions, was destroyed by an IRA bomb planted in the nearby Post Office Tower. The second version was much more sophisticated, using Pilkington's newly developed all-glass system.

The nature of architectural practice has changed almost beyond recognition since the day in 1967 when Norman and Wendy Foster established themselves as Foster Associates. They worked briefly from their flat in Hampstead before moving to Bedford Street in Covent Garden, the first of the sequence of London offices that the practice in its various incarnations has occupied over the years. After Covent Garden came Fitzrovia. First Fitzroy Street: a space characterised by lime green walls with submarine doors and yellow Herman Miller pinboards; and then Great Portland Street: an office with automatic sliding doors, and a raised metal floor – the kind of thing that in those days you only saw in clean rooms built for mainframe computers. Then in 1990 came the move to a Thameside site at Battersea.

The new studio building at Riverside – where Foster himself had an apartment – was a pioneer in reintroducing the idea of mixed-use development to London. By reopening the derelict dock and creating a network of pedestrian routes along the waterfront, the project also provided the catalyst for the longer-term regeneration of the area. Albion Riverside, completed in 2003, was a substantial next step, creating a mix of apartments, offices and galleries and a new piazza on the river. More recently, the Royal College of Art has relocated a number of departments there, to reinforce a thriving arts and residential community.

In the intervening decades, Foster + Partners itself has grown to become one of the largest private-sector employers in London. With that expansion, has come the growth of its own university-like campus on the waterfront. On an organisational level, the practice has transformed itself from a studio under the sole ownership of its founder, to become an entity with more than eighty individual shareholders, some still in their thirties.

Alongside the architects, the creative team comprises structural and environmental engineers, industrial designers, modelmakers, illustrators and graphic designers – the list goes on. Growth has allowed the practice to explore new areas of expertise and, significantly, to invest in research. There is a team devoted to studying issues of sustainability; a specialist computer-modelling group dedicated to exploring the applications and potential of complex geometries; a materials research team; a group that undertakes the management of projects; and a workplace consultancy, one of whose roles is to analyse a client organisation and help to define its future needs – an essential first step in ensuring that a project starts from the right brief. The most recent research team explores the factors which together define environmental comfort. It now follows up systematically the performance of completed projects.

It is an infrastructure that brings new possibilities to architectural practice. To have structural and environmental engineers working alongside the architects ensures that the design teams have an informed starting point when seeking to challenge accepted formulae, or trying to understand what might be fruitful new technologies to explore. Crucially, it enhances their potential to develop fully integrated, higher-performance design solutions. This input has expanded to the point where the practice can now offer its clients a wider single package of expertise. In that sense, as Foster himself points out, the practice is essentially returning to its roots.

1

2

3

It was the integrated nature of the design team that he created in the 1970s – bringing in key characters such as environmental engineer Loren Butt – that allowed Foster to devise buildings for Willis Faber & Dumas and the Sainsbury Centre for Visual Arts, in which space and structure, services and skin were considered holistically. Perhaps ironically, it was the Hongkong and Shanghai Bank, a project that marked a quantum shift in the practice's work, which forced a move towards using independent consultants.

Foster conceived the practice as a workshop in which the client comes to participate in the process, rather than to be the passive subject of a presentation.

Compared with the way they worked in the 1960s, the technical methods used by designers are of course very different. Ink and tracing paper, drawing boards and parallel motions have all been consigned more or less to the recycling bin. Lettering is no longer applied with a stencil, or rubbed down from a sheet of Letraset. Even the remarkably elegant drawing tables with the Lunar Lander style feet – the starting point for the Nomos table made by Tecno – that Foster designed for the Great Portland Street studio, have been discarded to become valuable collector's pieces.

New technology has had an enormous impact on the process of design, as well as on the vocabulary of architecture, in both obvious and less predictable ways. Painstaking cross-hatching applied in layer upon layer, to build up shadow and texture on a set of presentation drawings, is no longer the distraction from thinking about design that it once was. It can be laid down using a keyboard in minutes.

Digitalisation has also shifted architects away from their reliance on the traditional drawing skills and made possible new means with which architects are able to visualise and understand space. It has transformed the way that architects communicate their ideas to their clients and to the manufacturers and contractors who turn drawings into physical reality.

Until the last decade, very few people who commission architecture have been fully able to understand the significance of an architect's plan before it is built, just as very few non-musicians in a concert hall can imagine what the music they are about to hear will be like simply by being shown the composer's score. Even an axonometric projection baffles most people not familiar with its conventions. But the digital fly-through is not musical notation, or a cross-section or a mysterious projection convention. For the first time, digital rendering offers a straightforward way to convey to a non-expert what it will be like to move through an architectural space that has not yet been built.

The poignant presentation that the Foster team put together for their submission for the New York World Trade Center competition in 2003, tracing the journey of a child through the complex and down into the memorial that they proposed in the footprints of the lost Twin Towers, offered a moving demonstration of what is possible using sophisticated visualisation techniques. When the scope for an element of the unexpected in the translation from design to built reality is so reduced, the architect could be said to have rather less room for manoeuvre and for managing a client's expectations than in the past.

4. In 1981 the practice moved to a new office in Great Portland Street. The full-height glazing revealed a cavernous space, with islands of grouped plan chests forming plinths for models. The drawing tables were the precursors of the Nomos desking system.

5. The studio at Riverside, in Battersea, has been the practice's home since 1990. The studio's north-facing glass facade overlooks the River Thames. Along the outer edge, interspersed with models and mock-ups, are round tables for ad-hoc meetings. Everyone has a place at one of the long benches – modelmakers, secretaries and architects.

4

5

We have twenty-seven model makers and with support staff the group is over thirty. The original model shop in the studio is more than twenty years old, but it's still a good space to make things – it's easy for the architects to see what's happening and to come in and comment. When the office was a couple of hundred people it worked very well. But now there's a much greater demand, so the new model shop allows us to make more – and bigger – models. We're also trying to do more in-house so that we can better understand and translate what the architects are trying to achieve. Neil Vandersteen, of Foster + Partners, in conversation with the editor, 2011

These days there's a whole variety of weaponry at our disposal that allows people to understand projects more easily than drawings, for example, and modelling is a big part of that. No matter how much you think something is right, it's only when it's physically there that you can really judge. You learn a huge amount through modelling and small changes can sometimes make a massive difference. A little bit of that perspective comes from our product design experience because you're likely to make multiple models of things before they go into volume production; in architecture you only get one chance – once you've done it, that's it. David Nelson, in conversation with the editor, 2012

Digital and physical models can work very well together, but they're doing different things. With a digital model, you're not choosing your view – it is controlled by whatever digital media set player is on the screen. You can't walk around it, or bend down and study a certain view. If a model is on the table you can gather people around it and get them to engage with it more easily. You can't do that on screen. Diane Teague, of Foster + Partners, in conversation with the editor, 2011

1, 2. On a freezing morning in February 1996, twelve large crates were hoisted on to the north-east tower of the Reichstag. They contained the components of a 1:20-scale model of the dome and chamber, minutely detailed and large enough for three people to stand inside. For the first time, lighting designer Claude Engle was able to measure the light being reflected into the chamber, confirming that the mirrored cone at the heart of the dome worked perfectly. That winter's day was a landmark in the history of the project. It illustrates the central role that models play in design development.

The relationship between architect and patron has shifted and the client can potentially play a more informed role in the design process. Clearly this is a phenomenon whose impact on the practice of architecture can only grow. The architect's art will very likely become increasingly collaborative and more open to the involvement of the non-specialist in the process of shaping a building.

Yet, at the same time, the impact of digital techniques in conveying space and complex forms has not eliminated the need to evaluate a design through material means at key stages in the design process. Perhaps paradoxically it has encouraged the production of large-scale physical models, which as a working method are a particular Foster speciality. The more that architects can speculate freely about what architecture can be, using digital techniques, the more they need to be able to study the material implications of their speculations in three dimensions.

The extensive use of modelling is a thread that has run through every incarnation of the practice from the very beginning.

Visitors walking into the Foster studio pass an entire wall of models of all sizes, which echoes the collage of architectural fragments that packs every inch of Sir John Soane's house museum. These models have a seductive charm, but for the architect they are working tools – a means to explore the impact of design decisions, from the scale of the smallest detail up to the masterplan. Those projects that are in design development are represented by models lining the window wall of the studio, overlooking the Thames.

The wall of models is equally a reminder of the way in which Norman Foster conceived the practice as a workshop in which the client comes to participate in the process, rather than to be the passive subject of a presentation secluded in a conference room. There is no waiting room or reception seating in Battersea: clients are invited into the studio to be part of the action and this approach remains a key part of the way that the practice operates. For example, when the board of the Commerzbank visited the studio, they came away impressed by its open-plan nature and its potential to aid communication. It changed the way they had been thinking.

The extensive use of modelling is a thread that has run through every incarnation of the practice from the very beginning. In the design phase of the Hongkong Bank, in the early 1980s, Foster's Great Portland Street studio was temporarily transformed by the installation of full-size mock-ups of the diagonal structural solution the architects were then considering. It gave the design team an insight into what it would feel like to sit in an office in which views out would be shaped by structural members inclined at a 45-degree angle. A similar exercise was undertaken in the early 2000s during the design of the Swiss Re building. For several months passers-by could see a full-size section of the distinctive diamond-shaped structure through the studio's big riverside window.

Such mock-ups have been part of the working method of a select few architectural practices. Mies van der Rohe, for example, managed to lose a commission when his client decided on the basis of full-size elevations painted on canvas screens, that the house Mies was proposing was not quite what he wanted. But models are unusually important for Foster, and the precision of his work has its roots in the care with which every possible option is modelled or prototyped before a final decision is taken.

1

2

When Foster was working on the rebuilding of the Reichstag, for example, models of all kinds were made to test virtually every aspect of the design, from the character of the eagle, the symbol of the German Republic that dominates the debating chamber, to a representation of the cupola above it. A 1:20 model of the cupola – large enough for three people to stand up inside it – was made to test the impact of the ingenious lighting proposal and to gain a thorough understanding of its acoustic performance. In the depths of a freezing Berlin winter the model was hauled by crane on to the roof of the Reichstag – along with Foster and his colleagues – so that it could be tested in real-life environmental conditions.

This reliance on models ensures that the modelmaking workshops have due prominence in the Foster studio. The effect of their cutting and turning machines is to make parts of the space feel more like a particularly elegant factory than a conventional white-collar workplace. And within the wider campus, modelmaking facilities are becoming increasingly important, not less. A few minutes' drive from the studio there is a fully equipped industrial unit, where models can be built on an epic scale.

A recent example is a full-size study of one of the steel 'trees' that support the roof of the new winery for Château Margaux. Another space within the Riverside campus allows the architects themselves to build sketch models, using foam or card. But modelling techniques are also changing. The computer-controlled rapid prototyping process – in which the practice has made a considerable investment – has made extraordinarily intricate miniature representations of complex forms realisable at the touch of a mouse.

Digital analysis has changed not just the process of design, but also the way that buildings are made, and the nature of the forms they can assume. A digital file sent direct from the architect to the factory can form the basis of the pattern-cutting program that a manufacturer uses to produce the skin or bones of a building.

Elements as diverse as the laminated wooden frame of Chesa Futura and the steel deck and superstructure of Millau Viaduct were fabricated in this way. In each case the methodology allowed a degree of accuracy once unimaginable in the construction industry. An additional benefit of digital analysis is that it allows the architects to explore far more complex geometries than were once possible. Chesa Futura, for example, was modelled three-dimensionally from the outset.

Even in its early days, Foster's work was never defined entirely by the orthogonal geometry of say, the Pilot Head Office for IBM, completed in 1971: the Willis Faber building, with its sinuous curves, belongs to the same period. But the analogue systems of that era were very different from the digital technologies that enabled the complex shell forms of The Sage Gateshead music centre, designed some thirty years later.

Willis Faber's curves were achieved by using flat sheets of glass, and they followed a geometry that only curved in one plane. The Sage's complex cloud-like forms curve in two planes, and thus have an entirely different character, one that reflects the times in which they were designed and built – and perhaps also the impact of Foster's relationship with Buckminster Fuller, and his ideas about high-performance structural geometry and sustainability. Interestingly, one of Foster's early sketches for Willis Faber shows a bulbous form, with a note suggesting that it was probably too far ahead of its time to be realised quickly.

3. A self-contained model shop in Battersea, which complements the existing facility in the Riverside studio, allows models to be made on virtually an industrial scale. It has state-of-the-art equipment, including a large-format laser cutter and a three-dimensional CNC router. Four large tables in the centre of the room provide flexible workspace, below suspended power points, and a 'CAD bar' – a bench of standing workstations lining one wall – keeps technical information close to hand.

3

We have a young team and the studio is very cosmopolitan. The average age is a little over thirty and between us we speak something like forty-five languages. We have a 'world view', an ability to see local issues in a wider context that comes from long experience of working in many different countries and cultures. Allied to that is a strong commitment to a green agenda – finding new ways to improve energy efficiency and sustainability in both buildings and communities, wherever they might be in the world. Norman Foster, in conversation with the editor, 2012

Like most of my senior colleagues, I joined the office as a new graduate. Over more than two decades together we have grown with the practice, helped to shape it, and now guide its future direction. Mouzhan Majidi, in conversation with the editor, 2012

1. Scenes from daily life in the Riverside studio: here Norman Foster conducts a design review with Nigel Dancey and David Summerfield.

2. Spencer de Grey in a brief exchange with Mouzhan Majidi and Grant Brooker.

When Foster was working on Willis Faber's glass curtain wall he felt the need to refer to Jean Prouvé for advice on facade engineering. Today, in contrast, the Foster team has expertise in new materials and technologies that few can match. Equally, working in the context of historic buildings, the practice has expanded its vocabulary, detailing elegantly in stone, concrete and timber.

The scale of architectural practice compared with the 1960s is also different. Until quite recently fifty people constituted a substantial office. Now Foster + Partners is not the only firm in the world with a team numbering over a thousand; and the range of work it is able to address has also changed. At the time of writing it has projects under way, at various stages of development, which cover a spectrum from boats and bridges, aircraft and individual houses, to studies shaping entire cities.

Foster + Partners itself is a conscious response to the changing context for architectural practice. Just like an architectural project, the practice can be seen as the result of a careful design process, initiated by a self-generated brief. A guiding principle for Foster was to create the potential for evolutionary expansion and ensure the practice's long-term creative future by bringing a younger generation into senior management positions. At the heart of that move was his determination that it remains a practice run by architects and engineers, committed to architecture and the wider context of sustainable infrastructure.

Foster likes to point out that despite its forty years of experience it is still a youthful organisation – the average age is just thirty-two, exactly the same as it was in 1967. The veterans at its core bring an unmatched level of experience to bear alongside the continually refreshed stream of bright new talent, who can treat the practice as a form of graduate school.

Another key objective when the practice reconstituted itself was to release Foster himself from responsibility for the detailed management of the practice so that he could concentrate more on design. It also allowed him to expand the important ambassadorial role that he plays: a worldwide practice with a high degree of political involvement for its major projects demands a huge amount of travel for client presentations and meetings, and site visits to view progress and prototypes.

Foster likes to point out that despite its forty years of experience it is still a youthful organisation – the average age is just thirty-two, exactly the same as it was in 1967.

In order to do that, the company needed a management structure in which a chief executive could take over the day-to-day responsibilities, freeing Foster to become a very active chairman. Foster assigned the chief-executive role to Mouzhan Majidi, a post he took up formally in 2007, having begun to assume responsibilities the previous year. Like many of Foster's senior partners, Majidi joined the practice straight from university, in his case in 1987. Among many other projects, he played a key role in the design development of Stansted Airport and was responsible for realising Hong Kong's Chek Lap Kok airport, living in Hong Kong until it was completed. He now leads the practice in its strategic direction, but still remains closely involved in all aspects design. 'With my colleagues I review all the projects across the practice – that is the enjoyable part of being an architect', says Majidi.

1

2

The two heads of design, Spencer de Grey and David Nelson, have both been with Foster since the 1970s, cutting their teeth on projects as diverse as the Sainsbury Centre and the Hongkong Bank. Alongside them is a very experienced senior team. The practice is structured in a group system, with each group led by a senior partner. There are currently six architecture groups – led by Stefan Behling, Grant Brooker, Nigel Dancey, Gerard Evenden, Luke Fox and David Summerfield – and two structural and environmental engineering groups, led respectively by Roger Ridsdill Smith and Piers Heath, but the practice could scale up or down to operate with more or fewer groups, should conditions change.

Foster has tried to put in place a structure that allows the firm consistently to go on producing elegant and intelligent work. The key to that is the scrutiny of the design board and the guidance it offers to architects throughout the practice. The board is chaired by Foster and comprises de Grey, Nelson, Majidi and Behling. Together they will call on the heads of the architecture and engineering groups as required. The design board scrutinises every project and will insist on a fresh approach if it believes one is necessary.

As Foster says, 'the design board was created in the spirit of challenging and being challenged – it can initiate design as well as review it.' It is a method that has its origins way back in his past when as a young Masters student at Yale, he found himself asked to justify his work by Paul Rudolph – the endlessly demanding chairman of the architecture department – often in front of a jury of visiting critics. It is a strategy that encourages one group to learn from another, and allows the firm to maintain a unified approach to architecture and a sense of intellectual and aesthetic cohesion.

The evolution of the practice into its present form took several years to complete. Like any design process, it involved research, prototyping and testing a variety of models – and naturally some adjustment. 'In a small company you can expect to know everybody and be quite flexible in the way you organise yourselves. But beyond a certain size you need more focused management systems, which is where the group structure came from', says Majidi. Foster first mooted the idea in 2004, when the practice had approximately 600 staff: 'What we wanted was a structure that allowed us to have the best of both worlds – to have the strategic advantages that only size can bring, but with the attention to detail and close client relationships of a small atelier', he says.

The practice has its largest base in London, which is where the majority of the design work is carried out, but it also has long-established studios in Abu Dhabi, Hong Kong, Madrid and New York. Additionally, the firm has established a presence in every location in which it is building, wherever that might be. Currently, there are twenty-five Foster offices around the world. Typically, in any given period, some of these will be dedicated to a particular project, where the team charged with seeing the building through to completion will establish a base before construction starts. Importantly, that team will always comprise native language speakers – a consideration that has helped to forge strong client relationships over the years.

Innovation is another attribute of the studio that resonates with clients. Foster has tried hard to create the conditions that will ensure the practice's continuing creative energy. It is clear that he and the firm share a hunger for new forms, and new approaches to building. In its latest incarnation, Foster + Partners is coming to resemble not so much any previous large architectural practice, but more a cross between a leading school of architecture and a global research-based consultancy.

3. Norman Foster and Mouzhan Majidi in conversation during a break from a meeting.

4. David Nelson and Gerard Evenden in an impromptu meeting – just one of many such encounters that will take place throughout the day.

3

4

A willingness to challenge accepted responses or solutions is something that has always underpinned our work. It means trying to ask the right questions, allied with a curiosity about how things work – whether that is an organisation or a mechanical system. I have characterised that tendency to look at a problem afresh, from first principles, as 'reinventing'. It's a process that can often be seen to unfold through a series of projects. Norman Foster, in conversation with the editor, 2012

There's never been much of a desire in this place to just do what we did the last time. We certainly want to build on what we've done before, but we want to do it better, or differently. A lot of people come to us because of that. A lot of the time the parameters of the project shape the way in which we move forward: it's the client, the budget, the site – definitely the climate. All of that goes towards building a base from which a project can emerge and respond to a particular place. The best projects come out of the closeness of that engagement. David Nelson, in conversation with the editor, 2012

1. A design review in progress. These reviews take place under the direction of the design board. They are an essential part of the working method in the studio and are scheduled at key stages in the development of every project, both formally and informally. They can be crucial in determining the direction a design will follow.

2. Norman Foster and the project team on a site visit to Château Margaux to inspect a full-size mock-up of one the new winery's structural 'trees'. Mock-ups of this kind are also an essential part of the practice's working method.

'Encapsulating what we do in one sentence is difficult', says David Nelson: 'It has many strands. Partly, it's about communicating a sense of culture and quality – both within the studio and to others. We are also good at listening and learning – which means knowing how to ask the right questions. People come to us because they believe we can help them to quantify what they need – sometimes we've even helped them to clarify the nature of their own organisations. And then they recognise the value that we add.'

Frank A Bennack Jr, a former chief executive of Hearst, and one of Foster's clients for Hearst Tower, sums it up thus: 'Norman has a feel for what it is your business does. The dialogue is often not about architecture, but how does your business function, and how do people live in the space.' That degree of understanding is an essential prerequisite of great architecture.

Returning to the integrated structure that shaped the practice in its early days, has allowed the firm to address the impact on traditional architectural practice of what is now a worldwide market for architecture. Roger Ridsdill Smith, who came to the practice after seventeen years at Arup, where he worked on a number of Foster projects, including the Millennium Bridge, regards the arrangement as being positive for everyone:

'If the architects come up with an idea in one room and give it to their engineering team in another, that's ostensibly just an economic arrangement. Here we're working together on the same job at the same time. In a design meeting there is no hierarchy in terms of where an idea will come from. People are simply interested in finding the very best solution. That means you have to work at keeping sharp, at staying right at the forefront of your discipline.'

Piers Heath, whose environmental consultancy, PHA Consult, worked closely with Foster over a fifteen-year period before he and his colleagues joined the practice, offers another perspective: 'One of the strongest reasons for the integrated team is to ensure that you get joined-up thinking. That means communicating and testing ideas beyond the team itself – with the people that are going to implement them – and then following through when the building is finished and occupied to make sure that the systems are working correctly.'

The scale and organisation of the office allows it to invest in the kind of thinking time that is not easily come by in a traditional architectural practice. The design board is an important part of that – the stick, as it were: a controlling mechanism with the authority when needed to say that there is a better way to do things. The other strand is the carrot, the creation of a structure within the office that can encourage the architects and engineers and their specialist colleagues to do their best work at every level.

The effect of size on architectural practice is a phenomenon that has not as yet attracted enough critical attention and analysis. It may well yet turn out to be the most significant change of all in practice in recent years. There was a period when the ingrained ethos of the architectural community was that to become too big, or even just big, would undermine the intimacy and scale needed to encourage creativity and nurture a culture of design. While Foster was building the Hongkong Bank – his first major overseas project and the first high-rise building the practice had built – he deliberately restricted himself, declining offers of further work in Hong Kong. He wanted to avoid distractions so that the practice could prove itself; and having done so, he felt able to move on.

1

2

The challenge for the practice now that it is no longer a newcomer, but a landmark at the very centre of the architectural landscape – with the capability to address projects at the mega-scale – is to retain its freshness and its sense of openness to new fields of enquiry. Size offers a capacity for research and speculative thinking that is simply not possible in a small practice; it also means that the office can work effectively on the most dauntingly scaled programmes, constrained by apparently impossible deadlines, such as Beijing Airport, which was designed and built in just four years.

The scale and organisation of the Foster studio allows it to invest in the kind of thinking time that is not easily come by in a traditional architectural practice.

The practice now has experience on every continent and with every building type, from airports to skyscrapers, from schools to houses, hotels, bridges and boats. It has the resources to research the issues of energy consumption, transport and fabrication. In its work for Masdar City, in Abu Dhabi, the Foster team helped the Emirates to create an urban vision for life after oil. Just one of Foster's many experimental studies for Masdar was the development of a remote-controlled electric taxi to create the most innovative on-demand transport system in the world.

Closer to home, Foster has ploughed back the firm's accumulated knowledge and research capability to formulate plans for a new airport and transport hub in the Thames Estuary – part of a holistic, self-funded initiative that sets out a strategy for the renewal of the UK's transport, communications and energy infrastructure.

Masterplanning and infrastructure projects such as this require architects to think on the scale of an entire city and beyond. That development is reflected in the configuration of the meeting rooms on the mezzanine level of the Foster studio, in London, to allow for the enormous models required to represent urban masterplans and the groups of people needed to work on them together. The buildings themselves are also increasing in size. The Central Market in Abu Dhabi, for example, is 713,000 square metres; and the terminal at Beijing Airport is an almost unimaginable 1,306,000 square metres – by some measures the largest single building ever realised. Projects on this scale have given the practice a unique role, shaping the way in which an explosive period of change has evolved.

This phenomenon of seemingly ever-greater scale is in part an outcome of the rapid modernisation of the world's emerging economies, the so-called BRIC group – Brazil, Russia, India and China – which have witnessed the kind of explosive growth that Europe and North America have not seen since the Industrial Revolution; and it is these economies that have transformed architectural practice. Foster is busy in all these places.

3. The Personal Rapid Transit system (PRT) developed for Masdar City. Masdar is designed to be a pedestrian-friendly urban environment, without fossil-fuel cars. The driverless PRT system is available for longer journeys. Vehicles travel at up to 40kph and the longest routes will take just ten minutes.

4. A self-funded study – unique for its scale and strategic cross-sector thinking – the Thames Hub (2011-) offers a blueprint for future infrastructure development in Britain. The proposal brings together rail, freight logistics, aviation, energy production and transmission, flood protection and regional development. By recognising the synergies between these different strands, it reaps the benefits of their integration.

3

4

1. Masdar City, Abu Dhabi (2007-). This pioneering development explores sustainable technologies and the planning principles of the traditional walled Arab city to create a desert community that will be carbon neutral and zero waste. The surrounding land accommodates wind and photovoltaic farms, enabling the community to be energy self-sufficient.

In Moscow, the practice has played a major and inevitably – given the scale of the transformation of the city – sometimes controversial part in the creation of a new kind of Russian capital. They are working on some of the most symbolic projects in the city, including the remodelling of the Pushkin Museum. In India, Foster is involved with an equally striking transformation of those parts of the country that have detached themselves from the traditional idea of the sub-continent, to challenge the high-tech industries of Europe and North America.

Yet, at the other end of the scale Foster is designing and funding the construction of a school in Sierra Leone, which is just 295 square metres, and building a new winery for Château Margaux, which is just 1,200 square metres. He is also creating the set and costumes for a production of *Otello* at La Scala in Milan and curating an exhibition – *Norman Foster on Art* – to mark the twentieth anniversary of the Carré d'Art in Nîmes. As Foster says, 'When you look at what we do, there is no such thing as a typical project. We are engaged right across the spectrum – from the largest to the smallest.'

Foster Associates' first overseas work in the early 1970s was in Norway and on the Canary Island of Gomera. Both projects were the result of an ongoing connection with Fred Olsen, and represented a natural outgrowth of Foster's domestic practice. The Hongkong Bank was perhaps the last manifestation of a colonial connection, a commission that came from the other side of the world to supply an expertise that was not then locally available.

Since then, the nature of international practice has become very different. Those early projects reflected a one-way transaction, in which Britain was exporting expertise. But the more that Foster + Partners has worked outside Britain, the more it has become a two-way process. The architects are to some degree still exporting their skills, but at the same time they are, consciously or not, finding their world view transformed by the places in which they work and the projects they take on – learning through genuine collaborations with others. Once you have built a skyscraper in Shanghai, for example, it is impossible to see the world only through the perspective of the constraints and preconceptions of the City of London.

As Foster says, 'When you look at what we do, there is no such thing as a typical project. We are engaged right across the spectrum – from the largest to the smallest.'

The experience of working in cultures in which central governments are prepared to countenance radical new approaches to development, by connecting transport systems in an integrated way, or steering large-scale projects through a maze of competing interests, inevitably tends to transform perceptions of what the architect can achieve.

When Hong Kong countenanced the closure of the territory's old airport at Kai Tak and the construction of an entirely new one at Chek Lap Kok, it reclaimed the island site from the sea, connected it to the city centre via a brand new mass-transit link, building one of the world's longest suspension bridges in the process. And it did all that in just six years. It makes the reluctance of the authorities in Britain to consider Foster's similarly radical solution to the problem of overcrowding and noise pollution at Heathrow by relocating London's airport to the Thames Estuary seem self-defeatingly timid.

1

Much of our new work goes far beyond the way that architecture has been practised traditionally. These projects have moved beyond the scale of the individual building to encompass major infrastructure and city masterplanning. There is also a focus on the public realm – on transport, bridges, streets and squares – everyday places that are easily taken for granted but have a real impact on the way that we live. We really are at the point where it's possible to consider the design of the built environment as a totality – for the first time to be able to have a holistic approach to design. Mouzhan Majidi, in conversation with the editor, 2012

Design for me is all encompassing. It is about values. I believe that we have a moral duty to design well and responsibly – whether that is at the scale of a door handle or a regional or city masterplan. Design can explore the new and build on the past. It can transform patterns of health, living and working. To design is to question and to challenge. Norman Foster, in conversation with the editor, 2012

In its evolving incarnation, the Foster studio has to think about the big ideas, but also the details. In the settings in which it is now working, it must understand different tastes and preconceptions as well as the broader concerns of climate and culture. Stefan Behling, who has helped to develop the practice's research into sustainable environmental initiatives, says: 'Our buildings are rooted in the culture and the environment in which they are conceived and will operate. You can look at our current work and say that, twenty years ago, we would not have done something that looked like this or that.

'The truth is that the architectural landscape has changed quite radically. We are doing some of our largest projects in the desert, for example, in extreme climatic conditions, and that suggests a certain kind of response. With Masdar we began by looking at the regional vernacular – the "architecture without architects" that existed historically – and then aimed to build for zero carbon and zero waste, with the least amount of embodied energy.'

Certainly the work that Foster is building now has taken on some new characteristics. In forty years architectural preoccupations have moved on. There are new techniques and aesthetic expressions to work with.

However, the evolution of Foster's work is based on a sense of continuity, rather than the sudden lurch taken by some US architects towards Postmodernism in the 1980s. That was a moment in which the practices which had once shaped the development of modern architecture suddenly lost their compass and started conducting seminars to find a way forward. Foster + Partners is still clear about its architectural priorities and bearings, despite its capacity to embrace change.

Furthermore, while architects have always been ready to work all around the world, the potential of contemporary communications to allow Norman Foster to make a presentation in Abu Dhabi on a Sunday, return to London on Monday, to prepare for the opening of a gallery in Madrid on Wednesday, before moving on to New York, make architecture an activity very different from the one pursued by Edwin Lutyens with the requirement to spend weeks at sea and months at a time in India building New Delhi. Even in 1962, Jørn Utzon felt the need to relocate his studio to Sydney to build the Opera House when he won the competition for its design.

When Norman Foster established his office in 1967, there was a sense that architectural reputations were established primarily on the basis of the work that an architect would build within his or her own country. In the past there might have been a few projects overseas, but these were often understood as diversions from the main effort. That is no longer true. Architecture is now as universal as it was in the Middle Ages when groups of itinerant master masons went from cathedral site to cathedral site, and made the Gothic in France, Germany and England an integrated whole.

2. Norman Foster's preliminary sketches for the mixed-use Russia Tower in Moscow (2006).

3. A model of the Pushkin Museum of Fine Arts extension, Moscow (2007-). Building on the experience of projects such as the Carré d'Art, in which cultural buildings are explored as part of a wider urban programme, this masterplan aims to establish a thriving cultural quarter focused on the Pushkin. The project encompasses the restoration of the museum and the creation of new buildings to more than triple the Pushkin's exhibition and archive spaces.

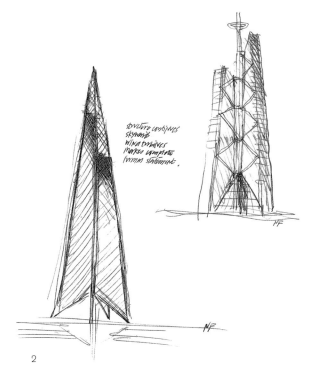

2

3

1-4. The studio's annual
Graduate Show is an eagerly
awaited fixture of the studio's
calendar. Norman Foster
leads the 'crit' with every
participant, and all the
senior partners take part.

Foster + Partners to date has built in more than thirty countries, and that experience has inevitably shaped the nature and ambition of the architecture it is building. The London studio has become a centre that attracts ambitious and gifted young architects from all around the world, eager to learn, and to work on the remarkable range of projects that the practice addresses. That diversity is reflected in the fact that collectively they speak some forty-five languages.

The world has changed too. The first of the landmarks of Foster's independent career was the Olsen Amenity Centre, long since demolished – like the Reliance Controls Electronics Factory, the building that bridged the close of Foster's career as a partner in Team 4 and the birth of his independent practice. Both buildings were, in their time, at the forefront of new thinking about architecture. Olsen was a breakthrough in social attitudes to the workplace. Reliance was also an attempt to break down the class distinctions – 'white-collar' versus 'blue-collar' – that once bedevilled the British workplace; at the same time it addressed the need to accommodate new production methods for the nascent electronics industry.

The leading edge of technology continually moves on, leaving architecture behind and posing questions about the preservation of buildings of historic significance from the recent past. There are already buildings designed by Foster that have been placed on the statutory list of buildings protected by the legislation for historic buildings. Interestingly, Willis Faber, now a Grade I-listed structure, was realised at a time when the economic climate was at least as sombre as it is at the time of writing, when inflation in Britain exceeded 20 per cent, and when power cuts, the three-day week, and the oil embargo imposed by OPEC in the wake of the Six Day War between Israel and the Arab world were threatening the economic order.

Realising Willis Faber was a very different task from the challenge of working in the construction bubble of the first decade of the twenty-first century, when the Chinese hunger for structural steel made the material so expensive that reinforced concrete had to be used as an alternative in many cases. Foster has shown the resolve and cool-headedness to operate effectively in both conditions. Those are just two of the qualities which characterise the practice.

Foster's London studio has become a centre that attracts ambitious and gifted young architects from all around the world, eager to learn, and to work on a remarkable range of projects.

Another quality is the capacity to work creatively in almost any context, anywhere in the world. Bringing civilised working conditions to the British factory floor may be a very different proposition from the challenge faced by architects working in former Soviet-Bloc nations emerging from decades of underdevelopment looking for international-standard buildings, but the practice's ability to grasp the demands of the contexts in which it operates has allowed it to manage the transition from East Anglia to Central Asia, and in different ways to transform expectations in both environments.

1

2

Architecture has become a kind of global early warning system. Follow the direction that architects are taking, and you have an understanding of the nature of the shifts in the world economy, and the changing balance of cultural power. When Norman Foster was a student, America was a place that exported architecture and architectural ideas around the world. In recent years, it has started to bring architects from elsewhere to inject a new energy into the country.

Hearst Tower in Manhattan is perhaps the most striking New York skyscraper to be built in the last thirty years. In designing it, the Foster team had learned the lessons of the nature of high-rise architecture to create a new model for dealing with a tall building in a city which believed that it had already tried all the permutations. Among a growing portfolio of recent US projects, the practice is designing a campus for Apple in California and an office tower on Park Avenue in Manhattan. In the last decade, it has completed a dazzling array of cultural buildings there, including the Sperone Westwater Gallery in Manhattan, the Art of the Americas Wing at the Museum of Fine Arts, Boston and the Winspear Opera House in Dallas. Foster is now addressing the challenges of the New York Public Library – a project that draws on the practice's considerable skills in designing within the context of historic buildings.

Foster + Partners has a global reach that poses interesting questions about how the firm is to be understood. Whether it is working in Abu Dhabi, Hong Kong or Kazakhstan, the practice is regarded as an international firm which is comfortable anywhere. Indeed, in Abu Dhabi and Hong Kong – and New York and Madrid and a host of other cities – it is virtually a 'local' firm. Winning the competition for the West Kowloon Cultural District, for example, demonstrated the depth of Foster's roots in the region – roots that can be traced back to the Hongkong Bank competition of 1979.

Reputations, of course, require constant nurturing, protection and replenishment. To ensure its long-term survival, the practice must maintain the high standards of organisation and performance on which it has based its identity. At the heart of the Foster ethos is a series of key projects that have measured out the development of contemporary architecture itself: from the very early work for industry and the arts, to the Hongkong Bank, which virtually reinvented the tall office building, and Stansted Airport which redefined the character of the modern airport terminal, to Masdar City – begun as a masterplan and with a physical legacy in the form of the Masdar Institute.

Masdar defines the office's revolutionary thinking as much as the Hongkong Bank once did. Its vision for a technically advanced, carbon-neutral settlement on a vast scale pushes to the limits of what is possible with known materials, techniques and transport strategies: and then beyond. Foster knows that to endure, architecture must be able to incorporate and benefit from technologies that we cannot yet imagine.

And so how does Foster foresee the practice in future? Certainly it has reached a point where it is far too large and sophisticated an operation to be understood as a vehicle for one individual. But Norman Foster is a remarkable architect, and in Foster + Partners he has created an organisation which can carry on the practice of architecture in a way that has the essence of Norman Foster, and his personal history and determination about it. As he says, 'the practice is the design project of which I am most proud.'

3

4

Foster + Partners

Previous pages: this team photograph was taken by Nigel Young on 9 October 2008 outside the Riverside studio in London.

The list of individuals given here represents the staffing and structure of the office at the time of going to press in July 2013. For details of those people who worked on the projects in this volume – some of whom have since left the practice – please refer to the Project Credits.

Founder and Chairman
Norman Foster

Chief Executive
Mouzhan Majidi

Senior Partners
Spencer de Grey
Head of Design

David Nelson
Head of Design

Grant Brooker
Design Director Group 1

David Summerfield
Design Director Group 2

Luke Fox
Design Director Group 3

Stefan Behling
Design Director Group 4

Gerard Evenden
Design Director Group 5

Nigel Dancey
Design Director Group 6

Matthew Streets
Chief Financial Officer

Andy Bow
Group 1

Brandon Haw
Head of Business Development

Paul Kalkhoven
Head of Technical Development

Roger Ridsdill Smith
Head of Engineering 1

Piers Heath
Head of Engineering 2

Mark Sutcliffe
Head of Management

Graham Young
Head of Information and Design Systems

Design Board
Norman Foster
Mouzhan Majidi
Spencer de Grey
David Nelson

Stefan Behling
Armstrong Yakubu

Partners

Anis Abou Zaki
Francis Aish
Mark Atkinson
Zak A Ayash
James Barnes
Gamma Basra
Simona Bencini
Rafe Bertram
Toby Blunt
John Blythe
Timothy Bodinnar
Chris Bubb
Keith Calder
Angus Campbell
Patrick Campbell
William Castagna
Martin Castle
Young Chiu
Chris Connell
Tony Cooper
Xavier De Kestelier
Rhian Deakin
Niall Dempsey
Ben Dobbin
Xiaonian Duan
Jon Fielding
Morgan Fleming
Colin Foster
Juan Frigerio
Irene Gallou
Mike Gardner
Edward Garrod
Michael Gentz
Martin Glover
Pedro Haberbosch
Russell Hales
Lee Hallman
Ulrich Hamann
Peter Han
Katy Harris
Robert Harrison
Richard Hawkins
Darron Haylock
Ken Hogg
Mike Holland
Stephen Holmes
Thouria Istephan
Mike Jelliffe

David Jenkins
Reinhard Joecks
Iwan Jones
Michael Jones
Arjun Kaicker
Anton Khmelnitskiy
David Kong
Jurgen Kuppers
Stuart Latham
Paul Leadbeatter
Alistair Lenczner
Nicholas Ling
Muir Livingstone
Nikolai Malsch
Luis Matania
James McGrath
Bobbie Michael
Laura Morales
Kate Murphy
Antoinette Nassopoulos
Michael WT Ng
Ross Palmer
Jonathan Parr
Divya Patel
Emily Phang
Tony Price
Bob Ramsden
Taba Rasti
Austin Relton
Giles Robinson
Filo Russo
Narinder Sagoo
Ricky Sandhu
Roland Schnizer
Owe Schoof
Ben Scott
Kirsten Scott
Cristina Segni
Dan Sibert
Barry Smith
John Smith
Andrea Soligon
Hugh Stewart
Diane Teague
Huw Thomas
Brian Timmoney
Dara Towhidi
Christopher Trott
Steve Trstenjak

Pablo Urango Lillo
Neil Vandersteen
Juan Vieira-Pardo
Karsten Vollmer
Wolfgang Wagener
Jeremy Wallis
Colin Ward
Chris West
Ian Whitby
Chris Williams
Michael Wurzel
Edson Yabiku
Armstrong Yakubu

Associate Partners

Harriet Abbott
Amer Altaf
Annamaria Anderloni
Sofia Arraiza Ruiz de Galarreta
Mike Bass
Aike Behrens
Jonathan Bell
Elena Bertarelli
Giovanni Betti
Doretta Bevilacqua
James Bishop
Robin Blanchard
Barrie Cheng
Emma Clifford
Jonathan Cox
Francois-Pierre Curato
Adam Davis
John Dixon
Shyamala Duraisingam
Tim Dyer
James Edwards
Abdelkader El-Chgar
Miriam Elwing
Rudy Espiritu
Tie Fan
Bassem Fawwaz
Jacopo Fiabane
Matthew Foreman
Michaela Fuchs
Anna Garreau
Carolyn Gembles
Gregory Gibbon
Sharon Giffen
William Gordon
Stephanie Gracies
Marc Guberman
Dominik Hauser
Matthew Hayhurst
Joost Heremans
Jens Hoffman
Darryn Holder
John Jennings
Aphrodite Kavallieraki
Kathryn Keen
Jeremy Kim
Andrew King
Angelika Kovacic
Hernan Kraviez

Ashley Lane
Tillmann Lenz
Randy Liekenjie
Franquibel Lima
Andy Lister
Sarah Lister
Neil MacLeod
Maria Mallalieu
Consuelo Manna
Colin McEvoy
Sebastian Mendez
Tony Miki
Nathan Millar
Bruno Moser
Michael Mueller
Wolfgang Muller
Carlo Negri
Rajesh Patel
Umesh Patel
Nick Paterson
Richard Pendlebury
Salvador Rivas Trujillo
Damiano Rizzini
Katy Roach
Martin Rolfe
Maddalena Sanvito
Gordon Seiles
Robert Seymour
Danny Shaw
Riko Sibbe
Marilu Sicoli
Paul Smith
Peter Sokoloff
Carlos Sole Bravo
Iwona Szwedo-Wilmot
Pearl Tang
Caroline Tarling
Martha Tsigkari
Stephanie Tunka
Robert Turner
Jorge Uribe Restrepo
Mark van der Byl
Stephan Verkuijlen
Kai Wertel
Vincent Westbrook
James White
Simon Windebank
Simon Wing
Sabrina Wisely

Rene Wolter
Anna Xu
Dion Young
Nigel Young
Zheng Yu
Daniel Zielinski
Maximilian Zielinski

Associates
O'Neil Alexander
Gregor Anderson
Enrico Anelli Monti
William Arbizu
Christopher Arnold
Seif Bahaa Eldin
Massimo Severo Barbera
Trevor Barrett
Ed Bartlett
Cely Bigando
Andrew Bigwood
Diogo Bleck
Katy Boehm
Stephan Bohne
Peter Brittain
Richard Brown
David Burton
Ricardo Candel Gurrea
Stefano Cesario
Kevin Chan
Athena Chau
Ho Ling Cheung
Saxbourne Cheung
Steven Chiu
Gabriele Coccia
Bryan Cory
Miguel Costa
Andrew Coward
Alicia Cox
Salmaan Craig
Paul Cristian
Patrick Crocock
Andrea Dallari
Kunal Dalvi
John De Maio
Federico De Paoli
Melinda De Wet
Upesh Dhanji
Tomas Elizalde
Derrol Euling
Hazel Eynon
Maria Farina
Manuel Fernandez
Andrea Fleming
Oliver Flindall
Iolanda Fortunato
Domingos Garcia
Jose Garcia Ares

Andrew Gardner
Claudia Gentili Spinola
Kashif Ghafoor
Ei-Kie Giam
Evangelos Giouvanos
Amanda Glover
Rupert Goddard
Jorge Gomez Bernal
Krzysztof Gornicki
Bernadette Greaney
Michelle Guthrie
Andy Haigh
Isabelle Hannig-Buchbinder
Takuji Hasegawa
Rie Hasloev
Klaus Heldwein
Stefanie Hickl
Timothy Hui
Rony Imad
Sidonie Immler
Panos Ioannou
Amer Ismail
Sophie Izon
Andrew Jackson
Mayoor Jagjiwan
Dirk Jantz
Erik Josefsson
Sam Joyce
Eleni Kalogeropoulou
Bela Kasza
Martin Kehoe
Paul Kennedy
Se Kwan Kim
Sejin Kim
Yong Bin Kim
Yung A Kim
Richard Klewer
Bojana Knezevic
Jedrzej Kolesinski
Luca Latini
Hwa-Seop Lee
Gibert Leygonie
Susie Lober
Susanne Loeffler
Ian Malcomson
Milena Marucci
Karl Mascarenhas
Joshua Mason
Rana Mezher

Cristiano Michelena
Gregor Milne
Ryan Mitchell
Sam Morgan
Jeng Neo
Adam Newburn
Michael Ng
Kristine Ngan
Brian Nolan
Eva O'Connell
Laszlo Pallagi
Nina Pari
Chan Ik Park
Bhavesh Patel
Nicky Patel
Michele Pecoraro
Laura Podda
Lorenzo Poli
Samuel Price
Stanley Pun
Jonathan Rabagliati
Florian Rieger
Emily Rix
Stephen Rock
Daniel Rogers
Ivo Sales Costa
George Salinas
Jillian Salter
Nicola Scaranaro
Ronald Schuurmans
Jayendra Shah
Sachen Shah
Steve Shaw
Bartenis Siaulytis
Sarah Simpkin
Parul Singh
Joanna Smith
Tan Sohanpall
Sunphol Sorakul
Lukas Sosna
Zoe Stokes
Hiroyuki Sube
Gary Taylor
Harsh Thapar
Charlotte Thomas
Lara Thrasher
Pedro Tiago de Sousa
Dina Timartseva
Damian Timlin

Yusuke Tsutsui
Diem Uong
Bram van der Wal
Gareth Verbiest
Sarah Villar-Furniss
Linjie Wang
Weina Wang
Michael Ward
Haruna Watanabe
Adrian Weidmann
Tony Wenban
Dave Wicker
Catherine Wilson
Dominic Wilson
Lawrence Wong
Dorothee Woollard
Katy Wu
David Yang
Tak Kei Yip
Kevin Yiu
Munehiko Yokomatsu
Juanjuan Zhang

Group One
Grant Brooker
Andy Bow

Sofia Arraiza Ruiz de Galarreta
Filippo Bari
Steven Baumann
Jonathan Bell
Richard Bevan
Chad Bishop
Clement Bois
Alisia Bourla
Peter Brittain
Luis Ramos Castro
Saxbourne Cheung
Young Wei-Yang Chiu
Kyuho Choi
Federica Ciocci
Francois-Pierre Curato
Peter Donegan
Sarah Fenner
Oliver Flindall
Raffaele Gavassa
Krzysztof Gornicki
Felicia Guldberg
Andres Harris
Robert Harrison
Takuji Hasegawa
Jens Hoffman
Aaron Holden
Brandon Hubbard
Rony Imad
Sandy Karagkouni
Raphael Keane
Hyun-Jin Kim
Yongcchun Kim
Jedrzej Kolesinski
David Kong
Angelika Kovacic
Jurgen Kuppers
Paul Leadbeatter
Insub Lee
Isabel Lopez Taberna
Andrew Macpherson
Adeline Morin
Antoinette Nassopoulos
Phakorn Nilwong
Anthonia Ogundeji-Peters
Jolanda Oud

Misza Boncza Ozdowski
Raffaella Panella
Prisca Pannone
Nick Paterson
Gaurav Powale
Alex Qian
Madelaine Raposas
Merino Ranallo
Madelaine Raposas
Santiago Rebolledo Pulgar
Damiano Rizzini
Martin Rolfe
Michael Rush
Orsolya Say
Owe Schoof
Leyre Senosiain Orense
Dan Sibert
Hugh Stewart
Benjamin Tate
Wendy Teo
Theodoros Themistocleous
Pedro Tiago de Sousa
Maria Sagrario M Torres
Paola Tuosto
Yusuke Tsutsui
Sarah Wai
Ian Whitby
Tomasz Wozny
Louise Yeung
Kevin Yiu
Emily Zhu

Group Two
David Summerfield
Chris Bubb

Rui Alves
William Arbizu
Gabriel Belli Butler
Rafe Bertram
Emily Bidegain
Megan Blaine
Anthony Cestra
Chris Connell
Madeleine Dahlstedt
Satyajit Das
German de la Torre
John De Maio

Niall Dempsey
Upesh Dhanji
Eva Diu
Claire Donnelly
Jeremy Dworken
James Edwards
Chris Farmer
Alda Fernandes de Jesus
William Villalobos Fernandez
James Freeman
Juan Frigerio
Camilo Garavito
Domingos Garcia
David Gillespie
Minaki Goto
Friso Gros
Marc Guberman
Pedro Haberbosch
Peter Han
Ross Harniman
Paloma Hendel
Rebekah Hieronymus
Jose Gad Peralta Iglesias
Amer Ismail
Mayoor Jagjiwan
Mike Jelliffe
John Jennings
Despina Kalapoda
Aphrodite Kavallieraki
Se Kwan Kim
Janggen Lee
Shuanglong Li
Brook Lin
Consuelo Manna
Karl Mascarenhas
John McCulley
Scott Moqueen
Sebastian Mendez
Gregor Milne
Shinji Miyazaki
Roger Molina-Vera
Marian Moravek
Mouzafer Ntagkala
Mario Ortiz Valverde
Maria Paez Gonzalez
Miguel Peralta Munoz
Jorge Pereira
Lucia Petrelli
Lorenzo Poli

Tandorn Prakobpol
Samuel Price
Rui Rabaca
Sunil Rajaratnam
Maro Riga
Daniel Rodrigues
Nielsen Rodrigues
Nathan St John
Rudrajit Sabhaney
George Salinas
David Santamaria
Ben Scott
Kirsten Scott
Cristina Segni
Robert Seymour
Claire Sharpe
Danny Shaw
Wendy Smith
Kit Smithson
Peter Sokoloff
Anthony Stahl
Robin Tandavanitj
Sherman Tang
Fabio Tellia
Charl Testa
Damian Timlin
Yasuhiro Tohdoh
Takashi Tsurumaki
Jorge Uribe Restrepo
Jose Vargas-Hidalgo
Francisco Waltersdorfer
Linjie Wang
Anina Weber Bach
Dominic Wilson
Vivienne Wong
Pui Kie Wu
Astrid Wulff
Michael Wurzel
Antonio Yeregui
Anna Xu

Group Three
Luke Fox
Angus Campbell
Jonathan Parr

Sarah Akigbogun
Sarah Ash

Mark Atkinson
Matt Ault
Zak A Ayash
Mina Ayoughi
Seif Bahaa Eldin
Thomas Bartram
Doretta Bevilacqua
Cely Bigando
Diogo Bleck
Shengfei Cao
Kevin Chan
Athena Chau
Martin Cheung
Steven Chiu
Won Suk Cho
Nicholas Chrispin
Howard Chung
Louise Clausen
Jonathan Drayton
Tim Dyer
Lea Faber
Tie Fan
David Ferment
Colin Foster
Etienne Fuchs
Andrew Gardner
Ulrich Geissler
Michael Gentz
Filipa Fonseca George
Ei-Kie Giam
Tim Gibbons
Sharon Giffen
Charles Gillespie
Daniel Glaessl
Inigo Garate Gomara
Alejandro Noe Guerrero Ortega
Isabelle Hannig-Buchbinder
Richard Hawkins
Asa Hjort
Huy Quang Ho
Vince Ho
Ken Hogg
Darryn Holder
Jade Ip
Martin Kehoe
Paul Kennedy
Anton Khmelnitskiy
Jeremy Kim
Sejin Kim

Sungji Kim
Vera Kleesattel
Eirini Kouka
Jekaterina Kowaltschuk
Hernan Kraviez
Renee Tsuen Yan Kwok
Celia Yixin Lai
Diana Lam
Marian Lee
Alistair Lenczner
Ka Man Leung
Lee Li
David Liang
Randy Liekenjie
Yuki Liu
Connie Luk
Theo Malzieu
Veronika Martykán
Tony Miki
Michael Mueller
Kin Wah Mui
Sofia Muzio
Carlo Negri
Michael Ng
Michael WT Ng
Phuc Minh Nguyen
Orlando Oliver
Kurtulus Oflaz
Michele Pecoraro
Patricia Peter
Francisco Pinto Basto
Sevil Pius
Stanley Pun
Sergio Reyes Rodriguez
Ivo Sales Costa
Juan Carlos Sanchez Rodriguez
Ricky Sandhu
Roland Schnizer
Jayendra Shah
Bartenis Siaulytis
Riko Sibbe
Soraya Somarathne
Rossella Stina
Hiroyuki Sube
Henry Suryo
Pearl Tang
Charlotte Thomas
Huw Thomas
Dina Timartseva

Brian Timmoney
Tsuyoshi To
Karsten Vollmer
Kai-Yi Wang
Qiaojuan Wang
Weina Wang
Colin Ward
Peter Webb
Vincent Westbrook
Kitti Wong
Lawrence Wong
Reine Kit Shun Wong
Katie Wu
Shu-Hao Wu
Meng Xia
Zhili Xu
David Yang
See Teck Yeo
Bong Yeung
Alexandra Young
Dion Young
Zheng Yu
Bo Zhang
Sonia Zhang

Group Four
Stefan Behling
Michael Jones

Diana Araya Munoz
Andrew Ballard
Maria-Cristina Banceanu
Ton Men Banh
Simona Bencini
Elena Bertarelli
Ergin Birinci
Keith Conrad Blaine
Robin Blanchard
Stephan Bohne
Dariusz Boron
Luca Carraro
William Castagna
Atisthan Charoenkool
Michael Chou
Christopher Christophi
Gabriele Coccia
Julia Eisman Cordero
Michael Cowen

Paul Cristian
Andrea Dallari
Kunal Dalvi
Federico De Paoli
Ben Dobbin
Erin Dwyer
Mohamad El Khayat
Afra Farry
Jacopo Fiabane
Jon Fielding
Katharina Fleck
Andrea Fleming
Morgan Fleming
Thomas Fryer
Michaela Fuchs
Daniel Gaertner
Christin Gegenheimer
Giuseppe Giacoppo
Rebeca Gonzalez Murillo
Philip Goodman
Florian Goscheff
Ulrich Hamann
Patrick Hamdy
Kylie Han
Rie Hasloev
Matthew Hayhurst
Darron Haylock
Klaus Heldwein
Stefanie Hickl
Sung Ho Hong
Dmitry Ivanoff
Dirk Jantz
Reinhard Joecks
Ben Johnson
Kadri Kaldam
Regine Kandan
Bela Kasza
Yung A Kim
Ignacio Larracoechea San Sebastian
Christopher Lee
Jean-Francois Lemay
Tillmann Lenz
Jeffrey Leopando
Philip Li
Maggie Liang
Li-Jun Lin
Hang Ling
Sarah Elizabeth Lucy
Petra Lui

James McGrath
Thomas Mahon
Nikolai Malsch
Simone Martin
Luis Matania
William Mathers
Lucas Mazarrasa Chavarri
Alberto Menegazzo
Rana Mezher
Antonio Moll Moliner
Diana Araya Munoz
Kate Murphy
James Murray
Ting Zhee Ng
Kristine Ngan
Laura Nieto Mendez
Yooju No
Thomas Oberniedermayr
Saran Oki
Laszlo Pallagi
James Patterson
Edward Pearce
Joshua Plourde
Amin Sadeghy
Jessica Sano
Joana Santos
Maddalena Sanvito
Kyle Schertzing
Gordon Seiles
Behdad Shahi
Samson Simberg
Parul Singh
Lukas Sosna
Krzysztof Szymanski
Nada Tayeb
Diego Alejandro Teixeira Seisdedos
Lara Thrasher
Kasia Townend
Stephanie Tunka
Wolfgang Wagener
Kai Wertel
Rene Wolter
Nicos Yiatros
Oskar Yip
Daniel Zielinski
Maximilian Zielinski

Group Five
Gerard Evenden
Stuart Latham

Enrico Anelli-Monti
Nicholas Arthurell
Lieselot Baert
Massimo Barbera
Jefferson Barnes
Aike Behrens
Toby Blunt
John Blythe
Aleksander Bociewicz
Martin Castle
Yang-Hen Chen
Barrie Cheng
Ho Ling Cheung
Assawin Choochottavorn
Emilio Cimma
Daniella De Almeida
Roberto Di Donato
Iolanda Fortunato
Sidonie Immler
Hisayo Kaneko
Yong Bin Kim
Andrew King
Giovanna Sylos Labini
Ashley Lane
Joliette Lange
Luca Latini
Won Suk Lee
Jiexin Li
Franquibel Lima
Wei Jie Liu
Muir Livingstone
Georgia McGowan
Martina Meluzzi
Ricardo Messano
Laura Morales
Irina Nazarova
Adam Newburn
Ross Palmer
Ill Sam Park
Chan Ik Park
Richard Pendlebury
Emily Phang
William Plowman
Laura Podda
Austin Relton

Florian Rieger
Jillian Salter
Daniele Sbaraglia
Ronald Schuurmans
Jie Shen
Marilu Sicoli
Sunphol Sorakul
Chris Storie
Iwona Szwedo-Wilmot
Dara Towhidi
Silvia Valeri
Bram van der Wal
Wen Wang
Hamish Watt
Dominic Williams
Simon Wing
Edson Yabiku
Munehiko Yokomatsu
Yantian Zhou

Group Six
Nigel Dancey
Giles Robinson

Ana Agag Longo
Adeel Ali
Chantal Aquilina
Anna Aversing
Alexios Bacolas
James Barnes
Jose Berg Aldoney
Federico Bixio
Juan Bourkaib Fernandez
de Cordoba
David Burton
Patrick Campbell
Veronique Castel-Branco
Elice Catmull
Sanhita Chaturvedi
Heidi Chi
Sze Nam Kenzaf Chung
Ben Coss
Miguel Costa
Danah Dib
Patricia Espejo Moreno
Manuel Fernandez
Luis Fuentes Arambula
Jose Garcia Alamar

Jose Garcia Ares
Carolyn Gembles
Jorge Gomez Bernal
Pablo Gonzalez-Valcarcel
Manzano-Monis
William Gordon
Xenia Gyftaki
Russell Hales
Dominik Hauser
Joost Heremans
Chris Johnstone
Iwan Jones
Sharat Kaicker
Go Kawakita
Akbar Khan
Kristine Krueger
Kathleen Laskin
Hwa-Seop Lee
Nicholas Ling
Yuan Hsin Lo
Naveed Mughal
Ahmed Mukhtar
Pablo Munoz Roca
Carmen Ortega Chamorro
Emilio Ortiz Zaforas
Gulnaz Ozbay
Eva Palacios
Nina Pari
Andreas Peyerl
Pip Phillips
Stefan Popa
Ivan Kaye Puertos
Isidora Radenkovic
Taba Rasti
Salvador Rivas Trujillo
Emily Rix
Katy Roach
Filo Russo
Paola Nena Sakic
Angel Sanchez Lazcano
Nicola Scaranaro
Eva Seo-Andersen
Carlos Sole Bravo
Paul Stanbridge
Milena Stojkovic
Zoe Stokes
Ramnika Subberwal
Catherine Thiemann
Steve Trstenjak

Pablo Urango Lillo
Jaime Valle
Juan Vieira-Pardo
Wenwen Wang
Chris West
Amber Wood
Jacqueline Yeung
Agnieszka Zych-Twadell

Engineering 1
Roger Ridsdill-Smith
Christopher Trott

James Bishop
Joseph Camajani
Ricardo Candel Gurrea
Davide Conti
Andrew Coward
Joseph Dimery
Xiaonian Duan
Carole Frising
Helene Huang
Rupert Inman
Arthur Lapeyrere
John Larkey
Pedro Manuel Martins Nave
Wolfgang Muller
Jeng Neo
Ilyas Pisirici
Laura Smith
Andrea Soligon
Bárbara Valente de Sousa Ramos
Babak Niai Tizkar
Antonio Villani
Michael Ward
Dorothee Woollard
James Wroot
Zhi Zhao

Engineering 2
Piers Heath
Edward Garrod

Anis Abou Zaki
Trevor Barrett
Keith Calder
Amanda Clemente

Emma Clifford
Baris Coskun
James Do
Ruth Dominguez Sanchez
Tomas Elizalde
Alex Fanzini
Evangelos Giouvanos
Sophie Halford
Tim Howarth
Andrew Jackson
Andrew Jones
Bojana Knezevic
Dimitra Kyrkou
Mauro Leuce
Peter Luczak
Mohammed Mautasimuddin
Tom McIntosh
Cristiano Michelena
Nathan Millar
Simon Oliphant
Rajesh Patel
Nirav Shah
Daniel Skidmore
John Smith
Bo Wang
Brenda Yang
Juanjuan Zhang
Lujun Zhou

Specialist Teams

Applied Research and Development
Francis Aish

Angelos Chronis
Adam Davis
Shuai Feng
Sam Joyce
Martha Tsigkari

Business Development
Brandon Haw

Communications
Katy Harris
David Jenkins

Mona Cheng
Matthew Foreman
Gregory Gibbon
Amanda Glover
Rupert Goddard
Stephen Huntley
Lexie King
Susie Lober
Jay Lopez
Gayle Mault
Zoë Simpson
Rebecca Roke
Elizabeth Shelton
Sarah Simpkin
Samuel Tomlyn
Annelise Tvergaard
Joe Wong
Nigel Young

Construction Review Group
Paul Kalkhoven

Philip Bonner
Jennifer Booth
Patrick Crocock
Mario Fasulo

Ana Gordon
Kristin Hoogenboom
Max Li
Bob Ramsden
Paul Smith
Stephan Verkuijlen
Haruna Watanabe
Michael Woodrow

Design Communications
Narinder Sagoo

Kacper Chmielewski
Georgina Fairhurst
Olga Rienda Sevilla
Tan Sohanpall

Design Systems
Stephen Holmes

Stefanie Borms
Derrol Euling
Robert Jones
Beth McLeod
Lee Schmidtchen

Industrial Design
Mike Holland

Stefan Bench
Pietro Gottardi
Harry Parr-Young
Francesco Sasia
Thomas Wagner
Adrian Weidmann
James White

Information Centre/MRC
Divya Patel

Erik de Laurens de Saint Martin
George Fereday
Anja Lucht

Information Technology
Graham Young
Barry Smith

Stevie Adefehinti
Olu Akin-kuoroye
Amer Altaf
Joana Antunes
Christopher Arnold
Matthew Bellingham
Bikramjeet Bhullar
Rylan Blackmore-Holness
Aba Dabi
Amek Ebele
Kashif Ghafoor
Timothy Hui
Sohail Iqbal
Kashif Khan
Noemi Klajbar
Andrew Leckie
Hui-Ting Liu
Renna McDonagh
Rajeev Mirchandani
Indren Naiker
Eva O'Connell
Chirag Patel
Mehul Patel
Mark Phillips
Lee Rance
Justin Scott
Neil Snowden
Gary Taylor
Sam Tincey
Kong Tse
Mark van der Byl
Anthony Watson
Wing Wong

Information Systems
Tony Price

Michelle Meyer
Bhavesh Patel
Nikhil Ramchandani
Giuseppe Rossitto
Mitesh Sachania

Interiors Group
Lee Hallman

Annamaria Anderloni
Mariana Castro Baquero
Stefano Cesario
Lydia Corfield
Tamika Kawabuchi
Andy Lister
Sarah Lister
Maria Mallalieu
Kate Mason
Alex Nevedomskis
Simona Rossi
Vladimir Shukhov
Karin Skoglund
Benjamin Stevenson
Caroline Tarling

Management Group
Mark Sutcliffe

Andrew Bigwood
Timothy Bodinnar
Claire Castledine
Melinda de Wet
Inés Puelles Dominguez
Jessica Fung
Michelle Guthrie
Thouria Istephan
Neil MacLeod
Colin McEvoy
Luke Moloney
Lisa Roston
Gemma White
Michael Woodrow

Model Shop
Neil Vandersteen
Diane Teague

James Algar
Gregor Anderson
Ed Bartlett
Richard Brown
Hannah Catt
Bryan Cory

John Dixon
Jamie Fallon
Kevin Garvey
William Griffin
Tarela Higson
Benjamin Jones
Matthew Mason
Pedro Vasconcelos Medeiros
Ryan Mitchell
Sam Morgan
Alexander Mortimer
Lochlann O'Suilleabhain
Daniel Rogers
Joseph Sant
Christopher Scillitoe
Alan Seall
Ralph Seller
Ryan Trimmer
Stavros Tsitsopoulos
Robert Turner
Adam Twigger
Gareth Verbiest
Simon Windebank

Project Management Group
Mike Gardner

Feride Basaran
Jaime de Paz
Shyamala Duraisingam
Abdelkader El-Chgar
Miriam Elwing
Rudy Espiritu
Bassem Fawwaz
Stephanie Gracies
Eleni Kalogeropoulou
Susanne Loeffler
Milena Marucci
Youwakim Nasr
Ebru Payne
Samantha So
Claudia Gentili Spinola
Yuka Uchijima
Lei Wang
Mei Xue

Specialist Modelling Group
Xavier de Kestelier
Irene Gallou

Giovanni Betti
Stefano Capra
Salmaan Craig
Miriam Dall'igna
Ivan Del Renzio
Golnaz Ighany
Erik Josefsson
Joshua Mason
Josef Musil
Daniel Piker
Dusanka Popovska
Jonathan Rabagliati
Robert Slater
Harsh Thapar
Arthur van der Harten

Sustainability Research
Stefan Behling
Rafe Bertram

Andy Haigh
Lukas Sosna

Urban Design
Bruno Moser

Maayan Ashkenazi
Dana Behrman
John Delfs

Visualisation
Gamma Basra

Emma Boal
Daniele Boldi Cotti
Jonathan Cox
Clark Denman
Hazel Eynon
Panos Ioannou
Nicolas Junco
Daniele Ludovisi
Alain Mehmet

Samuel Serridge
Laurent Shen
Stephen Teare
Ben Wakely

Workplace Consultancy
Arjun Kaicker

Harriet Abbott
Helena Croft
Martin Glover
Neil Gray
Emma Hutton
Natalie Latacz
Sarin Varadul
Lorenzo Vianello
Sarah Villar-Furniss
Nicholas Wong

Administration

Accounts
Chris Williams

Sharad Agarwal
Deanne Argue
Carlyn Aurelien
Iliya Bozhkov
Bernadette Greaney
Geoffrey Green
Sara Hunter
Gibert Leygonie
Ian Malcomson
Kamran Malik
Bobbie Michael
Nikki Nicolas
Brian Nolan
Nicky Patel
Sinem Sevket
Mital Dilip Shah
Sachen Shah
Joanna Smith
Kelly Smith
Diem Uong
Jeremy Wallis

Document Control
Dave Wicker

Ana Djenadija
Eleanor Dwyer
Garry Fairweather
Maria Farina
Jennifer Harvey
Christian Lawrence
Anakin Lee
Jeff Lewis
Hazel Quines
Stephen Rock
Agnes Szabo

Facilities
Tony Cooper

O'Neil Alexander
Boris Dehalu

Alan Foxwell
Richard Gayle
Brendan Hendy
Norman Johnson
Richard Klewer
Floyd Lee
Joseph Rosser
Billy Russell

General Counsel
Rhian Deakin

Hospitality
Alicia Cox

Lee Currier
Anne Hone
Nauris Vilcans

Human Resources

Iain Alembick
Gemma Barlow
Sarah Grant
Natalie Keymer
Rima Khanom
Alexandra Leptos
Vicki Tavener

Lord Foster's Office
Richard Dilworth
Aled Lewis

Postroom
Mark Hargrave
Richard Jenkins
Matthew Wilson

Printroom
Mike Bass
Tony Wenban

John Driver
Luke Nolan
Michael O'Donovan
Gary Ovenden
Jamie Sinton
Gerben van der Est

Reception
Anna Garreau

Samia Ablekimoglu
Janet Affran
Zandra Boyd
Amy Kerr
Shelly McGibbon
Laura Thomas
Wendy Verco
Kirby Watson

Secretarial
Kathryn Keen

Bethany Barnes
Georgia Barnes-Pilcher
Elisabet Barone
Bella Bin
Miranda Birkby
Katy Boehm
Heidi Brothers
Laura Carver
May Cheung
Ashley Collins
Emma Copeland
Polly Deng
Tessa Emslie
Nicole Garcia Saez
Rema Gargum
Maria Gea Velez
Helen Golding
Katherine Hernandez
Sophie Izon
Jane Lambert
Jasmine Lee

Fanny Ling
Hannah Manson
Katie Murphy
Erin Neil
Jessica Palandri
Shuyu Pan
Sophie Pell
Heather Penney
Teresa Pow
Rachel Prance
Tola Rebello
Kelly Ritchie
Silvia Romani
Victoria Sanz Luque
Saira Soarez
Aleksandra Stiglic
Tamar Suleiman
Sunny Wang
Rachel Wardlow
Hannah Wild
Catherine Wilson
Sabrina Wisely
Serena Zhu

Security
Steve Shaw

Lee Bethell
Geoff Cox
James Cunningham
Roger Da Costa
Antonio De Souza
Al Dionisio
Nigel Griffiths
Tim Hampton
Ross Hancock
Michael Jeffery
David Jones
Ahmed Oguntola
Mick Slavin
Luke Wynne-Sutton

Warehouse
Craig Edwards

Peter Porter
Stephen Street
Duarte Vaz

Project Credits

10 Gresham Street
London, England
1996-2003
Client
Standard Life Investments
Project Team
Cara Bamford
Grant Brooker
D'Arcy Fenton
Norman Foster
Jan-Carlos Kucharek
Yui San Law
Joon Paik
Giles Reid
Martin Rolfe
James Sandwith
Margaret Hoi Shan Lau
Ken Shuttleworth
James Thomas
Consultants
Structural Engineer: Waterman
Partnership
Quantity Surveyor: Davis
Langdon & Everest
Mechanical and Electrical
Engineer: Roger Preston
& Partners
Project Management: Buro
Four Project Services
Construction Manager: Bovis
Lend Lease
Principal Awards
2004 The Worshipful Company
of Chartered Architects New
City Architecture Award,
Commendation
2004 Civic Trust Award

33 Holborn
London, England
1993-2000
Client
Gemini Commercial Investments
Ltd
Tenant: J Sainsbury Plc
Project Team
Alice Asafu-Adjaye
Katharina Borsi
Angus Campbell
John Drew
Jason Flanagan
Norman Foster
Loretta Law
Sandra Loschke
Mateo Miyar Olaiz
Won Kyung Paik
Erik Ramelow
Christiana Schmidt
Ken Shuttleworth
Dan Sibert
John Silver
Paul Smith
Danni Tinero
Consultants
Structural Engineer: Yolles
Partnership Ltd
Mechanical and Electrical
Engineer: Hilson Moran
Partnership Ltd
Rights of Light Consultant:
Schatunowski Brooks
Cladding Consultant: Emmer
Pfenninger Partner AG
Fire Engineering: Fisec
Planning Supervisor: AYH
Partnership
Lighting Consultant: Claude
R Engle Lighting
Main Contractor: Bovis Lend
Lease

50 Finsbury Square
London, England
1997-2000
Client
Standard Life Investments
Project Team
Grant Brooker
D'Arcy Fenton
Norman Foster
John Jennings
Martin Riese
Martin Rolfe
Ken Shuttleworth
Joe Witchell
Consultants
Structural Engineer: Waterman
Partnership
Mechanical and Electrical
Services Engineer: Roger
Preston & Partners
Cost Consultant: Gardiner
& Theobald
Access Consultant: Lerch Bates
& Associates
Main Contractor: Schal
International Management Ltd

51 Lime Street
London, England
2001-2007
Client
The British Land Co plc;
Stanhope plc
Project Team
Jason Alderson
Sofia Arraiza
Matthew Austen
Thomas Austerveil
Jonathan Bell
Doretta Bevilacqua
Grant Brooker
Tara Brooks
Peter Buche
Hon Kong Chee
Svetlana Curcic
John Drew
Manuel Fernandez
Norman Foster
Robert Harrison

Tim Kemp
John Lacey
Randy Liekenjie
Marina Loeb
Anatoly Patrick
Damon Pearce
John Ross
Luis Santos
Anne-Marie Saul
Orsolya Say
Dan Sibert
Laura Stecich
Sanja Tiedemann
Tek Tsien Tan
Oliver Voss
Fenna Haakma Wagenaar
Martyn Weaver
Ian Whitby
Sam Wilson
Kevin Yiu
Consultants
Structural Engineer: Whitbybird
Quantity Surveyor: Davis
Langdon Mott Green Wall
Mechanical and Electrical
Engineer: Roger Preston
& Partners
Landscape Consultant: Charles
Funke Associates
Lighting Consultant: Equation
Lighting Design
Construction Manager: Mace Ltd
Principal Awards
2008 Council for Tall Buildings
and Urban Habitat, Best Tall
Building in Europe
2007 Worshipful Company of
Chartered Architects New City
Architecture Award

100 Wood Street
London, England
1997-2000
Client
Helical Bar plc
Project Team
Grant Brooker
John Drew
Norman Foster
Simon Peckham
Ken Shuttleworth
Hugh Stewart
Colin Ward
Ian Whitby
Consultants
Structural Engineer: Waterman
Partnership
Quantity Surveyor: Gleeds
Mechanical and Electrical
Services Engineer: Roger
Preston & Partners
Facade Consultant: Emmer
Pfenninger Partner AG
Facade Access and Maintenance
Consultant: Lerch Bates
& Associates
Main Contractor: HBG

Albion Riverside
London, England
1998-2003
Client
Hutchison Whampoa Property
Project Team
Ewan Anderson
Alice Asafu-Adjaye
Mark Atkinson
Timothy Bodinnar
Andy Bow
Mark Camillin
Simon Chadwick
Alan Chan
Chris Connell
Neil Crawford
Stephen Crawley
Gunnar Dittrich
Fabian Evers
Michel Foex
Nick Foster

Norman Foster
Ramses Frederickx
Juan Diaz-Llanos Garcia
Nathalie Gidron
Sophie Goldhill
Anthony Guma
Alice Hawthorn
Ken Hogg
Todd Hutton
Phyllis Fat Yin Lam
Stuart Latham
Andy Lister
Sarah Lister
Graham Longman
Peter McLaughlin
Joel Meersseman
Tony Miki
James Milne
Laura Morales
Kate Murphy
Pauline Murphy
Antoinette Nassopoulos
Max Neal
Douglas Newman
Justin Nicholls
Alex Peaker
Michael Pelken
Nadine Pieper Bosch
Catherine Ramsden
Sean Roche
Axel Rostock
Ken Shuttleworth
Michaela Smith
Azhar Sulaiman
Melinda Stamenkovic
Alasdair Travers
Tim Walpole-Walsh
Jin Watanabe
Chris White
Matthew White
Tracey Wiles
Nick Willson
Sam Wilson
Gordon Young
Consultants
Structural Engineer: Arup
Quantity Surveyor: Davis
Langdon

Project and Construction
Management: CM International
Logistics: Jolyon Drury
Landscape Architect: Townshend
Landscape Architects
Lighting Consultant: Speirs
+ Major
Management Contractor: Exterior
International plc
Principal Awards
2004 Concrete Society Award
Certificate of Excellence in
Building category
2005 National Home Builder
Design Awards, Best Apartment
Building
2006 Wandsworth Design Award
2006 Civic Trust Commendation

Asprey London
London, England
2001-2004
Client
Asprey & Garrard
Project Team
Norman Foster
Andries Kruger
Abel Maciel
Michael Ng
Graham Phillips
Giles Robinson
Filo Russo
Gloria Tsai
Ryan Von Ruben
Winky Wong
Raza Zahid
Consultants
Structural Engineer: Alan Baxter
& Associates
Mechanical and Electical
Engineer: Troup Bywaters
& Anders
Quantity Surveyor: Davis
Langdon & Everest
Interior Designer: David Mlinaric
Lighting Consultant: Kondos
Roberts
Principal Awards
2005 RIBA Award

Asprey New York
New York, USA
2002-2004
Client
Asprey & Garrard
Project Team
Matthew Abbott
Kevin Carrucan
Kathleen Feagin
Norman Foster
Marco Gamini
Guy Herschell
Michael Ng
Graham Phillips
Giles Robinson
Bernd Truempler
Gloria Tsi
Armstrong Yakubu
Consultants
Interior Furnishings: Mlinaric,
Henry and Zervudachi
Architect of Record: Leclere
Associates
Project Manager: Gardiner
& Theobald
Structural Engineer: Cantor
Seinuk Group
Mechanical and Electrical
Engineer: Thomas J Fiskaa
Engineering
Lighting Consultant: Kondos
Roberts

Beijing International Airport
Beijing, China
2003-2008
Client
Beijing Capital International
Airport Company Ltd
Joint Venture
NACO Foster Arup
Project Team
Mark Atkinson
John Ball
Cara Bamford
Alan Chan
Steven Chiu
Young Wei-Yang Chiu
Roberto Davolio
Rodrigo de Castro Pereira
Gunnar Dittrich
Wulf Duerrich
Andrea Etspueler
Tie Fan
Colin Foster
Norman Foster
Kristin Fox
Luke Fox
Marco Gamini
Michael Gentz
Richard Hawkins
Gabrielle Ho
Darryn Holder
Loretta Law
Da Chun Lin
Jun Luo
Mouzhan Majidi
David Nelson
Jonathan Parr
Sean Roche
Riko Sibbe
Danny Sze
Pearl Tang
Brian Timmoney
William Walshe
Joyce Wang
Irene Wong
Shyue-Jiun Woon
Zheng Yu
Jean Wenyan Zhu

Consultants
Airport Consultant: NACO
Structural and Mechanical
Engineer: Arup
Design Institute: BIAD
Landscape Architect: Michel
Desvigne
Lighting Consultant: Speirs
+ Major
Quantity Surveyor: Davis
Langdon
Baggage Handling Consultant:
BNP Associates Inc
APM and Airport Engineering
Consultant: Logplan GmbH
Fire Consultant: Arup Fire
Facade Maintenance Consultant:
Reef UK
Retail Consultant: Design
Solutions
Principal Awards
2007 Condé Nast Traveller
Award for Innovation and Design,
Winner Infrastructure category
2008 The Emirates Glass LEAF
Awards, Best Structural Design
of the Year
2009 Travel + Leisure Design
Award: Best Transportation
2009 Condé Nast Traveller
Readers' Travel Awards: Favourite
Airport
2009 RIBA International Award
2009 AJ100 Building of the Year

Bishops Square
London, England
2001-2005
Client
Corporation of London;
Hammerson plc; Spitalfields
Development Group
Project Team
Sofia Arraiza
Jonathan Bell
Holm Bethge
Doretta Bevilacqua
Grant Brooker
Peter Buche
John Drew
Norman Foster
Ash Goyal
Karsten Huneck
Richard Hyams
Tim Kemp
David Kong
Angelika Kovacic
Randy Liekenjie
Milena Marucci
Don Orike
Stuart Palmer
Nick Paterson
Anatoly Patrick
Damiano Rizzini
Ricky Sandhu
Owe Schoof
Heidrun Schuhmann
Paul Stanbridge
Tek Twien Tan
Catriona Tanner
Oliver Voss
Miriam White
Ian Whitby
Henk Wieringg
Sam Wilson

Consultants
Structural Engineer: Arup
Transport Consultant: Arup
Quantity Surveyor: Davis
Langdon
Cladding Consultant: Emmer
Pfenninger Partner AG
Specialist Lighting: Claude Engle
Mechanical and Electrical
Engineer: Hoare Lea
Planning Consultant: Montagu
Evans
Facade Access Consultant: Lerch
Bates & Associates
Landscape Consultant:
Townshend Landscape Architects
Fire Engineering: Hoare Lea
Access Consultant: Centre for
Accessible Environments
Principal Awards
2005 London Planning Awards,
Best Built Project contributing to
London's Future, Joint Winner
2006 Regeneration Awards,
Winner Best Commercial-led
Regeneration Project
2007 London Planning Awards,
Best New Public Space, Winner

Business Academy Bexley
Bexley, England
2001-2003
Sponsor
Sir David and Lady Garrard
Client
Garrard Educational Trust/
Tim Garnham
Project Team
Ian Bogle
Aike Behrens
Grant Brooker
Marlene Chausse
Sophie Coe
Spencer de Grey
Lulie Fisher
Norman Foster
Juan Frigerio
Christina Gresser
Henriette Hahnloser
Paul Kalkhoven
Josef Kaps
Steve Langman
Jorge Ortega Del Vecchio
Viktorie Smejkalova
Karsten Vollmer
Consultants
Quantity Surveyor: Davis
Langdon & Everest
Structural, Mechanical and
Electrical Engineer, Fire:
Buro Happold
Acoustics: Harris Grant
Associates
Access: Halcrow
Health and Safety: Osprey
Planning: Montagu Evans
Project Management: Second
London Wall
Main Contractor: Exterior
International plc
Principal Awards
2004 Civic Trust Commendation
2004 RIBA Award

Capital City Academy
London, England
2000-2003
Sponsor
Sir Frank Lowe
Client
The Capital City Academy Trust
(Sir Frank Lowe and DfES)
Project Team
Marco Acerbis
Simon Bowden
Spencer de Grey
Norman Foster
Paul Rogers
Phil Smith
Consultants
Quantity Surveyor: Davis
Langdon
Structural/Mechanical and
Electrical Engineer: Buro
Happold
Principal Awards
2004 Civic Trust Commendation

Central London Masterplan
London, England
1996-2002
Client
City of Westminster
Department for Culture, Media
and Sport
English Heritage
Government Office for London
The Houses of Parliament
London Transport
The Royal Parks Agency
Project Team
Andy Bow
Spencer de Grey
Norman Foster
Ike Ijeh
Max Neal
David Rosenberg
Filo Russo
Andrew Thomson
Consultants
Transport Planning: Halcrow Fox
Urban Space and Historic
Context: Civic Design Partnership
Movement and Spatial Analysis:
Space Syntax Laboratory
Cost Consultants: Davis Langdon
& Everest
Landscape Design: Peter Walker
& Partners
London School of Economics
Consultant: Richard Burdett

Chesa Futura
St Moritz, Switzerland
2000-2004
Client
SISA Immobilien AG (St Moritz)
Project Team (Foster + Partners)
Francis Aish
Stefan Behling
Kate Carter
Matteo Fantoni
Norman Foster
Jooryung Kim
Judit Kimpian
Tillman Lenz
Sven Ollmann
Cristiana Paoletti
Graham Phillips
Stefan Robanus
Carolin Schaal
Horacio Schmidt
Thomas Spranger
Anna Sutor
Michele Tarroni
Huw Whitehead
Project Team (Küchel Architects,
St Moritz)
Francesco Baldini
Vic Cajacob
Martin Hauri
Thomas Henz
Thomas Kaufmann
Richart Kevic
Arnd Küchel
Georg Spachtholz
Consultants
Structural Engineer: Edy Toscano
AG; Ivo Diethelm GmbH;
Arup
Mechanical and Electrical
Engineer: EN/ES/TE AG; R & B
Engineering GmbH
Quantity Surveyor: Davis
Langdon & Everest
Cladding Consultant: Emmer
Pfenninger Partner AG
Lighting: Reflexion AG
Principal Awards
2004 Holzbaupreis Graubünden,
Commendation

City Hall
London, England
1998-2002
Client
More London Development Ltd
Project Team
Sean Affleck
Alice Asafu-Adjaye
Louise Blackler
Andy Bow
Stefan Behling
Bruce Curtain
Frank Filskow
Elodie Fleury
Norman Foster
Sam Harvey
Ken Hogg
Richard Hyams
Tomer Kleinhause
David Kong
Attilio Lavezzari
Graham Longman
Niall Monaghan
Max Neal
Mario Pilla
Ken Shuttleworth
Consultants
Structural, Services and Acoustic
Engineer: Arup
Cost Consultant: Davis Langdon
& Everest
Planning Consultant: Montagu
Evans
Services Cost Consultant: Mott
Green & Wall
Construction Manager: Mace
Principal Awards
2003 Institution of Civil
Engineers London Association:
Merit Award

Dada Place Kitchen
2004
Client
Dada SpA
Project Team
Norman Foster
Todd Hutton
James Milne
John Small

Deutsche Bank Place
Sydney, Australia
1997-2005
Client
Investa Property Group
Prinicipal Tenant
Deutsche Bank Australia
Project Team
Arthur Branthwaite
Dirk Henning Braun
John Blythe
David Crosswaite
Daniela Dähn
Gerard Evenden
Alfredo de Flora
Glenis Fan
Norman Foster
Fleur Hutchings
Edmund Klimek
Thomas Lettner
Muir Livingstone
Fiona McLean
Alex Morris
Paul Morris
Carsten Mundle
David Nelson
Ross Palmer
Daniel Pittman
Sven Ollmann
Caroline Rabourdin
Eva Siebmanns
Nick Sissons
Carmel Thomas

Consultants
Collaborating Architect and
Landscape Architect: Hassell Pty
Ltd
Project Management and
Construction: Bovis Lend Lease
Structural Engineer: Lend Lease
Design; Arup
Quantity Surveyor: Rider Hunt
Australia
Mechanical and Electrical
Engineer: Norman Disney &
Young; Lincoln Scott; Roger
Preston & Partners
Fire Engineering: Stephen
Grubits & Associates Pty Ltd
Vertical Transportation: Norman
Disney & Young
Facade Consultant: Arup Pty Ltd
Principal Awards
2006 Australian Stone
Architecture Awards, Best
Commercial Interior
2006 ASI Steel Awards NSW
& ACT, Architectural Industrial &
Commercial Steel Design
category: High Commendation
2007 Property Council of
Australia/Rider Hunt Award,
Overall Winner
2007 Rider Hunt Award for
Office Developments

Djanogly City Academy
Nottingham, England
2002-2005
Sponsor
Sir Harry Djanogly
Client
Djanogly City Academy; Sir Harry
Djanogly & DfES
Project Team
Alex Barry
Simon Bowden
Spencer de Grey
Norman Foster
Robert Miles
Susanne Popp
Katherine Ridley
Consultants
Structural/Mechanical and
Electrical Engineer: Buro
Happold
Quantity Surveyor: Davis
Langdon
FF+E/ICT: Clarson Goff
Management
Main Contractor: Sol
Construction
Principal Awards
2005 The City of Nottingham
Lord Mayor's Award for Urban
Design, Commendation

Dresden Station
Dresden, Germany
1997-2006
Client
Deutsche Bahn AG Station
& Service
Project Team
Florian Boxberg
Spencer de Grey
Patricia Fairclough
Anja Flesh
Felix Forthmeyer
Norman Foster
Stanley Fuls
Christina Gresser
Christian Hallmann
Klaus Heldwein
Tom Mival
Yohko Mizushima
Virginie Mommens
Uwe Nienstedt
Sven Ollmann
John Prevc
Michael Richter
Axel Rostock
Diana Schaffranek
Marc Schwabedissen
Bernd Treide
Inge Tümmers
Consultants
Structural Engineer: Buro
Happold – Membrane Roof;
Schmitt Stumpf Frühauf &
Partner – Existing Building
Mechanical and Electrical
Engineer: Schmidt Reuter &
Partner – Membrane Roof; Zibell
Willner & Partner – Reception
Building
Cost Consultant: BAL GmbH;
Schmitt Stumpf Frühauf &
Partner
Project Management: AYH
Homola GmbH & Co KG –
Membrane Roof; Kaiser
Baucontrol – Reception Building
Historic Buildings Advisor: adb
Lighting Consultant: Speirs
+ Major

Principal Awards
2007 RIBA Stirling Prize Shortlist
2007 RIBA European Award
2007 BD International
Regeneration Award
2007 Structural Awards,
Heritage Award for Infrastructure
2007 Renault Traffic Future
Award
2008 Brunel Award
2008 Preis des Deutschen
Stahlbauer
2008 Deutsche Architekturpreis
2008 Chicago Athenaeum
International Architecture Award

**Electronic Arts European
Headquarters**
Chertsey, England
1997-2000
Client
Electronic Arts Europe Ltd; P&O
Developments/Connaught
Estates Ltd
Project Team
Catriona Borland
Chris Connell
Neil Crawford
Jon Fielding
Norman Foster
Katy Ghahremani
Tanya Griffiths
Darron Haylock
Sandra Loschke
Mateo Miyar Olaiz
Simon Peckham
Patricia Pires Neves
Ken Shuttleworth
John Silver
Catriona Tanner
Huw Turner
Cezanne Webber
Gavin Woodford
Andrew Yeoh

Consultants
Structural and Civil Engineer:
Whitbybird
Project Management: Rowney
Sharman; P&O Developments
Management Contractor: Exterior
International
Mechanical, Electrical, Acoustics
and IT Engineer: Oscar Faber
Quantity Surveyor: Wheelers
Specification Consultant:
Schumann Smith Ltd
Landscape Architect: Land Use
Consultants
Audio-Visual Consultant: Mark
Johnson Consultants
Fire Engineering: Jeremy
Gardner Associates
Electrical Services: T Clarke plc
Specialist Sound Studio:
Recording Architecture
Specialist Lighting: Claude Engle
Principal Awards
2000 RIBA Regional
Architecture Award
2000 The Times/Gestetner
Digital Office Collection Award,
Third Prize
2000 Runnymede Borough
Council Design Award,
Commercial Category
2000 Whitby Bird and Partners'
Structural Award
2001 Civic Trust Award
2002 Concours des Plus Beaux
Ouvrages de Construction
Metallique

Emeco 20-06 Chair
2006
Client
Emeco
Project Team
Norman Foster
Mike Holland
David Nelson
John Small
Dmitri Warner
Principal Awards
2007 Good Design Award
2008 Baden-Württemberg
International Design Award
'Focus Green', Gold Award

Foster 500/5 Series Sofas
2002-2005
Client
Walter Knoll
Project Team
Norman Foster
Todd Hutton
James Milne
Werner Sigg
John Small
Dmitri Warner
Principal Awards
2002 Red Dot Design Award
2004 Baden-Württemberg
International Design 'Focus in
Silber' Award
2004 Red Dot Design Award

Gerling Ring Karree
Cologne, Germany
1996-2001
Client
Baugemeinschaft Gerling Ring
GbR
Project Team
Daniela Daehn
Norman Foster
Reinhard Joecks
Paul Kalkhoven
Josef Kaps
David Nelson
Sven Ollmann
Consultants
Associate Architects: Buro
Polonyi & Partner
Structural Engineer: Dr Ing W
Naumann & Partner
Mechanical and Electrical
Engineer: Schmidt Reuter
Partner
Landscape Architect: Desvigne
& Dalnoky
Project Management: GKVM
Main Contractor: Höhler
+ Partner
Principal Awards
2003 Kölner Architekturpreis

Hearst Tower
New York, USA
2000-2006
Client
Hearst Corporation
Project Team (Building)
Bob Atwal
Nick Baker
John Ball
Una Barac
Gerard Evenden
Morgan Fleming
Norman Foster
Peter Han
Brandon Haw
Mike Jelliffe
Michaela Koster
Chris Lepine
Martina Meluzzi
David Nelson
Julius Streifeneder
Gonzalo Surroca
Michael Wurzel
Project Team (Fit-out)
Sandor Ambrus
Mandy Edge
Norman Foster
Peter Han
Brandon Haw
Mike Jelliffe
Nasrin Kalbasi
John Small
Ingrid Solken
Kathleen Streifender
Chris West
Michael Wurzel
Consultants
Associate Architect: shell and
core: Adamson Associates;
Fit-out: Gensler
Development Manager: Tishman
Speyer Properties
Structural Engineer: Cantor
Seinuk Group
Services/MEP: Flack + Kurtz
Vertical Transportation: VDA
Lighting: George Sexton (shell
and core); Kugler Associates
(fit-out)

Food Service: Ira Beer
Associates
Main Contractor: Turner
Construction
Principal Awards
2004 Wallpaper Design Awards
Winner Best Building Sites
2005 Global Green USA Green
Building Design Award
2006 Build New York Awards,
Winner New Project
2006 Emporis 'Best New
Skyscraper of the Year for
Design and Functionality'
2007 BCI International Award
2007 Business Week/
Architectural Record Citation for
Excellence for the Interiors
2007 RIBA International Award
2007 The Greater New York
Construction User Council
Outstanding Green Project
Award
2007 New York City MASterwork
Awards, Best New Building
2007 AIA New York Design
Honor Award in the Architecture
category
2008 International Highrise
Award, Winner
2008 XVI Concorde
Internationale Sistema d'Antore
Metra, Innovative Use of
Technology
2008 Chicago Athenaeum
International Architecture Award

Her Majesty's Treasury
London, England
1996-2002
Client
HM Treasury; Exchequer
Partnership; Stanhope plc; Bovis
Lend Lease; Chestertons
Project Team
Alexander Barry
Chris Bolland
Spencer de Grey
Christian Duerr
Philip Eichstadt
Suzanne Flau
Anja Flesch
Norman Foster
Julian Gilhespie
Andrew Henderson
Michael Naehrlich
Matthias Olt
Michael Pelken
Tim Quick
Kathy Ridley
Peter Ridley
George Stowell
Robin Tandavanitj
Huw Thomas
Jens Weiler
Zeya Winn
Consultants
Structural Engineer: Waterman
Partnership plc
Mechanical and Electrical
Engineer: JBB
Environmental Engineer: BDSP
Partnership
Space Planning: DEGW
Cost Consultant: Hanscomb
Partnership; Mott Green Wall
Acoustic Engineer: Hann Tucker
Landscape Consultant:
Gustafson Porter
Lighting Design: Speirs + Major
Historic Building Advisor: Fielden
+ Mawson
Artist: Per Arnoldi
Main Contractor: Bovis Lend
Lease

Principal Awards
    2003 British Construction
    Industry Awards Major Project
    Category, High Recommendation
    2003 British Council for Offices:
    National Refurbished Workplace
    Award
    2003 Public Private Finance
    Award, Best Design Project
    2003 British Council for Offices
    London Refurbished/Recycled
    Workplace Award
    2005 British Construction
    Industry Conservation Award
    2005 Urban Land Institute (ULI)
    Award for Excellence, Europe
    competition

Hyatt Tower
    Chicago, USA
    2000
Client
    Pritzker Realty Group/Higgins
    Development Partners
Project Team
    Lee Bennett
    Simon Blakemore
    Hayley Cross
    Norman Foster
    Brandon Haw
    Martin Lee
    Luis Moneo
    David Nelson
    Gerard Outram
    Phil Smith
    Robert Starsmore
    Julius Streifeneder
    Damian Timlin
    Armstrong Yakubu
Consultants
    Structural Consultant: Halvorson
    & Kaye
    Cost Consultant: Davis Langdon
    & Everest
    M&E Consultant: Environment
    Systems Designs

La Voile
    St Jean Cap Ferrat, France
    1999-2002
Client
    Confidential
Project Team
    William Castagna
    Jan Coghlan
    Michel Foex
    Norman Foster
    Tanya Griffiths
    James Johnson
    Pedro Garcia Martinez
    James Milne
    Robert Mirams
    Andrew Thomson
    Juan Vieira-Pardo
    Paul Wang
    Tracey Wiles
Consultants
    Structural Engineer: Arup
    Lighting Consultant: George
    Sexton

Leslie L Dan Pharmacy Building
    Toronto, Canada
    2002-2006
Client
    University of Toronto
Project Team
    James Barnes
    Stephen Best
    Nigel Dancey
    Lena Janine Feindt
    Norman Foster
    Joost Heremans
    Luis Matania
    David Nelson
    Alexandra Quantrill
    Danny Shaw
    Gabriel Tang
    Pietje Witt
Consultants
    Local Architect: Moffat Kinoshita
    Architects/Cannon Design
    Quantity Surveyor: Vermeulens
    Cost Consultants
    Structural Engineer: Halcrow
    Yolles
    Mechanical and Electrical
    Engineer: HH Angus
    & Associates Ltd
    Laboratory Consultant: Levine
    Lauzon Architects
    Landscape Architect: Diana
    Gerrard Associates
    Lighting Consultant: Claude R
    Engle Lighting
    Main Contractor: PCL
Principal Awards
    2006 Ontario Steel Design
    Award, Engineering category

Lighting Systems
iGuzzini Radial System
    2006
Client
    iGuzzini SpA
Project Team
    Norman Foster
    David Nelson
    Mike Holland
    Todd Hutton
    James Milne
    Werner Sigg
    John Small
Principal Awards
    2000 Industrie Forum Design
    Award
    2007 iF Product Design Award

Illium Light
    2006
Client
    Nemo SpA
Project Team
    Norman Foster
    Mike Holland
    Werner Sigg
    David Nelson
    John Small
    Dmitri Warner

OTO Spotlight System
    2001
Client
    Artemide SpA
Project Team
    Norman Foster
    Mike Holland
    James Johnson
    John Small

Three-Sixty Table Lamp
2005
Client
  FontanaArte SpA
Project Team
  Norman Foster
  Mike Holland
  David Nelson
  John Small
  Dmitri Warner

London Academy
Edgware, England
2002-2006
Client
  DfES and Barnet City Academy
Project Team
  Eleanor Baxter
  Stefan Behling
  Eike Danz
  Spencer de Grey
  Gilles Delage
  Jon Fielding
  Norman Foster
  Darron Haylock
  Paul Kalkhoven
  Peter Matcham
  Max Neal
  Joris Pauwels
  James Sandwith
  Anja Tassotto
  Alex Thomson
  Peter Tso
  Andrea Wu
Consultants
  Structural Engineer: Buro
  Happold
  Cost Consultant: Davis Langdon
  Mechanical and Electrical
  Engineer: Buro Happold

London City Racecourse
London, England
2000
Client
  Wiggins Group plc
Project Team
  Francis Aish
  Johan Belmans
  Anna Bergbom
  Xavier De Kestelier
  Norman Foster
  Tamara Hall
  Judit Kimpian
  Jacob Norlov
  Robin Partington
  Jason Parker
  Ken Shuttleworth
  Michiel Verhaverbeke
  Hugh Whitehead
Consultants
  Structural Engineer: Adams Kara
  Taylor
  Quantity Surveyor: Cyril Sweett
  Landscape Consultant: The
  Landscape Partnership
  Environmental Consultant:
  WSP Environmental
  Racing Consultant: Tom Clarke
  Ecology Consultant: Ecological
  Services Ltd
  Planning Consultant: Weatherall
  Green & Smith
  Acoustic Engineering: Acoustic
  Air Ltd
  Lighting Design: WSP
  Environmental
  Fire Engineering: Arup Fire

McLaren Production Centre
Woking, England
2009–2011
Client
  McLaren Group
Project Team
  Nigel Dancey
  Norman Foster
  Dominik Hauser
  Chris Johnstone
  Iwan Jones
  Kathleen Laskin
  Nina Linde
  David Nelson
  Nicholas Papas
Consultants
  Structural and Civil; Geothermic;
  Fire; Acoustics; and CDM
  Consultant: Buro Happold
  Services and Environmental
  Consultant: PHA Consult
  Landscape Architect and
  Planning Consultant: Terence
  O'Rourke
  Quantity Surveyor: Gardiner
  & Theobald
  Contractor: Kier Build Ltd
Principal Awards
  2012 MIPIM Awards, Best
  Industrial and Logistics
  Development
  2012 RIBA Award
  2012 Structural Steel Design
  Award: Commendation
  2012 LABC Award: Best Large
  Commercial Building

McLaren Technology Centre
Woking, England
1998-2004
Client
  McLaren Group
Project Team
  Mark Atkinson
  John Ball
  Jim Barnes
  Stefan Behling
  Stephen Best
  Adrian Boot
  Alastair Bowden
  Nigel Dancey
  Ulrich Dangel
  Rebecca Davis
  Alexander Dusterloh
  Lena Janine Feindt
  Sophie Filhol
  Norman Foster
  Carl Francis
  Ravinder Gill
  Russell Hales
  Lee Hallman
  Egon Hansen
  Fleur Hutchings
  Iwan Jones
  Malte Just
  Gunter Kohnlein
  Andreas Krause
  Nicholas Ling
  James Marks
  David Nelson
  Darren Purvis
  Alexandra Quantrill
  Alexander Schmid
  Danny Shaw
  Nick Sissons
  Neil Sterling
  David Summerfield
  Gaku Takahashi
  Gabriel Tang
  Steve Trstenjak
  Susanne Tutsch
  Jonas Upton-Hanson
  Tess Warburton
  Chris West
  Simon Whiting
  Pietje Witt

Consultants
    Structural Engineer and Acoustic
    Consultant: Arup
    Services Engineer: Schmidt Reuter
    Quantity Surveyor: Davis
    Langdon
    Project Management: Arlington
    Securities
    Planning and Landscape:
    Terence O'Rourke
    Highways, Infrastructure and
    Environmental Engineering: WSP
    Planning Supervisor: Intec
    Management
    Lighting Consultant: Claude R
    Engle Lighting
    Lake Consultant: Atelier Dreiseitl
    Services Engineer for CAT3:
    Amec
    Contractor: Kier Build Ltd
Principal Awards
    2005 Festival Automobile
    International Architecture Prize
    2005 British Association of
    Landscape Industries (BALI),
    National Landscape Grand
    Award
    2005 RIBA Stirling Prize,
    Channel 4 'People's Choice'
    Award
    2005 RIBA Award
    2005 The Royal Fine Art
    Commission Trust/ BSkyB
    Building of the Year Award
    2005 RTPI Planning Awards,
    Award for Planning for Business
    2006 Structural Steel Design
    Award

Molteni Sofa and Bed
    2006
Client
    Molteni SpA
Project Team
    Norman Foster
    Mike Holland
    David Nelson
    John Small

Moor House
    London, England
    1997-2005
Client
    Moor House Limited Partnership;
    Hammerson plc; Henderson
    Global Investors
Project Team
    Grant Brooker
    Sebastian Busse
    Filippo Cefis
    Tim Coleridge
    Andrew Drummond
    Norman Foster
    Trevore Grams
    Rainer Grelle
    Christopher Hammerschmidt
    Pablo Heredia
    Wolfgang Hochmuth
    Conrad James
    John Jennings
    Paul Leadbeatter
    Martin Lee
    Luis Matania
    Michael Nahrlich
    Gerard Outram
    Anna Pla
    Neil Pusey
    Martin Riese
    Martin Rolfe
    Anne Schneider
    Martina Barth Sedelmayer
    Ken Shuttleworth
    Hugh Stewart
    Caroline Tarling
    Joe Witchell

Consultants
    Structural Engineer: Arup
    Mechanical and Electrical
    Engineer: Arup
    Cost Consultant: Davis Langdon;
    Mott Green Wall
    Landscape Consultant: Charles
    Funke Associates
    Lighting Consultant: Claude
    Engle; Sector Light Design
    Facade Consultant: Arup
    Fire Engineering: Arup Fire
    Building Consultant: CBRE
    Property/Commercial Consultant:
    Jones Lang LaSalle
    Facade Access: Lerch Bates
    & Associates
    Archaeology: Mills Whipp
    Partnership
    Planning Consultant: Montagu
    Evans
    Space Analysis: Space Syntax
    Specialist Engineers: Bureau
    Veritas
Principal Awards
    2005 Deep Foundation Institute,
    Outstanding Project Award

More London – Masterplan
    London, England
    1998-2003
Client
    More London Development Ltd
Project Team
    Alice Asafu-Adjaye
    Glenis Fan
    Frank Filskow
    Norman Foster
    Stuart Fraser
    Sofia Karim
    Max Neal
    Ken Shuttleworth
    Matthew White

Consultants
    Planning Consultant: Montagu
    Evans
    Structural Engineer: Arup
    Cost Consultant: Davis Langdon
    & Everest
    Building Configuration and
    Space Planning: DEGW
    Landscape Architect: Townshend
    Landscape Architects
    Public Space Analysis: Space
    Syntax Ltd
    Townscape Impact Assessment:
    Feilden + Mawson
    Daylight and Sunlight Consultant:
    Gordon Ingram Associates
    Lighting Consultant: Equation
    Lighting
    Local History: Stephen
    Humphrey
    Public Consultation: URBED;
    Arup Economics; SRU (Strategic
    Regeneration Unit)
    Construction Manager: Mace Ltd

More London – Construction
    London, England
    2000-2010
Client
    More London Development Ltd
Project Team
    Sean Affleck
    Paul Allen
    Mark Atkinson
    Grant Brooker
    Gilles Delage
    Brian Ditchburn
    Denis Dixon
    Fabian Evers
    Tommaso Fantoni
    Norman Foster
    Ravinder Gill
    Jan Horst
    Richard Hyams
    David Kong
    Louis Lafargue
    Stuart Latham
    John Man
    Niall Monaghan

Max Neal
Marcin Panpuch
Jason Parker
Mario Pilna
Patricia Pires Neves
Tom Politowicz
Gary Rawlings
Harald Schönbrodt
Ken Shuttleworth
Daniel Smith
Robert Smith
Spiros Soulis
Sonia Villaseca
Matthew White
Consultants
Structural and Transport
Engineer: Arup
Cost Consultant and Contract
Administrator: EC Harris
Services Consultant: Mott Green
& Wall
Services and Lift Engineering:
Roger Preston & Partners
Planning Consultant: Montagu
Evans
Acoustic Consultant: Sandy
Brown Associates Ltd
Facade Access: Lerch Bates
Associates Ltd
Lighting Consultant: Claude R
Engle Lighting/Equation Lighting
Design Ltd
Landscape Architect: Townshend
Landscape Architects
Cladding Consultant: Sandberg
Fire Engineering: Roger Preston
Fire
Principal Awards
2004 British Council for Offices,
London Commercial Workplace
Award (Plot 1)
2004 Structural Steel Design
Award (Plot 1)
2005 LDSA Built in Quality
Awards, Winner Large
Commercial category (Plot 1)
2008 BCO Award, Best Fit-out
of Workplace, National and
London Winner (Plot 3)

The Murezzan
St Moritz, Switzerland
2003-2007
Client
AG Post und Merkatorium
Project Team
Matteo Fantoni
Tommaso Fantoni
Marco Ferri
Norman Foster
Kristin Fox
Roland Grube
Edmund Klimek
Tillmann Lenz
David Nelson
Carolin Schaal
Dorothea Schulz
Kirsten Scott
Cristina Segni
David Summerfield
Karsten Vollmer
Tavis Wright
Armstrong Yakubu
Consultants
Structural Engineer: Holzbau
Amann
Mechanical and Electrical
Engineer: Edwin Keller AG

National Police Memorial
London, England
1996-2005
Client
National Police Memorial Trust;
Michael Winner
Project Team
Jan Coghlan
Spencer de Grey
Norman Foster
Peter Ridley
Andrew Thomson
Consultants
Structural Engineer: Waterman
Partnership
Cost Consultant: Davis Langdon
Mechanical and Electrical
Engineer: Waterman Gore
Landscape Architect: Charles
Funke
Lighting Design: Speirs + Major
Facade Consultant: Arup
Facades
Project Manager: Bovis
Lend Lease
Water Feature: OCMIS
Artist/Graphic Designer:
Per Arnoldi
Main Contractor: Bovis
Lend Lease
Principal Awards
2006 RIBA Award

**Newbury Racecourse
Grandstand**
Newbury, England
1999-2000
Client
Newbury Racecourse plc
Project Team
Norman Foster
Michele McSharry
Ken Shuttleworth
Dominic Skinner
Viktorie Smejkalova
Matthew White
Consultants
Structural Engineer: Whitby
Bird & Partners
Services Consultant: Roger
Preston & Partners
Planning Consultant: Montagu
Evans Chartered Surveyors
Quantity Surveyors: Davis
Langdon & Everest
Construction Manager: Heery
International Ltd
Principal Awards
2002 Structural Steel Design
Awards, Commendation

New York Times Headquarters
New York, USA
2000
Client
The New York Times
Project Team
Lee Bennett
Hayley Cross
Norman Foster
Jan Güell
Brandon Haw
David Inwood
Martin Lee
Ken Shuttleworth
Phil Smith
Dara Towhidi
Armstrong Yakubu

Consultants
  Structural Consultant: Cantor
  Seinuk Group Inc
  Cost Consultant: Davis Langdon
  & Everest
  Landscape Consultant:
  Gustafson Partners Limited
  Lighting Consultant: Fisher
  Marantz Stone

One London Wall
  London, England
  1992-2003
Client
  London Wall Development
  Partnership Ltd; Kajima;
  Hammerson UK Properties plc
Project Team
  Grant Brooker
  Graham Collingridge
  John Drew
  Norman Foster
  Jurgen Kuppers
  Loretta Law
  Jonathon Scull
  Ken Shuttleworth
  Dan Sibert
  Colm Tamney
Consultants
  Structural Engineer: Waterman
  Partnership
  Cost Consultant and Employer's
  Agent: Davis Langdon & Everest
  Services Engineer: Hilson Moran
  Partnership Ltd
  Rights to Light/Party Wall:
  Schatunowski Brooks
  Planning Consultant: Montagu
  Evans
  Facade Access: Lerch Bates
  Cladding Consultant: EPP
  Lighting: Claude R Engle
Principal Awards
  2006 LDSA Built-in Quality
  Awards, Best Large Commercial
  Project

**Petronas University of
Technology**
  Bandar Seri Iskandar, Malaysia
  1998-2004
Client
  Universiti Teknologi Petronas
Project Team
  Jake Atcheson
  Toby Blunt
  Marc Buchmann
  Alan Chan
  Tina Che
  Ben Dobbin
  Brynley Dyer
  Norman Foster
  Michael Greville
  Jan Güell
  Fleur Hutchings
  Hannah Lehmann
  David Nelson
  Tony Miki
  Andy Miller
  Jonathan Parr
  Tom Politowicz
  Clive Powell
  Richard Scott-Wilson
  Michael Sehmsdorf
  Danny Shaw
  Jonathan Shaw
  Marilu Sicoli
  Robin Snowden
  Daniel Statham
  Peter Stuck
  Brian Timmoney
  Michael Wurzel
  Edson Yabiku

Consultants
  Collaborating Architect: GDP
  Architects
  Structural Engineer: Ranhill
  Bersekutu Sdn Bhd (Academic
  Buildings); Wimsa HSS
  Integrated (Resource Centre);
  Majid & Associates
  Mechanical and Electrical
  Engineer: Roger Preston &
  Partners (Concept); Majutek
  Perunding
  Laboratory Consultant: Research
  Facilities Design
  Acoustics: Sandy Brown
  Associates; Marshall Day
  Acoustics
  Signage: BDG McColl
  Quantity Surveyor: Jurukur
  Bahan Malaysia/KPK
  Project Manager: KLCC Projeks
  Sdn Bhd
  Landscape Architect: Shah PK
  & Associates
  Lighting: Vision Design Studio
  (Academic Buildings); Lightsource
  International (Asia) Ltd (Resource
  Centre)
Principal Awards
  2006 PAM Award for Best Public
  and Civic Building
  2007 Aga Khan Award for
  Architecture

Regent Place
  Sydney, Australia
  2003-2007
Client
  Greencliff (CPL) Developments
  Pty Ltd
Project Team
  John Blythe
  Fleta Burberry
  Martin Castle
  David Crosswaite
  Gerard Evenden
  Glenis Fan
  Norman Foster
  Giulia Galiberti
  Martina Meluzzi
  Laura Morales
  Antoinette Nassopoulos
  David Nelson
  Ross Palmer
  Dan Pittman
  Neville Smith
  Barbara Spano
  Karsten Vollmer
Consultants
  Collaborating Architect, Sydney:
  PTW Architects
  Quantity Surveyor: Rider Hunt
  Structural Engineer: Taylor
  Thompson Whitting; Robert Bird
  Group
  MEP/Lifts/Facade Engineer:
  Connell Mott MacDonald
  Fire/Hydraulics: Warren Smith
  & Partners

Riverside One
London, England
1998-1999
Client
 Confidential
Project Team
 Kevin Carrucan
 Brynley Dyer
 Norman Foster
 Mike Gardner
 David Keech
 Robert Mirams
 Graham Phillips
 Tim Quick
 Juan Vieira-Pardo
 Tomas Zenker
Consultants
 Main Contractor: Sisk
 Structural Engineer: Arup
 Quantity Surveyor: Davis
 Langdon
 Mechanical and Electrical
 Engineer: Roger Preston &
 Partners
 Lighting Consultant: Claude
 R Engle
 Landscape Architect: Michel
 Desvigne

RF1 Stacking Chair
2006
Client
 R Randers
Project Team
 Norman Foster
 Mike Holland
 James Milne
 Werner Sigg
 John Small
 Dmitri Warner

Smithsonian Institution Courtyard
Washington DC, USA
2004-2007
Client
 Smithsonian Institution
Project Team
 Doretta Bevilacqua
 Grant Brooker
 Graham Collingridge
 Spencer de Grey
 John Drew
 Norman Foster
 Jurgen Kuppers
 Nils Muenker
 Brady Peters
 Jonathan Scull
 Dan Sibert
 Alexander Thonicke
 Hiroko Uchino
Consultants
 Associate Architect/Architect
 of Record: Smith Group
 Landscape Architect: Gustafson
 Guthrie Nichol
 Structural Engineer: Buro
 Happold
 MEP Engineer: URS Corporation
 Lighting Designer: George
 Sexton Associates
 Acoustic Consultant: Sandy
 Brown Associates
 Cost Consultant: Davis Langdon
 Cladding Consultant: Emmer
 Pfenninger Partner
 Environmental Engineer: Battle
 McCarthy
 Stone Consultant: Sandberg
 General Contractor: Hensel
 Phelps
 Roof Contractor (Steel and
 Cladding): Josef Gartner USA
Principal Awards
 2008 Washington Building
 Congress Craftsmanship Award
 2008 World Architecture Festival,
 Winner Best 'New & Old'
 2008 Chicago Athenaeum
 International Architecture Award

Supreme Court
Singapore
2000-2005
Client
 The Supreme Court Singapore
Project Team
 Isabel Arellano
 Alfredo De Flora
 Gerard Evenden
 Norman Foster
 Mike Holland
 Thomas Lettner
 Robert McFarlane
 Andy Miller
 James Milne
 David Murphy
 David Nelson
 Marcin Panpuch
 Emily Phang
 Richard Scott-Wilson
 Marilu Sicoli
 Werner Sigg
 John Small
 Michaela Smith
 Sylvia Soh
 Peter Stück
 Alicia Tan
 Dmitri Warner
 Jin Watanabe
 Edson Yabiku
Consultants
 Local Collaborating Architect,
 Engineer, Quantity Surveyor and
 Project Manager: CPG
 Consultants PTE Ltd
 Interior Consultant: TID
 Associates PTE Ltd
 Landscape Consultant: Tierra
 Design
 Lighting Consultant: Lighting
 Planners Associates Inc
 Acoustics, AV and IT Consultant:
 CCW Associates PTE Ltd
 Fire Engineering: Colt
 International Ltd
 Facade Consultant: Arup Facade
 Engineering

Tower Place
London, England
1992-2002
Client
 Tishman Speyer Properties (UK)
 Ltd
Tenant
 Marsh & McLennan Companies
Project Team
 Stefan Behling
 Sundeep Bhamra
 Louise Blacker
 Ian Blaney
 Arthur Branthwaite
 Chris Bubb
 Penny Collins
 Neil Crawford
 Rebecca Davis
 Simon Davis
 John Drew
 Hester Edlmann
 Ken Faulkner
 Patrick Finney
 Jason Flanagan
 Norman Foster
 Luke Fox
 Ravinder Gill
 Rupert Goddard
 James Goodfellow
 Christina Gresser
 Ulrike Hammerschmidt
 Ken Hutt
 Richard Hyams
 Sofia Karim
 Lester Korzilius
 Martin Lee
 Sandra Loschke
 Benedict Marshall
 Tarek Merlin
 Mike Morgan
 Chris Mury
 Mateo Miyar Olaiz
 Won Kyung Paik
 Simon Peckham
 Tom Politowicz
 Stefan Redle
 Simon Reed
 Kristian Roberts
 Ken Shuttleworth

John Silver
Paul Simovic
Paul Smith
Catriona Tanner
Dara Towhidi
Suzanne Tutsch
Cezanne Webber
Erica West
Gavin Woodford
Miguel Woodhead
Gabriel Woods
Consultants
Structural and Services Engineer: Arup
Cost Consultant: EC Harris
Facade Engineering: Arup
Glass Needles Concept: James Carpenter Design Associates
Specialist Lighting: Claude R Engle
Landscape Architect: Townshend Landscape Architects
Archaeological Consultant: AOC Archaeology Group
All Hallows Church Architect: Caroe & Partners
Art: Anderson O'Day
Water Feature: The Fountain Workshop Ltd
Stone: Sandberg Consulting Engineers
Facade Access: Reef UK Ltd
Graphics: Pentagram Design
Specialist Signage: Richard Conn Associates
Construction Manager: Mace Ltd
Principal Awards
2003 Construct Award for Innovation and Best Practice
2004 Civic Trust Commendation

Trafalgar Square
World Squares for All Masterplan – Phases 1 and 1a
London, England
1999-2003
Client
Transport for London Street Management
Managers on behalf of the Crown
The Greater London Authority
Steering Group
Westminster City Council
The Department for Culture, Media and Sport
The Parliamentary Works Directorate
English Heritage
The Royal Parks Agency
London Transport Buses
Project Team
Spencer de Grey
Morgan Fleming
Norman Foster
Mike Holland
John Jennings
David Rosenberg
Abdou Sene
Consultants
Lead Consultant and Design Team Coordinator: Atkins Design Environment & Engineering
Transport Planning and Highways Engineering: Atkins Highways and Transportation
Conservation Architect: Feilden & Mawson
Lighting Consultant: Speirs + Major
Communication Design: GMJ Data Presentation
Project Manager: TPS Schal
Quantity Surveyor: Davis Langdon & Everest
Artist/Colour Consultant: Per Arnoldi
Access Consultant: JMU Access Partnership
Main Contractor: Fitzpatrick

Principal Awards
2003 Europa Nostra Award, Cultural Landscape Category, Diploma
2004 Civic Trust Special Award, Hard Landscaping
2004 RIBA Award
2004 RIBA London/English Heritage Award for a Building in a Historic Context
2005 RTPI Planning Awards, Commendation for Planning for City and Metropolitan Areas

The Walbrook
London, England
2005-2010
Client
Minerva plc
Project Team
Boguslaw Barnas
Peter Brittain
Grant Brooker
Norman Foster
Michaela Fuchs
Rafaelle Gavassa
Mathias Koester
Michael Krueger
Paul Leadbeatter
Misza Ozdowski
Merino Ranallo
Martin Rolfe
Laura Stecich
Caroline Tarling
Oliver Voss
Consultants
Structural Consultant: Arup
Quantity Surveyor: Davis Langdon LLP
Planning Supervisor: DP9
Project Manager: GVA Second London Wall
Engineer: PCM Safety
Building Services: Roger Preston & Partners

Wembley Stadium
London, England
1996-2007
Client
Wembley National Stadium Ltd
Architects
World Stadium Team (Foster + Partners and HOK Sport)
Project Team (Foster + Partners)
Zak Ayash
Nathan Barr
Angus Campbell
Norman Foster
Juan Frigerio
David Goss
Trevore Grams
Richard Hawkins
Edward Highton
Phyllis Fat Yin Lam
Alistair Lenczner
Richard Locke
Mouzhan Majidi
Tony Miki
Carlo Negri
Eyal Nir
Erik Ramelow
Jonathan Scull
Chee Huang Seah
Ken Shuttleworth
James Speed
Pearl Tang
Huw Thomas
James Thomas
Wing Sai Tsui
Colin Ward
Vincent Westbrook
Andrew Wood
Dion Young
Project Team (HOK Sport)
Megan Ashfield
Richard Breslin
Warrick Chalmers
Dale Jennings
David Manica
Alastair Pope
Rod Sheard
Ben Vickery

Consultants
  Structural and Civil Engineer:
  Mott Stadium Consortium
  Mechanical and Electrical
  Engineer: Mott Stadium
  Consortium
  Cost Consultant: Franklin
  + Andrews
  Specialist Lighting: Claude
  R Engle
  Disabled Access Consultant:
  Sinclair Knight Merz (Europe) Ltd
  Transport and Crowd Movement:
  Steer Davies Gleave
  Pitch Consultant: Sports Turf
  Research Institute
  Planning Consultant: Nathaniel
  Lichfield and Partners
  Planning Supervisor: Arup
  Catering Consultant: Mike
  Driscoll Associates
  Signage: Identica
  Main Contractor: Multiplex
Principal Awards
  2007 Vodafone Live Music
  Awards, Best Live Music Venue
  2008 LABC National Built-in
  Quality Awards, Best Commercial
  Project and Overall Winner
  2008 World Architecture Festival,
  High Commendation, Sport
  2008 RIBA National Award
  2008 RIBA Award

West London Academy
  London, England
  2002-2006
Sponsor
  Alec Reed
Client
  DfES and West London
  Academy Trust
Project Team
  Geoffrey Bee
  Robin Blanchard
  Simon Bowden
  Sebastian Busse
  Spencer de Grey
  Anne Fehrenbach
  Norman Foster
  Paul Kalkhoven
  Olga Michalopoulou
  Daniel Pittman
  John Prevc
  Gareth Pywell
  Gordon Seiles
  Julius Streifeneder
  Anja Tassotto
Consultants
  Structural Engineer: Buro
  Happold
  Quantity Surveyor: Davis
  Langdon
  Mechanical and Electrical
  Engineer: Buro Happold
  Main Contractor: Taylor Woodrow
  Construction Ltd
Principal Awards
  2008 Civic Trust Award,
  Commendation

World Trade Center
  New York, USA
  2002-2003
Client
  Lower Manhattan Development
  Corporation
Project Team
  Stefan Abidin
  Sean Affleck
  Mark Atkinson
  Gamma Basra
  Stefan Behling
  Yoon Choi
  Alan Chung
  Matt Clarke
  Bryan Corry
  Marcos de Andres
  Spencer de Grey
  Xavier de Kestelier
  John Dixon
  Jeremy Kim
  Richard Kulczak
  Norman Foster
  Ramses Frederickx
  Brandon Haw
  Judit Kimpian
  Anthony Lester
  David Nelson
  Graham Phillips
  David Picazo
  Tom Politowicz
  Joe Preston
  Agustina Rivi
  Narinder Sagoo
  Paul Scott
  Pearl Tang
  Diane Teague
  James Thomas
  Alex Thomson
  Damian Timlin
  Ken Shuttleworth
  Robert Starsmore
  Neil Vandersteen
  Gareth Verbiel
  Carsten Vollmer
  John Walden
  William Walshe

  Hugh Whitehead
  Chris Windsor
  Richard Wotton
Consultants
  Sculptor: Anish Kapoor
  Structural Engineer: Cantor
  Seinuk; Ysrael Seinuk
  Environmental Engineer: Roger
  Preston & Partners
  Vertical Transportation: Lerch
  Bates Associates Ltd
  Cost Planning: Davis Langdon
  & Everest
  Pedestrian Movement Analysis:
  Space Syntax

Project Bibliography

10 Gresham Street
Architects' Journal,
   10 September 2000, 'Foster
   march on City goes on'
   by David Taylor

33 Holborn
Architects' Journal (supplement
   Concrete Quarterly),
   4 September 2003, 'Filigree writ
   large in the urban web'
   by Sutherland Lyall
Building, 15 October 1999, 'Low
   Cunning' by Andy Pearson

50 Finsbury Square
Architects' Journal, 20 February
   2003, 'Working party – BCO
   award winners' by Barrie Evans
FX, September 2002, 'Lift off'
   by Sarah Brownlee

51 Lime Street
Building, 27 April 2007, 'Dancing
   with disaster' by Thomas Lane
Building Design, 12 July 2008,
   'Ahead of the curve' by
   Elaine Knutt

100 Wood Street
Building Design, 15 October 1999,
   'Lining up on the grid' by
   Peter Wislocki
The Observer, 18 February 2002,
   'This is primordial London calling,
   where no building lasts forever'
   by Deyan Sudjic

Albion Riverside
A&U, special issue: Housing
   Currents, June 2006,
   'Albion Riverside'
Architectural Design, November/
   December 2005, 'Home run'
   by Stephen Archer
Architecture and Urbanism,
   June 2006, 'Albion Riverside'

Baumeister, July 2004, 'Riverside
   Albion von Foster and Partners
   in London – dreidimensional
   gekrummte metall-
   dachkonstuktion' by Peter Gahr
Building, 18 October 2002, 'Foster's
   cover up' by Thomas Lane
Building, 27 February 2004,
   'As good as it's got' by
   Martin Spring
Building Design, 16 April 2004,
   'A building the Thames needs?'
   by Jeremy Till
Contract Journal, 6 November 2002,
   'Curves in all the right places'
   by David Bennett
Financial Times, 29-30 September
   2001, 'Down by the Riverside'
   by Anne Spackman
GA Document, June 2004,
   'Albion Riverside Development'

Asprey London
Building Design, 21 May 2004,
   'Shopping in style'
Casa Brutus, October 2004,
   'Asprey' by Megumi Yamashita
Esquire, June 2004,
   'Back in business'
Interior + Design (Russia), October
   2005, 'Asprey'
International Herald Tribune, 25 May
   2004, 'Asprey reopens with a
   splash on New Bond Street'
   by Suzy Menkes

Asprey New York
Architectural Digest, May 2004,
   'Asprey's American face' by
   Therese Bissell
Monument, August/September
   2004, 'Manhattan manor'
   by Zoe Ryan

Beijing International Airport
Architectural Record, July 2008,
   'Beijing Capital International
   Airport' by Jen Lin-Liu
Architectural Review, special issue:
   'Beijing Airport', August 2008,
Architecture and Design (China),
   June 2008, 'Poetry of flight:
   'Beijing Capital International
   Airport' by Jiang Yingying
Archithese, July/August 2008,
   'Bigger dragon' by Hubertus
   Adam
Arquitectura Viva, special issue:
   Pekin Olimpico, no 118/119,
   2008, 'Beijing International
   Airport'
Building, 7 April 2006, 'Forget T5,
   here's T-Rex' by Martin Spring
Building Design, 23 November 2007,
   'Racing towards tomorrow' by
   Ellis Woodman
Civil Engineering, October 2008,
   'Aerial gateway' by Robert L Reid
Detail, July 2008, 'Airport terminal
   in Beijing' by Holger Falter
Domus (China), April 2008,
   'Chinese speed'
FuturArc, special issue: Mobility,
   Transportation, vol 5 2007,
   'Beijing International Airport,
   Terminal 3'
GA Document, May 2008,
   'Beijing Capital International
   Airport'
Glas Architektur und Technik, no 4,
   2008, 'Terminal 3 –
   Internationaler Flughafen Peking'
L'Arca, May 2008, 'Foster +
   Partners' new International
   Terminal Beijing'
The New Yorker, 21 April 2008,
   'Situation terminal – Can anyone
   design a nice airport' by
   Paul Goldberger
Space, July 2008, 'Beijing
   International Airport'

Tatlin Plan, 3/5/63 (2008),
   'Beijing Airport'
Urbanism and Architecture (China),
   no 43, 2008, 'The new terminal
   building at Beijing International
   Airport'
Varium, January 2009, 'Celebrating
   the thrill of flight' by Daniella
   Loupatatzi
World Architecture, special issue:
   New Beijing Traffic Building,
   August 2008, 'Pivotal airport
   terminal for the future' by
   Weiping Shao

Bishops Square
Building, 16 September 2005,
   'The City marches east' by
   Martin Spring
Building Design, 14 October 2005,
   'City on the march' by
   Charlie Gates
Building Services, October 2005,
   'The City meets Spitalfields'
   by Stephen Kennett

Business Academy Bexley
Building, 13 June 2008, 'Qualified
   success' by Martin Spring
Building Design, 6 February 2004,
   'City slickers' by Mark Dudek

Capital City Academy
GA Document, June 2004,
   'Capital City Academy'
Ottagono, March 2005, 'A scuola
   di stile' by Eleonora Capelli

Chesa Futura
A&U, May 2002, 'Chesa Futura'
AD Architectural Design, May/June 2004, 'Blurring the lines: The Chesa Futura' by André Chaszar
Architects' Journal (Timber in Architecture supplement), 27 May 2004, 'Fostering invention at a Swiss ski resort' by Ruth Slavid
Architektur Wettbewerbe, special issue: Appartementhauser, September 2002, 'Chesa Futura'
Arkitektur, special issue: Nordic wood/international wood architecture, September 2006, 'Chesa Futura, St Moritz' by Ruth Slavid
Arup Journal, January 2005, 'Chesa Futura, St Moritz' by David Glover and Jan-Peter Koppitz
Building Design, 28 February 2003, 'Smashing pumpkin' by Amanda Birch
Dwell, November/December 2003, 'Tradition tempts technology' by Iain Aitch
The Financial Times, 13/14 April 2002, 'The steel man catches shingle fever' by Helen Kirwan-Taylor
The Financial Times, 28 January 2006, 'The final frontier for architecture' by Edwin Heathcote
GA Document, special issue: GA Document International 2003, April 2003, 'Chesa Futura'
Gebäudetechnik, January 2003, 'Norman Fosters holzhaus' by Margrit de Lainsecq
The Plan, September 2004, 'Chesa Futura Apartments'
La Repubblica, 17 May 2003, 'Un ufo a Sankt Moritz' by Sebastiano Brandolini
The Times, 22 March 2003, 'Foster builds "pumpkin palace" in the Alps' by Marcus Binney

City Hall and More London Riverside
The Architects' Journal, 8 July 1999, 'Foster gives GLA building a radical rethink' by Ruth Slavid
Architectural Record, February 2003, 'Seeking the shape of green' by Jayne Merkel
Architectural Review, August 2002, 'London calling'
Architecture Today, September 2002, 'Logic and language: Foster and Partners' City Hall' by Chris Wilkinson
Building, 10 May 2002, 'Twisted genius' by Martin Spring
de Architect, November 2002, 'Democratie transparent gemaakt' by Will Jones
Detail, September 2002, 'City Hall in London'
The Guardian, 6 May 2002, 'The helter-skelter from outer space' by Jonathan Glancey
Intra, September 2002, 'Mayor's nest' by Katherine Bateson
The Observer, 5 May 2002, 'The thriller on the river' by Deyan Sudjic
World Architecture, July/August 2002, 'Power house' by Naomi Stungo

Dada Place Kitchen
MD, August 2004, 'Sein rezept: Hightech'

Deutsche Bank Place
Architecture Australia, July/August 2006, 'Deutsche Bank Place' by Philip Vivian

Djanogly City Academy
Building, 13 January 2006, 'Class struggle' by Eleanor Cochrane and Martin Spring

Dresden Station
Architecture Today, January 2007, 'Material advantage' by Michael Vitzhum
Baumeister, January 2007, 'Sanierung des Hauptbahnhofs in Dresden' by Tanja Scheffler
Bauwelt, 7 December 2006, 'Ein Bahnhof, keine shopping mall' by Silke Reifenberg
Detail, November 2007, 'Refurbishment and renovation of Dresden's Central Station'
The Guardian, 23 November 2006, 'Light at the end of the tunnel' by Steve Rose

Electricity Pylon
The Guardian, 28 February 2000, 'Eye catcher' by Jonathan Glancey
L'Arca, April 2000, 'Eco-friendly pylons' by Michele Bazan Giordano
Wallpaper, March 2000, 'Poles apart' by Lee Marshall

Electronic Arts European Headquarters
Architects' Journal, 27 July 2000, 'Frameless wonder' by Austin Williams
Architecture Today, July 2000, 'External skin: ways of seeing'
Construire, December 2000, 'Aperta a tutto'
RIBA Journal, June 2000, 'Game on' by Peter Clegg

Hearst Tower
Architecture (New York), August 2006, 'Devil wears diagrid' by Julie Sinclair Eakin
Architecture Intérieure Créé, September/October 2006, 'Un intrus vert à Manhattan' by Anne-Laure Egg
Architectural Record, August 2006, 'Green by design' by Sarah Amelar
Architectural Record (Innovation supplement), November 2005, 'Norman Foster and the Hearst Corporation complete an 80-year-old vision' by Sara Hart
Architectural Review, November 2006, 'Foster takes Manhattan' by Michael Webb
Architektur Aktuell, May 2006, 'Hearst Tower' by Robert Temel
A&V Monografia, November/December 2006, 'Torre Hearst, Nueva York' by Paul Goldberger
Building, 23 June 2006, 'A midtown Xanadu' by Martin Spring
Building Services, February 2008, 'New York giants' by Will Jones
Casabella, November 2006, 'Una manierata barbarie' by Marco Mulazzani
Civil Engineering, April 2006, 'Landmark reinvented' by Brian Fortner
Detail, special issue: High-rise buildings, September 2007, 'Hearst Tower in New York'
Domus, November 2006, 'Lord of the spring' by Stefano Casciani
The Financial Times, 14 May 2006, 'The triumph of the diagonal' by Edwin Heathcote
GA Document, November 2006, 'Hearst Tower'
Moniteur Architecture AMC, December 2003, 'Concours Hearst' by Ingrid Taillandier
New York Times, 9 June 2006,

'Upward mobility, at last'
by Nicolai Ouroussoff
The New Yorker, 19 December
2005, 'Triangulation' by
Paul Goldberger
*Society of Architectural Historians
Journal*, June 2007, 'Scenography
and structural theatrics: Urban,
Foster, and the Hearst Tower'
by Stephen Rustow
Time, 15 May 2006, 'Love triangle'
by Richard Lacayo
Wallpaper, October 2005,
'Steeling beauty'

HM Treasury
Architects' Journal, 20 October,
2005, 'BCI Awards/
Conservation'

La Voile
Architectural Digest, October 2006,
'Taking on the sky and sea'
by Joseph Giovannini
MD, November 2007, 'Freiraum'
by Susanne Tamborini

Leslie L Dan Pharmacy Building
Azure, July/August 2006, 'Pod
Mod' by Brian Carter
Architectural Record, special issue:
Lighting, May 2007, 'For the
Leslie L. Dan Pharmacy building
Claude Engle bathes floating pills
in an array of bright colours' by
Tim McKeough
Building, 17 November 2006, 'Foster
joins the pod people' by
Thomas Lane

London Academy
Architects' Journal, 22 May 2008,
'Britain's schools: the vision
becomes reality' by
James Pallister
Architecture Today, October 2006,
'Bespoke making: London
Academy, Edgware' by
Chris Foges

London City Racecourse
Architects' Journal, 15 August 2002,
'Foster goes to the races'

McLaren Production Centre
Architects' Journal, 16 February
2012, 'Go Foster' by Felix Mara
Architecture Today, 17 February
2012, 'Factory finish' by Tim
Abrahams
Building Design, 20 January 2012,
'McLaren Production Centre'
Building Magazine, 25 November
2011, 'Driving force' by Ike Ijeh
Frame, March 2012, 'Petrol-head
heaven' by Jane Szita
The Guardian, 22 November
2011, 'Men from McLaren can
still set the pulse racing' by
Richard Williams
The Independent, 27 June 2012,
'Squeaky clean McLaren gearing
up for growth' by Tom Bawden
Interni, March 2012, 'La Fabbrica del
Futuro' by Antonella Galli
IOL Motoring, 27 June 2012,
'McLaren 12C factory like a
hospital' by Tom Bawden
The Manufacturer, 15 June 2012,
'Interview: Sheriff's law for MP4',
by Tim Brown
The New York Times, 12 November
2011, 'In the pursuit of excellence
– and elusive No. 1' by Brad
Spurgeon

McLaren Technology Centre
A+E, August 2004, 'Drive
for perfection'
A&U, special issue: Automobile
Architecture, July 2007, 'McLaren
Technology Centre'
Arca, April 2004, 'La metafora
dell'efficiencza' by Stefano
Pavarini
Architects' Journal, 4 March 2004,
'A machine for working in' by
Barrie Evans
Architects' Journal, 4 March 2004,
'Driving Force' by Isabel Allen
Architecture Intérieure Créé,
special issue: Centres de
recherche et de design
automobiles, September/October
2004, 'Pole d'excellence'
by Remi Rouyer
Architectural Design, January/
February 2006, 'McLaren
Technology Centre' by
Jeremy Melvin
Arquitectura Viva, special issue:
Parque Automovil, no 106, 2006,
'Lonja de precisión'
Bauwelt, 8 April 2004, 'Der Name:
Paragon' by Christian Brensing
Casabella, October 2006, 'Norman
Foster: McLaren Technology
Centre' by Federico Bucci
Dax, October 2005, 'McLaren
Technology Centre' by
Caroline Kruit
Detail, 19 No 5 2006, 'Light to
the interior' by Susan Dawson
Domus, special issue: Progetto
e material 1, September 2005,
'Una vittoria collettiva' by
Laura Bossi
GA Document, August 2004,
'McLaren Technology Centre'
The Guardian, 13 October 2004,
'Built to win' by Jonathan Glancey
Habitat Ufficio, August 2004,
'McLaren Technology Centre:
Uno spazio per l'innovazione e
l'invenzione' by Emilia Prevosti

Icon, November 2003, 'A machine
for working in' by Alex Wiltshire
Profile, no 2, 2004, 'McLaren
Technologie-Zentrum'

The Metropolitan
Arquitectura Viva, October 2003,
'The Metropolitan Office Building'
by David Crowley

Moor House
Architects' Journal, 6 May 1999,
'Foster puts curves into City of
London offices' by Jez Abbott
Ground Engineering, November
2002, 'First cut is the deepest' by
Paul Wheeler
New Civil Engineer, 4 September
2003, 'Repeat performance' by
Ruby Khan
New Civil Engineer International,
February 2003, 'Planning ahead'
by Paul Wheeler

The Murezzan
AD Architectural Design (Italy),
23 May 2006, 'La tradizione
diventa moderna' by
Riccardo Bianchi

National Police Memorial
The Guardian, 27 April 2005,
'Simple sentinel' by
Jonathan Glancey

**Newbury Racecourse
Grandstand**
Architects' Journal, 19 December
2002, 'Racing times' by
Susan Dawson
FMX, May 2001, 'Racing certainty'
by Katy Greaves
RIBA Journal, August 2000, 'United
We Stand' by Stephen Pacey

Petronas University of Technology
A&U, December 2007, '2007 Aga Khan Award for Architecture'
Arca, February 2008, 'The Aga Khan Award: 10th edition, 30th anniversary'
Architect (Washington DC), September 2007, '2007 Aga Khan Award for Architecture given to nine projects'
Architectural Design, special issue: On Green Design (part 3), January/February 2008, 'The basic premises for green design' by Ken Yeang
Architectural Review, November 2007, 'Aga Khan Award for Architecture 2007'
Architecture Malaysia, special issue: Centres of Learning, October 2006, 'Universiti Teknologi Petronas, Tronoh, Perak', by Ahmad Nizam Radzi
Arkitekten (Copenhagen), no 13 2007, 'Arkitektonisk mellemfolelighed' by Birgitte Kleis
Building Design, 4 September 2007, 'Foster university in Malaysia wins Aga Khan award' by Rory Olcayto
Intervention Architecture, Introduction by Homi K Bhabha, 2007

Regent Place
Monument, August/September 2004, 'Blinded by the light' by William Smart

Smithsonian Institution Courtyard
Architectural Record, March 2008, 'The Smithsonian Institute' by Russell Fortmeyer
Building, 2 February 2007, 'Gorgeous Washington' by Thomas Lane
Building Design, 11 April 2008, 'Smithsonian Institute' by Will Hunter
Detail, January 2009, 'The canopy at the Smithsonian Institution's Kogod Courtyard' by Klaus Lother and Wolfgang Rudolph
GA Document, special issue: GA Document International 2005, May 2005, 'Smithsonian Institution Patent Office Building courtyard enclosure'
GA Document, December 2007, 'Robert and Arlene Kogod Courtyard, Smithsonian Institute'
The Independent, 7 February 2008, 'The king's new court' by Ciar Byrne
Washington Post, 9 September 2005, 'A roof that's patently the best option' by Benjamin Forgey

Stacking Chairs – Emeco 20-06 and R Randers
The Architect's Newspaper, 10 May 2006, 'The shape of things to come' by Cathy Lang Ho
I:D, September/October 2006, 'From seat to shining seat' by Jayne Margolies
indesign, November 2006, 'New Foster Icons'

Supreme Court
Dialogue, October 2008, 'Supreme Court Singapore'
Singapore Architect, October 2005, 'Symbolic constructions: the new Supreme Court' by Chang Jiat Hwee
Structural Engineer (supplement), 18 July 2006, 'Singapore's new Supreme Court building – marrying form and function' by Dan Yap Tian Wee, Tan Kheng Soon, Lai Hoke Sai and Lim Peng Hong

Tower Place
AT Handbook, July 2003, 'Foster + Partners, Tower Place, London'
Building, 15 March 2002, 'Clear vision' by Andy Pearson
Building Design Envelope, October 2003, 'Tube tales' by Luke Lowings
Concrete (The Construct Award) January 2004, 'Creative car parking'
Construction News, 31 March 2002, 'Good neighbour' by Emma Forrest
Detail, July/August 2003, 'Tower Place in London'

Trafalgar Square
Building, July 2003, 'Revamped Trafalgar Square returns to public domain' by Martin Spring
The Observer, 29 June 2003, 'So, Nelson, what's your view?' by Deyan Sudjic
RIBA Journal, July 2003, 'The pigeons, my friend …' by Robert Elwall
Town & Country Planning, April 2000, 'Urban design – waking the sleeping giants' by Matthew Carmona

Wembley Stadium
Architecture Today, May 2007, 'Field of dreams' by Neven Sidor
Architektura & Sport, January 2007, 'Nowy Stadion Wembley' by Lidia Grzybowska-Kwieoinska
Building, 23 March 2007, 'Get in!' by Thomas Lane
Building Design, 10 June 2005, 'In detail: Wembley Stadium arch' by Graham Bizley
Building Design, 10 June 2005, 'In a league of its own' by Pamela Buxton
de Architect, August 2007, 'Architectonisch feestje' by Neven Sidor
Detail, August 2008, 'Wembley-Stadion in London' by Christopher Hill
FX, April 2004, 'Inside story' by Karen Glaser
The Guardian, 9 March 2007, 'We think it's all over…' by Jonathan Glancey
Impianti, August 2007, 'Il nuovo stadio di Wembley'
New Civil Engineer, 17 May 2007, 'Engineer's guide to the FA Cup' by Andrew Mylius
OfArch, December 2007, 'Il nuovo Wembley Stadium' by Christina Molteni
Stadia, July 2007, 'They think it's all over…' by Mark Bisson
Wembley Stadium: Venue of Legends, Prestel 2007, by Patrick Barclay and Kenneth Powell

World Squares for All Masterplan
Evening Standard, 20 January 1998, 'Let our squares breathe' by Paul Waugh
The Independent, 6 November 1997, 'A vision of the heart of London without traffic' by Nicholas Schoon
Planning in London, January 1998, 'Civilising Westminster's streets and squares' by Peter Heath

World Trade Center
Architectural Record, February 2003, 'Architects at the forefront as they show Ground Zero aspirations' by John E. Czarnecki
Architectural Record, February 2003, 'A defining moment for architecture' by James S. Russell
Domus, February 2003, 'Sette visioni di New York'

Contributors

Chris Abel is an architectural theorist, critic and lecturer. His books include two collections of his essays: *Architecture and Identity: Responses to Cultural and Technological Change* and *Architecture, Technology and Process*. He was assistant curator for the Royal Academy of Arts 2003 Summer Show exhibition, 'Sky High: Vertical Architecture', and is the author of the book of the same title.

'Beijing International Airport' is an edited version of a text first published in *The Architectural Review*, August 2008.

Gavin Blyth is a former assistant editor of the *Norman Foster Works* series and a regular contributor to books and magazines on architecture. After gaining an MA in architectural history and theory from the University of Essex he went on to edit UK photographic industry magazine *Image* before editing the University College London alumni magazine, *UCL People*.

Edward Bosley is director of the Gamble House in Pasadena, California. He is an authority on nineteenth- and early twentieth-century American architecture, particularly the American Arts and Crafts Movement. His many books include the definitive monograph on the work of the architects Greene & Greene.

Peter Buchanan worked as an architect, urban designer and planner for a decade before turning to writing, becoming deputy editor of *The Architectural Review* from 1983 to 1992. His books include *Renzo Piano Building Workshop: Complete Works*, Volumes 1 to 5, and *Ten Shades of Green*, the catalogue of an exhibition he curated in 2001. He has also taught short courses in universities in diverse parts of the world.

Francis Duffy is an architect and is one of the founders of the international practice, DEGW, which specialises in the programming and design of the working environment. He is a researcher, writer and critic in the field. He has been President of the Royal Institute of British Architects (RIBA) and the Architects' Council of Europe. From 2001 to 2003 he was based in DEGW's New York office and was a Visiting Professor at MIT. His most recent books are *The New Office*, *Architectural Knowledge* and *Work and the City*.

Joseph Giovannini is an architectural designer, critic and writer. He has been a contributor to the *Los Angeles Herald Examiner* and the *New York Times* and to a number of books on contemporary architecture and design, including *Graphic Design in America* and *Los Angeles at 25mph*.

Paul Goldberger has served as architecture critic for the *New Yorker* and the *New York Times*, where his work received the Pulitzer Prize. In 2012 he was named the winner of the Vincent Scully Prize, conferred by the National Building Museum in Washington, DC. He is the author of numerous books, including *Why Architecture Matters*. He holds the Joseph Urban Chair in Design and Architecture at the New School in New York City, and is a contributing editor at the magazine *Vanity Fair*.

Simon Inglis is an architectural historian and author of several books on stadiums, including *Football Grounds of Britain*, *The Football Grounds of Europe*, and *Sightlines, a Stadium Odyssey*. During the 1990s he edited a series of stadium design guidelines for various football and government bodies in Britain, including the fourth edition of the *Guide to Safety at Sports Grounds*. He is currently editor of *Played in Britain*, an English Heritage series on sporting architecture.

Nicola Jackson is a former editor of *World Architecture*. Her books include *Building the BBC: A Return to Form* and *The Story of Paternoster: A New Square for London*, as well as monographs on MJP Architects and van Heyningen and Haward Architects.

David Jenkins is editor of the *Norman Foster Works* series. He is a former buildings editor on *The Architects' Journal*, and was for seven years editorial director at Phaidon Press, responsible for architecture and design. He is the co-author of a monograph on the work of Pierre Koenig and the editor of numerous books, including: *On Foster – Foster On*, *Foster 40* and *Martin Pawley: The Strange Death of Architectural Criticism*.

Annette LeCuyer is an architect, critic and educator. A former Thurnau Professor at the University of Michigan, she is now professor at the State University of New York at Buffalo. She is the author of *Radical Tectonics*, co-author of *All-American: Innovation in American Architecture*, and a contributor to architectural publications in Europe and North America.

Thomas Leslie is Pickard Chilton Professor of Architecture at Iowa State University, where his teaching focuses on the integration of building technology and architectural design. Prior to teaching he spent seven years in the offices of Foster + Partners. He is the author of *Louis I Kahn: Building Art, Building Science* and a monograph on the Millau Viaduct.

Kenneth Powell is a writer and critic. A former architectural correspondent of the *Daily Telegraph*, he is the author of many books and contributes to newspapers and journals in Britain and abroad. He is an Honorary Fellow of the Royal Institute of British Architects. His many books include *New Architecture in Britain*, *The Jubilee Line Extension* and *Architecture Reborn: The Conversion and Reconstruction of Old Buildings*.

Libby Sellers is the founder of Gallery Libby Sellers, a roaming gallery that specialises in one-off and limited edition pieces. She studied history of art and journalism before obtaining a Masters degree in design history from the Royal College of Art. For six years she was curator for contemporary design at the Design Museum, London. A frequent public speaker and commentator on design and contemporary culture, she is also a regular juror for a number of international design awards.

Deyan Sudjic is director of the Design Museum in London. He is the founding editor of *Blueprint* magazine, a former editor of *Domus* and architectural correspondent for *The Observer*. The director of Glasgow 1999, he also directed the 2002 Venice Architecture Biennale. His many books include *The 100 Mile City* and *The Edifice Complex: How the Rich and Powerful Shape the World*.

Thomas Weaver is the editor of the Architectural Association's *AA Files* and a former assistant editor of the *Norman Foster Works* series. He has also worked as editor of *ANY* magazine, and has taught architectural history and theory at Princeton University and the Cooper Union in New York, while contributing essays on architectural criticism to a number of books and journals.

Richard Weston is professor of architecture at the Welsh School of Architecture, Cardiff University. An award-winning author and architect, his many books include *Utzon*, the first authorised monograph on the architect of the Sydney Opera House, *Materials, Form and Architecture*, *The House in the Twentieth Century*, *Alvar Aalto* and *Modernism*.

Norman Foster was born in Manchester in 1935. After graduating from Manchester University School of Architecture and City Planning in 1961, he won a fellowship to Yale University, where he gained a Masters degree in Architecture.

In 1963 he co-founded Team 4 and in 1967 he established Foster Associates, now known as Foster + Partners. The practice has its main studio in London, with project offices worldwide. Since its inception the practice has received more than 600 awards and citations for excellence and has won more than 100 national and international competitions.

Norman Foster was awarded the Royal Gold Medal for Architecture in 1983, the Gold Medal of the French Academy of Architecture in 1991 and the American Institute of Architects Gold Medal in 1994. Also in 1994, he was appointed Officer of the Order of Arts and Letters by the Ministry of Culture in France. In 1999 he became the twenty-first Pritzker Architecture Prize Laureate and in 2002 he was elected to the German Orden Pour le Mérite für Wissenschaften und Künste and awarded the Praemium Imperiale. In 2005 he was awarded the inaugural World Solar Prize; and in 2009 he became the twenty-ninth laureate of the Prince of Asturias Award for Arts.

He was granted a knighthood in the Queen's Birthday Honours List, 1990, and appointed by the Queen to the Order of Merit in 1997. In 1999 he was honoured with a life peerage in the Queen's Birthday Honours List, taking the title Lord Foster of Thames Bank.

Index

Credits

Drawings and Sketches
Birds Portchmouth Russum: 46-47, 64-65 (4), 92-93 (5), 101-102 (5), 114-115 (5), 122-123 (6), 126 (1), 138-139, 144-145 (1), 148-149 (1), 152, 195, 203 (4), 215 (4), 219 (4), 252-253, 298-299, 301, 322-323, 328-329 (5), 358-359 (8), 394 (1), 408 (2), 415 (6), 425 (2), 436-437 (4), 439 (5), 443 (4), 449 (4), 460-461 (1), 480-481 (1), 532-533 (5)
Mike Cook: 487 (top)
Gordon Cullen: 373 (top), 401 (top)
Nigel Dancey: 77 (5)
Norman Foster: 12 (1), 13 (3), 18 (1), 20 (1), 36, 37 (3), 39, 70, 71, 78, 79, 111 (3), 115 (5), 119 (3), 125 (2), 141, 142, 155 (6), 158 (2), 160 (3), 163 (2), 168 (6), 169 (7, 8), 170, 173 (3), 174 (3, 4), 175 (7), 176 (2), 177 (5), 185 (2, 3), 186-187, 192, 201 (3), 203 (top), 203 (5), 211 (2), 220 (1), 225 (4, 5), 226, 228, 229, 235 (7), 236, 237, 268, 269 (2-4), 273 (2), 291, 292 (4-8), 293 (12), 294 (3), 315 (4), 333 (3), 334 (top), 339 (5, 6), 345 (4), 355 (3), 363 (top, 2), 364, 377 (4), 378 (1), 387 (2, 3), 388 (4), 415 (top), 422 (top), 426 (top), 427 (2), 428 (2), 433 (5), 434 (2), 440 (1), 446 (3), 451 (6), 453 (2), 477 (2), 487 (4), 490-491, 498 (1-4)
Foster + Partners: 22 (1), 24, 40 (1), 41 (2), 48, 49, 54, 55, 66 (3), 72, 80 (2), 81 (3), 90, 91, 95, 99, 102 (top), 104 (1), 105 (2), 112, 127 (4), 136, 151, 164 (4), 179 (4), 196, 202 (2, 3), 216 (1), 223 (3), 225 (3), 230, 239 (5,6), 242, 244, 245, 271 (5, 7), 274 (1), 280 (1), 295 (4-8), 308, 312, 313 (5), 314 (2), 316-317, 318, 319, 334 (1,2), 336, 340 (1), 342 (2-4), 349, 358 (7), 377 (3), 390, 392 (7, 8), 393 (9-12), 397 (7), 403 (2-3), 407 (5), 410 (2), 412 (2), 421 (3-7), 428 (1,3,4), 434 (1,3), 440 (2-4), 446 (1, 2), 450 (2, 3), 451 (4, 5), 457 (6,7), 464-465 (2-4), 469 (3), 478 (top, 3), 478 (5), 484, 485 (2), 486 (1, 2), 492, 496, 497 (6-8), 500-501, 502 (3), 512-513, 514, 515-517, 520-521, 538, 540 (3), 559 (2)
Gregory Gibbon: 41 (top), 42-43, 84-85, 134, 234 (2), 241 (6), 246-247, 352-353, 504-505
© Hellman: 67 (top)
John Hewitt: 82 (1, 2), 182 (1, 2) 183 (3, 4), 238, 391 (3), 444 (2,3), 445 (4, 5), 540 (4), 542 (2)
Helmut Jacoby: 456 (1), 457 (5)
Ben Johnson: 154 (top)
Jan Kaplicky: 220 (top)
David Nelson: 76 (3)
Narinder Sagoo: 224 (1), 227, 274 (2, 3), 275 (4), 372 (1-4), 373 (5), 498 (1)

Every effort has been made to contact copyright holders. The publishers apologise for any omissions which they will be pleased to rectify at the earliest opportunity.

Editing: David Jenkins, Rebecca Roke
Picture research: Gayle Mault
Design: Thomas Manss & Company with
Per Arnoldi; Thomas Manss, Keira Yang,
Angela Pescolderung
Research: Matthew Foreman, Oliver Pawley
Cutaway drawings: Gregory Gibbon
Technical illustration: John Hewitt, William
McElhinney, Richard Portchmouth
Proofreading: Julia Dawson
Index: Hilary Bird
Production supervision: John Bodkin, Martin Lee
Reproduction: Dawkins Colour
Printed and bound in Italy